61st VOLUME

1993-1994

THE HIGLEY COMMENTARY

International Uniform
Sunday School Series

Editor
Wesley C. Reagan

Writers
Douglas Ezell, PhD
Ron Durham, PhD
Rod Kennedy, PhD
Bill Love, PhD
John Wright

Illustrator
Billy Ledet

"**Sparkles**" and "**Smiles**" are new features designed to add notes of insight, inspiration, and humor. "**Say it Right**" is an easy to use guide to the pronunciation of rare or unfamiliar words in the Bible. These added features make an old friend even more helpful. Thanks for your friendship with the HIGLEY COMMENTARY.

Higley Publishing Corporation
Post Office Box 5398
Jacksonville FL 32247-5398

PREFACE

When the editor of Higley Commentary asked me to write the Preface for the 1993-1994 volume I replied, "Who am I that you would want me?" We talked, he persisted and I gave in.

Well...who am I? I am a 67-year-old retired research scientist and author of lots of published technical material, but I don't believe he asked me because of that. I believe he asked me because he knows that I have taught Sunday School Classes of both adults and children and that I have a strong commitment both to the church and religious education.

Teaching may be in my genes. My father taught a Men's Bible Class of over a hundred men and many of my forebears were both Sunday School and Public School teachers. My mother often said that I was almost born in a Sunday School Class. My faith journey has been profoundly affected by Bible study and many capable and caring Sunday School teachers.

It may be more related to my career as research scientist than teaching in Sunday School, but I value very highly well researched basic information together with creative suggestions in formulating a lesson teaching plan. I also look for quality of work and credibility of authors. I am quite impressed by both the quality and quantity of material in Higley Commentary.

I suppose my favorite part of each lesson is "Seed Thoughts." The thoughts are stimulating in every lesson and serve well for use with any lesson plan. Another favorite section is "Memory Selection." I believe very strongly in the power of memorization to impart direction for our lives. I'm sure you will have your favorite part. Every part is excellent.

If you have concluded that I recommend Higley, you are right. All that I value as either teacher or student as extra resource material for The International Sunday School Lesson Series is in a compact, inexpensive publication--The Higley Commentary. I highly recommend it.

Truman Ward
Committed Christian
Sunday School Student & Teacher

FOREWORD

A Sunday School teacher might dream of having a staff of trained, Bible-loving people who would research the assigned text each Sunday. In his reverie, the teacher might imagine that the text might be broken down into its various components and studied as though under a microscope. Then, the dream might continue, the researchers would seek ways to apply the lesson in daily life and search for interesting ways to discuss it in class.

As the dream went on, the teacher might conceive of the research staff putting all the material together in a condensed form so it could be read in a short time.

Happily, that is not a dream but a reality for tens of thousands of Sunday School teachers that have discovered The Higley Commentary.

The writing staff of Doug Ezell, Ron Durham, Rod Kennedy, Bill Love, and John Wright burned midnight oil more than a year in advance so the material would be ready for any given Sunday. This carefully assembled group of writers is **your research team.** This is one dream which has become reality.

Our prayer is that the 1993-1994 Higley Commentary will be your faithful, helpful and encouraging companion all year long. May your Sunday School experience be one of peace, joy and vigorous growth in the understanding and practice of our Lord's way of life.

Wesley C. Reagan, Editor
The Higley Commentary

Lessons and/or Readings based on International Sunday School Lessons. The International Bible Lessons for Christian Training, copyright © 1990 by the Committee on the Uniform Series.

Copyright © 1993
Higley Publishing Corporation
ISBN 0-9614116-6-x Softcover
ISBN 09614116-7-8 Hardcover
ISBN 0-9614116-8-6 Adult Student

FALL QUARTER

God's Creation of and Relationship with Humankind
(Lessons 1-4)
The Beginning of a New Relationship
(Lessons 5-8)
The Promise is Transmitted
(Lessons 9-13)

<u>SUNDAY</u> <u>PAGE</u>

September 5   The Origin of the Universe 1
              Genesis 1:1-25

September 12 The Origin of Humankind 11
              Genesis 1:26-31; 2:4-9, 15-25

September 19 The Origin of Sin 21
              Genesis 3:1-13

September 26 God's Response to Humankind's Sin 31
              Genesis 3:14-24; 6:5-8, 11-27; 9:8-13

October 3   God's Commitment to Abram 41
              Genesis 12:1-3; 15:1-18

October 10   Sarai Attempts to Manipulate Events 51
              Genesis 16

October 17   God Establishes an Everlasting
              Covenant   Genesis 17 61

October 24   God Keeps His Promise 71
              Genesis 21:1-21

October 31   The Sons of Isaac 81
              Genesis 25:19-34

November 7   Jacob Steals the Blessing 91
              Genesis 27

November 14 Jacob's Experience with Laban 101
              Genesis 29:1-30

November 21 Jacob Is Reconciled with Esau 111
              Genesis 33

November 28 Jacob Blesses Joseph and His Sons 121
              Genesis 48

WINTER QUARTER
Luke: A Savior is Born
(Lessons 1-4)
Luke: Ministry in Galilee
(Lessons 5-9)
Luke: The Cross and the Resurrection
(Lessons 10-13)

SUNDAY		PAGE
December 5	Preparing the Way .... 131 Luke 1:5-25; 3:1-18	
December 12	Yielding to God's Will .... 141 Luke 1:26-56	
December 19	Born a Savior .... 151 Luke 2:1-20	
December 26	Testing a Commitment to Service .... 161 Luke 3:21-22; 4:1-15	
January 2	Jesus States His Mission .... 171 Luke 4:16-28	
January 9	Jesus Heals the Sick .... 181 Luke 4:31-43	
January 16	Jesus Teaches His Followers .... 191 Luke 6:17-36	
January 23	Jesus Calls and Commissions .... 201 Disciples Luke 9:51-10:12	
January 30	Jesus Tells Parables About the Lost .... 211 Luke 15	
February 6	Who Can Be Saved? .... 221 Luke 18:15-30	
February 13	God's Patience and Justice .... 231 Luke 20:1-19	
February 20	One Who Serves .... 241 Luke 22:1-30	
February 27	From Death to Life .... 251 Luke 23:32-47; 24:13-35	

SPRING QUARTER

Righteousness Through Faith
(Lessons 1-4)
Empowered by the Spirit
(Lessons 5-8)
Set Free by God's Grace
(Lessons 9-13)

SUNDAY		PAGE
March 6	The Power of God for Salvation Romans 1:1-17	261
March 13	God's Gift of Redemption Romans 3:21-4:25	271
March 20	The Gift of Life in Christ Romans 5	281
March 27	Deliverance from Sin Romans 6	291
April 3	A Glimpse of Glory Mark 16:1-8; Romans 8:12-27	301
April 10	Life in the Spirit Romans 8:1-11	311
April 17	Using Our Gifts in Serving Romans 12	321
April 24	Living for Others Romans 14	331
May 1	Delivered from Bondage Galatians 1-2	341
May 8	Adopted as God's Children Galatians 3:1-4:7	351
May 15	Given the Birthright of Freedom Galatians 4:8-31	361
May 22	Bear Fruit of the Spirit Galatians 5	371
May 29	Express Christ's Love in All Relationships Galatians 6	381

SUMMER QUARTER

Deliverance from Oppression
(Lessons 1-4)
Provisions for Present and Future
(Lessons 5-9)
Instructions for Life
(Lessons 10-13)

SUNDAY		PAGE
June 5	God Remembers	391
	Exodus 1-2	
June 12	God Calls and Moses Responds	401
	Exodus 3:1-4:17	
June 19	God Redeems Israel	411
	Exodus 6:2-9	
June 26	God Brings Victory	421
	Exodus 13:17-14:31	
July 3	Bread from Heaven	431
	Exodus 16	
July 10	Leadership for Meeting Needs	441
	Exodus 18	
July 17	A Covenant to Keep	451
	Exodus 19:1-20:17	
July 24	Restoration After Wrongdoing	461
	Exodus 32; 34:1-10	
July 31	God's Constant Presence	471
	Exodus 25:1-9; 29:38-46; 40:16-38	
August 7	Celebrate God's Ownership	481
	Leviticus 25	
August 14	Accept God's Guidance	491
	Numbers 13-14	
August 21	Love the Lord Your God	501
	Deuteronomy 6	
August 28	Choose to Obey	511
	Deuteronomy 28	

HOW TO USE SEED THOUGHTS

The Seed Thought feature, with its ten questions at the end of each lesson, is designed to stimulate class participation. Use the questions where they best apply in the course of developing the lesson. The suggested answers are really just starters and can be enlarged on as needed.

The duplicate questions on the outside portion of the page can be cut out and given to selected students the week before. The names of the students to whom questions have been assigned can be written on the teachers half of the Seed Thoughts page.

Also available from your Christian Bookstore:

CROSS and CARD

The cross in your pocket or handbag helps to remind you daily that Jesus Christ, the Son of God, died for you.

Invaluable as a conversation opener, its impact is long-lasting when given as a gift to a friend.

The reverse side of the card contains "Footprints" poem.

A perfect way to share your Christian experience with others.

ISBN 0-9614116-2-7
Price $1.00 + Shipping

Higley Publishing Corporation
P.O. Box 5398
Jacksonville, FL 32247-5398
904-396-1918

September 5, 1993

The Origin of the Universe

Genesis 1: 1-15

1 IN the beginning God created the heaven and the earth.
2 And the earth was without form, and void; and darkness was upon the face of the deep. And the Spirit of God moved upon the face of the waters.
3 And God said, Let there be light: and there was light.
4 And God saw the light. that *it was* good: and God divided the light from the darkness.
5 And God called the light Day; and the darkness he called Night. And the evening and the morning were the first day.
6 And God said, Let there be a firmament in the midst of the waters, and let it divide the waters from the waters.
7 And God made the firmament, and divided the waters which *were* under the firmament from the waters which *were* above the firmament: and it was so.
8 And God called the firmament Heaven. And the evening and the morning were the second day.
9 And God said, Let the waters under the heaven be gathered together unto one place, and let the dry *land* appear. and it was so.
10 And God called the dry land Earth; and the gathering together of the waters called he Seas: and God saw that *it was* good.
11 And God said, Let the earth bring forth grass, the herb yielding seed, and the fruit tree yielding fruit after his kind, whose seed *is* in itself, upon the earth: and it was so.
12 And the earth brought forth grass, *and* herb yielding seed after his kind, and the tree yielding fruit, whose seed *was* in itself, after his kind: and God saw that *it was* good.
13 And the evening and the moming were the third day.
14 And God said, Let there be lights in the firmament of the heaven to divide the day from the night; and let them be for signs, and for seasons, and for days, and years:
15 And let them be for lights in the firmament of the heaven to give light upon the earth: and it was so.

◀ **Memory Selection**
Genesis 1:1-3

◀ **Devotional Reading**
Isaiah 40: 21, 25-26, 28-31

◀ **Background Scripture**
Genesis 1:1-25

◀ **Printed Scripture**
Genesis 1:1-15

THE ORIGIN OF THE UNIVERSE

Teacher's Target

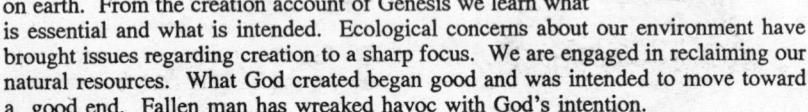

When we say we believe in creation, it is our faith confession that from the beginning God is the source of all structures on earth. From the creation account of Genesis we learn what is essential and what is intended. Ecological concerns about our environment have brought issues regarding creation to a sharp focus. We are engaged in reclaiming our natural resources. What God created began good and was intended to move toward a good end. Fallen man has wreaked havoc with God's intention.

Ask your students to discuss the following quote. Dwight L. Moody once said, "I look upon this world as a wrecked vessel. God has given me a life boat and said to me, 'Moody, save all you can.'" Is it a "wrecked vessel?" If so, in what way? What is our purpose as God's caretakers? What is our hope?

Lesson Introduction

Children are masters of wonder and awe. "Mama, where did I come from?" is a question familiar to any parent. Wondering how our universe came to be doesn't stop with children. Adults want to know sources, too. In Genesis 1 the Bible explains the origin of the world. God created all things. We may never comprehend the complexity of how and when of creation. God's ways are not our ways. He is Creator, we are creature. He is the author of all things, animate and inanimate. Thus, He is the authority over all things including us. He created all things good out of the core of His being which is love. Such love never gives up on what He created.

Our biblical understanding of creation does not set us at odds with science. What we object to is any view that rejects the Creator as the origin of all things.

Teaching Outline

I. First Day: Gen. 1:1-5
   A. God Moved: 1-2
   B. Light Appeared: 3
   C. Light and Darkness
      Appeared: 4-5
II. Second Day: Gen. 1:6-8
   A. Sky and oceans: 6-7
   B. Heaven: 8
III. Third Day: Gen. 1:9-13
   A. Earth and Sea: 9-10
   B. Plants and Trees: 11-13
IV. Fourth Day: Gen. 1:14-16
   A. Seasons, Days and Years: 14
   B. Sun and Moon: 15-16

Daily Bible Readings

Mon. In the Beginning, God
Gen. 1:1-2; John 1:1-5
Tue. Let There Be Light
Gen. 1:3-5; Jer. 31:35-37
Wed. God Made the Firmament
Gen. 1:6-8, 14-19
Thu. God Made the Earth and Sea
Gen. 1:9-10; Is. 40:21-26
Fri. Earth Produces Plants
Gen. 1:11-12, 29-30
Sat. Living Creatures of Seas
Gen. 1:20-22; Ps. 8:3-8
Sun. Living Creatures of Earth
Gen. 1:24-25; Is. 40:9-11

September 5, 1993

VERSE BY VERSE

I. First Day: Gen. 1:1-5

A. God moved: 1-2

1. In the beginning God created the heaven and the earth.
2. And the earth was without form, and void; and darkness was upon the face of the deep. And the Spirit of God moved upon the face of the waters.

Have you ever considered the great choice made by God to create? He did not have to create. He chose to create. Some might say that since God is love He had to create so He would have something to love. Nothing forces God. Love, even ours, can't be forced. It has to flow out of the core of one's being. After creating, God chose to love and make Himself responsible for the well being of what He created. This we call providence. Knowing this origin out of love, we cannot reduce the magnitude of creation to just a discussion of scientific facts.

However, incredible facts concerning the relationship between the earth and other planets, angles and axis, orbit and rotation, and other correspondences in nature make it harder to believe it all just happened than to believe one, creative, intelligent, loving God masterminded all that is.

Some ask what was before God? According to Scripture, God is the infinite one before all things. To ask for more explanation is like asking what is the highest number! The answer to that one is beyond our capacity. We must accept that some things are beyond US. our finite minds were not created to consume the infinite. If we could we would be greater than God who created us.

In verse two the phrase "the earth was without form and void" implies that God created out of His essence of being. We call this creating "ex nihilo" (out of nothing that was present). From this we can understand that God's being formed everything. Nothing is that does not bear the imprint of His being upon it.

"The Spirit of God moving upon the waters" is akin to the care of a mother hen for her small chicks. God didn't just wind the world up like a clock to let it run down in time. God has invested Himself in all that is, and is as jealous for its welfare as any mother for the life of her young.

We can learn much about God and ourselves from these opening verses of Genesis. About God: He is outside of all He created. He is infinite and eternal. He is creative love. About ourselves: Because God created all things, all things are valued by Him. This includes us, human beings.

B. Light appeared: 3

3. And God said, Let there be light; and there was light.

This verse is a good place to see how God permeates everything. God is light (John 8:12) and without His revealing we would know nothing. He has revealed in the material world so that we can see and appreciate His creation. He has revealed in the spiritual dimension so that we can experience, enjoy and serve a loving God. By giving us light, God says to us that His intent was for us to know and experience all things good including Himself to the fullest. It was never His intent, as the serpent claims in Genesis 3, to hide anything from us. God knew when and how to reveal to us what we needed to know and could appreciate.

C. Light and Darkness Appeared: 4-5

4. And God saw the light, that it was good: and God divided the light from the darkness.
5. And God called the light Day, and the darkness he called Night. And the evening and the morning were the first day.

Some people see the problems of the world since the Fall of man in Genesis 3 and conclude that God didn't do a very good job with His creation. Some say, how could He be God and let it get so out of hand?

The account of the beginnings in Genesis tell a different story. It can not be read without realizing that all was created in order. All was created the way God knew it would work best. Day for working, playing, enjoying what we see. Night for refreshing, rest and sleep. These are good examples of God's purposefulness and desire for order.

II. Second Day: Gen. 1:6-8

A. Sky and Oceans: 6-7

6. And God said, Let there be a firmament in the midst of the waters, and let it divide the waters from the waters.
7. And God made the firmament, and divided the waters which were under the firmament from the waters which were above the firmament: and it was so.

This is only an imaginative picture, but God having great fun like a child with paints reaching out His finger parting the waters, wrapping some of the water in clouds, and pushing other waters into the oceans? Both waters from above and waters from below, God used to make the earth fertile.

B. Heaven: 8

8. And God called the firmament Heaven. And the evening and the morning were the second day.

In Ezekiel 1:26 we are told that God has His throne in heaven. The visible sky above us is a reminder of the supremacy of God over all things. The distance from us and the expanse of the sky is a reminder of how God is so totally other than us. His glory is broader than the canopy of the skies. His providence is over and around us as the sky. Such providence declares that though different from us, God is with us. His purity of being has more splendor than the brilliance of a bright day.

III. Third Day: Gen. 1:9-13

A. Earth and Sea: 9-10

9. And God said, Let the waters under the heaven be gathered together unto one place and let the dry land appear: and it was so.
10. And God called the dry land Earth; and the gathering together of the waters called he Seas: and God saw that it was good.

After fashioning the light in the heavens and establishing the framework of His creation with the separation of the firmament, God goes to creative and playful work on the lower regions. Here man, His crowning glory of creation, is to live and be plentiful and have dominion. How thoughtfully God created mankind's home. Land is for human habitation. The waters of the seas are set within protective boundaries and limits. Both land and sea are for man's use. As God uncovered the earth from the waters so He is continually uncovering His good and gracious gifts to us as a blessing in our behalf.

B. Plants and Trees: 11-13

11. And God said, Let the earth bring forth grass, the herb yielding seed, and the fruit tree yielding fruit after his kind, whose seed is in itself, upon the earth: and it was so.
12. And the earth brought forth grass, and herb yielding seed after his kind, and the tree yielding fruit, whose seed was in itself, after his kind: and God saw that it was good.
13. And the evening and the morning were the third day.

Provision was made by God for every creature to be fed by the earth's bounty. God speaks and provision is assured. Through the ages, His speaking and providing does not change in its nature. God's nature is grace. When God spoke in the prophets and incarnated His word in Jesus Christ, His intent was to feed us once again but at an even more necessary level for life. The earth and the Word continue to create with an unwearied power and inexhaustible goodness. Though God's provisions often come through secondary causes we must not be deceived; still it is from His hand that we are fed.

IV. Fourth Day: Gen. 1:14-15

A. Seasons, Days and Years: 14

14. And God said, Let there be lights in the firmament of the heaven to divide the day from the night; and let them be for signs, and for seasons, and for days, and years.

There is no monotony with God. His creation is ever new and full of wonder. Seasons, days, years give us varied activities, new starts, and something to look forward to. With God there is order, but also much variety.

B. Sun and moon: 15

15. And let them be for lights in the firmament of the heaven to give light upon the earth: and it was so.

By means of sun and moon God has given us our signs for changes in weather, seasons and days. They allow us to order our activities with deliberation and foresight. They also set boundaries and limits to our work and play. Note that the lights of heaven do not shine for themselves; they are there for all plants and creatures. As the lights of heaven serve us, so they are a reminder of our calling from God to serve Him and others.

THE ORIGIN OF THE UNIVERSE

Evangelistic Emphasis

So many in our world seem to be lost within a meaningless fog of nothingness. Like gerbils on their exercise wheels, their lives move from crisis to crisis and back again—going nowhere. If it were not for the crises punctuating their cyclic journeys, there would be little or no sense of movement at all.

What a blessing it is for those who face life with an awareness of their origin and a vision of their destiny. God opened His Book with the best of good news, "In the beginning God..." He stands at the gateway of time providing life its start. All the nothingness and darkness preceding that beginning was intercepted by the loving work of God. "In the beginning God created.... " And so, *all that is* was begun.

God testifies to our origin, and so gives us identity. We did not merely emerge from the green algae of swamp slime as a chance fluke of nature. Our world is not simply the aftermath of a collision of randomly floating chunks of matter. It was created by God. With forethought and purpose God launched our world into process. Each of us shares in that overarching decision of God. We are the product and the beneficiaries of that fiat. All that we are or ever will be is inseparably linked to that.

Memory Selection

In the beginning God created the heaven and the earth. *Genesis 1:1*

The question that has intrigued the minds of the world's geniuses is answered so simply. Unfortunately, truth memorized by the child of three somehow often escapes his grasp before he is twenty-three.

Yet, we must be careful not to be hard on doubting young minds. Sometimes, before a man can believe, he must first doubt. Before a woman is able to embrace an idea, she must first stand at a distance and scrutinize its merits on her own. Much like when considering a new suit or dress, one carefully tries on each competing "answer" until the one is found that best fits. Only then is it "bought" and taken home. This person's faith is in no way inferior to the faith of the individual who "just believes." In fact, in the years that lie ahead, it may actually prove to be more strongly rooted because of the fact that it dared to test its foundation and proved to its own satisfaction that the foundation is true.

September 5, 1993

Weekday Problems

Angela is a young Christian mother. She has been quite attentive to what she perceives to be her responsibility to her two children, Tabitha and Matthew. She has nurtured them carefully throughout their preschool years. Prayer is something they learned even before they could talk, because Angela prayed with them. She sang to them in their crib. She read to them regularly from the great stories of the Bible. Church and Sunday School have always been regular weekly events—experiences in which Tabitha and Matthew have delighted.

However, it is now time for Tabitha to start to school. Angela has heard many frightening stories about the public school system, including its secular curriculum that leaves out God. There is no Christian school nearby, at least none that Angela trusts to be academically strong enough. She does not believe she is a candidate for home-schooling, although she knows some parents who have done that very successfully.

*What should Angela do? How can she protect Tabitha from what she has heard to be "brainwashing tactics of secular humanism"?

*What are some ways Angela's church could help? If starting a Christian school is not feasible at this time, what other methods of support can her church contribute?

*Are Angela's fears reasonable or merely the product of hysterical gossip? How can Angela find out what is true? How can she put her mind to rest regarding her decision?

Sparkles

LIGHT - This is a key word in Scripture. Light cleanses, illumines, heals. In the days of scripture there were no electric lights, not even flashlights. Often the only light for a journey on a dark night was a saucer shaped bowl containing a little oil with a lighted wick laying in the oil. Such a light gave only enough illumination for the next step into the darkness that surrounded the traveler. God's Word is such a light. He gives us enough light for our next step of faith. When that step is taken then we will see where to plant our foot for the next task. This way we won't hurry and we won't try to run ahead of God who knows what we need better than we know ourselves.

This Lesson in Your Life

GOD IS THE GIVER OF ALL

Any careful observation of life will show that we cycle in and out of economic recession. Never-endingly, there seem to come alternating periods of plenty and want. The times of plenty always seem to be briefer than those of want. Nevertheless we do cycle from one to the other.

Of course, "lean years" are almost always more taxing to our faith than "fat years." As we are forced to tighten our belts and to look for other sources of revenue, we are compelled also to think more carefully about what we have and what we need. Unscheduled sickness or unemployment can very quickly clean out whatever we might have stored away during those times of plenty. Once our storehouse is empty, then we begin to look beyond ourselves for rescue and supply. If that help is slow in coming, the true strength or fragility of our faith begins to show.

The bill collectors come. At first, they send nice notes reminding us that our account is overdue, notes with a much more stern message appear. Then, threats pound on the door of our security and self-sufficiency. Phone calls haunt day and night, threatening to take away the car, turn off the electricity, and to repossess the house. Where will the money come from to fill our need? A good name and a strong credit that once could have borrowed as much as was needed is now found to be worthless. When it was available it was not needed. Now that it is needed, it is no longer available. If one cannot go to his neighborhood banker for help, then to whom can he go?

Fortunately, there is an answer. Even though He may not rescue us from this immediate crisis *immediately,* our God will be there. He who brought light out of darkness can be counted on to give light to my present darkness. He who caused the barren earth to bring forth grass and fruit trees yielding fruit can cause a bountiful harvest to spring forth from the current desert of my life.

The question is not whether God *can* do these things, or even *whether* The will. The question is *how* He will do them and *what exactly* He will choose to produce. Will he place a greater priority on what he brings out of my emptiness for me or on what he uses that emptiness to produce within me? Which is more barren, my pantry shelves or the shelves of my heart? Which is more fragile, my consumer credit or my God-reliant trust?

These beginning verses ought never to be packed away in moth balls or even banished to "the children's department" of our church curriculum. These verses echo the words and truths that serve as the life-blood of faith.

During those times when it seems that life blows all the dark clouds of the universe into our personal world, these verses assure us that God created all and remains in control. His throne is not a visible one that I can go to see. But, it is no less real. Even amidst all the disorder and chaos of my broken life, the order of God's creation stands firm and predictable. It testifies endlessly to His own order and sovereignty that I so easily forget.

Most comfortingly, these verses speak to us during those painful nights when we toss and turn, haunted by our day's brokenness and failures. They remind us of our worth and of our inherent goodness by relating to us again that *God Himself* created us and declared us to be "good." All of my mistakes and failures may scream incessantly into my ears telling me that I am nothing. Even my own conscience may condemn me. But the light whisper of God is greater than all of these voices together. He speaks quietly from the opening verses of the Bible and tells me that I am the product of His hand.

Seed Thoughts

1. What was the origin of the universe from which God made the heavens and the earth?
The words, "God created the heaven and the earth," are general and inclusive in nature. In other words, "God created the universe."

2. Is it true that at first the earth was a dry and empty desert that contained no life?
No. The Bible says that "the Spirit of God moved upon the face of the waters." So, though lifeless, it was not at all dry.

3. Which did God create first "light" or "the sun" that is the source of our light?
God created light before he created the sun that serves as our immediate and primary light source.

4. What theological truth can we draw from this light-sun order of creation?
Without light there is no life, but the sun is not our primary light. Unlike ancient pagans, we do not worship the sun, but our God who provided light before there was a sun.

5. Which did God create first— land animals or sea animals?
God created sea animals before He created animals that live on the land.

(PLEASE TURN PAGE)

---

1. What was the origin of the universe from which God made the heavens and the earth?

2. Is it true that at first the earth was a dry and empty desert that contained no life?

3. Which did God create first "light" or "the sun" that is the source of our light?

4. What theological truth can we draw from this light-sun order of creation?

5. Which did God create first— land animals or sea animals?

6. Is it true that consistently the days of creation were measured from morning to evening

7. On what day did God separate the seas from the dry land?

8. What command did God give to the fish and fowl following his creation of them?

9. What evaluation did God make after each creation day?

10. What scientific observation can be made about the creation account of Genesis 1?

(SEED THOUGHTS--Cont'd)

The words, "God created the heaven and the earth," are general and inclusive in nature. In other words, "God created the universe."

No. The Bible says that "the Spirit of God moved upon the face of the waters." So, though lifeless, it was not at all dry.

God created light before he created the sun that serves as our immediate and primary light source.

Without light there is no life, but the sun is not our primary light. Unlike ancient pagans, we do not worship the sun, but our God who provided light before there was a sun.

God created sea animals before He created animals that live on the land.

No. The days of creation were measured from evening to morning.

The Bible says that God let the dry land appear on the third day of creation.

God commanded the fish to "be fruitful and multiply, and fill the waters in the seas," and to the fowl he instructed, "let the fowl multiply in the earth."

After each day of creation our God looked at His handiwork and "saw that it was good."

It can be noted that the Genesis 1 account is consistent with the known scientific information regarding the basic food chain and with the basic scientific account of origins.

6. Is it true that consistently the days of creation were measured from morning to evening
No. The days of creation were measured from evening to morning.

7. On what day did God separate the seas from the dry land?
The Bible says that God let the dry land appear on the third day of creation.

8. What command did God give to the fish and fowl following his creation of them?
God commanded the fish to "be fruitful and multiply, and fill the waters in the seas," and to the fowl he instructed, "let the fowl multiply in the earth."

9. What evaluation did God make after each creation day?
After each day of creation our God looked at His handiwork and "saw that it was good."

10. What scientific observation can be made about the creation account of Genesis 1?
It can be noted that the Genesis 1 account is consistent with the known scientific information regarding the basic food chain and with the basic scientific account of origins.

September 12, 1993

The Origin of Humankind

Genesis 1:26-28
26 And God said, Let us make man in our image after our likeness: and let them have dominion over the fish of the sea, and over the fowl of the air, and over the cattle, and over all the earth, and over every creeping thing that creepeth upon the earth.
27 So God created man in his *own* image, in the image of God created he him; male and female created he them.
28 And God blessed them, and God said unto them, Be fruitful, and multiply, and replenish the earth, and subdue it: and have dominion over the fish of the sea, and over the fowl of the air, and over every living thing that moveth upon the earth.

Genesis 2:18-25
18 And the Lord God said, *It is* not good that the man should be alone; I will make him an help meet for him.
19 And out of the ground the Lord God formed every beast of the field, and every fowl of the air; and brought *them* unto Adam to see what he would call them: and whatsoever Adam called every living creature, that *was* the name thereof.
20 And Adam gave names to all cattle, and to the fowl of the air, and to every beast of the field; but for Adam there was not found an help meet for him.
21 And the *Lord* God caused a deep sleep to fall upon Adam, and he slept: and he took one of his ribs, and closed up the flesh instead thereof;
22. And the rib, which the Lord God had taken from man, made he a woman, and brought her unto the man.
23 And Adam said, This *is* now bone of my bones, and flesh of my flesh: she shall be called Woman, because she was taken out of Man.
24 Therefore shall a man leave his father and his mother, and shall cleave unto his wife: and they shall be one flesh.
25 And they were both naked, the man and his wife, and were not ashamed.

◀ **Memory Selection**
Genesis 1:27

◀ **Devotional Reading**
Psalm 8:3-9

◀ **Background Scripture**
Genesis 1:26-31; 2:4-9, 15-25

◀ **Printed Scripture**
Genesis 1:26-28, 2:18-25

THE ORIGIN OF HUMANKIND

Teacher's Target

People often get confused about what it means to be created in God's image. Other scriptures point out our difference from God. List ways mankind is like God and ways we are different from Him. Notice in the text that neither man nor woman is created more in the image of God than the other. Discuss with the class why it takes both male and female to express the full image of God in human form. How can men and women enhance each other's expression of God's image? What ways have we learned from culture to depreciate each other?

Dominion is given to humans. What is the difference between having dominion and dominating?

Leaving home is difficult for some youth. How can parents facilitate this launching? How can the church family assist? How can the church family strengthen young couples?

Lesson Introduction

Scripture tells us God is Spirit (John 4:24). When the Bible speaks of His reaching out His hand or walking upon the earth, it is speaking anthropomorphically. This big word means using human analogies to communicate truth about God. Then we can make a connection between the visible and invisible. God does not have a body like ours since He is Spirit, but He is intelligent (has order), emotional (has feelings) and will (has a purposeful direction to His actions). Created in the image of God, humans have intellect, emotion and will.

Adam and Eve did not consider being human good enough. Out of this inferiority they grasped for control of their fate. They rebelled and lost control of intellect, emotion, and will. In Christ, restoration of proper use of these begins.

Teaching Outline

I. Humankind Created: Gen. 1:26
   A. God's Image: 26
   B. Humankind's Dominion: 26
II. Two Genders: Gen. 1:27; 2:18-25
   A. Male: 1:27; 2:18-20
   B. Female: 27; 2:21-25
III. God's Blessing: Gen. 1:28
   A. Be Fruitful: 28
   B. Replenish: 28
   C. Subdue: 28

Daily Bible Readings

Mon. Human Beings Created In God's Image
Gen. 1:26-31
Tue. God Breathed Life Into Man
Gen. 2:1-9
Wed. Man Not Made To Be Alone
Gen. 2:15-20
Thurs. God Created Woman
Gen. 2:21-25
Fri. Remember: Extol God's Work
Job 36:22-33
Sat. God Accomplished All Things
Job 37:1-13
Sun. God: Superior to Every Person
Job 38:1-11

September 12, 1993

VERSE BY VERSE

I. **Humankind Created: Gen. 1:26**

A. **God's Image: 26**

26. And God said, Let us make man in our image, after our likeness:

Human life has often been seen from a rather low vantage point in the latter half of this century. One has even said that humans are a walking sewer system with rather poor plumbing. Scripture has a loftier view of human beings. God is the author of our existence and nothing He creates is without a touch of His splendor. In the case of humans, the Scripture declares we are the only beings created in God's own image. In another place Scripture says we are only slightly lower than the angels (Ps. 8:5).

The viewpoint at which you begin your examination of mankind makes a great deal of difference in how you value yourself and others. Being created in God's image, having intellect, emotion and will, is a position of privilege and responsibility. In response to God's loving call we will either act in constructive and life respecting ways, or be the most destructive beings of all God's created order. It is here on the sixth day of God's creating that we can best learn about ourselves. it is good that God held off in His process of creating until the last to create man. In this way we could not in any way fool ourselves that we had any hand in the creative process. This should allow us to humble ourselves before our Creator. On the other hand, to be endowed with such splendor as to be created in His very image, should give us our sense of worth. The very way the Scripture introduces the creation of humankind seems to indicate an affectionate relationship established by God with us. This is not true to the same degree of the rest of creation. Before the creation of all other life it is recorded that God said "Let there be," but with humans the text reads "Let us make." The God-human relationship is special. Proverbs 8:31 may lend support to this. God is speaking and says, "My delights were with the sons of men." It is as if God said, "The supporting cast has been established and the stage set, now let us place the leading actors upon the scene."

Man was not made in the likeness of any animal but rather in the likeness of God. This is why it is so tragic that we have fallen from our lofty beginning and become more out of sync than any other part of the created order.

B. **Humankind's Dominion: 26**

26. and let them have dominion over the fish of the sea, and over the fowl of the air, and over the cattle, and over all the earth, and over every creeping thing that creepeth upon the earth.

How gracious is our God toward us. We neither thought up nor created a single thing in creation, yet our Father has given us charge over all He made. He has honored us and still we have not believed it to be enough. Blind to His generosity and honor of us, we either cringe in fear of our Maker or strike out on our own as if

13

we did not need Him at all.

Because of the Fall of mankind our dominion has often turned into domination. Having lost much of our understanding of how to be co-creators under God's guidance, we have raped and pillaged that which was entrusted to our care. Regaining respect for the good earth is necessary for our survival. This will take an acknowledgement of our littleness and need of guidance as well as our recognition of the greatness bestowed upon us by God. A "humbled grandeur" seems appropriate.

II. Two Genders: Gen. 1:27; 2:18-25

A. Male: 1:27; 2:18-20

27. So God created man in his own image, in the image of God created he him; male and female created he them.
18. And the Lord God said, It is not good that the man should be alone; I will make him an help meet for him.
19. And out of the ground the Lord God formed every beast of the field, and every fowl of the air; and brought them unto Adam to see what he would call them: and whatsoever Adam called every living creature, that was the name thereof.
20. And Adam gave names to all cattle and to the fowl of the air, and to every beast of the field; but for Adam there was not found an help meet for him.

Out of the earth God formed man. In this verse our connection with the earth is established. Many in our day have insisted that we are losing our souls because in our technological grandiosity we have lost touch with nature's rhythm. Artists are painting pictures of our cities without any signs of life in them. This is not because they are enamored with the architecture but to make a statement about the death that has settled upon the city dweller.

Man was made as the glory of the Father (1 Cor. 11:7), but he was not sufficient alone. Out of man's side the woman was created. This established that they were of one blood. Woman was to be man's glory (1 Cor. 11: 7).

B. Female: 1:27; 2:21-25

27. So God created man in his own image, in the image of God created he him; male and female created he them.
21. And the Lord God caused a deep sleep to fall upon Adam, and he slept: and he took one of his ribs, and closed up the flesh instead thereof:
22. And the rib, which the Lord God had taken from man, made he a woman, and brought her unto the man.
23. And Adam said, This is now bone of my bones, and flesh of my flesh: she shall be called Woman, because she was taken out of man.
24. Therefore shall a man leave his father and his mother, and shall cleave unto his wife: and they shall be one flesh.
25. And they were both naked, the man and his wife, and were not ashamed.

There was no suitable mate for man in the animal kingdom. Having created woman out of the side of man, God intended a deep love to be established between the two as she was bone of his bone and flesh of his flesh. God gloried in what He had created and ordained that man was to glory in woman (1 Cor. 11:7). This did not mean to worship her nor was she to worship man. Rather, as God had bestowed honor upon man, so man was to delight in, cherish, honor and cleave to woman as his equal whose gifts from the Father were as valuable and necessary as any bestowed upon man. Such love was to create a response of love. The Fall and the resulting war between the sexes has produced competition between, not complementing of, each other's attributes. Only in Christ can there be established the harmony of relationship God intended from the beginning. In Christ the distinction and distrusts of male and female are dissolved.

Also it is worth noting that whereas animals for the most part (wolves and cardinals being two exceptions) may have many mates, God intended one for man and woman for life. Breaking a union between two in marriage cannot be done lightly and always there is great pain.

III. God's Blessing: Gen. 1:28

A. Be Fruitful: 28

28. And God blessed them, and God said unto them, Be fruitful and multiply, and replenish the earth, and subdue it: and have dominion over the fish of the sea, and over the fowl of the air, and over every living thing that moveth upon the earth.

"Be fruitful" is more than just having children. Anyone without physical limitations can be a paternal or maternal parent. But fathering and mothering take time, surrender of self, energy and discipline to bestow a heritage of love and values upon children.

B. Replenish: 28

28. And as God Blessed them, and God said unto them, Be fruitful, and multiply, and replenish the earth, and subdue it: and have dominion over the fish of the sea, and over the fowl of the air, and over every living thing that moveth upon the earth.

"Replenish" has not only the character of multiplying in numbers but restoring, putting back into the creation those characteristics and values that enliven and enrich life. It is much like restoring the nutrients to the soil for future use and covering the fallow ground with a cover crop to prevent erosion.

C. Subdue: 28

28. And as God blessed them, and God said unto them, Be fruitful, and multiply, and replenish the earth, and subdue it: and have dominion over the fish of the sea, and over the fowl of the air, and over every living thing that moveth upon the earth.

"Subdue" does not mean crush or ravage in this context. There is no trampling under foot intended. What God intended was for humans to use their intelligence under His sovereignty to manage and order all that was inferior to him for the best possible fruitfulness and welfare of all creation.

Evangelistic Emphasis

It is not without cause that a high percentage of our people suffer from "a poor self-image." Quite predictably, a small child will come to doubt his worth if he is reminded repeatedly that he "was an accident." This problem is further compounded if indication is given that there was no subsequent anticipation of his arrival or delight once he had arrived.

As individuals we need to be needed. We need to see our lives as purposeful and productive of good. This is true not only for the believer but for the unbeliever, as well. One of the most powerful messages the doubting heart can hear is one that affirms his worth and value. Though self-help programs and psychology might have *something* to contribute to this need, they have little of substance to offer to the heartbeat of the problem.

The message is not only psychologically sound and spiritually right; it also taps at the deepest yearnings of the heart. We are driven, every one of us, to search compulsively for that which will fill the void in our souls. Far from being a liability in the cause of evangelism, the message of the creation of humanity is one of our richest assets. It tells us, one and all, that we are created in the image of God and were given dominion as rulers of God's great universe. Far from being an "afterthought" of His creative process, we were the crowning glory of it all. To humanity God gave the mantle of responsibility. To us all He assigned the scepter of commanding rule.

Memory Selection

God created man in His own image, in the image of God he created him; male and female he created them. *Genesis 1:27*

Was only the man created in the image of God, or the woman also? That may sound like a foolish question to those of us who reside in the late twentieth century, but there was a time when clergymen were not sure. Always, we struggle against the tide of the culture around us. Sometimes, it's difficult to know what ideas are those of our own mind and study and what are simply the echoes of the masses outside. Filtered through the polluted screens of pagan sexisms, even passages as clear as this one become blurred.

Yes. An emphatic yes! Woman was created in the image of God also. It has never been our gender that separated us from God. It has been our sin. Both male and female, we carry within our essence the very image of God. It is that divine origin that blesses us with inherent value. It is that truth that blesses us with the hope of possibly being redeemed.

September 12, 1993

Weekday Problems

Bert and Becky are young adults of the nineties. They bear all the marks common to their peers. "Home" incites mixed images for both of them. Bert's parents divorced when he was ten. He remembers quite keenly how upset he was at the time. Eventually, though, he adjusted to the fact that Dad was gone from his life (except for every other weekend) and that someone named "Bill" had come to take his place.

For Becky life was not so clearly delineated. Her parents never did "split up." They just never seemed ever to get it together. Life for them was an ongoing feud about nothing in particular. Now, as an adult, Becky finds the whole image of "marriage" pocked with the haunting scars of her painful past.

Both Becky and Bert find themselves trapped between their love for each other and their nagging fears of marriage. There is nothing they want more than a loving, nurturing home, and nothing they fear more than duplicating the misery of their parents. Though they are both believers, the increasingly popular lifestyle of "just living together" entices them.

*Certainly, many in our contemporary society see marriage as an archaic human institution which fails to meet the needs of modern humanity. They point to the escalating divorce rate as evidence of their position. Bert and Becky find themselves to be drawn to the "reasonableness" of this argument. Are they correct? Why or why not?

*How can the church use this text to provide foundational instruction for struggles such as are presently threatening Becky and Bert?

*What other measures can the church take to better equip families to deal with the stresses and social pressures of the mid-nineties?

Say It Right

Pison: Pie-sun

Havila: Have-i-lah

Gihon: Ge-hon

Ethiopia: Ee-thee-o-pee-ah

Hiddekel: Hid-duh-kel

Euphrates: U-fray-tees

This Lesson In Your Life
BREAKING AWAY

Jonathan was the pastor for a small church in Minneapolis. Not having a professional music staff, he relied completely on volunteers to lead the singing of worship. One Sunday morning he was finishing a four-lesson sermon series on Love. He had communicated with Randall, the young Law student who was to lead the singing that morning. He had given Randall both his sermon text and his theme title. This last sermon was addressing the subject, "Parental Love." The very last point of the sermon was an affirmation about parental love that, "Love Must Let Go."

As the congregation began the response song following the sermon, ripples of chuckles passed rapidly throughout the room. The song that had been chosen was none other than, "O Love That Will Not Let Me Go."

In spite of this pastor's very embarrassing moment, his affirmation is quite correct. If parents truly love their children, they must grow in their own maturity as parents to a point where they can gracefully let go.

No. I am not speaking of abandonment. I'm not suggesting that children be forsaken to drown in a sea of confusion and worldly pressures. However, I am asserting that if children are to develop and mature in a healthy way, their parents must learn to let them--encourage them--to "fly."

Usually, this is not something that happens all at once. Leaving father and mother begins before a toddler has ever gotten out of diapers. S/he cannot do everything alone, yet. But, the demand, "I want to do it all by myself!" comes before the words can even be spoken. Some children begin stretching the apron strings at birth. Other children must have the strings cut for them with the insistence that they venture out on their own.

Parents must neither be threatened by the independent child, nor timid with the reluctant one. It is only by the child's "breaking away" that maturity comes.

The writer of Genesis tells us in clear terms that God intended from the beginning that we mature and break away from the womb that gave us birth. According to His design, unless the home provides for this kind of alteration, the homes that would be formed cannot form.

Even within Christian families, this can be a struggle. Often a "leaving" never takes place, or if it does, it comes so late in the life of the "child" that a "cleaving" is unlikely, if not impossible. For others, there is a leaving of the homefires, but because of the turmoil accompanying the child's departure, there resides little or no security to blanket any newly-forming home.

Whose problem is it? Is the problem a product of the child's immaturity and unwillingness to grow into adulthood with appropriate responsibilities? Or is the problem the parents' immaturity and unwillingness to equip the child to be independent and separate from the parents' control?

Whichever it is, Genesis 2 makes it clear that if humanity is to function as God designed it, then family love must yield to the reality of severance so as to reproduce itself in the generations to come.

Christians talk a lot about "the breakdown of the family" and about "the humanist conspiracy against the home." But is it possible that the greatest threat to the family's future does not lie without the home, at all, but within. Is it possible that our fear of losing what is precious to us has caused us "overly to protect" it. Rather than *in faith* investing our love for our child in the unknown soil of the future, we've chosen *in fear* to hold on to that love, burying it in the tomb of our own "loving arms."

Seed Thoughts

1. **Has mankind fulfilled God's command to replenish the earth and subdue it?**
   This is about the only command that humanity has kept consistently.

2. **What was meant by the expression, "a help meet for him"?**
   "Help meet" is an archaic expression for "help suitable." The text is telling the reader that God made a mate that was suitable to the companionship needs of the man, Adam.

3. **What was to happen if Adam and Eve ate from the tree of knowledge of good and evil?**
   They were to die, for God said to Adam, "in the day that thou eatest thereof thou shalt surely die."

4. **What kind of death would Adam and Eve face if they disobeyed God?**
   At this point in the account, that is not clear. But, it becomes clear that they faced two kinds of death: (1) Spiritual death, immediately, and (2) Physical death, eventually.

5. **What was Adam to do in the garden?**
   The Bible says that it was Adam's responsibility to dress it and keep it.

(PLEASE TURN PAGE)

---

1. Has mankind fulfilled God's command to replenish the earth and subdue it?

2. What was meant by the expression, "a help meet for him"?

3. What was to happen if Adam and Eve ate from the tree of knowledge of good and evil?

4. What kind of death would Adam and Eve face if they disobeyed God?

5. What was Adam to do in the garden?

6. Why did God create man?

7. How did God create both a man and a woman "in his image"?

8. What did God put in the garden that He created?

9. Where do theologians think the Garden of Eden was located?

10. Why should a man leave his father and mother?

(SEED THOUGHTS--Cont'd)

This is about the only command that humanity has kept consistently.

"Help meet" is an archaic expression for "help suitable." The text is telling the reader that God made a mate that was suitable to the companionship needs of the man, Adam.

They were to die, for God said to Adam, "in the day that thou eatest thereof thou shalt surely die."

At this point in the account, that is not clear. But, it becomes clear that they faced two kinds of death: (1) Spiritual death, immediately, and (2) Physical death, eventually.

The Bible says that it was Adam's responsibility to dress it and keep it.

Genesis 2:5 seems to indicate that at least one of the reasons that God created man was to take care of his creation (i.e., "to till the ground").

Humanity is essentially neither male nor female. Humanity may be either, therefore the sex of a person is a secondary trait rather than a primary one.

God placed in the garden man, all kinds of fruit-bearing trees, the tree of life, the tree of knowledge of good and evil, creatures of all sorts and a river.

Usually the location of the Garden of Eden is estimated by referencing the rivers mentioned in the text.

The Bible says that a man is to leave his father and his mother in order to pursue a "one flesh" relationship with a wife.

6. Why did God create man?
Genesis 2:5 seems to indicate that at least one of the reasons that God created man was to take care of his creation (i.e., "to till the ground").

7. How did God create both a man and a woman "in his image"?
Humanity is essentially neither male nor female. Humanity may be either, therefore the sex of a person is a secondary trait rather than a primary one.

8. What did God put in the garden that He created?
God placed in the garden man, all kinds of fruit-bearing trees, the tree of life, the tree of knowledge of good and evil, creatures of all sorts and a river.

9. Where do theologians think the Garden of Eden was located?
Usually the location of the Garden of Eden is estimated by referencing the rivers mentioned in the text.

10. Why should a man leave his father and mother?
The Bible says that a man is to leave his father and his mother in order to pursue a "one flesh" relationship with a wife.

September 19, 1993

The Origin of Sin

Genesis 3:1-13

3 NOW the serpent was more subtil than any beast of the field which the LORD God had made. And he said unto the woman, Yea, hath God said, Ye shall not eat of every tree of the garden?
2 And the woman said unto the serpent, We may eat of the fruit of the trees of the garden:
3 But of the fruit of the tree which *is* in the midst of the garden, God hath said, Ye shall not eat of it, neither shall ye touch it, lest Ye die.
4 And the serpent said unto the woman, Ye shall not surely die:
5 For God doth know that in the day ye eat thereof, then your eyes shall be opened, and ye shall be as gods, knowing good and evil.
6 And when the woman saw that the tree *was* good for food, and that it *was* pleasant to the eyes, and a tree to be desired to make *one* wise, she took of the fruit thereof, and did eat, and gave also unto her husband with her, and he did eat.

7 And the eyes of them both were opened, and they knew that they *were* naked; and they sewed fig leaves together, and made themselves aprons.
8 And they heard the voice of the LORD God walking in the garden in the cool of the day: and Adam and his wife hid themselves from the presence of the LORD God amongst the trees of the garden.
9 And the LORD God called unto Adam, and said unto him, Where *art* thou?
10 And he said, I heard thy voice in the garden, and I was afraid, because I *was* naked; and I hid myself.
11 And he said, Who told thee that thou *wast* naked? Hast thou eaten of the tree, whereof I commanded thee that thou shouldest not eat?
12 And the man said, The woman whom thou gavest *to be* with me, she gave me of the tree, and I did eat.
13 And the LORD God said unto the woman, What *is* this *that* thou hast done? And the woman said, The serpent beguiled me, and I did eat.

◀ **Memory Selection**
Genesis 3:4-5

◀ **Devotional Reading**
Psalm 51:1-4, 6, 9-17

◀ **Background Scripture**
Genesis 3:1-13

◀ **Printed Scripture**
Genesis 3:1-13

THE ORIGIN OF SIN

Teacher's Target

This passage explains mankind's present circumstances in the world. Human nature's split between good and evil finds its origin here. Ask the class who said God didn't want Adam and Eve to know good and evil? Jesus knew good and evil. He was tempted but did not sin. Could humans have known good and evil more clearly, as Jesus did, had they listened only to God's instructions? Were God's instructions for the protection of His creation? Do we need boundaries?

List ways in which Jesus is like Adam and ways He is not (see Rom. 5:12-21, 1 Cor. 15:45-50). Notice that Jesus believed being human under the Father's guidance was good enough (Phil. 2:5-11). Adam believed human to be inferior. Is sin's root inferiority? Is rebellion the result?

Lesson Introduction

God knows us better than we know ourselves. He wanted Adam and Eve to enjoy the creation. God wanted life to be creative play. Wonder and awe would result. He knew what and when knowledge could be assimilated. God's timing and discretion would provide what was needed when it was needed.

Satan had another agenda. He determined to raise doubt, create discouragement, throw up a diversion, generate defeat and manifest delay. Doubt often questions God's goodness. Discouragement focuses us on a problem rather than provision. Blindsided by diversions the wrong things become attractive. A defeated spirit asks, "Why try?" Delay is interpreted as never. We lose motivation.

Jesus showed us the solution. Go to the Father with all things. Adam did not. He acted on his own. What if Adam had taken the temptation to God?

◆◆◆◆◆◆

Teaching Outline

I. Eve Deceived: Gen. 3:1-5
   A. The Serpent's Question: 1
   B. Eve's Response: 2-3
   C. The Serpent's Twist: 4-5
II. Adam and Eve's Sin: Gen. 3:6-7
   A. Eve Misled: 6
   B. Adam Succumbs: 6
   C. Shame Results: 7
III. God Approaches: Gen. 3:8-13
   A. God Comes: 8
   B. God Calls and Confronts: 9,11
   C. Adam and Eve Blush and Blame: 10, 12, 13

Daily Bible Readings

Mon. Temptations in the Garden
Gen. 3:1-6
Tue. God Seeks the Sinners
Gen. 3:7-11
Wed. Sinners Blame One Another
Gen. 3:12-13; Ps. 139:1-12
Thurs. Punishment for All
Gen. 3:14-19
Fri. How to Love God
Deut. 6:4-14a
Sat. Commit You Way to the Lord
Ps. 37:3-9; 27-31
Sun. Walk in God's Way
Ps. 119:1-8

September 19, 1993

VERSE BY VERSE

I. Eve Deceived: Gen. 3:1-5

A. The Serpent's Question: 1

1. Now the serpent was more subtil than any beast of the field which the Lord God had made. And he said unto the woman, Yea hath God said, Ye shall not eat of every tree of the garden?

Another word for subtle is crafty. The serpent began his strategy by getting Eve to doubt God's goodness. He pictured God as a master too strict, too stingy and too selfish. Eve's sight got focused only on what she didn't have. God's generosity and abundance were missed. The serpent had no "theology of enough," only an overreaching covetousness.

B. Eve's Response: 2-3

2. And the woman said unto the serpent, We may eat of the fruit of the trees of the garden:
3. But of the fruit of the tree which is in the midst of the garden, God hath said, Ye shall not eat of it neither shall ye touch it, lest ye die.

Eve began well with her answer. She stated the word of God clearly. Evidently she had not incorporated it into her being. By whose authority did the serpent speak? Eve didn't check with God or her mate. Her contentment was undermined and she acted impulsively. Unilateral decisions alienate us from God and significant others in our lives.

C. The Serpent's Twist: 4-5

4. And the serpent said unto the woman, Ye shall not surely die:
5. For God doth know that in the day ye eat thereof, then your eyes shall be opened, and ye shall be as gods, knowing good and evil.

Lies and half truths are the evil one's stock in trade. Hear the serpent. The lie: "You will not die." True, physical death did not come immediately, but spiritual death did. The half truth: God did not want mankind to become like Him.

The sincere motive of becoming like God is good. The serpent used this good motive against Eve. Becoming like God is not becoming Him.

Knowledge of good and evil is desirable too. But to leave God out is to become our own god. We get a distorted view of good and evil by doing evil. only Jesus rightly discerned between the two. He learned from God and doing good. Obeying our Heavenly Father we become like Him.

II. Adam and Eve's Sin: Gen. 3:6-7

A. Eve Misled: 6

6. And when the woman saw that the tree was good for food, and that it was pleasant to the eyes, and a tree to be desired to make one wise, she took of the fruit thereof, and did eat.

Where is your focus? Eve looked at the tree. Here the battle was lost. She focused on the earthly plane rather than the spiritual. We need God more than food. Jesus taught us this in His experience of temptation (Matt. 4:4 and Luke 4:4). Often, the temptation is to choose second best when the best is available.

Temptation will come (1 Cor. 10:13). If temptation is not fled (2 Tim. 2:22), it will spread. We are not islands unto ourselves. Sadly, the ones most affected by our sin are those most dear to us.

Eve involved Adam. Ironically, Adam, at Eve's invitation, transgressed the boundary He had taught her not to cross. Misery loves company. Maybe we think if enough of us do it, it won't be wrong anymore.

B. Adam Succumbs: 6

And when the woman saw that the tree was good for food, and that it was pleasant to the eyes, and a tree to be desired to make one wise, she took of the fruit thereof, and did eat, and gave also unto her husband with her; and he did eat.

Adam was told the boundaries of the garden before Eve was created. But when she came to him with the fruit of the tree, he forgot his source of life and acted on his own. Eve took the issue to her source. She had come out of the side of Adam and he had told her the rules. But Adam acted without regard for his creator.

The fate of creation was on the line. Adam showed off for Eve. He could have humbled himself in front of his mate and before God. He could have modeled need of the Father's guidance.

Physical strength is not the greatest strength. Jesus knew this. He did not hesitate in showing His need of the Father (John 5:19,30). He knew He could do nothing unless the Father gave it to Him to do. Pilate and Caiaphas, the high priest, had physical strength on their side. Jesus relied upon spiritual strength. Jesus has been shown to be strong. How different things might have been had Adam sought strength in God.

C. Shame Results: 7

7. And the eyes of them both were opened, and they knew that they were naked; and they sewed fig leaves together, and made themselves aprons.

We are prone to talk about guilt in regard to man's condition. But Scripture here and also in Paul's teaching seems to focus on human shame and helplessness. God is not nearly so concerned to point out our guilt as He is to make us aware of our helplessness and need of Him. Shame overcame Adam and Eve. They no longer felt adequate.

Physically nothing had changed. They still had their health, their minds and their physical strength. But their sense of being good enough was gone. Shame replaced security. Shame says, "Something is wrong with me." Guilt follows shame like a shadow and says, "Something is wrong with my actions." Such shame-based living causes us to rebel.

III. God Approaches:
    Gen. 3:8-13

A. God Comes: 8

8. And they heard the voice of the Lord God walking in the garden in the cool of the day: and Adam and his wife hid themselves from the presence of the Lord God amongst the trees of the garden.

Hiding is useless when it comes to spiritual matters. We can't escape God's gaze. Also, we have to take ourselves with us wherever we go. We know our undoneness. Hiding from God is like covering our eyes and believing that because we can't see, no one can see us. Confession is what cleanses us and puts us in the light (1 John 1:7-10).

B. God Calls and Confronts: 9, 11

9. And the Lord God called unto Adam, and said unto him, Where art thou?
11. And he said, Who told thee that thou wast naked? Hast thou eaten of the tree, whereof I commanded thee that thou shouldest not eat?

God wants fellowship with us. He longs to be with us. our shame causes us to fear fellowship with Him. Adam and Eve had moved. God had not. God asks, "Where art thou?" "The question is not about location. What is severed is spiritual connection. God is asking "Where are you in relation to Me and to yourself?" God is sensitive to the slightest movement by us away from Him. He is jealous to restore the relationship and bring about reconciliation. He confronts not to further alienate but to allow us to confess our need and be reconciled to Him. He is always reconciled to us. Jesus Christ has, by way of the cross, removed the curse and opened the way for us to return to the Father. This is unconditional love that offers total forgiveness for our faults.

C. Adam and Eve Blush and Blame: 10, 12, 13

10. And he said, I heard thy voice in the garden, and I was afraid, because I was naked and I hid myself.
12. And the man said, The woman whom thou gavest to me, she gave me of the tree and I did eat.
13. And the Lord God said unto the woman, What is this that thou hast done? And the woman said, The serpent beguiled me, and I did eat.

Avoiding responsibility for our own actions and blaming others is how fallen man deals with evil. So much for the serpent's prediction that we would become like God. Adam blamed Eve, even though he taught her the rules and knew them well. When it comes to temptation no one can lead us where we don't already want to go. Eve blamed the serpent, though she had been taught the rules by Adam. The book of James is quite clear. "Every man is tempted, when he is drawn away of his own lust and enticed; then when lust hast conceived it bringeth forth sin; and sin, when it is finished, bringeth forth death" (James 1:14,15).

THE ORIGIN OF SIN

Evangelistic Emphasis

Those who received their primary education a generation ago at Barrackville Elementary School, were blessed by the gifted and caring tutelage of "Mrs. Kyle." She was always creative with her instruction and impressively thorough. It was obvious to each of her students that she cared deeply about his growth. Her concern was not limited to the assigned curriculum. Most of her students had lived all of their lives in this small West Virginia mining town, as had their parents and grandparents before them. But, Mrs. Kyle brought to her sixth grade classroom the adventures of the world. Through carefully chosen books to be read for extra credit, occasional films, and challenging projects, Mrs. Kyle stretched the horizons of the young minds in her charge far beyond that small town encompassed by hills.

It was normal to begin the school day with the "pledge of allegiance," a reading from the Bible and prayer. Often, Mrs. Kyle would ask one of the boys to word the prayer. sometimes, she led it herself. When she prayed, there was one phrase that was always included. "Thank you, Lord, for our troubles as well as for our blessings," she prayed. "For without the troubles we would be unable to appreciate the blessings."

Much in that same spirit, it has been said that the Gospel must be "bad news" before it can be "good news." Before one can be receptive to the salvation of the Lord, he must first be aware of his need for it. Most assuredly, we must hear and be receptive to the message, "Jesus saves!" Yet, before we can receive that wonderful word, we must first hear that we are lost.

Memory Selection

The serpent said...God knows that when you eat of it your eyes will be opened, and you will be like God, knowing good and evil.
Genesis 3:4-5

It's strange, isn't it, that the first successful temptation, and the one that continues to nip at our heels, is the temptation to be "like God"? That is strange.

Don't you see, "to be like God" is the very goal of a Christian, or for that matter, the goal of anyone wishing to be identified with God. That's why we sometimes say about someone, "She's really a godly woman." We are testifying that she reflects God-like characteristics. We do not insult her by making such a remark. We honor her. Our great aspiration is to be like Him.

Yet, it was a cruel twist of this high aspiration that brought to an end the first paradise for man. Where we ought to seek God's humility and holiness and sacrificial love, we seek instead to equal His power and his rule. Perhaps, it's not so much that we want to be *like God* as it is that we want to *be gods*, ourselves.

September 19, 1993

Weekday Problems

Jean is an Area Sales Manager for a leading cosmetic firm. She has been with the company for more than twenty years. Her record both for sales growth and management success has been impressive. Numerous trophies decorate her office testifying to her exceptional success.

Recently, however, not everything has been so positive. Rather than increasing in sales, her area has shown a negative growth curve six months consecutively. Consequently, the home office has been leaning on her to turn things around. Her immediate supervisor, who is new to that position, has expressed the judgment that Jean is "incompetent" and "simply not proficient in the latest sales techniques" and "too old for the job."

Jean, on the other hand, doesn't know what to believe. A part of her blames her supervisor, who has dramatically changed a number of procedures. Also, the company has altered several of the products that her customers liked the best. And, the economy has been down, generally.

Being a Christian, and knowing how all-pervasive the temptation is to "pass the buck," Jean struggles with knowing how much is really "her fault" and how much of the blame lies elsewhere.

She truly does not want to ignore her rightful need for improvement. Yet, she has spent many late nights agonizing over this problem with little positive results.

*What can Jean do to help her know whether she is simply refusing to shoulder her rightful responsibility or whether she is being victimized by someone else who is doing that very thing?

*To what extent does our ability to see "the fault in others" blind us to our own fault?

*When negative things happen in our lives, is there always someone to be blamed?

Sparkles

The tree of life was in the Garden of Eden along with the tree of the knowledge of good and evil. These trees conveyed a reality in the spiritual realm. All is from God and in His timing. God's boundaries are always for our protection. When Adam and Eve had disobeyed, still God protected them. He stationed mighty angels with a flaming sword to prevent access to the tree of life. Why? Because God did not want us to remain in an eternal state of death. Had Adam and Eve eaten of the tree they would have lived eternally in a fallen state. In Scripture we do not find the tree of life in the midst of mankind again until Revelation 22. This is in the new heaven and the new earth after the resurrection.

This Lesson In Your Life

THE FIRST SIN

Billy was only in the first grade when he experienced his first sin. Oh, he had disobeyed his parents before that. Many times, beginning at about the age of three, he had gotten a spanking for straying out of the yard and into the nearby creek. He knew every time when his mother caught him that he would get another spanking because the creek was strictly off limits.

Yet, this time it was different, somehow. There was a consciousness of having done wrong that weighed heavily on him that had never burdened him at the creek. And, this time he hadn't even gotten caught.

Billy's sin was stealing pears on his way home from school one day. The pear tree, you see, was in the side yard of one of the houses that was adjacent to the school property. It was an old house that was much in disrepair. An elderly lady with snow white hair lived there. Most of the kids imagined her to be a witch. She was always coming out of the house waving her broom as she yelled for the kids to get away from her pears. Certainly, many of the school children had eaten them, and somehow the old woman's grouchiness and general "witchiness" made taking her pears seem OK.

For Billy it was not OK, though. From the moment he hurried away with that pear, he had a knot in his chest that wouldn't leave. He dreamed about it that night. It was not a pleasant dream. Nothing had changed when he awoke the next morning. His walk to school took him past the old house where the pear tree stood. His misdeed refreshed itself in his mind as if it had happened again.

For three long days and nights Billy anguished over his taking that pear. Finally, in a wave of tears he confessed to his mother what he had done. Then, with great fear and apprehension, but according to his mother's instruction, he knocked on the door of the old house and confessed to that woman, offering to pay for the pear.

To his surprise, she smiled and said, "That's OK. But, please just don't do it again." Somehow, she didn't look like a witch anymore, but more like an angel in an old lady's dress. Needless to say, he never stole a pear again.

It is not necessary for one to look closely to see the "Eve" in Billy. It stands out like a red flag blowing in the wind. True story though it is, it is only one of many such stories that could be told of "first sins." In truth, there is a little bit of Eve in every one of us. This text does not simply record for us a "fairy tale" that is remote from anything relevant to contemporary life. Rather, it records for us historical truth that is relived tangibly every day in the lives of God's children who stray.

Like Eve, we are susceptible to distorting voices that lure us away from God by altering the perception of reality in our minds. Somehow, it seems OK to deceive our boss who is "underpaying us" anyway. It seems acceptable to short-change the customer who "probably has more money than she will ever use." It seems justifiable to be unkind to those who appear to be so unkind, themselves. It seems reasonable for us to ignore the instructions of a God "whose primary goal is to take all of the excitement out of living and to find some reason to damn us in the end."

It wasn't so much that the serpent lied to Eve (though he did do that) as it was that he planted a seed of distrust in her mind. He skillfully altered ever so slightly the image she had of God. From a God who had gone to great lengths to protect her, he came to be perceived as a God who would go to all lengths to deprive her. From a God who created and gave everything, he came to be charged as the villain who wished to withhold the greatest prize of all. "Who really ought to care what such a god wanted, anyway?! That kind of god doesn't deserve either our obedience or our respect!"

Tragically, these are the same kinds of seeds of distrust that are still planted in the minds of men and women today. And, they grow and produce just as successfully as they did in the beginning.

Seed Thoughts

1. Where was the tree that was forbidden to Adam and Eve?
The Bible tells us that the tree of knowledge of good and evil was "in the midst of the garden."

2. Did the serpent lie or tell the truth when it said to Eve that she would not die?
The serpent lied when it told Eve that she would not die. Eve began her progression toward death that very day she ate of the fruit.

3. What was it about the forbidden fruit that made it appealing to Eve?
The fruit from the tree of the knowledge of good and evil looked good to eat and promised to make her wise. She was enticed by both of these factors.

4. How is that which tempts us today like that which tempted Eve in the beginning?
Almost always we humans are tempted by those things that look good and appear helpful. Rarely are we tempted by the ugly or the repulsive.

5. What happened to Adam and Eve after they ate the forbidden fruit?
After Adam and Eve ate the forbidden fruit, their eyes were opened and they knew that they were naked.

(PLEASE TURN PAGE)

---

1. Where was the tree that was forbidden to Adam and Eve?

2. Did the serpent lie or tell the truth when it said to Eve that she would not die?

3. What was it about the forbidden fruit that made it appealing to Eve?

4. How is that which tempts us today like that which tempted Eve in the beginning?

5. What happened to Adam and Eve after they ate the forbidden fruit?

6. Why did Adam and Eve hide from God when they heard Him walking in the garden in the cool of the day?

7. Whom did Adam and Eve blame for their sin?

8. Whom do we of the twentieth century usually blame for our sins?

9. Did Adam answer God's question, "Who told thee that thou wast naked?"

10. How do we sometimes hide from God when we have sinned?

The Bible tells us that the tree of knowledge of good and evil was "in the midst of the garden."

The serpent lied when it told Eve that she would not die. Eve began her progression toward death that very day she ate of the fruit.

The fruit from the tree of the knowledge of good and evil looked good to eat and promised to make her wise. She was enticed by both of these factors.

Almost always we humans are tempted by those things that look good and appear helpful. Rarely are we tempted by the ugly or the repulsive.

After Adam and Eve ate the forbidden fruit, their eyes were opened and they knew that they were naked.

Adam and Eve hid themselves from God because they had sinned and were aware of their nakedness.

Adam blamed Eve (and God who gave him Eve). Eve blamed the serpent for her sin.

Others. Usually we are not all that selective about whom we blame for our sins so long as the finger is pointing outward.

No. He quickly dodged that question so as to proceed with his decision to blame Eve for his wrong.

Often those who involve themselves in obvious sin will stop praying, cut themselves off from the community of faith, and "try to avoid making eye contact with God."

(SEED THOUGHTS--Cont'd)

6. Why did Adam and Eve hide from God when they heard Him walking in the garden in the cool of the day?
Adam and Eve hid themselves from God because they had sinned and were aware of their nakedness.

7. Whom did Adam and Eve blame for their sin?
Adam blamed Eve (and God who gave him Eve). Eve blamed the serpent for her sin.

8. Whom do we of the twentieth century usually blame for our sins?
Others. Usually we are not all that selective about whom we blame for our sins so long as the finger is pointing outward.

9. Did Adam answer God's question, "Who told thee that thou wast naked?"
No. He quickly dodged that question so as to proceed with his decision to blame Eve for his wrong.

10. How do we sometimes hide from God when we have sinned?
Often those who involve themselves in obvious sin will stop praying, cut themselves off from the community of faith, and "try to avoid making eye contact with God."

September 26, 1993

God's Response to Humankind's Sin

Genesis 3:22-24
22 And the LORD God said, Behold, the man is become as one of us, to know good and evil: and now lest he put forth his hand and take also of the tree of life, and eat, and live for ever.
23 Therefore the LORD God sent him forth from the garden of Eden, to till the ground from whence he was taken.
24 So he drove out the man; and he placed at the east of the garden of Eden Cher-u-bims, and a flaming sword which turned every way, to keep the way of the tree of life.

Genesis 6:5-8
5 And God saw that the wickedness of man was great in the earth, and *that* every imagination of the thoughts of his heart *was* only evil continually.
6 And it repented the LORD that he had made man on the earth, and it grieved him at his heart.
7 And the LORD said, I will destroy man whom I have created from the face of the earth; both man, and beast, and the creeping thing, and the fowls of the air, for it repenteth me that I have made them.
8 But Noah found grace in the eyes of the LORD.

Genesis 9:8-13
8 And God spake unto Noah, and to his sons with him, saying
9 And I, behold: I establish my covenant with you, and with your seed after you;
10 And with every living creature that *is* with you, of the fowl, of the cattle, and of every beast of the earth with you; from all that go out of the ark, to every beast of the earth.
11 And I will establish my covenant with you; neither shall all flesh be cut off any more by the waters of a flood; neither shall there any more be a flood to destroy the earth.
12 And God said, This *is* the token of the covenant which I make between me and you and every living creature that *is* with you, for perpetual generations:
13 I do set my bow in the cloud, and it shall be for a token of a covenant between me and the earth.

◆◆◆◆◆◆

◀ **Memory Selection**
Genesis 9:11

◀ **Devotional Reading**
Psalm 36:1-4, 7-9;
62:1-2

◀ **Background Scripture**
Genesis 3:14-24; 6:5-8,
11-27; 9:8-13

◀ **Printed Scripture**
Genesis 3:22-24;
6:5-8; 9:8-13

31

GOD'S RESPONSE TO HUMANKIND'S SIN

Teacher's Target

Scripture, both Old and New Testaments, establishes that God is for us. He created us good and desires our good. However, He did not create us as puppets or robots that He controls. Rebellion could and did occur. Self-rule and self-mastery resulted, but self-correction didn't. God's heart is grieved by such self-destruction. What did God do to protect Adam and Eve from an eternal state of death once they were removed from the garden (see Rev. 22:2)? Was God's decision to destroy the earth purely punitive or was He so grieved He chose to stop the carnage and wicked folly? God spared the earth from destruction because of one man. What does that tell us about God's willingness to save? God made a covenant with Noah. Does the text state anything for Noah to do?

Lesson Introduction

Humankind is adrift like a ship adrift. It started with listening to a serpent. We have been listening to lesser powers ever since. We are all derelicts. This word originated on the high seas to describe a ship with no captain and no crew. Seamen feared destruction from a collision with such a vessel. Humans are out of control when away from God.

God is not responsible for sin. This alien element entered our nature by way of an unauthorized union between two of God's creations, Satan and humankind.

In this text we find God protecting Adam and Eve from eternal death. Later, God repents (changes His mind and direction of action) with Noah. He graciously makes a covenant that will redeem mankind.

♦♦♦♦♦♦

Teaching Outline

I. God's Sentinel: Gen. 3:22-24
  A. The Need: 22
  B. The Remedy: 23-24
II. Sin Escalates: Gen. 6:5-8
  A. Man's Crimes: 5
  B. God's Grief: 6,7
  C. God's Grace: 8
III. A Promise of Assurance: Gen. 9:8-13
  A. The Covenant: 8-11
  B. The Sign: 12-13

Daily Bible Readings

Mon. Consequences of Pride *Gen. 3:20-24*
Tue. Persons Determine Their Future *Gen. 4:1-7*
Wed. Religious Jealousy Destroys *Gen. 4:8-17*
Thurs. Wickedness Causes Sorrow to God—*Gen. 6:1-8*
Fri. God Yearns For the Faithful *Gen. 6:11-22; 7:1*
Sat. God Covenants with Noah *Gen. 9:8-17*
Sun. Confess Your Transgressions *Ps. 32:1-11*

VERSE BY VERSE

I. God's Sentinel: Gen. 3:22-24

A. The Need: 22

22. And the Lord God said, Behold, the man is become as one of us, to know good and evil: and now, lest he put forth his hand, and take also of the tree of life, and eat, and live forever.

Prior to the Fall, Adam and Eve were not perfect. They were innocent. The book of Hebrews tells us Jesus was made perfect by obedience through the things He suffered (Heb. 5:8,9). Jesus, taking on human form (Phil. 2:5-11), did for us what Adam failed to do. By being made perfect and dying for our sin on the cross He removed the curse upon humankind and became the author of eternal salvation (Heb. 5:9). Adam's rebellion issued in death. Jesus' obedience brought about life (Rom. 5:17). At every moment Jesus was tempted like as are we yet without sin. As man, He proved Himself worthy by obedience to God and established His perfection and secured righteousness for those who believe (Rom. 5:19). This was God's plan from the foundation of the world: that we should be holy and without blame (Eph. 1:4). This Jesus accomplished through faith in the Father's word.

God made sure that death would not have the final word. God's instructions are always for our protection. His actions are also. God's first move toward us is for a saving purpose not for our condemnation. He knew humankind's weakness and the subtlety of the tempter. So, He made sure that a second failure by Adam would not be an eternal one.

B. The Remedy: 23-24

23. Therefore the Lord God sent him forth from the garden of Eden, to till the ground from whence he was taken.

24. So he drove out the man; and he placed at the east of the garden of Eden Cherubims, and a flaming sword which turned every way, to keep the way of the tree of life.

Had Adam been allowed into the garden to eat of the tree of life, he would have been in a state of eternal fallenness. God's love for humankind could not allow this to happen. Adam and Eve now knew good and evil but they didn't know how to use it. It was enough heartache to God that for all generations we would use our good for bad purposes and our bad motives would often turn out for good. Without God to guide us we may see what is good but to do it is beyond us.

So God stationed cherubim and a flaming sword to prevent access to the tree of life. Praise is due our God for protecting us from eternal alienation until the justifying and glorifying act of Jesus Christ upon the cross and in the resurrection could be accomplished (Rom. 8:30). God is not punitive but protective of His creatures in spite of their own acts of self-destruction. Providentially and redemptively He is constantly at work in humankind's behalf.

II. Sin Escalates: Gen. 6:5-8

A. Man's Crimes: 5

5. And God saw that the wickedness of man was great in the earth, and that every imagination of the thoughts of his heart was only evil continually.

Adam and Eve have fallen. Cain has slain Abel (Gen. 4:1-15). The atrocities multiplied as the population of the earth expands. Continually was the heart of man evil. But God was patient. He gave the people in the time of Noah 120 years to change and return to Him. But evil flooded their hearts while Noah built the ark on dry land. The offer of life, an opportunity to repent, and a coming judgment were all symbolized in the ark in their midst. The saving word of God always comes first. Judgment falls only after man persistently refuses grace. when it comes it is the consequence of man's sin for it is not God's will that any should perish (2 Pet. 3:9).

Today people still ignore God's ultimate sign of life, the cross and resurrection of Jesus Christ. Still we, like Noah, have to stay at the task of offering good news. The ark was offered in Noah's day and Christ died in the fullness of time for the ungodly (Rom. 5:6).

B. God's Grief: 6, 7

6. And it repented the Lord that he had made man on the earth, and it grieved him at his heart.

7. And the Lord said, I will destroy man whom I have created from the face of the earth; both man, and beast, and the creeping thing, and the fowls of the air; for it repenteth me that I have made them.

God was not sorry that He created man. He was grieved about what He saw the people doing to themselves and to each other. How far from the image of God our wickedness can carry us! This is a continual sorrow to the One who originally made us in His own image. The expression here in our text "it repented the Lord that He had made man" is much like a parent speaking of a child that has gone bad. Such a parent might be heard to say, "I rue the day that this my child was born." This by no means prevents the parent from longing for a return of the child, nor does it cut off the parent's love. Luke 15 tells us of God as the waiting Father. This passage might be a good commentary on our passage for today.

C. God's Grace: 8

8. But Noah found grace in the eyes of the Lord.

Noah was not perfect. He proves this later (Gen. 9:20-27). But verse nine tells us he was "righteous." This word means that the person or thing fulfills the purpose for which it was created. For example a teapot is righteous if it makes good tea. A chair is righteous if it holds us up when we sit down on it. People are righteous when they love God and enjoy Him. Noah loved God, His word, and sought to carry out God's will.

Grace is unmerited favor, a gift bestowed without price. God's grace had captivated Noah and he responded to God in righteousness. Noah's willing response to grace was a pleasure to God. Today God delights in our response to Him and lavishes the riches of His love upon us.

III. A Promise of Assurance: Gen. 9:8-13

A. The Covenant: 8-11

8. And God spake unto Noah, and to his sons with him, saying,

9. And I, behold, I establish my covenant wth you, and with your seed after you;

10. And with every living creature that is with you, of the fowl, of the cattle, and of every beast of the earth with you; from all that go out of the ark, to every beast of the

earth.

11. And I will establish my covenant with you; neither shall all flesh be cut off any more by the waters of a flood; neither shall there any more be a flood to destroy the earth.

When God gives His word it is like the final will of a person in our culture. No one has to second it. What He wills is done by one and given to the other party. He ratifies it within Himself. What God says He also does. What God does is for His glory and our good. We, like Noah and Abraham, can only open empty hands to praise God and receive His gifts of creation and redemption. The covenant here establishes that no flood will ever destroy all life, the seasons will come and go with regularity and a sign will be set in the heavens to assure us that God is true to His word.

B. The Sign: 12-13

12. And God said, This is the token of the covenant whch I make between me and you and every living creature that is with you, for perpetual generations:

13. I do set my bow in the cloud, and it shall be for a token of a covenant between me and the earth.

Humans are symbolic creatures. Flags, slogans, status symbols, mottos, state birds, mascots, state flowers and national emblems are all examples of our love of and need for symbols. God gave Noah a sign that would symbolize His faithfulness in providential care of His creation. When the clouds come, and the rains fall, the rainbow will follow as a sign of the promise that God made to Noah and all the earth for generations to come. This providential sign rejoices our hearts and calms our fears.

Greater still is the redemptive sign that God gave us in Jesus Christ. The cross and the empty tomb are an eternal reminder that God has broken the hold of the curse of sin upon us and given eternal life.

Evangelistic Emphasis

When the great redemptive scriptures are talked about, hardly ever is this one mentioned. The story of the flood is cited as evidence of the judgment of God, not of his mercy. "Because of God's aversion for the sin of man, he was willing to destroy the whole world in order to get rid of it," some are apt to say. It is true that the holiness of God recoils at the wickedness of humankind.

Is that the primary truth behind the destruction of the world by water? If that is so, wasn't God naive not to realize that it would just "get dirty all over again"? Typically, we have taken some gratification in the fact that "it must not be quite as bad as it was in the days of Noah, for He hasn't destroyed it as He did then." Yet, it is possible that our gratification may be misplaced.

There is another way to view this text that accentuates the goodness of God rather than our own "lack of badness." Was it that God "hated sin so much that he destroyed the whole world to get rid of it"? Or, did God love Noah so much that he was willing to give up everything he had created in order to save him? Just as Peter pointed to the flood as a forecast of baptism, so it is also quite clear that the total sacrifice made by God in that event was a preview of the Cross. Certainly, it is that very same kind of love that eventually motivated Him to surrender his Son so that salvation and redemption might finally become a reality.

◆◆◆◆◆◆

Memory Selection

I will establish my covenant with you, that never again shall all flesh be cut off by the waters of a flood, and never again shall there be a flood to destroy the earth. *Genesis 9:11*

Several great covenants have been made by our God. This is the first of them. Notice how it was made by God at his own initiative. Likewise, He bound Himself to keep it, without any prompting from those who were its beneficiaries. Notice, also, that this covenant was unconditional and all-inclusive. It did not rest on some responding agreement from mankind. In fact, the covenant was more encompassing than mankind. It even included the animals and livestock, also--"every living creature," the text says.

Question: Can God be trusted to keep His covenant?

Answer: Thousands of years have passed since that rainbow was placed in the sky sealing this promise of God. Not once since that day has our God broken His word. Not once has He allowed the waters of the earth to fall unrestrained since that day. Not once has His destruction overwhelmed all of life, as it did in that day. Yes! Our God is one who keeps His word. Truth is the very essence of His nature. He can most assuredly be trusted.

September 26, 1993

Weekday Problems

It seems to Bill as though he has always been "on the outside looking in." In contrast to many of his coworkers at the shoe factory, he is a Christian. Not a token church goer who shows up now and then, Bill is one who has been involved since he was a child. When the door is open, he is there. He has taken his turn at about every job available, except staffing the nursery. He even offered to do that once, but Sister Gertrude scoldingly informed him that that was no place for a man. Furthermore, Bill's Christianity is not left at church. He very diligently tries to live to the standard he professes.

There's just one problem. Bill has grown weary of being "odd." The jokes by the fellows at work who call him "Preacher" have gotten old. Desperately, he yearns to be included. More than anything he can think of, he wants to fit in.

Recently, he has begun to wonder if it's worth it all. More than once Bill has given thought to doing "whatever it takes" to establish his place among "the boys."

*Is what Bill is going through right now "normal?" or is he just "losing his faith"?

*What can Bill do to better respond to this longing within himself? How can he fortify his own resources to see this crisis through?

*How can Bill's fellow Christians most effectively help Bill? Or, does he have to go through this storm alone?

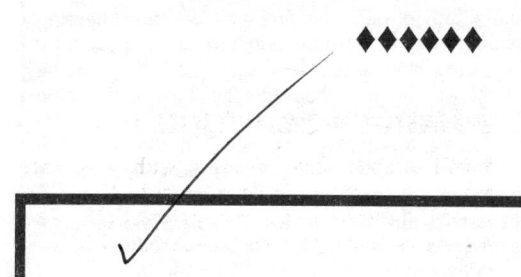

♦♦♦♦♦♦

Sparkle

A disciple asked a teacher to be his mentor. The teacher said, "You may live with me, but you cannot become a follower of me!"

Puzzled the disciple asked, "Whom, then, shall I follow?"

The response was, "No one. The day you follow someone you cease to follow Truth."

We must remember to always point beyond ourselves to Jesus Christ. He is the Truth, the Way, the Life.

GOD'S RESPONSE TO HUMANKIND'S SIN

This Lesson In Your Life

THE GRIEF OF GOD

During his earthly ministry, Jesus told a parable of a father whose son decided that he didn't wish to be forever under his father's thumb. He asked for his share of the inheritance in advance so that he could "hit the road" and be on his own. Of course, the father granted his wish, and the son left according to his plan.

We are not told how the father felt as he watch his son become a small speck on the horizon. Nor are we told what he thought about as he lay in his bed during the nights that followed while his son remained away. Those who are parents have a fairly good idea how he felt and the kinds of thoughts that haunted his sleeplessness.

Mothers become frantic when their daughters do not come home in the evening. Fathers' hearts break when their sons discard their instruction. Even the "normal" process of adolescence is usually a heavy burden to bear. But, to have one's son throw away everything one has worked a lifetime to provide, including his very family, is almost more than a parent can bear. Of course, Jesus was not just telling about some unknown father someplace. He was using a parable to teach about God, the Father of all.

Please notice that these scriptures relating the response of God to the sin of humankind do not stress His anger but His sorrow. The picture that is painted for the reader is not one of a holy tirade or of a lashing out for vengeance. Instead, we are shown a father who is so grieved by the waywardness of his children, so disappointed in the results of his creation, that he is ready to undo it all.

It's sad that we don't usually think of our sin in that way. We fear angering God. Images haunt us of the possibility of "pushing Him too far," or of sinning somehow so terribly that we are "beyond forgiveness." We may even be terrorized by the caricature of the warden-god who walks the balcony of heaven overlooking earth (thunderbolts in hand) just waiting for us to step out of line. Rarely do we think of our misdeeds as wounding God. We do not think of Him as the father lying awake on his bed at night with a broken heart because his children have rejected his love.

Yet, that is the image that Jesus paints for us in the "Parable of the Prodigal Son." That's the God who is revealed for us in these texts. Genesis 6:6 tells that the wickedness of humanity "grieved him at his heart." The New International Version reads, *"The Lord was grieved* that he had made man on the earth, and *his heart was filled with pain."*

Perhaps, if we thought more about the pain we bring to God when we sin, rather than His possible anger, we would be more responsive to His love. So often, we humans are preoccupied with the question, "How far can I go without being lost?" Or, "What's the most I can get by with, and still be saved?" "Will God forgive me once for that transgression? How about Twice? Seven times? After all, He said that we should forgive seventy times seven? Can He do any less?" Still, probably we don't fully believe all of our ramblings, and so shudder at the thought of His wrath.

To be sure, fear has its place as an incentive to repent, but anyone wishing to live a long life of righteousness needs a motivation that is more enduring than fear. We serve God best and most faithfully when our service is motivated by a heart filled with love. We avoid sin most, not because of our apprehension of punishment, but because of our desire not to wound Him.

Seed Thoughts

1. What was the serpent's punishment for having tempted the woman?
The serpent received a curse upon it that destined it to move upon its belly and to eat the dust of the earth from that day onward.

2. What was the woman's punishment for having eaten of the tree of the knowledge of good and evil?
The woman's sorrow in childbirth was multiplied and her husband ruled over her.

3. What was Adam's punishment for having eaten of the forbidden tree?
Because of Adam's sin, the ground was cursed so that in sorrow the man would eat through diligent labor.

4. In what way did the man become "like God" when he ate of the forbidden tree?
When the man ate of the forbidden tree, he became like God in that he now recognized the difference between good and evil.

5. Why did God feel that it was necessary to drive man out of the garden?
Adam and Eve were driven from the garden so that they could not eat of the tree of life and live forever.

(PLEASE TURN PAGE)

---

1. What was the serpent's punishment for having tempted the woman?

2. What was the woman's punishment for having eaten of the tree of the knowledge of good and evil?

3. What was Adam's punishment for having eaten of the forbidden tree?

4. In what way did the man become "like God" when he ate of the forbidden tree?

5. Why did God feel that it was necessary to drive man out of the garden?

6. Why was God grieved that He had made man?

7. Why did God make a bow in the clouds following the flood?

8. Why did God decide to destroy the earth?

9. What did God save on the ark?

10. What does God's covenant with Noah mean to those of us living today?

The serpent received a curse upon it that destined it to move upon its belly and to eat the dust of the earth from that day onward.

The woman's sorrow in childbirth was multiplied and her husband ruled over her.

Because of Adam's sin, the ground was cursed so that in sorrow the man would eat through diligent labor.

When the man ate of the forbidden tree, he became like God in that he now recognized the difference between good and evil.

Adam and Eve were driven from the garden so that they could not eat of the tree of life and live forever.

God was grieved that He had made man because of the pervasive wickedness that had come to characterize man.

God placed a bow in the sky following the flood as a token of the covenant between Himself and the earth that he would never again destroy the world with water.

God decided to destroy the earth because the wickedness of humanity was so pervasive that "a new start" was essential if the righteous were to survive.

On the ark God preserved two of each kind of animal, seven of each sacrificial animal, Noah, Noah's wife, Noah's sons and their wives.

The covenant that God made with Noah extended to all of creation including his descendants, us.

(SEED THOUGHTS--Cont'd)

6. Why was God grieved that He had made man?
God was grieved that He had made man because of the pervasive wickedness that had come to characterize man.

7. Why did God make a bow in the clouds following the flood?
God placed a bow in the sky following the flood as a token of the covenant between Himself and the earth that he would never again destroy the world with water.

8. Why did God decide to destroy the earth?
God decided to destroy the earth because the wickedness of humanity was so pervasive that "a new start" was essential if the righteous were to survive.

9. What did God save on the ark?
On the ark God preserved two of each kind of animal, seven of each sacrificial animal, Noah, Noah's wife, Noah's sons and their wives.

10. What does God's covenant with Noah mean to those of us living today?
The covenant that God made with Noah extended to all of creation including his descendants, us.

God's Commitment to Abram

Genesis 15:1-16

15 AFTER these things the word of the LORD came unto Abram in a vision, saying, Fear not, Abram: I *am* thy shield, *and* thy exceeding great reward.
2 And Abram said Lord GOD, what wilt thou give me, seeing I go childless, and the steward of my house is this E-li-e'-zer of Damascus?
3 And Abram said, Behold, to me thou hast given no seed: and, lo, one born in my house is mine heir.
4 And, behold, the word of the LORD *came* unto him, saying, This shall not be thine heir; but he that shall come forth out of thine own bowels shall be thine heir.
5 And he brought him forth abroad, and said, Look now toward heaven, and tell the stars, if thou be able to number them: and he said unto him, So shall thy seed be.
6 And he believed in the LORD; and he counted it to him for righteousness.
7 And he said unto him, I *am* the LORD that brought thee out of Ur of the Chal'-dees, to give thee this land to inherit it.
8 And he said, Lord GOD, whereby shall I know that I shall inherit it?
9 And he said unto him, Take me an heifer of three years old, and a she goat of three years old, and a ram of three years old, and a turtledove, and a young pigeon.
10 And he took unto him all these, and divided them in the midst, and laid each piece one against another but the birds divided he not.
11 And when the fowls came down upon the carcases, Abram drove them away.
12 And when the sun was going down, a deep sleep fell upon Abram; and, lo, an horror of great darkness fell upon him.
13 And he said unto Abram, Know of a surety that thy seed shall be a stranger in a land *that is* not theirs, and shall serve them; and they shall afflict them four hundred years;
14 And also that nation, whom they shall serve, will I judge: and afterward shall they come out with great substance.
15 And thou shalt go to thy fathers in peace; thou shalt be buried in a good old age.
16 But in the fourth generation they shall come hither again: for the iniquity of the Am'or-ites *is* not yet full.

◆◆◆◆◆◆

◀ **Memory Selection**
Genesis 12:2

◀ **Devotional Reading**
Genesis 11:31-32; 12:1-10; 15:1-7

◀ **Background Scripture**
Genesis 12:1-3; 15:1-18

◀ **Printed Scripture**
Genesis 15:1-16

GOD'S COMMITMENT TO ABRAM

Teacher's Target

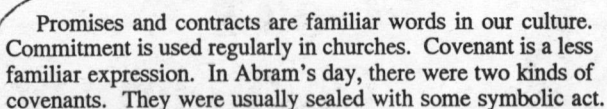

Promises and contracts are familiar words in our culture. Commitment is used regularly in churches. Covenant is a less familiar expression. In Abram's day, there were two kinds of covenants. They were usually sealed with some symbolic act.

As a class, define and discuss the words: promise, contract, commitment, and covenant. Here are some possible questions to ask: Have you ever broken a promise? Has anyone ever broken a contract with you? How is God's covenant different from a marriage contract between a man and a woman?

Lesson Introduction

A neighborhood full of children provided ample opportunity for trades and promises. Baseball cards, marbles and yo-yo's would be traded. Often deals would be regretted. Exclamations of "Indian giver!" would be shouted and the object returned. We also made alliances sealed with secret codes. Exclusive loyalties would last until the first dispute over a close call at the sandlot baseball game. In other words, humans were and are fickle.

God is not so. What He commits to, He carries through. God gave Abram hope with a promise. Abram's part was to believe (accept) the promise. This was counted as righteousness.

God ratified His promise within Himself. Through the continuous rebellions that accent Israel's history, God never reneged.

♦♦♦♦♦♦

Teaching Outline

I. God's Promise: Gen. 15:1-5
   A. Calms Fear: 1
   B. Listens Attentively: 2-3
   C. Speaks Reassuringly: 4-5

II. Abram's Faith: Gen. 15:6
   A. Believes God: 6
   B. Counted Righteous: 6

III. God's Seal: Gen. 15:7-16
   A. Faithfulness Recounted: 7
   B. A Sign Given: 8-12
   C. A Prophecy Shared: 13-16

Daily Bible Readings

Mon. Let Us Make a Name for Ourselves - *Gen. 11:1-9, 13-32*
Tue. God Gives Abram a Threefold Blessing - *Gen. 12:1-8*
Wed. People of Faith are God's Children *Gal. 3:2-9*
Thurs. Abram Meets Priest-King, Melchizedek - *Gen. 14:10-20*
Fri. The "Shield" of Abram *Gen. 15:1-6*
Sat. The Cutting of a Covenant *Gen. 15:7-11*
Sun. God Sets Boundaries for Abram *Gen. 15:12-18*

VERSE BY VERSE

I. God's Promise: Gen. 15:1-5

A. Calms Fear: 1

1. After these things the word of the Lord came unto Abram in a vision, saying, Fear not, Abram: I am thy shield, and thy exceeding great reward.

After a victory over Chedorlaomer and the recovery of Lot, Abram (later named Abraham) evidently began to fear. Many of us are great in the crisis and our feelings only catch up with us afterwards. The same happened to Elijah after his victory on Mount Carmel (1 Kings 18). Both Abram and Elijah recognized their vulnerability and weakness. Here, as in the case of Elijah, God responded to Abram's fear. In essence, God said, "You are right. You are weak. What you must not forget is that I, 'The I Am', will be your shield." We are inadequate for the trials and troubles of this world but God is sufficient. How many things He takes care of in a day we will never know about! As Paul declares, in our weakness, He is made strong. Man can make no armament to rival God as a shield. He is enough.

Notice God called Abram by name. What an honor! He calls each of us by name. Such personal relationship with God is reassurance enough in our times of fear.

B. Listens Attentively: 2-3

2. And Abram said, Lord God, what wilt thou give me, seeing I go childless, and the steward of my house is this Eliezer of Damascus?

3. And Abram said, Behold, to me thou hast given no seed: and, lo, one born in my house is mine heir.

Having an heir to carry on the family name was a great and continual concern to Abram. Note that Abram complained to God, not of God. Often God is the only one who can hear and receive our complaints and petitions. Humans will lose patience. God will listen and act. Even though God had already told Abram that he would become a great nation and his seed would be as numerous as the dust of the earth (Gen. 12:2; 13:16), he questioned. As the father of our faith, Abram makes a good illustration of how we are not faithless as long as we are bringing our concerns, questions and doubts to God.

Certitude is not ours in this age. Faith is. What we seek is certainty; what we receive is comfort in the midst of uncertainty. Though often delayed for reasons known only to God at the time, His promises will find fruition. Cast your cares upon the Lord for He cares for you (1 Pet. 5:7). This Abram did. God listened and responded.

C. Speaks Reassuringly: 4-5

4. And, behold, the word of the Lord came unto him, saying, This shall not be thine heir; but he that shall come forth out of thine own bowels shall be thine heir.

5. And he brought him forth

abroad, and said Look now toward heaven, and tell the stars, if thou be able to number them: and he said unto him. So shall thy seed be.

God made plain His promise to Abram. The heir would be of Abram's seed, not just an heir of one of his household servants. God's answer to us is always better than we had designed for ourselves and is greater than our fears. As one grandmother told her grandson in a time of his questioning God's slow response, "Son, God doesn't ever come when you want Him, but He is always on time." God showed Abram the numerous stars and said "so shall thy seed be." Abram wanted one son. God promised multitudes. Abram had to wait upon the Lord, but not without a promise to give him confidence and hope. Jesus Christ has come as the ultimate Son. He has promised forgiveness and eternal life. His cross and resurrection are our promise as we wait in hope.

II. Abram's Faith: Gen. 15:6

A. Believed God: 6

6. And he believed in the Lord; and he counted it to him for righteousness.

In Romans 4:19-21, Paul uses Abram as a prime example of faith, "He was not weak in faith; he staggered not at the promise; he was strong in faith; he was fully persuaded." God's irresistible love was the power that elicited such faith from Abram. God gave the revelation and Abram received it. The same Lord has given us Jesus Christ, the seal of a greater covenant, and we are to receive and embrace His word. Assurance and comfort come to those who receive by faith the promise. Opening empty hands to receive the gift is the appropriate response.

B. Counted Righteous: 6

6. And he believed in the Lord; and he counted it to him for righteousness.

Hebrews 11:4 declares that by faith Abram obtained witness that he was righteous. Before Abram had fulfilled obligations, His faith was counted as righteousness. God is righteous. We are ungodly. If righteousness becomes our possession we would have no need of God. Our faith, like Abram's, gives us access to God's righteousness. As the New Testament declares, Abram was justified by faith without works of the law (Rom. 4:3; Gal. 3:6). Abram had struggled with unbelief and conquered. Now faith was crowned with honor. Such acceptance and dependence upon God's promise gave Abram the right to all the blessings contained in the promise.

III. God's Seal: Gen. 15:7-16

A. Faithfulness Recounted: 7

7. And he said unto him, I am the Lord that brought thee out of Ur of the Chaldees, to give thee this land to inherit it.

God declared who He is, the "I AM." "I can give," the Lord declared, "because all that is, is mine; and I am before all that exists." Earthly rulers promise and cannot deliver. God always delivers exceedingly more than we can think or ask (Eph. 3:20). God recounts His mercy in delivering Abram out of Ur. It was an effectual and personal call to Abram. A Jewish tradition says that Abram was cast into a fiery furnace for refusing to worship idols and was miraculously rescued. Whether this is accurate or not, it is sure that God calls each of us out of our idolatries of this age to faith in Him. God's power and grace are effectual.

B. A Sign Given: 8-12

8. And he said, Lord God,

whereby shall I know that I shall inherit it?

9. And he said unto him, Take me an heifer of three years old, and a she goat of three years old, and a ram of three years old, and a turtle dove, and a young pigeon.

10. And he took unto him all these, and divided them in the midst, and laid each piece one against another: but the birds divided he not.

11. And when the fowls came down upon the carcases, Abram drove them away.

12. And when the sun was going down a deep sleep fell upon Abram; and, lo, an horror of great darkness fell upon him.

"How shall I know?" was Abram's question. We humans want evidence and God gives us signs. If we had "sight evidence" we would no longer be children of faith. So Abram received a sign and it was enough for him to go forward with the Lord. John the Baptist asked Jesus for proof of His sonship, and was given only His deeds which could be accepted or rejected (Matt. 11:2-5). God's signs can always be questioned and discounted. In the case of the resurrection of Jesus, some wanted to believe that Jesus' disciples had stolen the body. Only faith "sees."

The sign in our text was not an extraordinary event out of heaven but a sacrifice on earth. Abram had eyes to see God seal His own promise. Notice Abram was in great darkness. Faith is a way of light in the midst of darkness.

C. A Prophecy Shared: 13-16

13. And he said unto Abram, know of a surety that thy seed shall be a stranger in a land that is not theirs, and shall serve them; and they shall afflict them four hundred years;

14. And also that nation, whom they shall serve, will I judge: and afterward shall they come out with great substance.

15. And thou shalt go to thy fathers in peace;thou shalt be buried in a good old age.

16. But in the fourth generation they shall come hither again: for the iniquity of the Amorites is not yet full.

The way of the Lord often leads through trials, hardship, persecutions and temptations. But as Paul says in Rom. 8:18, "...the sufferings of this present time are not worthy to be compared with the glory which shall be revealed in us." Abram's seed learned this truth through the slavery in Egypt. The hope of the promise sustained them. God allows wounds and then heals. God allows humbling then exalts. God did not tell Abram this was a pronouncement of punishment. Rather it was preparing him and his seed for the trial and a comfort of His presence in it. Nothing befalls us of sorrow and grief that has not first pierced the heart of God Himself.

The Egyptian persecution was a judging of themselves. They revealed their wickedness. Their end is sure. The reward of the faithful far exceeds their temporary suffering.

Evangelistic Emphasis

It is common to think of the Christian life in terms of commitment. And of course, that is a natural thing to do. After all, Jesus did say, "Whosoever will come after me, let him deny himself, and take up his cross, and follow me." (Mark 8:34) So, it is impossible to consider being a Christian without thinking of it in terms of commitment. It is a life commitment. It is the kind of commitment that requires "laying it all on the line" to win or lose, to do or to die.

Yet this lesson is not one that stresses *our* commitment, but *God's*. Long before Abraham was declared "righteous" because of his faith in God, God had firmly placed his faith in Abraham. Long before He ever asks for us to give to the relationship, he first gives. Before He ever calls for our commitment, he commits His all to us.

Far from our religion being that of a cowering people serving the whimsical wishes of a tyrannical god, Christianity proclaims to the world the God who makes Himself the servant of his people. We seek not to appease His wrath, but to return His immeasurable love. The covenant He makes with us is always to our advantage and for our good. Christianity is not the religion of "God seekers." It is, instead, the faith community of those who have been found by the God who seeks his own. Being part of that fellowship indicates that you are named among the fortunate ones that have been found.

◆◆◆◆◆◆

Memory Selection

I will make of you a great nation, and I will bless you, and make your name great, so that you will be a blessing. *Genesis 12:2*

For a seventy-five year old man who was still childless, this seemed like a very fantastic promise. Before the answer of this promise was finally granted, it would seem impossible. Possibly with the completion of every year, Abraham wondered why God had not kept his promise. As each new year began, he and Sarah speculated, "Do you suppose if will happen this year?"

Yet, as month followed month and season succeeded season the report from the Abraham and Sarah home echoed the same, "She's still not pregnant." Together, they prayed and wondered, and perhaps, tried to figure out "What are we doing wrong?"

The answer was, "Nothing. The time has just not come, yet."

Eventually, the day did come, just as God had promised. Our God is one who keeps his promises, even if not according to our schedule. He keeps them just the same.

October 3, 1993

Weekday Problems

Jim and Linda are young Christians who were once unusually excited about living the Christian life. Though they each had been reared in the church, their faith had not really been *theirs* until the revival two years ago. For the first time in their lives, they became aware of and took hold of the promises of God.

One of the promises that impressed Linda and Jim the most was made by Jesus, "Give, and it shall be given unto you; good measure, pressed down, and shaken together, and running over, shall men give into your bosom" (Luke 6:38a). So much were they impressed by it, that they decided to test it.

Carefully, they looked around for the perfect opportunity to give in such a way. Finally, the day came. On the way home from work one Friday evening Jim picked up a hitch-hiker. Learning that he was living on the street, Jim took him home.

Much to her own surprise, Linda was as excited about their new house guest as Jim was. She prepared a special meal, gave him some of Jim's clothes to wear for the evening while she washed and pressed his. The next morning, Jim took a day's vacation while he helped his new friend look for a job.

Days passed. Then weeks. Three months later, Jim and Linda had their home to themselves again. Then they waited for the Lord's generous response.

It has now been more than a year, and they still have seen no answer to the Lord's promise, "... and it shall be given unto you." "Where is the Lord?" they asked their pastor last Sunday. "He promised, but He hasn't come through."

* How could Jim and Linda's pastor help them to better understand the ways of God by drawing from this passage?

* How can we instruct ourselves when we wonder about the promises of God When they don't seem to be receiving as much of God's attention as we had hoped, how can we more completely surrender our gifts to Him?

Say It Right

Abram: Ay-brum

Eliezer: El-ee-ay-zer

Chaldees: Chal-deez

Chedorlaomer: Ched-or-lay-oh-mer

Melchizedek: Mel-kiz-e-dek

This Lesson In Your Life
JUST ONE FAMILY!

As we near the end of the twentieth century the mood common to modern life is the feeling of insignificance. Every day we are reminded of the incredible sea of people that call this blue and green golf ball "home." As just one among billions it's easy to feel that, "I really can't make much of a difference!"

This is an increasingly troublesome attitude in the world of democracy where fewer and fewer feel compelled to vote. In community life, participation in neighborhood projects has diminished to a handful. P.T.A.'s across our country must fight for every single member. Even at church, committees often include only the chairperson, except in name only.

The problem is not a shortage of people. The world is increasing with people by the second. Rather, it is precisely our consciousness of that rapid increase of population that leaves us with the feeling of being unneeded and unimportant. Unfortunately, the impact of this "insignificance" spills over into virtually every realm of our Christian life.

"What difference does it make whether or not I am faithful to my Christian vow? I'm just one person. Nobody pays any attention to what I do." Of course, if it really doesn't make any difference, then all urgency or importance of fidelity and faithfulness is somehow reduced (at least in our own minds).

The truth is, though, it does make a difference. Just as one lone penny is absolutely significant in the compilation of a huge fortne, one person is significant to the ultimate outcome of the Kingdom of God. Did you realize that if you began the month with just one penny and had it doubled every successive day thereafter, you would finish a thrity-one day month with more than ten million dollars? Go ahead, get out your pocket calculator and test it. The exact yield is $10,737,418.24. It is difficult to believe, but it's true. Each and every penny is significant to a multimillion dollar fortune.

It is precisely in that way that God used Abraham to shape the direction of the world. One man faithful to God taught his family members to follow God, who then taught their families, also. In result, you and I are children of faith, children of Abraham.

Of course, you and I play no less a part in God's plan as we each become a building for the future. For how many generations, yet, will the world stand? Some believe that the Lord could return at any time. He could. But, suppose the Lord decides to allow the world to stand for a thousand more years. The impact of your one life or one family will be compounded for *fifty generations*. As your family faithfully passes on the treasures of God to succeeding generations, the darkness of the world is illuminated with His glory, and the decay of the world is retarded by the Christian salt. A thousand years from now there will be not just one family's torch of testimony but a whole nation of faithful children, because of you.

Suppose the world does not stand another thousand years. Is the faithfulness of your own children and grandchildren any less important to you? They need you to show them the way.

Seed Thoughts

1. Does the Bible teach that God always spoke to Abraham in the same way?
No. God used different ways to speak to Abraham. In this text, "a vision" was used. Later it is said that "the Lord appeared to Abram." Genesis 18 speaks of "three men" who seem to have been angels.

2. What primary concern did Abram express to God in this conversation?
Abram's primary concern was that he was still childless and that the one who would inherit his estate was Eliezer of Damascus.

3. Who had Abram anticipated would be the source of his offspring?
Abram had looked to the Lord as the giver of his offspring, for he said to the Lord, "Behold, to me thou hast given no seed."

4. What was the Lord's response to Abram's having given up on the idea of ever becoming a father?
The Lord told Abram that Eliezer would not be his heir, but rather his heir would be his own offspring.

5. To what did God compare the future descendants of Abraham?
The Lord told Abram to look at the stars in the heavens. His descendants would be as numberless as the stars.

(PLEASE TURN PAGE)

---

1. Does the Bible teach that God always spoke to Abraham in the same way?

2. What primary concern did Abram express to God in this conversation?

3. Who had Abram anticipated would be the source of his offspring?

4. What was the Lord's response to Abram's having given up on the idea of ever becoming a father?

5. To what did God compare the future descendants of Abraham?

6. How did Abram receive this rather incredible promise, considering his age?

7. What additional promise did the Lord make to Abram on this visit by way of a vision?

8. What follow-up question did Abram ask in response to the Lord's promise of the land?

9. How did the Lord confirm the land promise that He had just made to Abram?

10. As the Lord concluded His covenant with Abram, what condition was Abram in at the time?

No. God used different ways to speak to Abraham. In this text, "a vision" was used. Later it is said that "the Lord appeared to Abram." Genesis 18 speaks of "three men" who seem to have been angels.

Abram's primary concern was that he was still childless and that the one who would inherit his estate was Eliezer of Damascus.

Abram had looked to the Lord as the giver of his offspring, for he said to the Lord, "Behold, to me thou hast given no seed."

The Lord told Abram that Eliezer would not be his heir, but rather his heir would be his own offspring.

The Lord told Abram to look at the stars in the heavens. His descendants would be as numberless as the stars.

The Bible says that Abram "believed the Lord, and he counted it to him for righteousness." That is, the Lord counted Abram's faith as righteousness.

The Lord promised Abram that he would be given "this land" to inherit for his descendants.

Abram responded to the Lord's promise by asking, "Lord God, whereby shall I know that I shall inherit it?" or, in other words, "How can I be sure?"

The Lord responded by formalizing His promise with the shedding of blood. A covenant sacrifice sealed the promise that had been made.

The Bible says that "when the sun was going down, a deep sleep fell upon Abram; and, lo, an horror of great darkness fell upon him."

(SEED THOUGHTS--Cont'd)

6. **How did Abram receive this rather incredible promise, considering his age?**
The angel of the Lord told Hagar to return to her mistress and submit to her hand.

7. **What additional promise did the Lord make to Abram on this visit by way of a vision?**
The Lord promised Abram that he would be given "this land" to inherit for his descendants.

8. **What follow-up question did Abram ask in response to the Lord's promise of the land?**
Abram responded to the Lord's promise by asking, "Lord God, whereby shall I know that I shall inherit it?" or, in other words, "How can I be sure?"

9. **How did the Lord confirm the land promise that He had just made to Abram?**
The Lord responded by formalizing His promise with the shedding of blood. A covenant sacrifice sealed the promise that had been made.

10. **As the Lord concluded His covenant with Abram, what condition was Abram in at the time?**
The Bible says that "when the sun was going down, a deep sleep fell upon Abram; and, lo, an horror of great darkness fell upon him."

October 10, 1993

Sarai Attempts to Manipulate Events

Genesis 16:1-4

16 NOW Sarai Abram's wife bare him no children: and she had an handmaid, an Egyptian, whose name was Ha,-gar
2 And Sa-rai said unto Abram, Behold now, the LORD hath restrained me from bearing: I pray thee, go in unto my maid; it may be that I may obtain children by her. And Abram hearkaened to the voice of Sa'-rai.
3 And Sa-rai, Abram's wife, took Ha'-gar her maid the Egyptian, after Abram had dwelt ten years in the land of Canaan, and gave her to her husband Abram to be his wife.
4 And he went in unto Ha'-gar, and she conceived: and when she saw that she had conceived, her mistress was despised in her eyes.

Genesis 16:11-16

11 And the angel of the LORD said unto her, Behold, thou *art* with child, and shalt bear a son, and shalt call his name Ishmael; because the LORD hath heard thy affliction.
12 And he will be a wad man; his hand *will be* against every man, and every man's hand against him; and he shall dwell in the presence of all his brethren.
13 And she called the name of the LORD that spake unto her, Thou God seest me: she said Have I also here looked after him that seeth me?
14 Wherefore the well was called Be'-er-la-hai'-roi; behold, *it is* between Ka'-desh and Be'-red.
15 And Hagar bare Abram a son: and Abram called his son's name, which Hagar bare, Ishmael.
16 And Abram *was* fourscore and six years old, when Hagar bare Ishmael to Abram.

◆◆◆◆◆◆

◀ **Memory Selection**
Genesis 16:2
or Genesis 16:13
◀ **Devotional Reading**
Genesis 16:1-15

◀ **Background Scripture**
Genesis 16

◀ **Printed Scripture**
Genesis 16:1-4, 11-16

SARAH ATTEMPTS TO MANIPULALTE EVENTS

Teacher's Target

Have you ever heard the saying "You can't have two cooks in the kitchen?" Could you apply this to Sarai and Hagar? Our story for today is an example of manipulation that backfired. It also reveals our mistrust even of God. The ownership of "place" in a family and the fear of losing place become obvious. A class discussion of manipulation could help bring the text to life in the present. Also, ask the class if anyone close to them has ever misled or broken trust with them (parent, siblings, friend, workmate, boss)? Ask them to put yourselves in Sarai's place; in Hagar's place. Are our characters in this historical event so different from us? Help the class see how the evil we do so often arises out of our insecurity, fear, hurt, frustration, pain and shame.

Lesson Introduction

Sarai manipulates circumstances to assist God's promise in coming true. She is not so different from us. The Lord speaks. We begin to plan. Details of our own making replace God's directive. It is a part of our not knowing how to discern good and evil. We may know it ideally in our heads, but carrying it out is our problem.

The harm that presumptions and illusions can perpetuate upon ourselves and others becomes apparent in Sarai and Hagar. Abram, once again like Adam, demonstrates how prone we are to listen to those close to us. Doesn't God tell us not to lean on the arm of man (Jer. 17:5, Matt, 10:36)? We cannot serve God and mammon (Matt. 6:24). We cannot trust even our own hearts (Prov. 28:26, 2 Cor. 1:9). Peter states it, "we ought to obey God rather than men" Acts 5:29).

♦♦♦♦♦♦

Teaching Outline

I. Sarai's Manipulation:
Gen. 16:1-3
   A. Sarai's Problem: 1
   B. Sarai's Solution: 2-3
II. Abram's Compliance:
Gen. 16:2,4
   A. Abram Listens: 2
   B. Abram Acts: 4
III. Hagar's Plight and Promise:
Gen. 16:4, 6, 11-16
   A. Hagar's Contempt: 4
   B. Hagar's Plight: 6
   C. Hagar's Promise: 11-16

Daily Bible Readings

Mon. Hagar Felt Superior to Sarai
Gen. 16:1-5
Tue. God Promised Hagar
Numerous Progeny - *Gen. 16:6-10*
Wed. Hey God ... Where Are You?
Gen. 16:11-16
Thurs. God's Way of Looking at
Ishmael - *Gen. 21:13-17*
Fri. Arise, Lift Up the Lad (Ishmael)
Gen. 21:18-22
Sat. The Nature of Ishmaelites
Gen. 37:12-17, 25-28
Sun. What Are You Doing Here
(Elijah)?
2 Kings 19:9-19

October 10, 1993

VERSE BY VERSE

I. Sarai's Manipulation: Gen. 16:1-3

A. Sarai's Problem: 1

1. NOW Sa´-rai Abram's wife bare him no children: and she had an handmaid, an Egyptian, whose name *was* Ha´-gar.

Sarai had been blessed by God with beauty and a share in the possession of Abram. She was gifted to be a good wife. But one blessing had been withheld. She was without child. She wanted to please Abram and give him a child. Not knowing herself well nor the nature of the reaction of Hagar when she could bear a child and Sarai could not, Sarai sought to resolve her own problem without reference to God's direction.

When our hearts are too fixed upon a desire we are prone to manipulate circumstances and contrive solutions that short cut and/or thwart God's intent. Always our dreams and wishes must be under God's sovereignty. There is no implication that Sarai sought God's guidance. Prayer purifies our wishes. Such prayer could have saved Abram, Sarai and Hagar much heartache. Being descendants of Adam and Eve, as are we, the same flaw continued to plague humankind: disregard for God's counsel.

B. Sarai's Solution: 2-3

2. And Sa-´rai said unto Abram, Behold now, the Lord hath restrained me from bearing: I pray thee, go in unto my maid; it may be that I may obtain children by her. And Abram hearkened to the voice of Sa´-rai.

3. And Sa´-rai, Abram's wife, took Ha´-gar her maid the Egyptian, after Abram had dwelt ten years in the land of Canaan, and gave her to her husband Abram to be his wife.

Taking matters into our own hands is a common malady of humans. We are big on doing and short on patience. We leap before we look. We try to run before we can crawl. we can go out on a limb and saw it off behind ourselves. Accepting God's promises and waiting upon Him to fulfill His purposes in our lives comes to us slowly. How much grief we could spare ourselves if we were not so hasty in our actions. Time itself became the test of both Abram's and Sarai's patience in waiting for God to supply their need and desire.

Since Hagar was Sarai's handmaiden, she chose to use her as a surrogate to provide Abram with a son. Since Hagar was her servant, she was a gift from Sarai and in a sense the child would be hers because the handmaiden was her gift. This is convoluted reasoning. How twisted our thinking becomes when we seek to justify our own misguided ends.

II. Abram's Compliance: Gen. 12:2,4

A. Abram Listens: 2

2. And Sa´-rai said unto Abram, Behold now, the Lord hath restrained me from bearing: I pray thee, go in unto my maid; it may be that I may obtain children by her.

And Abram hearkened to the voice of Sa´-rai.

As in the case of Sarai, Abram was sincere in believing that this could fulfil what God had promised. After all, God had not yet told him the seed was to come from Sarai's body. He only knew the heir was to be his seed. Sincere? Yes! But sincerely wrong. Sincerity is not faith. The fair words of Sarai fostered a foul end. Like Adam, Abram listened to human persuading rather than taking the matter to God.

B. Abram Acts: 4

4. And he went in unto Ha´-gar, and she conceived: and when she saw that she had conceived, her mistress was despised in her eyes.

The One who had called Abram out of Ur of the Chaldees was God, not Sarai. Yet Abram acted upon her word to please her rather than God. The best wisdom on the human plane cannot comprehend God's ways and means. Abram's action in haste upon unauthorized advice brought sorrow for Sarai, Hagar and himself. How we want to blame God for our folly. With us, as with Abram, we act independently of God and open the door for trouble to enter. Abram and Sarai had only themselves to thank for their grief, shame and guilt that rushed in upon them.

III. Hagar's Plight and Promise: Gen. 16:4, 6, 11-16

A. Hagar's Contempt: 4

4. And he went in unto Ha´-gar, and she conceived: and when she saw that she had conceived, her mistress was despised in her eyes.

Hagar had pride in something that was not even hers. It was a gift. She had done nothing to be able to conceive, just as Sarai had done nothing to cause her inability to conceive. How humans to take pride in natural endowments. Vanity, vanity, all is vanity with humankind. Then we look down on those who do not measure up to an arbitrary standard established by man. Boasting of herself as a better woman than Sarai, Hagar would not submit as she had before to Sarai. How haughty and insolent the lowly can become when favored or advanced, if a spiritual change has not occurred. Even those accustomed to honor have great difficulty handling it humbly and justly. There is a saying, "The stone will return upon him that rolls it." How often we suffer at the hands of those we indulge in an inappropriate manner. Sarai learned her lesson the hard way.

B. Hagar's Plight: 6

Abram said unto Sarai, Behold, thy maid is in thy hand; do to her as it pleaseth thee. And when Sarai dealt hardly with her, she fled from her face.

Human nature is prone to retaliation when wronged. Sarai was no exception. Hagar had pride in a gift. She treated it as an accomplishment. Sarai used her power of station wrongly. Hagar had wronged her mistress with her insolence and dishonored Abram, her husband, by not honoring Sarai. How quickly we forget that the God who made us made the neighbor next to us.

Sarai, provoked to a passionate anger, abandoned the plan of her own devising. She banished Hagar bearing the child Sarai once envisioned as the heir to Abram.

C. Hagar's Promise: 11-16

11. And the angel of the LORD said unto her, Behold, thou *art* with child, and shalt bear a son, and shalt call his name Ish-ma-el; because the LORD hath heard thy affliction.

12. And he will be a wild man; his hand *will* be against every man,

and every man's hand against him; and he shall dwell in the presence of all his brethren.

13. And she called the name of the LORD that spake to her, Thou God seest me: for she said, Have I also here looked after him that seeth me?

14. Wherefore the well was called Be'-er-la-hai'-ri; behold, *it is* between Ka'-desh and Be'-red.

15. And Ha'-gar bare Abram a son: and Abram called his sons name, which Ha'-gar bare, Ish'-ma-el.

16. And Abram *was* fourscore and six years old, when Ha'-gar bare Ish'-ma-el to Abram.

God is not thwarted by our mistakes. He redeems them. Sarai ran ahead of God in her action. Abram went along with her. Hagar boasted and taunted Sarai. Though men and women may see only our flaws and failings, God bestows blessings in spite of and often even through our miscues and ill advised actions. Here, God promised to solve Hagar's problem. Likewise, later Abram and Sarai still received their son. God's arm is not shortened by humankind's plots and plans so that He cannot act.

Often it is when we recognize the affliction we have brought upon ourselves that we call out to God. The child's name Ishmael means "God will hear." He always does.

Though the promise of God contained a description of the child as a wild man and one who was against all men, his seed would not be removed from the earth. He would stand. Not only so, but even the wild ones can and will be tamed and their energy channeled for good by the grace of our Lord ultimately revealed in Jesus Christ.

The statement, "Have I also here looked after him that seeth me?" may mean Hagar saw the back parts of God as He moved away from her. She had communed with God. The name of the well means, "the well of the living one who sees me."

Evangelistic Emphasis

Well-intentioned people sometimes become obstacles between others and God. Not realizing how God is presently working in their lives to produce faith and response in others, they sometimes take inappropriate action "on their own." Their action, then, rather than producing faith and response, actually becomes an obstacle to the plan that God had in place.

It is difficult, often, to know exactly what role we play in God's sovereign will. We know that He used others to bring us to faith. We know that He has promised to work in our lives, too. Yet, as we come into contact with opportunity after opportunity, we're not just sure "which one God placed there just for me."

Perhaps, the best response we can make to the opportunities of God is to be prepared to "plant" or "water," whichever the occasion requires. At the same time, disciplining ourselves to remember that *it is God who gives the increase*, we permit the seed of God to produce naturally. We refuse to force artificially the harvesting hand of God. A young plant that is pulled out of the ground by its roots will not live. The plant that is appropriately watered and allowed to grow will push through the ground on its own and yield its fruit in its season. The key is not "idleness" on our part, but patience. It's not that we do nothing. Rather, like the farmer, we respond appropriately to the fertile soil with seed and water and loving care, and we wait for the Lord to produce His harvest.

◆◆◆◆◆◆

Memory Selection

Sarai said to Abram, "Behold now, the LORD has prevented me from bearing children; go in to my maid; it may be that I shall obtain children by her." *Genesis 16:2*

It is unlikely that Sarai was malicious in her suggestion to Abram. She was a wife who obviously loved her husband very much. Yet, she was now an old woman. At seventy-five she did not think it possible that she would yet give birth. It had even been ten years since the promise of God had come that they would have children.

"We must be doing something wrong," perhaps she thought. "Maybe we misunderstood what God meant. Perhaps, He never intended *me* to carry this child. Certainly, I can mother a child born to my own maid. Obviously, that's what God intended."

Like Sarai, we too presume wrongly the reasons or the plans of God. Jumping to conclusions as to why some accident was allowed to happen, why a child died, or what outcome God will bring to a given process, we speak hastily and foolishly.

October 10, 1993

Weekday Problems

Fred and Jill have been married for twelve years. During their early years of marriage, they were both in school and used birth control carefully so as not to begin their family prematurely. After Jill's graduation from college, she supported Fred while he finished law school. Finally, with law school behind them and the bar exams passed, Fred and Jill began to plan for children.

Much to their surprise, the children did not come. They had never considered even the possibility that they might have difficulty giving birth. Nor were they quick to face that reality. Month after month passed, but they did not give up easily. After four years of planning and dreaming and dusting their beautifully equipped nursery, they finally faced the fact that they needed help. Yet, even though they went to the best and highest paid specialists they could find, two years later they were still childless.

One day a few months ago, one of their many doctors raised the idea of contracting a surrogate mother. It seems that the problem is with neither Fred's nor Jill's lack of fertility, but with Jill's body blocking the impregnation from ever taking place. For a fee this surrogate mother would carry Jill's child, begun "in a test tube," until it was ready to be born. Once born, it would be Jill and Fred's child in every respect.

*Since money is not an obstacle, should Fred and Jill take this opportunity to have children, or should they consider Jill's barrenness as "God's will for them"?

*Are there moral or ethical implications of surrogate motherhood that Christians ought to avoid?

*What message, if any, ought Fred and Jill glean from this text for their dilemma?

♦♦♦♦♦♦

Say It Right

Abram:	Ay-brum
Sarai:	Say-ray
Hagar:	Hay-gar
Ishmael:	Ish-may-el
Beerlahairom:	Beer-lay-high-roy
Kadesh:	Kay-desh
Bered:	Bee-red

This Lesson in your life
TARNISHED HEROES

One of the refreshing traits of the Bible is its uncompromising honesty. Never, throughout all of its pages, are it's "heroes" protected from being seen, "warts and all." History's "greats" like Moses, Joshua, David, Peter and Paul are shown for what they were—imperfect humans who stumbled from time to time in their attempts to walk with God. Even Abraham, the father of faith, had feet of clay. Contrary to the pedestal that we would put him on, the biblical text dispels any false and unrealistic image we might build of him.

In contrast to popular imaginings about Abraham, the scriptures do not indicate an ongoing daily dialogue with God. The record seems to suggest that sometimes years separated God's messages. During those times of silence, Abraham had to act based on his faith in God just like any of the rest of us.

There were times when he was not really sure how God would carry out his promise. There were times when he did not seem to be sure what God wanted him to do. There were times when, it seems, doubt even entered into his mind. Abraham was a champion of faith, not because he was pampered and hand-led throughout his earthly pilgrimage. Very much to the contrary, he was a champion of faith because, in spite of the silence he heard, and in spite of the unanswered questions he had, and in spite of the yet unfulfilled promises, he still believed. That belief, then, prompted him to move on in the direction God had shown.

Where there was no light from God, Abraham groped in the darkness. At times he waited patiently. At other times he chanced a guess as to the direction that God wished him to go. Sometimes, he was wrong. Such was true when he agreed with Sarah to father a child by Hagar. The problem was not that he was "unfaithful to Sarah." He was unfaithful to God, even if it was a "well-intentioned" unfaithfulness. The long-lasting repercussions of that unfaithfulness haunted him and his family for generations to come. If Abraham was a hero in any sense, certainly it was a tarnished one.

Today also, the church can boast only "tarnished heroes." We make a strategic mistake when we pretend otherwise. This does not necessarily mean that our churches ought to flaunt the skeletons that are hidden in their closets. The display of unsightly skeletons usually does not encourage either conception or birth. But, whenever we pretend that those of faith have no faults or weaknesses in order to impress those we hope will come to faith, we compromise the truth and are guaranteed to reap embarrassment in the end.

In the truest sense of the word, the Bible has no heroes but God. He is presented as the Creator, the Redeemer, the forgiving Father, the Deliverer of all. There is no trophy gallery honoring men or women who ran the race without flaw. Only one pedestal stands with honor in the halls of biblical history. Only one pedestal will adorn the history of the church. God is our hero. Creator, Redeemer, Sacrifice, Savior, Judge and Lord. He is the origin of all. He is the sustainer of all. In one mighty, self-sacrificing act—a cross—He redeemed all. "To God be the glory. Great things He has done"

Seed Thoughts

1. Why would Sarai send her husband into the tent to consort with her handmaid?
Sarai "knew" that she was past the age of bearing children, and yet she was aware of the promise of God that Abraham would father children. This seemed to her to be the way to accomplish that.

2. Who was Hagar?
Hagar was Sarai's Egyptian handmaiden.

3. After Hagar conceived, why did she despise Sarai?
The Scriptures do not tell us. It seems, however, that she felt superior to her mistress in becoming pregnant when her mistress could not.

4. How did Sarai treat Hagar after Hagar conceived?
The Bible says that Sarai "dealt harshly" with Hagar (mistreated her), so much so that Hagar left.

5. Where did Hagar go when she ran away from Abram's house?
The angel of the Lord found Hagar at a spring in the wilderness by the road that leads to Shur. Apparently, she had set out to go to Shur.

(PLEASE TURN PAGE)

---

1. Why would Sarai send her husband into the tent to consort with her handmaid?

2. Who was Hagar?

3. After Hagar conceived, why did she despise Sarai?

4. How did Sarai treat Hagar after Hagar conceived?

5. Where did Hagar go when she ran away from Abram's house?

6. When the angel of the Lord found Hagar, what did he tell her to do?

7. What was the promise made to Hagar by the angel of the Lord?

8. Why was the well called "Beer Lahai Roi"?

9. Who gave Hagar's son his name?

10. What kind of man did the angel of the Lord say that Ishmael would be?

Sarai "knew" that she was past the age of bearing children, and yet she was aware of the promise of God that Abraham would father children. This seemed to her to be the way to accomplish that.

Hagar was Sarai's Egyptian handmaiden.

The Scriptures do not tell us. It seems, however, that she felt superior to her mistress in becoming pregnant when her mistress could not.

The Bible says that Sarai "dealt harshly" with Hagar (mistreated her), so much so that Hagar left.

The angel of the Lord found Hagar at a spring in the wilderness by the road that leads to Shur. Apparently, she had set out to go to Shur.

The angel of the Lord told Hagar to return to her mistress and submit to her hand.

The angel of the Lord promised Hagar, "I will multiply your descendants exceedingly, so that they shall not be counted for the multitude."

Beer Lahai Roi means "well of the Living One who sees me." God had seen her in the desert even though she was far away from home.

Hagar's son was named by the angel of the Lord. He instructed that he was to be named "Ishmael," which means "God hears."

The angel of the Lord said that Ishmael would be "a wild man" whose hand would be against every man.

(SEED THOUGHTS--Cont'd)

6. When the angel of the Lord found Hagar, what did he tell her to do?
The angel of the Lord told Hagar to return to her mistress and submit to her hand.

7. What was the promise made to Hagar by the angel of the Lord?
The angel of the Lord promised Hagar, "I will multiply your descendants exceedingly, so that they shall not be counted for the multitude."

8. Why was the well called "Beer Lahai Roi"?
Beer Lahai Roi means "well of the Living One who sees me." God had seen her in the desert even though she was far away from home.

9. Who gave Hagar's son his name?
Hagar's son was named by the angel of the Lord. He instructed that he was to be named "Ishmael," which means "God hears."

10. What kind of man did the angel of the Lord say that Ishmael would be?
The angel of the Lord said that Ishmael would be "a wild man" whose hand would be against every man.

October 17, 1993

God Establishes An Everlasting Covenant

Genesis 17:1-14

17 AND when Abram was ninety years old and nine, the LORD appeared to Abram, and said unto him, I *am* the Almighty God; walk before me, and be thou perfect

2 And I will make my covenant between me and thee, and will multiply thee exceedingly.

3 And Abram fell on his face: and God talked with him, saying,

4 As for me, behold, my covenant *is* with thee, and thou shalt be a father of many nations.

5 Neither shall thy name any more be called Abram but thy name shall be Abraham; for a father of many nations have I made thee.

6 And I will make thee exceeding fruitful, and I will make nations of thee, and kings shall come out of thee.

7 And I will establish my covenant between me and thee and thy seed after thee in their generations for an everlasting covenant, to be a God unto thee, and to thy seed after thee.

8 And I will give unto thee, and to thy seed after thee, the land wherein thou art a stranger, all the land of Canaan, for an everlasting possession; and I will be their God.

9 And God said unto Abraham, Thou shalt keep my covenant therefore, thou, and thy seed after thee in their generations.

10 This *is* my covenant, which ye shall keep, between me and you and thy seed after thee; Every man child among you shall be circumcised.

11 And ye shall circumcise the flesh of your foreskin; and it shall be a token of the covenant betwixt me and you.

12 And he that is eight days old shall be circumcised among you, every man child in your generations, he that is born in the house, or bought with money of any stranger, which *is* not of thy seed.

13 He that is born in thy house, and he that is bought with thy money, must needs be circumcised: and my covenant shall be in your flesh for an everlasting covenant.

14 And the uncircumcised man child whose flesh of his foreskin is not circumcised, that soul shall be cut off from his people; he hath broken my covenant.

◆◆◆◆◆◆

◀ **Memory Selection**
Genesis 17:7

◀ **Devotional Reading**
Genesis 17:1-15

◀ **Background Scripture**
Genesis 17

◀ **Printed Scripture**
Genesis 17:1-14

GOD ESTABLISHED AN EVERLASTING COVENANT

Teacher's Target

Man's decisions are mostly short-sighted. We tend to think only of the immediate or short term consequences. God sees from the perspective of eternity. When we plug into His decisions we are investing in events that will be consequential for generations to come. Abram misread his cues at times, but never wavered in going with God.

THERE ARE other leaders in the Christian faith who have had far reaching impact, like Abraham: Martin Luther, John Wesley, Charles Finney, Martin Luther King, Corrie Ten Boom, Mother Theresa, others. Reflect upon your own local church. Who in your community of faith has impacted your church?

Ask the class to write out five ways they believe they are to count for God. Discuss.

We make many contracts in our lives. What contracts has God made with you?

Lesson Introduction

Have you ever noticed how God takes the initiative with people? Even after his act of disobedience, Adam was sought by God. In his initial call (Gen. 12:1-3) and here, Abram is approached by God. Faith never knows where it is going. God is the orchestrator of faith life. Ours is not a life of knowing where we are going but knowing who is asking us to go.

Here it is well to notice Abram's silence before God. In awe, Abram fell on his face and listened.

Abram is not covenanting to keep his vows before God. Rather it is a matter of our relationship to God who covenants with us. It is God's honor that is on the line not ours. It is necessary for us steadfastly to refuse to promise anything and to give ourselves over to God's promise. Trusting in our trust is a sinking sand.

Teaching Outline

I. Offer and Awe: Gen. 17:1-3
   A. God's Offer: 1, 2
   B. Abram's Awe: 3
II. Fellowship and Fatherhood: Gen. 17:4-9
   A. Fellowship with God: 4
   B. Father of Nations: 5-9
III. The Sign and the Shame: Gen. 17:10-14
   A. Circumcised Heirs: 10-13
   B. Uncircumcised Posterity: 14

Daily Bible Readings

Mon. God Gives Abram a New Name *Gen. 17:1-5*
Tue. God's Covenant Includes: Land, Nations, Descendants *Gen. 17:6-10*
Wed. Circumcision: A Sign of the Covenant - *Gen. 17:11-14*
Thurs. Sarah Blessed as Mother of Sons/Kings - *Gen. 17:15-19*
Fri. A Blessing and a Covenant *Gen. 17:21-25*
Sat. Keeping Covenant Maintains Faith and Circumcision *Gen. 17:26-27; Heb. 6:13-20*
Sun. Be an Unashamed Worker for Christ - *2 Tim. 2:1-15*

VERSE BY VERSE

I. Offer and Awe: Gen. 17:1-3

A. God's Offer: 1, 2

1. AND when Abram was ninety years old and nine, the LORD appeared to Abram, and said unto him, I am the almighty God; walk before me, and be thou perfect.
2. And I will make my covenant between me and thee, and will multiply thee exceedingly.

God starts things and God ends things. our decision is whether we will be a part of the action of God. What Jesus said in the New Testament is what His Father said in the Old Testament, "Come with me." Abram didn't talk. He listened. Abram didn't plan. He wondered. Abram didn't propose. He received. Abram didn't take charge. He was guided. Abram didn't have certainty. He had faith in God's certainty.

These characteristics of listening and receiving are what make Abram the father of the faith. It is not that he did everything right. He didn't. For example, twice he tried to pass Sarai off as his sister to protect himself. What he did do, was continually go back to the Father for instruction. Slowly he seemed to learn to go to Him first.

In John 6 when Jesus asked His disciples would they also go away from Him, Peter responded, "To whom shall we go? You have the words of eternal life." Abram knew the same truth. Only God had the perspective, the plan and the power to meet his every need.

God promises that when we walk before Him we will be made perfect. It is never our perfection. It is His perfection bestowed upon us fully as we relate to Him.

B. Abram's Awe: 3

3. And Abram fell on his face: and God talked with him, saying,

It is the attitude of a child that reveals to us what awe and wonder really are like. This is the way Abram was before God. Mouth open, tongue silent, eyes wide and ears catching every sound as the Almighty encountered him and spoke. There is deep humility, confident trust and pure delight in being in God's presence. These are characteristics of faith in God.

There is a proper kind of waiting for God's direction. But often we have been given God's witness and are refusing to accept it. God has promised. Will you accept it? Self-idolatry would have us wait for more evidence. Abram did not hesitate. He flung himself before God and left the confirmation and consequences to God.

Often people tell themselves that they are waiting for God to speak when in truth they are refusing to accept and act on what God has clearly said. As one person once said, "My problem is not what I don't know, it is that I don't act on what I already know."

II. Fellowship and Fatherhood: Gen. 17:4-9

A. Fellowship with God: 4

4. As for me, behold, my covenant is with thee, and thou shalt be a father of many nations.

God talked with Abram. Whenever this occurs, the person's life is no longer about his own private agenda. Now Abram was caught up into God's universal purpose. His effectiveness as an instrument for God depended upon this fellowship with God. His self-interest dissipated. He was no longer a private road to carry the goods of me and mine. Now he was God's interstate for His purposes and good pleasure.

Do you ask permission of your hands to use them? No more so does God ask permission to use us for His ends. God and His will are our joy as well as our accepted duty. Now the impossible is possible. The supernatural power of God has come to us. we laugh with joy that God has made room in Himself for us and let us in on His incredible promise.

Joy does not mean there will be no more problems. Neither is joy something required as a sign that we are on our way to heaven. Joy is that exhilaration of knowing we are in fellowship with God. It is much like the joy of a child getting to go along with his dad to his job. The child gets to see and even work alongside his dad as he sees him do mighty deeds. What joy to be let in on the "big people's" world. So it is with us and our Heavenly Father.

B. Father of Nations: 5-9

5. Neither shall thy name any more be called Abram, but thy name shall be Abraham; for a father of many nations have I made thee.
6. And I will make thee exceeding fruitful, and I will make nations of thee, and kings shall come out of thee.
7. And I will establish my covenant between me and thee and thy seed after thee in their generations for an everlasting covenant, to be a God unto thee, and to thy seed after thee.
8. And I will give unto thee, and to thy seed after thee, the land wherein thou art a stranger, all the land of Canaan, for an everlasting possession; and I will be their God.
9. And God said unto Abraham, Thou shalt keep my covenant therefore, thou, and thy seed after thee in their generations.

Abram was given a new name, Abraham, which meant "father of nations." on what basis? He believed in the Heavenly Father and allowed Him to flow through his life. A new disposition was now in Abraham. Not the natural way which the Hagar episode represented, but the supernatural way which resulted from oneness with God. Continually the natural has to die as we, by faith, see more clearly that God's ways are not our ways.

"Father of nations" clearly referred in the first instance to the twelve tribes (or nations) of Israel. But God had more in mind as the New Testament tells us. Ultimately God intended to be the father of people from every tribe, every tongue, every people, every nation. These were to be God's kingdom of priests (Rev. 5:9,10). The "seed" through which this would become so was not Isaac. This seed was Jesus Christ as Paul explains in Galatians 3:16. How much broader is God's embrace than man's. How much deeper His meaning. How much richer His fulfillment.

How one sided are the blessings of God! He offers. He promises. He bestows. We marvel that He did it through us, frail vessels of clay.

III. The Sign and the Shame: Gen. 17:10-14

A. Circumcised Heirs: 10-13

10. This is my covenant, which ye shall keep, between me and you and thy seed after thee; Every man child among you shall be circumcised.

11. And ye shall circumcise the flesh of your foreskin; and it shall be a token of the covenant betwixt me and you.

12. And he that is eight days old shall be circumcised among you, every man child in your generations, he that is born in the house, or bought with money of any stranger, which is not of thy seed.

13. He that is born in thy house, and he that is bought with thy money, must needs be circumcised: and my covenant shall be in your flesh for an everlasting covenant.

Circumcision was an outward sign of God's sanctification (making holy) of that which is unholy (the whole human race and Abraham's descendants in particular at this point). The old nature of man is made one with a new nature by the action of God. The ignoble is declared and made noble by the presence and power of the great "I AM."

Notice God doesn't discard the natural. He doesn't deny historical and physical descent of generations. Even Jesus Christ came by way of humankind through Mary, His mother, in the virgin birth. That which is defiled is to be made holy. God is not calling us out to be pious prudes but pure persons. Now through God's action in Jesus Christ, Jews and Gentiles are heirs of the promise.

This receiving of circumcision was an unalterable identification with the children of Abraham. There was no turning back from the "cutting off" of the old life and purification of the heart toward God.

B. Uncircumcised Posterity: 14

14. And the uncircumcised man child whose flesh of his foreskin is not circumcised, that soul shall be cut off from his people; he hath broken my covenant.

The uncircumcised among the people were excluded from the promise. With circumcision, it was not just the removal of the foreskin that was involved. The outward act was a sign of an inner reality. Faith had been placed in the promises of God by the one circumcised. Also, the person had declared himself a member of the fellowship of those who desired to worship and serve God. There was nothing magical in the surgical processing any more than there is magic in the waters of baptism in the Christian faith. The refusal to receive circumcision was a declaration of refusal of God's promise. It was an action expressive of "un-faith."

Evangelistic Emphasis

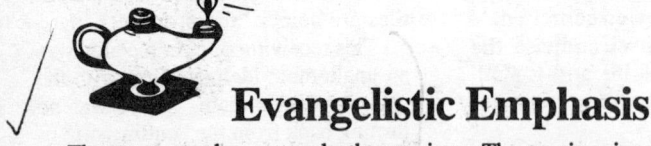

The ceremony does not make the marriage. The marriage is made by the vows that two people exchange and their commitment to keep them. Yet, the ceremony of a marriage is not without value. It provides the public arena where vows can be invoked before God and witnesses. In that setting the marriage vow is solemnized with love and devotion. If there is any failure to keep the vow, an accounting is called for. Marriages that fail do not fail because of a flaw in the ceremony, but rather because of a breaking of the commitment.

It is obvious from the biblical text that God values ceremony. Every time He made a vow with His people, He drove a peg at that point in history with a ceremony. The circumcision of Abram and the changing of his and Sarai's names to Abraham and Sarah was such a peg. Never again would they forget that day and the vow they made to God, nor the covenant He made with them. Until they went to their graves, they told the story of that day when God made His covenant with them. Their names reminded them every time they were introduced to a stranger or kissed each other good night. Abraham carried the mark of his agreement to the Lord's covenant on his body as long as he lived.

When we look at the church of today, we find ceremony. Some would call it, "meaningless ceremony." Yet, in most cases the ceremony present had significant meaning when it was initiated.

It continues to have meaning to those who prove faithful to the vow it signifies. when we find ceremony "meaningless," it is usually because we have not taken seriously the vow. The uninitiated will almost never fully appreciate the ceremony that disciples regard as priceless.

♦♦♦♦♦♦

Memory Selection

I will establish my covenant between me and you and your descendants after you throughout their generations for an everlasting covenant, to be God to you and to your descendants after you. *Genesis 17:7*

The phrase "you and your descendants after you" is rather inclusive and far-reaching. But, "everlasting" goes the limit and beyond. It is difficult to fathom the ultimate implications of such a promise. Our minds are trapped by time and limited by the extent of our own qualified experience.

Our God is not limited by such qualifications. Since He is the originator and author of the covenant, only the limits that He specifies apply. It was not Abraham's place to negotiate "terms of contract" with God. Instead, he was offered a covenant that was very much to his advantage. His choice was either to agree to it or to reject it. To all of his offspring was extended an open invitation to subscribe. As children of Abraham, the covenant was theirs for the receiving. If received, they were bound by all conditions therein and were beneficiaries of all promises. Circumcision was the symbol they received signifying their covenant status.

October 17, 1993

Weekday Problems

Herb was a grandfather when he became a Christian. All of his life he had scoffed at the "foolishness of religion." As far as he was concerned, "The weak and the ignorant might need a crutch to lean on," but he didn't. His children were taught from birth to avoid "religion pushers" much as other children are warned about those who deal drugs.

Now an old man, Herb sees life differently. It is as much of a surprise to him that he is a Christian as it is to anyone else. His only heartbreak is that his faith came so late. Of course, he is immeasurably thankful for the salvation he has found. But, his family life is already behind him. His wife died several years ago, an atheist like he had been. His children are all grown, each of them steeped in the antagonism to faith he had instilled within them. Desperately, he wants his family to share in what he now knows.

*What can Herb do to persuade his family that he is not insane, but rather more sane than he has ever been?

*How can Herb deal with his own past and the awareness that his children lack faith because of him?

*Is there any sense in which Herb's new covenant relationship with God offers a special open door of opportunity to his children and grandchildren?

*What special covenant privilege does your relationship with God offer to your children?

♦♦♦♦♦♦

Sparkles

How fickle we are. We want to be distinctive but not different. We want to be uniform but not united. Sometimes the more we try to be distinct the more we become alike. Fads make those who accept them look alike. There is no distinctiveness in that. We love uniforms, formal and informal, that make statements about our station or position.

Only God's distinctions can be worn without galling. Only He can transform our hearts and unite us as Jew or Greek, rich and poor, male and female, slave and free, at the foot of the cross where there is level ground.

This Lesson In Your Life

CONTRACTS AND COVENANTS

It is not unusual for American Christians to think of contracts and covenants in the same terms. We are, after all, very much a contract-oriented people. Though there was a time when a hand-shake was sufficient to seal a bond between two neighbors, it is not true anymore. Litigations and lawsuits have put an end to casual agreements based on the friendship of two people. Today, even the smallest business arrangement is "signed in triplicate" with attorneys on both sides scouring carefully every sentence for tricks, traps and loopholes.

Contracts, by their very nature, are agreements that rest heavily on the technical precision of the wording of the bond. In a sense, they are adversarial in nature and suspicious in tone.

Covenants, on the other hand, are a bit foreign to our culture, even though we make and participate in them commonly. Rather than resting on "wording precision," covenants rest on the strength of the relationship between the people of the covenant. Due to the fact that we tend to think in terms of "contract" instead of "covenant," even the covenants that we make are often treated more like contacts.

"Marriage" is a classic example of this. Though it is a covenant, based on the relationship shared by two people, it is often policed like a contract. Very commonly, the marriage is dissolved because of a "breach of contract." Though that phraseology is not often used, the essence of what takes place is precisely that. It is sad that this lack of distinction between covenant and contract has assaulted our homes. That which was intended to be tolerant (for better or for worse) and forbearing ('til death do us part) has come to be most intolerant and unforgiving.

Perhaps, even more unfortunate is that we often view the covenant of God in legalistic and contractual terms. Adversarially, God is perceived to be scouring carefully our record, seeking some error that might be cited against us at judgment day. Correspondingly, we hope to build our defense based on "legal loopholes," "technical righteousness" and "character witnesses." Seeking contract satisfaction, rather than covenant satisfaction, minimum requirements often define the limits of our response. This approach to religion endeavors more to *obligate God* to save us than to glorify God for having saved us.

Please notice that the covenant that God made with Abraham was very much rooted in a *relationship*. God himself initiated it and defined the terms thereof. It was not a negotiated agreement, but an accepted promise. That is, the promise was made by God and accepted by Abraham, according to the terms and blessings therein. The only obligations placed upon God were placed there by his own doing. God and Abraham were not adversaries but friends.

One of the privileges inherent in the Abrahamic covenant was the option of any of the descendants of Abraham to participate in the same. If they chose to do so, they participated according to the terms and blessing of the original pledge. In good faith the males of the family surrendered to the seal of circumcision. That seal documented the promise of God to accept this individual into His covenant and documented the promise of the participant to be loyal to God.

Seed Thoughts

1. What did Abram do when the Lord appeared to him?
When the Lord appeared to Abram, he fell on his face.

2. What was the covenant that God made with Abram?
The covenant that God made with Abram was two-fold. First, He promised that Abram would have many descendants. Second, he promised to give him Canaan as an everlasting possession.

3. To what did God change Abram's name? And why?
God changed Abram's name to "Abraham" because of his promise that Abraham would be the father of many nations. Abraham means "father of many."

4. What did God say he would give Abraham and to his seed?
The Lord told Abraham that he would give to him and to his descendants all the land of Canaan where he presently roamed as a stranger. It would be an everlasting possession.

5. How was Abraham to show his acceptance of the covenant?
The Lord designated circumcision as the sign of the covenant. Abraham and every male descendant thereafter was to be circumcised in order to signify his place in the covenant.

(PLEASE TURN PAGE)

---

1. What did Abram do when the Lord appeared to him?

2. What was the covenant that God made with Abram?

3. To what did God change Abram's name? And why?

4. What did God say he would give Abraham and to his seed?

5. How was Abraham to show his acceptance of the covenant?

6. Who all was to be circumcised?

7. What would happen to the uncircumcised man child?

8. What was to change about Sarai as a part of this new covenant arrangement?

9. What does the Bible say that the Lord did when he was through talking with Abraham?

10. How soon after this conversation with God did Abraham circumcise the males of his house?

When the Lord appeared to Abram, he fell on his face.

The covenant that God made with Abram was two-fold. First, He promised that Abram would have many descendants. Second, he promised to give him Canaan as an everlasting possession.

God changed Abram's name to "Abraham" because of his promise that Abraham would be the father of many nations. Abraham means "father of many."

The Lord told Abraham that he would give to him and to his descendants all the land of Canaan where he presently roamed as a stranger. It would be an everlasting possession.

The Lord designated circumcision as the sign of the covenant. Abraham and every male descendant thereafter was to be circumcised in order to signify his place in the covenant.

All males born in Abraham's house, all males bought from a stranger to be part of the household were to be circumcised according to the covenant that God made with Abraham.

According to the instruction of the Lord, every uncircumcised male would be cut off from his people.

The word of the Lord to Abraham regarding Sarai was that she would no longer be called Sarai, but Sarah. She would no longer be barren, but would give birth to a son.

The Bible says that "God went up from Abraham" when He had finished talking to him.

That very same day Abraham circumcised every male that lived in his house.

(SEED THOUGHTS--Cont'd)

6. Who all was to be circumcised?
All males born in Abraham's house, all males bought from a stranger to be part of the household were to be circumcised according to the covenant that God made with Abraham.

7. What would happen to the uncircumcised man child?
According to the instruction of the Lord, every uncircumcised male would be cut off from his people.

8. What was to change about Sarai as a part of this new covenant arrangement?
The word of the Lord to Abraham regarding Sarai was that she would no longer be called Sarai, but Sarah. She would no longer be barren, but would give birth to a son.

9. What does the Bible say that the Lord did when he was through talking with Abraham?
The Bible says that "God went up from Abraham" when He had finished talking to him.

10. How soon after this conversation with God did Abraham circumcise the males of his house?
That very same day Abraham circumcised every male that lived in his house.

October 24, 1993

God Keeps His Promise

Genesis 21:1-14
21 AND the LORD visited Sarah as he had said, and the LORD did unto Sarah as he had spoken.
2 For Sarah conceived, and bare Abraham a son in his old age, at the set time of which God had spoken to him.
3 And Abraham called the name of his son that was born unto him, whom Sarah bare to him, Isaac.
4 And Abraham circumcised his son Isaac being eight days old, as God had commanded him.
5 And Abraham was an hundred years old, when his son Isaac was born unto him.
6 And Sarah said, God hath made me to laugh, *so that* all that hear will laugh with me.
7 And she said, Who would have said unto Abraham, that Sarah should have given children suck? for I have born *him* a son in his old age.
8 And the child grew, and was weaned: and Abraham made a great feast the *same* day that Isaac was weaned.
9 And Sarah saw the son of Ha'-gar the Egyptian, which she had born unto Abraham, mocking.
10 Wherefore she said unto Abraham, Cast out this bondwoman and her son: for the son of this bondwoman shall not be heir with my son, *even* with Isaac.
11 And the thing was very grievous in Abraham's sight because of his son.
12 And God said unto Abraham, Let it not be grievous in thy sight because of the lad, and because of thy bondwoman; in all that Sarah hath said unto thee, hearken unto her voice; for in Isaac shall thy seed be called.
13 And also of the son of the bondwoman will I make a nation, because he *is* thy seed.
14 And Abraham rose up early in the morning, and took bread, and a bottle of water, and gave it unto Hagar, putting *it* on her shoulder, and the child, and sent her away: and she departed, and wandered in the wilderness of Beersheba.

◆◆◆◆◆◆

◀ **Memory Selection**
Genesis 21:2, 3

◀ **Devotional Reading**
Genesis 21:1-21

◀ **Background Scripture**
Genesis 21:1-21

◀ **Printed Scripture**
Genesis 21:1-14

Teacher's Target

God promises and fulfills. We make mistakes and suffer consequences. However, God may do mighty things with our mistakes.

Have the class list promises made to them by people. Ask them to check off the ones that have been kept.

Make a list of mistakes. Ask the class to put a check by the ones that seem to have no consequences and an "x" by those that had obvious consequences. When parents allow children to continue to behave in ways that are without discipline, what pitfall are they setting up for the child?

Ask the class about their feelings when promises are delayed; when they are not kept at all. Is there anything "on hold" in your lives right now?

Lesson Introduction

Can we believe God is good when providence seems to prohibit the fulfillment of what He has promised? Abraham is our greatest example of a yes answer to that question. "Abraham believed God" (Rom. 4:3). No one said that Abraham's life of faith didn't have its ups and downs. It was full of them, many of which could have been avoided if Abraham had remembered one fundamental fact: only the one who makes the promise can fulfill it.

Abraham, like us, was not big on waiting. He endured the long drought of Sarah's infertility. Waiting, which means going on in a settled certainty of faith in God's faithfulness, slipped away from his consciousness from time to time.

Remember, God is as honest as He ought to be. If He doesn't mean it; He doesn't say it. Abraham and Sarah will see.

Teaching Outline

I. Said and Did: Gen. 21:1, 2
   A. God Had Said: 1
   B. God Now Did: 2
II. Obedience and Laughter: Gen. 21:3-7
   A. Abraham's Obedience: 4, 5
   B. Sarah's Laughter: 6, 7
III. Mocking Grief and Consolation: Gen. 21:8-14
   A. Ishmael's Mocking: 8, 9
   B. Abraham's Grief: 10, 11
   C. God's Consolation: 12-14

Daily Bible Readings

Mon. Middle-Eastern Courtesy and Hospitality - *Gen. 18:1-8*
Tue. Sarah Laughs at Possible Pregnancy - *Gen. 18:9-15*
Wed. Abraham's Nephew Saved from Death - *Gen. 19:12-19a*
Thurs. Isaac's Birth Brings Sarah Laughter - *Gen. 21:1-7*
Fri. Sarah Almost Ruins a Festival *Gen. 21:8-11*
Sat. Abraham and Abimelech Make Covenant - *Gen. 21:22-27*
Sun. Friendly Agreements Replace War - *Gen. 21:28-34*

October 24, 1993

VERSE BY VERSE

I. Said and Did: Gen. 21:1, 2

A. God Had Said: 1

1. AND the LORD visited Sarah as he had said, and the LORD did unto Sarah as he had spoken.

Sarah had waited ninety years for this baby boy. When she was told she would have a child of her own, even though the word was from God, she laughed. Maybe not so much from lack of faith in what God could do, as from unbelief in what her body could be counted on to accomplish at her age. When confronted about her laughter she lied just as she had seen her husband do on many occasions. Revealing her true feelings was not something she desired. But Scripture does not question her faith. Hebrews 11:11 celebrates her faith.

God's speaking is always for an appointed time. This is always on His appropriate timetable. God is not subject to our agenda. We are subject to His.

B. God Now Did: 2

2. For Sarah conceived, and bare Abraham a son in his old age, at the set time of which God had spoken to him.

God's word, when seen from the side of fulfillment by His deed, always reveals that He knew best and caused a joy to occur within us that would not have been nearly as profound nor appreciated if done when we had expected it.

Promise of resurrection sustained Jesus during His ministry, though it did not stop His being hard pressed until it was over (Luke 12:50). On the other side of the resurrection we can see the necessity of His earthly life to demonstrate what life lived in the Spirit is about.

Abraham's life prior to the promise shows us what faith is like. Jesus' life shows us what the life continually in fellowship with God is like and what one who receives it can expect from the world (Phil. 2:5-11). True belief in the Father's word will enable us to do that which is beyond the power of human nature.

Notice that the child born to Sarah was an ordinary child. only faith can see the extraordinary nature here. The same was true of Jesus. God rarely comes in the way the world would detect. God is often so natural in His presence we can miss Him even in His most magnificent feats. For example, the birth of Isaac, the birth of Jesus, the crucifixion of Jesus.

II. Obedience and Laughter: Gen. 21:3-7

A. Abraham's Obedience: 4, 5

4. And Abraham circumcised his son Isaac being eight days old, as God had commanded him.

5. And Abraham was an hundred years old, when his son Isaac was born unto him.

Do you think Abraham might have wondered if he could stand to see Sarah suffering without a child of her

73

own? What about Sarah herself? Does such desolution come to us all when we submit our ambitions to God's transformation? Abraham, though he misinterpreted and acted rashly, never stopped listening to God.

B. Sarah's Laughter: 6, 7

6. And Sarah said, God hath made me to laugh, so that all that hear will laugh with me.
7. And she said, Who would have said unto Abraham, that Sarah should have given children suck? for I have born him a son in his old age.

"Hope but don't expect." That might have been Sarah's motto. She believed but could not conceive of how it could be possible for her to conceive a child. When such a scarcely expected promise is fulfilled she is filled with hilarious laughter. How can this thing be?

Do we not say the same thing even more emphatically, concerning Jesus? How can it be possible that God incarnated Himself and did this marvelous work for us?

Look who God used: a haughty Sarah and a humble peasant, Mary. Neither would have been voted most likely for God to honor. God appears so willy-nilly in His selection. Truly, He is no respecter of persons. He appears at the strangest times in the most unlikely places and persons.

III. Mocking Grief and Consolation: Gen. 21:8-14

A. Ishmael's Mocking: 8

8. And the child grew, and was weaned: and Abraham made a great feast the same day that Isaac was weaned.

Ishmael was like his mother before him. She had taunted Sarah. Galatians 4:25 gives us an interpretation of this verse by declaring that "he that was born after the flesh persecuted him that was born after the Spirit." The Septuagint (the Greek translation of the Old Testament) states that Sarah saw Ishmael playing with Isaac and in the playing mocking him." There was no movement made to cast Ishmael out until he became a disturbance and a grief to Abraham's household. Again, God is not in the punishment business but the protection and restoration business. The natural must be disciplined and turned into spiritual.

B. Abraham's Grief: 10, 11

10. Wherefore she said unto Abraham, Cast out this bondwoman and her son: for the son of this bondwoman shall not be heir with my son, even with Isaac.
11. And the thing was very grievous in Abraham's sight because of his son.

Were the natural not "cast out" (disciplined) it would not only perish itself; it would bring the whole house down with it. All of us have to heed God's word and discipline ourselves mentally, emotionally and spiritually. It was for Ishmael's good, as well as Isaac's, that God agreed with Sarah's assessment. The natural cannot be the master, but rather the servant of the spiritual. To God a strong will is not strength but grave weakness. Our pride and insolence will get us thrown out every time.

Jesus never exercised His will (John 5:19, 30), but He had more will than any who ever lived. He was teachable (meek) and obedient.

Here, Abraham was teachable and obedient. He did not follow His own inclinations.

C. God's Consolation: 12-14

12. And God said unto Abraham, Let it not be grievous in thy sight because of the lad, and because of thy bondwoman; in all that Sarah

hath said unto thee, hearken unto her voice; for in Isaac shall thy seed be called.

13. And also of the son of the bondwoman will I make a nation, because he is thy seed.

14. And Abraham rose up early in the morning, and took bread, and a bottle of water, and gave it unto Ha′-gar, putting it on her shoulder, and the child, and sent her away: and she departed, and wandered in the wilderness of Be′-er-she′-ba.

Our egocenteredness must be destroyed. By casting it out God could bring it back into right relationship with the spiritual above the natural. Our personhood is what God desires to recreate. Like Abraham, we may grieve the loss of the natural, but we know the outcome will be a life which knows no division between sacred and secular. Abraham would not let the good of the natural keep him back from God's best. Abraham had to believe that it was best for the mother and child of the natural to be subject to the spiritual. By casting it out God could bring it back into right relationship with the spiritual above the natural.

Evangelistic Emphasis

God must surely like laughter! Certainly, He has had His hand at provoking quite a bit of it through the ages. Just take a look at the baboon, sometime, or the platypus. Many of God's creatures strike a smile without so much as a word. Not a few times, God has enticed even rolling-on-the-floor laughter.

Such was the case when the Lord had it announced to Abraham and Sarah that Sarah was going have a baby. Gen. 17:17 tells us that "Abraham fell upon his face, and laughed..." Then, Gen. 18:12 says that "Sarah laughed within herself..." She was more discrete about it than her husband, but still she got the joke.

The joke was on Sarah and Abraham. God is one who keeps his word! Just as the Lord had promised, "Sarah conceived, and bare Abraham a son in his old age, at the set time of which God had spoken to him" (Gen. 21:2).

Have you noticed how God continues to make us laugh today? People we would have sworn would never enter a church door are to be found leading worship, teaching classes, or even preaching. Our God is the God of the impossible. His surprises never cease. Seemingly, He still enjoys making people laugh. He transforms the most lost drunkards into whole persons again. He melts the icy hearts of the contemporary Scrooges. He takes the broken pieces of my life and produces something beautiful and good.

◆◆◆◆◆◆

Memory Selection

Sarah conceived, and bore Abraham a son in his old age at the time of which God had spoken to him. *Genesis 21:2*

According to the TV series MASH, Radar's dad was sixty-three when Radar was born. In real life, Christian psychologist Paul Tournier was born in his father's seventy-first year. Unfortunately, his dad died two months later. according to family legend, the old man got so excited about fathering a child in his old age that his heart couldn't take it. He died with a smile on his face.

Abraham was one hundred years old! Perhaps more impressive than the old age of Abraham was the old age of Sarah. Long before "it ceased to be with Sarah after the manner of women." (Gen. 18:11) In other words, her body had ceased its monthly cycle in preparation for conception. Her body itself had given up the idea of ever birthing. It had completely shut down all reproductive systems.

Sarah's body did not have the last word. God did. He brought new life out of that body that was thought to be dead.

October 24, 1993

Weekday Problems

Harold and Sandy Jones have been married for eighteen years. For the past five years, Harold's mother has lived with them. With two teenage children and an "in-house mother-in-law," the stress at the Jones' house has become rather intense. It seems as though almost every day there is a big "blow up" about something. According to Sandy, Harold's mother is usually in the middle of it. It appears to Sandy as if her mother-in-law is a catalyst to a whole lot of negative communication. She seems to grow increasingly critical with age. Neither of the children ever seem to please her. There is a ready word of correction in response even to their best attempts.

Harold works long hours at the office and is gone often on business trips. He surmises that Sandy is "blowing things out of proportion." However, he's not sure. Last week, Sandy told Harold that she'd had all she could stand; his mother had to go.

*How can Harold carry out his duty both to his aged mother and to his wife and children? At what point does his responsibility to the one end and his responsibility to the other begin?

*How can this text bear light on Harold's dilemma? What "word from God" does the text have for Harold?

*What are some possible "other options" for Harold to see to his mother's needs as well as provide for the needs of his family?

♦♦♦♦♦♦

Smiles

There is no such thing as a bad short sermon.

A pessimist is a person who, when there is a choice of two evils, takes both.

An optimist can have more fun guessing wrong than a pessimist can have guessing right.

How can you spot a pessimist? He turns out the light to see how dark it is.

Optimist: happy-chondriac.

Believe only half of what you hear, but be sure it's the right half.

This Lesson In Your Life

SEPARATE BLESSINGS

Our competitive mind-set is such that usually we think in terms of "winners" and "losers." Even in an enviable setting such as where "the most beautiful girl in the world" is being chosen, our heart aches for the first runner-up because "she lost!" So, Miss Australia is a winner, while Miss America (the first runner-up) and all the others are "losers." How sad.

Such is true, also, at most of the sporting events in our culture. A golf pro may very well collect a fortune for his second-place position in the tournament, yet he gets with it the stigma of being "a loser" because he came in second rather than first. At a stock car track, a camera may be required to determine which of two cars actually won a 500 mile race. At the 11 o'clock news, the sportscaster informs us that "After 500 miles, A. J. Foyt *lost* by three hundredths of a second to Mr. Petty."

It is this same kind of thinking that is often brought to this story of Isaac and Ishmael. Somehow, it is seen as a "rival relationship" asking, "Who will get the blessing?" As we continue to read, we learn that "Isaac is the winner and Ishmael is the loser." There may very well be a sense in which that is true.

However, before we shed too many tears for Ishmael, and before we write him off as "rejected by God," we ought to read again the text. Verse 18 records God as saying of Ishmael, "... *I will make him a great nation,*" and verse 20 says, *"And God was with the lad; ... "*

It is true that Isaac was chosen as the son of Abraham through whom the Messiah would come. This is as had been planned all along. Ishmael proved to be an unplanned interruption of the process. It wasn't that Ishmael was not loved by God nor that he was somehow deemed unfit or undeserving of the role. Someone else had already been chosen.

It is clear from this scripture that Abraham was very much distressed over the matter. He anguished over sending Hagar and Ishmael away to fend for themselves. God, however, provided him with reassurance that they were not being abandoned, as it seemed. Ishmael may not have been the one chosen through whom the Messiah would come, but he was in no sense "rejected by God." Indeed, God was very much with him and would make him great.

The necessity to make choices is common to life. Sometimes, those choices are pressed upon us by others. The situation can be particularly distressing when there appears to be a conflict between our responsibilities on two different fronts. Fulfilling our responsibility at one point jeopardizes our faithfulness to a separate responsibility. It would be so much simpler "if no one forced the issue" and we could continue to fulfill partially our responsibility to both loyalties.

Yet, the demand for us to choose forces us to be more fully the human beings that God created us to be. Choices mature us. Tough choices make us strong. They compel us to decide our priorities, our goals, our identity. The demand placed upon us to make choices enables us to establish who we are in concrete terms.

It is helpful, though, when we come to realize that it is possible for you to be you and for me to be me (emphatically different) without that difference or distinction signifying rivalry.

Seed Thoughts

1. What happened to Sarah that was quite unusual for a woman of her age?
As the Lord promised, Sarah conceived and bore Abraham a son in his old age.

2. Why did Sarah laugh when she listened from behind the door to the men talking?
Sarah laughed because she overheard one of the visitors tell Abraham that she was going to give birth to a son. She was long past the age of childbirth.

3. What did Abraham do when Isaac was eight days old?
When Isaac was eight days old, Abraham circumcised him as the Lord had instructed him so that Isaac would be included in the covenant of the Lord.

4. What did Abraham do when Isaac was weaned?
The Bible says that on the same day that Isaac was weaned Abraham made a great feast.

5. What did Sarah want to be done with Ishmael?
Sarah insisted to Abraham that Ishmael, the son born to Hagar, be cast out.

(PLEASE TURN PAGE)

---

1. What happened to Sarah that was quite unusual for a woman of her age?

2. Why did Sarah laugh when she listened from behind the door to the men talking?

3. What did Abraham do when Isaac was eight days old?

4. What did Abraham do when Isaac was weaned?

5. What did Sarah want to be done with Ishmael?

6. Why did Sarah insist that Hagar and Ishmael be cast out?

7. How did Abraham feel about Sarah's request?

8. What was God's response to Sarah's request of Abraham?

9. How did God show his care of Ishmael?

As the Lord promised, Sarah conceived and bore Abraham a son in his old age.

Sarah laughed because she overheard one of the visitors tell Abraham that she was going to give birth to a son. She was long past the age of childbirth.

When Isaac was eight days old, Abraham circumcised him as the Lord had instructed him so that Isaac would be included in the covenant of the Lord.

The Bible says that on the same day that Isaac was weaned Abraham made a great feast.

Sarah insisted to Abraham that Ishmael, the son born to Hagar, be cast out.

Sarah insisted that they be cast out so that Ishmael could not be heir with her son, Isaac.

The matter distressed Abraham greatly because it concerned his son.

The Lord told Abraham to listen to whatever Sarah requested and to do accordingly.

God showed his care of Ishmael by promising Abraham that He would be with Ishmael and would make Ishmael into a great nation. God heard Ishmael's cry in the desert.

Growing into an adult, Ishmael became an archer and lived in the desert of Paran marrying a woman from Egypt.

(SEED THOUGHTS--Cont'd)

6. Why did Sarah insist that Hagar and Ishmael be cast out?
Sarah insisted that they be cast out so that Ishmael could not be heir with her son, Isaac.

7. How did Abraham feel about Sarah's request?
The matter distressed Abraham greatly because it concerned his son.

8. What was God's response to Sarah's request of Abraham?
The Lord told Abraham to listen to whatever Sarah requested and to do accordingly.

9. How did God show his care of Ishmael?
God showed his care of Ishmael by promising Abraham that He would be with Ishmael and would make Ishmael into a great nation. God heard Ishmael's cry in the desert.

10. What became of Ishmael as he grew into a man?
Growing into an adult, Ishmael became an archer and lived in the desert of Paran marrying a woman from Egypt.

October 31, 1993

The Sons of Isaac

Genesis 25:19-34

19 And these are the generations of Isaac, Abraham's son: Abraham begat Isaac:
20 And Isaac was forty years old when he took Rebekah to wife, the daughter of Bethuel the Syrian of Padanaram, the sister to Laban the Syrian.
21 And Isaac intreated the LORD for his wife, because she *was* barren: and the LORD was intreated of him, and Rebekah his wife conceived.
22 And the children struggled together within her, and she said, If *it be* so, why *am* I thus) And she went to enquire of the LORD.
23 And the LORD said unto her, Two nations are in thy womb, and two manner of people shall be separated from thy bowels; and *the one* people shall be stronger than *the other* people; and the elder shall serve the younger.
24 And when her days to be delivered were fulfilled, behold, *there were* twins in her womb.
25 And the first came out red, all over like an hairy garment; and they called his name Esau.
26 And after that came his brother out, and his hand took hold on Esau's heel; and his name was called Jacob: and Isaac *was* threescore years old when she bare them.
27 And the boys grew and Esau was a cunning hunter, a man of the field; and Jacob *was* a plain man, dwelling in tents.
28 And Isaac loved Esau, because he did eat of *his* venison: but Rebekah loved Jacob.
29 And Jacob sod pottage: and Esau came from the field, and he *was* faint:
30 And Esau said to Jacob, Feed me, I pray thee, with that same red *pottage*; for I *am* faint: therefore was his name called Edom.
31 And Jacob said, Sell me this day thy birthright.
32 And Esau said, Behold, I *am* at the point to die: and what profit shall this birthright do to me?
33 And Jacob said, Swear to me this day, and he sware unto him: and he sold *his* birthright unto Jacob.
34 Then Jacob gave Esau bread and pottage of lentiles; and he did eat and drink, and rose up, and went his way: thus Esau despised *his* birthright.

◆◆◆◆◆◆

◀ **Memory Selection**
Genesis 25:23

◀ **Devotional Reading**
Genesis 25:19-23

◀ **Background Scripture**
Genesis 25:19-34

◀ **Printed Scripture**
Genesis 25:19-34

THE SONS OF ISAAC

Teacher's Target

Being first born is a special place in any family. Not in the sense of "better than others," but in the sense that the parents are experiencing the wonder of childbirth for the first time. However, the first born is not always the favorite one. All kinds of dynamics happen in families.

In biblical times the first child was to receive the birthright. Esau sold his for a mess of pottage.

Discuss with the class their birth order in their family of origin. How did it feel to be there? How did you get along with siblings? Did you ever envy an older or younger child in the family?

Ask the class members what they have traded away for things you wanted. Have you ever lost something valuable while grasping for an immediate desire or supposed need?

Lesson Introduction

An old fable tells of a dog with a bone in its mouth going by a pond and seeing his reflection in the water. He stopped, moved closer, looked down into the water and saw a dog with a bigger bone staring back at him. Desiring the larger bone he opened his mouth to bite it only to see it disappear as the bone he had went "kerplunk!" in the water. The lesson is obvious.

We know the principle in the story, yet we betray ourselves. Esau is a good example. His immediate "want" caused him to shortchange himself for the future.

Jacob was cunning. He played upon his brother's weakness. Being hungry was not a sin. Letting the natural rule the spiritual was Esau's error. Long before this event Esau had relied upon his arm of flesh to carry him. Our appetites must not have mastery over us.

Teaching Outline

I. The Request Made:
   Gen. 25:19-21
   A. Rebekah Barren: 19, 20
   B. Isaac Prays: 21
II. Twins Born: Gen. 25:22-26
   A. In the Womb: 22
   B. In Promise: 23
   C. In Birth: 24-26
III. Siblings Struggle:
   Gen. 25:27-34
   A. The Difference: 27, 28
   B. The Betrayal: 29-32
   C. The Blessing: 33, 34

Daily Bible Readings

Mon. God Tests Abraham's Faith - *Gen. 22:1-13*
Tue. God Blesses Abraham's Progeny - *Gen. 22:14-19*
Wed. The Search for Isaac's Wife - *Gen. 24:7-18, 25-27*
Thurs. Isaac and Ishmael Bury Abraham - *Gen. 25:5-11*
Fri. Before Birth Rebekah's Twins Struggle - *Gen. 25:19-23*
Sat. Isaac Loved Esau; Rebekah Loved Jacob - *Gen. 25:24-28*
Sun. Esau Sells His Birthright to Jacob - *Gen. 25:29-34*

October 31, 1993

VERSE BY VERSE

I. The Request Made: Gen. 25:19-21

A. Rebekah Barren: 19, 20

19. And these are the generations of Isaac, Abraham's son: Abraham begat Isaac:
20. And Isaac was forty years old when he took Rebekah to wife, the daughter of Be-thu'-el the Syrian of Pa'-dan-a'-ram, the sister to Laban the Syrian.

Rebekah was a wife given in answer to prayer. Abraham's eldest servant, sent to find Isaac's bride, had asked for God to reveal the appropriate maiden. God was faithful. Like his father's wife before him, Isaac's wife, Rebekah, was barren. For twenty years after his marriage Isaac had no children. During the delay of the promise of an heir, Isaac did not, like his father, go into a handmaiden's chambers. He waited. Isaac was a man of contemplation rather than action. He spent his days in quietness and silence. God uses men of all temperaments and personalities. There is no blueprint for us to follow, only God.

Rebekah was "very fair to look upon" (Gen. 24:16) much loved by Isaac (Gen. 24:67). She was a person of determination and was not bashful about taking the initiative. These qualities, as with all our natural attributes when they are not yielded to God, brought conflict and heartache.

God's promises are sure. Often to us, His timing seems slow. He even appears to be thwarted by world events. However, this is the surface. Like a calm sea, beneath the appearance, much activity is in process. So it is with God. His work is obvious only to faith.

B. Isaac Prays: 21

21. And Isaac intreated the LORD for his wife, because she was barren: and the LORD was intreated of him, and Rebekah his wife conceived.

Isaac is an old Testament example of one who prayed without ceasing (Luke 18:1; 1 Thess. 5:17). He was sixty years old when his children were born. His faith had been tried. His patience exercised. His prayer answered. Long awaited mercies are often the occasions of our deepest joys and experiences of abundant life.

II. Twins Born: Gen. 25:22-26

A. In the Womb: 22

22. And the children struggled together within her; and she said, If it be so, why am I thus? And she went to enquire of the LORD.

An excessive amount of movement within Rebekah's womb made her apprehensive. Her concern could have been around the health of the life within her, or a sensing of a sign of things to come, or concern for her own health.

She had worried before their conception about her barrenness. Now she was troubled about the struggle in the womb. What we often most desire may be granted, but it may also bring with it trials and troubles we never envisioned in our ideal picturing of things prior to the actual event. To Rebekah's credit, she sought the Lord with her anxiety and questioning. An example for us all!

B. In Promise: 23

23. And the LORD said unto her, Two nations are in thy womb, and two manner of people shall be separated from thy bowels; and the one people shall be stronger than the other people; and the elder shall serve the younger.

God reassured Rebekah. He always does so when we focus on Him rather than let our circumstances get into our hearts and control us.

The fact that two nations were within her was the explanation God gave for the mysterious conflict. They were to be quite different. Their distinctiveness would clash and great conflict would result. Again, God promised heirs, but not without the reality of struggle and conflict which are part and parcel of this world.

C. In Birth: 24-26

24. And when her days to be delivered were fulfilled, behold, there were twins in her womb.
25. And the first came out red, all over like an hairy garment; and they called his name Esau.
26. And after that came his brother out, and his hand took hold on Esau's heel; and his name was called Jacob: and Isaac was threescore years old when she bare them.

The prophecy from God came true. Esau was rough and hairy as if grown. "Esau" means "made," as one reared already. He was a man of action. Jacob was fair and tender. Much of what we choose in life comes from our natural constitution and make up. As is not uncommon with God, He chose the weaker one through whom He would do His mighty acts.

From the first, Jacob was grasping to overtake and pass Esau. He grabbed his foot at birth. Jacob means "the supplanter." In time through deceit he would live up to his name.

III. Siblings Struggle: Gen. 25:26-34

A. The Difference: 27, 28

27. And the boys grew: and Esau was a cunning hunter, a man of the field; and Jacob was a plain man, dwelling in tents.
28. And Isaac loved Esau, because he did eat of his venison: but Rebekah loved Jacob.

In their manner, minds, interest, temperament and affections, Esau and Jacob were, to say the least, different. Esau was a man of the world, of the field. He was a hunter, gifted in the use of bow and arrow. Jacob was a man of the quieter life, a plain, unassuming tent dweller. As a shepherd he was more attached to the safe and silent pursuits. Esau was the rugged warrior.

Jacob was the statesman. Esau appeared to have been more outgoing. Jacob was more a searcher for solitude. There is the indication in other writings that a "man of the tent" was a seeker of spiritual things. Esau had lost the scent of such things out in the field. Esau is called profane in Hebrews 12:16.

B. The Betrayal: 29-32

29. And Jacob sod pottage: and Esau came from the field, and he was faint:
30. And Esau said to Jacob, Feed me, I pray thee, with that same red pottage; for I am faint: therefore was his name called E'-dom.
31. And Jacob said, Sell me this

day thy birthright.

32. And Esau said, Behold, I am at the point to die: and what profit shall this birthright do to me?

Often we miss the fact that there were two betrayals here. Jacob betrayed his brother by playing upon his weakness rather than helping him protect himself from his weakness. The natural inclination, apart from God's grace having worked in our lives, is to exploit, not protect another's weakness.

The second betrayal was Esau's betrayal of himself. His desire for the immediate satiation of his physical hunger led him to make one of history's most foolish bargains. Esau was led by his belly. He allowed the natural to have ascendancy over the spiritual. Though he had the reputation of being a cunning man, a simple and plain man conned him. Is this not the story of God choosing the foolish to confound the wise (1 Cor. 1:27)?

C. The Blessing: 33, 34

33. And Jacob said, Swear to me this day; and he sware unto him: and he sold his birthright unto Jacob.

34. Then Jacob gave Esau bread and pottage of lentiles; and he did eat and drink, and rose up, and went his way: thus Esau despised his birthright.

Being "penny wise and pound foolish," Esau relinquished his blessing. Jacob played upon Esau's faulty or weak reasoning and secured the blessing with a bowl of "red." The pottage had no meat in it but the red color drew him at this moment more than his own game had. He was drawn out of himself, as all of our appetites tend to do, and gave Jacob his birthright.

Jacob chose his time to strike the bargain well. Esau's strength had ebbed away. He secured an oath to seal the promise. He knew Esau's nature well. Later he would want to renege.

It may be true that Jacob was not so ambitious for the material things of the blessing as for the spiritual. Nevertheless, his coveting the blessing and his deception are no less to be denounced than Esau's folly.

Evangelistic Emphasis

"Election" is a difficult concept for the Christian to grasp. Historically, it is a topic that has provoked questions and debates regarding the justice of God. As the apostle Paul pointed out in his letter to the Romans when he wrote of Jacob and Esau, *"(For the children being not yet born, neither having done* any *good or evil, that the purpose of God according to election might stand, not of works, but of him who calleth;) It is said unto her [Rebekah], The elder shall serve the younger"* (Rom. 9:11-12). We ponder, "Why?"

Perhaps, it might be helpful if our approach to the whole matter of "election" were thought of in very practical terms. The truth is, there are many examples of election in the normal course of life. The fact that a baby is born in the late twentieth century gives to that baby opportunities and challenges that were not available to another baby born in A.D. 1500.

Some are born into poverty and ignorance on the same day that others are born to a life of wealth and privilege. Why? One infant girl will be born with black skin, while another infant girl will be born with white skin. One baby boy will be born with a high potential for learning. Another baby boy will enter into life with a grossly limited potential for learning. One will be born into a land where freedoms are plentiful. Another will start life under the thumb of a tyrant. Some, just because of birth and circumstances of life, will be blessed generously with the opportunity to hear God's message and to respond. Others will never hear.

In each situation the human child starting life is charged with the responsibility to "bloom where he is planted." As Christians, that too is our task.

Memory Selection

And the LORD said unto her, two nations are in thy womb, and two manner of people shall be separated from thy bowels; and the one people shall be stronger than the other people; and the elder shall serve the younger.
Genesis 25:23

During my graduate studies, I was privileged to survey a variety of "personality theories" that are used to interpret behavior and to provide therapy. one particular theory caught my interest, and to a large extent, my loyalty. It was the theory called "Tabula Rasa," or "Blank Slate." Basically, this theory postulates that every person is born into this life as a "blank slate." What a person becomes is the pure result of the circumstances to which he or she has been exposed. If it were possible to duplicate exactly the experience of life, the personality, likewise, would be duplicated exactly.

That sounded good to me! "Tabula Rasa" became *my theory* of personality development. For four years I never wavered. Then one day, my second child was born. Within the week I had trashed four years of loyalty to a theory as "pure hogwash!"

Child number two was clearly and radically different from child one from the moment she exited the birth canal.

What is noted in this text about Jacob and Esau is often the very experience of parents, even the parents of twins. We never cease to be amazed at how totally different our own children can be from each other.

October 31, 1993

Weekday Problems

Ivan is forty-eight years old. He has been a farmer all of his life, as was his dad before him. His own dad had gotten his start into farming as a sharecropper. Gradually, he saved his excess profits and bought a small piece of land. Then in the years that followed, he added to that land as the money came and as the land became available. When Ivan was old enough to set out on his own, his dad gave him a plot of land on which to begin. There he built a small house and started his family.

Ivan was one of four sons, all of whom were farmers given a start by their dad. When their dad died a few years ago, his remaining land was divided among them. It has not always been an easy life, but it has provided them with a comfortable living. Even a sizable college fund has been set up so as to allow the upcoming children the chance to be even more competitive by studying the science of agriculture.

There is but one problem. Of Ivan's three children (Nick, John and Traci), only John is interested in farming. From his childhood he showed excitement when the seed sprout pushed its stem up through the earth. Neither Nick nor Traci has shown even a slight interest. Ivan thought that with time the love for farming that he knew would come. To his great disappointment, it hasn't.

*How can Ivan best deal with this very real disappointment in his children's choices? Does this text provide any advice or warnings that Ivan would do well to consider?

*Even against Ivan's most determined will, he definitely feels *partial* toward John. He suspects that the children are aware of his favoritism. How can he deal with this bias in a constructive way?

♦♦♦♦♦♦

Sparkles

The Monkey and the Fish

The monkey was lifting the fish out of the water. A passerby asked, "What on earth are you doing?" As he placed the fish on the branch of the tree, the monkey replied, "I am saving it from drowning."

What is good for one is not always so for others. One man's junk is another man's treasure. The same sun that melts the wax hardens the clay.

This Lesson In Your Life
BIRTHRIGHTS, ETC.

We western Christians do not relate very well to the whole concept of "birthright." We understand "inheritance," but "birthright" and "inheritance," though related, are not exactly the same. It is therefore difficult for us to grasp either Esau's irreverence or Jacob's trickery.

Perhaps it would be easier for us to relate to the offense that would be felt by a family should a son bypass his right to the family business or the family home or, even worse, should he forsake the family name. Such choices are made by grown children, and usually they seem quite rational to the offspring. They are not likely to be understood by the parents.

A son was trying to make his way into the entertainment business. His agent told him that his name "Freidrick Heimer" must go. "It's not catchy enough," he said. "It is heavily laden with all kinds of ethnic baggage. It doesn't roll off the tongue easily. In these times of pro-American import-bashing, it doesn't sound American." So, after a thoroughly computerized analysis of Freidrick's career goals, the name "Bill Winters" was selected.

Bill was excited as he envisioned his career soon taking off. His call home to Dad to tell him his new name did not produce the same level of excitement in his father that he had experienced. His dad was furious! Actually, the word "hurt" would be a more accurate description. As far as Bill's dad was concerned, Freidrick had spurned his *birthright*--both his given name and his family name were frivolously discarded in pursuit of "an image." What's more, it was an image that Bill's father didn't even like.

It is this kind of lack of appreciation for one's heritage that was found in Esau. His immediate hunger seemed more important to him than his privileged position in the family or his posterity. What some men would kill for, Esau traded for a "pottage of lentils." It was more than just a double portion of the inheritance (Deut. 21:17) that Esau carelessly forfeited. The birthright carried with it a position of authority within the family, the responsibility for the future of the tribe, and immeasurable perennial honor. It is for this great forfeiture, that it is said of Esau, "Esau despised his birthright."

Most of us will never have to deal with the temptation to "sell our birthright," but we may be enticed to sell something else just as fundamental to our identity. Will it be our integrity? Integrity is sometimes sold for less than a bowl of pottage. It may be peddled to save face in a moment of potential embarrassment, or to avoid the risk of being associated with the unorthodox. Or, will it be our good name that is merchandised for a few extra pieces of silver to jingle in our pocket?

One's morality is sometimes sold in a moment of panic when truth might be painful and a lie promises momentary escape. One's chastity is exchanged for the illusive goal of "being accepted." One's fidelity is trashed for the seductive promise of feeling young again.

The truth is that most of us are unable honestly to "look down our nose" at the foolishness of Esau. At some point along the way, we have "sold our birthright," too. It's not that we don't know better. Rather, in our moments of weakness, we forget the richness of the value of the most precious treasures of life, the ingredients of our identity.

Seed Thoughts

1. What was Isaac's response to the awareness that Rebekah was unable to have children?
When Isaac learned that his wife was barren, he prayed to the Lord for her.

2. How many years passed after Isaac prayed to the Lord in behalf of Rebekah until the Lord granted the request of his prayer?
The Bible does not say specifically, but the flow of the text seems to indicate that the Lord granted the request of his prayer immediately.

3. What surprise awaited Rebekah when she went in to see the doctor for her first prenatal checkup?
After being anxious because she was barren, she was then surprised with the news that she was going to give birth to twins.

4. After God answered Isaac's prayer that his wife be enabled to conceive, why did Rebekah feel it necessary to petition the Lord again?
Rebekah was greatly troubled by the twins who struggled within her and asked the Lord why this was happening to her.

5. How did the Lord respond to Rebekah's enquiry as to the jostling within her?
The Lord told Rebekah that this was just the beginning. "Two nations are in thy womb, and two manner of people shall be separated from thy bowels," he warned.

(PLEASE TURN PAGE)

---

1. What was Isaac's response to the awareness that Rebekah was unable to have children?

2. How many years passed after Isaac prayed to the Lord in behalf of Rebekah until the Lord granted the request of his prayer?

3. What surprise awaited Rebekah when she went in to see the doctor for her first prenatal checkup?

4. After God answered Isaac's prayer that his wife be enabled to conceive, why did Rebekah feel it necessary to petition the Lord again?

5. How did the Lord respond to Rebekah's enquiry as to the jostling within her?

6. What additional word of prophecy did the Lord give to Rebekah that proved to be fateful in the years that lay ahead?

7. How long had Isaac and Rebekah been Married before they became parents?

8. What was unusual about Esau when he was born?

9. What was unusual about Jacob at his birth?

10. What was the price that Jacob requested for the serving of pottage Esau had asked for in his hunger?

When Isaac learned that his wife was barren, he prayed to the Lord for her.

The Bible does not say specifically, but the flow of the text seems to indicate that the Lord granted the request of his prayer immediately.

After being anxious because she was barren, she was then surprised with the news that she was going to give birth to twins.

Rebekah was greatly troubled by the twins who "struggled together within her," and so went to ask the Lord why this was happening to her.

The Lord told Rebekah that this was just the beginning. "Two nations are in thy womb, and two manner of people shall be separated from thy bowels," he warned.

While she was yet pregnant with her twins, Gold told Rebekah that the older child would serve the younger.

Isaac and Rebekah were married twenty years before they became parents. Isaac was forty when they married and sixty when the twins were born.

The Bible says that when Esau was born, he was red, all over like a hairy garment.

When the twins were born, Esau was born first but Jacob had hold of Esau's heel as he was born. This proved to be merely symbolic of the struggle between them that lay ahead.

Jacob seized the opportunity presented by Esau's hunger and offered to trade the pottage for Esau's birthright.

(SEED THOUGHTS--Cont'd)

6. What additional word of prophecy did the Lord give to Rebekah that proved to be fateful in the years that lay ahead?
While she was yet pregnant with her twins, Gold told Rebekah that the older child would serve the younger.

7. How long had Isaac and Rebekah been married before they became parents?
Isaac and Rebekah were married twenty years before they became parents. Isaac was forty when they married and sixty when the twins were born.

8. What was unusual about Esau when he was born?
The Bible says that when Esau was born, he was red, all over like a hairy garment.

9. What was unusual about Jacob at his birth?
When the twins were born, Esau was born first but Jacob had hold of Esau's heel as he was born. This proved to be merely symbolic of the struggle between them that lay ahead.

10. What was the price that Jacob requested for the serving of pottage Esau had asked for in his hunger?
Jacob seized the opportunity presented by Esau's hunger and offered to trade the pottage for Esau's birthright.

November 7, 1993

Jacob Steals the Blessing

Genesis 27:6-8
6 And Rebekah spake unto Jacob her son, saying, Behold, I heard thy father speak unto Esau thy brother, saying
7 Bring me venison, and make me savoury meat, that I may eat, and bless thee before the LORD before my death.
8 Now therefore, my son, obey my voice according to that which I command thee.

Genesis 27:15-27
15 And Rebekah took goodly raiment of her eldest son Esau, which *were* with her in the house, and put them upon Jacob her younger son:
16 And she put the skins of the kids of the goats upon his hands, and upon the smooth of his neck:
17 And she gave the savoury meat and the bread, which she had prepared, into the hand of her son Jacob.
18 And he came unto his father, and said, My father: and he said, Here *am* I; who *art* thou, my son?
19 And Jacob said unto his father, I *am* Esau thy firstborn; I have done according as thou badest me: arise, I pray thee, sit and eat of my venison, that thy soul may bless me.
20 And Isaac said unto his son, How *is it* that thou hast found it so quickly, my son? And he said, Because the LORD thy God brought *it* to me.
21 And Isaac said unto Jacob, Come near, I pray thee, that I may feel thee, my son, whether thou *be* my very son Esau or not.
22 And Jacob went near unto Isaac his father, and he felt him, and said, The Voice *is* Jacob's voice, but the hands *are* the hands of Esau.
23 And he discerned him not, because his hands were hairy, as his brother Esau's hands: so he blessed him.
24 And he said, *Art* thou my very son Esau? And he said, I *am*.
25 And he said, Bring *it* near to me, and I will eat of my son's venison, that my soul may bless thee. And he brought *it* near to him, and he did eat: and he brought him wine, and he drank.
26 And his father Isaac said unto him, Come near now, and kiss me, my son.
27 And he came near, and kissed him: and he smelled the smell of his raiment, and blessed him, and said, See, the smell of my son *is* as the smell of a field which the LORD hath blessed:

◆◆◆◆◆◆

◀ **Memory Selection**
Genesis 27:35

◀ **Devotional Reading**
Hebrews 12:14-17

◀ **Background Scripture**
Genesis 27

◀ **Printed Scripture**
Genesis 27:6-8, 15-27

JACOB STEALS THE BLESSING

Teacher's Target

The story of the Trojan horse, the story of the Fifth Column, the movie "The Sting" are examples of gaining advantage by deception. It's as old as the serpent speaking for God in the Garden of Eden. What is strange about our story here is that God blesses the deceiver. Maybe that is because deceivers are all He has to work with. We deceive ourselves and others. *HAVE YOU* ever been deceived. By whom? How did it feel? Have they ever done the same? Have they ever deceived themselves? When? What were the consequences? Did they feel really smart when they pulled off a trick or joke or deception on someone? Did they plot with others? Could they have done it without the strength of numbers?

Lesson Introduction

There were coalitions in Isaac's house. He favored Esau. Rebekah favored Jacob. Walking alongside a child in a special way for awhile to give him the confidence he needs to launch out on his own is one thing. Tying him so closely to you that you can get him to collude with you in a scheme against the other parent and a sibling is another. Here we have an example of the latter.

Rebekah's concern and Jacob's was not whether they were right or wrong, but getting caught. Whenever we are concerned about being caught in an action it should sound an alarm that it might not be the right move. We humans seem to be good at overriding our alarm systems.

Teaching Outline

I. The Plot: Gen. 27:6-8
   A. Rebekah Overhears: 6
   B. Jacob Enlisted: 7, 8
II. The Planning: Gen. 27:15-17
   A. The Clothes: 15
   B. The Smell and Touch: 16
   C. The Food: 17
III. The Act: Gen. 27:18-27
   A. Jacob Deceives: 18, 19
   B. Isaac Questions: 20-24
   C. Jacob Receives: 25-27

Daily Bible Readings

Mon. Isaac Seeks the Way of Peace *Gen. 26:12-22*
Tue. Isaac Joins Philistines in Covenant - *Gen. 26:23-29*
Wed. Isaac's Servants Dig Another Well - *Gen. 26:30-35*
Thurs. Isaac Prepares to Bless Esau *Gen. 27:1-4*
Fri. Rebekah Schemes to Bless Jacob *Gen. 27:5-17*
Sat. Isaac Unwittingly Blesses Jacob *Gen. 27:31-46*
Sun. Esau Weeps Bitterly: Hates Jacob - *Gen. 27:31-46*

November 7, 1993

VERSE BY VERSE

I. The Plot: Gen. 27:6-8

A. Rebekah Overhears: 6

6. And Rebekah spake unto Jacob her son, saying, Behold, I heard thy father speak unto Esau thy brother, saying,

Esau had promised his birthright to Jacob in a weak moment. Still the action of Rebekah was not justified. She overheard Isaac's instructions for the occasion of blessing Esau. She could not bear this action to be carried out and deprive her beloved Jacob of the birthright.

How important it is for parents to stand together. When the primary allegiance is not to each other, all manner of loyalties can come between couples. children need to know their parents are together. They do not need to be able to drive a wedge between father and mother. Such ability to divide the household gives a false sense of power that will bring great harm to the household and the child in later life. Jacob and Esau are good examples of such unsuspected mischief. How little we know of the damage we will cause when we change the course of things ever so slightly at the beginning.

B. Jacob Enlisted: 7, 8

7. Bring me venison, and make me savoury meat, that I may eat, and bless thee before the LORD before my death.
8. Now therefore, my son, obey my voice according to that which I command thee.

Rebekah called Jacob, the favored one in her affections, to plot the plan that would thwart the intended blessing of Esau. Rebekah could have gone to Isaac and told him of Esau's selling of the birthright to Jacob. Also, she could have pointed out that Esau forfeited his right to the blessing by marrying foreign wives. Possibly this would have been enough for Isaac to bestow the blessing upon Jacob. Instead she colluded with her son to supplant his brother by deceiving Isaac. She taught Jacob through example how to lie and deceive.

II. The Planning: Gen. 27:15-17

A. The Clothes: 15

15. And Rebekah took goodly raiment of her eldest son Esau, which *were* with her in the house, and put them upon Jacob her younger son:

Isaac had lost his ability to see. But still the clothing Esau wore was distinctively different from Jacob's clothing. Rebekah had thought out every detail necessary to pull off the deception. The disguise was flawless.

B. The Smell and Touch: 16

16. And she put the skins of the kids of the goats upon his hands, and upon the smooth of his neck:

Esau would have the smell of wild animals and his body was covered with hair. Jacob was fair and smooth. The skins of freshly killed young goats would provide the rough texture to his hands as well as the smell of one who had just killed game for a meal.

The cultural taboo against abuse of the elderly had to be overcome. Do you not think Jacob was full of foreboding? Rather than protecting his father from dangers caused by the deterioration of his faculties in old age, Jacob was going to play upon them to his father's shame and his brother's hurt.

C. The Food: 17

17. And she gave the savoury meat and the bread, which she had prepared, into the hand of her son Jacob.

The final piece in the puzzle was the meal. Rebekah made the meat savory. She knew Esau's way of preparing a meal for his father and she knew what pleased Isaac's palate. With all this planning and with his love of his mother, still Jacob was hesitant (Gen. 27:11,12). He knew he might be found out and receive a curse not a blessing. Rebekah was so determined she told Jacob that, if that should be the case, she would take his curse upon herself (Gen. 27:13).

Jacob's objection was a chance for Rebekah to change her mind. Instead, she dug her ditch of deceit deeper.

Rebekah had become so obsessed with her plan that the consequences no longer mattered. She would be willing to bear any curse just so Jacob received the blessing. How many parents are willing to push their children in a similar way without regard to the consequences to the children or themselves?

III. The Act: Gen. 27:18-27

A. Jacob Deceives: 18, 19

18. And he came unto his father, and said, My father: and he said, Here *am* I; who *art* thou, my son?
19. And Jacob said unto his father, I *am* Esau thy firstborn; I have done according as thou badest me: arise, I pray thee, sit and eat of my venison, that thy soul may bless me.

Jacob was his mother's son. When the deed was to be done, he carried it off masterfully. How quickly we learn that which is evil and how slowly we appropriate unto ourselves the good.

When asked who he was, Jacob lied. He claimed to be Esau. Isaac momentarily questioned the sound of the voice he heard. Upon touching the hairy hands he was confused. Again he asked if this was Esau. A second time Jacob lied and said, "I am."

Does it not seem that we are quick learners when it comes to evil? Sometimes it appears that some people had rather lie than tell the truth even when the truth would serve them better. Habits learned early are hard to break. This makes it so important for parents to model truth for their children in both word and action.

Jacob even brought God into the deception, claiming that He had enabled him to kill his prey so quickly. Many evils have been done while invoking the name of the Lord.

B. Isaac Questions: 20-24

20. And Isaac said unto his son, How *is it* that thou hast found it so quickly, my son? And he said, Because the LORD thy God brought *it* to me.
21. And Isaac said unto Jacob, Come near, I pray thee, that I may

feel thee, my son, whether thou *be* my very son Esau or not.

22. And Jacob went near unto Isaac his father, and he felt him, and said, The voice *is* Jacob's voice, but the hands *are* the hands of Esau.

23. And he discerned him not, because his hands were hairy, as his brother Esau's hands: so he blessed him.

24. And he said, *Art* thou my very son Esau? And he said, I *am*.

Isaac knew his sons. Especially did he know his favorite, Esau. Had Rebekah's planning not been so thorough and her cunning so ingenious the plot would have failed. Isaac questioned the voice, but having lost his sight, possibly he distrusted his other senses as well. He did not heed his ears. Often that which is our gut level instinct is correct. It is God's prompting and warning in many cases. Some have said Jacob had the voice of a saint but did the work of a sinner. Are we not all after the order of Jacob? Only the grace of God upon the ungodly redeems us.

C. Jacob Receives: 25-27

25. And he said, Bring *it* near to me, and I will eat of my son's venison, that my soul may bless thee. And he brought *it* near to him, and he did eat: and he brought him wine, and he drank.

26. And his father Isaac said unto him, Come near now, and kiss me, my son.

27. And he came near, and kissed him: and he smelled the smell of his raiment, and blessed him, and said, See, the smell of my son *is* as the smell of a field which the LORD hath blessed:

Jacob sat with his father through the meal. After Isaac had eaten his fill and drank his wine, he called Jacob near and asked for a kiss from his son. The smell in the clothing and the freshly killed kids was that of Esau. Isaac trusted his nose where he had discounted his ears. How often we can be misled by following the wrong sense.

Jacob received the blessing and was not cursed. However, his victory was not without cost. His mother died. His uncle, Laban, deceived him. His family was strife-ridden. The heirs of Esau and the lineage of Jacob became perennial enemies. What might have been had he and Rebekah waited for God's timetable to unfold?

Evangelistic Emphasis

The inability to be forgiven sometimes is not the problem. Even though forgiveness is received, complications remain that forgiveness will not fix. Unfortunately, too often we are painfully slow at learning that. Misunderstanding the whole matter of grace, we fantasize that we can "go on sinning for awhile" and then, before the curtain falls, repent and be forgiven. "God will then remove our sin, and all will be well," we say to ourselves.

Though there is *some* truth to our conception, it is fatally flawed. The flaw is to be found in the supposition that "all will be well." Basically, it mistakenly presumes that being forgiven removes all consequences of the sin. Though the guilt is taken away, the consequences remain.

Certainly, Esau could be forgiven for his lack of appreciation for his birthright. Most of us have been forgiven for worse transgressions than that. Unfortunately, what Esau could not do was reverse the flow of circumstances that were set into motion by that choice. As far as he was concerned, destiny had been altered. It would never be the same again.

Yet, this too Esau eventually dealt with in the years ahead. The anger that burned within him initially, refined his own spirit and made him a better man. So also, the painful consequences that come in result of our sin can serve in the molding hand of God as the blacksmith's forge for our holy shaping, if allowed to do so. We ask amiss when we pray that all consequences of our actions be removed, though that is a very natural prayer. Instead, we ought to pray that God will use our brokenness to make something beautiful and holy.

♦♦♦♦♦♦

Memory Selection

Your brother came with guile, and he has taken away your blessing. *Genesis 27:35*

We are informed, of course, that Esau had relinquished his right to the birthright by trading it for a bowl of soup. It seems, however, that he had hoped to retain somehow the blessing that accompanied the birthright. His hopes were dashed when he returned from the hunt to find that "his blessing" had already been given away.

Regardless of the fact that Esau had sold his birthright to Jacob, it was with cunning deception that Jacob managed to lay claim on the blessing. That deception was just as devastating to Isaac as it was to Esau. obviously, Jacob was not aware of the earlier agreement that had taken place between his twin sons. He had every intention of passing on the mantle of patriarchy to his favorite son. Even though his blessing was gained through dishonesty, having granted his blessing to his younger son, he could not take it back. Isaac sorrowed for having been deprived of passing on his legacy to the son of his love. Additionally, he sorrowed at the deceit of Jacob, his other son.

November 7, 1993

Weekday Problems

Disappointments come in all sizes. Some of them are "lifesize." For Ted the hurt and bitterness ran deep. At thirty years of age, he had been going with Linda for more than seven years. Oh, they had talked about marriage a time or two, but they never got past the talking stage. Invariably, something interrupted this line of discussion. At times it was an argument. Sometimes it was an unsettling awkwardness. Once when their discussion had continued for several weeks, Ted's mother died. They didn't get back to the subject for nearly a year.

Then one day Linda announced matter-of-factly that she and Ted's brother, Harold, were planning to be married. Ted was undone. He knew that they talked a lot when at family gatherings. They always seemed to be interested in the same things, but Ted had no idea that there was ever any romantic interest for either one of them.

Five years have now passed since that painful disclosure. Harold and Linda have a very happy marriage and two small children. It was a long time before Ted ever dated. About six months ago he met a woman of a kindred spirit. Not even six weeks were required for Ted to decide that he had found what he was looking for. Less than three months later they were married.

*Though Ted's anger toward Harold and Linda has disappeared, and though Ted can now acknowledge intellectually that he never had any "claim on Linda," he still deals with the feeling of having been betrayed. How can Ted better see what part he contributed to this "betrayal"?

*How can this text help Ted to grapple with his pain of rejection within the context of God's will for his life?

Sparkles

A man had lost his keys. A friend found him on his knees searching diligently. The friend asked, "What are you looking for?"

The man replied, "My keys, I seem to have lost them." The friend began to look for the keys as well.

Considerable time passed and the friend asked, "Where did you lose your keys?"

The man replied, "At home."

Puzzled, the friend asked, "Then why are you looking for them here?!"

"Because," the man responded, "There is more light here."

Do you ever find yourself looking for the truth where it is easiest to look: outside yourself?

This Lesson In Your Life

WHAT MEANS JUSTIFY AN END?

Esau was a real "man's man." It is not surprising that he was the favorite son of his father. He was an outdoorsman hunter, a man to be with men. He was rugged and could be depended upon to provide for the longings of his father. Not insensitive, he cared tenderly for his father, much as his father did for him. Jacob, on the other hand, spent his time among the tents with the women. He was not much for "manly pursuits." It is not surprising that Rebekah was closer to him, nor that he would plot with her in conspiracy.

There is something very tragic about this whole story. At the same time, there is something refreshingly triumphant! Certainly, at the beginning of the chapter, one would be hard-pressed to imagine how it could close with a happy ending. A scheming wife is plotting with her son the deception of her aged and blind husband in order to defraud her other son.

Successful in their attempt, both the aged husband and the wronged son are heart-broken. The wound is so intense that a death threat is vowed, brother against brother. How could Rebekah and Jacob do this to their family?! How could Rebekah justify such deception of her husband of so many years? Even considering the success of the ploy, was it really worth the pain that it brought to the family?

Yet, there is a more positive side. First, Isaac was "man enough" not to allow his anguish over Esau's loss prevent him from protecting the life of Jacob. It was Isaac who made it possible for Jacob to escape the anger of Esau. It was Isaac who provided the fatherly advice that Jacob needed in order to marry wisely.

Second, Jacob was man enough to listen to the words of wisdom from his aged father. What lay ahead of him was not easy. Even as he took advantage of his brother and father, he was, himself, exploited. Away from his mother's apron strings, Jacob was given the opportunity to be sifted by life. He had to make it on his own. He had to become a man.

It is probable that many times in the ensuing years, Jacob looked over his shoulder in fear that his brother would appear to carry out his death threat. What would he do if he ever encountered his brother? How would he respond if his brother hunted him down? Being a skilled hunter of wild beasts, Esau certainly possessed the ability to track him. Pity on Jacob if he did.

Life can be unsettling when our past lurks ominously in the shadows of our present. When wrongs have not been righted, and the court of justice has not yet arrived at a decision, it is difficult to get on with life. An aspiring politician is hounded by the wild oats sown in his youth. The respectable family man tries to forget about that other family he left in Viet Nam, about which "no one knows." The Christian wife and mother of three has sleepless nights wondering what ever happened to that baby born to her when she was fifteen, even though it's been twenty years. The upwardly mobile assistant manager cringes with every annual review, fearing that someone might have turned up his earlier termination for embezzlement.

The quality of life is simply diminished and compromised by the skeletons that collect dust in our closets. It was none the less so for Jacob. Yet, in the end, he would be a better man. Tried by the fires of life that he helped kindle, Jacob would be purified and remolded into a shape that God Himself would provide.

Seed Thoughts

1. What could not be said of Isaac in his old age that was later said of Moses? (hint: Deut. 34:7)
It could not be said of Isaac in his old age as it was later said of Moses, "his eye was not dim, nor his natural force abated."

2. What prompted Isaac to request the venison meal from his son, Esau?
Isaac was quite advanced in years, blind, and apparently in fear of dying. He wanted to have one last good meal of Esau's venison and set his estate in order before he died.

3. How did Rebekah learn of the request that her husband, Isaac, made of their son, Esau?
Rebekah had been eavesdropping on the conversation between her husband and her eldest son.

4. In her plot with Jacob for deceiving blind Isaac, what was substituted for the venison that Isaac had requested?
Rebekah substituted two kid goats for the venison, apparently seasoning the meat in such a way that the taste would be similar to the taste of deer.

5. How did Rebekah disguise Jacob so as to make his father think that he was his twin brother, Esau?
Rebekah dressed Jacob in Esau's finest clothes and covered his hands and the smooth part of his neck with the goat hides.

(PLEASE TURN PAGE)

---

1. What could not be said of Isaac in his old age that was later said of Moses? (hint: Deut. 34:7)

2. What prompted Isaac to request the venison meal from his son, Esau?

3. How did Rebekah learn of the request that her husband, Isaac, made of their son, Esau?

4. In her plot with Jacob for deceiving blind Isaac, what was substituted for the venison that Isaac had requested?

5. How did Rebekah disguise Jacob so as to make his father think that he was his twin brother, Esau?

6. What one thing about Jacob could Rebekah not disguise successfully?

7. What was Esau's response when he learned that his blessing had been given to his brother, Jacob?

8. How did Isaac respond to Esau's question, "Hast thou but one blessing, my father?"

9. What threat did Esau pronounce against his brother, Jacob?

10. Who first warned Jacob of his brother's vow?

(SEED THOUGHTS--Cont'd)

It could not be said of Isaac in his old age as it was later said of Moses, "his eye was not dim, nor his natural force abated."

Isaac was quite advanced in years, blind, and apparently in fear of dying. He wanted to have one last good meal of Esau's venison and set his estate in order before he died.

Rebekah had been eavesdropping on the conversation between her husband and her eldest son.

Rebekah substituted two kid goats for the venison, apparently seasoning the meat in such a way that the taste would be similar to the taste of deer.

Rebekah dressed Jacob in Esau's finest clothes and covered his hands and the smooth part of his neck with the goat hides.

His voice. Isaac's response to Jacob was, "The voice is Jacob's voice, but the hands are the hands of Esau."

The Bible says that when Esau learned of the deception, "He cried with a great and exceeding bitter cry, and said unto his father, 'Bless me, even me also, O my father.'"

In an indirect way, Isaac answered Esau's desperate question with a "yes." He had only one blessing to give, even though that saddened him as much as it did Esau.

Esau hated his brother because of what he had done and promised himself that after his father was dead, he would kill his brother, Jacob.

Rebekah first warned Jacob of his brother's threat to kill him. She anticipated that Esau's anger would pass in a matter of "a few days."

6. What one thing about Jacob could Rebekah not disguise successfully?
His voice. Isaac's response to Jacob was, "The voice is Jacob's voice, but the hands are the hands of Esau."

7. What was Esau's response when he learned that his blessing had been given to his brother, Jacob?
The Bible says that when Esau learned of the deception, "He cried with a great and exceeding bitter cry, and said unto his father, 'Bless me, even me also, O my father.'"

8. How did Isaac respond to Esau's question, "Hast thou but one blessing, my father?"
In an indirect way, Isaac answered Esau's desperate question with a "yes." He had only one blessing to give, even though that saddened him as much as it did Esau.

9. What threat did Esau pronounce against his brother, Jacob?
Esau hated his brother because of what he had done and promised himself that after his father was dead, he would kill his brother, Jacob.

10. Who first warned Jacob of his brother's vow?
Rebekah first warned Jacob of his brother's threat to kill him. She anticipated that Esau's anger would pass in a matter of "a few days."

November 14, 1993

Jacob's Experience with Laban

Genesis 29:15-30

15 And Laban said unto Jacob, Because thou *art* my brother, shouldest thou therefore serve me for nought? tell me, what *shall* thy wages *be?*

16 And Laban had two daughters: the name of the elder *was* Leah, and the name of the younger *was* Ra´-chel.

17 Leah *was* tender eyed: but Ra´-chel was beautiful and well favoured.

18 And Jacob loved Ra´-chel; and said, I will serve thee seven years for Ra´-chel thy younger daughter.

19 And Laban said, *It is* better that I give her to thee, than that I should give her to another man: abide with me.

20 And Jacob served seven years for Ra´-chel; and they seemed unto him *but* a few days, for the love he had to her.

21 And Jacob said unto Laban, Give *me* my wife, for my days are fulfilled, that I may go in unto her.

22 And Laban gathered together an the men of the place, and made a feast.

23 And it came to pass in the evening, that he took Leah his daughter, and brought her to him; and he went in unto her.

24 And Laban gave unto his daughter Leah Zil´-pah his maid *for* an handmaid.

25 And it came to pass, that in the morning, behold, it *was* Leah: and he said to Laban, What *is* this thou hast done unto me? did not I serve with thee for Ra´-chel? wherefore then hast thou beguiled me?

26 And Laban said, It must not be so done in our country, to give the younger before the firstborn.

27 Fulfil her week, and we will give thee this also for the service which thou shalt serve with me yet seven other years.

28 And Jacob did so, and fulfilled her week: and he gave him Ra´-chel his daughter to wife also.

29 And Laban gave to Ra´-chel his daughter Bill-hah his handmaid to be her maid.

30 And he went in also unto Ra´-chel, and he loved also Ra´-chel more than Leah, and served with him yet seven other years.

♦♦♦♦♦♦

◀ **Memory Selection**
Genesis 29:25

◀ **Devotional Reading**
Psalm 130

◀ **Background Scripture**
Genesis 29:1-30

◀ **Printed Scripture**
Genesis 29:15-30

JACOB'S EXPERIENCE WITH LABAN

Teacher's Target

"Live by the sword, die by the sword" is certainly true. However, it applies to more than just warring. In Jacob's case one could say, "live by deceit, die by deceit." For here we have occasion to see that the way he had gained his birthright is turned back upon him by his uncle, Laban. This deceit cost Jacob an extra seven years in service to Laban.

All of us have areas where we have allowed the evil one entrance. We are weakened in our inner selves in these areas. It might be a habit of lying, an appetite unchecked, a disposition continued, a habit repeated. Allow time for each member in the class to silently reflect upon himself and his area of continual attack by the enemy of faith. These silent reflections need not be shared. The lesson will address the matter.

Lesson Introduction

Do you remember a time in your life when an older and wiser youth made a "swap" with you and got the better of the deal? Or were you the older person who benefitted? Probably each of us can remember an occasion like this in youth.

Jacob struck a bargain for Rachel's hand in marriage. He was to work for seven years in his uncle's service. Then he could marry Rachel. Laban pulled a switch. A veiled Leah, Rachel's older sister, was presented to Jacob. The next morning he awoke to the trickery.

Here is true romance. Jacob's love for Rachel was so great, he consented to serve Laban seven more years for her hand in marriage. How would you respond to such trickery? Are you willing to wait beyond the time expected for something you desire?

Teaching Outline

I. A Contract Made: Gen. 29:15-20
   A. The Offer: 15
   B. The Reward: 16-18
   C. The Agreement: 19, 20
II. The Trick: Gen. 29:21-25
   A. The Request: 21
   B. The Switch: 22-24
   C. The Discovery: 25
III. A New Deal: Gen. 29:26-30
   A. The Explanation: 26
   B. The Bargain: 27, 28a
   C. The Prize: 28b-30

Daily Bible Readings

Mon. Isaac Sends Jacob to Laban - *Gen. 28:1-5*
Tue. Esau Resentfully Seeks Foreign Wives - *Gen. 28:6-9*
Wed. Jacob's Dream and Promise to God - *Gen. 28:10-22*
Thurs. Jacob Meets Shepherds Who Know Laban - *Gen. 29:1-8*
Fri. Jacob Meets Rachel, Laban's Daughter - *Gen. 29:9-14*
Sat. Bright-eyed Rachel vs. weak-eyed Leah - *Gen. 29:15-30*
Sun. Wealthy Jacob Plans to Return Home - *Gen. 30:25-36, 43*

VERSE BY VERSE

I. A Contract Made: Gen. 29:15-20

A. The Offer: 15

15. And Laban said unto Jacob, Because thou art my brother, shouldest thou therefore serve me for nought? tell me, what shall thy wages be?

Jacob was a guest in Laban's home. While visiting one day they made a fair contract for Jacob's service to Laban. Possibly Laban had seen Jacob's initiative and willingness to put his hand to a task. He showed Jacob that he is a just man by not allowing him to work for nothing. Jacob asked for Rachel to be his wife at the end of seven years of service.

Laban presented himself as just. However, he was not totally honest about local customs or his own intentions as we will see. Withholding information can be as much a lie as telling something untrue.

B. The Reward: 16-18

16. And Laban had two daughters: the name of the elder was Leah, and the name of the younger was Ra'-chel.
17. Leah was tender eyed; but Ra'-chel was beautiful and well favoured.
18. And Jacob loved Ra'-chel; and said, I will serve thee seven years for Ra'-chel thy younger daughter.

Two daughters were part of Laban's treasure. Leah, the older was "tender eyed." This is understood differently by interpreters. Some believe Leah's eyes had a weak appearance. Others, like the Living Bible interpret the description to mean she had lovely eyes. Whichever, it is clear that the overall appearance and countenance of Rachel had captivated Jacob. She was his preference. To him, she was well worth seven years of labor for his uncle.

C. The Agreement: 19, 20

19. And Laban said, It is better that I give her to thee, than that I should give her to another man: abide with me.
20. And Jacob served seven years for Ra'-chel; and they seemed unto him but a few days, for the love he had to her.

Laban was a good judge of who could take care of his daughter. He accepted the terms of the contract. Seven years for a fair maiden.

Jacob was so smitten with love for Rachel that the time passed as though it had been only a few days. He was willing to earn Rachel as a token of his love for her. Love makes long and often difficult work seem short and easy. Paul calls for such love for God in response to his gift of Christ. The trials of this age cannot compare to the joy and glory that is to be ours (Rom. 8:18). Is not this story a good example of a labor of love (1 Thess. 1:3)?

II. The Trick: Gen. 29:21-25

A. The Request: 21

21. And Jacob said unto Laban, Give me my wife, for my days are fulfilled, that I may go in unto her.

Though a deceiver, Jacob had the good qualities of loyalty and duty. He was loyal to his mother to his own hurt, and now he had been loyal to Laban. He did his duty and made his request for Rachel. The bargain struck had been kept. Now he expected justice in payment from Laban.

B. The Switch: 22-24

22. And Laban gathered together all the men of the place, and made a feast.
23. And it came to pass in the evening, that he took Leah his daughter, and brought her to him; and he went in unto her.
24. And Laban gave unto his daughter Leah Zil'-pah his maid for an handmaid.

Laban was a deceiver as clever as Rebekah. Some say no one is as easy to con as a con man. In this case it proved true. Whether this was a custom prohibiting the younger daughter to marry before the older may not be true. However, it is true that it was an embarrassment to the older daughter for this to occur. If customary, Laban should have told Jacob from the start.

How could Jacob be so easily fooled? First, Leah probably wore a veil over her face. Second, lighting was not what it is today and it was night. Third, Jacob saw what he wanted to see. His projection upon this one after seven years of nursing it in his heart may have been so strong that he missed reality all together. He was not the last who has had his eyes opened only after the illusion has crumbled.

C. The Discovery: 25

25. And it came to pass, that in the morning, behold, it was Leah: and he said to Laban, What is this thou hast done unto me? did not I serve with thee for Ra'-chel? wherefore then hast thou beguiled me?

Panic, rage, disappointment and puzzlement consumed Jacob in the light of daybreak. His question was full of pathos. Not only had Laban wronged Jacob but both of his daughters. Rachel was deprived of being the bride of the one she loved. Leah was placed in a position of conspiracy as Jacob had been with Rebekah. Why she went along with it, knowing she was not the desired one, is a good question to ponder. She was not blameless in this affair.

As mentioned, Laban's excuse was a lame one. However, the deed was done. Do you think maybe Jacob had a flashback to his own act of deception?

III. The New Deal: Gen. 29:26-30

A. The Explanation: 26

26. And Laban said, It must not be so done in our country, to give the younger before the firstborn.

Laban dealt treacherously with Jacob from the first. He withheld information, he used Jacob's love for Rebekah as leverage, he plotted a solution to his own problem. His true character was exposed. What is done in the dark will be exposed in the light. The truth will come out. often it takes a long time for a person's true colors to show through their disguise and defenses. Probably Jacob had seen Laban's character in dealing with others during the seven years. Still, gullible like we all can be, he believed Laban would not do the same to him. However, leopards don't change their spots. What is in the heart is what will come out (Matt. 15:16-20).

B. The Bargain: 27, 28a

27. Fulfil her week, and we will give thee this also for the service which thou shalt serve with me yet seven other years.
28. And Jacob did so, and fulfilled her week:

How crestfallen Jacob must have been. Another seven years longing for the affection of the one he loved. How hard for Leah to know she was not desired. She paid dearly for her cunning. Now two wives would be taken. This did not make for tranquility in Jacob's life. Loyalty once again showed itself in Jacob. He did not forsake Rachel. He would serve another seven years. Jacob did not seek revenge. Possibly because he saw himself in Laban. Often it is this seeing ourselves in others that God uses to teach us acceptance and forgiveness. Jacob didn't seem to lick his wounds for long. He did what he could to salvage some good from a bad situation. When we are caught in self-pity or revenge we seldom see God's bigger picture and redeeming plan.

C. The Prize; 28b-30

and he gave him Ra'-chel his daughter to wife also.
29. And Laban gave to Ra'-chel his daughter Bil'-hah his handmaid to be her maid.
30. And he went in also unto Ra'-chel, and he loved also Ra'-chel more than Leah, and served with him yet seven other years.

At long last Rachel was to be wed to Jacob. It is said that we can learn to love people. However, when our affections are focused and fixed upon one individual the effort of learning to love is seldom exerted. Jacob's affections and emotions were with Rachel. He would not be blocked from his goal. He was persistent, maybe even stubborn, in his purpose.

Having taken care of his and Leah's embarrassment, to Leah's hurt, now Laban followed through on the second deal. Jacob and Rachel were united. However, they were not one. Leah was very much present.

In this whole experience with Leah and Rachel, God has been at work. It is revealed in Scripture that God shaped Jacob into a man He could entrust with His purposes. Later this is revealed in Jacob ("the supplanter") being renamed Israel ("one who has power with God").

Evangelistic Emphasis

There is something precious about meeting someone of common roots when a great distance from home. Perhaps you are on a vacation at the Grand Canyon and spot a family from your home town. Or, you're on a cruise in the Carribean and get to chatting with another guest only to learn that the two of you are distant cousins. Or, you learn that you and your new friend that you just met on the plane went to the same college. Instantly, there is a tangible bonding that takes place, a bonding that might never have happened had you not been so far from home.

Such may have been part of the attraction that so quickly demonstrated itself between Jacob and Rachel. They were kin! Even more significantly, they worshipped the same God. Their devotion was linked beyond the clouds to one who guarded their nights and listened to their prayers. So many of the potential mates for either of them were deeply entangled in webs of polytheism. Not only did they not worship only one God, they didn't even understand those who worshiped only one God.

Today, there is a similarly instant bonding between believers of like faith. This is especially significant when a great distance from familiar surroundings. Somehow, finding one whose heart beats as one with yours removes the loneliness of the soul and makes even "this strange place" seem like home. Kinship for the Christian is found just as strongly in the faith ties as it is in the blood ties, and often more so. In these times when relationships tend to gravitate toward the superficial and when hearts yearn for "connectedness," this special bond in the life of the Christian carries valuable dividends.

♦♦♦♦♦♦

Memory Selection

What is this you have done to me? Did I not serve with you for Rachel? Why then have you deceived me? *Genesis 29:25*

None of us likes to be deceived. A small boy responds to an ad on a serial box for a "camping tent." The measurements are said to be "nine feet square." The price is *unbelievable!* Yet, he believes. After weeks of painful waiting, the package arrives. The "camping tent" is *nine square feet* or three feet square. It was made to fit over a small card table, hardly suitable for camping.

Listening from the conditioning of our culture, it's difficult to imagine how Laban's trickery was carried out so successfully. It wasn't until the next morning, after the wedding night, that Jacob realized that he had been victimized. After the wedding night, it was too late to complain. His wife was now his wife. A small boy's dad might intervene and send back the fraudulent "camping tent," but Jacob could not send back Leah. The marriage had been consummated. Jacob and Leah were married for keeps. The results of Laban's deception were just as irreversible as Jacob's deception of his own father had been earlier.

November 14, 1993

Weekday Problems

Sandra met Richard at a Christian college in Tennessee. She had gone to that particular college because of her desire to be bathed in an ocean of faith and immersed in a sea of Christians. She was especially interested in meeting strong Christians of the male variety. The small town in which she was reared had only a few, and not one of them had much impressed her.

Richard caught her eye early in the college adventure and never did let go. Not only was he handsome, he was obviously dedicated to his faith. His involvement rivaled the that of the "Bible majors" who were expected to be that way.

As it often happens, interest turned into attraction, and attraction turned into head-over-heels love. Richard and Sandra were married. What a beautiful wedding! Richard was truly the man of Sandra's dreams, she thought.

The morning after the wedding was Sunday. Sandra rolled over and kissed her new husband to wake him to dress for worship. *"I'm not going,"* he informed her. *"Not, going?"* she asked. *"Never again!"* was his shocking reply.

As the truth gradually and painfully came out, Richard was not sure that he believed in God. He had only gone to a Christian college because his parents insisted. He had put on a show of righteousness because he realized the kind of man that would interest her, and he wanted her.

*Like Jacob with Leah, as far as Sandra was concerned, the marriage had been sealed. It was irrevocable. Given that fact, what were her best options at that point?

*How could Sandra's family and church best help her to deal with this painful disappointment of life?

*What advice can parents give to their own marriageable children that might help ward off such disappointments?

Sparkles

One disciple asked his teacher how one could distinguish true spirituality from false. Being wise, his teacher responded, "How do you distinguish between a person who is truly asleep and one who is faking?"

The puzzled disciple replied, "There is no way. Only the sleeper knows when he is faking sleep."

The teacher smiled and said, "The trickster can delude others but he cannot delude himself. But unfortunately, the one with false spirituality can delude both others and himself."

This Lesson In Your Life

GOD OF THE UNDERDOG

It was Moses who affirmed, "The LORD your God is God of gods, and Lord of lords, a great God, a mighty, and a terrible, which regardeth not persons, nor taxeth reward: He doth execute the judgment of the fatherless and widow, and loveth the stranger, in giving him food and raiment" (Deut. 10:16-17). Numerous times thereafter this same truth is affirmed by a variety of God's prophets.

David lifted up praise to God for his exceptional equity, "Lord, thou hast heard the desire of the humble: thou wilt prepare their heart, thou wilt cause thine ear to hear; To judge the fatherless and the oppressed, that the man of the earth may no more oppress" (Ps. 10:17-18).

God has declared Himself clearly to be the God of the disadvantaged. Any man who attempts to exploit the helpless had better prepare himself to take on God, also. For surely, he has placed himself directly in opposition to God in his attack on the weak.

This truth about God is demonstrated even in this telling of the marriages of Jacob. Although, there is no indication that Jacob actively wronged Leah, she was a pawn, caught in the middle of painfully negative circumstances. Jacob was not the only one who had been wronged by Laban's sly trickery. Leah was just as much a victim as he.

The wedding had been a grand occasion, an event she had anticipated with "school-girl dreams" as long as she could remember. That night, she felt the embrace of loving warmth with excitement and delight. A dream came true that she had feared would never be realized. All was well when the night's sleep fell gently into her eyes.

Then came morning. Abruptly, her dream-world vanished with the morning dew. *"Aaaaak! It's Leah!"* rang out loudly through the village, echoing endlessly in her ears. The warm embrace of the night before turned into stone. The residual excitement of the marriage feast bled disappointment all over Jacob's face. Jacob's delight was now fury--the worst she had ever seen.

It is obvious that Jacob felt terribly wronged, and rightfully so. Yet, there is no indication that he ever gave thought to Leah and how she had been wronged, too. It is quite clear that his protest was in behalf of himself, only. Perhaps, his pain was too intense for him to consider the pain of any other.

God didn't forget Leah. "And when the LORD saw that Leah was hated, he opened her womb;" the text says "but Rachel was barren" (v. 31). Rachel had the advantage of Jacob's love. Therefore, Leah was given the advantage of Jacob's children. The God of justice, the protector of the disadvantaged, showed his presence and brought equality to a very unfair and unequal situation. It wasn't that Rachel had sinned some awful sin that caused God to punish her with a barren womb. Rather, in order to bring about an equality between Leah and Rachel as Jacob's wives, Leah was blessed with fertility as superior to Rachel's as Rachel's place of preference in Jacob's eyes was superior to Leah's.

The American Declaration of Independence optimistically declared that "all men are created equal." "That may be true," a wag later corrected, "but some are more equal than others!" Where blatant inequality is being exploited, one can rest assured that God will be there, defending the cause of the disadvantaged. Why does He do that? Because He has accepted the mission of being the protector of the weak. That's just the kind of God He is.

Seed Thoughts

1. Why did Jacob weep when he met Rachel?

Jacob's tears were tears of joy. He had made a long journey, and finally Rachel wore the face of "family." He was happy to be with "his own people" again.

2. What was it about Rachel that attracted Jacob to her romantically?

The Bible describes Rachel as "beautiful and well favored."

3. What kind of "deal" did Jacob make with his uncle, Laban?

Jacob agreed to serve Laban for seven years for his younger daughter, Rachel. At the end of the seven years, Jacob was to receive Rachel for his wife.

4. When the seven years of service had been completed, how did Laban defraud Jacob?

Without forewarning him, Laban gave to Jacob Leah to be his wife instead of Rachel.

5. When did Jacob find out that he had been tricked by Laban?

Jacob learned the next morning, after he had consummated the marriage, that he had been given the wrong woman.

(PLEASE TURN PAGE)

---

1. Why did Jacob weep when he met Rachel?

2. What was it about Rachel that attracted Jacob to her romantically?

3. What kind of "deal" did Jacob make with his uncle, Laban?

4. When the seven years of service had been completed, how did Laban defraud Jacob?

5. When did Jacob find out that he had been tricked by Laban?

6. What excuse did Laban give for the exchange?

7. What adjustment did Laban hasten to make with Jacob in order to keep him happy?

8. How did Jacob respond to this second offer?

9. What did Laban give in addition to his two daughters to Jacob?

10. How were Jacob's feelings for Rachel different from his feelings for Leah?

Jacob's tears were tears of joy. He had made a long journey, and finally Rachel wore the face of "family." He was happy to be with "his own people" again.

The Bible describes Rachel as "beautiful and well favored."

Jacob agreed to serve Laban for seven years for his younger daughter, Rachel. At the end of the seven years, Jacob was to receive Rachel for his wife.

Without forewarning him, Laban gave to Jacob Leah to be his wife instead of Rachel.

Jacob learned the next morning, after he had consummated the marriage, that he had been given the wrong woman.

Laban's excuse for having made the switch was that in his country the younger daughter never marries before the older daughter.

Laban told Jacob that after he had completed his marriage week with Leah, he could then have Rachel to wed also, provided that he would agree to serve another seven years.

Having no better option, Jacob accepted the terms that Laban negotiated.

To Leah, Laban gave Zilpah for a handmaid, and for Rachel, he gave Bilhah to be her handmaid.

It is said that "he loved also Rachel more than Leah." These proved to be words reflecting a truth that brought much pain to the family.

(SEED THOUGHTS--Cont'd)

6. What excuse did Laban give for the exchange?
Laban's excuse for having made the switch was that in his country the younger daughter never marries before the older daughter.

7. What adjustment did Laban hasten to make with Jacob in order to keep him happy?
Laban told Jacob that after he had completed his marriage week with Leah, he could then have Rachel to wed also, provided that he would agree to serve another seven years.

8. How did Jacob respond to this second offer?
Having no better option, Jacob accepted the terms that Laban negotiated.

9. What did Laban give in addition to his two daughters to Jacob?
To Leah, Laban gave Zilpah for a handmaid, and for Rachel, he gave Bilhah to be her handmaid.

10. How were Jacob's feelings for Rachel different from his feelings for Leah?
It is said that "he loved also Rachel more than Leah." These proved to be words reflecting a truth that brought much pain to the family.

November 21, 1993

Jacob is Reconciled with Esau

Genesis 33:1-14

33 AND Jacob lifted up his eyes, and looked, and, behold, Esau came. and with him four hundred men. And he divided the children unto Leah, and unto Ra'-chel, and unto the two handmaids.
2 And he put the handmaids and their children foremost, and Leah and her children after, and Ra'-chel and Joseph hindermost.
3 And he passed over before them, and bowed himself to the ground seven times, until he came near to his brother.
4 And Esau ran to meet him, and embraced him, and fell on his neck, and kissed him: and they wept.
5 And he lifted up his eyes, and saw the women and the children; and said Who *are* those with thee? And he said, The children which God hath graciously given thy servant.
6 Then the handmaidens came near, they and their children, and they bowed themselves.
7 And Leah also with her children came near, and bowed themselves: and after came Joseph near and Ra'-chel, and they bowed themselves.
8 And he said, What *meanest* thou by all this drove which I met? And he said, *These are* to find grace in the sight of my lord.
9 And Esau said, I have enough, my brother, keep that thou hast unto thyself.
10 And Jacob said, Nay, I pray thee, if now I have found grace in thy sight, then receive my present at my hand: for therefore I have seen thy face, as though I had seen the face of God, and thou wast pleased with me.
11 Take, I pray thee, my blessing that is brought to thee; because God hath dealt graciously with me, and because I have enough. And he urged him, and he took *it.*
12 And he said, Let us take our journey, and let us go, and I will go before thee.
13 And he said unto him, My lord knoweth that the children *are* tender, and the flocks and herds with young *are* with me: and if men should overdrive them one day, all the flock will die.
14 Let my lord, I pray thee, pass over before his servant: and I will lead on softly, according as the cattle that goeth before me and the children be able to endure, until I come unto my lord unto Se'-ir.

◆◆◆◆◆◆

◀ **Memory Selection**
Genesis 33:10

◀ **Devotional Reading**
Matthew 5:23-26

◀ **Background Scripture**
Genesis 33

◀ **Printed Scripture**
Genesis 33:1-14

JACOB IS RECONCILED WITH ESAU

Teacher's Target

Reconciliation is God's major goal in all things. He was in Christ reconciling the world unto Himself (2 Cor. 5:19). In our passage Jacob and Esau are reconciled. Ask the class to write down some definitions of reconciliation. Share experiences of reconciliation with family members, neighbors or friends. Role playing this scene of two brothers reconciling after a long time of resentment, anger and hurt would give class members a chance to see themselves in both characters. Put the name of Jacob on a sheet of paper and the name of Esau on another. Place these on opposite walls of the room. Ask the class members to go stand by the one they identify with. Let as many as desire tell you why they identify with Jacob or Esau.

Lesson Introduction

Some people say people can't change. "Leopards don't change their spots." But, when God gets in our hearts it causes much change.

One factory worker in England converted under John Wesley was interviewed by a reporter. The reporter said, "If you are a follower of Christ you must know a great deal about Him. Where was He born? How many sermons did He preach? How old was He when He died?"

To all of these the man said, "I don't know." Then he said, "But, this I do know: Before I was in debt, I drank up our family's living and my wife and children dreaded me returning home each day. Now we have furniture in the house, food on the table and bills are paid. Also, my wife and children look forward to my coming home." God changes things and people.

Teaching Outline

I. The Reunion: Gen. 33:1-4
   A. Esau Sighted: 1
   B. Jacob Bowed: 2, 3
   C. Esau Embraced: 4
II. The Reception: Gen. 33:5-11
   A. Family Recognized: 5
   B. Family Introduced: 6, 7a
   C. Blessing Bestowed: 7b-11
III. The Journey: Gen. 33:12-14
   A. Brothers Collaborate: 12
   B. Children Considered: 13
   C. Mercy Shown: 14

Daily Bible Readings

Mon. God Orders Jacob's Return
Gen. 31:1-8, 15-18
Tue. Laban and Jacob Covenant Together - *Gen. 31:36-37, 44-54*
Wed. Jacob Prepares to Meet Esau
Gen. 32:3-8, 13-18
Thurs. Jacob, in Fear, Seeks Appeasement - *Gen. 32:19-32*
Fri. Jacob's Family Introduced to Esau - *Gen. 33:1-7*
Sat. Jacob and Esau Are Reconciled
Gen. 33:8-14
Sun. Jacob Buys Land and Builds
Gen. 33:15-20

November 21, 1993

VERSE BY VERSE

I. The Reunion: Gen. 33:1-4

A. Esau Sighted: 1

1. AND Jacob lifted up his eyes, and looked, and, behold, Esau came, and with him four hundred men. And he divided the children unto Leah, and unto Ra´-chel, and unto the two handmaids.

Put yourself in Jacob's shoes. You stole your brother's birthright. You have been tricked by your uncle. You have decided to return home. How will you be received? Then you see your brother coming with 400 men. What is in your brother's heart? Will he forgive and forget? How will God answer Jacob's prayer? Will he prevail with his brother (Gen. 32:28)? How bitter he was when you left (Gen. 25:29-34). Jacob arranged his family in a way that would present no threat and also protect his immediate family as best he could, if Esau's intent was harm.

Note the contrast. Esau with 400 men. Jacob followed by a train of women and children. Yet it was Jacob who had the birthright and the promise of God. How different are the ways of God from the ways of humankind!

B. Jacob Bowed: 2, 3

2. And he put the handmaids and their children foremost, and Leah and her children after, and Ra´-chel and Joseph hindermost.
3. And he passed over before them, and bowed himself to the ground seven times, until he came near to his brother.

Though he had the birthright and God's promise, Jacob was not haughty in the presence of his brother. Surely he was scared, but there is more there than just that. He showed respect for his older brother. He humbled himself and was dutiful as an expression of his desire for peace. Humble respect often turns away wrath. As has been said, "the bullet passes over the one who stoops."

Humility does not imply a lack of strength. Nor is humility a sign of a lesser station in life. Humility recognizes that God is creator and we are creature. Also, it declares that the person is no better or worse than any other person. We especially recognize we are on level ground when we stand at the foot of the cross.

C. Esau Embraced: 4

4. And Esau ran to meet him, and embraced him, and fell on his neck, and kissed him: and they wept.

Esau embraced Jacob. More so, he ran to meet his brother. No rage, no anger was expressed, only the demonstration of love. The men with him showed his status was now forgotten, for there was no longer any need for ascendancy between brothers regardless of who had the right. The same is true in the church. There can be no ascendancy between brothers and sisters in Christ, regardless of who is given the responsibility of leading. God answered Jacob's prayer. He changed Esau's heart.

Esau erred as a young man. He relinquished much but he did not remain bitter. He honestly expressed his feelings before God, released the situation to God, forgave the one who wronged him and was content with the blessings God had given him.

Both men wept tears of relief. Jacob and Esau were both released from their grief and shame. These tears were also mingled with the joy of forgiveness and restoration. Their tears had washed their souls like a spring shower.

II. The Reception: Gen. 33:5-11

A. Family Recognized: 5

5. AND he lifted up his eyes, and saw the women and the children; and said, Who are those with thee? And he said, The children which God hath graciously given thy servant.

That Jacob had an estate, Esau knew (Gen. 32:5). Jacob had not mentioned his children. Maybe he withheld this for fear of what Esau might do for revenge. Notice Jacob's answer to Esau's question, "Who are those with you?" He gave credit to God for blessing him with children. How rich we are when we are given the joy of the presence of children. Though they take much care, time, money and instruction, they bring much laughter, fun, wonder, insight, joy and appreciation.

B. Family Introduced: 6, 7a

6. Then the handmaidens came near, they and their children, and they bowed themselves.

7. And Leah also with her children came near, and bowed themselves:

Like the head of the family, Jacob, the whole family showed similar respect to Esau. It is well for us to respect those who are respected by others in whom we have confidence.

How much Esau must have rejoiced at the great increase in family to love and be loved by. How rich an experience can be that of an uncle or aunt who cherishes not only his or her own, but also the children of siblings. It takes more than one model of male and female for children to receive a grounding in who they are.

C. Blessing Bestowed: 7b-11

and after came Joseph near and Ra'-chel, and they bowed themselves.

8. And he said, What meanest thou by all this drove which I met? And he said, These are to find grace in the sight of my lord.

9. And Esau said, I have enough, my brother; keep that thou hast unto thyself.

10. And Jacob said, Nay, I pray thee, if now I have found grace in thy sight, then receive my present at my hand: for therefore I have seen thy face, as though I had seen the face of God, and thou wast pleased with me.

11. Take, I pray thee, my blessing that is brought to thee; because God hath dealt graciously with me, and because I have enough. And he urged him, and he took it.

Esau declared that he did not need this present bestowed by Jacob. He had enough.

This is a good statement. How good it would be if more of us sought to develop a theology of enough. Also, Esau did not want his reception to be interpreted as based upon being bought off. His love and welcome were from the heart.

God had been faithful to his promise. Esau had the fat of the land. To his credit also it appears that he was not covetous. Still Jacob insisted that he be allowed to bestow the gift as an expression of love and desire for a genuine relationship with his brother.

III. The Journey: Gen. 33:12-14

A. Brother's Collaborate: 12

12. And he said, Let us take our journey, and let us go, and I will go before thee.

Esau offered to be a guide and companion to Jacob. Reconciliation had been accomplished. Now Jacob and Esau were together and for each other in a way they never had been before. often mother and/or father, or both in this case, can set up alliances with children that divide siblings and set up bitter rivalries. With both parents gone, some maturity, and the work of God, these two brothers are establishing harmony in their relationship.

B. Children Considered: 13

13. And he said unto him, My lord knoweth that the children are tender, and the flocks and herds with young are with me: and if men should overdrive them one day, all the flock will die.

Jacob declined the offer in order not to slow Esau or deter him from his pursuits or to overpress his children and his animals by moving at too quick a pace. Esau had no children or livestock with him. He could move swiftly. He was the hunter. Jacob was the shepherd. His consideration was for the children and the flocks under his care. He could not drive them too fast. It is well for us all to remember not to push our children in activity or developmental tasks at a pace that is beyond their developmental capacity.

C. Mercy Shown: 14

14. Let my lord, I pray thee, pass over before his servant: and I will lead on softly, according as the cattle that goeth before me and the children be able to endure, until I come unto my lord unto Se'-ir.

Jacob did not tie Esau to his task or pace. Esau offered his men to assist. Both men were seeking to show their respect and interest in each other. There is mercy here. Jacob did not shame Esau for his reliance upon his men. He, however, knew the care of God was with him. He did not need the strength of men to protect him. He asked only for a gracious acceptance of him by Esau. There can be nothing of riches or power better than the good will of God and the good will of our fellow man.

Evangelistic Emphasis

Esau and Jacob had been separated for years. The bulk of their adult lives had been lived in absence of any knowledge of the state of the other. The only Esau that Jacob could remember was an angry Esau of long ago who vowed to kill him. Jacob's fears came to life again when he heard of the approaching of Esau. He imagined the resurrection of Esau's anger.

Just as God had been at work in the life of Jacob throughout those intervening years, so also He had been at work in the life of Esau. Jacob was much more a man of faith than he had been when he left his father's house so many years before. Esau was much more a man of love. As God had humbled Jacob's cunning pride, so also He had cooled Esau's anger.

We sometimes forget that God is working in the lives of others. As we approach the whole matter of evangelism, it is priceless to remember that "just as God has been at work in my life bringing me to this point where I am about to witness in behalf of Christ, so also He has been at work in the lives of these to whom I am about to witness, preparing them for this occasion."

Before the Lord ever dispatched Ananias to approach Saul of Tarsus with the gospel of Jesus Christ, the Lord Himself had been at work in the life of Saul preparing his heart to receive the message. So also today, God does not leave us alone in the task of evangelism. Jesus said quite plainly, "Lo, I am with you always, even unto the end of the world."

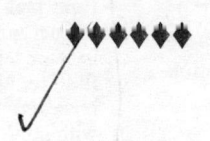

Memory Selection

If I have found favor in your sight, then accept my present from my hand; for truly to see your face is like seeing the face of God, with such favor you have received me. *Genesis 33:10*

Such an interesting analogy this is that Jacob made to Esau. It entices one to explore the intended implications of his words. What does he mean by this awesome remark, *"to see your face is like seeing the face of God?"*

Is he meaning to imply, "You look like what I imagine God must look like?" Or is he saying, "Your gracious reception is really an answer to prayer!" Either one of these is possible, though the latter is the more likely of the two.

Perhaps what Jacob said speaks as much about his perception of God as it does of Esau's welcome. Perhaps, he is saying, *"Your greeting is so exceptionally pleasant, that it must be similar to the grand reception we anticipate receiving from God."* In other words, it surely has no equal among mortals. To come even close, one must think in terms of the hospitality of God. That also reflects a very positive image of the greeting of God.

November 21, 1993

Weekday Problems

Imagined danger is often much greater than the real thing. The small boy hears a rustle in the bushes as he walks down a deserted street after dark and promptly imagines a most horrible monster stalking him. A moment later, a kitten runs from the bushes chasing a june bug.

Frank is not a small boy any longer, yet his imagination provides him with just as frightening "monsters" of a different kind. His biggest monster is "rejection." You see, Frank has been out of work for more than six months. An engineer whose whole career has been built around the petrochemical industry, Frank recently discovered that his career is one with a shaky future. This is something that he had never envisioned happening. When he signed on for an engineering major, he thought that he was setting up himself for life. Of course, there are other kinds of engineering jobs, but both Frank's training and his work record have been focused exclusively toward this one emphasis.

Frank's greatest liability is not his narrow job experience. Frank's greatest liability is his fear of rejection. He imagines being thrown out of the personnel office with great ridicule and frightening aggression, while all his friends and family watch. The thought of such humiliation is almost more than he can bear. So, when Frank enters the office of a prospective employer, he carries the baggage of his fearful dread with him. That baggage, then, becomes an obstacle between him and every desirable job.

*How can Frank replace his fear with faith that trusts in the hand of God to be paving the way for his provision?

*As with Jacob, what kind of peace offering can Frank offer to quiet this fancied monster?

Smiles

Here are some bloopers from church bulletins:

Youth choir cook-out by the creek. Time of praise and sin-a-long! (Guitar players to teach us a new song.)

A loudspeaker system has been installed in the church. It was given by one of our members in honor of his wife.

The church dinner was like Heaven. Many we expected to see were absent.

On Senior day: Members of the senior class are not to pass out until the pastor finishes speaking.

JACOB IS RECONCILED WITH ESAU

This Lesson In Your Life
RESPONDING TO GHOSTS OF THE PAST

When Esau and Jacob parted ways years earlier (Lesson 10), some things seemed certain. *It seemed certain* that their relationship as brothers was ended. It *seemed* certain that if they were ever to meet again, one of them would die. It seemed certain that Jacob would be "the great one" under the blessing of God, while Esau was destined to a life of insignificance. In reality none of those things that seemed so certain were as they seemed.

True, Jacob had gained the birthright and the deathbed blessing that would have belonged to Esau. Yet, Esau did not simply lie down and die. He did not allow his disappointment to place on him the label, "failure," and forever limit what he could become and do. It is wrong to think of Esau as "abandoned by God." Quite the contrary, it is clear that he was blessed abundantly. No, he did not carry the birthright, but he was still the son of Isaac, who was the son of Abraham, the friend of God.

This is made clear in Genesis 32:6, when Jacob learned that Esau was coming to meet him with 400 men with him. This was his army of men. Esau was in command, perhaps, much as Abraham had been in command of the 318 trained servants when he rescued Lot from his captors two generations earlier.

There is no evidence that Esau came with 400 men with the forethought of doing Jacob harm, only to be appeased by his gifts. Verse nine seems to make it clear that he regarded himself as a highly blessed man who had no reason for envy or a grudge. Instead, Esau came with his 400 men to show his long-estranged brother the genuine heart-felt honor it was to see him again.

Jacob responded to the images of his angry brother that he had carried with him for the past many years. They were old images, quite out of date. They did not allow for the time and the healing and the change that had taken place. He had no way of knowing what all had blessed Esau in these intervening years. Preparing for the worst, Jacob set his strategy to (1) attempt to appease Esau's wrath with gifts, and (2) divide his party into groups so that if the appeasement didn't work, perhaps some would be able to escape.

The gracious reception Esau extended was beyond Jacob's wildest imagination. Never in a thousand years would he have expected that. He was operating exclusively from the image of his brother that was a ghost of their past.

We sometimes do that. Offended, we pull away from friends or family members and do not see them again for years. When we do see them, we often find ourselves surprised at how much they've changed. We forget that the memory tape we've been playing is thirty years old!

Or we leave the church where we grew up, gleefully discarding all of its restrictive baggage that so defined it. Many years pass, but still when we think of that church, it is locked inside of that image we etched in our mind twenty years before. Though the preacher has changed several times, all of the leaders have been replaced, the building has been renovated, and hardly any of those original members are still there, we nevertheless, expect it to be the same as it was when we left.

Sadly, often that obsolete image dominates, and we never allow ourselves to know the church of today. Only the fortunate ones are blessed one day by the surprising encounter with the church they abandoned. It is their blessing to learn that, as with themselves, God has been at work in that church, too.

Seed Thoughts

1. What was Jacob's reaction when he learned that his brother, Esau was coming toward him with 400 men?

Jacob panicked. His most recent memory of his brother was quite distant and filled with much fear. His brother had threatened to kill him the next time he saw him.

2. When this perceived danger arose, how did Jacob demonstrate his preference for Rachel and Joseph?

Jacob placed the handmaids and their children foremost, Leah and her children next and Rachel and Joseph in the rear, where they would be the farthest from danger.

3. Why had Jacob sent ahead of him an assortment of gifts to greet Esau?

It was his intent to "find grace" in the eyes of Esau. He wished to appease his wrath from their earlier confrontation.

4. Did Jacob's shower of gifts work?

The Bible does not indicate that Esau intended to do Jacob any harm. Apparently, the 400 men with Esau were simply to enlarge the greeting.

5. What reason did Esau give for refusing Jacob's gifts?

Esau's initial rejection of Jacob's gifts was due to the fact that he already had plenty.

(PLEASE TURN PAGE)

---

1. What was Jacob's reaction when he learned that his brother, Esau was coming toward him with 400 men?

2. When this perceived danger arose, how did Jacob demonstrate his preference for Rachel and Joseph?

3. Why had Jacob sent ahead of him an assortment of gifts to greet Esau?

4. Did Jacob's shower of gifts work?

5. What reason did Esau give for refusing Jacob's gifts?

6. With whom did Jacob compare Esau's face, and why?

7. Did Esau finally accept the gifts, and why?

8. Why did Esau not carry out his vow that he had made years before to kill his brother, Jacob?

9. How does life experience between siblings today sometimes parallel that of Esau and Jacob?

10. What was Esau's generous offer to Jacob?

Jacob panicked. His most recent memory of his brother was quite distant and filled with much fear. His brother had threatened to kill him the next time he saw him.

Jacob placed the handmaids and their children foremost, Leah and her children next and Rachel and Joseph in the rear, where they would be the farthest from danger.

It was his intent to "find grace" in the eyes of Esau. He wished to appease his wrath from their earlier confrontation.

The Bible does not indicate that Esau intended to do Jacob any harm. Apparently, the 400 men with Esau were simply to enlarge the greeting.

Esau's initial rejection of Jacob's gifts was due to the fact that he already had plenty.

Jacob told Esau that to see his face was "as though I had seen the face of God, and thou wast pleased with me."

Yes. Esau eventually accepted the gifts because Jacob insisted so.

Apparently, his anger had diminished through the years. God had blessed him with a good life in spite of what Jacob had taken from him.

Time still has a way of healing wounds. Sibling rivalry can often be quieted by distance and time.

Esau offered to provide escort to Jacob and his company for their travel.

(SEED THOUGHTS--Cont'd)

6. With whom did Jacob compare Esau's face, and why?
Jacob told Esau that to see his face was "as though I had seen the face of God, and thou wast pleased with me."

7. Did Esau finally accept the gifts, and why?
Yes. Esau eventually accepted the gifts because Jacob insisted so.

8. Why did Esau not carry out his vow that he had made years before to kill his brother, Jacob?
Apparently, his anger had diminished through the years. God had blessed him with a good life in spite of what Jacob had taken from him.

9. How does life experience between siblings today sometimes parallel that of Esau and Jacob?
Time still has a way of healing wounds. Sibling rivalry can often be quieted by distance and time.

10. What was Esau's generous offer to Jacob?
Esau offered to provide escort to Jacob and his company for their travel.

November 28, 1993

Jacob Blesses Joseph and His Sons

Genesis 48: 9-19

9 And Joseph said unto his father, They *are* my sons, whom God hath given me in this *place*. And he said, Bring them, I pray thee, unto me, and I will bless them.
10 Now the eyes of Israel were dim for age, *so that* he could not see. And he brought them near unto him; and he kissed them, and embraced them,
11 And Israel said unto Joseph, I had not thought to see thy face: and, lo, God hath shewed me also thy seed.
12 And Joseph brought them out from between his knees, and he bowed himself with his face to the earth.
13 And Joseph took them both, E'phra-im in his right hand toward Israel's left hand, and Ma-nas'-seh in his left hand toward Israel's right hand, and brought *them* near unto him.
14 And Israel stretched out his right hand, and laid *it* upon E'-phra-im's head, who *was* the younger, and his left hand upon Ma-nas'-seh's head, guiding his hands wittingly, for Ma-nas'seh *was* the firstborn.
15 And he blessed Joseph, and said, God, before whom my fathers Abraham and Isaac did walk, the God which fed me all my life long unto this day.
16 The angel which redeemed me from all evil, bless the lads; and let my name be named on them, and the name of my fathers Abraham and Isaac; and let them grow into a multitude in the midst of the earth.
17 And when Joseph saw that his father laid his right hand upon the head of E'-phra-im, it displeased him: and he held up his father's hand, to remove it from E'-phra-im's head unto Ma-nas'-seh's head.
18 And Joseph said unto his father, Not so, my father for this *is* the firstborn; put thy right hand upon his head.
19 And his father refused, and said, I know *it*, my son, I know *it*: he also shall become a people, and he also shall be great: but truly his younger brother shall be greater than he, and his seed shall become a multitude of nations.

◆◆◆◆◆◆

◀ **Memory Selection**
Genesis 48:19

◀ **Devotional Reading**
Psalm 103:14

◀ **Background Scripture**
Genesis 48

◀ **Printed Scripture**
Genesis 48:9-19

Teacher's Target

Humans are big on tradition, position and protocol. In the passage before us today, Jacob (Israel) is going to give the greater blessing to Joseph's younger son, Ephraim. Joseph objects, but Jacob said that God had shown him that the younger would be the greater. God is not bound by human tradition, position or protocol.

Ask the class to think of ways we may restrict and hinder God with traditions and protocol in the church. Do you have examples of how children in a family exceed family labels and/or expectations? Have you ever been fooled by appearances of what "seems to be" or "what ought to be?" Make a list of traditions that class members desire to have explained to them.

Lesson Introduction

Jacob (Israel) is near the time of his death. He has given instructions about his burial. Jacob is sick. Joseph, along with his two sons, goes to visit him. Jacob adopts the two boys and takes them as his own. He gives a blessing to each, but blesses the younger son with a greater blessing. This was contrary to tradition. Joseph objects, but Jacob holds firm. He gives the blessing knowingly, with no deceit on the part of the recipient. He declares that it was in a spirit of prophecy that he gave Ephraim the greater blessing.

How unexpected was the reversal of station! Surely, both boys were surprised. Joseph's response shows that he was caught off guard. How often God does the unexpected.

Teaching Outline

I. The Visit: Gen. 48:9-11
   A. The Introduction: 9
   B. The Embrace: 10
   C. The Exhilaration: 11
II. The Blessing: Gen. 48:12-16
   A. Sons Positioned: 12-14
   B. Joseph Blessed: 15
   C. Sons Blessed: 16
III. The Objection: Gen. 48:17-19
   A. Joseph Displeased: 17
   B. Joseph Protested: 18
   C. Jacob Explained: 19

Daily Bible Readings

Mon. Joseph Holds No Resentment
Gen. 45:1-9
Tue. "Thus Says Your Son Joseph"
Gen. 45:10-20
Wed. Jacob Yearns to See Joseph
Gen. 45:21-28
Thurs. Aged Jacob Blesses Pharaoh
Gen. 47:1-12
Fri. Joseph Ushers in Land Reform
Gen. 47:13-26
Sat. Jacob Adopts Ephraim and Manasseh - *Gen. 48:1-7*
Sun. Jacob Blesses Manasseh, then Ephraim - *Gen. 48:8-14, 17-22*

November 28, 1993

VERSE BY VERSE

I. The Visit: Gen. 48:9-11

A. The Introduction: 9

9. And Joseph said unto his father, They are my sons, whom God hath given me in this place. And he said, Bring them, I pray thee, unto me, and I will bless them.

Joseph went to see his dying father. He took his sons along. They needed to see their grandfather and learn how to face death, both to see how to be with the dying and to see how a godly man dies. Often grandparents can communicate things to children that parents cannot. Also, what is said to children in such focused moments such as times of death can have a profound effect upon their lives.

Joseph introduced Manasseh, the eldest, and Ephraim to Jacob. He was proud of them. His having them with him was a blessing in itself. He desired his father's blessing and also a blessing for his sons. How important it is to bless our children, to call out their good qualities rather than to curse them by highlighting their flaws and failures. It is good to remember that the "blessing" comes long before the final words before death are spoken. The blessing is a process in the midst of living with our children day by day.

B. The Embrace: 10

10. Now the eyes of Israel were dim for age, so that he could not see. And he brought them near unto him; and he kissed them, and embraced them.

Jacob could hardly see. Age had taken its toll. Joseph was requested to bring the boys near. He did so and Jacob bestowed great affection upon them. How good it is for sons to be blessed not only by their father but also grandfathers and uncles. There are few joys greater for a grandchild than to receive the affection and blessing of grandparents. Along with this passage being a high moment in the spiritual history of the nation Israel, it is a moving expression of family dynamics and affection.

C. The Exhilaration: 11

11. And Israel said unto Joseph, I had not thought to see thy face: and, lo, God hath shewed me also thy seed.

Jacob was overjoyed. He had not expected to see Joseph again before his death and now he was doubly blessed. His grandsons had come as well. For so long Joseph had been away from Jacob in Egypt. These sons had been born in Egypt. Now Jacob was able to see them, embrace them, visit with them. Even at this late hour in his life, Jacob was receiving blessings from God.

How it must have heartened him to be surrounded by a family that loved and respected him at the time of his death.

II. The Blessing: Gen. 48:12-16

A. Sons Positioned: 12-14

12. And Joseph brought them out from between his knees, and he bowed himself with his face to the earth.
13. And Joseph took them both, E'-phra-im in his right hand toward Israel's left hand, and Ma-nas'-seh in his left hand toward Israel's right hand, and brought them near unto him.
14. And Israel stretched out his right hand, and laid it upon E'-phra-im's head, who was the younger, and his left hand upon Ma-nas'-seh's head, guiding his hands wittingly; for Ma-nas'-seh was the firstborn.

Verse 13 describes how Joseph placed Manasseh in position to receive the greater blessing since he was the oldest. Verse 14, however, depicts for us Jacob's reversal of the expected. He switched his right hand to Ephraim's head and his left hand rested upon Manasseh. How programmed for the expected we are! Change throws us off. We desire protocol to be set so that we know our roles. How frequently God thrusts us into situations that break our molds and redefine our roles.

B. Joseph Blessed: 15

15. And he blessed Joseph, and said, God, before whom my fathers Abraham and Isaac did walk, the God which fed me all my life long unto this day.

Before blessing Joseph and his sons, Jacob recounted how gracious and generous God had been to him. As he looked back over his life, he was mindful of God's continual care all along his journey. God had provided daily bread for him both physically and spiritually. God had visited him with special communion on occasion (Gen. 48:3), but always He had been near and watching over Jacob. How good to come to the end of our days and to be able to look back and see how all of it, both the good and the bad, have been woven together by God for our good and His glory (Rom. 8:28)!

C. Sons Blessed: 16

16. The angel which redeemed me from all evil, bless the lads; and let my name be named on them, and the name of my fathers Abraham and Isaac; and let them grow into a multitude in the midst of the earth.

Not only had God visited and cared for Jacob, but the angels of God had redeemed him from all evil. God, through His ministering angels, had set Jacob's feet on a steady course under His guidance rather than his own wilful nature. Jacob realized what disaster he had been delivered from. Can you imagine the impact that this testimony of their grandfather recorded in verses 15 and 16 would have on Manasseh and Ephraim?

Now Jacob claimed the two boys as his own. Though born in Egypt, they would not be cut off from the heritage of Abraham, Isaac, and Jacob. Joseph had power in Egypt but these two sons would have the heritage of the promise of Abraham, a far more precious gift than power bestowed by humankind.

III. The Objection: Gen. 48:17-19

A. Joseph Displeased: 17

17. And when Joseph saw that his father laid his right hand upon the head of E'-phra-im, it displeased

him: and he held up his father's hand, to remove it from E′-phra-im's head unto Ma-nas′-seh's head.

Joseph saw that Jacob had crossed his hands upon the sons' heads. He was displeased, thinking the older should receive the greater blessing. He wanted to be fair according to custom, but grace does not follow the course of nature or custom. Often what we think "ought to be" is in direct opposition to what God is working. Sometimes this is the case in instances when normally God would have agreed with tradition or custom. For example, Israel was normally first, but in refusal to accept Jesus Christ, the first shall become last.

Notice how often the younger received distinguished favor in God's covenant relationship: Abel above Cain, Shem above Japheth, Abraham above Nabor and Haron, Isaac above Ishmael, Jacob above Esau, Judah and Joseph above Rueben, Moses above Aaron, David and Solomon above their elder brothers. Here it was Ephraim above Manasseh.

B. Joseph Protested: 18

18. And Joseph said unto his father, Not so, my father: for this is the firstborn; put thy right hand upon his head.

The protest was not a lack of respect for his father and his right to do as he pleased with his blessing. It was a protest in line with custom and the normal bestowal of favor upon the first born. There is nothing wrong with order, nor with a tradition of bestowing greater favor upon certain roles or positions. All are not honored the same, either in nature or grace. God often bestows more gifts and responsibility upon one than on another, but God never fails to bless us all in the way that is good for us and for His purpose. In our human understanding we cannot know what is best for us and especially not for others. Jacob gave his blessing under the guidance of God. Joseph in his human reasoning was not better at knowing God's desire than any of us when we are leaning upon human faculties alone for guidance.

C. Jacob Explained: 19

19. And his father refused, and said, I know it, my son, I know it: he also shall become a people, and he also shall be great: but truly his younger brother shall be greater than he, and his seed shall become a multitude of nations.

Jacob would not be reversed in his decision. He may have been old, feeble, almost blind and very weak; yet, he was not ready to relinquish his leadership to his son just now. His spirit was still in tune with God. He was rich in communion with God and in a spirit of prophecy made his blessing upon the younger, Ephraim. Both sons were blessed. Both would be great. But as Jacob prophesied, Ephraim would become the larger nation than Manasseh. Manasseh was divided one half on one side of the Jordan and the other half on the other side. This division alone made Manasseh less powerful.

JACOB BLESSES JOSEPH WITH HIS SONS

Evangelistic Emphasis

Jacob did not face death with fear, anguish and turmoil. His body was weak but not his soul. He knew the voice of God, and placed his trust in Him. There is absolutely no indication that Jacob ever recoiled from death as if he might somehow escape it or prevent it. Neither do there seem to have been any heroic measures taken by any of Jacob's family members or doctors attempting to delay the inevitable.

Jacob was about to die, and he was quite ready for it. He made valuable use of that knowledge by setting his house in order before his death. Once those details had been taking care of he was ready to die.

Often Christians are even surprised, themselves, by their absence of fear of dying. It hasn't always been that way for them. Perhaps, in their youth the thought of dying struck terror in their hearts. Nevertheless, having walked with God for a half dozen or more decades, they have grown to love and trust Him immeasurably. It's not that these Christians have grown courageous in their old age. Courage has nothing to do with it. Instead, their lives have become so intertwined with God that they can no longer remember anything to fear.

The unbeliever may look at this demonstration of faith without full comprehension of what he sees. Perhaps he is bewildered by it. It may be that he will assume that this Christian is brave. one thing is certain, he has no scorn in his eyes now, only envy.

♦♦♦♦♦♦

Memory Selection

His younger brother shall be greater than he, and his descendants shall become a multitude of nations. *Genesis 48:19*

This seems to be a mere echo of an earlier statement regarding Esau and Jacob. Most of us realize, of course, that we each have our strengths. Not all of us are gifted the same. Not all have even the same level of intellect. Some are superior. Some are average. Some are inferior. I speak not of worth but of aptitude.

This reality can often be a difficult fact to accept. This is especially true if our sights are set on goals beyond our abilities. Yet, it is not our task to be what we are not. It is our task to be the best of what we are. If we come to accept this calling, we will find both success and happiness. For us not to accept it is for us to sentence ourselves to a lifetime of frustration and defeat.

126

November 28, 1993

Weekday Problems

Ed and Loretta are the parents of four children, three daughters and one son. It is very important to them that their children be blessed by a healthy interaction with their grandparents. They both treasure priceless memories of the way that their own grandparents made them to feel special, served as their mentors and helped to shape their values.

However, a problem has arisen that has created some very hard feelings in their home. Gradually, over the course of several years, it has come to be apparent that Ed's parents favor one of the grandchildren over the others. Though Ed has spoken with his parents several times about this, their very obvious favoritism has not diminished. In fact it has come to be a major point of contention among the children.

*What should Ed and Loretta do if these grandparents continue to be uncooperative about this matter?

*How can Ed and Loretta best help their children to deal with this matter wholesomely?

*How can one know when the allegation of "playing favorites" is justified and when it is not?

*Is there ever a legitimate reason for grandparents to show favoritism toward one grandchild over another? If so, when does it cease to be acceptable?

♦♦♦♦♦♦

Sparkles

Husband: "You know, Honey, I'm going to work hard, plan right and save. Someday we are going to be rich."

Wife: "Darling, we are already rich. We have each other. Someday maybe we will have money."

Where your treasure is, there will you heart be also.

JACOB BLESSES JOSEPH AND HIS SONS

This Lesson In Your Life
ACCEPTING OUR LOT

The middle years of life are often difficult to endure. Half of one's expected life is behind, and the indelible ink of time forces a confrontation with reality. The youth of life was characterized by dreams, ideals, ambitions, and fantasies. Many of the obstacles encountered were overcome by the force of sheer persistence and irresistible faith. Defeats of considerable magnitude left the spirit undaunted due to the underlying conviction that "tomorrow we will prevail!" Other fine ambitions simply were postponed "until tomorrow."

Midlife forces upon us the reality that the bank of tomorrows is running out. Postponed dreams may outnumber the anticipated years. Looking backward, one's victories can look small, while the defeats appear large. Dreams have a way of turning sour when they have been on the shelf too long. This is especially true when their reason for being there is linked somehow to one's inherent personal limitations.

In middle-life we are usually better able to assess our potential than we were in youth. Unfortunately, sometimes that more accurate appraisal can be painful. How does one accept his lot in life when it tramples upon his dreams?

Perhaps there is just not enough time to do all that one thought could be done. It takes a whole lot longer to accomplish one's goals than had been planned. Consequently, some of those goals will never make it to completion. Any scaling back of goals brings a torturous compromise of one's dreams.

Often, money is the primary wall between a dreamer and his dreams. More is required to supply the day-to-day needs of the family, leaving little for banking toward even the smallest dream. Also there are those unexpected setbacks that siphon off much of the funds that otherwise could be tucked away. Somehow, it's just not turning out the way it was anticipated in one's youth.

Of course there are other limitations that can prove to be far more devastating because of the "personal" way they pronounce judgment. A crippling accident leaves one but a fraction of the physical specimen that she was. A mental breakdown comes during medical school, trashing seven years of hard work and a lifetime of dreams. The unexpected divorce virtually ends one's career as a pastor. The tumor shows up on the doctor's X-ray and pronounces a much earlier termination date than had been anticipated. Consistent testing evidence reveals that one's mental capacity will not support the aggressive academic program that he had planned to pursue. Repeated failure at one's task slowly convinces him that he really ought to be doing something else, even though this is what he dreamed about doing all of his life.

Accepting the "cards that one has been dealt" is never easy. Especially, for the habitual dreamer, facing reality can be like turning one's back on everything she's been living for her whole life. Yet, accepting our lot in life is part of what life in the Lord is all about. It has to do with faith and hope and eternity.

Seed Thoughts

1. Why did Joseph happen to go to visit his father at this particular time?
Joseph had been told that his father was ill.

2. Whom did Joseph take with him when he went to visit his father?
Joseph took his two oldest sons, Manasseh and Ephraim.

3. What did Jacob mean by his words about Ephraim and Manasseh when he said, "now thy two sons...are mine"?
As far as the division of his estate was concern, Ephraim and Manasseh were to be counted as his sons. In a sense, he was adopting them for his own.

4. Where did Jacob say that he had buried his wife, Rachel?
Jacob said that Rachel had died "by me in the land of Canaan in the way unto Ephrath: and I buried her there in the way of Ephrath" (on the road to Ephrath, or Bethlehem).

5. As a matter of aging, how was Jacob like his father had been?
As with Isaac, Jacob's eyes were failing him. Apparently, he could still see a little but not much.

(PLEASE TURN PAGE)

---

1. Why did Joseph happen to go to visit his father at this particular time?

2. Whom did Joseph take with him when he went to visit his father?

3. What did Jacob mean by his words about Ephraim and Manasseh when he said, "now thy two sons...are mine"?

4. Where did Jacob say that he had buried his wife, Rachel?

5. As a matter of aging, how was Jacob like his father had been?

6. Why was it important which son was presented to which hand of Jacob?

7. How did Jacob surprise his son and grandsons?

8. How did Joseph respond to his father's surprise?

9. Who retained "the upper hand" in this disagreement between father and son?

10. What promise did Jacob make to Joseph?

Joseph had been told that his father was ill.

Joseph took his two oldest sons, Manasseh and Ephraim.

As far as the division of his estate was concern, Ephraim and Manasseh were to be counted as his sons. In a sense, he was adopting them for his own.

Jacob said that Rachel had died "by me in the land of Canaan in the way unto Ephrath: and I buried her there in the way of Ephrath" (on the road to Ephrath, or Bethlehem).

As with Isaac, Jacob's eyes were failing him. Apparently, he could still see a little but not much.

According to their age and rank, the eldest son ought to have received the right-hand blessing, so Jacob moved the boys toward their grandfather in that position.

Jacob crossed his hands and gave the right-hand blessing to the younger of the two boys.

It displeased him. He attempted to remove his father's right hand from Ephraim's head and to place it onto Manasseh's.

Jacob did. He refused to comply with his son's wishes, insisting that the younger of the two boys would be the greater of the two.

Jacob promised Joseph that God would be with him and would eventually bring them back to the land of their fathers.

(SEED THOUGHTS--Cont'd)

6. Why was it important which son was presented to which hand of Jacob?
According to their age and rank, the eldest son ought to have received the right-hand blessing, so Jacob moved the boys toward their grandfather in that position.

7. How did Jacob surprise his son and grandsons?
Jacob crossed his hands and gave the right-hand blessing to the younger of the two boys.

8. How did Joseph respond to his father's surprise?
It displeased him. He attempted to remove his father's right hand from Ephraim's head and to place it onto Manasseh's.

9. Who retained "the upper hand" in this disagreement between father and son?
Jacob did. He refused to comply with his son's wishes, insisting that the younger of the two boys would be the greater of the two.

10. What promise did Jacob make to Joseph?
Jacob promised Joseph that God would be with him and would eventually bring them back to the land of their fathers.

December 5, 1993

Preparing the Way

Luke 3:2b-4, 7-17

2 An'-nas and Ca'-ia-phas being the high priests, the word of God came unto John the son of Zach-a-ri'-as in the wilderness.

3 And he came into all the country about Jordan, preaching the baptism of repentance for the remission of sins;

4 As it is written in the book of the words of E-sa'-ias the prophet, saying, THE VOICE OF THE ONE CRYING IN THE WILDERNESS, PREPARE YE THE WAY OF THE LORD, MAKE HIS PATHS STRAIGHT.

7 Then said he to the multitude that came forth to be baptized of him, O generation of vipers, who hath warned you to flee from the wrath to come?

8 Bring forth therefore fruits worthy of repentance, and begin not to say within yourselves, We have Abraham to *our* father: for I say unto you, That God is able of these stones to raise up children unto Abraham.

9 And now also the axe is laid unto the root of the trees: every tree therefore which bringeth not forth good fruit is hewn down, and cast into the fire.

10 And the people asked him, saying, What shall we do then?

11 He answereth and saith unto them, He that hath two coats, let him impart to him that hath none; and he that hath meat, let him do likewise.

12 Then came also publicans to be baptized and said unto him, Master, what shall we do?

13 And he said unto them, Exact no more than that which is appointed you.

14 And the soldiers likewise demanded of him, saying, And what shall we do? And he said unto them, Do violence to no man, neither accuse *any* falsely; and be content with your wages.

15 And as the people were in expectation, and all men mused in their hearts of John, whether he were the Christ, or not;

16 John answered, saying unto *them* all, I indeed baptize you with water; but one mightier than I cometh, the latchet of whose shoes I am not worthy to unloose: he shall baptize you with the Holy Ghost and with fire:

17 Whose fan *is* in his hand, and he will thoroughly purge his floor, and will gather the wheat into his garner; but the chaff he will burn with fire unquenchable.

◆◆◆◆◆◆

◀ **Memory Selection**
Luke 3:4

◀ **Devotional Reading**
Matthew 1:18-25; 2:1-12

◀ **Background Scripture**
Luke 1:5-25; 3:1-18

◀ **Printed Scripture**
Luke 3:2b-4, 7-17

PREPARING THE WAY

Teacher's Target

John broke a 400-year silence. Once prophets had been numerous and powerful. After the Babylonian captivity prophecy had ceased. A rigid enforcement of the Law had emerged. Now, a strange figure out of the desert, wearing camel hair and eating locusts and wild honey appeared. His voice thundered for the religious to repent. A distant memory stirred in the people. Prophetic voices from their past echoed in their ears. John the Baptist paper-clipped the people to their prophetic past, pointed them to God in the present, and prophesied their hope for the future.

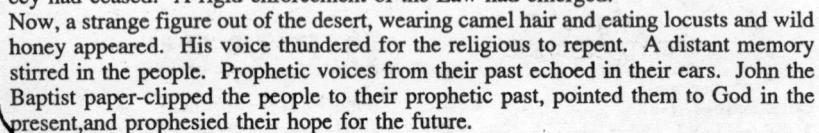

How would you have reacted to this strange prophet? Are we comfortable with the unfamiliar? Have the class members write down their definition of repentance. Is repentance the work of God or of man?

Lesson Introduction

The Jews were under Roman rule. Even the choice of their high priest was out of their hands. Rome had replaced Annas, the Jewish-appointed high priest, with Caiaphas, his son-in-law. The dream of a return of the golden age of David was far from being realized. Conquered and ruled, still they were determined to preserve their traditions.

Now John, the son of a priest, at thirty, was ready to be admitted to serve in the temple. Instead, he challenged the very foundation and structures of religious order.

John was not calling people to do more. Already the people were doing plenty. More activity would not suffice.

John's message was not man-centered. He called for the people to come home to God. Religious posturing was futile. Hearts had to change. God alone was John's solution for the bondage to world powers.

Teaching Outline

I. The Messenger and Message: Luke 3:2b-4
   A. God's Call: 2
   B. God's Message: 3
   C. God's Sovereignty: 4
II. John's Proclamation: Luke 3:7-9
   A. A Question: 7
   B. An Exhortation: 8
   C. A Prophecy: 9
III. The Response and an Explanation: Luke 3:10-17
   A. The People: 10-11
   B. The Publicans and Soldiers: 12-14
   C. The Explanation: 15-17

Daily Bible Readings

Mon. Zechariah Chosen for Priestly Duties - *Luke 1:5-9*
Tue. God Responds to Zechariah's Prayers - *Luke 1:10-17*
Wed. Gabriel Challenges Zechariah *Luke 1:18-25*
Thurs. The Word Comes to John *Luke 3:1-6*
Fri. John Preaches Baptism of Repentance - *Luke 3:15-22*
Sat. John Baptizes Jesus *Luke 3:15-22*
Sun. Jesus Affirms John *Luke 7:18-28*

December 5, 1993

VERSE BY VERSE

I. The Messenger and Message: Luke 3:2b-4

A. God's Call: 2

2. An´-nas and Ca´-ia-phas being the high priests, the word of God came unto John the son of Zach-a-ri´-as in the wilderness.

John's right to be a priest came from his lineage. His call to prophecy came from God. He was not man-commissioned, but God-called. His message was not from mankind but to mankind.

How the call came is not made clear. John had no doubt about who called or who he would serve.

The wilderness had been a place where God had often spoken to His people. In this lonely place God transacted business with His servants. There John faced himself and His God without distractions or amenities.

B. God's Message: 3

3. And he came into all the country about Jordan, preaching the baptism of repentance for the remission of sins;

John's was a mission of repentance. A repentance kind of baptism symbolized the work of God done in them. God called John. God offered baptism. God affected change in people.

Repentance was God's work, not another work of man. Judaism was overflowing with man's works. God worked beyond their religious, cultural, economic, political, and social norms and mores. This was not a call to more morals. Judaism was already such a movement that failed. God through John was calling for a commitment of relationship with Him.

Repentance means "a change of mind, direction, will and action." Apart from God's power and intervention, humankind was not capable of such change. Repentance, faith and remission of sins were a gift from God.

C. God's Sovereignty: 4

4. As it is written in the book of the words of E-sa´-ias the prophet, saying, THE VOICE OF ONE CRYING IN THE WILDERNESS, PREPARE YE THE WAY OF THE LORD, MAKE HIS PATHS STRAIGHT.

Long ago God spoke through Isaiah (Isaiah 40:3). Now He spoke again after a long silence. God was not subject to times appointed by men. Men plotted and planned, but God moved at His own pace.

In the meantime, Israel had become a "religious wilderness." Still God had His witnesses. Zechariah and Elizabeth, Joseph and Mary, Simeon and Anna, were a few who sought God and not religious posturing. Now John the Baptist would be the vehicle to rally His people to Himself.

II. John's Proclamation: Luke 3:7-9

A. A Question: 7

7. Then said he to the multitude

that came forth to be baptized of him, O generation of vipers, who hath warned you to flee from the wrath to come?

Matthew 3:7-10, a parallel passage, states that the Pharisees and Sadducees were present also. John still did not flinch. He would serve God and not man. He neither catered to the mighty nor coddled the common man. John confronted all with the truth and challenged all to receive the Word from God.

This generation, John declared, was no different from the people in the day of the prophets. They too were a brood of vipers. God endured with patience and kindness the misguided striving of humankind. In John, He came with a question. Will you hear and heed the Living God or men?

B. An Exhortation: 8

8. Bring forth therefore fruits worthy of repentance, and begin not to say within yourselves, We have Abraham to our father; for I say unto you, That God is able of these stones to raise up children unto Abraham.

Neither numbers nor lineage were of any consequence before God. Many children of Abraham were in the land. Few were children of God. John declared that their actions revealed this.

Being religious and being in synagogues did not give standing before God. A changed heart and life through the efficacious grace of Jesus Christ could transform "viper-ism" into true virtue.

John made it clear. Abraham's actions wouldn't count for them. Their actions would disclose who they were. Genealogy, appearances and works of merit would not make God's honor roll. Only God's work of grace could bestow honor.

C. A Prophecy: 9

9. And now also the axe is laid unto the root of the trees: every tree therefore which bringeth not forth good fruit is hewn down, and cast into the fire.

Already, John declared, the dividing line was drawn. It was in his very words. The people would hear the saving word of God or they would translate it into a condemning word by their rejection of it.

God always comes with a saving word first. Like a man on the roadside calling to cars loaded with people headed toward a washed out bridge the protective warning came. No scolding and denouncing, only warning. In John, God sought to save the lost.

Condemnation would come only if the saving word was refused. Rejected grace could not work its desired effect and God would weep (Matt. 23:37).

III. The Response and an Explanation: Luke 3:10-17

A. The People: 10-11

10. And the people asked him, saying, What shall we do then?
11. He answereth and saith unto them, He that hath two coats, let him impart to him that hath none; and he that hath meat, let him do likewise.

God desired renewal. Humankind wanted ritual. God was concerned with spirit. Humankind was concerned with structure and form. Always spirit over structure, Luther said.

John wanted the people to know God desired their character to reflect His. God gave His best in creation and redemption. He wanted His people to do the same with each other. There was to be no hoarding in God's

Kingdom, only an economy of enough for all. If one had more it was to be put to use for others. God was not gluttonness but giving.

B. The Publicans and Soldiers: 12-14

12. Then came also publicans to be baptized, and said unto him, Master, what shall we do?

13. And he said unto them, Exact no more than that which is appointed you.

14. And the soldiers likewise demanded of him, saying, And what shall we do? And he said unto them, Do violence to no man, neither accuse any falsely; and be content with your wages.

As God required mercy rather than sacrifice, He loved justice rather than oppression. John taught not to defraud the prince nor destroy the people.

The soldiers were told not to abuse people or put them into fear, entrap people with false witness, chafe about wages or try to make up what they thought they were worth by bribes or fraud or payoffs.

Notice that neither the tax collector nor the soldier were told to give up his position. God knew that taxes would have to be solicited and people protected. He knew then and now the nature of people and the insidiousness of sin.

C. The Explanation: 15-17

15. And as the people were in expectation, and all men mused in their hearts of John, whether he were the Christ, or not;

16. John answered, saying unto them all, I indeed baptize you with water; but one mightier than I cometh, the latchet of whose shoes I am not worthy to unloose: he shall baptize you with the Holy Ghost and with fire:

17. Whose fan is in his hand, and he will throughly purge his floor, and will gather the wheat into his garner; but the chaff he will burn with fire unquenchable.

Judaism taught that when the Messiah came, prophecy would once again come forth. Here was John prophesying! "Could this be the one?" people asked.

John explained his role. He was a preparer of the way. He was not the way. He called them to God. He was not God.

He used water of preparation. The coming one would wash them in the very Holy Spirit of God.

God, like the farmer, was concerned with the wheat. That chaff would be burned was a second thought, not the primary point. The wheat is ready for harvest. That's the point!

Evangelistic Emphasis

The story of John the Baptist connects the coming of Jesus to the Old Testament. Our faith is a product of the Old Covenant and the New Covenant. As an old Testament prophetic figure, John the Baptist not only preaches about building the King's highway, but is himself a bridge between the Old Testament and the New Testament. Any attempt, therefore, to understand the evangelistic message of Luke begins in what was foretold in the biblical history of Israel.

One of Luke's themes indeed seems to be that Christianity is the logical continuation of Judaism. The God of the old Testament has one ultimate missionary purpose: the salvation of all peoples. (Recall Solomons' prayer of dedication that the temple would be a place of prayer for everyone.) The same God, with the same salvation purpose, has now sent John to make final preparations for the coming of the King.

Therefore, with John the Baptist we see a continuity of purpose and proclamation carried over from the Old Testament. God, then and now, wants and wills salvation for all who receive Him. Along with the old Testament prophets, John the Baptist, Jesus and the apostles, we stand in the prophetic line of evangelistic preaching: "The voice of one crying in the wilderness, Prepare ye the way of the Lord, make his path straight."

Do you see that the world's salvation is up to us? A whole wilderness of people depends upon our faithful construction of the King's highway. Remember that the work of the evangelist is always wilderness work.

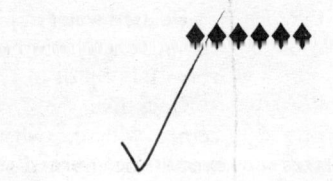

Memory Selection

The voice of one crying in the wilderness: Prepare the way of the Lord, make his paths straight. *Luke 3:4*

Building a highway in the desert is not an original sermon idea for John the Baptist. The ancient Hebrew prophet, Isaiah, first coins the imagery. Isaiah's road comes up out of Babylon, the land of captivity for God's people. For years they suffer the harshness of virtual imprisonment. Then comes Isaiah's message of hope. God plans an intervention. A great highway is being prepared through the desert. God will deliver His people from slavery.

John the Baptist takes up the sermon of Isaiah and says that it applies to the coming of Jesus. The King is coming. The world has to get ready for God.

Do you understand what Luke is telling us through John's preaching? We have to prepare the way for the King. Some hard, constant work has to be done, and the work will have to be repeated again and again. The rough ways have to be made smooth. Pot holes have to be filled. Curves have to be straightened. In other, more literal words: "Preach . . . be instant in season, out of season . . ." (2 Tim. 4:2).

December 5, 1993

Weekday Problems

John attended church recently for the first time since he was twelve years old. The preacher warned of the flames of hell for all unbelievers. He preached a message of fire and brimstone. Like a modern day, wild-eyed John the Baptist, the preacher shouted and ranted for over an hour.

John found the message demeaning and insulting to his intelligence. He told his best friend, Robert, all about his negative experience. "I'm never going to church again," said John. "I felt bad when I got to church, and I felt worse when I left."

*What would you say to John?

*In what ways could you balance the preacher's negative message with other, more positive biblical texts?

*Without denying the validity of negative biblical texts, are there more appropriate ways of presenting these difficult biblical truths? If yes, how?

◆◆◆◆◆◆

Sparkle

Theodore of Pherme, a desert father, was approached by one of the elders. He said to Theodore, "Look how such and such a brother has returned to the world."

Wisely, Theodore answered, "Does that surprise you? No, rather be astonished when you hear that someone has been able to escape the jaws of the enemy."

Theodore also said, "In these days, many take their rest before God gives it to them."

PREPARING THE WAY

This Lesson In Your Life

John is a loud, fiery preacher standing on the banks of the Jordan River. The wind blows his long hair. His mouth twists and twitches out the awful word: REPENT! REPENT! His deep-set eyes and dramatic rhetoric suggest a preacher conscious of the ways of God with men; a preacher unconcerned with his Neilson ratings, the amount of money in the offering, or the Sunday attendance; a preacher oblivious to establishing rapport with his audience. Why, he calls them a brood of vipers!

I whisper to John: "That's no way to win friends and influence people. You'll just turn them off. They'll never hear a word you say. Can't you see that people want to hear about God's grace and mercy, about love and forgiveness, and the assurance of eternal life?"

John, however, is not listening to me. He is too intense about his message, too worked up over our sins to keep quiet: "Who warned you to flee from the wrath to come? Bear fruits worthy of repentance."

Make no mistake. The intent of John's message is clear. John claims that people, the people of God, have gone soft. They are outwardly religious, but inwardly arrogant about their religious pedigree. The preacher seems to read their minds as he tells them that God can make children of Abraham out of stones.

There is much here for us by way of application. Do not begin to say, "We are Americans," or in "God we trust." Too many of us wear American flags where our crosses should be. There's a certain smugness on our face when we brag about being Americans. Don't you know? This is God's country. This is America--the home of the free and the brave--the world's leading exporter of bombs.

I look closely at John and imagine him loose in our churches. He is such an anachronism in our complex society, a throwback to the old days. I am sad that old John would not last long in our churches. His offended congregation will tell him to mind his own business and then hold back the money until he leaves town. Then they will find a preacher who will put them to sleep every Sunday with sweet Jesus songs and positive thinking therapy and pop psychology lessons. Poor John! He can't last out the year telling people to repent and be responsible.

The odd thing is that John's message rings so true. We can argue that people are too cultured and too sophisticated for such preaching. We can pretend they won't understand or that they'll just get mad, but that doesn't make the message any less true. Something Karl Menninger once wrote jumps into my mind: "Moral leadership languishes, and upon moral leadership we still rely for salvation. Whose job is it to cause society to repent if not the preacher's?"

Repentance is still our greatest need. Our salvation depends upon it. The sounds I hear in America, however, are not those of a people beating their chests, confessing and repenting of sin. No the sounds are those of a cacophony of voices all screaming for their rights.

Here then are two conflicting images. John preaches repentance while Americans demand their rights. Perhaps it is too late to save our nation. Perhaps we are not willing to repent of our infatuation with rights.

Listen: John is preaching to us. We can not long survive whining about rights. John has another way for us. Repent and be responsible. I call to John to tell him that his scary message is true after all; but he is gone. I am left with the echo of his words. Repent.

Seed Thoughts

1. What is the significance of the family background of Zacharias and Elizabeth?
   Both Zacharias and Elizabeth were members of the priestly families with a long tradition of devotion to God.

2. What are the major character traits of Zacharias and Elizabeth?
   They were both righteous and blameless.

3. What was probably the greatest disappointment in Elizabeth's life?
   She did not have a baby. "Elizabeth was barren."

4. What Old Testament couple was in a similiar circumstance to that of Zacharias and Elizabeth?
   Abraham and Sarah. Both couples were old and without children.

5. Why did Gabriel take away Zacharias' power of speech?
   Zacharias did not believe the promise of God. He thought only in the restricted patterns of rational thought.

(PLEASE TURN PAGE)

---

1. What is the significance of the family background of Zacharias and Elizabeth?

2. What are the major character traits of Zacharias and Elizabeth?

3. What was probably the greatest disappointment in Elizabeth's life?

4. What Old Testament couple was in a similiar circumstance to that of Zacharias and Elizabeth?

5. Why did Gabriel take away Zacharias' power of speech?

6. When the people realized that Zacharias could not speak, what did they think?

7. What does the birth of John and the lack of faith on the part of Zacharias teach us about God?

8. Where did John start his preaching mission and what is the significance of this place?

9. What was the content of John the Baptist's message?

10. How did John preach to the crowds?

Both Zacharias and Elizabeth were members of the priestly families with a long tradition of devotion to God.

They were both righteous and blameless.

She did not have a baby. "Elizabeth was barren."

Abraham and Sarah. Both couples were old and without children.

Zacharias did not believe the promise of God. He thought only in the restricted patterns of rational thought.

The people correctly assumed that Zacharias had seen a vision in the temple.

God does things His own way. We can be part of God's plan or we can stand on the side as unfaithful people, but God always completes His promises.

John preached at the Jordan River, the crossing place of Israel into the promised land.

John preached repentance for the forgiveness of sin.

John preached with honest, hard words the truth of God.

(SEED THOUGHTS--Cont'd)

6. When the people realized that Zacharias could not speak, what did they think?
The people correctly assumed that Zacharias had seen a vision in the temple.

7. What does the birth of John and the lack of faith on the part of Zacharias teach us about God?
God does things His own way. We can be part of God's plan or we can stand on the side as unfaithful people, but God always completes His promises.

8. Where did John start his preaching mission and what is the significance of this place?
John preached at the Jordan River, the crossing place of Israel into the promised land.

9. What was the content of John the Baptist's message?
John preached repentance for the forgiveness of sin.

10. How did John preach to the crowds?
John preached with honest, hard words the truth of God.

December 12, 1993

Yielding to God's Will

Luke 1: 26-38

26 And in the sixth month the angel Gabriel was sent from God unto a city of Galilee, named Nazareth,
27 To a virgin espoused to a man whose name was Joseph, of the house of David; and the virgin's name *was* Mary.
28 And the angel came in unto her, and said, Hail, *thou that art* highly favoured, the Lord *is* with thee: blessed *art* thou among women.
29 And when she saw *him*, and what manner of salutation this should be.
30 And the angel said unto her, Fear not, Mary: for thou hast found favour with God.
31 And, behold. thou shalt conceive in thy womb and bring forth a son, and shalt call his name JESUS.
32 He shall be great, and shall be called the Son of the Highest: and the Lord God shall give unto him the throne of his father David:
33 And he shall reign over the house of Jacob for ever, and of his kingdom there shaft be no end.
34 Then said Mary unto the angel, How shall this be, seeing I know not a man?
35 And the angel answered and said unto her, The Holy Ghost shall come upon thee, and the power of the Highest shall overshadow thee: therefore also that holy thing which shall be born of thee shall be called the Son of God.
36 And, behold, thy cousin Elisabeth, she hath also conceived a son in her old age: and this is the sixth month with her, who was called barren.
37 For with God nothing shall be impossible.
38 And Mary said, Behold the handmaid of the Lord; be it unto me according to thy word And the angel departed from her.

◆◆◆◆◆◆

◀ **Memory Selection**
Luke 1:38

◀ **Background Scripture**
Luke 1:26-56

◀ **Devotional Reading**
Luke 1:57-80;
Isaiah 11:1-15

◀ **Printed Scripture**
Luke 1:26-38

YIELDING TO GOD'S WILL

Teacher's Target

Many of God's leaders did their best work when they were older. Moses, Abraham, David, Paul, John, Peter and many more. However, they were connected with God early in life. Mary was young when the angel Gabriel appeared to her. There was much she was not ready for and did not understand, but she was faithful to God. It was who she knew that held her true, not what she knew.

Ask the class what they would do if an angel appeared to them. Have them share when and how they have heard and do continue to hear from God. Is God still doing mighty things with people in our day? Are miracles less prevalent today or are we less likely to believe them because of our faith in our technology and scientific way of thinking? Does a scientific model of thinking limit our vision as surely as an unscientific way of perceiving?

Lesson Introduction

Nothing out of the ordinary usually happened in Mary's hometown of Nazareth, especially nothing about God. In fact, Galilee was a region traditionally seen as the habitation of trollops, tramps and thieves. Nathaniel spoke a rather popular expression, "Can anything good come out of Nazareth?" (John 2:46).

Suddenly an angel appeared and talked! Mary was "troubled." Gabriel calmed her, and announced her favor. She would be the mother of one named Jesus. Mary questioned. How could this be when she was not married? God would overshadow her was the answer. Then the angel clinched his argument, "With God nothing is impossible." In faith, Mary yielded to her Lord, let it be! What an extraordinary day in the life of an ordinary young lady! How unpredictable and full of wonder was her God!

Teaching Outline

I. The Arrival: Luke 1:26-29
   A. Where: 26
   B. Who: 27
   C. Why: 28-29
II. The Announcement: Luke 1:30-33
   A. A Birth: 30-31
   B. A King: 32-33
III. The Astonishment: Luke 1:34-38
   A. Puzzlement: 34
   B. Power: 35-36
   C. Possible: 37-38

Daily Bible Readings

Mon. Mary Will Bear a Son
Luke 1:26-31
Tue. Born Holy
Luke 1:32-37
Wed. Mary and Elizabeth Rejoice
Luke 1:36-45
Thurs. Mary Sings the Magnificat
Luke 1:46-56
Fri. His Name is John
Luke 1:57-66
Sat. Prophet of the Most High
Luke 1:67-80
Sun. The Refiner's Fire Purifies
Malachi 3:1-5; 4:5-6

December 12, 1993

VERSE BY VERSE

I. The Arrival: Luke 1:26-29

A. Where: 26

26. And in the sixth month the angel Gabriel was sent from God unto a city of Galilee, named Nazareth,

Nazareth was a remote city in a remote area called Galilee. There were no literary centers in Galilee, no prominent political families, no religious citadels. The one prophet that was Galilean by birth was Jonah, and he had been a reluctant prophet to Gentiles, not his own people. Now, much later, Jesus would be rejected by His own and heard by the Gentiles.

The very place of Jesus' birth conveyed the little concern God has for pomp and circumstance, class status, social position, financial or political power. God came to a common young lady in a common place because we are all common. We are only human, no matter how we seek to primp and posture as if we were more. God was doing His most uncommon acts of grace, mercy and reconciliation in the most common ways and places. He worked through and for those who were most aware of their commonness.

B. Who: 27

27. To a virgin espoused to a man whose name was Joseph, of the house of David; and the virgin's name was Mary.

Gabriel came to Mary, a virgin. She was espoused ("engaged" comes close in our day) to Joseph. He was, like Mary, of the line of David, but neither of them was prominent in any way. Her unassuming and simple trust in God was her honor.

Other women who were married (Elizabeth for example) were as faithful as Mary and as cherished by God. However, for her task Mary needed to be a virgin. Jesus was to come into human nature by the supernatural work of God. His birth, life, death and resurrection were to be the beginning of a new humanity. He was to be the firstborn of the new creation (Col. 1:18). This event was to be a new beginning in the midst of the old and dying order.

C. Why: 28-29

28. And the angel came in unto her, and said, Hail, thou that art highly favoured, the Lord is with thee: blessed art thou among women.

29. And when she saw him, she was troubled at his saying, and cast in her mind what manner of salutation this should be.

Was Mary washing clothes? Cooking a meal? Mending a dress? Cleaning house? We don't know. What we do know is that she was taken by surprise. She was not accustomed to such attention, especially from a messenger from God!

143

Mary was of low estate in the society. Now she was being told by an angel that she was highly favored. It is as if she were being told, "Mary, you are being exalted to an important task by God himself."

Mary was shifted from seeing herself as unknown and uninvolved in the great events of history to a vision of herself as blessed among all women of all generations. How could she handle such news? "The Lord is with thee," was the assuring, strengthening and sustaining word that made her receptivity possible.

Mary was not puffed up. She was puzzled. Nothing in herself merited such recognition. Nothing in her family, circumstance or life preparation had any hint of things of such magnitude.

II. The Announcement: Luke 1:30-33

A. A Birth: 30-31

30. And the angel said unto her, Fear not, Mary: for thou hast found favour with God.

31. And, behold, thou shalt conceive in thy womb, and bring forth a son, and shalt call his name JESUS.

That Jesus would "come from above" rather than "out of" the earth was important. Jesus would be aligned with God and the heavenly order rather than the ways of humankind and worldly order. He would be man in every way. Yet His ways would be directed not by Adam's seed but by God's word.

Jesus means "God saves." God would come to us in real humanity. No play acting here. He was really God and really man. Paul made this clear in Philippians 2:5-11.

Mary's honor was not material. Her status in the world did not change. There was no clamor for her autograph. She received no sudden wealth; in fact her life would be full of puzzlement and pain. She could not justify her condition nor explain the outcome. She would have to wait for God's finished work to justify her. Still, she would be available to Him.

B. A King: 32-33

32. He shall be great, and shall be called the Son of the Highest: and the Lord God shall give unto him the throne of his father David:

33. And he shall reign over the house of Jacob for ever; and of his kingdom there shall be no end.

David had been promised a kingdom that would last forever. The Jewish kingdom had not only disappeared, but his descendants were an occupied and dominated people. They longed for and believed God would restore the golden age of David. However, God would not go backward. They were not ready for the kind of Kingdom God had in mind. Jesus would be greater than David; His Kingdom more inclusive; His authority more conclusive. His Kingdom would be eternal. God's promise to David would be kept (2 Sam. 7:16) but not as the Jews expected.

III. The Astonishment: Luke 1:34-38

A. Puzzlement: 34

34. Then said Mary unto the angel, How shall this be, seeing I know not a man?

That many were puzzled by the virgin birth should surprise no one. Mary herself was astonished at the thought. Faith, not credulity, was necessary to accept this miracle. Never had Mary heard of such a possibility. But a God who can create the heavens and the earth from nothing and would raise His son from the dead could surely activate the life force to conceive a child in Mary's womb. What is impossible with men is possible with God.

This second and last Adam (Rom. 5:14-19) was born innocent as Adam was created innocent. The hovering Spirit of God accomplished both feats.

Mary's human puzzlement was understandable. God's accomplishment was understandable only to faith. Proofs that will satisfy sight will not be offered by God in this age. Faith could see that which would blind sight.

B. Power: 35-36

35. And the angel answered and said unto her, The Holy Ghost shall come upon thee, and the power of the Highest shall overshadow thee: therefore also that holy thing which shall be born of thee shall be called the son of God.

36. And, behold, thy cousin Elisabeth, she hath also conceived a son in her old age: and this is the sixth month with her, who was called barren.

Adam brought sin into the world through his unholy and unauthorized relationship with Satan. God's desire and determination (purpose and plan) was to break the hold of this union over His creation. The power of the Holy Spirit would begin a new work of God. Jesus' life, death and resurrection would break humankind's bondage to sin and inaugurate a new creation.

Jesus would start as Adam had with a clean slate. Sin would be possible to Him since He would be tempted in all ways as a human being. However, He would avail himself to His access to God whereas Adam had not.

Born of the Holy Spirit and not of Adam's seed, Jesus would be free to hear the Father. Only a new beginning could affect a new reality.

C. Possible: 37-38

37. For with God nothing shall be impossible.

38. And Mary said, Behold the handmaid of the Lord; be it unto me according to thy word. And the angel departed from her.

How easily fear arose in the hearts of the people. The Jews lived in a world ruled by fear, as is true of all ages. Mary transcended all avenues of fear. She accepted the impossible possibility. Why? Because she realized who she was dealing with--the God of all possibilities. She did not know how. She did not know what Joseph would do. She did not know the change in her life that was to come. What she did know was who had called her out. This was enough. She would trust His tender mercies toward her.

Evangelistic Emphasis

We live in a world where people have it made and don't know it. The lack of wholistic living can be traced to our inability to know and to do God's will. If people can discover and carry out God's will they find life loaded with meaning.

Take the young Hebrew maiden Mary, for example. An angel appeared to her and told her she was going to have a son. Mary, troubled and confused, did not know what to make of the strange pronouncement of Gabriel, God's spokesperson. Isn't that just like us? We too are often confused by the word from God. Perhaps the word sounds too good to be true or too miraculous for rational human explanation. Whatever the reason, like Mary, we are often frightened by the Word of God that announces the will of God for us.

Mary's questioning of the angel is not to be cast in a negative light. To struggle with the will of God is an ancient and acceptable behavior. The questioning spirit often leads to deeper answers. Gabriel explained to Mary that the Holy Spirit would come upon her. Then Gabriel told Mary something that God had already done, something similar to what He wanted to do for Mary. Elisabeth, Mary's cousin, was also going to have a baby.

Confronted with the promise of the Holy Spirit and the evidence of God's power through Elisabeth, Mary uttered words of commitment to God's will: "Behold the handmaid of the Lord; be it unto me according to thy word." Mary offered herself as the servant of God.

♦♦♦♦♦♦

Memory Selection

Mary said, "Behold, I am the handmaid of the Lord; let it be to me according to your word."
Luke 1:38

Mary heard with the ears of faith and saw with the eyes of hope. How else could she have made such a positive and total commitment of herself to the will of God. Here we have one of those triumphant expressions of human greatness. Couched in sincere humility, these words indicate the appropriate response to the Lord.

All she had to go on was the word of an angel. That, however, proved to be enough. Mary, on the heels of hearing that with God nothing shall be impossible, gave herself without reservation to God. "I belong to the Lord, body and soul," Mary replied.

Isn't that the essence of the Christian experience? We belong to God not to ourselves. We are the slaves of God. Remember what St. Paul told us to do? "I beseech you therefore, brethren, by the mercies of God, that ye present your bodies a living sacrifice, holy, acceptable unto God, which is your reasonable service" (Rom. 12:1). Mary models for us all this kind of obedience to God.

December 12, 1993

Weekday Problems

Mary Sue has experienced a growing desire for spiritual depth and understanding. Having dropped out of the institutional church years ago, she now finds herself experimenting with alternative spiritual expressions. She saw an ad on cable television for a spiritual psychic. Intrigued by the claims, she called the 1-900 number that appeared on her screen.

After spending hundreds of dollars and finding no lasting spiritual guidance, Mary Sue felt more alone and depressed than ever. She mentioned her experience to Cindy, a colleague at work. Cindy, a Christian and member of a local church, invited Mary Sue to attend church with her. "No," said Mary Sue, "I tried church once years ago. I don't understand a thing they're saying."

*How can Cindy be a more effective witness to Mary Sue?
*Do most people have spiritual longings at one time or another? Why does this happen?
*Can you think of some ways to be alert to people who are hungry for spiritual experience?
*How can you help others find spiritual depth in the church?

◆◆◆◆◆◆

Sparkles

John's gospel reads, "The Word became flesh; and dwelt among us, full of grace and truth." John calls the Word the true light that enlightens every man. He declares that all things were created by Him and all that lives is alive because of His life. This light, John says, shines in the darkness and cannot be put out.

Two things, yea three, stand out in this profound teaching by John. First, the Word became flesh. Why are we always trying to turn flesh back into words? Is it because we can argue and debate words? Second, if you look into the darkness long enough you will see the light. Third, if all things find their source in His life, then in all living things we can see and learn of God, like Jesus did with sheep, fig trees, seeds and vineyards.

YIELDING TO GOD'S WILL

This Lesson In Your Life

There is only one appropriate response to the invitation to participate in the will of God: PRAISE. Mary made that response when she understood that God was at work in her life to carry out His missionary purpose. Now, praise can be treated in trite and little ways, but not by Mary, and especially not in the Bible. No, in the Bible praise is an attitude, an affirmation, and a way of life.

From the very beginning the religion of the Bible has been a religion of praise. Such religion was born under the praise of Moses and Miriam as they sang of the delivering power of God. The Psalms are the praise book of Israel. God is praised for bringing His people safely out of slavery, for His mighty right hand of power, for His loyal, steadfast love, for keeping His word, for bestowing mercy and forgiveness upon His people and for being with and for His people.

Praise for God is everywhere in the Bible. It follows that we can best fulfill ourselves when we learn, like Mary, to take part, in praise. The season of Christmas is a great time for songs of praise. Mary burst into song because she had every reason to praise the Lord. She believed the promises of God even when all around her people rejected her. No wonder she sings and magnifies the Lord.

If we are going to experience the inner meanings and nuances of Christmas, we have to spend time with Mary's song of praise. Nothing is closer to the heart of Christmas than praise. Mary, then, can tutor us in praise and teach us how not to let the routine of life become a rut of sameness, show us that the criticism and pessimism of other people should not kill off our praise. She can alert us to the constant surprises of God.

Praise is a fragile gift that requires care, else it will be killed off by despair. Mary refused to lose her gift of praise. She magnified the Lord. In a world that belittled God, Mary celebrated God's greatness. This woman has received the promises of God and experienced His affirmation and grace. No wonder she magnified the Lord. Are we caring for our gift of praise?

Another way of defining Mary's praise is to say that she took delight in the Lord. The gift of delight is a way of saying that we welcome God into our lives. It means that we accept all of God's will. There are no strings attached. Applied to our relationship with God, in what ways do we take delight in the Lord. Do we love Him? Is He accepted and welcomed in our world? Will we share all of life with Him?

These are by no means questions with automatic "yes" answers. This is where our struggle comes. God is working behind the scenes to make His promises come true. While those promises often seem postponed or delayed, our songs of praise and our taking delight in the Lord keep these promises alive. As long as people will praise the Lord, we will be able to look beyond the way this world is to the way God calls this world to be. Praise, then, as magnifying and taking delight in, remains the most appropriate response of the Christian to the God who comes at Christmas.

Seed Thoughts

1. In what way did God communicate the news to Mary that she would have a child?
God's messenger, the angel Gabriel, brought the good news to Mary.

2. How did Mary respond to the initial message from Gabriel?
She was afraid and confused.

3. What difficulty with the idea of having a baby does Mary express?
Thinking only in human terms, she tells Gabriel that she has never been with a man.

4. How does Gabriel deal with Mary's objection?
Gabriel tells Mary that the Holy Spirit will enable her to conceive the child.

5. What would you consider the most important theological teaching in Luke 1?
The birth of Jesus is of the Holy Spirit. With God nothing is impossible.

(PLEASE TURN PAGE)

---

1. In what way did God communicate the news to Mary that she would have a child?

2. How did Mary respond to the initial message from Gabriel?

3. What difficulty with the idea of having a baby does Mary express?

4. How does Gabriel deal with Mary's objection?

5. What would you consider the most important theological teaching in Luke 1?

6. Where does Mary go after Gabriel departs?

7. In what way does Mary respond to the news about the coming birth of Jesus?

8. How does Elizabeth receive the news of Mary's expected child?

9. What is one of the principal teachings of Mary's song of praise?

10. How long does Mary stay with Elizabeth?

(SEED THOUGHTS--Cont'd)

God's messenger, the angel Gabriel, brought the good news to Mary.

She was afraid and confused.

Thinking only in human terms, she tells Gabriel that she has never been with a man.

Gabriel tells Mary that the Holy Spirit will enable her to conceive the child.

The birth of Jesus is of the Holy Spirit. With God nothing is impossible.

Mary rushes to the home of Elizabeth.

She praises and magnifies the Lord.

With utmost faith Elizabeth says, "Whence is this to me, that the mother of my Lord should come to me?"

God, in the birth of Jesus, reverses the standards of the world.

Three months.

6. Where does Mary go after Gabriel departs?
Mary rushes to the home of Elizabeth.

7. In what way does Mary respond to the news about the coming birth of Jesus?
She praises and magnifies the Lord.

8. How does Elizabeth receive the news of Mary's expected child?
With utmost faith Elizabeth says, "Whence is this to me, that the mother of my Lord should come to me?"

9. What is one of the principal teachings of Mary's song of praise?
God, in the birth of Jesus, reverses the standards of the world.

10. How long does Mary stay with Elizabeth?
Three months.

December 19, 1993

Born a Savior

Luke 2:4-20

4 And Joseph also went up from Galilee, out of the city of Nazareth, into Judea unto the city of David, which is called Bethlehem, (because he was of the house and lineage of David,)
5 to be taxed with Mary his espoused wife, being great with child.
6 And so it was, that, while they were there, the days were accomplished that she should be delivered.
7 And she brought forth her firstborn son, and wrapped him in swaddling clothes, and laid him in a manger; because there was no room for them in the inn.
8 And there were in the same country shepherds abiding in the field, keeping watch over their flock by night.
9 And, lo, the angel of the Lord came upon them and the glory of the Lord shone round about them; and they were sore afraid
10 And the angel said unto them, Fear not: for, behold, I bring you good tidings of great joy, which shall be to all people.
11 For unto you is born this day in the city of David a Saviour, which is Christ the Lord.
12 And this *shall be* a sign unto you; Ye shall find the babe wrapped in swaddling clothes, lying in a manger.
13 And suddenly there was with the angel a multitude of the heavenly host praising God, and saying,
14 Glory to God in the highest, and on earth peace, good will toward men.
15 And it came to pass, as the angels were gone away from them into heaven, the shepherds said one to another, Let us now go even unto Bethlehem and see this thing which is come to pass, which the Lord hath made known unto us.
16 And they came with haste and found Mary and Joseph, and the babe lying in a manger.
17 And when they had seen *it*, they made known abroad the saying which was told them concerning this child.
18 And all they that heard *it* wondered at those things which were told them by the shepherds.
19 But Mary kept all these things, and pondered *them* in her heart
20 And the shepherds returned glorifying and praising God for all the things that they had heard and seen, as it was told unto them.

◆◆◆◆◆◆

◀ **Memory Selection**
Luke 2:10-11

◀ **Devotional Reading**
Isaiah 9:2-7

◀ **Background Scripture**
Luke 2:1-20

◀ **Printed Scripture**
Luke 2:4-20

BORN A SAVIOR

Teacher's Target

One of the hardest things to do is to make familiar stories come alive in new ways. We become habituated to the familiar and often miss the message. This can happen even with Scripture. Helping the class become a part of the story may help. For example, how do you think you would have reacted if you were the innkeepers? Do you think Joseph and Mary took it personally, or were they just one of many refused a room?

Look also at the shepherds. How would you have reacted to such an amazing announcement by a choir of angels? Did you know shepherds were ceremonially unclean and could not go to the temple? Now the "temple" so to speak comes to them!

Why a stable for Jesus' birthplace? Where was dignity and royalty? Today, would television reporters cover this event?

Lesson Introduction

Today Jesus' birth is celebrated worldwide. Yet, it was unacclaimed and unannounced when it occurred. A little town of Bethlehem, a peasant family numbered among the multitudes, a birth of another Jewish child; all of these were as ordinary as olive trees.

Like all other events of God's activity, one had to have eyes to see it for what it was. It could be missed completely or sentimentalized to insignificance. For example, too much could be made of the "babyness" of this story. Jesus was a baby, but too many would keep Him so. Then Jesus could be controlled or coddled. The amazing reality was that God entrusted His Son vulnerably to human care. That God allowed Jesus to be helpless or powerless from the beginning is the point of His birth.

Teaching Outline

I. The Registry: Luke 2:4,5
   A. Where: 4
   B. Why: 5
II. The Birth: Luke 2:6-7
   A. His Station: 6, 7
   B. His Location: 7
III. The Shepherds: Luke 2:8-20
   A. The Announcement: 8-14
   B. The Visitation: 15-19
   C. The Exaltation: 20

Daily Bible Readings

Mon. Luke Contrasts Caesar and Jesus - *Luke 2:1-7*
Tue. Angels Appear to Lowly Shepherds - *Luke 2:8-14*
Wed. Shepherds Find Joseph, Mary and Jesus - *Luke 2:15-19*
Thurs. Named By the Angels; "Jesus" - *Luke 2:20-24*
Fri. Simeon Blessed God, Mary, and Joseph - *Luke 2:25-35*
Sat. Joseph and Mary Think Jesus Lost - *Luke 2:41-45*
Sun. Jesus Amazes His Teachers *Luke 2:46-52*

December 19, 1993

VERSE BY VERSE

I. The Registry: Luke 2:4, 5

A. Where: 4

4. And Joseph also went up from Galilee, out of the city of Nazareth, into Judea, unto the city of David, which is called Bethlehem, (because he was of the house and lineage of David,)

Jesus' humiliation did not start on the cross. He humbled himself even in the manner in which He entered history. He was born in the city of David, Bethlehem. Micah 5:2 had foretold the arrival of one who would rule Israel. His hometown would be Bethlehem, a town small among the tribes of Israel. In the day of Jesus' birth the city had no status or prestige of any note.

Jerusalem was also called the city of David (2 Sam. 5:7). However, God did not choose the city of power and prestige for His son's place of birth, but rather the lowly place of David's origins. As David had been born in lowliness to be a shepherd, so Jesus came into history meek and lowly to shepherd the world.

Notice how God used secular events to accomplish His purposes. It was a registry for taxation that brought Joseph and Mary to Bethlehem. With God there was no secular and sacred. All of life was of one piece with God.

B. Why: 5

5. to be taxed with Mary his espoused wife, being great with child.

Joseph and Mary went to Bethlehem, they thought, to be registered. This was a seventy mile trip for them just to pay their taxes. Mary, though pregnant, had to go with Joseph. This manner of the registry was partly due to the Jews' desire to preserve the distinction of their tribes. However, Rome ordered the enrollment of the Jews as an acknowledgement that they were vassals of the state. Rome foolishly held to power authorized by this world. The Jews clung slavishly to old religious forms and missed the substance of God's Kingdom. Both Rome and Judaism were shattered by the power and presence of the true authority of God. This eternal authority was manifest through the death of a Jewish peasant Messiah crucified upon a Roman cross. God used both Judaism and Rome to break the old wine skins of a dead world. The new wine of Jesus Christ could be contained by neither.

II. The Birth: Luke 2:6-7

A. His Station: 6, 7

6. And so it was, that, while they were there, the days were accomplished that she should be delivered.

7. And she brought forth her firstborn son, and wrapped him in swaddling clothes, and laid him in

a manger; because there was no room for them in the inn.

Later in His ministry Jesus said, "Foxes have holes and birds of the air have nests, but the Son of Man has no place to lay His head" (Matt. 8:20). From the beginning this was so. Being born in the stable of an inn was by no means the usual place of birth. Inn stables were not then, nor now, permanent quarters. They were for wayfarers, sojourners, "passers through."

Jesus came to pass through life like a pied piper, gathering those who would follow Him to the Father's house which was not of this world (Heb. 11:13-16). Jesus' station in life has always been with those who know themselves to be lowly, poor in spirit, in need of God's assistance.

He was the firstborn of Mary and the firstborn of the new creation. In this world the new creation has no standing. This age has been infiltrated by God's Kingdom, but this age is not His Kingdom. One day Jesus' true station will be revealed. Until then He will be trampled by the world system, hated and taunted by His enemies, His truth ignored and His love spurned.

B. His Location: 7

7. And she brought forth her firstborn son, and wrapped him in swaddling clothes, and laid him in a manger; because there was no room for them in the inn.

A manger or stable substituted for a cradle. "Swaddling clothes" means "to tear." Jesus was wrapped in torn cloth, from a dress or robe perhaps. No royal palace. No royal robes. No political clout. No parents with pull. The poor and lowly had to fend for themselves.

Since He came for the outcasts of the world, He himself was located with them even by the place of His birth. The lame, the blind, the deaf, the widow, the orphan, the poor, the prisoner, the needy, the tax collectors and sinners, the nobodies that sustain the world but receive no honor--these He was positioned with by family and place of birth.

Having had no worldly glory, Jesus could and did show us where the true treasures were to be found. These treasures are love, joy, peace, patience, kindness, goodness, faithfulness, gentleness and self-control (Gal. 5:22,23). These could not be bought. No number of titles or credentials will bestow these upon a person. These will come only through the King of the Kingdom that has no permanent location in this age.

III. The Shepherds: Luke 2:8-20

A. The Announcement: 8-14

8. And there were in the same country shepherds abiding in the field, keeping watch over their flock by night.

9. And, lo, the angel of the Lord came upon them, and the glory of the Lord shone round about them, and they were sore afraid.

10. And the angel said unto them, Fear not: for, behold, I bring you good tidings of great joy, which shall be to all people.

11. For unto you is born this day in the City of David a Saviour, which is Christ the Lord.

12. And this shall be a sign unto you; Ye shall find the babe wrapped in swaddling clothes, lying in a manger.

13. And suddenly there was with the angel a multitude of the heavenly host praising God, and saying,

14. Glory to God in the highest, and on earth peace, good will toward men.

How would you announce the birth of a Savior? Who would you announce it to? Notice God lavishes His most extravagant announcement of His son's birth on the most unlikely audience. Shepherds in the field, ceremonially unclean and unable to enter the temple, received the heavenly singing telegram.

The shepherds expected no visitors, much less angels from God. Their first thoughts seemed to be of foreboding. Do you not imagine that all of their misdeeds and sins could have passed through their minds?

The angel calmed their fears and announced good news instead. It will always be this way with God. They were full of fear; He was full of grace and good tidings. He did not come to them through the angels to condemn them but to seek and to save them.

How will we know Him? they asked. He will be wrapped in swaddling cloths in a manger. Another shock. Surely such a one would be found in the best home in town. But no, God's Kingdom is an upside down Kingdom.

B. The Visitation: 15-19

15. And it came to pass, as the angels were gone away from them into heaven, the shepherds said one to another, Let us now go even unto Bethlehem, and see this thing which is come to pass, which the Lord hath made known unto us.

16. And they came with haste, and found Mary and Joseph, and the babe lying in a manger.

17. And when they had seen it, they made known abroad the saying which was told them concerning this child.

18. And all they that heard it wondered at those things which were told them by the shepherds.

19. But Mary kept all these things, and pondered them in her heart.

The shepherds had gotten the message. There was little hesitation. They made their plans quickly. They would honor what the Lord had spoken to them through His messengers. The child and parents were found. This wonderful news was confirmed. Don't you know that Joseph, Mary and the shepherds had a lot to share about the amazing visitations they had from God?!

C. The Exaltation: 20

20. And the shepherds returned, glorifying and praising God for all the things that they had heard and seen, as it was told unto them.

The shepherds had shared the good news of what they were told and had seen. The people had marveled at what they heard. Mary had taken all the wonderful and mystifying events into her heart to ponder their meaning and significance for her life and the life of the world.

Mary meditated upon these matters. The shepherds proclaimed them. Both were legitimate responses. The shepherds were moved to praise. God will always be found in the praise of His people.

Evangelistic Emphasis

In a world full of bad news, the good news of Jesus Christ often gets lost. Perhaps our familiarity with the gospel has dulled the edges for us. After all, we have sitting before us the preaching of the gospel for over 2,000 years. No wonder we often lose our sense of wonder at the nature of the original proclamation of the good news.

To see and hear once again the good news, imagine for a moment the sense of exhilaration that new parents feel when their first child is born. Dad is on the phone to everyone he knows. "We have a boy!" "She's the most beautiful girl ever born!" The sheer excitement, the giddy joy of the birth needs to be accented. Sometimes we stop total strangers on the street: "We have a boy!"

Well, that is the nature of the angel's announcement of the birth of Jesus. Could it be that we are so used to the story that we have lost the joy of our evangelism? Perhaps we need to reimage the birth of Jesus again and again to remind ourselves of the joy of the evangelistic message.

As we rejoice over the birth of a child, let us also rejoice over the birth of our Savior. Maybe a big sign in front of your church this Christmas could read: "It's a boy! Come and celebrate the birth of the Savior."

Memory Selection

Behold, I bring you good news of a great joy which will come to all the people; for to you is born this day in the city of David a Savior, who is Christ the Lord. *Luke 2:10-11*

St. Luke, with his ever-present concern for the universal nature of the gospel, proclaims from the outset that the good news is for "all the people." The exclusive nature so prevalent in Judaism is thus challenged by the baby of Bethlehem. Everything that God's chosen people had failed to become, Jesus now would be. Christ the Lord was the Savior for all persons and all seasons.

A second important aspect of St. Luke's message appears in the angelic proclamation: joy. Not only is the good news for all people; also, the good news produces joy in the lives of those who accept the gospel. There is so little joy in our world. In addition, much that passes for joy is artificially produced, especially at the time of the year when the birth of Christ is celebrated. Somewhere in the world there ought to be a group of people who specialize in the production of authentic joy. Shouldn't that group be those who follow Jesus Christ. Let us spread the joy of the gospel everywhere we go to as many people as we can.

A third important aspect of St. Luke's message is the announcement that Jesus Christ is Lord. Here in embryonic form is the first creed of the Church: "Jesus is Lord." The message of salvation is incomplete without the affirmation of the Lordship of Jesus Christ. Let us make Him our Lord.

December 19, 1993

Weekday Problems

Every year during the Christmas season, Nell watched the classic movie, "It's a Wonderful Life." She loved watching the story unfold with all of the poignancy that Hollywood could muster. She always cried when the whole town came together at the end to save their hero. The story was just too good to be true. Yet Nell always loved watching the movie.

This Christmas, however, Nell was going through a time of life that seemed too bad to be true. "It's a Wonderful Life" appeared to be a fairy tale. Her own life was anything but wonderful. Bill, her husband of twenty-five years had left her for a younger woman. She was unemployed and had five children. Christmas this year would not be sentimental. There was too much harsh reality to face.

*Do people sometimes use Christmas as an escape from the realities of life?
*Why are there more suicides right after Christmas than at any other time?
*How can Christians help people who are having a tough time at Christmas?

◆◆◆◆◆◆

Sparkles

Theodora was one of only a small number of desert mothers. There were many desert fathers. On one occasion she said, "Neither asceticism, nor vigils nor any kind of suffering are able to save us, only true humility can do that." She told this story:

A holy man was able to banish demons. On one occasion, he asked the demons what made them go away. "Is it fasting?" he asked.

"No, we do not eat or drink," they replied.

"Is it vigils?" he asked.

"No, we do not sleep."

"Is it separation from the world?"

"No, we live in the deserts."

"What is it then?"

The demons said, "Nothing can overcome us, but only humility."

"Do you see how humility is victorious over the demons?" Theodora asked.

BORN A SAVIOR

This Lesson In Your Life

The contrast Luke draws is severe: Caesar and Christ. The context of the birth of Jesus is the Roman peace. Yet the Roman period of peace was upheld by military force. At the manger in Bethlehem the Prince of Peace enters the world, not with an artificial peace but with the peace the world can not give.

Jesus is born in lowly and humble circumstances against the background of Caesar's majesty and renown. Luke knows, however, that the day is coming when every knee shall bow and every tongue confess that Jesus is Lord. The great reversal of fortune is characteristic of Luke's theology. It serves to remind us that our battle against principalities and powers will at the last be won by our Christ and Lord.

For those who look closely at the scene there is evidence that the chosen Messiah has come; not, of course, the expected military ruler, but the Son of God. Notice that Jesus is wrapped in cloth bands, reminding us of Moses' birth. He is born in the town of David, not in a lodge like a stranger, but in the manger of the Lord, who is the sustainer of His people. His birth announcement is given to shepherds, reminding us that David himself was a shepherd. Now a king greater than David is born. Isn't it just like God to come to Bethlehem in the form of a baby, instead of to Jerusalem as a mighty military general? In our lives should we not be alert to the presence of God in the ordinary experiences of life?

Luke also tells us that Joseph and Mary come to Bethlehem for a worldwide census ordered by the emperor. With characteristic emphasis, Luke gently reminds his readers of the worldwide significance of the birth. Caesar's edict pales into obscurity over against the angel's message. The King of kings is born. The Prince of Peace is come. The Savior of the world Arrives. No wonder there is joy unspeakable as the angels sing. In our lives should we not be alert to the opportunity for joy in the ordinary experiences of life?

Those privileged to be present in the birth scene have various reactions to the newborn King. The shepherds show us a spontaneous faith. They rush to Bethlehem, see the baby and tell everybody the good news. The Church often moves forward only on the wings of spontaneous outbreaks of faith and testimony. We would all be impoverished if not for those with the enthusiasm to respond immediately to the good news. Let us always be open to the moving of the Holy spirit in ways we do not expect.

Those who hear the message of the shepherds respond in awe and wonder. In a world as crass and cold as ours, we need people who know how to maintain a sense of wonder. We should always be open to God's surprises and reversals. Wonder is a marvelous gift. The very act of worship is enhanced when people gather in awe and wonder and adoration. Let us always be open to the experience of wonder.

Mary treasures and ponders over all that happens. She tries to hit upon the meaning of all her experiences. Luke lets us in on the secret that Mary is not sure of the significance of the birth of Jesus. She does not know everything. Yet she is open to understanding. To ponder the eternal truth of God is one of our greatest privileges. Let us always be open to new understandings. The picture of the Church pondering and treasuring the truth of God is an exciting one. May it always be true of us.

Seed Thoughts

1. What does Luke mean by "all the world should be taxed?"
The Roman Empire of Caesar covered most of the known world of the first century.

2. Why did Joseph leave Nazareth?
The government issued a decree requiring everyone to return to his home town.

3. Where was Jesus born?
In a stable that belonged to the Bethlehem innkeeper.

4. Who first heard the good news of the birth of Jesus?
A group of local shepherds outside Bethlehem.

5. What were the basic attitudes of the angels?
Great joy and praise to God.

(PLEASE TURN PAGE)

---

1. What does Luke mean by "all the world should be taxed?"

2. Why did Joseph leave Nazareth?

3. Where was Jesus born?

4. Who first heard the good news of the birth of Jesus?

5. What were the basic attitudes of the angels?

6. What might be the significance of the birth announcement being given first to shepherds?

7. What was the message of the angel choir?

8. Where did the shepherds go after the angels departed?

9. After leaving Bethlehem, what did the shepherds do?

10. How did Mary respond to these events?

(SEED THOUGHTS--Cont'd)

The Roman Empire of Caesar covered most of the known world of the first century.

The government issued a decree requiring everyone to return to his home town.

In a stable that belonged to the Bethlehem innkeeper.

A group of local shepherds outside Bethlehem.

Great joy and praise to God.

The greatest news of history went to the lowest social class in Palestine. God's Good News is for everyone.

Peace on earth and good will to men.

To Bethlehem to see the baby for themselves.

They told everyone and became the first evangelists.

She pondered them in her heart.

6. **What might be the significance of the birth announcement being given first to shepherds?**
The greatest news of history went to the lowest social class in Palestine. God's Good News is for everyone.

7. **What was the message of the angel choir?**
Peace on earth and good will to men.

8. **Where did the shepherds go after the angels departed?**
To Bethlehem to see the baby for themselves.

9. **After leaving Bethlehem, what did the shepherds do?**
They told everyone and became the first evangelists.

10. **How did Mary respond to these events?**
She pondered them in her heart.

December 26, 1993

Testing A Commitment to Service

Luke 4:1-15

4 AND Jesus being full of the Holy Ghost returned from Jordan, and was led by the Spirit into the wilderness,
2 Being forty days tempted of the devil. And in those days he did eat nothing: and when they were ended, he afterward hungered.
3 And the devil said unto him, If thou be the Son of God, command this stone that it be made bread.
4 And Jesus answered him, saying, it is written, THAT MAN SHALL NOT LIVE BY BREAD ALONE, BUT BY EVERY WORD OF GOD.
5 And the devil, taking him up into an high mountain, shewed unto him all the kingdoms of the world in a moment of time.
6 And the devil said unto him, All this power will I give thee, and the glory of them: for that is delivered unto me; and to whomsoever I will I give it.
7 If thou therefore wilt worship me, all shall be thine.
8 And Jesus answered and said unto him. Get thee behind me, Satan: for it is written, THOU SHALT WORSHIP THE LORD THY GOD, AND HIM ONLY SHALT THOU SERVE.
9 And he brought him to Jerusalem, and set him on a pinnacle of the temple, and said unto him, If thou be the Son of God, cast thyself down from hence:
10 For it is written, HE SHALL GIVE HIS ANGELS CHARGE OVER THEE, TO KEEP THEE:
11 AND IN *THEIR* HANDS THEY SHALL BEAR THEE UP, LEST AT ANY TIME THOU DASH THY FOOT AGAINST A STONE.
12 And Jesus answering said unto him, It is said, THOU SHALT NOT TEMPT THE LORD THY GOD.
13 And when the devil had ended all the temptation, he departed from him for a season.
14 And Jesus returned in the power of the Spirit into Galilee: and there went out a fame of him through all the region round about.
15 And he taught in their synagogues, being glorified of all.

◆◆◆◆◆◆

◀ **Memory Selection**
Luke 4:8

◀ **Devotional Reading**
Matthew 4:1-11

◀ **Background Scripture**
Luke 3:21-22; 4:1-15

◀ **Printed Scripture**
Luke 4:1-15

TESTING A COMMITMENT TO SERVICE

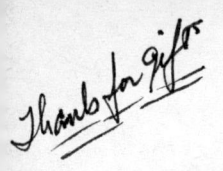

Thanks for gifts

Teacher's Target

The usual direction people turn is away from God. We are all like our father and mother, Adam and Eve. God knows our weakness and has never ceased seeking to show us a better way. Jesus gives us the example in His temptation.

After long striving with His people Israel, God sent His son to do for them what they couldn't do, overcome sin and death. Israel fell continually. Jesus withstood the tempter at his best and most furious. He began His stand for the Father at the outset of His ministry. *a couple of questions* ~~After reading the text, ask the class how Jesus did it.~~ *(Jesus)* What did He use to combat the evil one? How was this different from Adam and Eve? In the first temptation, who did Jesus declare He would be? Write down ~~areas where you know yourself to be weak.~~ How do you guard against falling?

Lesson Introduction

The temptation of Jesus tells the whole story of His ministry. The entire time of the incarnation Jesus was tempted (Luke 12:50). From the first, Jesus established who would be His authority. Also, He declared who He would be. He would be man. In the first temptation, Jesus was asked to use His divine power to meet His human need. Jesus declared, "Man shall not live by bread alone, but by every word of God." Then the tempter offered Him a short cut to His goal. Again, Jesus would only worship and serve God. Once He had declared that He would be the Son of God, the tempter challenged Him to prove it by casting Himself down from the temple. Jesus responded by declaring He would not tempt God. Each temptation was a challenge for Him to give up His humanity. Any act apart from His Father's direction would be to give up His Messiahship.

Teaching Outline

I. The First Temptation:
   Luke 4:1-4
   A. The Setting: 1-2
   B. The Attack: 3
   C. The Counter: 4
II. The Second Temptation:
    Luke 4:5-8
    A. The Setting: 5-6
    B. The Attack: 7
    C. The Counter: 8
III. The Third Temptation:
     Luke 4:9-15
     A. The Setting: 9
     B. The Attack: 10-11
     C. The Counter: 12-15

Daily Bible Readings

Mon. John Baptized for Moral Action
Matthew 3:1-10
Tue. God's Beloved Son
Matthew 3:11-17
Wed. Temptations: Bread, Power and Glory - *Luke 4:1-8*
Thurs. Display of Power
Luke 4:9-15
Fri. Wise Men Seek Jesus
Matthew 2:1-6
Sat. Wise Men Worship Jesus
Matthew 2:7-12
Sun. Pleased by the Beloved Son
Isaiah 42:1-9

December 26, 1993

VERSE BY VERSE

I. The First Temptation: Luke 4:1-4

A. The Setting: 1-2

1. AND Jesus being full of the Holy Ghost returned from Jordan, and was led by the Spirit into the wilderness,
2. Being forty days tempted of the devil And in those days he did eat nothing: and when they were ended, he afterward hungered.

Jesus, after His baptism, was led by the Holy Spirit into the desert. Luke 4:2 says He was tempted for forty days. The desert was a lonely place. No one was there to assist Him in this hour of trial. Alone with Himself, the tempter came. Jesus relied upon God's presence with Him.

Notice how different the setting was for Jesus from that of Adam. The Garden of Eden was lush. The desert was barren. Jesus came into a fallen world. He met Satan on his own ground. His weapons? Prayer, the word of God and His union with the Father would be sufficient. Scripture revealed quite a contrast between Adam and Christ.

B. The Attack: 3

3. And the devil said unto him, If thou be the Son of God, command this stone that it be made bread.

Jesus was hungry. He had fasted as a sign of His reliance upon the Father's provision. Adam had all his physical needs met, and still He did not properly appreciate the Father's care. The tempter attacked Jesus at humankind's point of weakness. The temptation was to distrust the Father's care, to be relevant and do something in the present moment to take care of Himself.

Satan wanted Jesus to show that He had the power to do relevant things for Himself and for others apart from the Father. "Aren't you hungry, Jesus," the tempter taunted. "Aren't others hungry? Don't you want people to see you are the Messiah by feeding the hungry? Start with yourself." But even later in His ministry, Jesus would not succumb to such a temptation, even from the people (John 6:25-34).

C. The Counter: 4

4. And Jesus answered him, saying, it is written, THAT MAN SHALL NOT LIVE BY BREAD ALONE, BUT BY EVERY WORD OF GOD.

Jesus would make a difference, not by being relevant, but by being human. He would show that man was meant to depend on God. He would show that man was first a spiritual being and only secondarily a physical being. "Man (human beings) live not by bread alone, but by every word that comes from the mouth of God."

What humans need first is God, not bread. The breath of life comes

163

first to a newborn, then the need for bread.

The world and Satan wanted Jesus to agree with them that He could take care of Himself. There was to be no acknowledgement of a need for God. Jesus chose to remain misinterpreted as irrelevant. He chose to enter into humankind's anguish.

II. The Second Temptation: Luke 4:5-8

A. The Setting: 5-6

5. And the devil, taking him up into an high mountain, shewed unto him all the kingdoms of the world in a moment of time.

6. And the devil said unto him, All this power will I give thee, and the glory of them: for that is delivered unto me; and to whomsoever I will I give it.

Now Satan tested Jesus' allegiance to God's authority. "Don't you want people to think you are powerful, Jesus?" the tempter taunted. Control was the issue. Satan thought a short cut to gaining control would sweeten the pot. So, he took Jesus to a high mountain and showed Him all the kingdoms of the world and their glory.

The world's glory did not impress Jesus. He had been in the presence of the Father's glory. There was no comparison. Jesus knew He couldn't serve humankind with the power of the world. World power served only itself and crushed people. Jesus saw the weariness of the world and the shabbiness of its pseudo-splendor.

B. The Attack: 7

7. If thou therefore wilt worship me, all shall be thine.

Whatever power was to be His as He walked this earth, Jesus knew would come from the Father. Satan had only so many tricks. They had worked with Adam and Eve, surely they would work again. Satan assumed Jesus would respond like Adam and Eve.

Listen to the attack amplified. "Why, with power you could really make things happen. You could go anywhere, dictate behavior, set up and enforce the right rules. Don't forget about money, either. With money you could feed the poor, clothe the needy, house the homeless, build hospitals, take care of the lepers. You do want the best for all these people, don't you Jesus?"

Building empires had never solved the peoples' ills. Empires rose and fell. The poor remained.

C. The Counter: 8

8. And Jesus answered and said unto him, Get thee behind me, Satan: for it is written, THOU SHALT WORSHIP THE LORD THY GOD, AND HIM ONLY SHALT THOU SERVE.

Making deals with Satan, or making alliances with the world never worked. Jesus knew Israel's fate. Even now they were an occupied people. They had worshiped power and not God. Look what it had brought them.

Adam's thirst for power multiplied over the centuries. Despair and heartache of humans continued. Worshiping God would mean a life of love not power. Jesus would choose a cross over control. He would choose love over political or religious prowess.

Jesus would live out intimacy with God. Power fears intimacy and vulnerability. Love bears all things, believes all things, hopes all things, endures all things (1 Cor. 13:7). Lo and behold, love overcomes the world!

III. The Third Temptation: Luke 4:9-15

A. The Setting: 9

9. And he brought him to Jerusalem, and set him on a pinnacle of the temple, and said unto him, If thou be the Son of God, cast thyself down from hence:

Now Satan went for Jesus' strength. Satan challenged Him to do something spectacular. Surely Jesus would be seen as a messenger from heaven if He would float down in the arms of angels from the top of the temple. Ironically, Jesus' true ministry would be the downfall of the temple.

B. The Attack: 10-11

10. For it is written, HE SHALL GIVE HIS ANGELS CHARGE OVER THEE, TO KEEP THEE:
11. AND IN THEIR HANDS THEY SHALL BEAR THEE UP, LEST AT ANY TIME THOU DASH THY FOOT AGAINST A STONE.

Having failed with bread and power, now Satan offered Jesus a following of people. He used Scripture for this attack. He did not misquote the Scripture, but he misinterpreted it. In its original context in Psalm 91, the passage was meant to show God's protection of His people in their everyday course of life. Never was it intended to be used as a proof text for doing ridiculous things and expecting God to intervene and stop the consequences of foolish acts.

C. The Counter: 12-15

12. And Jesus answering said unto him, It is said, THOU SHALT NOT TEMPT THE LORD THY GOD.
13. And when the devil had ended all the temptation, he departed from him for a season.
14. And Jesus returned in the power of the Spirit into Galilee: and there went out a fame of him through all the region round about.
15. And he taught in their synagogues, being glorified of all.

Jesus would not be a side show for the people to gaze at with fascination. Jesus wanted to declare who man is. He did not have to prove Himself. Humankind's glory was to be in being God's supreme creation, and in worshiping the One who created them. Man could have only a reflected glory from the Father.

Jesus knew that He did not have to test the limits of His boundaries. He knew that freedom was in the boundaries set by the Father. No tightrope act across the Niagara Falls was necessary. He would draw the chosen by His grace, mercy, forgiveness and love.

The spectacular drew crowds, but Jesus would not tempt God by swallowing fire, walking on coals, jumping from high buildings or putting His head in the lion's mouth. The common would be His way.

Evangelistic Emphasis

The evangelistic invitation always includes a call to absolute obedience. When the free grace of God is emphasized, however, there is a temptation to omit the call to obedience. As John Killinger points out, "This age knows far more about being free than about obeying."

The temptation experience of Jesus underscores the requirement of total obedience. When Jesus was baptized, God said, "Thou art my beloved Son." Jesus' mountaintop experience is somewhat analogous to a person's conversion experience. There is a tendency to believe that the confession of faith completes the process of salvation.

Life, however, teaches us that the mountain experience is usually followed by the wilderness experience. There in the wilderness, up against the power of satan for forty days, Jesus struggled with His own identity as the Suffering Servant of God. Likewise, neophyte Christians battle the temptation to be less than absolutely obedient to God.

Salvation is always a step followed by a walk. It is a choice followed by commitment. It is a moment of conversion followed by a life time of conversions. Salvation, then, always includes absolute obedience to God. Whenever we are tempted to forsake our faith, to abort our mission as a Kingdom person, we can take heart from the example of Jesus. He shows us how to go beyond the mountaintop spiritual experience to the everyday walk in the wilderness. He demonstrates absolute obedience to God. Nothing has a greater priority for the Christian than such obedience.

♦♦♦♦♦♦

Memory Selection

You shall worship the Lord your God, and him only shall you serve. *Luke 4:8*

Worship and serve God. Jesus insists in this verse that the obedient children of God will have two poles of existence: worship and service. one without the other simply will not do. It takes both to equal obedience to God.

One pole of the Christian experience is worship. This is the most basic experience of the Christian: to worship God. Regular, consistent, faithful worship is a necessity or growing Christians. To worship God is to allow the Holy Spirit to recreate our spiritual energy supply.

The other pole of Christian experience is service. Those who sing and pray and hear the gospel are also called to service. Service to neighbor follows naturally the worship of God. We love God through worship; we love our neighbors through service.

Worship without service can lead to excess emotionalism. Service without worship can lead to a dead, dry social activism. So let us do both: worship and serve.

December 26, 1993

Weekday Problems

Barry, a young executive with a master's degree in Business Administration, has been with his company for fourteen years. He and his wife, Carol, have three children. They are active in their church and community, and have just purchased a new home in the best area of town.

Then Barry's company takes bankruptcy, and Barry is laid off. For three months he looks for a job in the area. He and Carol do not want to move. Just when he is about to give up, he gets a call from a major distribution company, offering him twice his old salary plus a large end-of-the-year bonus. There is only one problem. The company is a regional beer distributor. Barry can take the job and he and his family can continue to live in their new home.

*If Barry asked you for advice, what would you say?
*How do people decide personal questions with large ethical dimensions to them?
*Does the experience of Jesus in the wilderness have anything to say to Barry?

♦♦♦♦♦♦

Sparkles

A wise man once said, "The acquisition of Christian books is necessary for those who can use them. For the mere sight of these books renders us less inclined to sin, and incites us to believe more firmly in righteousness."

He also said, "Reading the Scriptures is a great safeguard against sin, and ignorance of the Scripture is a precipice and a deep abyss."

Remember: God sells righteousness at a very low price to those who wish to buy it: a little piece of bread, a cloak of no value, and a cup of cold water (Matt. 25:31-46).

TESTING A COMMITMENT TO SERVICE

This Lesson In Your Life

The temptation faced by Jesus may be the most reassuring experience recorded in the Bible. The writer of Hebrews alludes to the validity of such an assumption: "For we have not an high priest which cannot be touched with the feeling of our infirmities; but was in all points tempted like as we are, yet without sin" (Heb. 4:15).

First of all, we have the assurance that temptation is not an alien experience. There is nothing that can attack us or seduce us that has not already been faced by our Savior. Jesus never asks or expects us to walk through any dark valleys or dry wildernesses that He has not already traversed. He was tempted in every way, just like us.

Second, we have the assurance that Jesus will help us with our temptation. No wonder the writer of Hebrews says, "Let us therefore come boldly unto the throne of grace, that we may obtain mercy, and find grace to help in time of need" (Heb. 4:16). As Jesus found power in the written Word of God, so do we find power in that Word of God who is Jesus Christ. He is present whenever the evil one tries to attack. He is present whenever there is danger for one of His children. That presence is our alliance as well as our assurance. That presence gives us power to resist temptation.

Third, following the example of Jesus, we have the assurance of God's Word contained in Holy Scripture. Notice that every attack of Satan is immediately counterattacked with a verse of scripture by Jesus. Perhaps St. Paul was thinking of Jesus' effective use of Scripture to fight off the devil when he wrote to the Ephesians, "And take . . . the sword of the Spirit, which is the word of God" (Eph. 6:17).

Those who follow Jesus Christ need to be students of the Word of God. We are all candidates for moral destruction. Once a person declares allegiance to Christ, he is going to have to battle with those who are on the side of evil. Jesus contended with a very real opponent, an evil power that attacked him. We have to face that same enemy and struggle against that evil power. In that war we need a weapon of defense, and that weapon is the Word of God.

That is why the Word of God is often called a sword. With that sword Jesus beat back the attacks of the devil. The battle unfolds before our eyes in Luke's Gospel.

The devil begins his attack with these words: "If you are the Son of God, command this stone that it be made bread." Immediately Jesus counterattacks: "It is written, Man shall not live by bread alone, but by every word of God."

Satan attacks Jesus at the point of His hunger with the temptation to make bread out of stones. Perhaps Satan was offering Jesus a way to win the approval of people. "Give them bread and satisfy their physical appetites," whispers the evil one, "and they will follow you anywhere." Jesus, however, sees through the offer and refuses to reach for popularity. Protected by his wisdom and by the word of God, Jesus knew that bread would only make people come back for more bread the next day and not for the truth from God. Later in his ministry Jesus would see His understanding of people verified.

The second attack by the devil was an offer of power and rulership over all the kingdoms of the world. Satan promised Jesus the world if He would fall down and worship him. Perhaps no temptation has more appeal in our age. Yet Jesus seemed to know that power is a corrupting influence. Once again he parried with the sword of God's Word: "Get thee behind me, Satan: for it is written, Thou shalt worship the Lord thy God, and him only shalt thou serve."

The final attack was directed at Jesus' faith. Jesus was tempted to put God to the test, make Him prove Himself, and therefore make faith unnecessary. Jesus, however, thrust back with the sword: "Thou shalt not tempt the Lord thy God."

Here then are our assurances: Jesus has already entered the wilderness ahead of us; Jesus has promised to be with us; Jesus has given us the Word of God as a weapon of defense. It would be foolish of a Christian not to know how to make use of these assurances; especially the Word of God.

Seed Thoughts

1. What happens to Jesus immediately after his baptism?
   He is led by the Spirit into the wilderness where he is tempted by Satan.

2. How do you suppose the Gospel writer found out about Jesus' wilderness experience?
   Jesus Himself told the disciples, and they told Luke.

3. What was Jesus doing during His wilderness time?
   Praying, fasting and seeking God's will.

4. What is the perceived advantage Satan enjoys in the first temptation?
   Jesus, after fasting for forty days, is hungry, and Satan tempts him to turn stones into bread.

5. How does Jesus defend Himself against the temptations of Satan?
   In all three temptations Jesus uses the Word of God to help him ward off temptation.

(PLEASE TURN PAGE)

---

1. What happens to Jesus immediately after his baptism?

2. How do you suppose the Gospel writer found out about Jesus' wilderness experience?

3. What was Jesus doing during His wilderness time?

4. What is the perceived advantage Satan enjoys in the first temptation?

5. How does Jesus defend Himself against the temptations of Satan?

6. During the second temptation, Satan and Jesus leave the wilderness. Where do they go?

7. What false claim does Satan make in the third temptation concerning the kingdoms of the world?

8. What is the basic issue in the temptations?

9. Is this the last temptation Jesus will face?

10. For how long will Satan leave Jesus?

He is led by the Spirit into the wilderness where he is tempted by Satan.

Jesus Himself told the disciples, and they told Luke.

Praying, fasting and seeking God's will.

Jesus, after fasting for forty days, is hungry, and Satan tempts him to turn stones into bread.

In all three temptations Jesus uses the Word of God to help him ward off temptation.

They go to Jerusalem, to the pinnacle of the temple.

Satan claims that all the kingdoms of the world belong to him.

The kind of Messiah Jesus would be.

No. He will face many more.

He departed from him for a season.

(SEED THOUGHTS--Cont'd)

6. During the second temptation, Satan and Jesus leave the wilderness. Where do they go?
They go to Jerusalem, to the pinnacle of the temple.

7. What false claim does Satan make in the third temptation concerning the kingdoms of the world?
Satan claims that all the kingdoms of the world belong to him.

8. What is the basic issue in the temptations?
The kind of Messiah Jesus would be.

9. Is this the last temptation Jesus will face?
No. He will face many more.

10. For how long will Satan leave Jesus?
He departed from him for a season.

January 2, 1994

Jesus States his Mission

Luke 4:16-28

16 And he came to Nazareth, where he had been brought up: and, as his custom was, he went into the synagogue on the sabbath day, and stood up for to read.
17 And there was delivered unto him the book of the prophet E-sa'-ias. And when he had opened the book, he found the place where it was written,
18 THE SPIRIT OF THE LORD *IS* UPON ME, BECAUSE HE HATH ANOINTED ME TO PREACH THE GOSPEL TO THE POOR; HE HATH SENT ME TO HEAL THE BROKEN-HEARTED, TO PREACH DELIVERANCE TO THE CAPTIVES, AND RECOVERING OF SIGHT TO THE BLIND, TO SET AT LIBERTY THEM THAT ARE BRUISED,
19 TO PREACH THE ACCEPTABLE YEAR OF THE LORD.
20 And he closed the book, and he gave *it* again to the minister, and sat down. And the eyes of all them that were in the synagogue were fastened on him.
21 And he began to say unto them, This day is this scripture fulfilled in your ears.
22 And all bare him witness, and wondered at the gracious words which proceeded out of his mouth. And they said, Is not this Joseph's son?
23 And he said unto them, Ye will surely say unto me this proverb, Physician, heal thyself: whatsoever we have heard done in Ca-per'-naum, do also here in thy country.
24 And he said, Verily I say unto you, No prophet is accepted in his own country.
25 But I tell you of a truth, many widows were in Israel in the days of E-li'-as, when the heaven was shut up three years and six months, when great famine was throughout all the land;
26 But unto none of them was E-li'-as sent, save unto Sa-rep'-ta, *a city* of Si'-don, unto a woman *that was* a widow.
27 And many lepers were in Israel in the time of El-i-se'-us the prophet; and none of them was cleansed saving Na'-a-man the Syrian.
28 And all they in the synagogue, when they heard these things, were filled with wrath.

◆◆◆◆◆◆

◀ **Memory Selection**
Luke 4:18-19

◀ **Devotional Reading**
Isaiah 61:1,2; 58:6

◀ **Background Scripture**
Luke 4:16-28

◀ **Printed Scripture**
Luke 4:16-28

JESUS STATES HIS MISSION

Teacher's Target

Going against the tide, planing against the grain; these are expressions we use to talk about people who go against custom or traditional attitudes or beliefs. Jesus had to do this in His own hometown. He even said on this occasion that a prophet is not accepted in His own country.

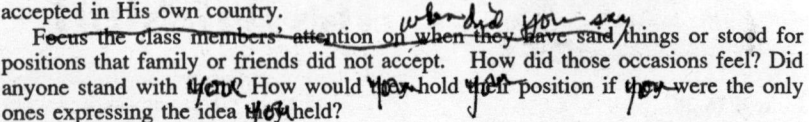

Focus the class members' attention on when they have said things or stood for positions that family or friends did not accept. How did those occasions feel? Did anyone stand with them? How would they hold their position if they were the only ones expressing the idea they held?

Also discuss how institutions can become fixed and rigid, not allowing new insights. What causes us to become closed to other views? How can we test our views to see if they are correct?

Lesson Introduction

In Jesus' day, the synagogue had become an established place of worship. Instituted during the Babylonian exile, a synagogue could be organized where there were at least ten Jewish families. The synagogue continued after the rebuilding of the temple.

Jesus' custom was to go to the synagogue. He had no intention of being a rebel. On this day Jesus, a visiting rabbi, was asked by the leader of the synagogue to read the Scripture and teach.

All was going well until He emphasized that outsiders, non-Jews, received the ministry of Elijah and Elisha. This infuriated the people who applied these promises of Isaiah 61:1-2 to themselves. Jesus had stopped short of the last of verse two which read, "and the day of his wrath to their enemies." Instead, Jesus spoke of God's ministry to outsiders.

Teaching Outline

I. The Occasion: Luke 4:16-17
   A. The Place: 16
   B. The Text: 17
II. The Prophecy: Luke 4:18-22
   A. The Promise: 18-19
   B. The Fulfillment: 20-21
   C. The Reaction: 22
III. The Interpretation:
   Luke 4:23-28
   A. The Present Prophet: 23-24
   B. The Application: 25-27
   C. The Rage: 28

Daily Bible Readings

Mon. Good News for Those in Need
Luke 4:15-19
Tue. No Prophet is Acceptable at Home - *Luke 4:20-24*
Wed. Jesus Condemned Arrogance and Pride - *Luke 4:25-30*
Thurs. He Feeds His Flock
Isaiah 40:1-11
Fri. God's Laws Written on Our Hearts - *Jeremiah 31:29-34*
Sat. Good Tidings for the Afflicted
Isaiah 61:1-6
Sun. Righteousness and Praise Spring Forth - *Isaiah 61:7-11*

January 2, 1994

VERSE BY VERSE

I. The Occasion: Luke 4:16-17

A. The Place: 16

16. And he came to Nazareth, where he had been brought up: and, as his custom was, he went into the synagogue on the sabbath day, and stood up for to read.

Jesus went home. Where better to declare His mission? He had gained a reputation in other cities. Don't you know that He hoped this would break down the "hometown boy" indifference? There was probably great pride at first on the part of the home folks. One of their own had gained notoriety. Now they would hear Him and see His ministry firsthand.

The people gathered in the synagogue. They were there for worship. They would not be preoccupied with work and daily activities. Jesus would have their ear. Here He would declare who He was and what His mission would be.

B. The Text: 17

17. And there was delivered unto him the book of the prophet E-sa'-ias. And when he had opened the book, he found the place where it was written,

The lesson for the day was from Isaiah 61. Jesus had been invited to read and teach from that text. How interesting that the text for the day was about the Messiah! God's providence?! The message of the text was about good news to the poor, healing for the brokenhearted, deliverance of captives, sight for the blind and liberty to the bruised.

The Spirit of the Lord was upon Jesus. He knew the meaning God intended the people to receive. They had long awaited the jubilee year of God--the time when all wrongs would be righted, lands returned to the original tribes and all debts canceled. Now Jesus proclaimed that the acceptable year of the Lord had come.

II. The Prophecy: Luke 4:18-22

A. The Promise: 18-19

18. THE SPIRIT OF THE LORD IS UPON ME, BECAUSE HE HATH ANOINTED ME TO PREACH THE GOSPEL TO THE POOR; HE HATH SENT ME TO HEAL THE BROKENHEARTED, TO PREACH DELIVERANCE TO THE CAPTIVES, AND RECOVERING OF SIGHT TO THE BLIND, TO SET AT LIBERTY THEM THAT ARE BRUISED,

19. TO PREACH THE ACCEPTABLE YEAR OF THE LORD.

The people had heard Isaiah 61:1-2 read many times. They had waited in hope for its fulfillment. Now Jesus brought in His own person and ministry the long awaited promise.

The "poor" was probably a general title for all the poor of the world, whether poor in physical ways or spiritually poor as meek and humble people, they would be ministered to on this day.

The poor were shunned and looked down on with contempt by many Jewish teachers and leaders. However, Jesus probably saw all His people, the Jews, as poor. They had been captives more than once. They had been blind to God's intent with His word. They had been hurt by pursuing other gods. Their hearts had been broken and they knew no freedom even now. Jesus hoped the lost house of Israel would hear His teaching as a release for them as well as the outsiders.

How quick they, like we, were to seek a way to make themselves superior even in their poverty. Arrogance has no class distinctions. It gripped rich and poor alike. How easily they missed Jesus' point.

B. The Fulfillment: 20-21

20. And he closed the book, and he gave it again to the minister, and sat down. And the eyes of all them that were in the synagogue were fastened on him.

21. And he began to say unto them, This day is this scripture fulfilled in your ears.

Jesus sat down to teach, as was the common practice of rabbis. He had not read the latter portion of Isaiah 61:2 aloud. There had been no mention of wrath toward the enemies of God's people. Jesus came to offer salvation to all. There was no exclusion of any in regard to access to God. Wrath would be a problem only for those who rejected the gift of grace Jesus brought.

The people were glued to His gaze and waited for His teaching. They knew the Scripture. Surely they wondered about His omission of part of the text.

C. The Reaction: 22

22. And all bare him witness, and wondered at the gracious words which proceeded out of his mouth. And they said, Is not this Joseph's son?

The people showed themselves to be the poor by the way they received His word. They needed the gracious words, though they would be offended to be placed with the outsider. Yet the truth was they had not truly heard their need of the grace of God. They had great need and yet were blind to it. They began to doubt Jesus' authority and power. Those were good words all right. It was nice for Him to say that the Scripture was fulfilled in their day, but wasn't this just Joseph's son talking?

III. The Interpretation: Luke 4:23-28

A. The Present Prophet: 23-24

23. And he said unto them, Ye will surely say unto me this proverb, Physician, heal thyself: whatsoever we have heard done in Ca-per'-na-um, do also here in thy country.

24. And he said, Verily I say unto you, No prophet is accepted in his own country.

By the saying, "Physician heal thyself," Jesus could have been addressing the question, If you are only Joseph's son, how is this miraculous thing going to be done so that you and we benefit?

Jesus went on to another truism. The Jews had rejected, stoned and killed their prophets before Him. Now the Prophet was in their midst and they would do the same to Him. How hard it was for them to see beyond appearances. If only He would do some miraculous thing, and not just speak words. Again Jesus was faced by His own people with the temptation to do something spectacular so they would believe.

B. The Application: 25-27

25. But I tell you of a truth, many widows were in Israel in the days of E-li'-as, when the heaven was shut up three years and six months, when great famine was throughout all the land;
26. But unto none of them was E-li'-as sent, save unto Sa-rep'-ta, a city of Si'-don, unto a woman that was a widow.
27. And many lepers were in Israel in the time of El-i-se'-us the prophet; and none of them was cleansed, saving Na'-a-man the Syrian.

Jesus took two examples of God's grace and mercy from the ministry of two of Israel's greatest prophets, Elijah and Elisha. Both accounts were of God's grace flowing through the two prophets to foreigners rather than to their own people. Elijah saved a widow of Sidon from starvation (1 Kings 17:9-16). Elisha had cleansed Naaman of leprosy (2 Kings 5:1-19). All along God had wanted Israel to be the priests to the nations (Ex. 19:6). They were His chosen people to take the message of His love and grace to all. Instead they refused all His striving with them. Never did they become ready vessels to pour out God's grace upon the world. Only a few in Israel heard the truth and ministered as Elijah and Elisha did.

C. The Rage: 28

28. And all they in the synagogue, when they heard these things, were filled with wrath,

The anticipation and excitement about a hometown boy of some reputation returning home to minister to His own people had passed. Good words had been said but there was no spectacular sign in their midst that would confirm for them that the acceptable year of the Lord had come. This was only Joseph's son. Now He had insulted them. He had told them they were not special. God loved outsiders as much as He loved them. He had grouped them among the poor and outcast. Rage was kindled in their hearts. All the gracious words had gone from them. If only they had responded with faith when grace reached out to them in Jesus. The Kingdom was in their midst and they missed it.

Evangelistic Emphasis

Sometimes the longest trip in the world is the one from knowing something to really knowing. Known as the journey from the head to the heart, this may also be the most difficult journey. The Jews from Jesus' home town of Nazareth fit these two concepts of knowing.

At one level, the hearers were impressed with their hometown boy. He read so well. Smiles covered the synagogue as corporate credit was taken for the obviously good job they had done with Jesus. They knew him because he was one of their own. They knew him well.

They also knew the Scriptures he read so well. For generations they had been reading of the Holy Word. They could close their eyes and repeat the passages from memory. Their knowledge of the Word of God was quite extensive.

When Jesus interpreted the Word from God in terms of His divine ministry, they also knew those Scriptures. They knew all about Naaman the leper from Syria and the foreign widow. Knowing, however, is not the same as knowing.

The hearers of Jesus' words did not want to know in their hearts that God accepts all persons. They were not ready to hear an inclusive message. Therefore they shut out the message of Jesus. In so doing they were angered by the words of Jesus. Then they tried to take it out on Jesus. Isn't it ironic that sometimes the more we know about Jesus the less we want to know in our hearts?

◆◆◆◆◆◆

Memory Selection

The Spirit of the Lord is upon me, because he has anointed me to preach good news to the poor. He has sent me to proclaim release to the captives and recovering of sight to the blind, to set at liberty those who are oppressed, to proclaim the acceptable year of the Lord. *Luke 4:18-19*

Jesus' announcement contains at least four significant theological thoughts. First, this ministry is one authorized and empowered by the Spirit of God. Political and military might are of no consequence.

Second, Jesus has been anointed by the Holy Spirit. His ministry has the blessing and direction of God. He stands in the prophetic line of anointed one. He is Prophet, Priest and King.

Third, the method of bringing in the Kingdom is preaching. The power of the Word should never be underestimated. The creative Word of God will bring about a new world.

Fourth, the good news is for all persons. A new world without boundaries is coming. Everyone is accepted and welcome. This is the coming Kingdom.

Weekday Problems

George has been attending a small church in the rural community where he lives. The people are friendly, and have welcomed him into their fellowship. One Sunday, however, George brings one of his Afro-American friends to church with him. He notices that at least six people got up and walked out of church as George and his friend sat down.

On Monday morning, one of the leaders of the church pays George a visit. He tells George that his black friend is not welcome. "There's a black church right up the road," he tells George. "Your friend should go to church with his own kind." As the church leader is leaving George's house, he tells George "I'll see you in church on Sunday."

*What should George do?
*What are your attitudes about persons of other races attending your church?
*Would persons of other races be welcome as members of your congregation?
*What does the Bible teach about our relationship with persons of other races and cultures?

♦♦♦♦♦♦

Say It Right

Nazareth:	Naz-uh-reth
Esaias:	Eh-say-yes
Capernaum:	Ca-per-nay-um
Elias:	Ee-ly-us
Eliseus:	El-i-see-us
Sidon:	Sy-dun
Sarepta:	Suh-rep-tuh
Naaman:	Nay-a-mun
Syrian:	Sear-i-un
Israel:	Iz-ray-el

This Lesson In Your Life

Jesus preaches in His hometown synagogue. The excitement in the synagogue catches up the whole crowd. They know this young man. This is Joseph and Mary's son. He was a hometown boy, one of their own. They are so proud of Him. He reads so well.

Have you ever dreamed of being there with Jesus? Wouldn't it have been great to hear Jesus' homecoming sermon? We would have believed if we we could have been there. Surely being there would have made it easier.

The problem though is not one of time and distance. Being there would not have made any difference. The Jews were there and they did not open their hearts to Jesus. Neither do we. The problem is one between the people of God and their memory. Memory can be a wonderful capacity enabling us to recall our faith. It can also be a debilitating capacity, especially when we practice selective retention. When Jesus spoke to the crowd from their own Scriptures, they didn't respond at first.

They just nodded their heads at the recognition of Isaiah's familiar words. They knew those words already. They had been sitting before the readings from Isaiah all their lives. Everyone felt comfortable. After all, these were their words, their Scriptures, their young preacher.

The reading of the ancient words was a nostalgic trip for God's people. We do that all the time don't we? The advertisers and the politicians make money and secure votes by appealing to our nostalgia. That's why they make their messages simple and sentimental, with no complications. We see and we hear and we nod in agreement. We remember the good old days, just like the folks listening to Jesus.

When Jesus finished the reading, everyone was pleased. They complimented His gracious words. Why didn't He leave well enough alone? Everybody had enjoyed the performance and was ready to go home. The proclamation of God's Word, however, is never just a performance. Therefore, Jesus interpreted the reading with two familiar stories about Elijah and Elisha.

These stories did not fit well with the selective memory, the nostalgic magic in the air, the preconceived notions about being God's chosen people. With no intention of remembering the stories, the crowd turned a stone wall of silence to the words of Jesus. Theirs was the silence of judgment, the silence of prejudice, the silence of hypocrisy.

Now, the church and all of us, stand judged by these same, old stories. We've heard it all before. Have we really heard the word from God? Have we opened our hearts to his message?

Much of the time the answer is No, because Jesus asks us to remember what we already know--that God does not play by our rules, and that God's kingdom is open to all. No one race, no one nation, no one people has a monopoly on God's grace.

Each Sunday at church the Sunday School teacher and the preacher remind us of what we already know. They trouble our memory. They put us there in the synagogue to hear the uncomfortable words of Jesus. Believing those words has nothing at all to do with being there. It has to do with our memory, and with our willingness to be open to new expressions of God's grace. Somehow we need to get back our whole memory of the Word of God, not just the part we want to retain. May the Lord enable us to have a full memory of His grace in this world.

Seed Thoughts

1. What is the significance of Jesus' preaching in Nazareth?
   Nazareth is His home town.

2. What important habit of Jesus does Luke reveal to us in 4:16?
   Jesus went to the synagogue to worship every Sabbath.

3. As Jesus read from the Scriptures, what was his text?
   He read from Isaiah 61.

4. How is Jesus to carry out His mission?
   By the preaching of God's Word.

5. What is the audience's initial reaction to Jesus?
   They are impressed with the hometown boy.

(PLEASE TURN PAGE)

---

1. What is the significance of Jesus' preaching in Nazareth?

2. What important habit of Jesus does Luke reveal to us in 4:16?

3. As Jesus read from the Scriptures, what was his text?

4. How is Jesus to carry out His mission?

5. What is the audience's initial reaction to Jesus?

6. What two examples does Jesus use that upset the congregation?

7. How does the audience react to the sermon?

8. What happens to Jesus after He preaches?

9. How does Jesus avoid being killed by the mob?

10. Where does Jesus go after leaving Nazareth?

(SEED THOUGHTS--Cont'd)

Nazareth is His home town.	**6. What two examples does Jesus use that upset the congregation?** Jesus uses the stories of the widow of Sidon and Naaman the Syrian.
Jesus went to the synagogue to worship every Sabbath.	**7. How does the audience react to the sermon?** They are filled with wrath.
He read from Isaiah 61.	**8. What happens to Jesus after He preaches?** The congregation tries to throw Him over a ledge and kill Him.
By the preaching of God's Word.	
They are impressed with the hometown boy.	**9. How does Jesus avoid being killed by the mob?** St. Luke tells us that Jesus passed through the midst of them.
Jesus uses the stories of the widow of Sidon and Naaman the Syrian.	**10. Where does Jesus go after leaving Nazareth?** He went to Capernaum.
They are filled with wrath.	
The congregation tries to throw Him over a ledge and kill Him.	
St. Luke tells us that Jesus passed through the midst of them.	
He went to Capernaum.	

January 9, 1994

Jesus Heals the Sick

Luke 4:31-43

31 And came down to Ca-per′-na-um, a city of Galilee, and taught them on the sabbath days.
32 And they were astonished at his doctrine: for his word was with power.
33 And in the synagogue there was a man, which had a spirit of an unclean devil, and cried out with a loud voice,
34 Saying, Let *us* alone; what have we to do with thee, *thou* Jesus of Nazareth? art thou come to destroy us? I know thee who thou art; the Holy one of God.
35 And Jesus rebuked him, saying, Hold thy peace, and come out of him. And when the devil had thrown him in the midst, he came out of him, and hurt him not.
36 And they were all amazed. and spake among themselves, saying, What a word *is* this! for with authority and power he commandeth the unclean spirits, and they come out.
37 And the fame of him went out into every place of the country round about.
38 And he arose out of the synagogue, and entered into Simon's house. And Simon's wife's mother was taken with a great fever, and they besought him for her.
39 And he stood over her, and rebuked the fever; and it left her: and immediately she arose and ministered unto them.
40 Now when the sun was setting, all they that had any sick with divers diseases brought them unto him; and he laid his hands on every one of them, and healed them.
41 And devils also came out of many, crying out, and saying, Thou art Christ the Son of God. And he rebuking *them* suffered them not to speak, for they knew that he was Christ.
42 And when it was day, he departed and went into a desert place: and the people sought him, and came unto him, and stayed him, that he should not depart from them.
43 And he said unto them, I must preach the kingdom of God to other cities also: for therefore am I sent.

◆◆◆◆◆◆

◀ **Memory Selection**
Luke 4:40

◀ **Devotional Reading**
Mark 6:1-6a; 9:1-18

◀ **Background Scripture**
Luke 4:31-43

◀ **Printed Scripture**
Luke 4:31-43

Teacher's Target

Jesus came to deliver humankind from death. During His ministry, the ravages of the evil one were challenged. His acts of healing were a sign of not only physical release, but spiritual health. He did not heal everyone. Even Paul was not released from his "thorn in the flesh." Whether Paul's "thorn" was physical, emotional or spiritual can be debated. Regardless, it was not removed. However, Jesus' ministry declared that He was Lord over death and all its temporal expressions.

Ask the class if they have ever experienced a healing. Does God use medical means to heal as well as direct intervention? What would be the reason Jesus did not heal everyone's illness? Does it take as much faith to accept not being healed as to experience a healing?

Lesson Introduction

Jesus once again was in the synagogue. This time He was in Capernaum. He had done mighty acts here before (Luke 4:24). Jesus, by doing these acts of mercy for the sick and demon possessed, declared His power to be greater than Satan's. Jesus had entered the strongman's arena and was binding him. Satan's stronghold would fall. God Himself entered history to heal creation's wounds. God did not leave His people to themselves nor to the ravages of the evil one.

Jesus' deeds did not automatically produce faith, neither were they a confirmation of the faith of the person healed. Only those who had eyes to see by faith would recognize what was happening. When people were healed, fed, or released from demons it did not automatically produce faith (the ten lepers, Matthew 17:12; the feeding of the 5,000, John 6:1-66).

Teaching Outline

I. The Encounter: Luke 4:31-37
   A. Authority and Resistance: 31-34
   B. Resistance Rebuked: 35
   C. Astonished Response: 36-37
II. The Authority Manifest: Luke 4:38-41
   A. Physical Healing: 38-40
   B. Spiritual Deliverance: 41
III. The Restful Retreat: Luke 4:42-43
   A. Departure: 42
   B. Interference: 42
   C. Mission: 43

Daily Bible Readings

Mon. Jesus Acts With Authority - *Luke 4:31-36*
Tue. Jesus Laid Hands on Everyone - *Luke 4:37-41*
Wed. Jesus Comes to Preach Good News - *Luke 4:42-5:3*
Thurs. Fishers Catching People - *Luke 5:4-11*
Fri. Jesus Healed One With Leprosy - *Luke 5:12-16*
Sat. Power to Heal - *Luke 5:17-26*
Sun. Jesus Heals Sinners - *Luke 5:27-39*

VERSE BY VERSE

I. The Encounter: Luke 4:31-37

A. Authority and Resistance: 31-34

31. And came down to Ca-per'-na-um, a city of Galilee, and taught them on the sabbath days.
32. And they were astonished at his doctrine: for his word was with power.
33. And in the synagogue there was a man, which had a spirit of an unclean devil, and cried out with a loud voice,
34. Saying, Let us alone; what have we to do with thee, thou Jesus of Nazareth? art thou come to destroy us? I know thee who thou art; the Holy One of God.

The conflict of authorities was clearly revealed at Capernaum. This conflict continued throughout Jesus' ministry. God or mammon, God or Satan, God or the world; however it would be stated by Jesus during His ministry, it was the same conflict. The question was, Who has the real authority over the created order?

Jesus spoke with authority because He was connected with the Father, the Creator and Redeemer God. This connection came through in His teaching and His deeds.

Every time there was an expression of God's authority, there was a counterattack by Satan and his minions. The greater the expression, the greater the counter. Satan did not want his hold on the world broken. He attacked the presence of God.

Jesus' power was greater. Where Jesus was present, demons were threatened and would attack. But where Jesus was (and is) demons could not stay for long.

B. Resistance Rebuked: 35

35. And Jesus rebuked him, saying, Hold thy peace, and come out of him. And when the devil had thrown him in the midst, he came out of him, and hurt him not.

The demons knew the goal of Jesus' mission. He came to destroy the power of Satan. They tried to expose Jesus in such a way that He would be rejected on grounds of blasphemy. Jesus knew that the time for His identity was the Father's decision. By the power and authority of the Father, Jesus silenced the demons' attempts to expose Him beforehand.

Here the devil threw a man down in the midst of the people. A simple command by Jesus broke his hold. The man was not harmed.

The devil continues, though defeated at the cross, to scare us with his pretense of power, to hold us in bondage to illusions that have no true power. Often, the power is there because we have listened to Satan's lies and half truths. When Jesus speaks to our hearts and we hear His voice, the demonic clutches of Satan's hold is broken and he must release us. Thanks be to God for His redeeming and releasing grace.

C. Astonished Response: 36-37

36. And they were all amazed, and spake among themselves, saying, What a word is this! for with authority and power he commandeth the unclean spirits, and they come out.

37. And the fame of him went out into every place of the country round about.

The people had long despaired of their inability to resist the minions sent by Satan. They were bound in their passions, compulsions and appetites. For all mankind's boast of power, people knew their weakness and continual defeats. All attempts at self-mastery failed. Without the truth they were helpless.

Jesus' authority over the evil that permeated their world amazed them. Later, they would fear that Jesus' authority wouldn't hold for them. Then they became angry that Jesus was stirring the demonic forces to a fever pitch. Could or would Jesus really protect and provide for them? For now, the wonder and awe of such a display of victory caused the people to carry news of Jesus everywhere they went.

II. The Authority Manifest: Luke 4:38-41

A. Physical Healing: 38-40

38. And he arose out of the synagogue, and entered into Simon's house. And Simon's wife's mother was taken with a great fever; and they besought him for her.

39. And he stood over her, and rebuked the fever; and it left her: and immediately she arose and ministered unto them.

40. Now when the sun was setting, all they that had any sick with divers diseases brought them unto him; and he laid his hands on every one of them, and healed them.

The demonic loosed in the world by humankind's failure to listen to the Father (first in the Garden of Eden) had given Satan the foothold he needed to take over. He did! Satan held sway over the lives of people so strongly that even Israel with all that God had done for them never in all her history was faithful to God. Continually the people were led astray by alien voices. They rebelled. They practiced spiritual adultery toward God.

Such giving over, such helplessness had allowed the demonic to bind people in muteness, deafness, blindness, and even insanity. Jesus began the revelation of His authority where the people lived, in the flesh. He performed physical healings that could be seen. He began in His own circle of disciples with Peter's mother-in-law. Jesus met the people on their level, spoke their language, healed where they knew they hurt. Later, He could take them deeper. First, as with us, He had to get on their wave length. Like us, they tended to focus on the physical and not the spiritual dimension of things.

B. Spiritual Deliverance: 41

41. And devils also came out of many, crying out, and saying, Thou art Christ the Son of God. And he rebuking them suffered them not to speak: for they knew that he was Christ.

Not only infirmities of the body, but deep splits and fragmentations of the very souls of multitudes of people had occurred. Rollo May, noted psychiatrist, has said that all psychological problems are ultimately spiritual problems. Jesus knew this well. He rebuked the fragmenting and tormenting demonic presence and brought people to wholeness in body, mind and spirit.

There was a report in one psychiatric hospital of patients coming to wholeness by gazing day after day at a picture of Jesus hung on their ward. Often religion had made them sick, but Christ healed them. The Jews were very religious and in bondage. Jesus was full of love and compassion and released them.

III. The Restful Retreat:
Luke 4:42-43

A. Departure: 42

42. And when it was day, he departed and went into a desert place: and the people sought him, and came unto him, and stayed him, that he should not depart from them.

No one, not even Jesus, could be in the harness and at labor, especially spiritual labor, all the time. He was depleted, drained and in need of time to replenish His spirit. This He did through time alone with the Father. Jesus knew how and when to rest. He also knew when it was time to leave people with what He had said and done so that they could grow in faith. He would not let them use Him as a crutch. Avoiding growth in faith was not allowed.

Notice Jesus sought a place away from people. He did not draw His life from them. He drew His life from the Father. Then He had something to give to the people.

B. Interference: 42

42. And when it was day, he departed and went into a desert place: and the people sought him, and came unto him, and stayed him, that he should not depart from them.

Who wants to grow up if he doesn't have to?! The people in Capernaum wanted to hold on to Jesus as their own and use Him for personal ends, not an uncommon malady in any day. So, they sought to prevent His departure.

Jesus knew what was best for them and for Himself. He also knew that others were in need of the same ministry. He could not be owned or manipulated for the purposes of any private interest group.

C. Mission: 43

43. And he said unto them, I must preach the kingdom of God to other cities also: for therefore am I sent.

How clear was Jesus' vision! How single-minded was His resolve! Neither mother, brother, friend, crowds, authority, religious or secular, could deter him from His mission. The Kingdom of God was for all. He must broaden the circle, not close it. He was sent to the world for the world.

Jesus was life and light for the whole world. Jesus was authority over all that destroys individuals, communities and cultures. His mission was to break the stronghold of the evil one. The very gates of hell could not prevail against Him.

Evangelistic Emphasis

In an age of powerlessness, the Church has lost confidence in the power of the spoken word. Yet in the world of advertising and politics, talk and appearance are everything. Preoccupation with appearances and name brands stifles our creativity. Obsession with political consultants and sound bites dominates our campaigns. Somehow the Church has to find a way to transcend both illusions: that the word is powerless when preached and that the word is all powerful in the world.

For Jesus the Kingdom of God was not about image and appearance. There was nothing artificial about Christ. He was a person of integrity. His Kingdom was coming in power, not pretense; reality not rhetoric.

His words possessed power because they were backed by the creative power of God. His preaching was backed up by acts of healing. He not only announced the coming Kingdom, He also ushered it in with authority.

His was a Word of authority. Now the Church needs to realize that our preaching is a continuation of the preaching of Jesus. His authority has been given to us. His power can enable us to speak with confidence. There is still power in the Word, but it is not the artificial power of sound bites. It is the power of the Holy Spirit speaking through Christians.

♦♦♦♦♦♦

Memory Selection

All those who had any that were sick with various diseases brought them to him; and he laid his hands on every one of them and healed them. *Luke 4:40*

Paul Tournier, in The Whole Person in a Broken World, says, "It is not necessary to be a great scholar to see that our world today is not in good health. It is a broken world. Its ills are innumerable. It writhes in pain" (p.1). Almost 2,000 years earlier Jesus offered the same diagnosis of our world's ills. If you were to read the charts of the people of our world, all the sin-sick persons of our society, you would see that they are dying from disease, a lack of spiritual wholeness. Jesus knew that instinctively.

Part of the ministry of the Church is a healing ministry. While we may be turned off by the extravagant claims of some faith healers, that is no reason to abandon our healing ministry. The church becomes God's agent of healing, but all healing is from God. Helping people be whole is always part of the church's mission.

January 9, 1994

Weekday Problems

Bill was concerned about an announcement his pastor made in the Sunday morning worship. According to the preacher, the church was having a healing and wholeness service on Wednesday evening at 7 p.m. All Bill could think of was the rather bizarre news accounts of so-called faith healers. He was not comfortable with healing services in his church.

In a later conversation with his pastor, Bill learned that the healing and wholeness service was not a claim that people would be healed from blindness or lameness. In fact, according to the pastor, the purpose of the service, was to help people know the prayers and support of the church were with them. There would be prayers for healing, laying on with hands, and anointing with oil. Still Bill felt a little uncomfortable.

*Are Christians often uncomfortable with matters such as healing services? Why?
*What does the Bible teach about the laying on of hands and anointing with oil?
*Jesus' ministry was one of healing. In what ways can the church be involved in healing ministries?

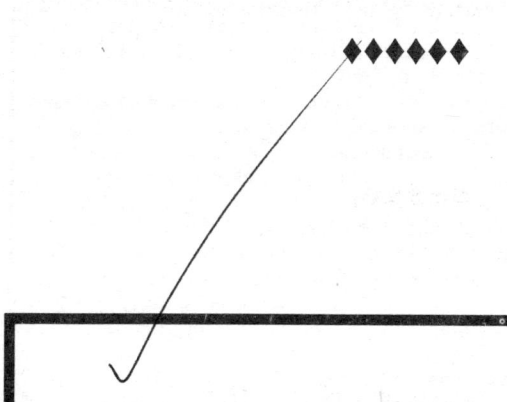

◆◆◆◆◆◆

Sparkles

A very distressed person came to a great saint for help and prayer. The saint said to the person, "Do you really want to be cured?"

The person replied, "If I did not want a cure, would I bother to come to you?"

"Oh, yes," the saint responded, "most people do."

"What on earth for?" the seeker asked.

"Not for a cure. That's painful. For relief," was the saint's answer. Then he turned to his disciples and said, "People want a cure so long as they can have it without pain, and they desire spiritual progress provided they can have it without change."

JESUS HEALS THE SICK

This Lesson In Your Life

Jesus confronts for the first time a man who was possessed with an unclean spirit. The occasion marks the initial confrontation of Jesus with the surrogates of the evil one. That the battle takes place in church may sound strange to some, while others may believe the devil is quite at home in such sacred halls. Although the demon probably came to church as complacent as the rest of the crowd, he was about to discover that this was no ordinary Sabbath, and Jesus was no ordinary preacher.

Trying to get the upper hand by making a bold move, much like the challenger in a chess match, the unclean spirit cried out, "Let us alone, what have we to do with thee, thou Jesus of Nazareth? Art thou come to destroy us? I know thee who thou art; the Holy one of God." The surrogate devil pleads to be left alone in a desperate cry of honesty. His next words, however, reveal his true pedigree as a son of the father of lies as he pretends that he has nothing to do with Jesus and that he has done nothing wrong.

There is one puzzle in the confrontation that defies our understanding. How is it that the demon recognized Jesus while religious people did not have a clue to his identity? Perhaps we are so much in touch with our worldliness that we have lost touch with that spiritual reality inhabited by the Son of God. We are judged by our inability to know Jesus when He comes to us in different and surprising ways.

Jesus, having just come from forty days of tense temptations, had no trouble recognizing the enemy. He has neither the time nor the patience to put up with the babblings of a minor underling of evil: "Hold thy peace," Jesus shouted. The bold cry of Christ called the bluff of evil.

While we still battle the forces of evil as if they have the upper hand, Jesus demonstrates for our benefit His power to silence our worst enemies. Has the Church lost its confidence in the face of unrelenting evil? If so, let us watch the Master in action as he routs the enemy with the word of authority. We know that the strongest man is on our side, and the ultimate victory belongs to us.

After church, and all the excitement there, Jesus went home with Simon for sabbath dinner. When the group arrived home they found Simon's mother-in-law "taken with a great fever." Luke is the only Gospel writer to present so many vignettes of Jesus' compassion for women. in this case, Jesus comes to the rescue of the most lowly of women in the ancient world, the mother-in-law. Luke tells us that Jesus "rebuked the fever."

What amazing power! Any doctor would be envious of the man who can simply scare fever away with a few words. With all our medical technology and miracle drugs, we still are not sure about the causes and cures of diseases. Jesus, however, goes straight to the source and commands the fever to leave. Without benefit of technology, just the presence of ultimate goodness, Jesus objected to the presence of the fever, and sent it away.

What then are we to make of the two episodes? Jesus dismisses both demons and diseases. His power and authority extend into all realms. Why then is the Church sometimes embarrassed about Jesus' power over devils and diseases? Is it evidence of our own lack of spiritual sensitivity? Can't we see that the power of pure goodness simply refuses to tolerate the cancerous presence of debilitating badness?

The main lesson for us is that we must go on making the redeeming, healing power of Jesus available to those who are emotionally and physically and spiritually sick. The Church has the responsibility to offer the healing power of Christ to a broken, sin-sick, diseased world.

Seed Thoughts

1. Why were people astonished by the preaching of Jesus?
His doctrine and the power of His word amazed them.

2. Who disrupted the service in the synagogue?
A man with an unclean spirit.

3. In what terms did the man address Jesus?
He called Him Jesus of Nazareth and the Holy One of God.

4. What is the significance of Jesus casting out the evil spirit?
Jesus demonstrates the power of God over Satan.

5. How does the reaction of the Capernaum crowd differ from that of the crowd in Nazareth?
In Capernaum they are amazed at His power and authority, but in Nazareth they show Him no respect.

(PLEASE TURN PAGE)

1. Why were people astonished by the preaching of Jesus?

2. Who disrupted the service in the synagogue?

3. In what terms did the man address Jesus?

4. What is the significance of Jesus casting out the evil spirit?

5. How does the reaction of the Capernaum crowd differ from that of the crowd in Nazareth?

6. What effect does the miracle have on Jesus' reputation?

7. Where did Jesus stay while He was in Capernaum?

8. What miracle does Jesus perform at Simon's house?

9. How did Jesus heal all the sick people that came to Him at Simon's house?

10. How did the people react when Jesus left town?

| *(SEED THOUGHTS--Cont'd)*

His doctrine and the power of His word amazed them.

6. What effect does the miracle have on Jesus' reputation?
His fame spread all over the region.

A man with an unclean spirit.

7. Where did Jesus stay while He was in Capernaum?
At the house of Simon Peter.

He called Him Jesus of Nazareth and the Holy One of God.

8. What miracle does Jesus perform at Simon's house?
He heals Simon's mother-in-law of a fever.

Jesus demonstrates the power of God over Satan.

9. How did Jesus heal all the sick people that came to Him at Simon's house?
He laid hands on them and healed them.

In Capernaum they are amazed at His power and authority, but in Nazareth they show Him no respect.

10. How did the people react when Jesus left town?
They followed Him into the desert.

His fame spread all over the region.

At the house of Simon Peter.

He heals Simon's mother-in-law of a fever.

He laid hands on them and healed them.

They followed Him into the desert.

January 16, 1994

Jesus Teaches His Followers

Luke 6:20b-36

20 And he lifted up his eyes on his disciples, and said, Blessed *be ye* poor: for yours is the kingdom of God.
21 Blessed *are ye* that hunger now: for ye shall be filled. Blessed *are ye* that weep now: for ye shall laugh.
22 Blessed are ye, when men shall hate you, and when they shall separate you *from their company,* and shall reproach *you,* and cast out your name as evil, for the Son of man's sake.
23 Rejoice ye in that day, and leap for joy: for, behold, your reward is great in heaven: for in the like manner did their fathers unto the prophets.
24 But woe unto you that are rich! for ye have received your consolation.
25 Woe unto you that are full! for ye shall hunger. Woe unto you that laugh now! for ye shall mourn and weep.
26 Woe unto You, when all men shall speak well of you! for so did their fathers to the false prophets.
27 But I say unto you which hear, Love your enemies, do good to them which hate you,
28 Bless them that curse you, and pray for them which despitefully use you.
29 And unto him that smiteth thee on the *one* cheek offer also the other, and him that taketh away thy cloke forbid not *to take thy* coat also.
30 Give to every man that asketh of thee; and of him that taketh away thy goods ask *them* not again.
31 And as ye would that men should do to you, do ye also to them likewise.
32 For if ye love them which love you, what thank have ye? for sinners also love those that love them.
33 And if ye do good to them which do good to you, what thank have ye? for sinners also do even the same.
34 And if ye lend *to them* of whom ye hope to receive, what thank have ye? for sinners also lend to sinners, to receive as much again.
35 But love ye your enemies, and do good, and lend, hoping for nothing again; and your reward shall be great, and ye shall be the children of the Highest: for he is kind unto the unthankful and to the evil.
36 Be ye therefore merciful, as your Father also is merciful.

◆◆◆◆◆◆

◀ **Memory selection**
Luke 6:36

◀ **Devotional Reading**
Matthew 5:3-12, 38-42; 7:12, 24-27; 8:1-4

◀ **Background Scripture**
Luke 6:17-36

◀ **Printed Scripture**
Luke 6:20b-36

JESUS TEACHES HIS FOLLOWERS

Teacher's Target

Kingdom values are not like earthly values. In fact, the Kingdom of God is an "upside down Kingdom." What the world values winds up on the bottom of God's list. What the world despises or rejects winds up on the top.

Every world society is based upon money, power and law. The Kingdom of God is based upon love, peace and grace. Judgment is the rule in the world. Forgiveness is the rule in the Kingdom of God.

As a class activity, cut out pictures from magazines and newspapers that represent both the world and the Kingdom of God. Make two poster board picture collages, one of the world, the other of the Kingdom of God. Who fulfilled the image presented by Jesus in this passage? It was Jesus Himself wasn't it?

Lesson Introduction

Teaching is an activity hard to measure. Even if a student gives the right answer, it doesn't mean that the material has been incorporated into the person's life. Until the learner decides the teaching is needed, it often isn't applied.

Jesus knew this. He hoped to break through the people's defenses with a word that would come to their remembrance in life situations. He didn't give them too much at once. He presented His truth in capsule-size doses. As a master teacher, Jesus tied His truth to everyday experiences and events in the lives of His hearers.

This lesson on the plain in Luke is parallel to Matthew's Sermon on the Mount. This teaching was to be heard as a promise of what the Spirit is going to work in us, not as a "new law" more difficult than the Ten Commandments.

Teaching Outline

I. The Blessings: Luke 6:20b-23
   A. The Poor: 20
   B. The Hungry: 21
   C. The Despised: 22-23
II. The Woes: Luke 6:24-26
   A. The Rich: 24
   B. The Full: 25
   C. The Well-Received: 26
III. Loving Enemies: Luke 6:27-36
   A. Do Good and Bless: 27-33
   B. Lend and Love: 34-35
   C. Be Merciful: 36

Daily Bible Readings

Mon. Jesus is Lord of the Sabbath
Luke 6:1-5
Tue. Jesus Heals on the Sabbath
Luke 6:6-11
Wed. Jesus Chooses Twelve
Luke 6:12-16
Thurs. Healings and Blessings
Luke 6:17-23
Fri. Love and Prayer for Enemies
Luke 6:24-31
Sat. Ways to Show Our Love
Luke 6:32-38
Sun. Be Like Your Teacher
Luke 6:39-49

January 16, 1994

VERSE BY VERSE

I. The Blessings: Luke 6:20b-23

A. The Poor: 20b

20. And he lifted up his eyes on his disciples, and said, Blessed be ye poor: for yours is the kingdom of God.

These beatitudes (Latin for "blessings") are kingdom values. Only those in Christ can have the power to move toward their fulfillment. Just as Christ saves us, so Christ has to empower us. Left to ourselves we would never become like Him. This teaching is not a new law to keep, but a new promise to cling to with hope. God through Christ by the power of the Holy Spirit is working this new character into our being.

"The poor" was a term used for all who were outcast in the society of Jesus' day. The physically poor were certainly a portion of those outcast. Their need was obvious to them. Jesus was desirous for all to see their need of God's provision as clearly as the physically poor could see theirs.

B. The Hungry: 21

21. Blessed are *ye* that hunger now: for ye shall be filled. Blessed are ye that weep now: for ye shall laugh.

The hungry could feel their need in the emptiness of their stomachs. How God longed for all His people to feel "hunger pangs" for His presence with them.

The Jews turned to self-righteousness to fill them. The Gentiles turned to their passions to fill them. Both were starving as surely as those that hungered for food. Nothing out of self was going to fill the emptiness of self. Jesus knew: self cannot fill self, neither with self-righteousness nor self-indulgence of the passions.

C. The Despised: 22-23

22. Blessed are ye, when men shall hate you, and when they shall separate you *from their company*, and shall reproach *you*, and cast out your name as evil, for the Son of man's sake.

23. Rejoice ye in that day, and leap for joy: for, behold, your reward is great in heaven: for in the like manner did their fathers unto the prophets.

Jesus presented exactly what was going to happen to Him. He would be hated, cast out of the people's company, reproached and called evil. "If you really hear my teaching," Jesus declared, "you will be treated likewise." Why? Because the world did not and does not want Kingdom values.

II. The Woes: Luke 6:24-26

A. The Rich: 24

24. But woe unto you that are rich! for ye have received your consolation.

Riches would be the only reward for those seeking wealth, Jesus said. A god could only give what that god had to give, was His point. For example, if one worshipped alcohol or drugs, all he would receive was a temporary escape from reality. When the high or the "buzz" was gone, reality would still be with him. Riches were the same. The other part of this sad truth was that each time it took more of whatever "treasure of this world" the person made his god, in order to get the high. There are no limits to the demands of the flesh.

Ultimately the person would die for something he made a god, something that was and always had been of lesser value than the person himself.

B. The Full: 25

25. Woe unto you that are full! for ye shall hunger. Woe unto you that laugh now! for ye shall mourn and weep.

Filled with themselves, food, riches, power, fame, self-professed righteousness, etc. People were unable to see their need. The principle was simple. Full left no room for God.

J. Paul Getty, at the time of his death, was the richest man in the world. Not long before his death, he was interviewed and asked if his wealth had made him happy. His response was a resounding No. He said he didn't know who really cared about him, and his family was divided over who would receive the inheritance. Also, he had always to be concerned about how to prevent losing what he had amassed.

C. The Well-Received: 26

26. Woe unto you, when all men shall speak well of you! for so did their fathers to the false prophets.

In the Old Testament the prophets (false to be sure) who told the kings and rulers what they wanted to hear were well-received and honored. Those who spoke the truth often stirred the ire of the one in power. Many true prophets were cast out and their reputations were ruined.

It is not men and women that we serve, Jesus declared. His disciples did not owe obedience to the world of humankind. It was God whom they needed to be attuned to and obey, not because He has to be pleased and appeased like a worldly ruler, but because He and He alone had the Words of life.

III. Loving Enemies: Luke 6:27-36

A. Do Good and Bless: 27-33

27. But I say unto you which hear, Love your enemies, do good to them which hate you,

28. Bless them that curse you, and pray for them which despitefully use you.

29. And unto him that smiteth thee on the *one* cheek offer also the other, and him that taketh away thy cloke forbid not to *take thy* coat also.

30. Give to every man that asketh of thee; and of him that taketh away thy goods ask *them* not again.

31. And as ye would that men should do to you, do ye also to them likewise.

32. For if ye love them which love you, what thank have ye? for sinners also love those that love them.

33. And if ye do good to them which do good to you, what thank have ye? for sinners also do even the same.

The Jews were an occupied people. They despised the Romans who mistreated and oppressed them. Jesus knew this. Still He called for the people to do good to those who hated them and pray for those who used them.

Loving enemies was not native to the way of the world. The world's way was to despise and turn into an enemy any who threaten one's own security and standing.

Acting in the best interest of their enemies must have hit the Jews' ears as strange sounds. Turn the other cheek, give them your coat also, treat them the way you want to be treated. Strange sounds indeed!

Everybody loved those like themselves. That was no big accomplishment. But loving those who were different, even those who were evil to them?! This was truly a hard saying!

B. Lend and Love: 34-35

34. And if ye lend *to them* of whom ye hope to receive, what thank have ye? for sinners also lend to sinners, to receive as much again.

35. But love ye your enemies, and do good, and lend, hoping for nothing again; and your reward shall be great, and ye shall be the children of the Highest: for he is kind unto the unthankful and to the evil.

Love is more than a word. It is action. Jesus was in the business of doing what humans only say. Banks will lend for profit. Love gives expecting nothing in return. Lending, not looking for anything back, was just one example of love in action. The question: What is really of value to us? Persons or profit?

Jesus knew that hearts and lives would be changed only by love. The world was in short supply of this commodity. Only God in Christ could love His enemies, Jews and Gentiles. On the cross, Jesus said, "Father, forgive them for they know not what they do."

C. Be Merciful: 36

36. Be ye therefore merciful, as your Father also is merciful.

Mercy was a word seldom lived out by the world. Judgment, eye for an eye, tooth for a tooth, retaliation, retribution, punishment that befits the crime; those were the world's ways.

In Colossians 3:14, love is described as the bond of perfectness. In Matthew 5:48 we are told to be perfect as our Heavenly Father is perfect. Here in this passage we have a parallel statement. Be merciful as your Father also is merciful. Loving our enemies is the way to be perfect as our Father in heaven is perfect. Thus, love and perfection equal the extension of mercy toward those who would deserve no mercy if judged by worldly standards. How perfect we can become if we are merciful! Isn't it strange that keeping rules of "do" and "don't" appeal to us more than mercy?

JESUS TEACHES HIS FOLLOWERS

Evangelistic Emphasis

As Jose Ortega y Gasset puts it, "The characteristic of the moment is that the mediocre mind, aware of its own mediocrity, is bold enough to affirm the rights of mediocrity and to impose them everywhere."

The imposing of mediocrity upon Christian discipleship does not square with the teaching of Christ. instead of the minimum, Jesus insists on the maximum. The Christian lives by a higher, holier standard.

For example, Jesus tells us to love our enemies. Such a demand transcends all other ethical teachings. Clarence Jordan points out that basically people have treated each other in four ways: unlimited retaliation, limited retaliation, limited love and unlimited love. The first, unlimited retaliation, was uncivilized and barbaric: "You kill my dog, and I will kill your dog, your horse and your wife." The second is from the old Testament: an eye for an eye. The third is a rather modern ethic that says we should love only our own family and kind. The fourth, the ethic of Jesus, goes beyond all of these previous, less-than-adequate approaches.

The Christian loves with the love of God. How else would you expect it to be? After all, this is the same God who loved us while we were still His enemies. Therefore we are to love our enemies. Of such is the Kingdom of God.

◆◆◆◆◆◆

Memory Selection

Be merciful, even as your Father is merciful.
Luke 6:36

Jesus calls His disciples to a life of mercy. In fact, His whole sermon is summed up in the command to be merciful. That is certainly not the characteristic lifestyle of most people in our world. We, however, are to show mercy.

In contrast, Jesus suggests that we express sympathy, empathy, understanding, tolerance and patience with others. To love in such a way means to be conscious of others in at least three specific ways: awareness, attention and acceptance.

Awareness is a gift that enables us to think of others and their needs instead of ourselves. Some people live in a self-enclosed world that has room only for their needs and their desires. The person who cultivates awareness will know when people are hurting.

Attention is the second step in showing mercy. When we are aware of the needs of others, we pay attention to those needs. Steps are taken to meet the needs that have come to our conscious attention. Only when we are unselfish are we able to pay attention to the needs of others.

The third step in showing mercy is acceptance. When we are able to accept people with all their differences and limits, we are able to show mercy. In this case mercy is the opposite of judgment.

January 16, 1994

Weekday Problems

Beverly was a radiant Christian woman. A Sunday school teacher for thirty years, she knew her Bible better than most preachers. Every Sunday she could be found serving her church. she was a blessing to her pastor and the whole congregation.

Beverly's brother-in-law, a deacon in the same church, cheated Beverly's husband in a business deal. The two brothers fell out with one another. To everyone's surprise, however, the person who developed the most unforgiving spirit was Beverly. Soon she quit coming to church. She resigned her Sunday School teaching position. After a few months, she stopped going anywhere. Her entire life was consumed by the growing spirit of bitterness and unforgiveness.

*Why was Beverly's bitterness so incompatible with her church relationship?

*By refusing to forgive her brother-in-law, what was Beverly doing to God's ability to forgive her?

*Is there any help for Beverly in our lesson for today?

♦♦♦♦♦♦

Smiles

The Sunday School teacher was teaching a lesson on creation to a class of children.

"Now children," she said, "Who can tell me what makes the flower spring from the seed?"

"God does it," answered one little girl, "but fertilizer helps."

A small boy's prayer: "Dear God, I hope you take care of yourself. 'Cause if anything happens to you, we would all be in a terrible mess."

This Lesson In Your Life

In the beatitudes, Jesus does not put the divine seal of approval on our carefully crafted social structures. He commands us to alter our usual ways of relating to others--ways based on social approval and social barriers. Jesus' whole approach to life was a refusal to bless usual human behavior toward others. Remember how Jesus ate with sinners and tax collectors. Remember how Jesus put making people well over the rules of the Sabbath.

At the apex of His popularity, Jesus even challenged the temple to transcend the idolatries of herdity, nationality and tradition. He routed those who had turned God's house into a gathering of the privileged rather than a meeting place with God. His challenge, however, was directed just as much at our tenacious inclinations to draw lines, set up boundaries, establish hierarchies and maintain discriminations. That challenge, like a gauntlet thrown down, judges us severely.

Jesus is insisting that our usual ways of doing business with one another are unacceptable in His Kingdom. Yet our practices are sometimes like a particular bird's nesting habits. The mother bird builds her nest on the ground. After laying the eggs, she makes a circle around the nest. When her baby birds hatch, she feeds only those inside the circle. The siblings try to push one another outside the circle. Sounds like us doesn't it? We keep coming up with creative ways to push away outsiders. Even churches create their own religious and social barriers.

Religious persons across the centuries have gone to inordinate lengths to maintain barriers and keep out the unwelcome. Archaeologists have recovered a sign that hung in the temple at Jerusalem: "No foreigner may enter within the fence and enclosure surrounding the sanctuary area. Whoever is caught so doing will have only himself to blame for the death which follows."

Think of the unwritten messages that churches still send in the same manner of the temple zealots. How ironic, that we Gentiles, the beneficiaries of Jesus' attack on the temple, have spent much of our energy restoring the temple warning that strangers are not always welcome. How many churches have invisible signs that everyone recognizes: "Only white people welcome here." "Only black people welcome here." "Only stable families welcome here." "Only Bible believers welcome here." "Only the well-dressed welcome here."

We're so adept at building these silent signs that become walls that we rarely notice their presence. With silent looks and whispers we keep outsiders in their place. We are thus surprised to see Jesus, sledge-hammer in hand, slamming away at our walls: "Love, do good, bless, pray," Jesus says. For whom? Why our enemies and our strangers of course. Jesus says that all the walls have to go, even the socially accepted ones.

What then are we supposed to do? We can practice love for enemies, goodness for those who hate us, blessings for those who curse us and prayer for those who abuse us. These commands are clear and concise. We know exactly what Jesus is saying. We are not all there yet when it comes to obedience.

We must be members of God's welcoming committee. Exclusion has no place among us. In its place is a whole new attitude of welcome. As Letty Russell says, "The church is a community of Christ, where everyone is welcome ... and worship ... includes the daily practice of hospitality or table fellowship with the stranger."

Seed Thoughts

1. What more famous sermon of Jesus does the sermon on the plain parallel in some respects?
The sermon on the mount found in Matthew 5-7.

2. In what sense are the poor blessed?
Jesus grants to the poor the Kingdom of God.

3. Is there any reward for those who are persecuted?
Jesus says their reward in heaven is great.

4. In a series of three woes, whom does Jesus warn?
He warns the rich, the full and those spoken well of by all men.

5. What does Jesus command His followers to practice?
He commands them to practice unconditional love.

(PLEASE TURN PAGE)

---

1. What more famous sermon of Jesus does the sermon on the plain parallel in some respects?

2. In what sense are the poor blessed?

3. Is there any reward for those who are persecuted?

4. In a series of three woes, whom does Jesus warn?

5. What does Jesus command His followers to practice?

6. What forms does such love assume?

7. How are Christians to treat others?

8. In what ways can Christians show their difference from sinners?

9. By what title does Jesus call those who do more than sinners?

10. What verse serves as the theme of Jesus' sermon?

| (SEED THOUGHTS--Cont'd)

The sermon on the mount found in Matthew 5-7.

Jesus grants to the poor the Kingdom of God.

Jesus says their reward in heaven is great.

He warns the rich, the full and those spoken well of by all men.

He commands them to practice unconditional love.

Love for enemies and those who hate us, those who curse us and despitefully use us, those that strike us and those who steal from us.

As we want to be treated.

By loving our enemies, doing good and lending without hoping to get a return.

The children of the Highest.

Verse 36: "Be ye therefore merciful, as your Father is merciful."

6. What forms does such love assume?
Love for enemies and those who hate us, those who curse us and despitefully use us, those that strike us and those who steal from us.

7. How are Christians to treat others?
As we want to be treated.

8. In what ways can Christians show their difference from sinners?
By loving our enemies, doing good and lending without hoping to get a return.

9. By what title does Jesus call those who do more than sinners?
The children of the Highest.

10. What verse serves as the theme of Jesus' sermon?
Verse 36: "Be ye therefore merciful, as your Father is merciful."

January 23, 1994

Jesus Calls And Commissions Disciples

Luke 9:57-10:12

57 And it came to pass, that, as they went in the way, a certain *man* said unto him, Lord, I will follow thee whithersoever thou goest.
58 And Jesus said unto him. Foxes have holes, and birds of the air *have* nests; but the Son of man hath not where to lay *his* head.
59 And he said unto another, Follow me. But he said, Lord, suffer me first to go and bury my father.
60 Jesus said unto him, Let the dead bury their dead. but go thou and preach the kingdom of God.
61 And another also said Lord. I will follow thee; but let me first go bid them farewell which are at home at my house.
62 And Jesus said unto him, No man, having put his hand to the plough, and looking back, is fit for the kingdom of God.
10 AFTER these things the Lord appointed other seventy also, and sent them two and two before his face into every city and place, whither he himself would come.
2 Therefore said he unto them, The harvest truly is great, but the labourers *are* few: pray ye therefore the Lord of the harvest, that he would send forth labourers into his harvest.
3 Go your ways: behold, I send you forth as lambs among wolves.
4 Carry neither purse, nor scrip, nor shoes: and salute no man by the way.
5 And into whatsoever house ye enter, first say, Peace *be* to this house.
6 And if the son of peace be there, your peace shall rest upon it: if not, it shall turn to you again.
7 And in the same house remain, eating and drinking such things as they give: for the labourer is worthy of his hire. Go not from house to house.
8 And into whatsoever city ye enter, and they receive you, eat such things as are set before you:
9 And heal the sick that are therein, and say unto them, The kingdom of God is come nigh unto you.
10 But into whatsoever city ye enter, and they receive you not, go your ways out into the streets of the same, and say,
11 Even the very dust of your city, which cleaveth on us, we do wipe off against you: notwithstanding be ye sure of this, that the kingdom of God is come nigh unto you.
12 But I say unto you, that it shall be more tolerable in that day for Sodom, than for that city.

◆◆◆◆◆◆

◀ **Memory Selection**
Luke 9:62

◀ **Devotional Reading**
Matthew 8:18-22; 9:38; 10:1-15

◀ **Background Scripture**
Luke 9:51 - 10:12

◀ **Printed Scripture**
Luke 9:57 - 10:12

JESUS CALLS AND COMMISSIONS DISCIPLES

Teacher's Target

Being a disciple of Jesus sounded like a great adventure to many until the actual time for decision came. Some things would have to be given up, other things left behind. An unknown way of life stretched before them. No certainties of being received, no reservations in advance for a motel room, no guarantee that the next meal would be provided. Only faith in God was offered as security.

Share with each other about when you went to your first job, off to college or to a new town or a new job. Consider each other's fears, uncertainties, excitements, enthusiasms, expectations and hesitancies. How are you stepping out in faith today for God? What grips your life enough that you would make such a commitment as is called for in the text today? Does Jesus so grip you?

Lesson Introduction

Jesus taught by example the cost of following Him. Here some disciples were sent ahead to a Samaritan village to reserve rooms for the disciples. They were turned away. When the word got back to James and John, they wanted to call down fire from heaven to burn up the village. Jesus rebuked them and He and His company of followers went on to another village.

The central lesson about retaliation was that vengeance belonged to God and not to people. God most often acts like He did with Jonah and Nineveh. He forgave Ninevah. The other lesson was that even provisions and protection were in God's hands.

Jesus seized the opportunity to teach about the cost of discipleship. He also instructed disciples as to how to carry out their mission.

Teaching Outline

I. Priority: Luke 9:57-62
   A. Foxes and Birds: 57-59
   B. The Dead: 60
   C. Hand and Plough: 61-62
II. Commission: Luke 10:1-9
   A. Harvest and Laborers: 1, 2
   B. Lambs and Wolves: 3
   C. Peace and Provisions: 4-9
III. Warning: Luke 10:10-12
   A. Not Received: 10
   B. Shake the Dust: 11
   C. Unwanted Fate: 12

Daily Bible Readings

Mon. A Centurion Shows Great Faith
Luke 7:1-10
Tue. Women Who Were With Jesus
Luke 8:1-3; 23:55-56
Wed. Twelve Receive Power and Authority - *Luke 9:1-6*
Thurs. Jesus Turns Toward Jerusalem
Luke 9:51-56
Fri. Priorities of Discipleship
Luke 9:57-62
Sat. Peace Be to This House
Luke 10:1-7
Sun. The Kingdom Comes Near
Luke 10:8-12

January 23, 1994

VERSE BY VERSE

I. Priority: Luke 9:57-62

A. Foxes and Birds: 57-59

57. And it came to pass, that, as they went in the way, a certain *man* said unto him, Lord, I will follow thee whithersoever thou goest.

58. And Jesus said unto him, Foxes have holes, and birds of the air *have* nests; but the Son of man hath not where to lay *his* head.

59. And he said unto another, Follow me. But he said, Lord, suffer me first to go and bury my father.

A man came to Jesus offering to follow Him wherever He went. He evidently had envisioned a great service, but had not counted the cost of such an offer. Words were cheap and still are. He was rash and hasty in his decision and Jesus brought him to reality with an analogy. Jesus told the man not to expect the trappings with which the world surrounds royalty. Rather expect poverty and rejection from the world. The world provided holes for foxes and nests for birds, but the Son of Man would not be received by the world nor would His followers. His home was in heaven with God.

Calling Himself "Son of Man," Jesus identified with humanity and the prophets who Israel rejected. Jesus would not ask of those who followed Him anything that He had not experienced a hundredfold.

B. The Dead: 60

60. Jesus said unto him, Let the dead bury their dead: but go thou and preach the kingdom of God.

Prioritize your life. This we have heard often. Jesus was in the process of making His disciples do that very thing. It was not that Jesus was callous toward family responsibilities, but He knew humankind's penchant for earthly loyalties over God's truth. Truth was the highest priority, loyalty second. Putting second best over the first would not suffice.

This passage can literally be translated, "but wanted to wait for his father's death." If this is so, then possibly the man was wanting to wait until he received his inheritance at his father's death. Then he could go with Jesus. In effect, what Jesus said was, "Man, if you cling to the things of this age they are all dead already. I am offering you the way of life eternal." There are always plenty of the spiritually dead who will attend to the dead.

C. Hand and Plough: 61-62

61. And another also said, Lord, I will follow thee; but let me first go bid them farewell, which are at home at my house.

62. And Jesus said unto him, No man, having put his hand to the plough, and looking back, is fit for the kingdom of God.

This man seemed to want the Kingdom, but was hesitant to cast himself fully upon the grace and mercy of God. Maybe he was wanting his cake while eating it too. Always, many concerns and cares of this world will clamor for attention. Jesus was saying that you can't get all your ducks in a row before you follow me. "Follow me," Jesus said, "and have faith that God will provide for what was needed." This passage is much like Jesus' teaching in Matthew 6 about seeking first the Kingdom of God and all the things necessary shall be added.

If you have ever plowed behind a mule or a horse or even on a tractor, you know that looking back means crooked rows, possibly even plowed up crops! You have to look straight ahead and forget what is behind. The past was past, Jesus said. It was unchangeable. Jesus warned us to keep stepping ahead into the Kingdom's light. Trusting God's sufficiency was the call.

II. Commission: Luke 10:1-9

A. Harvest and Laborers: 1-2

1. AFTER these things the Lord appointed other seventy also, and sent them two and two before his face into every city and place, whither he himself would come.

2. Therefore said he unto them, The harvest truly is great, but the labourers *are* few: pray ye therefore the Lord of the harvest, that he would send forth labourers into his harvest.

There had been many following Jesus. Now seventy would be commissioned to go out two by two in the name of the Kingdom of God. These were not special people with greater gifts than others. They were only those who had caught the vision.

The harvest Jesus could see was enormous. The task could have been overwhelming. The whole world needed salvation. Jesus knew that one alone would falter so He sent them by twos. He also told them to concern themselves with only their little part of the field. No one or two could harvest the whole crop. Hoe your own row; pray for other laborers, Jesus admonished.

B. Lambs and Wolves: 3

3. Go your ways: behold, I send you forth as lambs among wolves.

In an agricultural environment Jesus' hearers had often seen what wolves could do to a lamb. Their strength against the world would be no greater than a lamb against a wolf. They could not defeat the wolves, much less convert them in their own strength. They would have to trust the Great Shepherd's care of them (John 10).

Their role would not be to call down fire nor retaliate against the cruelty of the world. The wolves would howl and threaten. The disciples were to be peaceable and patient and without guile. In reality, Jesus was saying to them they would have to go forth as He had come forth from the Father.

C. Peace and Provisions: 4-9

4. Carry neither purse, nor scrip, nor shoes: and salute no man by the way.

5. And into whatsoever house ye enter, first say, Peace *be* to this house.

6. And if the son of peace be there, your peace shall rest upon it: if not, it shall turn to you again.

7. And in the same house remain, eating and drinking such things as they give: for the labourer

is worthy of his hire. Go not from house to house.

8. And into whatsoever city ye enter, and they receive you, eat such things as are set before you:

9. And heal the sick that are therein, and say unto them, The kingdom of God is come nigh unto you.

No purse, no money, no extra shoes, no wasting time along the way; these were the instructions. Most people considered these things essential for a journey. But Jesus was teaching a lesson in faith and God's providence.

They were to live off of the generosity of those that received the Kingdom. They were to carry the message and presence of peace into every city where they were sent. Where they were received they were to stay, accept accommodations and food without murmuring.

Notice also that where they were received and provided for, an even greater provision was given to those who received them. Their sick were healed and the Kingdom of God came to them. No ministry to God's messengers goes unnoticed or unrewarded, although this was not to be the motive for reception of the disciples.

III. Warning: Luke 10:10-12

A. Not Received: 10

10. But into whatsoever city ye enter, and they receive you not, go your ways out into the streets of the same, and say,

Jesus was realistic at every turn. he knew all would not receive His message nor His disciples. He knew that unless the disciples departed such places they would be harmed. He knew also that there was no need to waste time on non-reception when others were prepared to receive His word.

B. Shake the Dust: 11

11. Even the very dust of your city, which cleaveth on us, we do wipe off against you: notwithstanding be ye sure of this, that the kingdom of God is come nigh unto you.

The practice of shaking off the dust from their shoes was a sign that those whom they left had no part in their company or family. It also was a sign that the disciple wanted none of the rejecting attitude or spirit to cling to him.

Notice that the same message of peace was brought to all. God did not have one message for those who received and a different message for those who rejected. God always comes with a saving Word. What was done with the same message was the difference. God did not condemn anyone. They condemned themselves through their rejection of His gift of grace.

C. Unwanted Fate: 12

12. But I say unto you, that it shall be more tolerable in that day for Sodom, than for that city.

Sodom was an evil city that was destroyed by its sinfulness (Gen. 19). Sodom had become a synonym for wickedness. Jesus warned the people that a greater gift than was ever offered to Sodom had come among them. To reject such a gift would be flirting with a greater disaster than what befell Sodom. To see the Messiah, to experience His mighty deeds, to hear His compassionate and convicting words and then to turn away would be a strong statement of unbelief.

JESUS CALLS AND COMMISSIONS DISCIPLES

Evangelistic Emphasis

Urgency, commitment, joy--these are the words that describe the mission of the seventy disciples. What happens here is of intense and lasting consequence, not only for the seventy but for all future followers of Christ. Anyone who takes seriously the evangelistic mission of Christ will have about him urgency, commitment and joy.

Notice the urgency of the mission. There is not much time. There are not enough workers. No one can go back home to make preparations. All systems are go. No provisions are to be carried. These disciples are like soldiers on a mission behind enemy lines. They have to strip down and travel light. In addition they were to survive on the hospitality of the people they visited. Believe me, carrying the message of salvation to the world is urgent business.

The commitment required of disciples is found in Luke 9:57-62. The proclaiming of the Kingdom had to take priority over personal needs and family considerations. There is time only for spreading the message.

The seventy returned from their preaching with joy. They learned that faithful proclamation has power even over Satan! The disciples were excited, turned on to what God was doing! Here is a theme that we need to hear again and again: Satan has fallen, is falling and will finally fall. We have only to keep preaching and telling the good news.

♦♦♦♦♦♦

Memory Selection

No one who puts his hand to the plow and looks back is fit for the kingdom of God. *Luke 9:62*

Looking backward is a constant temptation for would-be disciples. The Israelites, only a few hours out of Egypt, looked back and begged Moses to take them back. There seems to be a constant pull in a backward direction. Perhaps it is true that known hells are preferable to uncertain heavens.

In any event, the desire to look back, to go back or to turn back, has no place in the Christian life. While Jesus uses a metaphor from farming that may sound foreign to city-dwellers, anyone can figure that plowing while looking backward is a dangerous business.

A person plowing with a mule has to keep his eyes straight ahead so he can plow in a straight direction. Thus, following Jesus means leaving behind security, duty and even family loyalty.

January 23, 1994

Weekday Problems

Jimmy had always been a follower. All the way through school and into adulthood, he did what everybody else did. If someone came along with charisma and leadership ability, Jimmy was an easy mark for him.

On Sunday morning, before going to church, Jimmy watched a televangelist on cable television. The preacher was charismatic in personality and dynamic in his preaching. He appealed to his listeners to send him large sums of money. In return he promised them the blessings of God. Jimmy thought the world of this particular preacher. Every week he sent his check. Then he waited for the riches to start falling out of the sky. He believed every word this preacher told him. Equating faith with fortune seemed to be as good a way to get rich as any other.

*What is the relationship between faith and fortune?

*If the only preaching we heard for the next fifty years was that of televangelists, what kind of churches would we have?

*Is it possible that Jimmy's motivations in giving were not of the highest order?

♦♦♦♦♦♦

Sparkles

"What kind of person is produced by the words of Jesus?" one disciple asked.

The teacher responded, "To be public-spirited and belong to no party, to move without being bound to any given course, to take things as they come, have no remorse for the past, no anxiety for the future, to move when pushed, to come when dragged, to be like a mighty gale, like a feather in the wind, like weeds floating on a river, like a millstone meekly grinding, to love all creation equally as heaven and earth are equal to all."

One disciple, deeply troubled by this teaching said, "This sort of teaching is not for the living but the dead." He walked away and followed no more. Are you dying to self?

JESUS CALLS AND COMMISSSIONS DISCIPLES

This Lesson In Your Life

Do you ever feel overloaded by the number of commitments you have made? Do you remember trying to be in two places at the same time? When we are thinking straight, we know that the quality of our lives depends upon the quality of our commitments. We even remember that commitment is the fiber that binds a collection of individuals into a caring community.

Make no mistake. Jesus is not conducting a public relations campaign. If anything, Jesus is too blunt. The requirements He sets forth are straightforward and severe. He is not trying to win a popularity contest, improve His standings in the polls or get elected to any office. "Let the dead bury their own dead," and "No one who puts a hand to the plow and looks back is fit for the kingdom of God." Believe me, a commitment to follow Jesus is no picnic. When Jesus says, "Follow me," he is not fooling around.

Jesus is looking straight at us, at our busy, cluttered lives. We are people of broken promises and broken words. Somehow the "I will" is replaced with "I'll try, but don't count on me," or "I'm too busy." What happens? How does "we will" become "we won't?" Why are there so many broken promises?

Jesus models for us the making and keeping of commitments. "He set his face to go to Jerusalem." That's how Luke puts it. Jesus made up his mind in advance. He was determined to carry out His mission. He affirmed His intention to keep His promises. Our church needs persons who know that a commitment is an affirmation. "I affirm my intention to be a faithful church member." No matter what happens I will stay on course--keep my word--live up to my promises. No matter who the preacher is, no matter who mistreats me or is rude to me, I will maintain my relationship to the church. The church needs affirmation-makers, people who feel personally responsible for the well-being and growth of the congregation.

Meanwhile, commitment is more than affirmation. It is also taking action. Commitment is more than an old promise; it is present-tense performance. We renew our commitment every Sunday as we gather for worship. We keep our commitments by arranging our lives around our center: Jesus Christ.

Arrangement of our priorities then is the second half of commitment. One basic question determines our priorities: How do we spend our time?

Perhaps in our busy lives we have misplaced a very important biblical principle: the sabbath rest principle. God made a special day for worship and rest, for the recreation of our energies. In worship we are able to renew our vows, center our lives and reorder our priorities and tasks. The time you spend in worship each week is the most important time of your entire week. We tend to get so confused and so disoriented. Through worship we touch base with God who calms our fears and redirects our energies for goodness. Worship is an experience of rest and re-creation.

We church people are called to make and to keep commitments. In a world of broken promises we are called to show the discipline of Kingdom life. We are a people of Christ with a clear directive to keep all our vows. No more flimsy excuses. No more putting Christ and the church second. A straightforward keeping of our vows will be our style, so help us God.

Seed Thoughts

1. Jesus had reached a conclusive decision about the direction of His ministry. Where then is He headed?
   "He set his face to go to Jerusalem."

2. Why did the Samaritans not receive Jesus?
   Racial and religious prejudice against Jews.

3. What did James and John propose to do to the Samaritans?
   They wanted to call down fire from heaven to consume them. No wonder they were called "the sons of thunder."

4. In what way did Jesus respond to James and John's request for the destruction of the Samaritan town?
   Jesus rebuked them and reminded them that His mission was to save, not to destroy.

5. What excuses did the three would-be followers give Jesus?
   The first gave no excuse, the second wanted to bury his father and the third wanted to say farewell.

(PLEASE TURN PAGE)

---

1. Jesus had reached a conclusive decision about the direction of His ministry. Where then is He headed?

2. Why did the Samaritans not receive Jesus?

3. What did James and John propose to do to the Samaritans?

4. In what way did Jesus respond to James and John's request for the destruction of the Samaritan town?

5. What excuses did the three would-be followers give Jesus?

6. How did Jesus respond to these would-be disciples?

7. How many disciples did Jesus send out on mission?

8. Why did Jesus send out his disciples?

9. What were the disciples to do when people would not receive them?

10. How were they to go forth on their mission?

(SEED THOUGHTS--Cont'd)

"He set his face to go to Jerusalem."	**6. How did Jesus respond to these would-be disciples?** With a harsh command Jesus told them that they were not worthy unless they went all the way.
Racial and religious prejudice against Jews.	**7. How many disciples did Jesus send out on mission?** He sent seventy disciples.
They wanted to call down fire from heaven to consume them. No wonder they were called "the sons of thunder."	**8. Why did Jesus send out his disciples?** The harvest was great and needed laborers.
Jesus rebuked them and reminded them that His mission was to save, not to destroy.	
The first gave no excuse, the second wanted to bury his father and the third wanted to say farewell.	**9. What were the disciples to do when people would not receive them?** Wipe the dust from their feet on the streets.
With a harsh command Jesus told them that they were not worthy unless they went all the way.	**10. How were they to go forth on their mission?** As lambs in the midst of wolves.
He sent seventy disciples.	
The harvest was great and needed laborers.	
Wipe the dust from their feet on the streets.	
As lambs in the midst of wolves.	

January 30, 1994

Jesus Tells Parables About the Lost

Luke 15:11-24

11 And he said, A certain man had two sons:
12 And the younger of them said to *his* father, Father, give me the portion of goods that falleth *to me*. And he divided unto them *his* living.
13 And not many days after the younger son gathered all together, and took his journey into a far country, and there wasted his substance with riotous living.
14 And when he had spent all, there arose a mighty famine in the land; and he began to be in want.
15 And he went and joined himself to a citizen of that country; and he sent him into his fields to feed swine.
16 And he would fain have filled his belly with the husks that the swine did eat: and no man gave unto him.
17 And when he came to himself, he said, How many hired servants of my father's have bread enough and to spare, and I perish with hunger!
18 I will arise and go to my father, and will say unto him, Father, I have sinned against heaven, and before thee,
19 And am no more worthy to be called thy son: make me as one of thy hired servants.
20 And he arose, and came to his father. But when he was yet a great way off, his father saw him, and had compassion, and ran, and fell on his neck, and kissed him.
21 And his son said unto him, Father, I have sinned against heaven, and in thy sight, and am no more worthy to be called thy son.
22 But the father said to his servants, Bring forth the best robe, and put *it* on him, and put a ring on his hand, and shoes on *his* feet:
23 And bring hither the fatted calf, and kill *it;* and let us eat, and be merry:
24 For this my son was dead, and is alive again; he was lost, and is found. And they began to be merry.

◆◆◆◆◆◆

◀ **Memory Selection**
Luke 15:2

◀ **Devotional Reading**
Isaiah 40:9-11;
Ezekiel 34:1-6, 11-12,
15-16

◀ **Background Scripture**
Luke 15

◀ **Printed Scripture**
Luke 15:11-24

Teacher's Target

One crisis in our culture today is the break-up of the family. What is desired is a family that provides boundaries and teaches healthy values. Young children especially need family. Even when youth think they do not need parents, when they chafe under discipline, good parents provide needed security and protection. As children grow into adolescence they often decide to rebel. Such rebellion is not true independence. It also is not a safe way to test limits. There is a time to leave home. Done wisely, one can return to be friends with those who once disciplined his behavior.

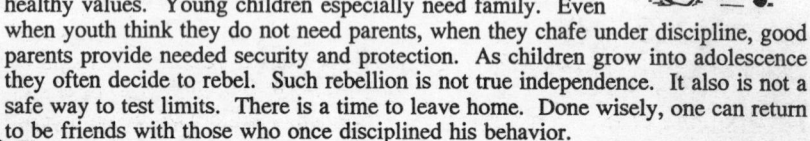

Consider these questions: As a child did you ever run away from home? Did you ever think your parents were unfair? Have you ever wished you had your inheritance now? Are your parents more important to you than what they can give you?

Lesson Introduction

Knowing something of the background of customs and thought at the time of Jesus will help make this passage come alive. First, the Pharisees had a theology that said there would be joy in heaven over every sinner that was condemned. Also, they believed that if sinners crawled, begged and pleaded God might perhaps forgive them. Feeding pigs as a Jewish boy not only made you ceremonially unclean, but their law said, "Cursed is every man who feeds swine." To say to his father, as the younger son did, "Give me my share of the inheritance now," was to treat him as if he were dead.

This story of a longing parent's anxiety and wayward children is all too common in our day. Listen closely to how God treats our rebellious nature.

Teaching Outline

I. The Rejected Father:
   Luke 15:11-16
   A. Home Rejected: 11-12
   B. Values Rejected: 13
   C. Inevitable Fall: 14-16
II. The Waiting Father:
   Luke 15:17-20
   A. Son Comes to Himself: 17
   B. Son Turns Home: 18-19
   C. Father Runs: 20
III. The Reconciling Father:
   Luke 15:21-24
   A. No Put Down: 21
   B. New Start: 22
   C. Much Joy: 23-24

Daily Bible Readings

Mon. How to Inherit Eternal Life
Luke 10:25-37
Tue. Mary Chooses the Better Part
Luke 10:38-42
Wed. Proper Place for Treasures
Luke 12:13-21, 32-33
Thurs. Rejoice When Lost Are Found
Luke 15:1-7
Fri. Finding Lost Coins and Sons
Luke 15:8-24
Sat. Envy Destroys Love
Luke 15:25-32
Sun. Last Will Be First
Luke 13:22-30

January 30, 1994

VERSE BY VERSE

I. The Rejected Father:
   Luke 15:11-16

A. Home Rejected: 11-12

11. And he said, A certain man had two sons:
12. And the younger of them said to *his* father, Father, give me the portion of goods that falleth *to me*. And he divided unto them *his* living.

The boy was safe and secure at home. All he had to do was acknowledge his father's authority. But something was eating at him. He saw the tinsel glitter that decorated life on the world's terms. If only his father were dead. He could have his inheritance and be free to explore the other side of the street for awhile. It looked greener over there. He knew the passage in Deuteronomy 21:17 that stated that the younger son would get one third of the father's inheritance. It would be enough. He would treat his dad as if he were dead and ask for it all right now. He got his way. The old man had been an easy touch. Now he could be on his way.

B. Values Rejected: 13

13. And not many days after the younger son gathered all together, and took his journey into a far country, and there wasted his substance with riotous living.

The journey to the far country didn't seem to take long. It never does when you have big plans and bright dreams. People at home never did know how to live. Now he would really show them what living was all about. They were always talking about values back home. "Trying to scare us young folks with how we would get hurt if we listened to the way of the world. This riotous living sure looks like fun to me."

It was . . . until the money was all gone. Then all the merrymakers began to drift away from him. He couldn't borrow a cent from anyone, though everyone had helped him spend. Strange ways, the way of the world.

C. Inevitable Fall: 14-16

14. And when he had spent all, there arose a mighty famine in the land; and he began to be in want.
15. And he went and joined himself to a citizen of that country; and he sent him into his fields to feed swine.
16. And he would fain have filled his belly with the husks that the swine did eat: and no man gave unto him.

Had he really wasted it? he asked himself. There had been some laughs and some feelings he had never experienced before. But now, what did he have to show for it? "They say the country is in for a famine. Where is my next meal coming from in the days ahead? I know--I'll get a job."

It wasn't easy finding someone to hire a Jewish boy in this far country.

213

"If my folks saw me feeding swine they would disown me. I know what the Scripture said about feeding swine, but I had to have a job. But I'm still not eating. My stomach is drawn up and aching. I tried eating the pods the swine ate, but my stomach won't digest them. Only a pig could stomach that stuff.

"What am I going to do? I never meant to get here. How did it happen to me? I thought I was smarter than that!"

II. The Waiting Father: Luke 15:17-20

A. Son Comes to Himself: 17

17. And when he came to himself, he said, How many hired servants of my father's have bread enough and to spare, and I perish with hunger!

We often call this parable the parable of the prodigal son, but the story is really about a waiting and forgiving father. How often he must have looked down the road on which his boy left, longing to see him returning. How often he must have wondered what was happening to his boy. Was he okay? Had he been robbed? Murdered? Could he take care of himself? The boy knew nothing of the far country's ways.

All this time the son was seeking answers, and the greatest compliment was paid to humankind in verse 17, "He came to himself." The son is representative of all of us. "Coming to ourselves" means to realize our helplessness and want to listen to the truth we thought we did not need.

Hired servants were the lowest on the payroll. Yet this son remembered that even they had bread to spare.

B. Son Turns Home: 18-19

18. I will arise and go to my father, and will say unto him, Father, I have sinned against heaven, and before thee,

19. And am no more worthy to be called thy son: make me as one of thy hired servants.

He was hungry, disillusioned, shamed, humiliated, broken in spirit; all of it by his own doing. No illusions were cluttering his mind now. He could think clearly now that necessity was upon him. Necessity had invented a repentant heart.

He rehearsed what he would say as he turned toward home. He would acknowledge his unworthiness. He would ask just to be given the chance of a hired servant.

C. Father Runs: 20

20. And he arose, and came to his father. But when he was yet a great way off, his father saw him, and had compassion, and ran, and fell on his neck, and kissed him.

The father was waiting—he had been since the boy left. Each morning, at noon, at the close of a day's work, he squinted his eyes and looked down that road longing to see his boy coming home. On this particular day he looked once again, half-hoping, half-doubting that there would be anything beside an empty road before his eyes.

Then, he took a second look. There was a figure on the road way off in the distance. As he got closer he saw there was something familiar about that person. "That's my boy! He doesn't look like he did when he left. His head is down, not thrown back. His shoulders are bowed. His chest isn't thrown out, but that's my boy! I know it is! My boy has come home!"

Then he did a thing not done by old men in the day of Jesus. He ran! Old men didn't run! They were not to allow their robes to come up above their ankles. To run was a sign of a lack of dignity. But who cared? The boy that was lost was found! The father didn't care about dignity. He cared about his boy!

God doesn't have any false dignity either. He comes to us in all our sin because He cares for us and not His dignity.

III. The Reconciling Father: Luke 15:21-24

A. No Put Down: 21

21. And his son said unto him, Father, I have sinned against heaven, and in thy sight, and am no more worthy to be called thy son.

Notice the boy began his confession but didn't get to finish what he had rehearsed. He was able to get out the part about his sinning and his own sense of unworthiness but he wasn't allowed to say what he thought his just reward for such behavior should be. "Make me as one of thy hired servants," was never uttered. If it had been, it would have pleased the Pharisees that were murmuring in Luke 15:1 about Jesus eating with tax collectors and sinners. However, God isn't like the Pharisees. This father in the parable treated his son as if he had never been away from home. The father didn't care what the boy had wasted. He only cared about what he could give to the boy and that the boy was home with him. It is easier to come home to God than to men and women.

B. New Start: 22

22. But the father said to his servants, Bring forth the best robe, and put *it* on him; and put a ring on his hand, and shoes on *his* feet:

How surprised this boy must have been. God is the God of new starts. We can always begin again and we have to do so over and over again in different areas of our lives as we grow in Christ.

The elder brother in Luke 15:25-31 thought the prodigal had gotten by with something. He didn't see the scars. He wouldn't remove the labels he placed upon his brother.

C. Much Joy: 23-24

23. And bring hither the fatted calf, and kill *it;* and let us eat, and be merry:

24. For this my son was dead, and is alive again; he was lost, and is found. And they began to be merry.

The fatted calf was killed. The celebration was on. Merriment reigned. The father represented God celebrating with sinners when they come home. There is always joy in heaven when that which is lost is found, when that which was dead is alive again. God wants to celebrate our victory in coming to ourselves and coming out of the far country.

Evangelistic Emphasis

Luke's story is usually called the parable of the prodigal son. The subject, however, of the story is actually the Father. The waiting father, symbolizing God, is the key to the story. Evangelism does not begin with our sin nor with the bad news about a misbehaving son. Evangelism begins in the heart of God.

We have no way of knowing the inner thoughts of the prodigal son, but we are shown the inner character of his father: warm, understanding, benevolent, gracious, forgiving, rejoicing. The father's passionate waiting for his son speaks volumes about the Father's desire that all His lost children come home. The story then is a perfect picture of the father who woos all his children home.

That the father waits for the son to return should not be interpreted as a lack of interest or a loss of concern. The waiting is an active looking and longing after the lost boy. All of the parables in Luke 15 are alive with imagery of the seeking God, the God who finds US. Even when the son was lost in the far country, it was the unseen presence of the father that caused him to be homesick. Indeed all of the lost ones are homesick. The message of our evangelism is: "You can come home again to the father. He waits to welcome you." Such is the gospel for us all.

♦♦♦♦♦♦

Memory Selection

This my son was dead, and is alive again; he was lost, and is found. *Luke 15:24*

"Amazing grace . . . that saved a wretch like me! I once was lost, but now am found . . ." Do you suppose John Newton had the words of the prodigal son's father in mind when he penned the opening verse of "Amazing Grace" in 1779? Whether he did or not, both the father's words and the words of Newton trumpet the "middle C" note of the entire gospel keyboard. Here the grace of God plays a melody that brings the dead to life and the lost to home.

A famous novelist claims we cannot go home again. Robert Frost suggests that home is the place where they have to take you in. Jesus insists, however, that home is where the waiting father welcomes the lost back with open arms. Home is where the prodigal finds the freedom he thought only the far country could provide. Everything he left home to find had been there for him all along.

January 30, 1994

Weekday Problems

James Jackson is a successful businessman. He has provided generously for his family--a wife and three children. He is active in his church as a Sunday School teacher. Everything in his life seems to be working beautifully. The only exception is his youngest daughter, Melissa, a 19-year-old sophomore at the university.

Melissa and her dad have clashed for years. James always demands the best from her. If she makes five As and one B, he wants to know why Melissa didn't make all As. He never compliments her and has trouble expressing his love. As a result he and Melissa are constantly fighting. There is a great distance between them.

*Are the standards James set for his daughter unreasonable?

*In what ways could we help James relate to his daughter in more positive ways?

*Compare and contrast the behavior pattern of James with that of the prodigal son's father.

♦♦♦♦♦♦

Sparkles

One disciple complained to his teacher that he could not tolerate his limitations. The teacher said, "Yes, you are limited, indeed we all are, but have you noticed you can do things today that you would have thought impossible fifteen years ago? What do you think changed?"

The disciple responded, "My talents changed."

"No," said the teacher, "you changed."

"Isn't that the same thing?" asked the disciple.

"No, you are what you think you are. When your thinking changed, you changed."

This Lesson In Your Life

Eugene O'Neil was a playwright, not a preacher, but he had opinions about religion. O'Neil said: "God will forgive. That's his business." Read the parable of the prodigal son and you probably agree. Here is a father killing the fatted calf for the return of a worthless wastrel of a son. Any way you look at it, forgiveness is written all over the narrative. Is that really what Jesus is trying to tell us?

Unfortunately, we often take God's forgiveness for granted. We act as if God forgives as a matter of course. "God will forgive. That's His business." Well, take another look at the story. This time ignore the prodigal son. Concentrate on the father, especially on his feelings.

Only when we look in the face of the father and see his pain, will we begin to understand the nature of forgiveness. If you live long enough, chances are you will be hurt by someone you love. That is exactly what happened to the father in our story. He received an unexpected, unfair hurt from his own son. Why do we always hurt those we love?

The son was probably oblivious to his father's hurt. He saw only what he wanted. And so he blurted out: "Give me my share."

Children often hurt their parents with their thoughtlessness, immaturity and poor judgment. Growing up is hard to do. Parents are sometimes the victims of the pain that washes over from the problems of children trying to grow up. The prodigal son hurt his father deeply. Have we forgotten the hurt that precedes forgiveness? I want us to spend time in the pain and hurt of the father so we can appreciate again the cost of forgiveness.

What is the nature of the father's hurt? He suffers rejection. The son no longer wants to be part of the father's house. Do you suppose that God is happy when he drops by His house and finds so many of his children missing?

The father also experiences anxiety. He never hears from his son. He doesn't know whether the boy is dead or alive. How many parents sit up and wait for children to come home at night? How would you feel if they were late and didn't call? How do you suppose God feels when we never pray, never take the time to develop a strong relationship of faith?

When we see the hurt on the father's face, we begin to understand. Good heavens, all along have we been thinking of forgiveness as a natural expression of God, something easy, a piece of cake.

In God's Kingdom forgiveness is costly. As a writer in <u>Weavings: A Journal of the Christian Spiritual Life</u> puts it: "To forgive is to make a conscious choice to release the person who has hurt us from the sentence of our judgment. Forgiveness constitutes a decision to call forth and rebuild that love which is the only authentic ground of any relationship." That is what the Father has done.

Notice closely the action of the forgiving father. Jesus tells us that he saw his son coming. He had been waiting for his son's return. There is all the love in the world in the picture of the waiting father.

The father calls for the son to be given a robe, a ring and some shoes. These were the symbols of sonship. The father is forgiving, but he is expecting the son to accept responsibility for living as a faithful son in his father's house. Forgiveness is free but it is never cheap. When people have been forgiven everything, they owe everything in return. Forgiven people have awesome responsibilities in the Father's house. We are the forgiven ones.

Seed Thoughts

1. **In the three parables of Luke 15 what three things are lost?**
   A coin, a sheep and a son.

2. **Why does Jesus tell these parables?**
   Because the Pharisees complained that Jesus associated with sinners.

3. **What is the constant refrain of Luke 15?**
   The joy over sinners who repent.

4. **Who is the central character in the story of the two sons?**
   The waiting father, who symbolizes God.

5. **Where does the younger son go with his fortune?**
   To the far country.

(PLEASE TURN PAGE)

---

1. In the three parables of Luke 15 what three things are lost?

2. Why does Jesus tell these parables?

3. What is the constant refrain of Luke 15?

4. Who is the central character in the story of the two sons?

5. Where does the younger son go with his fortune?

6. What is the significance of the son ending up among the swine?

7. What happened to the younger son in the far country?

8. How did the father see his son coming from so far?

9. What action does the father take when his son returns?

10. How does the older brother feel?

(SEED THOUGHTS--Cont'd)

A coin, a sheep and a son.

Because the Pharisees complained that Jesus associated with sinners.

The joy over sinners who repent.

The waiting father, who symbolizes God.

To the far country.

His degradation and failure were complete. Nothing was more offensive to Jews than swine.

He came to himself. In other words, he repented.

Obviously, the waiting father had been watching for his son.

He throws a big party for the prodigal. The robe, the ring and the fatted calf are given to the son.

He is jealous. He is not in favor of parties for prodigals.

6. What is the significance of the son ending up among the swine?
His degradation and failure were complete. Nothing was more offensive to Jews than swine.

7. What happened to the younger son in the far country?
He came to himself. In other words, he repented.

8. How did the father see his son coming from so far?
Obviously, the waiting father had been watching for his son.

9. What action does the father take when his son returns?
He throws a big party for the prodigal. The robe, the ring and the fatted calf are given to the son.

10. How does the older brother feel?
He is jealous. He is not in favor of parties for prodigals.

February 6, 1994

Who Can Be Saved?

Luke 18:15-30

15 And they brought unto him also infants, that he would touch them: but when *his* disciples saw *it,* they rebuked them.
16 But Jesus called them *unto him* and said, Suffer little children to come unto me, and forbid them not: for of such is the kingdom of God.
17 Verily I say unto you, Whosoever shall not receive the kingdom of God as a little child shall in no wise enter therein.
18 And a certain ruler asked him, saying, Good Master, what shall I do to inherit eternal life?
19 And Jesus said unto him, Why callest thou me good? none *is* good, save one, *that is,* God.
20 Thou knowest the commandments. Do not commit adultery, Do not kill, Do not steal, Do not bear false witness, Honour thy father and thy mother.
21 And he said, All these have I kept from my youth up.
22 Now when Jesus heard these things he said unto him, Yet lackest thou one thing: sell all that thou hast, and distribute unto the poor, and thou shalt have treasure in heaven: and come, follow me.
23 And when he heard this, he was very sorrowful: for he was very rich.
24 And when Jesus saw that he was very sorrowful, he said, How hardly shall they that have riches enter into the kingdom of God!
25 For it is easier for a camel to go through a needle's eye, than for a rich man to enter into the kingdom of God.
26 And they that heard *it* said, Who then can be saved?
27 And he said, The things which are impossible with men are possible with God.
28 Then Peter said, Lo, we have left all, and followed thee.
29 And he said unto them, Verily I say unto you, There is no man that hath left house, or parents, or brethren, or wife, or children, for the kingdom of God's sake,
30 Who shall not receive manifold more in this present time, and in the world to come life everlasting.

◆◆◆◆◆◆

◀ **Memory Selection**
Luke 18:17

◀ **Devotional Reading**
Matthew 19:13-30

◀ **Background Scripture**
Luke 18:15-30

◀ **Printed Scripture**
Luke 18:15-30

WHO CAN BE SAVED?

Teacher's Target

Children, riches, kingdom of God, one thing lacking, camels and needles' eyes; Jesus' speech was peppered with such metaphors and cryptic comments so full of meaning. Have the class define each of these thoughts in their own words. Let them state what they believe the "one thing lacking" might be.

Remember that the Kingdom of God is upside down. That is to say, for example, that there are riches in the Kingdom of God, but they are not the riches the world seeks. Diamonds, gold, silver, property, land, houses, livestock, merchandise, factories, oil wells--these are worldly riches. What do the riches of the Kingdom of God look like?

When Jesus tells us to be like children, does He want us not to grow up? Is there a difference between childlikeness and childishness? Explain.

Lesson Introduction

Jesus' disciples were much of this world. He often wondered how long it would be before they caught on to what He was really about. Here their worldly thinking showed itself. To them, Jesus was an important rabbi. He didn't have time for little children who had no power. They could do nothing to further Jesus' fame or bring in the great Kingdom. The return of the golden age of David was the people's dream. Once again splendor and grandeur would be restored by Jesus.

Jesus flipped everything topsy turvy. Children were important. Keeping all the commandments wasn't enough! Maybe not even important at all! Rich men, thought to be blessed, might not get into heaven. What kind of Kingdom was Jesus talking about? Who can be saved? Who will want to be in such a Kingdom?

Teaching Outline

I. The Children: Luke 18:15-17
   A. Rebuke: 15
   B. Reception: 16
   C. Likeness: 17
II. A Ruler: Luke 18-18-23
   A. The Question: 18
   B. The Answer: 19-22
   C. The Response: 23
III. The Kingdom: Luke 18:24-30
   A. Camels and Needles: 24-25
   B. The Impossible Possible: 26-27
   C. Kingdom Riches: 28-30

Daily Bible Readings

Mon. Praising the Steward's Prudence
Luke 16:1-9
Tue. Be Worthy of True Riches
Luke 16:10-15
Wed. Rich Man and Lazarus
Luke 16:19-31
Thurs. One Healed of Leprosy Thanks Jesus - *Luke 17:11-19*
Fri. Power of Persistent Prayer
Luke 18:1-8
Sat. Humility Better Than False Piety
Luke 18: 9-29
Sun. Basic Needs For Eternal Life
Luke 18:15-30

February 6, 1994

VERSE BY VERSE

I. The Children: Luke 18:15-17

A. Rebuke: 15

15. And they brought unto him also infants, that he would touch them: but when his disciples saw it, they rebuked them.

There was a double rebuke here. The disciples rebuked the parents for bothering their leader. He had bigger fish to fry than to mess with their small fries. Anybody should have been able to discern this.

Then Jesus rebuked the disciples for judging things by the world's standards. They were keeping points as to who was worthy and who was not worthy to be with Jesus. What Jesus said was that grace and acceptance was for the least, even losers. Those who could do nothing for Him but needed much from Him were the ones He came to save.

Grace was not easy to sell. In fact, Jesus could hardly give it away. Grace made everyone a loser, not a winner. Nobody wanted to stand in that line.

B. Reception: 16

16. But Jesus called them unto him, and said, Suffer little children to come unto me, and forbid them not: for of such is the kingdom of God.

In our generation with a rather romantic view of children and childhood (that is, that it is a wonderful and delightful state and not a nightmare of being a pygmy-size person looking at a world of kneecaps), we have a hard time understanding Jesus' point here. For most of history childhood has been seen as a condition to move out of as soon as possible. Such a powerless state was not to be desired. Children were little noticed and definitely not exalted. After all, they contributed nothing to their own support or to society.

What Jesus thought was important was very different. Jesus said, "If you are going to be my disciple you will have to admit your helplessness and need of God." Jesus did not come to save "successful" lives. He came to accept "unsuccessful" losers. This acceptance of children was an acted parable of grace.

C. Likeness: 17

17. Verily I say unto you, Whosoever shall not receive the kingdom of God as a little child shall in no wise enter therein.

Hearers shunned the truth of Jesus' teaching. All had sinned, come short, lost. The people held to works of morality. All manner of restrictions and self-improvement techniques were tried. Anything to cover the truth of their true state as losers.

Disciples, Pharisees and others wanted their own dark success rather than the light of revealing and redeeming grace. Jesus' message was: judgment had already fallen upon success images. Lose your life and you will save it.

II. A Ruler: Luke 18:18-23

A. A Question: 18

18. And a certain ruler asked him, saying, Good Master, what shall I do to inherit eternal life?

A walking success story appeared. A ruler who was rich and had kept all the commandments. He was our classic good guy.

Still he lacked something. "What shall I do to inherit eternal life?" He was thinking of a good deed he could do. That was the problem. He couldn't give up trying to win on his own terms.

B. The Answer: 19-22

19. And Jesus said unto him, Why callest thou me good? none is good, save one, that is, God.
20. Thou knowest the commandments, Do not commit adultery, Do not kill, Do not steal, Do not bear false witness, Honour thy father and thy mother.
21. And he said, All these have I kept from my youth up.
22. Now when Jesus heard these things, he said unto him, Yet lackest thou one thing: sell all that thou hast, and distribute unto the poor, and thou shalt have treasure in heaven: and come, follow me.

Jesus stopped him short with, "Nobody is good." Even Jesus' goodness looked to people like badness, so much so, that they had to get rid of Him. He made them sick.

"Give up the goodness search," Jesus said. "One thing is lacking. own your losing." Receive it from God as gift, but first, own your need of help."

How driven this one was by successful achievement: financial success, moral success, intellectual success, emotional success, popularity success, etc.

Jesus called for an acknowledgement of emptiness. Sawdust filling made from achievement would not nourish. Husks of the world would fill, and being filled felt better than empty. However, only grace could fill and nourish.

C. The Response: 23

23. And when he heard this, he was very sorrowful: for he was very rich.

The ruler was sorrowful. Giving up success was beyond him. It was his success! The sadness in Jesus arose from knowing the truth: that eventually all of the successes would be gone. Then the emptiness that could not be admitted would be very visible.

Jesus had emptied Himself (Phil. 2:5-11). He knew the cost. His trust in the Father had filled Him. He knew the gain: emptiness exchanged for nutrition. Knowing this, how sad to watch another walk away from it.

III. The Kingdom: Luke 18:24-30

A. Camels and Needles: 24-25

24. And when Jesus saw that he was very sorrowful, he said, How hardly shall they that have riches enter into the kingdom of God!
25. For it is easier for a camel to go through a needle's eye, than for a rich man to enter into the kingdom of God.

Jesus acted a parable with the children. He acted a second parable with the ruler. Still His disciples (like us) could not let go of the world's view of success. He gave them a hyperbole of camels and eyes of needles, or

224

he may have been referring to the fact that a fully loaded camel could not go through a particular passage in Jerusalem called the "Eye of the Needle." In either case, Jesus' point was clear. The great, the first, the successful, the proud and the rich were not what the Kingdom of God is about. The least, the last, the poor, the needy, the blind, the lame, the deaf, the dumb, the sick, the little, the dead--these were the heirs of the Kingdom of God.

Jesus was describing here, not prescribing. He was not prescribing the doom of some and the salvation of others. He was describing what it means to "let go" of everything except our lastness and lostness.

B. The Impossible Possible: 26-27

26. And they that heard it said, Who then can be saved?
27. And he said, The things which are impossible with men are possible with God.

The disciples got a glimpse of themselves on the success treadmill of the rat race. Like squirrels inside a cage, it went nowhere. Such truth prompted a question: "Who then can be saved?"

They saw the impossibility of riches or morality to save. They saw that they had been willing to buy anything but grace. That would mean giving up power.

Jesus took power to its death on the cross by giving up power. By His action, what was and is impossible with man became possible with God. Grace, the free gift of God's love that cost the death of His Son on the cross, was made possible for all, even the rich, the first, the winners, the proud, the successful. That is the truth. The question: Will they let go and accept His grace?

C. Kingdom Riches: 28-30

28. Then Peter said, Lo, we have left all, and followed thee.
29. And he said unto them, Verily I say unto you, There is no man that hath left house, or parents, or brethren, or wife, or children, for the kingdom of God's sake,
30. Who shall not receive manifold more in this present time, and in the world to come life everlasting.

The disciples were slow on the uptake. Now, Peter got a hint of the truth. "Lo, we have left all (success as fishermen, family men, upstanding citizens, civic leaders, religious leaders) and followed you." He couldn't hold this course but for now he saw it. The Holy Spirit would bring it to his remembrance after the resurrection.

Jesus responded by saying, "You've got it." No one who leaves house, parents, brethren, wife, children for the kingdom of God's sake will fail to receive manifold riches now and in the world to come. The principle is that grace works only by loss.

In the parallel passage in Mark 10:29-31, Jesus states that we will be blessed in this age while also experiencing persecution. God will not save us from this world's persecutions, but He will save us in them and through them.

Evangelistic Emphasis

"Who then can be saved?" ask the disciples of Jesus. The question cries out for an answer. First, however, we must look at the circumstances giving rise to the question. Jesus has just announced that camels can go through the eyes of needles easier than rich folks can enter into heaven.

The obvious overstatement involving camels and needles leaves the disciples feeling despondent. The criteria for salvation seem beyond their reach. While some commentators enjoy building a case for Jesus' supposed great sense of humor out of this story, I think there is a far more serious purpose here.

Entry into the Kingdom of heaven is impossible for anyone who will not put God first. The rich ruler put his riches first and therefore could not enter into eternal life. Money, fame, success, prestige, status and a whole host of other illusions can make salvation impossible. A camel going through the eye of a needle is more likely.

The good news is that Jesus gives the disciples a magnanimous answer. "The things which are impossible with men are possible with God." The wooing, loving Spirit of God can cause a person to give up riches and other priorities.

◆◆◆◆◆◆

Memory Selection

Whoever does not receive the kingdom of God like a child shall not enter it. *Luke 18:17*

The Kingdom of God is like a child, Jesus says. How could we have missed this truth? We should never overlook the little ones. Our Christian theology is rooted in the birth of a child. Remember the promise of Isaiah that a shoot would come forth from the chopped-down, left-for-dead Jesse stump? To speak of the Kingdom of God is to speak of children.

To become as a child means being open to all of life. The child possesses such creativity, such inquisitiveness, such wonder. These are the qualities Jesus seeks. Note that He insists on childlikeness, not childishness. The Church is often better known for the latter, much to our loss.

To become as a child means seeing each new day, each new experience as if for the first time. By no means is it ever easy to keep open all the windows of the soul to the movement of God. Yet this is exactly what a child is capable of doing.

February 6, 1994

Weekday Problems

George was the richest man in his city. He was a faithful member of his church. In addition, he was a person who believed in tithing. Every month he gave ten percent of his net income to the church. Everyone knew that George was the largest contributor to the church in the whole community.

One Sunday, the pastor preached a sermon on the rich young ruler. George came home from that sermon mad at his pastor. He fumed to his wife, "That preacher thinks that having money is the work of the devil. I guess he'll only be happy if we are in the poor house."

George's pastor probably did not mean exactly what George thought he meant. Preachers and Christians often have difficulty understanding the proper relationship between faith and money.

*How could you help George and his pastor better understand the relationship between faith and money?
*What does the Bible teach about having money and material possessions?
*Is money evil? or is it the love of money that is evil?
*What is your relationship with your material goods?

♦♦♦♦♦♦

Smiles

The pastor was teaching a class of boys. His lesson was about like a sermon. The story was about Philip and the eunuch. Anxious to impress the boys with the joy of becoming a Christian, he asked, "Why did the eunuch go on his way rejoicing?"

One boy answered promptly, "Because Philip quit preaching."

After church one Sunday morning, a seven year old boy and his nine year old sister were arguing.

"Sibling rivalry?" asked an armchair psychiatrist.

"No," replied the mother, "sible war!"

This Lesson In Your Life

Plenty of people think that the good life will be found in wealth and success. Then at the close of life they are left with illusions empty of any reality. Having anticipated a great sense of fulfillment and meaning, they are now loaded with regrets.

Why do you suppose that people often find out about life's deepest meaning at the end rather than the beginning? Couldn't we live better lives if we discovered on the front side what life is all about, rather than having to find out on the back side?

These questions bother the edge of my consciousness as I read the pronouncement story about a rich man looking for the meaning of life. At least he is looking for life. That's how the story begins.

A certain man wants to inherit eternal life. His level of interest, however, may have been rather casual. Judging from Jesus' response, the rich man may have only wanted to engage in mild religious discussion. Perhaps he was just curious.

In any event, Jesus went ahead and told him everything he needed to know about life. That is the good news in our story. Even when we approach God casually, He treats us seriously. He knows how much we need eternal life, not only for assurance for the future, but for living today. He knows that we are mostly dissatisfied and are not really living joyfully. The good news of Jesus is that everlasting life is not confined to heaven or the hereafter. Everlasting life is a kind of life available here and now as a life in which believers receive power over all that afflicts them. Even when we are only mildly interested, Jesus holds out the offer of a meaningful life to all of us. We do not have to wait until the end to discover the meaning of life. We can know now.

Knowing how to have life is not the same, however, as having life. We have to make some arrangement to receive the gift of everlasting life. If this story has any value at all, it is there to reveal that if we are not prepared to rearrange our priorities, if we are not ready to make a full commitment to Jesus Christ, we will not receive everlasting life. The truth is we already know the meaning of life.

For 2,000 years we have been sitting before the gospel of Jesus. We know the way to eternal life. Knowing is not our problem. Waiting, postponing and treating everlasting life as a ticket we punch at death is our problem. Until then our lives are often cluttered with substitutes for everlasting life.

Even when we know about eternal life, even when we slowly realize that all of life's successes and pleasures are only side dishes and not the main course, we still hesitate before the offer of everlasting life. We hesitate to rearrange our priorities. The rich man could not bring himself to put God first over wealth. Having money is not wrong; money having us is what's wrong. Jesus asks the rich man to get rid of what was keeping him from life. He asks the same of us. Put God first and all other matters second.

That's not a bad place to start in making a life. Take whatever is first and most important in your life and replace it with devotion to Jesus. This is the way to discover the meaning of life at the beginning of the journey instead of the end. Here is real life instead of a life of regrets.

The rich man walked away from life, reminding us that the decision to let God define what a successful life is for us is never an easy one. We can, however, choose to shape our lives according to God's definition of life. The people who do so will find meaning.

Seed Thoughts

1. How did the disciples react to the children being brought to Jesus?
They rebuked the parents for bothering Jesus.

2. Did Jesus approve of the disciples' action?
By no means. Jesus said, "Suffer little children to come unto me."

3. What does being a child have to do with entering the kingdom of God?
A child is open, honest, aware, trusting, all these qualities are essential in the kingdom.

4. What is the question of the rich ruler?
"What shall I do to inherit eternal life?"

5. When Jesus tells the ruler to keep the commandments, how does the young man respond?
He insists that he has always kept them.

(PLEASE TURN PAGE)

1. How did the disciples react to the children being brought to Jesus?

2. Did Jesus approve of the disciples' action?

3. What does being a child have to do with entering the kingdom of God?

4. What is the question of the rich ruler?

5. When Jesus tells the ruler to keep the commandments, how does the young man respond?

6. In what way does Jesus challenge the young ruler?

7. How does the rich ruler respond to Jesus' invitation?

8. If actions speak louder than words, what was the rich ruler saying with his actions?

9. What analogy does Jesus use about rich men?

10. Who then can be saved?

| (SEED THOUGHTS--Cont'd)

They rebuked the parents for bothering Jesus.

By no means. Jesus said, "Suffer little children to come unto me."

A child is open, honest, aware, trusting, all these qualities are essential in the kingdom.

"What shall I do to inherit eternal life?"

He insists that he has always kept them.

He tells him to get rid of his riches.

With regret and sorrow he turns away.

That his money was more important than eternal life.

It is easier for a camel to go through the eye of a needle than for a rich man to be saved.

With God all things are possible. Whosoever will may come.

6. **In what way does Jesus challenge the young ruler?**
He tells him to get rid of his riches.

7. **How does the rich ruler respond to Jesus' invitation?**
With regret and sorrow he turns away.

8. **If actions speak louder than words, what was the rich ruler saying with his actions?**
That his money was more important than eternal life.

9. **What analogy does Jesus use about rich men?**
It is easier for a camel to go through the eye of a needle than for a rich man to be saved.

10. **Who then can be saved?**
With God all things are possible. Whosoever will may come.

February 13, 1994

God's Patience and Justice

Luke 20:9-19

9 Then began he to speak to the people this parable; A certain man planted a vineyard, and let it forth to husbandmen, and went into a far country for a long time.
10 And at the season he sent a servant to the husbandmen, that they should give him fruit of the vineyard: but the husbandmen beat him, and sent *him* away empty.
11 And again he sent another servant: and they beat him also, and entreated *him* shamefully, and sent *him* away empty.
12 And again he sent a third: and they wounded him also, and cast *him* out.
13 Then said the lord of the vineyard, What shall I do? I will send my beloved son: it may be they will reverence *him* when they see him.
14 But when the husbandmen saw him, they reasoned among themselves, saying, This is the heir: come, let us kill him, that the inheritance may be ours.
15 So they cast him out of the vineyard, and killed *him*. What therefore shall the lord of the vineyard do unto them?
16 He shall come and destroy these husbandmen, and shall give the vineyard to others. And when they heard *it*, they said, God forbid.
17 And he beheld them, and said, What is this then that is written, THE STONE WHICH THE BUILDERS REJECTED, THE SAME IS BECOME THE HEAD OF THE CORNER?
18 Whosoever shall fall upon that stone shall be broken; but on whomsoever it shall fall, it will grind him to powder.
19 And the chief priests and the scribes the same hour sought to lay hands on him; and they feared the people: for they perceived that he had spoken this parable against them.

◆◆◆◆◆◆

◀ **Memory Selection**
Luke 20:17

◀ **Devotional Reading**
Matthew 21:23-27, 38-46

◀ **Background Scripture**
Luke 20:1-19

◀ **Printed Scripture**
Luke 20:9-19

Teacher's Target

In this parable Jesus addressed Israel's disregard toward God and His prophets. Like God, the owner of the vineyard showed great patience. He wanted to work with the husbandmen. Finally the husbandmen left him no choice but removal.

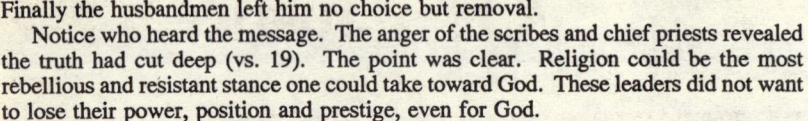

Notice who heard the message. The anger of the scribes and chief priests revealed the truth had cut deep (vs. 19). The point was clear. Religion could be the most rebellious and resistant stance one could take toward God. These leaders did not want to lose their power, position and prestige, even for God.

What power in the family, church or community do you hold that would threaten your allegiance to God? What makes yielding our worldly values and positions to God so unappealing? Are prophets received any better in our day?

Lesson Introduction

Parables are powerful vehicles for communicating truth because they by-pass our defenses. The story catches us and the truth slips in before our wall of resistance goes up. Denial, pride, position, power, posturing, possessions, projection, manipulation, suppression and repression are ways we disguise our powerlessness and need of an authority (ultimately God).

In this parable, Jesus revealed the sham of humankind's false allegiance to God. Ironically, church people often fail to see themselves as sinners. Yet Jesus pointed to the religious as most resistant to God.

In the Old Testament, Israel was referred to as God's vineyard (Isa. 5:7). Interestingly, Israel was always called a wild vine and never a good vine. Israel continually resisted God's authority.

Teaching Outline

I. The Parable: Luke 20:9-16
   A. The Husbandmen and Servants: 9-12
   B. The Husbandmen and the Son: 13-15
   C. The Owner's Response: 16
II. The Teaching: Luke 20:17-18
   A. The Scripture Quoted: 17
   B. The Result of Rejection: 18
III. The Reaction: Luke 20:19
   A. Chief Priests and Scribes: 19
   B. Their Anger: 19
   C. Their Fear: 19

Daily Bible Readings

Mon. An Argument About Authority
Luke 20:1-8
Tue. Parable of the Vineyard
Luke 20:9-18
Wed. Caesar's Tribute and God's
Luke 20:19-26
Thurs. God of the Living, Not the Dead - *Luke 20:27-38*
Fri. Beware of False Piety
Luke 20:39-47
Sat. Renewed in Spirit and Mind
Ephesians 4:22-32
Sun. Imitate God by Walking in Love
Ephesians 5:1-10

VERSE BY VERSE

I. The Parable: Luke 20:9-16

A. The Husbandmen and Servants: 9-12

9. Then began he to speak to the people this parable; A certain man planted a vineyard, and let it forth to husbandmen, and went into a far country for a long time.
10. And at the season he sent a servant to the husbandmen, that they should give him fruit of the vineyard: but the husbandmen beat him, and sent *him* away empty.
11. And again he sent another servant: and they beat him also, and entreated him shamefully, and sent *him* away empty.
12. And again he sent a third: and they wounded him also, and cast *him* out.

Jesus' parable was quite clear. Israel was the vineyard. The husbandmen were the religious leaders of Israel. The servants who were sent to check on the vineyard were prophets. The son was the Messiah, Jesus.

In Luke 20:1-8 Jesus' authority had been challenged by the religious leaders. Here in an indirect way He answered their questioning. Jesus revealed their true attitude toward God and their desire to kill Jesus Himself.

The owner continually sent out servants at the time of harvest. He was patient with the husbandmen's refusal to acknowledge his ownership. The husbandmen's lack of respect for the owner was reflected in their treatment of his messengers.

B. The Husbandmen and the Son: 13-15

13. Then said the lord of the vineyard What shall I do? I will send my beloved son: it may be they will reverence *him* when they see him.
14. But when the husbandmen saw him, they reasoned among themselves, saying, This is the heir: come, let us kill him, that the inheritance may be ours.
15. So they cast him out of the vineyard, and killed *him* What therefore shall the lord of the vineyard do unto them?

Finally, in a last attempt to make peace with the husbandmen, the owner sent his son. At this point the parable took a turn. The blind and obstinate stance of the religious leaders was exposed. Jesus wanted them to see the folly of their rejection of God's authority, generosity and patience.

Jesus knew that the authorities were no different from the authorities in former days. The prophets and Jesus were a dangerous nuisance to the plans and power of the religious leaders.

The absurdity of the leaders was reflected in the parable by the husbandmen's reasoning that if they killed the son they would inherit the vineyard. What owner would respond in this way to the loss of his son?

Did the husbandmen believe the owner was so distant they could make their profit and escape before retribution could come?

C. The Owner's Response: 16

16. He shall come and destroy these husbandmen, and shall give the vineyard to others. And when they heard *it*, they said, God forbid.

The authorities expected a Messiah like themselves, one who would use the means they favored: power, fame, money and law. Jesus was a paradoxical pretender in their eyes. Love, grace, mercy and peace were not their style. A retributive, violent Messiah who would once again put Israel on the top would have been acceptable.

The only vindicating judgement that would come would not be upon the outsiders. It was to come upon the leaders themselves! The basis of the judgment would be about their stewardship of the owner's affairs. "Did you tend to the harvest and manage my affairs well?" was the owner's concern.

Jesus asked his hearers what they thought the owner would do when he came. Then He said, "He shall come and destroy these husbandmen, and shall give the vineyard to others." What others? The poor, the needy, the weak, the sick, the lame, the deaf, the dumb, the blind, the possessed. The stewardship of the mystery of salvation would be taken from those who thought they controlled it. The ones the authorities believed had no part would receive it. What a reversal!

II. The Teaching: Luke 20:17-18

A. The Scripture Quoted: 17

17. And he beheld them, and said, What is this then that is written, THE STONE WHICH THE BUILDERS REJECTED, THE SAME IS BECOME THE HEAD OF THE CORNER?

Jesus quoted to them the passage in Psalm 118:22-23. He pressed home the point that all who trusted in the One sent by God would stand approved by God. The only thing necessary was trust (faith). Jesus' offer was to all, even the husbandmen. They too could be reconciled but they disqualified themselves by refusing to accept the authority and power of a loving God. The justice of God was manifest by allowing the people to choose their own fate.

B. The Result of Rejection: 18

18. Whosoever shall fall upon that stone shall be broken; but on whomsoever it shall fall, it will grind him to powder.

The cornerstone of their salvation was Jesus in their midst, truth in human form. He offered peace and acceptance to all. To refuse the offer would be to be broken by the very stone they rejected.

No work or attitude could evoke God's acceptance. Such acceptance issued from God's generous nature. The religious accountants were keeping score of merits and demerits. They would have justice their way on their terms. Jesus said their way was no way at all. All were lost and all would be offered salvation on the same grounds: trust in God.

Paul declared that Jesus Christ would be a stumbling block to the Jews and foolishness to the Greeks (1 Cor. 1:23). Here the chief priests and scribes tripped over the cornerstone. Their irrelevant rule-making and score-keeping was shown to be of no substance. Trust (faith) was full of substance and would survive all trials and attacks.

III. The Reaction: Luke 20:19

A. Chief Priests and Scribes: 19

19. And the chief priests and the scribes the same hour sought to lay hands on him; and they feared the people: for they perceived that he had spoken this parable against them.

Chief priests were prominent priests. Often they were relatives of the high priests or priests of special ability in interpreting the Law. Some had special political influence. The scribes were professional interpreters of the Law. They emphasized the traditions of Judaism. Many of the scribes were Pharisees. Both chief priests and scribes were committed to a worldly view of judgement based upon works rather than faith. The world of self-justification believed God was more impressed with good behavior than simple trust. Such a position made God a threat not a friend. Free salvation was alien to them. They did not want grace. They wanted law. Paul later noted that many Christians became just as legalistic.

B. Their Anger: 19

19. And the chief priests and the scribes the same hour sought to lay hands on him; and they feared the people: for they perceived that he had spoken this parable against them.

Self-justification was the criterion by which the religious leaders lived. They could not stand the outsiders in their presence. Surely God could not deem such people worthy of His presence. Jesus' teaching knocked the props from under their teaching concerning divine retribution. Jesus said faith alone mattered. There would be no scorekeeping on God's part. God's grace was sufficient.

The leaders were desperate to stop the power that would treat all equally. Such power would expose their sham and reveal their ungodliness. They would be placed alongside the riff raff of the day. For God to want only trust produced rage in them.

C. Their Fear: 19

19. And the chief priests and the scribes the same hour sought to lay hands on him; and they feared the people: for they perceived that he had spoken this parable against them.

What stopped them from carrying out their desire to destroy Jesus on the spot? It was the fear of losing their reputation with the people. They would do anything to rid themselves of this annoying presence, but not with people around to see their deed and to condemn them. Also, to cause such a public upheaval would bring the Roman authorities down on them. This would jeopardize their political alliances with the secular power.

Fear of people and fear of the government prevented their action. They would have to get them on their side. Then they could act. When they did, they crucified Jesus.

Evangelistic Emphasis

Luke's evangelistic message comes across in bold colors in the parable of the wicked servants. In one succinct story from Jesus a microcosm of human response to God is presented.

The theme, prevalent in Jesus' preaching, is that of an absentee landowner leaving his property in the care of a group of tenants. Left alone, with no supervision, man tends to claim ownership of the whole universe. The illusion of independence takes over and drives people to a giddy feeling of being able to live without God.

God, however, is not content to leave man to his illusions. Servants are sent to hold the tenants responsible. There is an expected level of stewardship required. In keeping with our history, the tenants ignore the servants and mistreat them.

Then, the landlord decides to send his own son. Having attempted to get across the message through others, the owner now allows the son to undertake the journey. Instead of respecting the son, the greedy tenants see their opportunity to take over the whole operation. They kill the son. But they are not in the clear. Accountability remains. Whatever illusions we embrace, accountability always remains.

♦♦♦♦♦♦

Memory Selection

The very stone which the builders rejected has become the head of the corner. *Luke 20:17*

The memory verse about the rejected stone is from Psalm 118:22-23, and was a favorite text among early Christians. Luke uses the verse once again in Acts 4:11, in the sermon of Peter before the high priests, scribes and elders. Obviously the rejected stone symbolizes Jesus rejected and crucified, who becomes the risen Lord.

The cornerstone was crucial to the whole structure. While the experienced builders had rejected this particular stone, God chose it to be the head of the corner. God's choice of the marred stone is shown by raising Jesus from the dead. The resurrection then constitutes a new Israel. Those who rejected Jesus found themselves rejected by God. The chief priests and elders own choice ended in the same judgment being passed upon them, i.e., rejection.

February 13, 1994

Weekday Problems

Linda was crying when her husband, George, came home from work. He asked her what was wrong. She told him that her best friend, Jennifer, had said some hurtful things to her at lunch. Linda was not only hurt by Jennifer's remarks, she was also very mad.

George, without very much awareness of his wife's feelings, started lecturing her. "You know what the Bible says about forgiveness. We should forgive those who hurt us. You should call Jennifer right now and tell her she is forgiven." Linda can not believe what she is hearing. Her own husband is taking sides with Jennifer. Now she is really mad. She says nothing to George the rest of the evening.

Linda loves both Jennifer and George. With the passing of a little time and the healing of the hurts, she will forgive both of them. She is not, however, ready to forgive them right now.

*Do you believe that true forgiveness sometimes takes time and requires patience?
*In what ways has God demonstrated His patience in forgiving us?
*Does it do any good to forgive someone through clenched teeth?

♦♦♦♦♦♦

Sparkles

A disciple asked his teacher, "What is love?"
The teacher responded, "The total absence of fear."
Then the disciple asked, "What is it we fear?"
"Love," said the teacher.

On another occasion the disciple observed the teacher being very gracious to university and seminary professors. However, the teacher would never respond to their questions or be drawn into their theological speculations.

The disciple asked his teacher about this behavior. The teacher replied, "Can one talk about the ocean to a frog in a well--or about the divine to people who are restricted by their concepts?"

This Lesson In Your LIfe

Servants or owners? Is this not the perennial conflict in our souls? Confronted by what appears to be the absence of God, we blindly assume everything now belongs to us. The entire focus of the biblical message, that we are servants, gets trampled in the rush to claim everything for ourselves. Perhaps we suffer amnesia. We have forgotten that we are not our own and we are not the owners. No one is self-made. All are indebted to others.

Somehow the image of faithful, responsible servanthood has to be recovered. The way to the Kingdom of God is not grasping for our independence but accepting our dependence. We are always servants, never owners in the Kingdom.

The tenants in our story forgot that the land was not theirs. They blocked out the reality that they worked on somebody else's property. Even in the church we have trouble with ownership and control issues. If our attorney did a title search, the exhaustive process would end at last with these words, not recorded in the local courthouse deed book, but in the Book of books: "In the beginning God created the heavens and the earth...." Those words make up the title to the universe. At our best we have always known that the earth is the Lord's. When, however, we suffer from spiritual amnesia, we start thinking we are the owners.

For example, listen to Church members talk about the Church. What do you hear but people who talk and act as if they own the Church. The Church belongs to Jesus Christ. He is the head of the Church. No amount of posturing on our part can change the title: The Church of Jesus Christ. We are not our own. Remember? We have been bought with a price. Like slaves we work on somebody else's property. There are no rights here but only privileges and responsibilities.

As servants we work for someone else. No wonder the Church falters in our time. In our haste to claim property and goods for ourselves, we've forgotten the One we're working to please. Our servant identity has been misplaced. If we live in a "What can the Church do for us?" world, then we have certainly forgotten that we exist to minister to the needs of others. In fact, like the wicked tenants, we have forfeited our place on the property. Faith in God is not a matter of watching but a matter of working. We are not critics or customers; we are servants of God. Do we come to church as a passive audience or as actors? Are we spectators or participants? So what does God say to us? God says, "Serve! Serve the church: Serve the world!"

If we are going to follow after Jesus, service will be our focus. Remember He is the one who came to serve, not to be served. Jesus is our model. The servant-leader model is everywhere in Scripture. From the portrait of the wounded doctor in Isaiah to Jesus washing the feet of His disciples, the model is always one of service. "Let this mind be in you, which was also in Christ Jesus: Who, being in the form of God, thought it not robbery to be equal with God: but made himself of no reputation and took upon him the form of a servant..." We are His servants.

Seed Thoughts

1. Why did the priests and scribes question Jesus?
They hoped to trap Him in His words and thus have Him killed.

2. Why were the priests and scribes afraid to answer the question about John the Baptist?
Either way they would look bad.

3. What did Jesus do when the priests and scribes refused to answer His question?
He refused to tell them the nature of His authority.

4. In the parable what happened to the servant who came to collect the rent?
The dishonest husbandmen beat the servant and sent him away empty.

5. After repeated efforts to get the husbandmen to pay the rent, what final action did the landlord take?
He sent his own son to collect the payment.

(PLEASE TURN PAGE)

---

1. Why did the priests and scribes question Jesus?

2. Why were the priests and scribes afraid to answer the question about John the Baptist?

3. What did Jesus do when the priests and scribes refused to answer His question?

4. In the parable what happened to the servant who came to collect the rent?

5. After repeated efforts to get the husbandmen to pay the rent, what final action did the landlord take?

6. Did the husbandmen have respect for the son?

7. What is the major implication of the parable?

8. How did the chief priests and scribes react to Jesus' parable?

9. What was the strategy of the chief priests?

10. To what does Jesus compare Himself in verse 17?

They hoped to trap Him in His words and thus have Him killed.

Either way they would look bad.

He refused to tell them the nature of His authority.

The dishonest husbandmen beat the servant and sent him away empty.

He sent his own son to collect the payment.

No. They killed the son of the landlord.

The servants represent the prophets, and the son represents Jesus. The wicked husbandmen are the Jewish religious leaders.

They conspired to have Him put to death.

They sent out spies and tried to trap Jesus.

To the stone which the builders rejected.

(SEED THOUGHTS--Cont'd)

6. Did the husbandmen have respect for the son?
No. They killed the son of the landlord.

7. What is the major implication of the parable?
The servants represent the prophets, and the son represents Jesus. The wicked husbandmen are the Jewish religious leaders.

8. How did the chief priests and scribes react to Jesus' parable?
They conspired to have Him put to death.

9. What was the strategy of the chief priests?
They sent out spies and tried to trap Jesus.

10. To what does Jesus compare Himself in verse 17?
To the stone which the builders rejected.

February 20, 1994

One Who Serves

Luke 22:14-30

14 And when the hour was come, he sat down, and the twelve apostles with him.
15 And he said to them, With desire I have desired to eat this passover with you before I suffer.
16 For I say unto you, I will not any more eat thereof, until it be fulfilled in the kingdom of God.
17 And he took the cup, and gave thanks, and said, Take this, and divide *it* among yourselves:
18 For I say unto you, I will not drink of the fruit of the vine, until the kingdom of God shall come.
19 And he took bread, and gave thanks, and brake *it,* and gave unto them, saying, This is my body which is given for you: this do in remembrance of me.
20 Likewise also the cup after supper, saying, This cup *is* the new testament in my blood, which is shed for you.
21 But, behold, the hand of him that betrayeth me is with me on the table.
22 And truly the Son of man goeth, as it was determined: but woe unto that man by whom he is betrayed!
23 And they began to enquire among themselves, which of them it was that should do this thing.
24 And there was also a strife among them, which of them should be accounted the greatest.
25 And he said unto them, The kings of the Gentiles exercise lordship over them; and they that exercise authority upon them are called benefactors.
26 But ye *shall* not *be* so: but he that is greatest among you, let him be as the younger, and he that is chief, as he that doth serve.
27 For whether *is* greater, he that sitteth at meat, or he that serveth? *is* not he that sitteth at meat? but I am among you as he that serveth.
28 Ye are they which have continued with me in my temptations.
29 And I appoint unto you a kingdom, as my Father hath appointed unto me;
30 That ye may eat and drink at my table in my kingdom, and sit on thrones judging the twelve tribes of Israel.

◆◆◆◆◆◆

◀ **Memory Selection**
Luke 22:26

◀ **Devotional Reading**
Mark 14:1-2, 10-25, 42-45

◀ **Background Scripture**
Luke 22:1-30

◀ **Printed Scripture**
Luke 22:14-30

ONE WHO SERVES

Teacher's Target

Success is a big issue in our culture. Society's definition and God's are quite different. Jesus said it is so different one cannot serve God and mammon. He will love one and hate the other, He said. Those are strong words. Most of us struggle with how to fulfill this truth in our lives.

Paul said it in a slightly different way. Live in the world but be not of the world. This is not a deed done once and forgotten. It is a part of taking up our cross daily.

Some questions that arise from this are: What is the meaning of power in our lives? How do we use power? What is really useful in this world for the Kingdom of God? How did Jesus define power by His words and actions? What kind of power is it to die on a cross? How can we appropriate Kingdom of God power? Is serving better than being served? Can confrontation be serving?

Lesson Introduction

That last meal must have been something. Jesus reinterpreted ancient symbols and rituals of the Passover meal in terms of Himself. He even talked about betrayal of His leadership and authority. Already His disciples' heads were reeling. Then He defined greatness, not in terms of His sitting at the head of the table, but in terms of serving at the table!

In our fleshliness, we yearn to be seated at the highest place of honor. Jesus said to take the lower seat lest we be embarrassed when the master of the banquet calls another to the place of honor and asks us to move.

Such "continuing with Christ" in His temptation is not without its reward now and hereafter. Now we can live in love and joy and peace for we are forgiven. Hereafter we will eat and drink at the heavenly table with Jesus.

Teaching Outline

I. The Meal: Luke 22:14-20
   A. Desire and Promise: 14-16
   B. The Cup: 17-18, 20
   C. The Bread: 19
II. The Betrayal: Luke 22:21-23
   A. The Pronouncement: 21
   B. The Warning: 22
   C. The Wondering: 23
III. True Greatness: Luke 22:24-30
   A. The Quarrel: 24
   B. The Contrast: 25-27
   C. The Benefit: 28-30

Daily Bible Readings

Mon. The Widow's Gift
Luke 21:1-5
Tue. Signs of the End
Luke 21:10-24
Wed. Peter and John Prepare the Passover - *Luke 22:1-8*
Thurs. Finding the Upper Room
Luke 22:9-13
Fri. Breaking Bread Together
Luke 22:14-20
Sat. Jesus Serves
Luke 22:21-27
Sun. Jesus Prays for Simon
Luke 22:28-34

VERSE BY VERSE

I. The Meal: Luke 22:14-20

A. Desire and Promise: 14-16

14. And when the hour was come, he sat down, and the twelve apostles with him.
15. And he said to them, With desire I have desired to eat this passover with you before I suffer.
16. For I say unto you, I will not any more eat thereof, until it be fulfilled in the kingdom of God.

Jesus wanted this final symbol of His self-giving love to be etched deeply into their souls. Jesus was about to suffer death. Time was precious. Much needed to be communicated. This occasion of His last meal with His disciples could not be wasted on the superfluous.

Jesus addressed the heart of the matter. He was going to His death. The disciples would be left alone. There would be no Jesus in the flesh to lead and protect them. The task once His would become theirs. This supper would call to remembrance that task every time they observed it. Also, as Jesus served them, so they were to be servants to each other. No one would be master over another. The message also contained a promise. They would see Jesus again and be with Him again in the Kingdom of God.

B. The Cup: 17-18, 20

17. And he took the cup, and gave thanks, and said, Take this, and divide *it* among Yourselves:
18. For I say unto you, I will not drink of the fruit of the vine, until the kingdom of God shall come.
20. Likewise also the cup after supper, saying, This cup *is* the new testament in my blood, which is shed for you.

Luke is the only one of the synoptic Gospels (synoptic means "to see alike") that records that there were two cups at the meal. Matthew and Mark record only one. At the traditional Passover meal wine was served four times. The statement about Jesus not drinking of the fruit of the vine again until the Kingdom of God shall come was spoken prior to the final cup. The statement about the cup symbolizing the new covenant in His blood was made at the time of the final cup.

Christian Communion services differ in various denominations in regard to the details. However, all Christians agree that the Lord's Supper commemorates Christ's death on the cross for the sins of the whole world. Also, there is agreement that it points to and celebrates the hope of Christ's coming in glory. To partake of this Supper is to express acceptance by faith in Christ's work on the cross in our behalf. Our faith and our hope are fed in this commemorative meal. Another aspect of the Lord's Supper is that our task as servants to one another is highlighted.

C. The Bread: 19

19. And he took bread, and gave thanks, and brake *it*, and gave unto them, saying, This is my body which is given for you: this do in remembrance of me.

The bread was broken and given just as Jesus' body was given up to physical suffering, spiritual agony and death in our behalf. He, like the paschal lamb at the time of the Exodus, would cover for our sin. The sacrifices under the Law of the Old Covenant were called "the bread of God" (Levit. 21:6, 8, 17). Jesus declared that He would become that bread (sacrifice) not only for Israel but for the whole world.

We are to feast upon the bread of life, Jesus. He will nourish and satisfy us. The Lord's Supper reminds us of our need and His sufficiency for our need.

II. The Betrayal: Luke 22:21-23

A. The Pronouncement: 21

21. But, behold, the hand of him that betrayeth me is with me on the table.

All the disciples' hands were with Jesus on the table (vs. 21) The eleven not plotting the betrayal were confused as to Jesus' meaning. However, the one for whom the word was intended heard it with clarity. All that was said by Jesus was not always intended for all. The word meant for each to hear would be heard. When heard, Jesus' word would either be heeded or rejected.

B. The Warning: 22

22. And truly the Son of man goeth, as it was determined: but woe unto that man by whom he is betrayed!

Nothing occurred that was outside the purview of God. Jesus made it clear, God was sovereign and the prime actor in this drama. No one would be taking His life. He would be laying it down for the world that sought to take it from Him.

Though this was so, Jesus warned that humankind was responsible for its actions. Woe to the man who would betray the son of man. Though God would allow and use this betrayal for His own ends, it did not lessen the sin nor the consequent suffering of the one who committed the betrayal. Judas could not live with his action. It troubled him to such a degree that he hanged himself.

C. The Wandering: 23

23. And they began to enquire among themselves, which of them it was that should do this thing.

The other eleven disciples wondered about themselves. Even a word not intended for them specifically caused them to search themselves. Such searching indicated a degree of sensitivity and a measure of willingness to practice self-examination. However, their dullness of understanding would be magnified in the next verse.

III. True Greatness: Luke 22:24-30

A. The Quarrel: 24

24. And there was also a strife among them, which of them should be accounted the greatest.

The disciples moved quickly from self-examination to self-exaltation. Jesus had just shared with them that He was going to suffer and one of them was going to betray Him. Still, the disciples could not shift their focus from themselves. Their response represented the self-centeredness of humankind. How easy it is to miss key moments because we are focused on our position, our standing or our image in the eyes of others.

B. The Contrast: 25-27

25. And he said unto them, The kings of the Gentiles exercise lordship over them; and they that exercise authority upon them are called benefactors.
26. But ye *shall* not *be* so: but he that is greatest among you, let him be as the younger, and he that is chief, as he that doth serve.
27. For whether *is* greater, he that sitteth at meat, or he that serveth? *is* not he that sitteth at meat? but I am among you as he that serveth.

When we look at the world's standards for deciding who is great we see a stark contrast to Jesus' teaching. World leaders battle for the top, clawing and scratching all the way. Jesus' followers were to lead by serving. He is a great leader who serves best, Jesus said.

There were many styles of leadership even among Jesus' disciples, but all must be practiced in service to the whole body. Personal advancement or recognition was not to be the priority consideration. Jesus called for a shepherd's heart, a servant's heart, among His disciples. This would be the mark of greatness. Worldly honors would wax and wane on the fickleness of humankind. With God there would be no thought of ascendancy. He would consistently honor service

and sacrifice. Jesus' life example brought the folly of worldly pomp and power into stark relief.

C. The Benefit! 28-30

28. Ye are they which have continued with me in my temptations.
29. And I appoint unto you a kingdom, as my Father hath appointed unto me;
30. That ye may eat and drink at my table in my kingdom, and sit on thrones judging the twelve tribes of Israel.

Jesus knew the trials His disciples had already been through and what trouble the future held for them. In the face of this and the illusion of grandeur and honor that the world would tempt them with, Jesus promised His followers a place at His table in His kingdom and an authority like His. This authority was one of love, mercy, peace and forgiveness.

David had once asked in Psalm 73 why the arrogant seemed to prosper. He came to himself and questioned how he could have ever thought that way. After all, God held David's hand, guided him and would not fail him.

Jesus was saying, "I know what it looks like sometimes. Those who reject me fare better than you. Also, I know the tribulation you bear. But don't be fooled. What is any of that in comparison to your position with God? What are worldly thrones when you are assured a place at the throne of the only true God?"

Evangelistic Emphasis

Listen to evangelistic appeals, and more often than not there is the implication that becoming a Christian is easy and simple. Evangelists often punctuate their invitations with the word "just." "Just trust in the Lord." "Just open your heart to Jesus."

Is there something wrong in these appeals? Well, perhaps a better suggestion is that something is missing. No matter how you read the lesson from St. Luke, the word "just" does not seem appropriate. Jesus is offering Himself for His disciples. The bread and the cup represent His body and His blood, which is given for them. "Just" implies there is not much to it. Well, there's everything to the sacrifice of Jesus.

Note that Jesus promises the kingdom to those who "have continued with me in my temptations." Following Jesus, while never boring, is certainly never easy. There is a certain tenacity and persistence required of those who will "sit on thrones judging the twelve tribes of Israel."

A full gospel of evangelism makes room not only for the appeal to trust in Jesus, but also for the reality of following Jesus. Salvation is a step followed by a walk; salvation is a moment followed by a life. Never try to make Christianity appear easy and simple. To do so not only cheapens the grace of God, and makes a mockery of the death of Jesus.

◆◆◆◆◆◆

Memory Selection

Let the greatest among you become as the youngest, and the leader as one who serves. *Luke 22:26*

In God's Kingdom only servants become leaders. What sounds contradictory in our status-crazed world is the norm for God's people. God's Kingdom is a servant world where all Christians model their lives after the perfect servant-leader, Jesus Christ. We may have to adjust our attitude in order to live in God's world.

Our normal world recognizes leaders according to a pecking order: the more people serving under you, the greater leader you are. Not so in God's world. Jesus turns the pyramid of human status upside down. Now the more people you are serving, the greater leader you are.

If we fail to comprehend our servant role, the church will flounder. We will become spectators rather than participants. We'll be an audience of religious critics instead of active servants in the ministry. We'll live in a "What can the church do for us?" instead of living to minister to the needs of others. We are servant-leaders.

February 20, 1994

Weekday Problems

For 40 years Albert has faithfully served a small church in an insignificant little town. When Albert died last month, the whole town showed up for his funeral. The minister handling the service had a time of testimony. He asked people whose lives had been changed, helped or otherwise touched by Albert to come forward and say a few words. The response was overwhelming. Albert would never have dreamed that he had helped so many people.

Yet, one by one they came forward to testify to Albert's love, patience and faithfulness to them in their hour of need. Albert, the poor, unknown, unheralded preacher of the small town lived and died without success in the world's eyes.

*Do you believe Albert was a success? In what sense?
*What is the difference between the world's success and success in the eyes of God? Are the two always incompatible with one another?
*What is your understanding of success?

♦♦♦♦♦♦

Sparkles

A prominent man of the world came to the teacher and put to him this question, "How would spirituality help a man of the world like me?"
The teacher answered, "It would help you have more."
"How can that be?" the worldly man asked.
"By teaching you to desire less," said the teacher.

ONE WHO SERVES

This Lesson In Your Life

Memories of meals play an important part in Jewish and Christian faith. Our religious past is full of stories of meals. Adam and Eve eating the forbidden meal open the human saga. The people of God at the marriage supper of the Lamb close out our narrative. In between we remember Abraham entertaining three angels, preparing a meal for them and expressing hospitality to them. We recall the Passover meal of the newly-liberated Hebrews. Memories of meals are written everywhere in the human experience.

As we reflect upon the Last Supper of Jesus with his disciples, there are three images of past meals, representing meanings of the Lord's Supper. All of these images are interrelated: the meal at Matthew's house, the Passover meal of Jesus and the disciples and the meal with Simon Peter by the sea.

The first image comes from a meal in the home of Levi, the tax-collector. Jesus, having called Levi as a follower, now accepts an invitation to be the guest of honor at a banquet in Levi's house. The meal, as one might expect, causes quite a stir in town. The scribes question, "Why does he eat with tax collectors and sinners?"

Why indeed? The image of the Savior eating with tax collectors and sinners often disturbs. Yet it is true to the Christian experience. Our God eats with sinners. The table of the Lord is not for the perfect. The invitation is for sinners saved by grace.

The Lord's Supper is for everyone like Matthew. Walt Whitman says, "Not 'til the sun excludes you do I exclude you." The Church should say as much. God knows there is no place for religious snobbery in the Church. Exclusiveness has no place among the people of Jesus. The truth is that none of us are good enough, but all of us are invited. The gospel song reads, "He invited me." One of Charles Wesley's early hymns puts well the dinner invitation. "Come, sinners, to the gospel feast; let every soul be Jesus' guest; ye need not one be left behind, for God hath bidden all mankind."

The second image comes from the last meal Jesus shares with all His disciples. Luke's account is filled with pathos as the conspiracy of Judas is told in bold starkness along side of the amazing love of Jesus. Spend some time lingering over the great desire of Jesus to share this last meal with His disciples. Perhaps we can learn much from Jesus wanting to spend His last moments in table fellowship rather than in preaching or teaching.

Jesus having dinner with His disciples on the eve of His death remains one of the most essential pictures in all of Christian experience. Jesus makes such a difference when He is present with His people. Remind your students that bread and wine are common, ordinary food and drink. Yet in the common and ordinary we experience the presence of Christ.

The third image comes from breakfast by the sea with Jesus and Simon Peter. Jesus, in the course of the meal, asks Peter if he loves with the gift-love of God. Peter responds that he loves with the love of a friend. Again Jesus poses the same question and receives the same answer. Finally, Jesus asks, "Do you love me as a friend?"

Here is the gospel of forgiveness. Jesus comes to where Simon is and offers him forgiveness. He offers us that same forgiveness. Whatever faith we possess will be enough. What love we offer, Jesus accepts. He takes us as we are, where we are, and helps us become all we can become.

Seed Thoughts

1. One of the disciples conspired with the chief priests. Who was he and what did he do?
   His name was Judas, and he betrayed Jesus to the chief priests.

2. Why did they want Judas to betray Jesus away from the crowds?
   The chief priests were afraid of the people.

3. What is Jesus doing while the conspiracy against Him unfolds?
   He is making plans to celebrate the Passover.

4. By what sign were the disciples to know they had found a house to celebrate the Passover?
   When they saw a man carrying a pitcher of water, that was to be their sign.

5. Where did the Last Supper take place?
   The Last Supper was held in a large upper room in the house of an unnamed man.

(PLEASE TURN PAGE)

---

1. One of the disciples conspired with the chief priests. Who was he and what did he do?

2. Why did they want Judas to betray Jesus away from the crowds?

3. What is Jesus doing while the conspiracy against Him unfolds?

4. By what sign were the disciples to know they had found a house to celebrate the Passover?

5. Where did the Last Supper take place?

6. Does Jesus know what is about to happen to Him?

7. What are the ordinary elements Jesus uses to celebrate His last meal with the disciples?

8. What are the disciples doing during the meal?

9. What does Jesus tell His disciples about greatness?

10. Who will inherit the kingdom with Jesus?

| *(SEED THOUGHTS--Cont'd)*

His name was Judas, and he betrayed Jesus to the chief priests.

The chief priests were afraid of the people.

He is making plans to celebrate the Passover.

When they saw a man carrying a pitcher of water, that was to be their sign.

The Last Supper was held in a large upper room in the house of an unnamed man.

Yes. His heart is heavy, but He is determined.

Jesus uses bread and wine.

They are wondering who the betrayer is, and arguing over which of them is the greatest.

The great ones are the ones who serve others.

Those who have continued with Him in temptations.

6. Does Jesus know what is about to happen to Him?
Yes. His heart is heavy, but He is determined.

7. What are the ordinary elements Jesus uses to celebrate His last meal with the disciples?
Jesus uses bread and wine.

8. What are the disciples doing during the meal?
They are wondering who the betrayer is, and arguing over which of them is the greatest.

9. What does Jesus tell His disciples about greatness?
The great ones are the ones who serve others.

10. Who will inherit the kingdom with Jesus?
Those who have continued with Him in temptations.

February 27, 1994

From Death to Life

Luke 23:32-46

32 And there were also two others, malefactors, led with him to be put to death.
33 And when they were come to the place, which is called Calvary, there they crucified him, and the malefactors, one on the right hand, and the other on the left.
34 Then said Jesus, Father, forgive them; for they know not what they do. And they parted his raiment, and cast lots.
35 And the people stood beholding. And the rulers also with them derided *him*, saying, He saved others; let him save himself, if he be Christ, the chosen of God.
36 And the soldiers also mocked him, coming to him, and offering him vinegar,
37 And saying, If thou be the king of the Jews, save thyself
38 And a superscription also was written over him in letters of Greek, and Latin, and Hebrew, THIS IS THE KING OF THE JEWS.
39 And one of the malefactors which were hanged railed on him, saying, If thou be Christ, save thyself and us.
40 But the other answering rebuked him, saying, Dost not thou fear God, seeing thou art in the same condemnation?
41 And we indeed justly; for we receive the due reward of our deeds: but this man hath done nothing amiss.
42 And he said unto Jesus, Lord, remember me when thou comest into thy kingdom.
43 And Jesus said unto him, Verily I say unto thee, Today shalt thou be with me in paradise.
44 And it was about the sixth hour, and there was a darkness over all the earth until the ninth hour.
45 And the sun was darkened, and the veil of the temple was rent in the midst.
46 And when Jesus had cried with a loud voice, he said, Father, INTO THY HANDS I COMMEND MY SPIRIT: and having said thus, he gave up the ghost.

Luke 24:33-34

33 And they rose up the same hour, and returned to Jerusalem, and found the eleven gathered together, and them that were with them,
34 Saying, The Lord is risen indeed, and hath appeared to Simon.

◆◆◆◆◆◆

◀ **Memory Selection**
Luke 24:34

◀ **Devotional Reading**
Mark 15:33-37

◀ **Background Scripture**
Luke 23:32-47, 24:13-35

◀ **Printed Scripture**
Luke 23:32-46; 24:33-34

FROM DEATH TO LIFE

Teacher's Target

We have all heard the saying, "It is darkest just before the dawn." This certainly applied to Jesus' crucifixion and resurrection. Jesus was alone between two criminals on the cross. Spectators gawked. Many mocked. one criminal scoffed; one asked for mercy. Jesus forgave all and death came. This was definitely dark, but it was not the end of the story.

On the third day Jesus arose. Dawn could not have been brighter. God had been faithful to His word and raised Jesus from the dead. Now life and not death would reign both here and hereafter.

Discuss times in life when class members have had dark days and nights in their lives. Ask how they got through them. Also ask them to describe their own "dawn" experience after the darkness.

Lesson Introduction

It is better to step into the risk than to stay with the familiar and die. Jesus knew this. Judaism was destroying people with burdens too heavy to bear. Jesus risked living in scorn of the consequences. This is the meaning of faith. Such living earned Him a cross. It also gained Him a resurrection. Many mocked on the day of His crucifixion. Since then millions have named Him Lord.

Our decisions have consequences. Also, if we turn back too soon we miss the blessing. Faith enables us to stay with our commitment. Jesus removed our debt on the cross. In the resurrection, He revealed that God is trustworthy and faithful. Taking risks and stepping into our fears--this is the way of life. Indecision, hesitation, stagnation, fear of failure, playing it safe--this is death.

Teaching Outline

I. The Setting: Luke 23:32-33
   A. Three on Crosses: 32
   B. The Place: 33
II. The Acts: Luke 23:34-43
   A. Jesus Forgives: 34
   B. People Mock: 35-38
   C. Criminal's Conversation: 39-43
III. The End: Luke 23:44-46; 24:33-34
   A. The Final Scene: 23:44-45
   B. The Curtain Closes: 23:46
   C. The Curtain Call: 24:33-34

Daily Bible Readings

Mon. Praying on the Mount of Olives
Luke 22:39-46
Tue. Judas Led a Crowd to Jesus
Luke 22:47-53
Wed. Peter Said, "I Don't Know Him!" - *Luke 22:54-62*
Thurs. "He Stirs Up the People"
Luke 23:1-12
Fri. Pilate Says, "Not Guilty!"
Luke 23:13-25
Sat. Three Men Die on Crosses
Luke 23:32-47
Sun. The Amazing Walk to Emmaus
Luke 24:13-35

February 27, 1994

VERSE BY VERSE

I. The Setting: Luke 23:32-33

A. Three On Crosses: 32

32. And there were also two others, malefactors, led with him to be put to death.

Three were to die on that day. one of them, however, was a substitute or a replacement. Earlier the crowd cried for Barrabas' release. A criminal on the streets was preferred to Jesus in their midst. Jesus was given the center cross as if He were the vilest of the offenders. What irony! He had the chief seat among criminals while His accusers had the chief seat in the synagogues.

How strange is the way of the world. Give us a crook, for we know how to live with them. Don't give us one who knows us yet loves us. He makes us know our helplessness and our need. The people always want Barrabas and not Christ. Barrabas is one of us, a sinner!

B. The Place: 33

33. And when they were come to the place, which is called Calvary, there they crucified him, and the malefactors, one on the right hand, and the other on the left.

Golgotha meant "the place of the skull." The skull was the ultimate symbol of death. Jesus was placed on this ignominious location of death as the site for His triumph of life over death. Ultimate Life, suffering death, was bearing away death forever.

II. The Acts: Luke 23:34-43

A. Jesus Forgives: 34

34. Then said Jesus, Father, forgive them; for they know not what they do. And they parted his raiment, and cast lots.

Bound with nails to a cross, jeered by people, mocked by soldiers, sarcastically labelled, Jesus conferred freedom on all. Soldiers who watched saw the truth (Matthew 27:54). Priests of Judaism were converted later (Acts 6:7). All manner of sinners would come to faith. This is why Jesus came. He would break the bondage of humankind to sin and death by taking sin and death upon Himself. "Father, forgive them." Sin blinded and still blinds humankind. The cross exposed the sin and healed it at the same time. So long as sin had its hold upon people they did not know what they were doing. The crucifiers were more bound than the ones crucified.

B. People Mock: 35-38

35. And the people stood beholding. And the rulers also with them derided him, saying, He saved others; let him save himself, if he be Christ, the chosen of God.

36. And the soldiers also mocked him, coming to him, and offering

him vinegar,

37. And saying, If thou be the king of the Jews, save thyself.

38. And a superscription also was written over him in letters of Greek, and Latin, and Hebrew, THIS IS THE KING OF THE JEWS.

The King was being stripped of His Kingdom, shamed and executed in public, or so it seemed. This was what was meant by the sign over Jesus' head on the cross. How the people gloated at seeing the fall of another, especially one who claimed power with God. If He was so powerful let Him show that it is so by saving Himself. In reality Jesus' Kingdom was beginning and the prince of this age was being defeated.

God's economy and God's justice are such that they confound the wisdom of the world. By dying Jesus gained and gave life. God is so righteous that His justice saves the ungodly while showing the sham and hypocrisy of the pious who think they have merit or privilege as a claim on God's righteousness.

C. Criminal's Conversation: 39-43

39. And one of the malefactors which were hanged railed on him, saying, If thou be Christ, save thyself and us.

40. But the other answering rebuked him, saying, dost not thou fear God, seeing thou art in the same condemnation?

41. And we indeed justly; for we receive the due reward of our deeds: but this man hath done nothing amiss.

42. And he said unto Jesus, Lord, remember me when thou comest into thy kingdom.

43. And Jesus said unto him, Verily I say unto thee, To day shalt thou be with me in paradise.

James and John had asked Jesus to allow them to sit on His right and His left in His Kingdom. Jesus had told them they didn't know what they asked (Mark 10:35-39). At the inaugural of the Kingdom condemned men were on either side of Him. This was a picture not to be forgotten, of the cost to sit with Jesus. Being a follower of Jesus would mean to be willing to suffer and die. This scene taught that the way of the cross leads home.

As they died, one criminal raged at Jesus. Trouble did not change this one's heart. It seemed only to irritate the wound within him. Pain did not purify.

The other malefactor rebuked his fellow sufferer. He asked for mercy from Jesus. That was all it took. Just a request was sufficient. Jesus responded with the assurance of a better seat with Him in paradise.

At the moment, this criminal had more faith than Jesus' disciples (Luke 24:21). To all appearances it appeared the Kingdom was over. This one saw through the appearance of things to the glory that was present in Jesus.

III. The End: Luke 23:44-46; 24:33-34

A. The Final Scene: 23:44-45

44. And it was about the sixth hour, and there was a darkness over all the earth until the ninth hour.

45. And the sun was darkened, and the veil of the temple was rent in the midst.

Extreme darkness fell upon the earth. Was this the sign of all creation mourning what the Son of God was suffering in its behalf? Here at what would be twelve o'clock noon, darkness had fallen. It continued for three hours.

The curtain in the temple was rent. This was the curtain that hung in front of the Holy of Holies. This rending of the curtain symbolized free and fearless access to the very presence of God for all. No longer would an earthly priest be needed to intercede. Now Jesus would be the one High Priest and all would have access to God through Him. Then He had called His followers to be priests to each other. As Luther said, "a priest at every elbow," a priesthood of believers.

Now there is no barrier between God and man. Nor is there a barrier between believers. There is neither slave nor free, rich nor poor, male nor female, Gentile nor Jew in Jesus. They are all one in Him.

B. The Curtain Closes: 23:46

46. And when Jesus had cried with a loud voice, he said, Father, INTO THY HANDS I COMMEND MY SPIRIT: and having said thus, he gave up the ghost.

Jesus' final word on the cross, the last of the seven statements He made while being crucified, was, "Father, into Thy hands I commend my spirit." With this statement Jesus declared His faith in the Father. Only the Father's word that He would raise Jesus on the third day was left to rely upon. That was enough. He would give Himself up to the sufficiency of the one true God that He had asked others to trust during His ministry. Jesus declared His own trust that the Father would be faithful to His word and not fail His son.

C. The Curtain Call: 24:33-34

33. And they rose up the same hour, and returned to Jerusalem, and found the eleven gathered together, and them that were with them,

34. Saying, The Lord is risen indeed, and hath appeared to Simon.

Just when it seemed all the stage of history had gone black and God's drama was over, Jesus made His curtain call. How sad, confused and disillusioned were His disciples. Then came the resurrection. A long section from Luke 24:13-35 describes Jesus' encounter with two disciples on the road to Emmaus.

In the two verses before us, the two disciples returned to Jerusalem and recounted to the eleven gathered together that Jesus had risen indeed. One of their items of good news was that Jesus had appeared to Peter. Paul also recorded in 1 Corinthians 15:5 that Jesus had appeared to Peter alone. There is no description of this meeting in any of the gospels. It is probable that Jesus showed a special concern for Peter. After his denial Peter felt totally unworthy. Also, Peter was to be the spokesman, the rock, for building the Church. He needed reassurance that he was still trusted for the task. This ministry he fulfilled in the first half of the book of Acts.

The point might well be that by appearing to Peter, Jesus revealed that He had come to those who felt themselves most unworthy, the ungodly. Upon Peter and others who knew their emptiness, Jesus would bestow His righteousness. He had risen indeed!

Evangelistic Emphasis

Is the word of the cross relevant to our world? This question has to be asked because critics are always demanding relevance of the Church. Worldly wisdom suggests that salvation can be found in psychotherapy, positive thinking, urban renewal or the sexual revolution. No wonder the story of a Jew crucified on a cross sounds strange and irrelevant.

People trying to hang on to the word of the cross are considered old-fashioned. Relevance is demanded. I ask, relevant to what? Relevant means to be related, to be appropriate, to be suitable. Before we write off St. Luke's story of the cross as unsuitable and inappropriate, a closer look is warranted.

The word of the cross is relevant to human need. Real problems are addressed and valid answers are given in the biblical, evangelistic message of the cross. The wisdom of the world is no match for the evangelism of the church. In the cross of Christ, God does for us what we cannot do for ourselves; He saves us. That is relevance. In other words, the cross is God's ultimate remedy. The cross is the power of God in a weak world. As evangelists we must not be ashamed to proclaim that message.

♦♦♦♦♦♦

Memory Selection

The Lord has risen indeed! *Luke 24:34*

Every Easter the church gathers around the empty tomb of Jesus. We hear again the most astounding words in all of history: "The Lord has risen indeed!" At least part of the reason for our Easter gathering is to regain our lost confidence. Those who have lost their sense of victory, those who have forgotten how to live joyfully, those who produce no evidence of the power of the gospel, can rediscover their confidence and faith during the days of Easter.

Carlyle Marney, after working with more than 8,000 laymen and ministers concluded that we are suffering from a loss of nerve, a loss of direction, erosion from culture, confusion of thought, exhaustion. "They have become shaken reeds, smoking lamps, earthen vessels, . . . spent arrows. They have lost heart. But they can be revived."

That is precisely the hope of the words of the memory verse. All of Scripture points us beyond the grave because the power of God resurrected Jesus from the dead. Despite the difficult times in which we live, we can have conquering confidence.

February 27, 1994

Weekday Problems

Three months ago, Jack's wife of sixty-five years died. During the time since her funeral, Jack has been lost in a fog of forgetfulness and despair. He has always been a good Christian. Yet now, when he seems most to need his faith, there is no external evidence that his faith is working.

He no longer comes to church, mostly because he forgets when Sunday comes. His voice is soft and lonely on those rare times when he speaks at all. He has lost the love of his life.

His pastor and fellow church members are doing everything they know to do. Jack seems to appreciate their visits and their prayers, but nothing changes. He just sits in the chair and stares out the window. At night he prays for the Lord to take him so he can join his wife. His grief goes deep because his love went so deep.

*How did you feel as you read about Jack's grief?

*Jack's faith is deeper than it appears, but don't we usually judge only on external appearances?

*In what ways could you be of help to Jack?

♦♦♦♦♦♦

Smiles

Mrs. Smith asked her Sunday school class to draw pictures of their favorite Bible stories. When Johnny finished, he showed his teacher the picture. Mrs. Smith saw that he had drawn an airplane with three people in the cockpit. "What is your picture about, Johnny?" she asked.

"The Flight Out of Egypt," Johnny responded.

"I see," Mrs. Smith said smiling. Then she pointed to two of the people pictured in the cockpit. "Who are they?" she asked.

"Mary and Joseph," Johnny said.

"And who is this one in the middle?" Mrs. Smith continued as she pointed to the person in the center of the cockpit.

Johnny looked at Mrs. Smith in disbelief, for he thought she should certainly know the answer to that question. Then he said confidently, "That's Pontius the Pilot!"

FROM DEATH TO LIFE

This Lesson In Your Life

Christianity depends on the most improbable event of all time--the resurrection of a dead man. We did not see it happen. No one did. We only know of resurrection by word of mouth. Still our whole religion comes down to the claim that in Christ Jesus we conquer death.

St. Luke tells us that the two disciples left Jerusalem and headed for Emmaus. Locating Emmaus has thus far proved to be an impossible task. No one knows where the biblical town was situated. Thus we have two disappointed disciples on the road to nowhere, the road to oblivion. They certainly do not believe in the resurrection of the dead; at least they do not yet believe.

The two disciples wear the reality of death as a deep scar in their psyche. We can understand. We live on gigantic burial mounds of past civilizations. Death haunts us like a pale rider following daily from a distance. Everywhere all humans live under the death penalty. As the disciples move toward Emmaus, their minds fill with the fact of death.

Perhaps if we could look back over our shoulders, back in time, the two disciples from Emmaus would come into our view. There see those two slump-shouldered, sad-faced men wandering aimlessly. The strain on their faces speaks of helplessness. We understand. Death crowds us as time rushes past. High tech medicine saves thousands of lives every year, but we are just kidding ourselves if we think medicine can stay the hand of death. We are helpless in the face of death. Like a silent terrorist, death holds the whole planet hostage. All the money in the world cannot stop the coming of death. The powerful and the weak, the rich and the poor all die. Ask the doctor or the preacher about our helplessness. They stare into the cold eyes of death more than others. They know better than all the rest the face of death. However you cut it, we, like the disciples moving toward Emmaus, are helpless.

Our only hope is the word of resurrection. That one word is all that stands between us and destruction. Resurrection tends to sound more like gossip than gospel. Yet Jesus explains to the disciples the meaning of the Scriptures. Resurrection belief, however, never comes easy, not even in the Church. The word of resurrection comes to those who are disappointed, overwhelmed and helpless. It is the only word we have, but what a word. Christ is risen!

Above the ruins of all our cemeteries strides One to whom all power is given. We have a living Lord and we can count on Him. Why? Because we have His Word.

In the presence and power of His Word, our hearts are strangely warmed. We realize that the living Christ is with us. We are talking the power of God! God alone rolls away the stone. Here is the good news that sweeps away our disappointment. The fear of death, the threat of death and the power of death are overthrown by the power of God.

Christ calls us back from Emmaus, the road to nowhere. His call, presented in His Word, is all we have to go on, but all we need. If we do not believe His Word, we have nothing. Notice that the disciples on the road to Emmaus received the Word and the bread from Jesus. The resurrection comes alive in the preaching of the Word and the celebration of communion.

Remember then the words of Jesus. Go on remembering and proclaiming the resurrection. The validity of the resurrection is the faithful proclamation of the Church.

Seed Thoughts

1. Who else was crucified with Jesus?
Two malefactors, whose crimes are not listed, were crucified with Jesus.

2. What is the name of the place where Jesus died?
The name of the place is Calvary.

3. According to Luke, what are Jesus' first words from the cross?
Jesus prays for His crucifiers to be forgiven.

4. What is the crowd doing during Jesus' prayer?
They are gambling over his clothing.

5. The people and the rulers are verbally abusing Jesus. What is their charge?
Jesus saved others but cannot save Himself.

(PLEASE TURN PAGE)

---

1. Who else was crucified with Jesus?

2. What is the name of the place where Jesus died?

3. According to Luke, what are Jesus' first words from the cross?

4. What is the crowd doing during Jesus' prayer?

5. The people and the rulers are verbally abusing Jesus. What is their charge?

6. What did the soldiers offer Jesus to drink?

7. What was the superscription written over Jesus?

8. Did both of the malefactors plead for mercy?

9. One of the malefactors asked for Jesus' help. What was his request?

10. What happened at Calvary during the sixth hour?

| (SEED THOUGHTS--Cont'd)

Two malefactors, whose crimes are not listed, were crucified with Jesus.

6. What did the soldiers offer Jesus to drink?
They offered Him vinegar.

The name of the place is Calvary.

7. What was the superscription written over Jesus?
In Greek, Latin, and Hebrew: "THIS IS THE KING OF THE JEWS."

Jesus prays for His crucifiers to be forgiven.

8. Did both of the malefactors plead for mercy?
No. One of them mocked Jesus.

They are gambling over his clothing.

9. One of the malefactors asked for Jesus' help. What was his request?
He asked Jesus to remember him in paradise.

Jesus saved others but cannot save Himself.

10. What happened at Calvary during the sixth hour?
The day turned to night and the veil of the temple was rent in the midst.

They offered Him vinegar.

In Greek, Latin, and Hebrew: "THIS IS THE KING OF THE JEWS."

No. One of them mocked Jesus.

He asked Jesus to remember him in paradise.

The day turned to night and the veil of the temple was rent in the midst.

March 6, 1994

The Power of God for Salvation

So for my part I am ready to preach the gospel to you... Romans 1:15

Romans 1:1, 3-17

1 Paul, a servant of Jesus Christ, called *to be* an apostle, separated unto the gospel of God.
3 Concerning his Son Jesus Christ our Lord, which was made of the seed of David according to the flesh;
4 And declared *to be* the Son of God with power, according to the spirit of holiness, by the resurrection from the dead:
5 By whom we have received grace and apostleship, for obedience to the faith among all nations, for his name:
6 Among whom are ye also the called of Jesus Christ:
7 To all that be in Rome, beloved of God, called *to be* saints: Grace to you and peace from God our Father, and the Lord Jesus Christ.
8 First, I thank my God through Jesus Christ for you all, that your faith is spoken of throughout the whole world.
9 For God is my witness, whom I serve with my spirit in the gospel of his Son, that without ceasing I make mention of you always in my prayers;
10 Making request, if by any means now at length I might have a prosperous journey by the will of God to come unto you.
11 For I long to see you, that I may impart unto you some spiritual gift, to the end ye may be established;
12 That is, that I may be comforted together with you by the mutual faith both of you and me.
13 Now I would not have you ignorant, brethren, that oftentimes I purposed to come unto you, (but was let hitherto,) that I might have some fruit among you also, even as among other Gentiles.
14 I am debtor both to the Greeks, and to the Barbarians; both to the wise, and to the unwise.
15 So, as much as in me is, I am ready to preach the gospel to you that are at Rome also.
16 For I am not ashamed of the gospel of Christ: for it is the power of God unto salvation to every one that believeth; to the Jew first, and also to the Greek.
17 For therein is the righteousness of God revealed from faith to faith: as it is written, The just shall live by faith.

◆◆◆◆◆◆

◀ **Memory Selection**
Romans 1:16

◀ **Devotional Reading**
Romans 1:18-25

◀ **Background Scripture**
Romans 1:1-17

◀ **Printed Scripture**
Romans 1:1, 3-17

THE POWER OF GOD FOR SALVATION

Teacher's Target

Paul declared that he had been separated out of his family culture to be a servant of Christ. How unfamiliar and often lonely his road must have been. In Jewish tradition when one became a Christian his family had a funeral for him and he was treated as if he were dead. His or her name was never spoken again in the family.

Paul longed for the comradeship of others who had placed their faith in Christ. He cherished them as new family.

In the face of all adversity Paul declared he was not ashamed of the gospel. He knew its power. Only Christ could have so revolutionized his life.

What has your faith in Christ cost you? Do you cherish your Christian brothers and sisters as family? When have you had to stand for Christ in the face of adversity and/or rejection?

Lesson Introduction

Paul had never been a slave. Now he "chained" himself to Christ. He renounced his position, his fame, his future in Judaism to be a slave to a peasant king from Galilee. To the world he appeared to be a fool. Once he had it all. Now Christ had him.

Only Christ was center stage for Paul now. He saw himself as chattel for the Master's use. He longed for fellowship with fellow Christians in Rome. They were precious to him and he defined his relationship to them as a peer relationship with only Christ exalted.

Paul was clear about where the power resided. It was the gospel that changed his affections and gave him life. The cross and resurrection of Christ, the finished work of God, provided salvation to Jew and Greek alike. Only in Christ was the righteousness of God revealed fully and finally.

Teaching Outline

I. An Introduction: Romans 1:1, 3-6
   A. The Person: 1
   B. The Message: 3-4
   C. The Results: 5-6
II. A Greeting: Romans 1:7-13
   A. A Blessing: 7
   B. A Thanksgiving: 8-9
   C. A Longing: 10-13
III. A Debt: Romans 1:14-17
   A. The Creditors: 14
   B. The Repayment: 15-16
   C. The Profit: 17

Daily Bible Readings

Mon. Jesus Christ: Truly Human, Truly God - *Romans 1:1-7*
Tue. Thanksgiving for the Romans' Faith - *Romans 1:8-12*
Wed. Through Faith the Righteous Shall Have Life - *Romans 1:13-17*
Thurs. God Loathes the Suppression of Truth - *Romans 1:18-23*
Fri. Suppression of Truth Dishonors Persons - *Romans 1:24-32*
Sat. Salvation Comes Only Through God - *Acts 4:5-13*
Sun. Are You Ready for Salvation *Romans 13:8-14*

March 6, 1994

VERSE BY VERSE

I. An Introduction: Romans 1:1, 3-6

A. The Person: 1

1. **Paul, a servant of Jesus Christ, called to be an apostle, separated unto the gospel of God.**

Paul counted servanthood to Christ as honor. What an upside down way of thinking. Slavery to Christ was the highest honor. Paul lorded nothing over the people, rather he saw himself as a steward in God's household. He would lead as his Lord Jesus Christ led.

He had authority as "one called out" or "one called for," an apostle. But, he served as one having no authority. The power of truth was his authority. This he served and shared.

Paul was not separated from the people. He was separated from former allegiances. Now he was a bond servant to Christ Jesus his Lord. Now his slavery was chosen. His obedience and complete dependence was upon his master. This one who once persecuted those who claimed the name of Jesus Christ had become a slave to Christ and servant to those he persecuted.

B. The Message: 3-4

3. **Concerning his Son Jesus Christ our Lord, which was made of the seed of David according to the flesh;**
4. **And declared to be the Son of God with power, according to the spirit of holiness, by the resurrection from the dead:**

God's own Son was Paul's Lord. God had promised He would send Him (Rom. 1:2). Jesus Christ was no alien to the Jewish heritage. He was of the seed of David. He was no pretender. His cross and resurrection validated His sonship to God. By the power of the Spirit of holiness, Jesus had been raised from the dead as the final undeniable sign and effectual power of His Sonship.

David had been given a promise concerning the Messiah. The Messiah would be a King of his seed with a Kingdom of great power established by God and not man (2 Sam. 7:12). Unlike the former kingdom of Israel, this one established through Christ would include Gentiles.

C. The Results: 5-6

5. **By whom we have received grace and apostleship, for obedience to the faith among all nations, for his name:**
6. **Among whom are ye also the called of Jesus Christ:**

The apostles would be a laughing stock in the world. They would lead a life of toil, hardship, trouble and hazard. Still Paul claimed this role as his honor. Because of the grace he had received, Paul desired to call all people everywhere to the obedience of faith. He knew that only here could persons find life more abundant.

Faith is obedience. That was Paul's message. Not works, not rules, not rituals, not rigorous bodily abuse, but faith alone in the finished work of Christ was counted as righteousness.

Not only the apostles but all believers were called out by God. Each had his or her own gift of grace and call to service. To be baptized into Christ was to be baptized into ministry.

II. A Greeting: Romans 1:7-12

A. A Blessing: 7

7. To all that be in Rome, beloved of God, called to be saints: Grace to you and peace from God our Father, and the Lord Jesus Christ.

Paul paid the Roman Christians a grand compliment. How deeply people needed to hear and claim what Paul called them, "Beloved of God, called to be saints." What a blessing! Believers are God's beloved children, heirs just like Christ to all His promises through Christ. In a world of rejection and hatred of Christ's followers, what a truth for the believers to hold on to and relish.

Each Christian, Paul said, was a saint. No special heroics were required. Simple faith was sufficient for one to be "set apart" for God's delight.

B. A Thanksgiving: 8-9

8. First, I thank my God through Jesus Christ for you all, that your faith is spoken of throughout the whole world.

9. For God is my witness, whom I serve with my spirit in the gospel of his Son, that without ceasing I make mention of you always in my prayers;

The Roman Christians' faith was spoken of all over the world. Though despised and persecuted, they were not insignificant. God through Paul let the people know that their faith had great importance and power. What was done in a corner of the world was being heralded around the world.

Paul was thankful for such a witness of faith. He prayed for them continually. He knew their peril and their need. He knew the evil one would not rest in his desire to devour them. He also knew God's faithfulness to sustain His people and to answer their prayers exceedingly beyond what they thought or asked.

C. A Longing: 10-13

10. Making request, if by any means now at length I might have a prosperous journey by the will of God to come unto you.

11. For I long to see you, that I may impart unto you some spiritual gift, to the end ye may be established;

12. That is, that I may be comforted together with you by the mutual faith both of you and me.

13. Now I would not have you ignorant, brethren, that oftentimes I purposed to come unto you, (but was let hitherto,) that I might have some fruit among you also, even as among other Gentiles.

Paul needed fellowship. He needed to be nourished and nurtured by the faith and life of others in Christ. He also knew he had something of spiritual value to share with his fellow believers. Paul hoped to experience mutual comfort in Rome (vs. 12). No dominance of position was in Paul's heart. A humble acknowledgement that God had entrusted him with truth was all he claimed. He also acknowledged that others had truth to share with him.

Paul knew he was not indispensable. He also knew God might have other plans than his. His hope, however, was to be allowed some time in Rome.

III. A Debt: Romans 1:14-17

A. The Creditors: 14

14. I am debtor both to the Greeks, and to the Barbarians; both to the wise, and to the unwise.

Even in the natural human sphere of things, Paul was a debtor. Many had contributed to his life. He had learned both from Jewish rabbis and Greek philosophers. He had been instructed and edified by Jewish peasants and Greek commoners. All had been his instructors.

Paul wanted to repay his debt. Now he had a gift to give that surpassed all gifts. He would endure any hardship, any trial or persecution to convey the message of salvation to all men everywhere.

Paul's debt was ultimately to Christ for his own salvation. The gift was not for him alone. He could repay his Master and his fellowmen in no better way than to introduce them to Christ.

B. The Repayment: 15-16

15. So, as much as in me is, I am ready to preach the gospel to you that are at Rome also.

16. For I am not ashamed of the gospel of Christ: for it is the power of God unto salvation to every one that believeth; to the Jew first, and also to the Greek.

How could a debt so enormous as Paul's conversion be repaid? What convinced Paul of the power of the gospel? The second question must be answered first.

Paul knew that if the gospel could transform his life it could have power with anyone. No one fought against the gospel any harder than Paul prior to his conversion. Now he was free from the bondage of sin, law and death. How could such a gift be withheld from anyone? Only this good news could impart to people what they truly needed. Only this gospel of grace could reconnect persons with their Creator and with one another in love.

C. The Profit: 17

17. For therein is the righteousness of God revealed from faith to faith: as it is written, The just shall live by faith.

Habakkuk 2:4 had declared that faith was the access to righteousness. Paul continually pointed his hearers to the reality that even in the Old Testament faith, not law, was the way to righteousness and life. This was made especially clear in the book of Galatians.

What was the profit of faith over law? Paul declared it was the righteousness of God. This could not be earned, only given by God. Grace bestowed righteousness. Faith acknowledged inability to save self and accepted God's work in Christ. By faith, Gentiles and Jews could become what the Jews never could be under the Law.

Evangelistic Emphasis

The gospel is bad news and good news. In Romans 5 Paul says there are times our lives when we are all helpless. The good news is that, even while we were helpless, Christ died for us. The doctor says the tumor is malignant. After surgery the report is, "We believe we got it all. No further treatment seems to be indicated." Everyone sighs with relief and there is a wonderful sense of joy and thanksgiving. The cure was only possible because the one who was ill was brave enough or desperate enough to admit the problem and seek help.

That's the way it is with the gospel. Many never know the joy of salvation because they will not endure the pain of honesty about their spiritual sickness. Some see their moral failures as merely a phase in their development, something like a childhood disease. The biblical faith says our problem is more serious; we are God's good creation spoiled and marred by our own pride. We are fallen from perfection. This realistic view of human nature and of our own failure is necessary before the gospel is good news. What a joy! The perfect God is no perfectionist. He loves and redeems all of us who will accept the bad news and the good news of the gospel.

◆◆◆◆◆◆

Memory Selection

For I am not ashamed of the gospel of Christ: for it is the power of God unto salvation to every one that believeth; to the Jew first, and also to the Greek. *Romans 1:16*

Paul was ashamed of Jesus the first time he heard of Him. He was ashamed that Israel could have produced such an embarrassment to the ancient faith. Everyone knew that Jesus of Nazareth never spent a day in seminary, never sat at the feet of the great teachers like Gamaliel. But the news on the streets was that thousands went out to the countryside or crowded the marketplace to hear Him teach. Worse still, He regularly criticized the Scribes and Pharisees. He called them hypocrites and whited sepulchres.

The young Saul of Tarsus was, no doubt, chagrined that a mere carpenter from the hill country could command so much attention and attract such a following. Most of all, he was scandalized by reports that this popular religious leader had ended on a criminal's cross! By the time he wrote the letter to the Romans, Paul was no longer ashamed of Christ and the word of His cross. That power which had turned his life right side up could revolutionize the world.

March 6, 1994

Weekday Problems

Martha tried every way possible to win Sue to the Lord. She expressed admiration for her appearance, her work and her view of life. She was the first one to Sue's apartment when her mother died of cancer. They talked into the small hours, and shared some of the most meaningful experiences and feelings of their lives.

When Martha's church had a special series of evangelistic meetings for singles she invited Sue to join her in attendance. The meetings were good. The theme was: "Christ, The Answer For Your Every Need." Specific problems discussed included: loneliness, professional ethics, relationships with one's parents, money management, dating and sexual morality, survival in a world designed for couples, etc.

The answer given for these real needs was the church: its programs, its fellowship, its Bible studies, its worship and its service to the community. Martha was disappointed with Sue's reaction. "All of that was nice," Sue said, "but why should I join your church any more than any other organization? Isn't it just people caring about people?"

*To what are we introducing those whom we would lead to the Lord?
*What was missing in the church's proclamation to Sue?

◆◆◆◆◆◆

Smiles

A noted clergyman was asked why the loud, shouting messages of his earlier days had given way to a more gentle, quieter, persuasive manner of speech.

"When I was young," he replied, "I thought it was the thunder that killed people, but as I grew older I discovered it was lightning. So I determined that in the future I would thunder less and lightnin' more!"

The rabbi finally decided he must talk to the richest member of his congregation about a problem, no matter how much it hurt or cost.

"Why," asked the rabbi, "do you fall asleep in the service right when I begin my message?"

The rich man answered, "Would I fall asleep if I didn't trust you?"

This Lesson In Your Life

We want our children to know many things. We want them to learn manners so they can negotiate life in our culture. They should have a basic understanding of American history, of mathematics, of English grammar and literature. They should learn to read the papers daily and keep up with what's going on in the world. We want them to learn their professions, to be good at what they choose to do.

Critical to their success is their education about human nature, we want them to understand people. They should learn that one must keep up professionally, it takes dedication to keep abreast. On a deeper level we want them to learn integrity, honesty and honor. There is so much to learn it takes a lifetime just to begin.

For Christians none of these kinds of learning takes first place. On the cross Jesus prayed, "Father, forgive them, for they know not what they do." This kind of ignorance is not cured by a night course at the university or in the college of hard knocks over a thirty-year career. It has to do with a relationship. Jeremiah the prophet spoke for the Lord to His wayward people. These are words we do well to ponder. "Thus says the Lord: Do not let the wise boast in their wisdom, do not let the mighty boast in their might, do not let the wealthy boast in their wealth; but let those who boast boast in this, that they understand and know me, that I am the Lord; I act with steadfast love, justice and righteousness in the earth, for in these things I delight, says the Lord" (Jer. 9:23, 24).

This language about boasting is echoed by Paul in his letter to the Galatian churches. "May I never boast of anything except the cross of our Lord Jesus Christ, by which the world has been crucified to me, and I to the world" (Gal. 6:14). Early in his academic and professional life, young Saul of Tarsus took great pride in his heritage, his training, his knowledge about the God of Israel and His Law. But he discovered who God really was when he encountered the crucified and risen Christ on the road to Damascus. From that point on, the world was crucified to Paul. Nothing in the world held him captive. From that moment on, his own ego was brought under tight control--it would no longer set his agenda. Near the end of his life he would say: "But I am not ashamed, for I know the one in whom I have put my trust, and I am sure that he is able to guard until that day what I have entrusted to him" (2 Tim. 1:12).

The gospel is not a set of rules. It is not a 10,000 page book of theology. Least of all is it a sensational feeling that I am a pretty adequate fellow in and of myself. The gospel of which Paul was not ashamed was his own personal relationship with and knowledge of God. Israel's God had revealed Himself most fully in Jesus of Nazareth. In knowing Him, both Jew and Gentile could find forgiveness, reconciliation and life.

Seed Thoughts

1. **Paul described himself as a "servant of Jesus Christ." Did he have low self esteem?**
   No, Paul saw it as the world's greatest honor to work as a slave to Jesus in proclaiming His love to the world.

2. **What was the gospel Paul was called to proclaim?**
   That "in Christ God was reconciling the world to himself" (2 Cor. 5:18).

3. **How could Paul give thanks for the Romans' faith when they were so mixed up?**
   Because, however proud and confused they were, they still looked to Jesus Christ as their Savior.

4. **Why did Paul say he longed to see the Romans and be with them?**
   He needed their fellowship and encouragement as much as they needed his.

5. **In what sense did Paul feel obligated to preach the gospel to everyone?**
   God had forgiven him in Jesus Christ, had called him to proclaim forgiveness to all.

(PLEASE TURN PAGE)

---

1. Paul described himself as a "servant of Jesus Christ." Did he have low self esteem?

2. What was the gospel Paul was called to proclaim?

3. How could Paul give thanks for the Romans' faith when they were so mixed up?

4. Why did Paul say he longed to see the Romans and be with them?

5. In what sense did Paul feel obligated to preach the gospel to everyone?

6. What is so powerful about the gospel?

7. Why did Paul stress to the Romans that the gospel was for all?

8. What, according to today's lesson, is the prerequisite for salvation in Christ?

9. In the book of Romans what does the word "righteousness" mean?

10. What does Paul mean by "the righteous will live by faith"?

No, Paul saw it as the world's greatest honor to work as a slave to Jesus in proclaiming His love to the world.

That "in Christ God was reconciling the world to himself" (2 Cor. 5:18).

Because, however proud and confused they were, they still looked to Jesus Christ as their Savior.

He needed their fellowship and encouragement as much as they needed his.

God had forgiven him in Jesus Christ, had called him to proclaim forgiveness to all.

One's life can be changed when he realizes that God came here to live and die to restore fellowship with us.

The little church at Rome was torn by strife between Jewish and Gentile Christians. All had sinned, all were saved in Christ.

That one truly believe the gospel and accept it.

Not moral perfection, but right standing with God.

By trusting in God, not by one's own goodness, knowledge or works we are made right with Him.

(SEED THOUGHTS--Cont'd)

6. **What is so powerful about the gospel?**
One's life can be changed when he realizes that God came here to live and die to restore fellowship with us.

7. **Why did Paul stress to the Romans that the gospel was for all?**
The little church at Rome was torn by strife between Jewish and Gentile Christians. All had sinned, all were saved in Christ.

8. **What, according to today's lesson, is the prerequisite for salvation in Christ?**
That one truly believe the gospel and accept it.

9. **In the book of Romans what does the word "righteousness" mean?**
Not moral perfection, but right standing with God.

10. **What does Paul mean by "the righteous will live by faith"?**
By trusting in God, not by one's own goodness, knowledge or works we are made right with Him.

March 13, 1994

God's Gift of Redemption

Romans 4:13-25

13 For the promise, that he should be the heir of the world, *was* not to Abraham, or to his seed, through the law, but through the righteousness of faith.
14 For if they which are of the law *be* heirs, faith is made void, and the promise made of none effect:
15 Because the law worketh wrath: for where no law is, *there is* no transgression.
16 Therefore it is of faith, that *it might be* by grace, to the end the promise might be sure to all the seed; not to that only which is of the law, but to that also which is of the faith of Abraham; who is the father of us all,
17 (As it is written, I have made thee a father of many nations,) before him whom he believed, *even* God, who quickeneth the dead, and calleth those things which be not as though they were.
18 Who against hope believed in hope, that he might become the father of many nations, according to that which was spoken, So shall thy seed be.
19 And being not weak in faith, he considered not his own body now dead, when he was about an hundred years old, neither yet the deadness of Sarah's womb:
20 He staggered not at the promise of God through unbelief, but was strong in faith, giving glory to God;
21 And being fully persuaded that, what he had promised he was able also to perform.
22 And therefore it was imputed to him for righteousness.
23 Now it was not written for his sake alone, that it was imputed to him;
24 But for us also, to whom it shall be imputed, if we believe on him that raised up Jesus our Lord from the dead:
25 Who was delivered for our offences, and was raised again for our justification.

◆◆◆◆◆◆

◀ **Memory Selection**
Romans 4:13

◀ **Devotional Reading**
Romans 2:4b-16

◀ **Background Scripture**
Romans 3:21-4:25

◀ **Printed Scripture**
Romans 4:13-25

GOD'S GIFT OF REDEMPTION

Teacher's Target

A young man went to his minister one day talking about "his" righteousness. The minister listened closely. After a time of hearing lots of "me," "mine" and "I," the minister spoke. "Your righteousness! You don't have any righteousness. It is always God's righteousness. You and I only get to share in it through Christ." The young man was taken aback, but got the point. We are ungodly. Righteousness is imputed to us. It never becomes our possession. We can't just put it in our hip pocket and claim ownership of it.

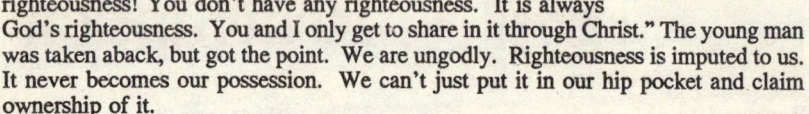

What is the danger of claiming righteousness as our possession? What group (or groups) in the Scripture believed righteousness was theirs by right or achievement? Do we really remain sinners all the days of our lives?

Lesson Introduction

Paul's major emphasis in Romans was justification by faith. Grace clothed believers in righteousness. However, no person within himself was righteous, no not one, Paul said.

This included Paul's prime example of faith, Abraham. He was called the father of our faith. However, when you read about his life after his acceptance of God's grace, you see him faltering and missing the mark. For example, twice he lied about Sarah being his wife. He was a human being, fallen and broken just like us. His righteousness was God's grace-gift, not Abraham's possession by right of right action. He slowly realized how much he needed to depend upon God. Slowly, he gave up the territory of his heart to God. He did it as grudgingly as the rest of us. Because of this Abraham made a wonderful illustration of faith righteousness.

Teaching Outline

I. The Promise: Romans 4:13-16
   A. Of an Heir : 13
   B. By Faith: 13,16
   C. Not Law: 14-15
II. The Fulfillment: Romans 4:17-21
   A. Father of Nations: 17-18
   B. Faith not Weak: 19-21
   C. Imputed Righteousness: 22
III. The Lineage: Romans 4:23-25
   A. Not Abraham Only: 23
   B. All Believers: 24
   C. Offenses Justified: 25

Daily Bible Readings

Mon. The Wicked Can Be Redeemed *Romans 2:3-11*
Tue. Practice What You Preach *Romans 2:12-21*
Wed. Righteousness Through Faith in Jesus - *Romans 3:22-26*
Thurs. All Are Justified by Their Faith - *Romans 3:27-31*
Fri. Abraham's Faith Reconciled Him *Romans 4:1-5*
Sat. Abraham Father of All Who Believe - *Romans 4:6-19*
Sun. Jesus Raised For Our Justification - *Romans 4:20-25*

VERSE BY VERSE

I. The Promise: Romans 4:13-16

A. Of An Heir: 13

13. For the promise, that he should be the heir of the world, was not to Abraham, or to his seed, through the law, but through the righteousness of faith.

"Heir of the world" was some inheritance! Abraham himself never received more than a small portion of land in comparison to such a promise. His "seed" would possess the earth as God's chosen. The first reference must surely be to Isaac; then to Israel, the physical descendants of Abraham. They were intended to be priests to all the world and claim the world for God. This role of privilege and responsibility was never fulfilled.

Jesus Christ fulfilled what Israel refused. He was Abraham's ultimate seed (see Gal. 3:16). He placed His faith, as had Abraham, in God and was obedient to God's voice. By His obedience even unto death on the cross Jesus became heir to the whole world.

B. By Faith: 13, 16

13. For the promise, that he should be the heir of the world, was not to Abraham, or to his seed, through the law, but through the righteousness of faith.

16. Therefore it is of faith, that it might be by grace, to the end the promise might be sure to all the seed; not to that only which is of the law, but to that also which is of the faith of Abraham; who is the father of us all,

In some ways Paul was like a "Johnny-One-Note." He continually pressed home that the blessing of God came only through faith alone by grace alone. Abraham was his prime example. The blessing had come to Abraham by faith long before the Law was given to Moses.

The Law could have been a benefit to Israel had they used it right. As it turned out it became a burden. But God never intended only the people of the Law to be heirs of His promise. Now in the revelation of Jesus Christ it had been made clear that the whole world could benefit from God's blessing through faith (see Gal. 3:14).

C. Not Law: 14-15

14. For if they which are of the law be heirs, faith is made void, and the promise made of none effect:

15. Because the law worketh wrath: for where no law is, there is no transgression.

Like the One who gave it, the Law was good. However, fallen humanity, full of arrogance, pride and rebellion, could not use it as a mirror of undoneness and turn to God for help. Instead, because of sin that clung to Adam's posterity, the Law was turned into a ladder of achievement in an attempt to reach God, or more accurately to become our own god. Humankind preferred a ladder, not a cross.

Paul declared that if the Law were the means of becoming an heir then it would nullify the blessing being a promise, a gift given by God and not achieved.

Because of how people used the Law, it worked wrath. it exposed failure, people experienced guilt and instead of calling out for mercy began to seek a means to justify themselves. Knowing themselves to be transgressors they could only fear that wrath would be their fate.

II. The Fulfillment: Romans 4:17-22

A. Father of Nations: 17-18

17. (As it is written, I have made thee a father of many nations,) before him whom he believed, even God, who quickeneth the dead, and calleth those things which be not as though they were.

18. Who against hope believed in hope, that he might become the father of many nations, according to that which was spoken, So shall thy seed be.

Paul's argument continued. If only those who practiced the Law were Abraham's heirs, how could he be the father of other nations? The answer was that faith in God through Jesus Christ was the universal access to God. Faith like Abraham's always had been the means to a relationship with God.

Though generation upon generation were between Abraham and Jesus, God had not forgotten His promise. He had blessed the nations through Abraham by sending Jesus Christ in his linage and as his heir to the promise. Through Jesus the promise had become the inheritance of all nations.

Abraham had believed against all hope in God's faithfulness. Jesus had also believed against all evidence that God would raise Him on the third day. God had been faithful to both men in the resurrection. Abraham became the father of nations and Jesus was exalted as Lord over all the world.

B. Faith Not Weak: 19-21

19. And being not weak in faith, he considered not his own body now dead, when he was about an hundred years old, neither yet the deadness of Sarah's womb:

20. He staggered not at the promise of God through unbelief, but was strong in faith, giving glory to God;

21. And being fully persuaded that, what he had promised he was able also to perform.

Abraham was over 100 years old and Sarah's womb was dead when she conceived and Isaac was born. Paul declared that Abraham was persuaded that if God promised something He would deliver on the promise. God did not just talk. He performed. Such faith in God was imputed to Abraham as righteousness.

Jesus had also believed and acted upon God's promise. By faith in the Father's word He endured the cross not knowing He would he raised on the third day, but believing in the Father's promise. On the third day God raised Him up!

Abraham went out not knowing whither God would lead him. Jesus went to the cross not knowing God would raise Him. Both believed the Father's word. Both men's faith was vindicated.

C. Imputed Righteousness: 22

22. And therefore it was imputed to him for righteousness.

What does imputed righteousness mean? First it means humankind has no righteousness in and of itself. Also, it means human beings cannot make themselves righteous, nor can they gain righteousness by achieving something.

Jesus Christ is righteous. His righteousness is experienced (not owned or possessed) by faith in His finished work on the cross. Believers are "in Christ." The righteousness is always Christ's righteousness and never ours. His righteousness is shared with us "as if" we were righteous. We are treated as righteous though we are not. This is imputed righteousness. Paul at the end of his days could see and say he was the chief of sinners. Abraham sinned all his days. Paul sinned all his days. Jesus' righteousness covered for their sin. Thanks be to God for Jesus Christ and His righteousness imputed to us.

III. The Linage: Romans 4:23-25

A. Not Abraham Only: 23

23. Now it was not written for his sake alone, that it was imputed to him;

God knew humankind was universally trapped, imprisoned, snared in the strong man's grip which leads to sin. They had no savior. They could not save themselves from their strong desire for things other than God. In fact, this is what sin is: to desire and long for other things more than we desire God.

Paul declared that what Jesus Christ had done was not done for Abraham only. What God had accomplished in Christ was for everyone. By faith all believers are in the linage of Abraham and heirs of the same righteousness.

B. All Believers: 24

24. But for us also, to whom it shall be imputed, if we believe on him that raised up Jesus our Lord from the dead:

Jesus Christ died for our sins, but not for ours only but for the sin of the whole world (1 John 2:2). His grace was offered to all. By faith in the one who raised up Jesus our Lord from the dead, all could appropriate this grace (Rom. 4:24). All that was required was to lift up empty hands to receive the gift.

C. Offenses Justified: 25

25. Who was delivered for our offences, and was raised again for our justification.

Paul's words revealed how strange and wonderful beyond our comprehension were the ways of God. Humankind had committed the offenses. They were the condemned ones by their very own actions. They had no excuse. Even their righteousness was as filthy rags. Yet, God took it all upon himself in Christ Jesus. Instead of humankind being delivered up Jesus was. For such obedience and sacrifice God raised Jesus up *for us*. Condemned for humankind's offenses; raised for their justification. How gracious is our God!

Evangelistic Emphasis

Karl Barth (pronounced Bart), the respected Swiss theologian, said that Christian fellowship is based first on a negative. When we come to know that we are all sinners, we can come to know that we are all brothers. "Sin" in that statement is not so much evil deeds we have done as it is a distorted relationship with God. We are out of relationship with Him, lost in the woods, full of guilt and shame.

There is such a thing as false guilt; but there is authentic guilt also. Christians are not sinless people, they are forgiven and reconciled to God in the cross of Christ. Too often Christians, with the very best of intentions, approach unbelievers with an air of superiority. The basis of evangelism should be our common need and God's grace for us all. There is an old saying, "Evangelism is nothing more than one beggar telling another beggar where to find a square meal."

If we cannot admit our own sin we come across as arrogant and spiritually superior. most people are turned off, not by the gospel but by the messenger. However, some will respond to the appeal of spiritual elitism. If our arrogance appeals to the arrogance in the unbeliever it should be no surprise that he will disturb the fellowship when he becomes a part of the church. We should carry a humble and thankful spirit into every conversation for Christ.

♦♦♦♦♦♦

Memory Selection

For the promise, that he should be the heir of the world, was not to Abraham, or to his seed, through the law, but through the righteousness of faith. *Romans 4:13*

Abraham was not a perfect man. Twice he lied to save his own neck because he feared foreign kings would take his beautiful wife and do away with him. But when God told him to pack up and leave Ur of the Chaldees he did just that. When God said "Go with me...you don't need a map or an itinerary...I'll take care of you...," Abraham moved out. When God asked that the long awaited son of the promise, Isaac, be sacrificed in worship, Abraham was prepared to follow through. The old couple had waited for decades for the prophecies of a son to be fulfilled. God's assurance that Abraham would be the father of a great nation hinged on it.

It was Abraham's trust in God, not his moral or intellectual perfection, which became the basis of his acceptance before God. Although we live in a totally different world, it is still true that the only way we will ever have true peace with God is by His grace and our trust in Him.

March 6, 1994

Weekday Problems

Henry had just the opposite of the Midas Touch. Everyone to whom he witnessed turned away. He just couldn't understand it. Henry grew up in a home where neither parent knew the Lord. There was no Bible or mention of God. Two decades after leaving home someone shared his faith with him and he became a Christian. He had never known such peace! No association had ever come close to the Christian fellowship he knew at church. His whole life took on new meaning and fulfillment.

He was so eager to share his faith! Henry thought about his friends, prayed for them, visualized their confessions of faith and baptisms. But every time he got beyond the sports and the weather they turned away. Henry could not imagine what he was doing wrong. Typically he said things like this: "You just have to come to our church, it's not like all the others. The people there really love the Lord and the minister is sincere and honest about what he says from the pulpit." "I had a problem like yours before I became a Christian. Never had enough time and was always frantic. Now I spend the first thirty minutes each day in prayer and reading the Bible. Now I find time to do what needs doing." "I'm praying for you, that you will find what I've found, that your life can be turned around and you will find the peace I know in Christ!"

*What was Henry's problem?
*Didn't the Lord urge us to let our lights shine? Is that not what Henry was doing?

♦♦♦♦♦♦

Smiles

A Sunday school teacher, driving his five-year-old daughter to church, began thinking aloud the ideas he expected to present to his college class that morning.

Susie listened for a moment, then asked, "Daddy, are you talking with me, or without me?"

What do a game of golf and a committee meeting have in common? You go around and around for hours and end up where you started.

This Lesson In Your Life

What is the connection between our theology, our understanding of the Bible and our relationships? Do we relate to people at home differently depending on our religious beliefs? To people in the church? Aren't religion and interpersonal relations really just two separate subjects? Paul didn't believe so. He was convinced that the interpersonal problems between Jewish and Gentile Christians in the church at Rome were rooted in defective theology. Specifically, their problems were due to a distorted view of how they stood before God, the method by which they had got right with Him. If one is not sure he or she is acceptable with God, or if one believes acceptance is based on merit or status, then person-to-person relationships will be affected.

So it was for a very practical purpose that Paul retold the story of Abraham and Sarah and how they got right with God. The Abraham story was important for two reasons. First, because all Jewish Christians looked to Abraham as the father of the faithful, the prototype of what real faith meant. Second, because legalists were claiming position and privilege in the church based on seniority, religious performance and pedigree. After all, Abraham was their father, and he was acceptable to God because he was a better man than the pagans around him.

Paul explained it differently. Abraham and Sarah lived on promises. They were promised a land of their own, a family which would be numerous and a blessing to all nations, and a special relationship with God. God had not called them to establish an exclusive Country Club, but as examples of people faithful to Him. He wanted all His runaway children back home. Abraham and Sarah were childless. They received the promise of a child when they were well past the age when a couple receives the first advertisements from the AARP. They pointed up the absurdity of it all to God. Couples in their eighties and nineties do not bear children. It would take a miracle, something never seen before. If they believed the promise it would just be upon His word, His word alone.

When the child was born they named him "Isaac," meaning laughter. Hope beyond hope had been realized! It was God's doing! That was clear for all to see. Human beings in their own power could not make such a thing happen. God had approved Abraham, not because he was good, but because he trusted. One text says that when God spoke Abraham said "Amen" and moved out on the strength of God's promise.

If the proud legalistic elitists were focusing on Abraham's goodness they were missing the main point of the story. The very point of Abraham's life was not his goodness but God's. When one looks to God, believes the promises, accepts the gifts in joy and gratitude then he is in the best position to deal with others. Spiritual pride puffs us up and makes us impossible to live with. Believing in God, confessing our dependence on Him, giving Him the glory and the praise prepare our hearts for fellowship. As God's happy children we lose nothing when we confess the limits of our own wisdom and goodness. When we trust Him for forgiveness, peace and a new relationship with Him, we are redeemed. Redeemed in our human relationships as well as in our relation with God.

Seed Thoughts

1. How did Abraham come by his acceptance with God?
God spoke, Abraham listened, trusted and obeyed God. God granted acceptance because of his faith.

2. What made Abraham tough and steadfast enough to obey and wait upon God?
He believed it was God who spoke to him and he trusted Him.

3. What single fact do we share with all human beings who have ever lived everywhere?
We have all sinned and fallen short of what God originally intended human beings to be.

4. Why should second and third generation Christians not feel superior to new converts?
Because acceptance with God is not based on seniority, but upon His grace.

5. Why did Paul spend so much time on Abraham and Sarah's case?
Because Jewish Christians at Rome thought Abraham was justified by his goodness and so they should run the church.

(PLEASE TURN PAGE)

---

1. How did Abraham come by his acceptance with God?

2. What made Abraham tough and steadfast enough to obey and wait upon God?

3. What single fact do we share with all human beings who have ever lived everywhere?

4. Why should second and third generation Christians not feel superior to new converts?

5. Why did Paul spend so much time on Abraham and Sarah's case?

6. How can we modern Christians be a part of Abraham's family and bring others to God?

7. What were the "facts of the case" that made Abraham's hope for a child look dim?

8. Since we are not Jews, what does "salvation by law" mean to us?

9. Are we kidding ourselves when we say we are righteous when we know that we constantly fall short of real goodness?

10. Why do we have such trouble believing and remembering that we are right with God in Christ?

(SEED THOUGHTS--Cont'd)

God spoke, Abraham listened, trusted and obeyed God. God granted acceptance because of his faith.

He believed it was God who spoke to him and he trusted Him.

We have all sinned and fallen short of what God originally intended human beings to be.

Because acceptance with God is not based on seniority, but upon His grace.

Because Jewish Christians at Rome thought Abraham was justified by his goodness and so they should run the church.

By trusting Him on His word and launching out to see His saving grace in the world.

He and Sarah were old, well beyond childbearing years.

We are always tempted to try to save ourselves by perfect law-keeping rather than accepting His grace.

No, we have right standing with God because He is good and gracious, not because we have achieved perfect goodness.

Two reasons: it's too good to be true and we're too proud to let another save us.

6. **How can we modern Christians be a part of Abraham's family and bring others to God?**
By trusting Him on His word and launching out to see His saving grace in the world.

7. **What were the "facts of the case" that made Abraham's hope for a child look dim?**
He and Sarah were old, well beyond childbearing years.

8. **Since we are not Jews, what does "salvation by law" mean to us?**
We are always tempted to try to save ourselves by perfect law-keeping rather than accepting His grace.

9. **Are we kidding ourselves when we say we are righteous when we know that we constantly fall short of real goodness?**
No, we have right standing with God because He is good and gracious, not because we have achieved perfect goodness.

10. **Why do we have such trouble believing and remembering that we are right with God in Christ?**
Two reasons: it's too good to be true and we're too proud to let another save us.

March 20, 1994

The Gift of Life in Christ

Romans 5:6-17

6 For when we were yet without strength, in due time Christ died for the ungodly.
7 For scarcely for a righteous man will one die: yet peradventure for a good man some would even dare to die.
8 But God commendeth his love toward us, in that, while we were yet sinners, Christ died for us.
9 Much more then, being now justified by his blood, we shall be saved from wrath through him.
10 For if when we were enemies, we were reconciled to God by the death of his Son, much more, being reconciled, we shall be saved by his life.
11 And not only so, but we also joy in God through our Lord Jesus Christ, by whom we have now received the atonement.
12 Wherefore, as by one man sin entered into the world, and death by sin and so death passed upon all men, for that all have sinned:
13 (For until the law sin was in the world: but sin is not imputed when there is no law.
14 Nevertheless death reigned from Adam to Moses, even over them that had not sinned after the similitude of Adam's transgression, who is the figure of him that was to come.
15 But not as the offence, so also *is* the free gift. For if through the offence of one many be dead, much more the grace of God, and the gift by grace, *which* is by one man, Jesus Christ, hath abounded unto many.
16 And not as *it was* by one that sinned, *so is* the gift: for the judgment *was* by one to condemnation, but the free gift *is* of many offences unto justification.
17 For if by one man's offence death reigned by one; much more they which receive abundance of grace and of the gift of righteousness shall reign in life by one, Jesus Christ.)

◆◆◆◆◆◆

◀ **Memory Selection**
Romans 5:8

◀ **Devotional Reading**
Colossians 1:9-14, 21-23

◀ **Background Scripture**
Romans 5

◀ **Printed Scripture**
Romans 5:6-17

THE GIFT IN LIFE OF CHRIST

Teacher's Target

Being told we are weak is not something we relish. Yet Paul makes a habit of telling us this. Here Paul declares we are without strength (Rom. 5:6). Another thing that seems to be hard for us is receiving help from someone else. Our beliefs in our independence, ability to provide, do it ourselves, make our own way are all deeply ingrained in us. One illustration of our dislike of helplessness and lack of control might be to reflect upon how we feel when we have to be hospitalized for tests or illness. Our finitude and fragility stare us square in the face at such times.

What weakness are you willing to admit? Does this weakness cause fear in you? How readily do you accept help? Who knows more and better than you? How do you feel when you are not needed? Ask someone to share about a time when they felt helpless.

Lesson Introduction

For Paul there were two pivotal characters in history. Adam began God's purpose in history. Jesus Christ fulfilled God's purpose in history. Adam refused to listen to God. Jesus listened to God at every moment. Adam's transgression brought sin into the world, and through sin entered death. Christ Jesus was obedient and through death restored eternal life to mankind. Judgment came by one to condemnation for all. By the other the free gift covered many offenses and brought justification. By one death reigned. Now by the other grace reigned unto life.

Much of Paul's teaching was to explain how God in Christ had corrected the fall of Adam. In a sense, Romans is a commentary on Genesis 1-3. God's remedy for Adam's disobedience was Jesus' cross.

Teaching Outline

I. The Gift: Romans 5:6-11
  A. The Need: 6,7
  B. The Love: 8
  C. The Justification: 9-11
II. The Contrast: Romans 5:12-17
  A. One Sinned: 12-13
  B. Many Died: 14-17
  C. One Justified: 15-17

Daily Bible Readings

Mon. Justification by Faith Grants Us Peace - *Romans 5: 1-5*
Tue. Christ Died for Us *Romans 5: 6-10*
Wed. Righteousness Brings Justification - *Romans 5: 11-16*
Thurs. As Sin Increased, Grace Abounded More - *Romans 5: 17-21*
Fri. God Redeemed My Soul, Offering Light - *Job 33: 23-28*
Sat. God Gives Sinners Life in Christ *Ephesians 2: 1-6*
Sun. "The Word of God is Not Fettered" - *2 Timothy 2: 8-15*

VERSE BY VERSE

I. The Gift: Romans 5:6-11

A. The Need: 6, 7

6. For when we were yet without strength, in due time Christ died for the ungodly.

7. For scarcely for a righteous man will one die: yet peradventure for a good man some would even dare to die.

Like light through a prism, the variety of expressions of the original offense of Adam had multiplied into a thousand varied manifestations. The worst part was that all were helpless to change. The need was great and undeniable.

The signs of our helplessness were everywhere evident. Denial could not block out the reality.

B. The Love: 8

8. But God commendeth his love toward us, in that, while we were yet sinners, Christ died for us.

It was not the need and definitely not the worthiness of the human race that caused God to act. The initiative came from within God Himself. God prompted Himself. God is love (1 John 4:8) and his actions flowed from Himself as a river flows from its source.

God's ultimate expression of His love was manifest in His sending Jesus Christ to die for us. Jesus did not act to appease an angry God. The love of the Father initiated the act, participated in it and provided the power for it.

C. The Justification: 9-11

9. Much more then, being now justified by his blood, we shall be saved from wrath through him.

10. For if, when we were enemies, we were reconciled to God by the death of his Son, much more, being reconciled, we shall be saved by his life.

11. And not only so, but we also joy in God through our Lord Jesus Christ, by whom we have now received the atonement.

"Justified" and "reconciled" are powerladen concepts. Justified means to be declared or treated as if one were righteous when in fact one is not. It took the power that raised Jesus from the grave to justify humankind. That power to live out a new life of love like that of Jesus was what had come in justification.

Reconciliation meant that once again man was in union with God. The relationship broken by Adam's disobedience has been restored by Christ's obedience.

God had always been reconciled to mankind. He never moved nor reneged on His promise. Humankind was not reconciled to God. Being human was not believed to be good enough. So, mankind sought to be like God. Humankind broke itself on its own grasping, arrogance and determination to know all.

The blood of Christ justified us.

This death covered us as surely as the blood of lambs on the lintel covered the Israelites in Egypt. The death angel passed their homes without killing the first born. So Christ's blood covered all who believed and reconciled them to God.

By the death of Jesus came reconciliation. By His resurrection came eternal life (Rom. 5:10). Reconciled to God by His death, we shall be saved for eternal life by His resurrection life.

The wrath of God was never against humankind. It was never God's will that any should perish (2 Pet. 3:9). God's wrath was against those things that would destroy His creation: Satan, sin, death and "the world"). Only so long as one refused the gift of God in Christ did a person remain under the wrath. In Christ God's will had been accomplished. Now there would be only justification and reconciliation offered by God.

II. The Contrast: Romans 5:12-17

A. One Sinned: 12-13

12. Wherefore, as by one man sin entered into the world, and death by sin and so death passed upon all men, for that all have sinned:

13. (For until the law sin was in the world: but sin is not imputed when there is no law.

Adam was a prototype of us all. His act is repeated by us all. Our solidarity with him is proved out and confirmed by our sins, which are only multiple variations of this original refusal to listen to God.

As Adam acted in the stead of all humanity, so Jesus the last Adam (1 Cor. 15:45) acted in the stead of all humanity. As there was a solidarity with Adam by our birth, so there is a solidarity with Christ by the new birth (John 3:3-8). What happened to Adam had fallen out to all his posterity. The stream was polluted at its source and had continued to "muddy up" as it flowed through history.

Adam and Satan formed an unholy union, one humankind could not handle. Once let in, Satan ruled. Now the enemy could kill, destroy, steal and despoil all creation. Death became the infectious disease that would be the universal fate of all.

Death, not life, became the monarch. It reigned over all creation. Paul showed that death was on the scene long before the Law. Obedience to the Law could not and did not break the rule of death. Death reigned, even over those who died in infancy, long before the Mosaic Law. There was something wrong in creation long before the Law. It only made specific and clear the transgression arising from humankind's refusal to listen to God.

B. Many Died: 14-17

14. Nevertheless death reigned from Adam to Moses, even over them that had not sinned after the similitude of Adam's transgression, who is the figure of him that was to come.

15. But not as the offence, so also is the free gift. For if through the offence of one many be dead, much more the grace of God, and the gift by grace, which is by one man, Jesus Christ, hath abounded unto many.

16. And not as *it was* by one that sinned, *so is* the gift: for the judgment was by one to condemnation, but the free gift *is* of many offences unto justification.

17. For if by one man's offence death reigned by one; much more they which receive abundance of grace and of the gift of righteousness shall reign in life by one, Jesus Christ.)

Death was inside the camp after Adam's choice of the serpent over God. once in the door, all were exposed to its effects. Like a cancer in the bloodstream and lymphatic system of an individual, so death spread throughout the body politic of humankind. The disobedience of one resulted in the death of many.

C. One Justified: 15-17

15. But not as the offence, so also is the free gift. For if through the offence of one many be dead, much more the grace of God, and the gift by grace, which is by one man, Jesus Christ, hath abounded unto many.
16. And not as *it was* by one that sinned, *so is* the gift: for the judgment was by one to condemnation, but the free gift *is* of many offences unto justification.
17. For if by one man's offence death reigned by one; much more they which receive abundance of grace and of the gift of righteousness shall reign in life by one, Jesus Christ.)

That which hindered justification and reconciliation had to be removed. Then salvation could follow. Disobedience had ruined the human race. Now an obedience could effect a righteousness that would restore a right relationship between man and God.

It was not a punishment that brought about this reconciliation. it was an obedience that brought it about. Jesus was wounded for our transgressions, it is true. But His obedience was the source of reconciliation. The punishment or death of Christ was the last and ultimate weapon of the evil one to attempt to shake Jesus' faith in and obedience to the Father. Satan was taking his best shot. God the Father was not beating up on His Son.

In this one act by Christ the gift of righteousness entered the stream of humanity. As the sin was by one, so the free gift was offered through one. As shame, guilt and death were communicated by one, likewise righteousness and life were communicated by one. As all are the seed of Adam, so all who believe are the spiritual seed of Christ, the firstborn of the new creation (Col. 1:18).

As strong as the serpent's poison was, the antidote was greater still. Through Christ we have been reinstated at a higher plane and with greater privileges than our former state in Adam prior to the fall.

Evangelistic Emphasis

"All I ever wanted was a little peace," said Anna Karenina in Tolstoy's novel. She said it just before she threw herself in front of a train. Many who do not know the Lord would say the same. Our lives are a jumble of bells, horns and whistles. We have schedules to keep, deadlines to make, challenges to master. More desperate still, when we are still we are somehow still at war. We spend enormous amounts of time and money trying to find peace, trying to dull the pain of our restlessness. We try to deny our emptiness, our futility, the pointlessness of our lives.

Many have never heard, many of us Christians have forgotten that Paul wrote in Romans 5:1, "Since we are justified by faith we have peace with God through our Lord Jesus Christ." Paul spoke not of peace of mind, but of peace with life and the God Who gave it to us. He spoke of a cessation of hostilities. We have peace, not because we were clever enough to arrange it. We have peace because "while we were yet sinners Christ died for us" and God offered us peace "signed, sealed and delivered," awaiting only our signature.

◆◆◆◆◆◆

Memory Selection

But God commendeth his love toward us, in that, while we were yet sinners, Christ died for us.
Romans 5:8

Many of us have fears deep down that we will never really win God's approval. His standards are so high, our performance so spotty, how can He possibly accept us? Does God grade on the curve?

"I'm afraid I haven't done enough," an elderly Christian woman said on her deathbed. Family and friends wanted to reassure her that she had lived a wonderful, unselfish life, far beyond average. But in her heart she knew the conflict most of us feel. Every good thought, word and deed could be offset by a selfish and hurtful thought, word and deed. After seventy or eighty years, who can keep an accurate count? Very logically, the woman was afraid.

If one is accepted by God on the basis of performance there is cause for alarm. on the other hand, if we could have been good enough to demand God's acceptance on our own record, Christ need never have come. Paul says it in an arresting way: "God proved His love for us in that while we were helplessly mired in self-centeredness Christ gave himself up for us."

March 20, 1994

Weekday Problems

Bernice was critical of everyone. She had worked as a third grade teacher in this school for twenty-two years. But that wasn't really the problem. Actually, her feelings about the job and the people around her had remained the same over all those years. No one could ever satisfy her. She was continually in conflict. She hated coming to school. The librarian never got the books she ordered fast enough. The custodians were careless in cleaning her classroom. The principal played favorites with other faculty. Her students were lazy, stubborn and uncooperative. The crossing guards held her up too long at the corner and made her late.

Her greatest resentment was the parents who were always blaming her for their children's emotional, social and intellectual problems. When she got home in the evening her husband seemed never to care about her problems, or even to listen to her frustrations. In short, Bernice was surrounded by ill-tempered, selfish and dull people. She dreamed of living in another place where people had their act together. Everyone around her dreamed of her living in another place also. They dreaded meeting her every day.

*Where should Bernice start to work out her problem?
*What does her Christian faith offer her which she has not found yet?

♦♦♦♦♦♦

Smiles

Two men of the world spotted one of the old saints of the church as she came down the street. Her acts of charity, cheerful generosity, and open acceptance of all riled them greatly. One pointed toward her.

"I'll bet you can't mention anybody that old lady can't find something good to say about," he said to the other.

"I'll take that bet," was the response.

"Good morning, Miss Thompson," the second man said, "what do you think about the devil?"

Miss Thompson cocked her head to one side, got a twinkle in her eye and said, "Well, there is one good thing about him. He is always on the job."

THE GIFT OF LIFE IN CHRIST

This Lesson In Your Life

Ralph Waldo Emerson taught Americans self-reliance. Why should we have to rely for everything both physical and intellectual from England? Why could we not think for ourselves, develop our own arts, build our own universities and create our own industry?

Self-reliance is a primary American value. That's a blessing in many ways. We have developed our own economy, our own educational system, our own arts and sciences. We have developed our own versions of Christianity.

But how painful is the lesson we are learning now, after more than a century of self-reliance! We find ourselves more and more interdependent with the rest of the world. On a personal level many of us have gone out on our own, made something of our selves and by ourselves, and yet we are still unhappy and unfulfilled. We need others.

Young Saul of Tarsus left home while still a beardless youth to find his career in Jerusalem. Was he to become a great scholar and teacher? A leading rabbi? Perhaps one of the leaders in Israel's Supreme Court, the Sanhedrin. Whatever his destiny, his first step was schooling in Jerusalem. He excelled in his studies, surpassed his peers and learned how to please his teachers. No doubt, he was learning self-reliance and discovering his own formula for success. Morally he had no large problem; he was not a "sinner," he was an achiever full of high hopes. Nothing could stop him.

Then, when on the fast track, he met Jesus of Nazareth on the Damascus road. The same Jesus who died on a Roman cross as a criminal and blasphemer just a while before. He was the same carpenter which His followers now proclaimed to be the long-expected Messiah. Young Saul had dismissed these claims as the ravings of an extremist, ignorant fringe group.

After his encounter with the crucified and risen Lord it took young Saul three years on a retreat in Arabia to sort through his view of life. His name had been changed to Paul. His formula for self-reliance and success had been shattered. By the time Paul the Christian missionary wrote Romans he could celebrate what God had done for him and for the whole world in Jesus Christ. "We have peace with God through our Lord Jesus Christ," he wrote. "While we were helpless...while we were sinners Christ died for us." Young Saul of Tarsus would have choked on that word, "helpless." His time with Jesus had changed everything.

Perhaps recent challenges to American superiority and self-reliance are not all bad. If they drive us into a closer relationship with the Lord, help us to know our dependence on Him, make us grateful for His grace then we will be blessed in the long run.

Seed Thoughts

1. Why does Paul say we have peace with God in Jesus Christ?
Because Jesus died on the cross as a covering for our sins and a reconciliation with God.

2. How can I know I have peace with God when I feel anything but peaceful?
The peace mentioned in Romans 5 is not a feeling, it is an armistice arranged on Golgotha.

3. How can peace with God lead me to peace with others and with myself?
Much of our conflict with others and self is rooted in guilt and fear of judgment. God takes these away once and for all in His gift.

4. According to today's lesson, what is the root cause of humanity's fear and restlessness?
Alienation from God the Creator and Lord of history.

5. What can I do to patch things up with God?
Nothing. He has done it all, and it's more than merely "patched up." Can you believe and accept the gift?

(PLEASE TURN PAGE)

---

1. Why does Paul say we have peace with God in Jesus Christ?

2. How can I know I have peace with God when I feel anything but peaceful?

3. How can peace with God lead me to peace with others and with myself?

4. According to today's lesson, what is the root cause of humanity's fear and restlessness?

5. What can I do to patch things up with God?

6. How does Paul prove God's love for us?

7. What special comfort should Christians know since they are now at home with God?

8. Why should Christians not be terror-stricken about death?

9. Why do we have trouble accepting the free gift of salvation?

10. Why do we have trouble understanding how all humans could "die in one man" and "be made alive" in another?

(SEED THOUGHTS--Cont'd)

Because Jesus died on the cross as a covering for our sins and a reconciliation with God.

The peace mentioned in Romans 5 is not a feeling, it is an armistice arranged on Golgotha.

Much of our conflict with others and self is rooted in guilt and fear of judgment. God takes these away once and for all in His gift.

Alienation from God the Creator and Lord of history.

Nothing. He has done it all, and it's more than merely "patched up." Can you believe and accept the gift?

"While we were helpless...while we were still sinners Christ died for us."

If Christ loved us enough to die for us, Paul says, how much more do we know His love now that He lives and intercedes for us with the Father.

Because one's separation from God caused by Adam's sin and our human nature has been overcome in Christ.

Because we hate to think that we need saving and can't do it ourselves.

Because our culture's stress on self-reliance had blurred for us the fact that we are connected in humanity.

6. How does Paul prove God's love for us?
"While we were helpless...while we were still sinners Christ died for us."

7. What special comfort should Christians know since they are now at home with God?
If Christ loved us enough to die for us, Paul says, how much more do we know His love now that He lives and intercedes for us with the Father.

8. Why should Christians not be terror-stricken about death?
Because one's separation from God caused by Adam's sin and our human nature has been overcome in Christ.

9. Why do we have trouble accepting the free gift of salvation?
Because we hate to think that we need saving and can't do it ourselves.

10. Why do we have trouble understanding how all humans could "die in one man" and "be made alive" in another?
Because our culture's stress on self-reliance had blurred for us the fact that we are connected in humanity.

March 27, 1994

Deliverance From Sin

Romans 6:3-14

3 Know ye not, that so many of us as were baptized into Jesus Christ were baptized into his death?
4 Therefore we are buried with him by baptism into death: that like as Christ was raised up from the dead by the glory of the Father, even so we also should walk in newness of fife.
5 For if we have been planted together in the likeness of his death, we shall be also *in the likeness* of *his* resurrection:
6 Knowing this, that our old man is crucified with *him*, that the body of sin might be destroyed, that henceforth we should not serve sin.
7 For he that is dead is freed from sin.
8 Now if we be dead with Christ, we believe that we shall also live with him:
9 Knowing that Christ being raised from the dead dieth no more; death hath no more dominion over him.
10 For in that he died, he died unto sin once: but in that he liveth, he liveth unto God.
11 Likewise reckon ye also yourselves to be dead indeed unto sin, but alive unto God through Jesus Christ our Lord.
12 Let not sin therefore reign in your mortal body, that ye should obey it in the lusts thereof.
13 Neither yield ye your members *as* instruments of unrighteousness unto sin: but yield yourselves unto God, as those that are alive from the dead, and your members *as* instruments of righteousness unto God.
14 For sin shall not have dominion over you: for ye are not under the law, but under grace.

Romans 6:20-23

20 For when ye were the servants of sin, ye were free from righteousness.
21 What fruit had ye then in those things whereof ye are now ashamed? for the end of those things *is* death.
22 But now being made free from sin, and become servants to God, ye have your fruit unto holiness, and the end everlasting life.
23 For the wages of sin *is* death; but the gift of God *is* eternal Life through Jesus Christ our Lord.

◆◆◆◆◆◆

◀ **Memory Selection**
Romans 6:23

◀ **Devotional Reading**
Colossians 3:1-4, 5-11, 12-15b

◀ **Background Scripture**
Romans 6

◀ **Printed Scripture**
Romans 6:3-14, 20-23

DELIVERANCE FROM SIN

Teacher's Target

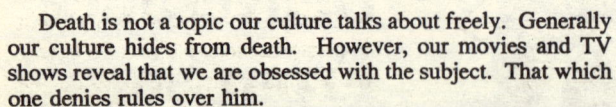

Death is not a topic our culture talks about freely. Generally our culture hides from death. However, our movies and TV shows reveal that we are obsessed with the subject. That which one denies rules over him.

Scripture states that we have to face our death before we can really live. Until a person has owned his or her own finitude, the preciousness and fragile nature of life does not become apparent.

Unless we lose our life we cannot save it. The sad irony is that by not losing our lives we are already dead in our sin. If we lose our lives God will give us life in Christ.

How do you die to self? Does this happen just once? What is meant by living unto God? What are the wages of sin? What is the fruit of righteousness? Why is "wages" plural and "fruit" singular in our passage?

Lesson Introduction

Someone had raised the question: If we are saved by grace from our sin, should we keep on sinning more so that God can show more grace? Paul answered this question in Romans 6. No, was his answer. Believers were not just saved <u>from</u> something, they were saved <u>to</u> something. Once they had no power to overcome sin. At that time they were free from righteousness. Now God had through Christ given believers a power to live out righteousness. God never gave an imperative without having provided the indicative. That is to say, God only commanded people to do something after He had given them the power to accomplish it. Only in Christ did anyone have the power to live unto God and not unto sin. Paul declared: become what you are, new creatures in Christ.

Teaching Outline

I. Dead unto Sin: Romans 6:3-7
   A. Baptized into Christ: 3-5
   B. Crucified with Christ: 6
   C. Freed from Sin: 7
II. Alive Unto God: Romans 6:8-12
   A. Dead with Christ: 8
   B. Death No Dominion: 9
   C. Alive Through Christ: 10-12
III. Instruments of Righteousness: Romans 6: 13-14,20-23
   A. Yield to God: 13
   B. Live under Grace: 14
   C. Bear Fruit: 20-23

Daily Bible Readings

Mon. Walk in the Newness of Life *Romans 6:1-5*
Tue. Freedom from Moral Enslavement - *Romans 6:6-11*
Wed. Let Not Sin Reign *Romans 6:12-16*
Thurs. Set Free from Immorality *Romans 6:17-21*
Fri. Wages of Sin <u>versus</u> Eternal Life - *Romans 6:22-23;7:1-4*
Sat. Immoral Persons Sin Against Their Bodies - *1 Corinthians 6:13-20*
Sun. Fruit of the Spirit *Galatians 5:16-25*

March 27, 1994

VERSE BY VERSE

I. Dead Unto Sin: Romans 6:3-7

A. Baptized Into Christ: 3-5

3. Know ye not, that many of us as were baptized into Jesus Christ were baptized into his death?
4. Therefore we are buried with him by baptism into death: that like as Christ was raised up from the dead by the glory of the Father, even so we also should walk in newness of fife.
5. For if we have been planted together in the likeness of his death, we shall be also in the likeness of his resurrection:

In the early church adult baptism was a symbol of burial with Christ in His death. Jesus had died to remove sin from us. He even called the cross His "baptism" (Matt. 20:22; Mark 10:39; Luke 12:50). Baptism was the symbol of believers dying to their old way of life. The way of sin and death was buried with and in Jesus at the cross.

B. Crucified With Christ: 6

6. Knowing this, that our old man is crucified with him, that the body of sin might be destroyed, that henceforth we should not serve sin.

That the old man had already been crucified at the cross is Paul's point. No person could crucify the "old man" within him by and of himself. No group observance of rules and rituals could restrain or destroy this old nature in humankind. The sin nature would express itself even through the very rules and rituals that were used to control or destroy it.

Paul declares that the body of sin was destroyed once and for all in Christ's death. No longer is serving sin inevitable and unavoidable. Sin was nailed to the cross and could not be charged against any in Christ (Col. 2:14). Since it was dead in Christ it no longer had to he served.

C. Freed From Sin: 7

7. For he that is dead is freed from sin.

A corpse cannot move. Dead men do not walk. Once sin had life. Now sin had been crucified in Christ. Sin was dead in Him.

Sin would still tempt us but no longer are we under its power. Now believers are under Christ's power. Before they were "alive to," or slaves to sin. Now they are alive to, or slaves to Christ.

The old man was and is truly dead. He died at the cross. Now, as Romans 6:11 stated, humankind has the choice "to reckon" itself dead to sin.

II. Alive unto God: Romans 6:8-12

A. Dead with Christ: 8

8. Now if we be dead with Christ, we believe that we shall also live

with him:

The cross was the place of sin and death's end. Both died as powers of influence there. Being dead in and with Christ, a believer becomes a corpse to sin. Now only Christ reigns. Sin and death reign no more. The despair and destination of sin and death cannot demoralize and debilitate people any longer. God has acted in behalf of His creation.

As with Adam, all were made alive to sin and death. Now with Christ all are made alive to righteousness and life. Believers now have the power not to obey the passions of the flesh: gluttony, avarice, impurity, depression, anger, vain glory, pride.

B. Death No Dominion: 9

9. Knowing that Christ being raised from the dead dieth no more; death hath no more dominion over him.

Dominion means the power or right to govern or control; to have sovereign authority. A second definition means a territory under a single ruler. Both definitions are implied in Paul's thought here. Death has no right in the life of those in Christ. Death was defeated at the cross. Death was not defeated at the point of a person's belief. The defeat was all God's work in Christ. It was then offered to all.

Death has no territory to claim as its own now that Christ has defeated sin and death. At the cross, death had been exposed as the intruder it had always been. Death now has no authority. Death now has no territory.

C. Alive Through Christ: 10-12

10. For in that he died, he died unto sin once: but in that he liveth, he liveth unto God.

11. Likewise reckon ye also yourselves to be dead indeed unto sin, but alive unto God through Jesus Christ our Lord.

12. Let not sin therefore reign in your mortal body, that ye should obey it in the lusts thereof.

Christ lived to God. In Christ, believers were alive to God. This was the Christian's assurance.

Sin has not gone anywhere. It is still lurking around in this age. Sin will still seek to draw people back into the world as it did Demas (2 Tim. 4:10). But Paul in verse twelve called for steadfastness. Now defeat at the hands of sin does not have to occur. Why? Because sin and death have no real power. They have been dethroned and stripped of all power in Christ. Now believers can conquer what once conquered and destroyed them, sin and death. Lusts of the mortal body can call out commands but these can be ignored. Christ through the work of the Holy Spirit has given to believers the power and the privilege to obey and live to God.

III. Instruments of Righteousness: Romans 6:13-14, 20-23

A. Yield to God: 13

13. Neither yield ye your members as instruments of unrighteousness unto sin: but yield yourselves unto God, as those that are alive from the dead, and your members as instruments of righteousness unto God.

Yielding is hard work. Why? Because humankind works so hard at holding on to its own way. Sin and death had left their tracks like wagon wheel ruts in our muddy roads, and we followed these ruts to the same weary destinations. Why? Because we yielded to sin and death long before we ever yielded to God. The imprint of sin was with us.

Cutting new paths was a long and hard process. Not because God's hand was shortened so that He couldn't perform, but because we were so reluctant to allow Him to perform. Faith was the victory but it was not won easily. What God had declared easy, we had made hard.

Yielding means to concede or surrender, to relinquish as to a superior force. This we did to sin readily. Letting go to God we resisted. Now sin and death really no longer have any claim to our territory. In reality they never did. It belongs and belonged always to God. Now in Christ we have the power to yield our territory to God.

B. Live Under Grace: 14

14. For sin shall not have dominion over you: for ye are not under the law, but under grace.

Sin worked through the law. Grace worked through Christ. Under the law and sin, people were compelled to sin. They were a slave to do the bidding of sin. Now under the grace of God in Christ, humankind is set free from the compulsion to sin which was prompted and reinforced by the law.

Believers are free *from* something and free *to* something. They are free from the old tired way of sin, free to the new and fresh way of life. Shackled to the law, sin was our master. We were prisoners. Bound to Christ, we have been given our sonship with God.

C. Bear Fruit: 20-23

20. For when ye were the servants of sin, ye were free from righteousness.

21. What fruit had ye then in those things whereof ye are now ashamed? for the end of those things is death.

22. But now being made free from sin, and become servants to God, ye have your fruit unto holiness, and the end everlasting life.

23. For the wages of sin is death; but the gift of God is eternal Life through Jesus Christ our Lord.

Dead fruit trees can't produce fruit. Being dead in sin one could not produce any fruit either. What good was in people was dead under the power of sin. The parasite, sin, produced its work of darkness through people instead.

Now believers are alive under grace. Jesus Christ has made them alive. Now they can produce fruit of the Spirit. Dead bodies have had life breathed back into them.

There can be no neutrality. There were two who vied for our obedience. Each paid in its own coin. The wages of sin is death. The gift of God is eternal life. One issued in works of the flesh which hurt the worker and all others around. The other issued in fruit of the Spirit that blesses the bearer and those nearby.

Evangelistic Emphasis

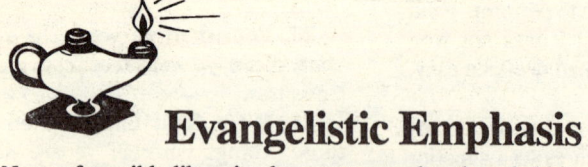

News of possible liberation has great appeal to those held in a prison camp. The method of the communication, the expertise of the messenger, his personal charm and good intentions, the technique and style are not what counts. They are not the good news. What fills the heart with joy and the eyes with tears is the promise of freedom.

Most people have an innate sense of justice which dictates that one will get what's coming to him. Consequently, they are in bondage to fears for their future. One cannot undo what he has done. How can he hope to escape the natural and just rewards of his own selfishness? The Christian messenger cannot deliver tormented souls held in the prison of their own failure and guilt. But he or she can tell of the Liberator, the one who came to this earth to set the captives free. On the basis of his goodness, not the merits of the captives, freedom is provided.

This story makes the difference in life and death. As we share our faith in the crucified and risen God we are not the heroes of the piece. The real focus is not to be on us, our gifts, our abilities, our knowledge, our techniques, our goodness. The focus in sharing faith must remain constantly on Jesus Christ.

♦♦♦♦♦♦

Memory Selection

For the wages of sin is death; but the gift of God is eternal life through Jesus Christ our Lord.
Romans 6:23

The problem with the Roman Christians in the first century, the problem with us modern American Christians, is our independent mindset. We take enormous pride in our self-sufficiency. "There is no free lunch." "No welfare for me, I make my own way!" We accept no free gifts, we collect our well-earned wages. Paul agreed with the psalmist: "God does not deal with us according to our iniquities."

If we were paid just what we have earned we would know separation from God, spiritual death. The fact that we Christians have been reconciled with God is not our doing. Salvation is not fair wages for work done. It is an outright gift of the goodness and mercy of God. So long as we think in terms of our own goodness, of earning our right standing with God, we have no hope of seeing how truly gracious He was to us in Jesus Christ.

Weekday Problems

Everyone at work knew Arnold was proud of being his own man. "No one owns me, I worked my way up every step of the way." He liked to tell all who would listen how he started twenty years ago at the bottom of the ladder and climbed his way up to supervisor. He had claimed no special privileges, asked no favors, was not the boss's nephew. He had not slid in half the way up the scale like some had done with their fancy college degrees.

Since he had earned all the success he enjoyed, he believed he owed no one anything. The trouble with Arnold's freedom was that it seemed to vanish unless he talked about it and tried to convince others of his achievement. At lunch, during afternoon break, at the foremen's meetings--everywhere he found it necessary to recall how he had worked his way up the hard way. Everyone but Arnold could see that he was not really free, he was enslaved to his own story. Talking or not talking about it was no longer an option. He had to explain his success and independence to everyone he met.

*Why do achievements relished tend to enslave us?
*Can Arnold be helped? How would you approach the problem?

♦♦♦♦♦♦

Sparkles

One of the desert fathers named Isaiah once said, "When God wishes to take pity on a soul and it rebels, not bearing anything and doing its own will, He then allows it to suffer that which it does not want, in order that it may seek Him again."

Who wants sin and death? Yet we serve both until we become sick of them. Jesus has the same gift we first refused waiting for us still. Grace, grace, marvelous grace!

Theodora, another desert father, said, "Give the body discipline and you will see that the body is for Him who made it."

DELIVERANCE FROM SIN

This Lesson In Your Life

In recent years we have read about it in the papers, we have seen it on the television news. Hostages have been taken by foreign powers. Sometimes they have spent months or even years in captivity. In our history books we have read about the slave trade in America before the Civil War. The slave was owned by another man. He or she had no self-determination. Every circumstance and every choice was controlled by another person. There was no court of appeal.

We cannot relate first-hand to these situations. But we do know a much more insidious form of captivity. We know an imprisonment which lasts, not for weeks, months, or years but for a whole lifetime. It is slavery to self. Many do not even realize they are held captive. But the chains are real and strong. Every enterprise prompts the question, "What's in it for me?" Every danger is met with, "What are the risks in this for me?"

Another is honored and we complain, "Why is it that some people are recognized and others never get noticed? Just once it would be nice to be honored." Another injures us and we know it was a calculated personal attack. "He knew perfectly well that he was hurting me, why else would have done such a thing? He is just mean and vindictive!" He or she who lives in such a world is held hostage just as surely as any political prisoner or any slave ever was.

We cannot just spring free from this slavery to self by our own initiative and power. Paul gives us the answer. He centers his whole theology, his entire hope, on the person of Jesus Christ. More specifically, the cross and resurrection of Jesus were the great liberating events of all time. Here in Romans 6 the whole struggle with self is framed in the wood from Golgotha's tree. Paul reminded his readers that they had been baptized into the death of Christ, had been raised with him to walk a new life. If we can focus on him, identify with him, trust him we can be free! Our runaway pride can be nailed to a cross while we are set free to get out of ourselves and care about others.

We are slaves to whatever we serve without reservation. The irony is in the nature of Christian freedom. We do not free ourselves any more than we baptize ourselves. Another does it for us in both cases. We are free, not by having no master, but by choosing the right Master. Martin Luther struggled with the problem of Christian freedom all his life. He stated the truth paradoxically. "The Christian is a perfectly free lord of all, subject to none; a Christian man is a perfectly dutiful servant of all, and subject to all." The reason is that the Christian's freedom springs from the person, work and example of Jesus Christ.

Seed Thoughts

1. Why should Christians not see liberty in Christ as carte blanche to live as they choose?
Because Jesus did not see His own liberty as freedom to do only what He wanted. He prayed, "Not my will but thine be done."

2. What is the meaning of Christian baptism?
Baptism symbolizes death to sin, and initiates us into the family of God.

3. What does baptism have to do with Christian ethics?
One should not accept a free and priceless gift and then slap the Giver in the face.

4. Does "newness of life" mean moral perfection?
No, the letter of Romans was written to Christians who continued to need the grace of God in their lives.

5. Why would one agree to the pain of "dying to" his or her own self?
Because Christ promises freedom from slavery of self and a new and free life in him.

(PLEASE TURN PAGE)

---

1. Why should Christians not see liberty in Christ as carte blanche to live as they choose?

2. What is the meaning of Christian baptism?

3. What does baptism have to do with Christian ethics?

4. Does "newness of life" mean moral perfection?

5. Why would one agree to the pain of "dying to" his or her own self?

6. Why would Paul become so earthy as to care what the Roman Christians did with the "members" of their bodies?

7. Why does Paul speak of being "slaves to righteousness?"

8. Why does Paul continually refer to the death, burial and resurrection of Jesus?

9. According to Romans 6, what is the mainspring of Christian ethics?

10. According to Paul, what is the best safeguard against "cheap grace" and loose, libertine ethics?

(SEED THOUGHTS--Cont'd)

Because Jesus did not see His own liberty as freedom to do only what He wanted. He prayed, "Not my will but thine be done."

Baptism symbolizes death to sin, and initiates us into the family of God.

One should not accept a free and priceless gift and then slap the Giver in the face.

No, the letter of Romans was written to Christians who continued to need the grace of God in their lives.

Because Christ promises freedom from slavery of self and a new and free life in him.

Because we serve whatever master we choose with our whole beings, with our whole bodies.

Because every human being serves something or someone as worthy of ultimate devotion.

Because he, like all the New Testament writers, saw the passion of Christ as the fountainhead of grace.

Gratitude for the love of God given for us in Jesus Christ.

To focus on Jesus Christ and to accept with thankfulness the priceless gift of life we have in Him.

---

6. Why would Paul become so earthy as to care what the Roman Christians did with the "members" of their bodies?
Because we serve whatever master we choose with our whole beings, with our whole bodies.

7. Why does Paul speak of being "slaves to righteousness?"
Because every human being serves something or someone as worthy of ultimate devotion.

8. Why does Paul continually refer to the death, burial and resurrection of Jesus?
Because he, like all the New Testament writers, saw the passion of Christ as the fountainhead of grace.

9. According to Romans 6, what is the mainspring of Christian ethics?
Gratitude for the love of God given for us in Jesus Christ.

10. According to Paul, what is the best safeguard against "cheap grace" and loose, libertine ethics?
To focus on Jesus Christ and to accept with thankfulness the priceless gift of life we have in Him.

April 3, 1994

A Glimpse of Glory

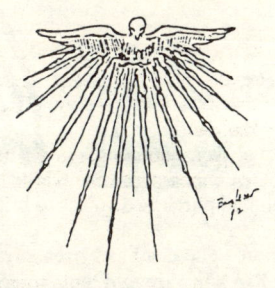

Mark 16:1-8

16 AND when the sabbath was past, Mary Mag-da-le-ne, and Mary the *mother* of James, and Sa-lo'-me, had bought him sweet spices, that they might come and anoint him.

2 And very early in the morning the first *day* of the week, they came unto the sepulchre at the rising of the sun.

3 And they said among themselves, Who shall roll us away the stone from the door of the sepulchre?

4 And when they looked, they saw that the stone was rolled away: for it was very great.

5 And entering into the sepulchre, they saw a young man sitting on the right side, clothed in a long white garment; and they were affrighted.

6 And he saith unto them, Be not affrighted: Ye seek Jesus of Nazareth, which was crucified: he is risen; he is not here: behold the place where they laid him.

7 But go your way, tell his disciples and Peter that he goeth before you into Ga-lilee: there shall you see him, as he said unto you.

8 And they went out quickly, and fled from the sepulchre; for they trembled and were amazed; neither said they any thing to any *man*; for they were afraid.

Romans 8:12-17

12 Therefore, brethren, we are debtors, not to the flesh, to live after the flesh.

13 For if ye live after the flesh, ye shall die: but if ye through the Spirit do mortify the deeds of the body, ye shall live.

14 For as many as are led by the Spirit of God, they are the sons of God.

15 For ye have not received the spirit of bondage again to fear, but ye have received the Spirit of adoption, whereby we cry, Ab'-ba, Father.

16 The Spirit itself beareth witness with our spirit, that we are the children of God:

17 And if children, then heirs; heirs of God, and joint-heirs with Christ; if so be that we suffer with *him*, that we may be also glorified together.

◆◆◆◆◆◆

◀ **Memory Selection**
Romans 8:16-17

◀ **Devotional Reading**
Luke 24:1-11

◀ **Background Scripture**
Mark 16:1-8; Romans 8:12-27

◀ **Printed Scripture**
Mark 16:1-8; Romans 8:12-17

A GLIMPSE OF GLORY

Teacher's Target

Every culture has its own rituals to honor the dead. In our culture we place flowers on the grave. In Jesus' day, anointing the body of the dead with sweet-smelling spices was a sign of love. After the Sabbath had ended, the women had purchased spices to bring to Jesus' tomb early on the first day of the week.

They were startled by a strange phenomenon. The dead had risen. Jesus was not in the tomb, but a messenger sat where Jesus had lain. He told them to go to Galilee. They would see Jesus there.

How do you express grief and your goodbyes to loved ones who have died? What would you feel if you went to the graveside and the grave was empty? Can you place yourself in the place of these women? Have you ever experienced a mysterious event? Who believed you? Can you believe these women?

Lesson Introduction

The women who loved Jesus were shocked by His death. Now they were in for a second shock. Bearing spices to anoint Jesus' body, they found no body in the tomb. Jesus, the friend of those who had little power in the culture, was gone. No one had ever honored and appreciated them as He did. Jesus neither worshiped women nor abused them. He accepted and appreciated them for themselves. The women felt the void of this different kind of love.

Now they were twice shocked. He wasn't dead. He had risen! He had gone before them into Galilee. They fled from the tomb trembling with amazement. They were afraid. Who wouldn't have been! What could it all mean? What were they to do with this new information? But first how could they process it themselves?

Teaching Outline

I. Burial Ritual Planned:
   Mark 16:1-6
   A. Preparation: 1
   B. The Journey: 2-4
   C. The Messenger: 5,6
II. Overruled by Resurrection:
   Mark 16:7-8
   A. Instructions: 7
   B. Response: 8
III. Resurrection Meaning:
   Romans 8:12-17
   A. No Debt to Flesh: 12-13
   B. Led by the Spirit: 14-16
   C. Joint Heirs with Christ: 17

Daily Bible Readings

Mon. Shocking News: He has Risen!
Mark 16:1-8
Tues. Who Are the Children of God?
Romans 8:12-18
Wed. The Work of the Spirit
Romans 9:26-32
Thurs. More Than Conquerors
Romans 8:33-39
Fri. The Glory of the Lord
Isaiah 6:1-8
Sat. Visions of God
Ezekiel 1:15-28
Sun. Commissioned to Prophesy
Ezekiel 2:1-7

April 3, 1994

VERSE BY VERSE

I. Burial Ritual Planned: Mark 16:1-6

A. Preparation: 1

1. AND when the sabbath was past, Mary Mag-da-le-ne, and Mary the mother of James, and Sa-lo′-me, had bought him sweet spices, that they might come and anoint him.

The plan was to honor the dead. The Sabbath had been a sad one. The disciples of Jesus, male and female, were full of grief and fear. No one was sure how safe it was to go near the tomb. But they wanted to express their love.

The women brought sweet spices after the Sabbath ended. Maybe if they went early in the morning no one would see them. Maybe if only the women went they would not be accosted or arrested. The last services to the body of Jesus had been interrupted by the Sabbath. Now this last expression of love and affection could be shown to Him. There was no expectation of a resurrection. The women's attitude was one of a last tribute to the dead. The disciples, the eleven especially, had an attitude that said everything had ended like a Greek tragedy.

B. The Journey: 2-4

2. And very early in the morning the first day of the week, they came unto the sepulchre at the rising of the sun.
3. And they said among themselves, Who shall roll us away the stone from the door of the sepulchre?
4. And when they looked, they saw that the stone was rolled away: for it was very great.

There was no sense of joy or victory in the hearts these women. Without the resurrection of Jesus neither joy, courage nor victory would have come to Jesus' followers. They were despondent, with little hope, full of great sorrow over a relationship of deep love that had been cut short. Theirs was a sad march to the grave.

It was sunrise when they arrived at the tomb. As they moved toward the tomb, they realized they had brought no one with them who could roll away the stone from the entrance. Their combined effort would not be sufficient.

Still they would not turn back. Their love and devotion to Jesus drew them on to do this one final gesture of their honor and love for Him.

C. The Messenger: 5, 6

5. And entering into the sepulchre, they saw a young man sitting on the right side, clothed in a long white garment; and they were affrighted.
6. And he saith unto them, Be not affrighted: Ye seek Jesus of Nazareth, which was crucified: he is risen; he is not here: behold the

303

place where they laid him.

They went out to anoint a dead man and were met by one sent from God, an angel. Like the shepherds in the field at Jesus' birth, the women were afraid when the angel was present. No one would have expected this in a field or at a tomb.

What unexpected comfort! A messenger from God with news, good news, that Jesus had risen from the dead. Yes, He was crucified. Yes, He died. Yes, He was buried there. But now they were to go and tell His disciples what they had seen. The place where He was laid is empty.

II. Overruled by Resurrection: Mark 16:7-8

A. Instructions: 7

7. But go your way, tell his disciples and Peter that he goeth before you into Galilee: there shall you see him, as he said unto you.

The angel had helped them calm down. He had made sure they saw the empty tomb. Later there would be no mistaking this experience for a grief-laden, hysterical illusion. Now they were assured that their emotions and senses were not playing a trick on them, they were ready for their victory orders.

They were to go quickly and tell the disciples and Peter. The women had been the first there to serve Jesus. They would be the first to be sent out in His service.

Why was Galilee the place Jesus wanted to meet? Possibly because it was there that Jesus had told His disciples He would make them fishers of men (Matt. 4:19). From the accounts of the Gospels it appears that Jesus had to meet the disciples first in Jerusalem (Luke 24:36). They were behind locked doors out of fear of the authorities. Later Jesus did meet them in Galilee. It might be worthy of note that all the meetings with Jesus were by His own appointing, not the bidding of the disciples. He will not forget His appointments and He will meet His disciples where they are.

B. Response: 8

8. And they went out quickly, and fled from the sepulchre; for they trembled and were amazed; neither said they any thing to any man; for they were afraid.

The women left quickly. They had experienced too much too fast. From death to life, from grief to joy, from despondency to encouragement, all in three short days.

They, like we, had been enemies to their own faith. They had heard words but they had not truly heard Jesus when He spoke of rising on the third day. Had they truly heard they would have been more expectant. Who can fault them without pointing to himself.

The women left and would tell no one along the way. They were in shock. They weren't sure what had happened. They would do as they were told and see what transpired from that point on.

III. Resurrection Meaning: Romans 8:12-17

A. No Debt to Flesh: 12-13

12. Therefore, brethren, we are debtors, not to the flesh, to live after the flesh.
13. For if ye live after the flesh, ye shall die: but if ye through the Spirit do mortify the deeds of the body, ye shall live.

The women at the tomb were privileged, it is true. Yet they only got a glimpse of glory. Their witness and the witness of Scripture give us an even clearer picture of the meaning of Jesus' resurrection.

Jesus was not just a character in a book or in history. He was and is a presence alive in our midst. Jesus was not a memory. A memory fades with time. Jesus was a real presence that became more certain to believers with time. Believers do not just know about Jesus, but because of the resurrection they know Him.

Believers do not live for the flesh. A life lived in service of the flesh is a life lived for death. By the power of the Spirit believers mortify the deeds of the flesh. Now a new power overcomes the power of the flesh. Spirit has replaced flesh as the ruler and enabler in life. Flesh is owed no allegiance to follow its destructive way.

B. Led by the Spirit: 14-16

14. For as many as are led by the Spirit of God, they are the sons of God.
15. For ye have not received the spirit of bondage again to fear, but ye have received the Spirit of adoption, whereby we cry, Ab'-ba, Father.
16. The Spirit itself beareth witness with our spirit, that we are the children of God:

Jesus in the Lord's prayer addressed God as "Abba." This was a term of deep endearment much like our word "Daddy." No Jewish man had ever addressed God so intimately. Yet Jesus taught that God was "Daddy." What could be sweeter to a parent's ears than for a child to crawl into his arms and say, "Daddy" or "Mama?"

Here Paul states once again that we have been adopted through Christ into the family of God. We are given the privilege to cry, "Abba, Father" when we address God. "The Spirit itself beareth witness with our spirit, that we are the children of God" (Rom. 8:16).

In Roman culture an adopted child had all the rights of a natural heir. He was considered a full heir to his father's estate. Likewise, we who claim Christ as our Savior gain the privileges and responsibilities of Christ, God's true Son.

C. Joint Heirs With Christ: 17

17. And if children, then heirs; heirs of God, and joint-heirs with Christ; if so be that we suffer with him, that we may be also glorified together.

No longer are believers slaves of sin. Now they are children of the Master. All that was His is theirs.

This means responsibility as well as privilege. Paul states in verse 17 that believers will suffer with Him for His name sake. The final word is they will also be glorified together with Him.

Evangelistic Emphasis

One of the greatest barriers to Christian witness is the fear in our hearts. We are afraid of rejection, afraid we are not good enough examples of Christian living, afraid we might be asked questions we cannot answer. We even ask if fearful Christians can ever come to witness as they should to their Lord.

Mark's story of Jesus is helpful just here. Why did the three women at Jesus' empty tomb leave and say nothing to anyone? Mark explains: "for they were afraid" (Mk. 16:18). All the way through Mark's story of Jesus various ones of his disciples wanted to go out and tell what had happened. Jesus restrained them several times, saying, "Don't tell anyone about this." Perhaps they didn't have the full story yet. Not until the open tomb was the story complete. Even then the women lacked courage. They were not exceptions. None of the disciples was brave enough to tell what happened. They witnessed boldly only after they were filled with the Holy Spirit on Pentecost.

To be an effective witness we need more than the facts. We need to pray for a better understanding of the meaning of those facts and to pray for God's Presence in our hearts to help us bear testimony to our risen Lord.

◆◆◆◆◆◆

Memory Selection

The Spirit itself beareth witness with our spirit, that we are the children of God: and if children, then heirs; heirs of God, and joint heirs with Christ; if so be that suffer with him, that we may be also glorified together. Rom. 8:16-17

Many Christians are insecure about their standing in God's family. How do we know that we are reconciled and back home with God? Whose word do we take for it? Is it on merits we have won, or on what basis? Are we in one day, out the next, back in on a third day?

In Romans 8 we are assured that we belong in God's family if we have "put on Christ." We have been given life (vs. 11). We are the adopted brothers and sisters of Christ and so heirs with him (vss. 16, 17). We know it is true because the Holy Spirit prompts us to be uninhibited children and cry out "Abba, Father" (v.15).

One day when we are in heaven we will see plainly that we are loved and belong at home with Him. In the meanwhile, by the gift of God's spirit, He assures us that we are accepted into the family circle.

April 3, 1994

Weekday Problems

Fred was a terror to himself, his classmates, his high school principal and most of all to his family. He disrupted every class he attended, drove his car at excessive speeds around town, and frequently left the house in the middle of the night to go out drinking. Three times in the last year he had been in jail. On the third occasion Fred was charged with stealing money from the cash register where he worked to buy drugs.

The judge warned Fred that he was on a dangerous downward spiral and would end up in serious trouble unless he changed his ways. But he did not have an idea of how to change. His mother was in her third marriage. None of her men had accepted Fred, much less shown any real concern for his welfare. His father whom he had never seen had married and divorced since he left Fred's mother and was now living with a girlfriend. Fred had declared war on the world. Friends tried to understand, counselors attempted to reach out, teachers tried to make contact. No one could get to first base with him.

*What is the good news of the gospel for Fred?
*What could the youth group at church mean to Fred?

♦♦♦♦♦♦

Sparkles

A disciple asked, "What must I do to attain a holy life?"
The teacher said, "Follow your heart."
The disciple was pleased with the answer and was about to leave satisfied when the teacher spoke again in a low voice that caused the disciple to pay close attention, "To follow your heart, you are going to need a strong constitution."

Another disciple asked how to distinguish a true teacher from a false one. The teacher did not hesitate but responded, "A good teacher offers practice; a bad one offers theories."

Hedging a bit from the answer, the student asked, "But how shall I know good practice from bad?"

The teacher replied, "In the same way the farmer knows good cultivation from bad."

This Lesson In Your Life

It's a life and death matter, according to Paul. Your life and death. And mine. Ours together. If we live "according to the flesh" we will die spiritually. He's not just talking about drunkenness, embezzlement of funds and sexual immorality. "According to the flesh" means living life on our own, by our own wits, in business for ourselves. (See for example the wide variety of self-centered attitudes mentioned in Gal. 5:16-26.)

On the other hand, how can we "walk by the Spirit?" What is the formula? Are some Christians especially good, sincere and serious about their religion and so God gives them the Spirit? What does it meant to walk according to the Spirit anyway?

In Gen. 1:1 we meet the basic biblical understanding of the Spirit. The Spirit of God moved over the face of the waters creating order where there was only chaos, shedding light in the darkness and bringing life to a lifeless waste. In the Bible the Holy Spirit does many things. He inspires the prophets, sets kings upon their thrones, empowers the first disciples to announce the gospel, sometimes grants special gifts of tongues, prophecy and teaching. But in all of this the view set forth in the first verse of the Bible holds primary: the Holy Spirit is God here with us, creating order, light and life. In creation. In the church. In our own personal lives.

According to Peter's promise (Acts 2:38) when we believe in Jesus the crucified and risen Lord, turn from our sins to him and are baptized into his name we are forgiven our sins and given God's Spirit to create new life in us. The extent to which we are conscious of and dependent on God's creative Presence in us is limited only by our own openness to Him.

For many of us Christians the first step is to remember our birth into Christ, to trust the promise that we have the Creator living in us and to claim the joys, benefits, responsibilities and privileges as God's children in His family. Since we are the adopted children of God we have an inheritance waiting for us. Whatever joys we know in the Lord here and now, they are nothing compared to what we have waiting for us! So meanwhile, we accept suffering and heartaches as workers with Him in His redeeming mission. We cry out, sometimes with grief so deep we cannot find words. The Spirit helps us, prays for us. When we accept the fact that we are God's children, that He lives in our hearts, all life is transformed.

Seed Thoughts

1. Why do Christians sometimes feel that we are captives to Satan, bound to slavery in sin?
Because we have not accepted the fact that we have God's life in us and belong to Him.

2. If one who bakes for a living is a baker, one who gardens is a gardener, how can I not be a sinner since I continually sin?
Because your new life and new identity is "child of God" who sometimes sins.

3. How can I feel like a slave if, in fact, I am a child of God?
If a child of God chooses bondage to Satan he can certainly know the burden of that life.

4. Does "living according to the Spirit" mean I'm exempt from temptation and sin?
No, we live both in "this age" and in "the age to come" as Paul would say.

5. If I am a child of God and Jesus is my brother, am I presuming to be equal with Jesus?
No, Jesus is God's only son, the only one of a kind. We are adopted into the family.

(PLEASE TURN PAGE)

---

1. Why do Christians sometimes feel that we are captives to Satan, bound to slavery in sin?

2. If one who bakes for a living is a baker, one who gardens is a gardener, how can I not be a sinner since I continually sin?

3. How can I feel like a slave if, in fact, I am a child of God?

4. Does "living according to the Spirit" mean I'm exempt from temptation and sin?

5. If I am a child of God and Jesus is my brother, am I presuming to be equal with Jesus?

6. Why do Christians accept suffering for Christ as a normal part of life?

7. What does our promised family reunion in heaven have to do with our suffering now?

8. What does Paul mean when he says the whole creation longs for redemption?

9. When I hurt too bad to pray should I feel guilty?

10. If I do not feel the Holy Spirit working in my heart does this mean I am dead spiritually?

Because we have not accepted the fact that we have God's life in us and belong to Him.

Because your new life and new identity is "child of God" who sometimes sins.

If a child of God chooses bondage to Satan he can certainly know the burden of that life.

No, we live both in "this age" and in "the age to come" as Paul would say.

No, Jesus is God's only son, the only one of a kind. We are adopted into the family.

Because Jesus suffered to do God's work and we are called to be his helpers.

Paul said our present struggles are nothing compared to what we have waiting for us.

Our biblical faith says all of creation fell short when man fell short and all will be redeemed together one day.

No, God hears the Spirit who communicates even the groanings of our hearts.

Do you sometimes cry out to God, call out for help, for understanding, for strength to cope? Paul says you are a living child of God.

(SEED THOUGHTS—Cont'd)

6. Why do Christians accept suffering for Christ as a normal part of life?
Because Jesus suffered to do God's work and we are called to be his helpers.

7. What does our promised family reunion in heaven have to do with our suffering now?
Paul said our present struggles are nothing compared to what we have waiting for us.

8. What does Paul mean when he says the whole creation longs for redemption?
Our biblical faith says all of creation fell short when man fell short and all will be redeemed together one day.

9. When I hurt too bad to pray should I feel guilty?
No, God hears the Spirit who communicates even the groanings of our hearts.

10. If I do not feel the Holy Spirit working in my heart does this mean I am dead spiritually?
Do you sometimes cry out to God, call out for help, for understanding, for strength to cope? Paul says you are a living child of God.

April 10, 1994

Life In The Spirit

Romans 8:1-11

1 THERE is therefore now no condemnation to them which are in Christ Jesus, who walk not after the flesh, but after the Spirit.
2 For the law of the the Spirit of life in Christ Jesus hath made me free from the law of sin and death.
3 For what the law could not do, in that it was weak through the flesh, God sending his own Son in the likeness of sinful flesh, and for sin, condemned sin in the flesh:
4 That the righteousness of the law might be fulfilled in us, who walk not after the flesh, but after the Spirit.
5 For they that are after the flesh do mind the things Of the flesh; but they that are after the Spirit the things of the Spirit.
6 For to be carnally minded is death; but to be spiritually minded is life and peace.
7 Because the carnal mind is enmity against God: for it is not subject to the law of God, neither indeed can be.
8 So then they that are in the flesh cannot please God.
9 But ye are not in the flesh, but in the Spirit, if so be that the Spirit of God dwell in you. Now if any man have not the Spirit of Christ, he is none of his.
10 And if Christ be in you, the body is dead because of sin; but the Spirit is life because of righteousness.
11 But if the Spirit of him that raised up Jesus from the dead dwell in you, he that raised up Christ from the dead shall also quicken your mortal bodies by his Spirit that dwelleth in you.

◆◆◆◆◆◆

◀ **Memory Selection**
Romans 8:2

◀ **Devotional Reading**
Romans 8:26-28, 35-39

◀ **Background Scripture**
Romans 8:1-11

◀ **Printed Scripture**
Romans 8:1-11

LIFE IN THE SPIRIT

Teacher's Target

Shame and guilt are two aspects of humankind's fallen condition. For this Jesus was sent. In Jesus' finished work on the cross and in the resurrection shame and guilt were removed far from us. As far as east is from west. Thus, in Christ there is no condemnation, only forgiveness and righteousness are bestowed where once shame and guilt reigned.

In the flesh (the fallen or lower nature) no one could please God. God knew this. He did for us what we could not do. Then He offered the new possibility of making us pleasing to Him in Christ. The power of this new life is the indwelling Holy Spirit.

Explain the difference between flesh and Spirit? What does it mean to be carnally minded?

Lesson Introduction

In Romans 1-7 Paul had been painting a clear and unmistakable picture. Whether people lived in sinful rebellion running from God, or sinful Law-keeping trying to be their own god, humankind was hopelessly lost. All were ungodly and there was none righteous, no not one.

In Romans 8 Paul declared the remedy. Jesus Christ had taken the curse of humanity's iniquity to the cross, nailed it there and declared the guilty were acquitted in Him.

Paul knew that though he was no longer condemned, the old nature still clung to him. Only by faith could he live out any of Romans 8. Otherwise he would live in Romans 1-7. Though sin raged within, no longer did believers have to listen. New life in the power of the Spirit was possible.

Teaching Outline

I. Free from Sin and Death: Romans 8:1-4
   A. Free from the Law: 1-2
   B. Sin Condemned: 3
   C. Righteousness in the Spirit: 4
II. Minding the Things of the Spirit: Romans 8:5-9
   A. Carnally Minded: 5-8
   B. Spiritually Minded: 6-9
III. Raised Up With Jesus: Romans 8:10-11
   A. Body Is Dead: 10
   B. Spirit Is Life: 10
   C. Quickened by the Spirit: 11

Daily Bible Readings

Mon. Free! Free! I'm Free at Last! *Romans 8:1-5*
Tue. Mind on Flesh or Spirit? *Romans 8:6-11*
Wed. Children and Heirs of God *Romans 8:12-17*
Thurs. A Vision of the Exalted God *Revelation 4*
Fri. There Shall Be Showers of Blessings - *Ezekiel 36:22-26*
Sat. Even Maidservants Shall Prophesy - *Acts 2:14-21*
Sun. God Gives a Heart of Flesh *Ezekiel 11:14-21*

April 10, 1994

VERSE BY VERSE

I. **Free from Sin and Death: Romans 8:1-4**

A. **Free from the Law: 1-2**

1. **THERE is therefore now no condemnation to them which are in Christ Jesus, who walk not after the flesh, but after the Spirit.**
2. **For the law of the the Spirit of life in Christ Jesus hath made me free from the law of sin and death.**

The ultimate fear of the human race was death, non-existence. The question asked by philosophers and men in the street alike down through the ages had been: was there an answer? Could man do more than just exist in the present? And in the beyond would there be life?

Paul declared that in Jesus Christ the answer had been given by God. All had broken the Law of God. No one had been obedient. But in Christ, who did obey God, humankind had been acquitted. Jesus nailed the Law and its handwritten ordinances against us to the cross in His death. He carried our accuser in His victory train. Satan was stripped of any power to condemn us again (Col. 2:13-15). In Christ humankind was set free from all condemnation.

B. **Sin Condemned: 3**

3. **For what the law could not do, in that it was weak through the flesh, God sending his own Son in the likeness of sinful flesh, and for sin, condemned sin in the flesh:**

What was condemned in Christ was not humankind but sin. This alien intruder into the nature of man had been challenged, conquered and condemned in Christ. Now rather than people being dead, sin was dead. Through Christ, people could come to life once again.

Jesus Christ walked not after the way of the flesh (the way of disobedience). He was obedient (which means "give ear to"). He gave His ear to the Father. Jesus listened only for His voice in all situations. When He listened to the Father, the Spirit flowed in Him and He did not obey the law of sin and death.

"The law of the Spirit of life" was to listen to the Father. Only Jesus had ever done this completely and continually. Humankind's yes to Jesus was their passport to freedom.

C. **Righteousness in the Spirit: 4**

4. **That the righteousness of the law might be fulfilled in us, who walk not after the flesh, but after the Spirit.**

At creation the Holy Spirit was present (Gen. 1:2). Humankind was at that time innocent, not perfect. Adam fell and all after him. Now, in Christ, once again humankind was declared innocent though guilty. How? Because the one man, Jesus Christ, did for all what not one of the all could do. He lived out righteousness (which means to fulfill the function for which a person or thing was created). This righteousness He bestowed on believers as a gift. The ungodly had been declared righteous by Jesus. By faith the Holy Spirit entered the believer's life and the believer then had the power to live out what he had been declared to be, righteous in Christ.

II. Minding the Things of the Spirit: Romans 8:5-9

A. Carnally Minded: 5-8

5. For they that are after the flesh do mind the things Of the flesh; but they that are after the Spirit the things of the Spirit.

6. For to be carnally minded is death; but to be spiritually minded is life and peace.

7. Because the carnal mind is enmity against God: for it is not subject to the law of God, neither indeed can be.

8. So then they that are in the flesh cannot please God.

Paul knew that just because by grace through faith the believer had been declared righteous, the battle was not over. The ultimate victory was assured, but claiming the inner territory of each person's life would be a daily warfare. The power of sin could not be underestimated without grave consequences. The old nature's propensity to believe that its own willpower could stand against the tempter was strong. Peter had believed this and he denied his Lord three times.

Relying upon self was to be carnally minded. The mind of the believer must be focused on the kingdom of God revealed in Jesus Christ (Matt. 6:33). He was their strength (Phil. 4:13). All are carnally minded. Only Christ can empower us to be spiritually minded.

B. Spiritually Minded: 6-9

6. For to be carnally minded is death; but to be spiritually minded is life and peace.

7. Because the carnal mind is enmity against God: for it is not subject to the law of God, neither indeed can be.

8. So then they that are in the flesh cannot please God.

9. But ye are not in the flesh, but in the Spirit, if so be that the Spirit of God dwell in you. Now if any man have not the Spirit of Christ, he is none of his.

Carnally minded, that is self-willed and self-indulgent, was death. Self did not know the way. Only faith could access the way. Faith didn't know, faith believed. The Holy Spirit would disclose the way to faith but not in advance. As Paul said in 1 Corinthians 13 faith sees only through a glass darkly. In fact, the focus was not to be on the outcome of things. The focus was to be on Christ (Col. 3:1-3). Christ was the new lens through which all things were accessed and interpreted.

Only Christ is not at odds with God. The carnal mind always was. Only by being subject to God can we know life and peace. The flesh (lower nature) was carnal (has its mind on self's way). The Spirit was life (has its mind on God's way). Let the Spirit rule (have the guiding role) in your life was the exhortation of Paul.

III. Raised With Jesus: Romans 8:10-11

A. Body is Dead: 10

10. And if Christ be in you, the body is dead because of sin; but the Spirit is life because of righteousness.

How well the believers knew the body was not dead! But the Scripture said it was?! How could this apparent contradiction be reconciled? "Body" as used here by Paul meant the lower nature of mankind. Paul knew that because of sin in the corporate body of humanity, all the ways of humankind when unaided by God's revelation in Jesus Christ would lead to death. This death Paul knew to be physical and spiritual. The earthly body would die. But more importantly the spiritual reality of man would be dead as long as it obeyed sin. But this death of body and spirit had not been God's intent and it would not be the final word.

A life begun in the natural body led to death. Starting over in the Spirit through Christ led to a new body. The natural body was connected with death. The spiritual body is connected with eternity.

B. Spirit is Life: 10

10. And if Christ be in you, the body is dead because of sin; but the Spirit is life because of righteousness.

The Holy Spirit had been given as a down payment of all that was to come (Eph. 1:1314). People used to speak of someone giving them "earnest money." By that they meant they had received a down payment as a promise that the person would come through with the rest that was to be paid. God has given us "earnest money" in the form of the Holy Spirit. He has given us this witness within us that reassures our hearts that God will come through with the fruit of the Spirit, the resurrection body and eternal life.

C. Quickened by the Spirit: 11

11. But if the Spirit of him that raised up Jesus from the dead dwell in you, he that raised up Christ from the dead shall also quicken your mortal bodies by his Spirit that dwelleth in you.

Eternal life and peace were not just for the age to come. Their mortal bodies, the very ones that were dying, had now through faith in Christ been enlivened by "the new man." The old man (mortal body) was dying daily. But the new man (spiritual nature) was being renewed daily. The eternal life had begun now. The believers' mortal bodies are actually being instilled with new life to be used for the glory of God.

Evangelistic Emphasis

Most people in our society live under a cloud of condemnation. It's easy to see in the case of the Christian legalist. He tries to live up to the demands of legal perfection. The day will come when he either rationalizes his failures and pronounces himself perfect or faces up to the brutal fact that he is not really good enough in himself to win God's approval.

Less obvious is the situation of the grace-oriented Christian. She has learned that it is not by her perfect works that she is justified. She also knows that she should respond appropriately to the gracious gift of God in Jesus Christ. But how does one really live in a way appropriate to that unspeakable gift?

The grace-oriented Christian also experiences a nagging sense of failure. Even those who have no religious convictions, who scoff at the Christian faith, live under condemnation. Why? Because every human being has some sense of what he or she should be. No one perfectly measures up. No one can meet his or her own expectations, production standards and highest ideals. Paul was correct: "all have sinned and fallen short of God's glory." The only answer is to discover Jesus' perfect performance on our behalf which is credited to our account when we believe. What good news we have to share!

◆◆◆◆◆◆

Memory Selection

For the law of the Spirit of life in Christ Jesus hath made me free from the law of sin and death.
Romans 8:2

Paul finished chapter seven of Romans in utter despair so far as human goodness is concerned. A perfect law, imperfect performance--justice demanded a penalty. Unless something intervenes, sin leads to alienation and death. Someone had intervened.

That's why Paul could begin chapter eight with the shout of victory, "Now there is no condemnation to those who are in Christ Jesus!" Two laws are mentioned in our memory verse. One cannot live under both. One cannot claim a right standing with God based on both. Either one claims reconciliation on the basis of his own record of performance, or one accepts it as a free gift on the basis of the cross of Christ. In the former case he is on his own, and it is up to him to measure up. But if one accept salvation in Christ he is still called to live a good life. The difference is he is not alone; God's Spirit lives within him. One is free from the yoke of self-salvation when he accepts Christ's salvation and His Spirit.

April 10, 1994

Weekday Problems

Sandra could never measure up. Everyone told her she was a fine actress, one of the finest young talents to appear off Broadway in years. The more they praised her, the more miserable she became. Every time she received rave notices she remembered her first high school play. In her dreams she relived it again and again, the forgotten line. She lived in terror of forgetting again, her preparation was always obsessive.

Her high school drama career had been outstanding. Even then people talked about her unusual talent and the probability of a professional acting career. In college her acclaim grew stronger and stronger. It was unusual if she was not given the most thunderous applause at curtain calls. But for some reason Sandra was full of fear and self-doubt. She could tell you every mistake she ever made in any play. The more she received approval the more pressure she felt. She knew what a perfect performance should be and she had never even approached perfection.

*Aside from what psychological counseling could offer Sandra, what does our Christian faith say to her?

*Have you given up on your perfect performance? Why or why not?

♦♦♦♦♦♦

Sparkles

The wise man in the community was asked, "What does it mean to follow the narrow and hard way?"

The old sage answered, "The narrow and hard way is this: to control your thoughts and focus upon the things above and strip yourself of your own willfulness for the sake of God. This is also the meaning of the sentence, "Lo, we have left everything and followed you" (Matt. 19:27).

The same sage was asked which is better, to be loyal or to seek the truth. He answered, "If someone were very dear and special to me, but I realized that he was leading me to do something less good, I should put him from me."

This Lesson In Your Life

Sometimes we elevate the apostles in our minds to semi-divine status. As a result, we lose much of the inspiration their stories could provide our lives. Often we think they had special experiences which removed them from the ranks of regular human beings. "If I could just know Jesus as John did I could write about love like he did." "If I had seen Jesus on the Mount of Transfiguration and after the resurrection like Peter did I could witness boldly like he did on Pentecost." "If the Lord had appeared to me as he did to Paul on the Damascus Road I could write: 'I can do all things in Christ who strengthens me.'" We miss the point which could mean so much to us: these were all human beings like ourselves, dependent on God's grace.

Paul was not perfect. At this point in his life when he wrote Romans he no longer felt the necessity of being perfect. But he did want to give himself wholly to Christ in gratitude for his salvation. Paul had the joy and freedom that comes only when we see and accept the truth that our right standing with God does not depend on our perfect performance but on what God has perfectly done in Jesus Christ.

Christians have life in God's Spirit, not in themselves. Not that the victory in Jesus is realized and felt every moment of the day. The joy sometimes gives way to feelings of anxiety, guilt and fear. Living in the spirit does not mean we are never torn between God's will and our own. In Romans 7 Paul confessed the confusion, anxiety and failure he felt every time he took the perfect law and tried to win God's approval by living up to it perfectly. It was always that way, before and after Paul met Christ and accepted the Spirit into his life. Defeat and despair always follow self salvation efforts. We Christians lapse from time to time into self-salvation thinking. "If I can just pull this off I will be okay with God."

What freedom and joy we experience at those times when we see that the merit is Christ's, not ours. Perfection is in His cross, not in our efforts. Life is found only in God's Spirit and never in our own achievements.

Even when we cannot accept these truths they are still true. Even if we go through our whole lives trying to win God's love we are never saved that way. He has loved us fully and forever at Golgotha. There and there alone we are reconciled to God, accepted and welcomed back home with Him. That is why Paul could utter the great shout of victory: "There is therefore now no condemnation to those who are in Christ Jesus... !"

Seed Thoughts

1. Should Christians just quit talking about sin, guilt and judgment since they are under grace?
No, we should be honest about our sin and God's holiness.

2. What is the difference between grace and the popular idea that we are adequate in ourselves?
Grace takes seriously our limitations, pride and sin, and offers an honest answer.

3. If I am free in Christ why do I not feel free?
It took a while before news of the Emancipation Proclamation reached the slaves. They were free but hadn't heard.

4. Was Paul advocating the abolition of all laws, of God's Law given at Sinai?
No, he was talking about the means of justification. We are never saved by the Law.

5. If "living according to the flesh" brings death, should Christians resign their jobs, leave their families and live the ascetic life?
No, "the flesh" refers to our self-centeredness. It always prays "not thy will by mine be done."

(PLEASE TURN PAGE)

---

1. Should Christians just quit talking about sin, guilt and judgment since they are under grace?

2. What is the difference between grace and the popular idea that we are adequate in ourselves?

3. If I am free in Christ why do I not feel free?

4. Was Paul advocating the abolition of all laws, of God's Law given at Sinai?

5. If "living according to the flesh" brings death, should Christians resign their jobs, leave their families and live the ascetic life?

6. If it's true that "anyone who does not have the Spirit of Christ is none of his," am I out of His good graces when I'm down?

7. What does Jesus' resurrection have to do with my daily struggles?

8. If we are "raised with Christ," why do we continue to struggle day to day?

9. Why do so many Christians get so nervous about talk of the Holy Spirit?

10. According to the Bible, who or what is the Holy Spirit?

No, we should be honest about our sin and God's holiness.

Grace takes seriously our limitations, pride and sin, and offers an honest answer.

It took a while before news of the Emancipation Proclamation reached the slaves. They were free but hadn't heard.

No, he was talking about the means of justification. We are never saved by the Law.

No, "the flesh" refers to our self-centeredness. It always prays "not thy will by mine be done."

No, the "Spirit of Christ" is not your own feelings. It's God's Presence in your heart.

The same One who, by His Spirit, raised Jesus is living and working in your daily life.

One day we will be raised complete in Him. Meanwhile He helps us with our struggles along the way.

Many destructive doctrines have been taught under the heading of the Holy Spirit.

He is God present here on earth creating life, order and light (Gen. 1:1-3).

(SEED THOUGHTS--Cont'd)

6. If it's true that "anyone who does not have the Spirit of Christ is none of his," am I out of His good graces when I'm down?
No, the "Spirit of Christ" is not your own feelings. It's God's Presence in your heart.

7. What does Jesus' resurrection have to do with my daily struggles?
The same One who, by His Spirit, raised Jesus is living and working in your daily life.

8. If we are "raised with Christ," why do we continue to struggle day to day?
One day we will be raised complete in Him. Meanwhile He helps us with our struggles along the way.

9. Why do so many Christians get so nervous about talk of the Holy Spirit?
Many destructive doctrines have been taught under the heading of the Holy Spirit.

10. According to the Bible, who or what is the Holy Spirit?
He is God present here on earth creating life, order and light (Gen. 1:1-3).

April 17, 1994

Using Our Gifts in Serving

Romans 12:1-18

1 I BESEECH You therefore, brethren, by the mercies of God, that ye present your bodies a living sacrifice, holy, acceptable unto God, *which is* your reasonable service.
2 And be not conformed to this world: but be ye transformed by the renewing of your mind, that ye may prove what *is* that good, and acceptable, and perfect, will of God.
3 For I say, through the grace given unto me, to every man that is among you, not to think *of himself* more highly than he ought to think: but to think soberly, according as God hath dealt to every man the measure of faith.
4 For as we have many members in one body, and all members have not the same office:
5 So we, *being* many, are one body in Christ, and every one members one of another.
6 Having then gifts differing according to the grace that is given to us, whether prophecy, l*et us prophesy* according to the proportion of faith;
7 Or ministry, *let us wait* on *our* ministering: or he that teacheth, on teaching;
8 Or he that exhorteth, on exhortation: he that giveth, *let him do it* with simplicity; he that ruleth, with diligence; he that sheweth mercy, with cheerfulness.
9 *Let* love be without dissimulation. Abhor that which is evil; cleave to that which is good.
10 *Be* kindly affectioned one to another with brotherly love; in honour preferring one another.
11 Not slothful in business; fervent in spirit; serving the Lord;
12 Rejoicing in hope; patient in tribulation; continuing instant in prayer;
13 Distributing to the necessity of saints; given to hospitality;
14 Bless them which persecute you: bless, and curse not.
15 Rejoice with them that do rejoice, and weep with them that weep.
16 *Be* of the same mind one toward another. Mind not high things, but condescend to men of low estate. Be not wise in your own conceits.
17 Recompense to no man evil for evil. Provide things honest in the sight of all men.
18 If it be possible, as much as lieth in you, live peaceably with all men.

◆◆◆◆◆◆

◀ **Memory Selection**
Romans 12:6

◀ **Devotional Reading**
Philippians 2:1-4, 14-16
4:8-9

◀ **Background Scripture**
Romans 12

◀ **Printed Scripture**
Romans 12:1-18

USING OUR GIFTS IN SERVING

Teacher's Target

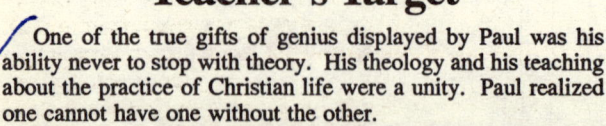

One of the true gifts of genius displayed by Paul was his ability never to stop with theory. His theology and his teaching about the practice of Christian life were a unity. Paul realized one cannot have one without the other.

One of our culture's defense mechanisms against seeing reality and having to deal responsibly with everyday life is intellectualizing. We tell ourselves, "If I understand it in my head I know it." That is not true. The longest journey in the world is from our head to our heart. Getting what we know in our heads into our being and doing it is no simple task. It takes a lifetime.

How do you avoid putting into practice what you know? How does what you believe match with what you live out? Have we turned the "word become flesh" back into words?

Lesson Introduction

Paul called for believers to be "living sacrifices." His intent was for believers to become expressions of Jesus' life. None could become Jesus. Paul knew this. one crucifixion per world was sufficient. What he envisioned was a living expression of a life yielded to God's grace and guidance. Willfulness would be surrendered. Self and others would be loved as God loves.

Only the power of Christ could accomplish this. The meaning and message of the cross and resurrection was the source of power. In the practical section of his writing, Paul described what a yielded life looked like. Being a living sacrifice would mean taking up your cross daily. Such living would produce the fruit of the Spirit. Freedom from bondage of self and others would result.

Teaching Outline

I. Transformed: Romans 12:1-3
   A. World Conformation: 1-2
   B. Mind Transformation: 1-3
   C. Sober Thinking: 3
II. One Body : Romans 12:4-15
   A. Many Members: 4-5
   B. Different Gifts: 6-8
   C. Common Life: 9-15
III. Same Mind : Romans 12:16-18
   A. Humble: 16
   B. Honest: 17
   C. Peaceable: 18

Daily Bible Readings

Mon. Depths of God's Riches, Wisdom, - *Romans 11:25-36*
Tue. Many Gifts, One Body *Romans 12:1-8*
Wed. Outdo One Another in Showing Honor - *Romans 12:9-13*
Thurs. Live Together in Integrity and Harmony - *Romans 12:14-21*
Fri. "Love Your Neighbor as Yourself" - *Romans 13:5-10*
Sat. Salvation Is Near to Us *Romans 13:11-14*
Sun. To God Be Glory Through Jesus Christ - *Romans 16:17-27*

April 17, 1994

VERSE BY VERSE

I. Transformed: Romans 12:1-3

A. World Conformation: 1-2

1. I BESEECH You therefore, brethren, by the mercies of God, that ye present your bodies a living sacrifice, holy, acceptable unto God, which is your reasonable service.

2. And be not conformed to this world: but be ye transformed by the renewing of your mind, that ye may prove what is that good, and acceptable, and perfect, will of God.

Daily life is where living has its depth and its specificity. What we do not live out in the reality of everyday existence is just our pious nature speculating about what could be. Paul knew that the world talked a good game. What the world couldn't do was walk out what it talked. The world's message was heard and practiced so long it became habit. Only a miracle could redirect life. That miracle was the cross and resurrection of Jesus Christ (Rom. l-11). Now Paul described what that miracle looked like in everyday life.

B. Mind Transformation: 1-3

1. I BESEECH You therefore, brethren, by the mercies of God, that ye present your bodies a living sacrifice, holy, acceptable unto God, which is your reasonable service.

2. And be not conformed to this world: but be ye transformed by the renewing of your mind, that ye may prove what is that good, and acceptable, and perfect, will of God.

3. For I say, through the grace given unto me, to every man that is among you, not to think of himself more highly than he ought to think: but to think soberly, according as God hath dealt to every man the measure of faith.

Be a living sacrifice. Be holy. Be acceptable unto God. These were tall orders. Paul did not call for this without first making the people aware they now had the power to live it out. Jesus Christ was that power living in them through the indwelling of the Holy Spirit. This indwelling presence would renew their minds.

When Paul talked about proving what is good, acceptable and perfect he was not talking about proving it to God as if this were necessary for our salvation. What Paul was declaring was that if we allow our minds to be renewed and shaped by the divine Word of God, our living will follow suit and prove to all around us that what God had called us to be and become was the better way of life.

C. Sober Thinking: 3

3. For I say, through the grace given unto me, to every man that is among you, not to think of himself more highly than he ought to think: but to think soberly, according as God hath dealt to every man the measure of faith.

Paul knew us well because he knew himself well. He knew the struggle with pride, power and pomposity of every man and woman. Facing this was a humbling experience.

A look at faith's walk reveals that God gives a certain measure of faith for each believer to fulfill His specific assignment for Christ. What will be needed for the task will be given. God knows His sheep. God gives the faith--believers do not work it up. He gives them the place where He needs them and where their faith can best serve. The believer is to learn to be content with his measure of faith.

II. One Body: Romans 12:4-15

A. Many Members: 4-5

4. For as we have many members in one body, and all members have not the same office:
5. So we, being many, are one body in Christ, and every one members one of another.

Every Christian received the Spirit at conversion and baptism. There is in the church a universal priesthood. It is called the priesthood of believers. All are to be priest to each other. As Luther said, "a priest at every elbow."

Because we are many we do not all have the same office. There is diversity in our unity. Difference does not mean division, nor distinction of one over another. No one is to dominate, manipulate or intimidate another. When this occurs, the church ceases to be Christ's Body, and turns back into a religious organization. Christian oneness is in seeking the same goal as the Father and the Son: to glorify God, in all things and love our neighbors as ourselves.

B. Different Gifts: 6-8

6. Having then gifts differing according to the grace that is given to us, whether prophecy, let us prophesy according to the proportion of faith;
7. Or ministry, let *us* wait on our ministering: or he that teacheth, on teaching;
8. Or he that exhorteth, on exhortation: he that giveth, let him do it with simplicity; he that ruleth, with diligence; he that sheweth mercy, with cheerfulness.

Every Christian has grace-gifts (charisma means grace gift) and the gift was to be verified in daily life. These were not possessions of the individual. They were the effect of God's grace in the community. Everyone was not suited for everything. Some things were harder for some than for others, but none made the others superfluous. Each assisted the other in the face of the world's scorn.

Every grace-gift was a specific share of grace with a specific orientation and with specific deficiencies. All were fragile vessels of our Lord's triumph. All were earthly signs of God's justification of the ungodly. Brotherliness was to be sought and preserved. None were to claim a privilege at the expense of the whole but all were to practice restraint in the interest of others.

C. Common Life: 9-15

9. Let love be without dissimulation. Abhor that which is evil; cleave to that which is good.
10. Be kindly affectioned one to another with brotherly love; in honour preferring one another
11. Not slothful in business; fervent in spirit; serving the Lord;
12. Rejoicing in hope; patient in tribulation; continuing instant prayer;
13. Distributing to the necessity of saints; given to hospitality.
14. Bless them which persecute you: bless, and curse not.
15. Rejoice with them that do rejoice, and weep with them that weep.

Gifts of the Spirit could be falsified but the fruit of the Spirit could not. By their fruits you will know them, Jesus said. Believers could not be left to their own cleverness. God had to rule in their hearts. Even the believers' "wisdom of the world" had to be shattered. None could escape this shattering. Living by law had to be unlearned. In the midst of each situation the Holy Spirit would direct and confirm the right stance to take. No predetermined rule could be imposed on all situations. Thus, the leading of the Spirit could always be open to misinterpretation and misunderstanding.

Paul declared that lukewarm commitment was the worst offense (vs. 11). Also, hope for Paul was not expectation of better circumstances. Hope was for Paul peace and joy in the midst of circumstances. The hope of the age to come was the prevailing atmosphere even in adversity (vs. 12). Hatred of evil was enjoined but not cursing of evil (vs. 9). Believers were to bless their persecutors. Also, believers were the same in their need of God. This accepted, they could weep and rejoice together.

III. Same Mind: Romans 12:16-18

A. Humble: 16

16. Be of the same mind one toward another. Mind not high things, but condescend to men of low estate. Be not wise in your own conceits.

Being of one mind did not mean for Paul that all would think the same thoughts. This he knew would seldom be realized. In fact, it would not even be desirable. Diversity in thoughts, feelings, ideas and actions would be a strength to the community. What if the human body was all eyes or all ears or all mouth?

This humble orientation of one mind meant that all were directed toward a single goal of the community united in grace (see Philip. 2:5-11). This "one mind" found expression in avoidance of strife and the service of peace, but did not advocate resignation. There could he conflict and confrontation without condemnation or castigation.

B. Honest: 17

17. Recompense to no man evil for evil. Provide things honest in the sight of all men.

Never seek retribution, Paul declared. Let honesty be your best policy. Paul was concerned with living, not theorizing. Enthusiastic feelings or heavenly thoughts did not, for Paul, constitute an expression of the heavenly nature. Deeds in earthly opportunities would reveal Christ's nature in believers.

C. Peaceable: 18

18. If it be possible, as much as lieth in you, live peaceably with all men.

The practice of peace was not theory. It was relationship to God expressed in the relation to an actual neighbor. It was what was necessary in a given situation. Jesus did not behave the same with all. He sought to express in word and action what would issue in the greatest peace for the person He was relating to at the time. What Jesus did with the Pharisees was not the same as what he did with the woman at the well nor with Zacchaeus.

Evangelistic Emphasis

The real world is often more like a jungle than a loving family. "Survival of the fittest," every person is out for himself or herself. For our services and products we charge "what the market will bear" more often than what the fair price should be. People use people and value things. The name of the game is power and prestige. We have learned to seek control and position. Success is measured by money, social standing and the number of people who answer to us. Appearances and image are everything, substance is of little importance.

In this kind of world the Lord's church should stand out in stark relief. When outsiders visit they should notice a difference. They should detect that something is controlling the conflict of egos. Each person cares for the others, has a realistic view of his or her own gifts, performs loving acts for the good of all, and even puts up with the others in love and for the good of the kingdom. Nothing is a more powerful evangelistic witness than a true church of Christ where his Spirit sets the agenda. When that is the case we are eager to bring an unbelieving friend with us to church. "By this will they know that you are my disciples," Jesus said, "that you love one another."

◆◆◆◆◆◆

Memory Selection

Having then gifts differing according to the grace that is given us, whether prophecy, let us prophesy according to the proportion of faith. *Romans 12:6*

Some gifts are for treasuring, keeping or at least storing. Everyone knows the experience of receiving a Christmas present and not knowing what to do with it: the tie he would never choose for himself, or that awful picture she is asked to hang in her living room. sometimes Christians are not happy with the gifts God has given them. They would quarrel around the Christmas tree with the others who got what they really wanted.

We are asked, in this area as in every aspect of the Christian life, to walk by faith. When we do not appreciate the gift we are given we are called to use it anyway, trusting God with the outcome. So often we see later what a blessing our gift has been to others, what a glory it was to the one who gave it. Our gifts were not given us to put on a shelf and admire or to hide in a closet in embarrassment. They were given us to be used in faith that God will bless the lives of others.

April 17, 1994

Weekday Problems

Henry and George, just by themselves, keep the church in turmoil. Henry is chairman of the Finance ministry. He has served faithfully in that role for twenty-three years. There have been several times when he steered the church through stormy financial waters. He has a hard-nosed, realistic view of income and outgo. In church meetings he often says, "Yes, that's a wonderful idea. We should be doing that just as soon as we can fund it. But where would we find the money in next year's budget?" Henry even sometimes hints that he might resign his role in the financial planning if his advice is ignored.

George was a charter member of the church. He and a few others' dreamed the original dream. "You have to think big, plan big, pray hard and launch out with courage and faith," he often says. He is head of the Adult Education Ministry and leader of long-range planning for the church as a whole. He feels completely capable of assigning the appropriate priorities for church expenditures, of setting goals, of choosing ambitious objectives for the church. Henry and George often have conflict, even in meetings of the church as a whole. Even visitors at worship services sometimes sense the conflict between the two and their respective followings.

*What would you say to Henry? To George?
*What verses of Romans 12 speak to these two Christian brothers?

♦♦♦♦♦♦

Smiles

"My boy," asked the young man's boss, "do you believe in life after death?"
"Yes, sir, I do!" responded the boy.
"Then that makes everything just fine," the employer continued, "because about an hour after you left yesterday to attend your grandfather's funeral, he came by the store to see you."

The teacher smiled at the Sunday School class and exclaimed, "All right, class, all who want to go to heaven raise your hands."
Everybody in the class had their hand up except one boy. "Don't you want to go to heaven, Johnny?" the teacher asked.
"Oh, yes ma'am, but I can't. My mother said for me to come straight home."

This Lesson In Your Life

At home, at work, in the church the challenge is the same. We are to value ourselves without devaluing others. We are to make our contributions and encourage others to make theirs. We should do our part without taking ownership of all the parts. We should find great joy and contentment in making a contribution without needing to make the biggest or most important contribution. For many of us the struggle to strike these balances goes on continually. We are jealous of our prerogatives, threatened by the roles of others. We get puffed up and then knocked down. We are inflated when others brag on us and deflated when they don't. How can we get on top of this problem?

Four teachings from Paul's epistles can prove helpful. First, those statements that we are not to live and die by the ratings of others are good medicine. In Galatians 1: 10 he asked, "Am I now seeking human approval ... or God's approval? ... If I were still seeking to please people I would not be a servant of Christ." Young Saul of Tarsus was running hard to please his superiors when he was arrested on the road to Damascus by the crucified and risen Lord. Since that time the focus of Paul's life had changed. Here in Romans 12 he begins by saying that Christians should give themselves, body and soul, as a thank offering to God. Such gratitude truly worships and pleases God. Paul says the primary focus should be on knowing God's approval, not the approval and applause of others.

Second, he reminds us that each of us has gifts, opportunities and assignments given by God Himself. Others in the church did not decide which gifts should be given to which persons. God's Holy Spirit made those assignments (1 Cor. 12:4-11). We should not be ungrateful and deny our own gifts. We are to be grateful, recognizing our abilities as gifts and using them to God's glory and for the good of His people. If our gifts are assigned by the Spirit we have no reason to boast. We have not earned these gifts. They are a sacred trust, given us to be a blessing to God's people.

Third, there is a large range of ministries for which we never have enough help: loving and promoting the good, showing mutual affection, rejoicing in hope, showing patience in tribulation, returning good for evil, etc. (Rom. 12:9-13). While Christians quibble over the spectacular gifts these important ministries are often neglected.

Fourth, we celebrate the whole body with all its appointed members, gifts and mutual ministry (Rom. 12:1-12). We should ask ourselves soberly and honestly whether we could do all the jobs that need to be done. Can we not see that God's appointments are wise and beautiful as the Body works together in love? Paul has furnished us the guidelines for a healthy view of ourselves and others in the Lord's Church.

Seed Thoughts

1. "I appeal to you therefore ... to present your bodies a living sacrifice..." What did Paul mean by "therefore"?
By the "mercies of God" detailed in Rom. 1-11.

2. Why did Paul say "present your bodies" instead of "present your spirits" or "present your souls"?
Because the Judeo-Christian faith sees the whole person wrapped up in the body.

3. Paul said giving ourselves body and soul is "spiritual worship." How is it worship?
It is given to God for His praise, honor and glory.

4. Why did Paul admonish Christians to let themselves be transformed in their hearts and minds?
Because we are naturally conformed and conforming to the world, not God's will.

5. What is the safeguard for the haughty attitude: "I know it all. If they would just let me I could run it all!"?
Trust that God is in control, has assigned the gifts and roles, and will make the Body healthy in His own way.

(PLEASE TURN PAGE)

---

1. "I appeal to you therefore ... to present your bodies a living sacrifice..." What did Paul mean by "therefore"?

2. Why did Paul say "present your bodies" instead of "present your spirits" or "present your souls"?

3. Paul said giving ourselves body and soul is "spiritual worship." How is it worship?

4. Why did Paul admonish Christians to let themselves be transformed in their hearts and minds?

5. What is the safeguard for the haughty attitude: "I know it all. If they would just let me I could run it all!"?

6. "Do not think more highly of yourself than you ought to think." How highly should we think of ourselves?

7. What keeps us reminded of our place in the Body?

8. How can I respect the brother or sister who is different in personality, perspective and gifts?

9. What is the basis and incentive for life in the Body of Christ?

10. Why are we Christians not to avenge wrongs done us?

By the "mercies of God" detailed in Rom. 1-11.

Because the Judeo-Christian faith sees the whole person wrapped up in the body.

It is given to God for His praise, honor and glory.

Because we are naturally conformed and conforming to the world, not God's will.

Trust that God is in control, has assigned the gifts and roles, and will make the Body healthy in His own way.

Led by faith that God has placed within each of us some gift for his glory, we are to respect ourselves without haughty arrogance.

That Christ died for it, is its Head and God assigned the roles.

God designed us differently for different roles. If we were all alike, many functions of the Body would not be fulfilled.

The "mercies of God" given exposition in Romans 1-11.

Because vengeance belongs only to God.

(SEED THOUGHTS--Cont'd)

6. **"Do not think more highly of yourself than you ought to think." How highly should we think of ourselves?**
Led by faith that God has placed within each of us some gift for his glory, we are to respect ourselves without haughty arrogance.

7. **What keeps us reminded of our place in the Body?**
That Christ died for it, is its Head and God assigned the roles.

8. **How can I respect the brother or sister who is different in personality, perspective and gifts?**
God designed us differently for different roles. If we were all alike, many functions of the Body would not be fulfilled.

9. **What is the basis and incentive for life in the Body of Christ?**
The "mercies of God" given exposition in Romans 1-11.

10. **Why are we Christians not to avenge wrongs done us?**
Because vengeance belongs only to God.

April 24, 1994

Living For Others

Romans 14:7-19

7 For none of us liveth to himself, and no man dieth to himself.
8 For whether we live, we live unto the Lord; and whether we die, we die unto the Lord: whether we live therefore, or die, we are the Lord's.
9 For to this end Christ both died, and rose, and revived, that he might be Lord both of the dead and living.
10 But why dost thou judge thy brother? or why dost thou set at nought thy brother? for we shall all stand before the judgment seat of Christ.
11 For it is written, As I LIVE, SAITH THE LORD, EVERY KNEE SHALL BOW TO ME, AND EVERY TONGUE SHALL CONFESS TO GOD.
12 So then every one of us shall give account of himself to God.
13 Let us not therefore judge one another any more: but judge this rather, that no man put a stumblingblock or an occasion to fall in *his* brother's way.
14 I know, and am persuaded by the Lord Jesus, that *there is* nothing unclean of itself: but to him that esteemeth any thing to be unclean, to him *it is* unclean.
15 But if thy brother be grieved with *thy* meat, now walkest thou not charitably. Destroy not him with thy meat, for whom Christ died.
16 Let not then your good be evil spoken of:
17 For the kingdom of God is not meat and drink; but righteousness, and peace, and joy in the Holy Ghost.
18 For he that in these things serveth Christ *is* acceptable to God, and approved of men.
19 Let us therefore follow after the things which make for peace, and things wherewith one may edify another.

◆◆◆◆◆◆

◀ **Memory Selection**
Romans 14:19

◀ **Devotional Reading**
Romans 15:1-17

◀ **Background Scripture**
Romans 14

◀ **Printed Scripture**
Romans 14:7-19

LIVING FOR OTHERS

Teacher's Target

Being strong does not rule out being sensitive to others. Not only so, none of us is strong in every aspect of our lives. The strong and weak brothers and sisters keep switching places depending on the need, the circumstance and the gifts required. One believer may be insensitive. Another may he overly scrupulous. One may misuse freedom in too lax an application of boundaries, and another may offend by too strict an application of rules and regulations. None is perfect, nor is any one right all the time.

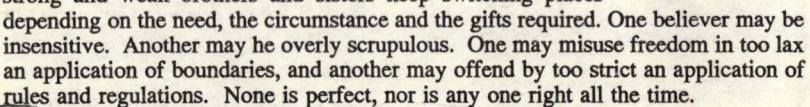

Ask class members to list their own weaknesses and strengths. Ask them to share a strength and tell where they think it could be used to benefit the whole community of faith. Discuss different weaknesses that are common and elicit suggestions on how to address them.

Lesson Introduction

Paul was deeply concerned about mutual acceptance in the church. Though Paul had not been with the church in Rome he had information about the church. Though the problems were not totally the same as in the Corinthian church, Paul addressed the issue of the "strong" and the "weak" in the church at Rome as well. It could be that Paul desired to head off similar conflicts in Rome as had occurred in Corinth (see 1 Cor. 8-10).

The recognition of true brotherhood was Paul's concern. He was not advocating tolerance of any who would reject the core truth of the gospel message. The weak in faith had some doubt about the limits of the exercise of Christian liberty. The strong, believing that there was nothing unclean in and of itself, had not always considered the consequences of their actions in regard to those more scrupulous.

Teaching Outline

I. Live unto God: Romans 14:7-9
  A. No One Lives to Self: 7
  B. All Believers Are God's: 8
  C. Christ Died for This: 9
II. Judge No One: Romans 14:10-13
  A. No Discounting Persons: 10
  B. Bow to God Only: 11-12
  C. Be No Stumbling Block: 13
III. Make Peace : Romans 14:14-19
  A. Nothing Unclean of Itself: 14
  B. Good Can Be Seen As Evil: 15-16
  C. Follow Things That Edify: 17-19

Daily Bible Readings

Mon. The Strong and the Weak
Romans 14:1-4
Tue. Honor God at all Times
Romans 14:5-10
Wed. The Weak and the Strong
Romans 14:13-23
Thurs. Bear No Pleasure in Failings of Weak - *Romans 15:1-6*
Fri. "Praise the Lord, All Gentiles!"
Romans 15:7-13
Sat. Paul's Ministry to the Gentiles
Romans 15:14-21
Sun. Paul Seeks the Romans' Prayers
Romans 15:22-33

VERSE BY VERSE

I. Live unto God: Romans 14:7-9

A. No One Lives to Self: 7

7. For none of us liveth to himself, and no man dieth to himself.

Different lifestyles based upon different traditions and mores could be tolerated. However, Paul was also well aware that all were not at the same stage of faith in their understanding. It was not faith that was sectarian, but the thought-structure and practices in which it was expressed.

Some had begun to make distinctions between themselves and others. An air of superiority, of greater privilege due to greater faith or deeper understanding, had developed. In reality it was more of a difference of perspective than a sign of greater or lesser value, growth, knowledge or practice. Their judgment and criticism of each other reflected that neither group had grown too much. True growth, Paul declared, would be reflected in a deep realization that we do not live unto ourselves.

B. All Believers Are God's: 8

8. For whether we live, we live unto the Lord; and whether we die, we die unto the Lord: whether we live therefore, or die, we are the Lord's.

Only God decides whether the place assigned to a person has been kept or abandoned. All believers belong to Him, not to each other in any possessive sense. This relationship is much like that of children who belonged to parents and were related to each other.

Paul knew that friendliness would not and could not defuse the conflict. Nor could it be dismissed by just acknowledging everyone's good intentions. Also, there could be no theological condemnation of others. This would break fellowship in either judgement or contempt. Both the strong and the weak had to remain patient and allow some room for each to maneuver, change and grow. Such an openness and nonjudgmental posture could be attained only in a relatedness to God, not a rigid adherence to one's own understanding.

C. Christ Died For This: 9

9. For to this end Christ both died, and rose, and revived, that he might be Lord both of the dead and living.

For the cause of redeeming all, Jesus died and rose. He returned to heaven to be Lord of all. He gave none the right to judge or despise others, as if he were their lord and master. Others were not to make it their business to please a particular group and to stand or fall by their judgments and sentences of doom. Christ was their Master. He had already made His ruling. In Him all were saved. He did not come to condemn but to seek and to save the ungodly. All, weak and strong alike, were ungodly.

333

II. Judge No One: Romans 14:10-13

A. No Discounting Persons: 10

10. But why dost thou judge thy brother? or why dost thou set at nought thy brother? for we shall all stand before the judgment seat of Christ.

In serving, the good pleasure of the Lord was found. He took no pleasure in believers judging each other. All things were lawful as long as they remained under Christ's lordship (Rom. 12:1, 1 Cor. 3: 21-22). That was the point, believers must see the limit of any gift conferred by God, and not use it to destroy the Body of Christ.

Infinite possibilities of expression of the Christian life were open to the Church. Where this was not allowed, Christianity broke up into sects. Christ's Body suffered distortion. When uniformity was enforced, there was an uncritical subjection to conventions. On the other hand there was an unmovable limit. If life activities no longer manifested that the ultimate connection was with the Lord Jesus Christ, existence became godless. No persons in the community were to be discounted either by our tolerance or restrictions. God is the Judge.

B. Bow to God Only: 11-12

11. For it is written, AS I LIVE, SAITH THE LORD, EVERY KNEE SHALL BOW TO ME, AND EVERY TONGUE SHALL CONFESS TO GOD.

12. So then every one of us shall give account of himself to God.

All clashing, contradicting and censuring of each other's practice of the faith was an affront to God. Christ will be the judge. All will have to give an account before Him. Only He has authority and ability to determine one's eternal state or the value of any of his decisions and actions in this age.

None will be called on to give an account for others. Each will be called only to account for himself. What is despised or judged in others is most often an unacknowledged aspect of the one judging. Denial is a universal malady.

C. Be No Stumbling Block: 13

13. Let us not therefore judge one another any more: but judge this rather. that no man put a stumblingblock or an occasion to fall in his brother's way.

Paul insists that if the believers would put as much energy into avoiding putting a stumbling block in each other's way as they did in judging one another the problem would resolve itself. We "pass sentence," we "condemn," we "think critically" of each other out of our old nature. To invest in such self examination as to remove ourselves as a possible stumbling block is the work of the indwelling Spirit of Christ (see Matthew 18:16-17).

III. Make Peace: Romans 14:14-19

A. Nothing Unclean of Itself: 14

14. I know, and am persuaded by the Lord Jesus, that there is nothing unclean of itself: but to him that esteemeth any thing to be unclean, to him *it is* unclean.

In 1 Timothy 4:4 Paul declared, "every creature of God is good and nothing is to be refused if it be received with thanksgiving." It was not being in this party or having that persuasion that would commend them to God. The believer would not be asked whether he was a conformist or a non-conformist. He would be asked if he named Jesus Christ as Lord and Savior. He was saved by his faith not his theology or his convictions. Paul realized nothing could destroy true Christianity as surely as placing it in modes, forms, rituals and causes that eat away at the essentials. As C.S. Lewis once said, "The measure of a true Christian is not whether he is as good a person as he could or should be, but is he a better man than he would have been if he had never met Christ."

B. Good Can Be Seen As Evil: 15-16

15. But if thy brother be grieved with thy meat, now walkest thou not charitably. Destroy not him with thy meat, for whom Christ died.

16. Let not then your good be evil spoken of:

Both our freedoms and our restraints could be seen as evil. Pious religious rules or unexamined liberty turned license could bring ruin to a brother or sister in Christ.

Paul used eating meat offered to idols to illustrate. Do not follow your bellies, was his injunction. The quest was not material but spiritual. Make nothing of this world ultimate and *Do not believe that one way is the only way*

absolute. Salvation canceled self-assertion and inaugurated love of neighbor. Do not destroy a brother over that which will pass away.

C. Follow Things That Edify: 17-19

17. For the kingdom of God is not meat and drink; but righteousness, and peace, and joy in the Holy Ghost.

18. For he that in these things serveth Christ *is* acceptable to God, and approved of men.

19. Let us therefore follow after the things which make for peace, and things wherewith one may edify another.

Righteousness, peace and joy-against such there is no law and the practice of these is without limit. Through these, Christ's reign would be seen in the community. These are the anticipatory characteristics of the fulfilled Kingdom of God at Christ's return.

The Holy Spirit does not take believers out of the world nor allow them to demonstrate faith by asceticism or indulgence of earthly things. Righteousness is not right action, but divine power. Peace is now openness to everyone. Joy is the realization that we stand under an open heaven with free access to God through Christ.

Evangelistic Emphasis

Many features of the Christian faith attract unbelievers. In the first century many Gentiles came to the Jewish faith because of the high ethical standards and moral behavior of Israel. That same attraction brought many into the Christian church. Others found in the Judeo-Christian faith a refreshing view of God. The Creator of the universe was also the Father of Jesus Christ and of all mankind. The sharp contrast with the capricious gods of the pagans was winsome.

One of the most magnetic aspects of Christianity was its acceptance of all men and women as equals before God. When unbelievers observed on what basis Christians accepted one another they were moved to take another look at this new religion. The same is true today. Students are invited into the honor society if their grades are good enough. Trade unions require members to be licensed practitioners of their various crafts. Country Clubs accept only those who qualify by vocation, financial and social standing. But Christians are to accept one another as they are acceptable to God. It is not because of anything they have achieved, but because He has loved them in Jesus Christ. What a powerful and magnetic witness it is when unbelievers actually see Christians accept one another on that basis!

◆◆◆◆◆◆

Memory Selection

Let us therefore follow after the things which make for peace, and things wherewith one may edify another. *Rom. 14:19*

Peace between Christians is not a given. Over the centuries, from the fellowship of Jesus' first disciples on, followers of Jesus have had conflict and division. Differences in doctrine often played a significant part in these tensions. Invariably, personal egos and agendas were also involved. The most persistent question which has stressed the Body of Christ over the centuries was neither the nature of the Trinity, nor the divinity and humanity of Christ, nor the free will of man versus the sovereignty of God. The most persistent question which has torn the Church apart over the centuries is that same concern the first disciples had: "Who is greatest in the Kingdom?" Our job is not to create the peace, but to treasure and maintain what has been given us. That which made peace between us and God is the same and only instrument of peace between us. When we all stand gratefully before the cross of Christ we look into one another's eyes with a new caring and love for peace.

Weekday Problems

Wes and Sandra went to the minister because they had a problem. Not the wedding plans themselves. This problem was more serious, it was a question of their happiness after the wedding. Wes came from a Roman Catholic home and Sandra from a Baptist family. They deeply loved each other and were completely serious about the vows they were to take. The largest unresolved area in their relationship was their religion. Each tried to understand the other's tradition, they attended worship in both places, they spent countless hours discussing their differences.

Their friends told them they were making too much of the problem. Wes and Sandra did not really believe them. They thought their hopes, their plans for children and home, their own relationship could be damaged by their deeply held differences. The minister made two observations. First, such differences are significant and can be destructive. Second, he encouraged them to begin at the center of their faith and to work their way out from there. "Every day, read from the Gospels together and ask the Lord you both follow to lead you through these problems."

*Did Wes and Sandra have a real problem, or were they just experiencing the prewedding jitters?

*Evaluate the minister's advice. What would you say to them?

♦♦♦♦♦♦

Smiles

Two men were talking. One said to the other, "Listen carefully, because I can only tell this once. I promised I wouldn't repeat it."

Some people will believe anything if they happen to overhear it.

Believe only half of what you hear, but be sure it is the right half.

A rumor goes in one ear and out many mouths.

Secret: Something which is hushed about from place to place.

LIVING FOR OTHERS

This Lesson In Your Life

Many people are miserable all their lives because they cannot get others to perform according to their specifications. In Rom. 14 Paul urges us to welcome someone who is different from us into the Christian community, "but not with the idea of arguing over his scruples." In their case, Jewish and Gentile Christians came with different backgrounds regarding keeping special days and eating meats which had been sacrificed to idols. Each group judged the other harshly, perhaps even to the point of wanting to exclude one another from the Christian fellowship.

People come with various backgrounds, perspectives and viewpoints. What is a matter of opinion to one person is a subject of deep conviction to another. Since all are justified by faith in Jesus Christ crucified (Rom. 5:1), none stands on his or her own record for justification before God. How much less does each Christian have to satisfy the wishes of other Christians.

In his Life Of Samuel Johnson, James Boswell related a conversation the two of them had one morning after a dinner at the Crown and Anchor Tavern. "Well, we had a good talk," Johnson said in satisfaction with the previous evening's experience. "Yes, sir," replied Boswell, "you tossed and gored several persons."

Some of the best of us "toss and gore" people on a regular basis. Gossip and harsh criticism of others is a habit not easily broken. Recall how, even after Peter had denied the Lord three times and endured painful reinstatement ("Do you love me? Do you love me? Do you love me?"), almost immediately he asked Jesus what would become of John. "What is that to you?" Jesus replied, "You follow Me" (John 21:15-22).

The Last Judgment is always God's. We are called to make tentative judgments of one another— "by their fruits you shall know them." Life demands that we make such daily working judgments. But our appraisals are only provisional in nature. Jesus forbids us to pronounce on the essential worth, acceptability to God or eternal destiny of any person. "Judge not that you be not judged..."

The phrase "Last Judgment" has a double meaning. God's judgment is both the last one and the highest one. After all is said and done He alone will decide about each person. "Last Judgment" also means that God's judgment is above our judgments at every moment. Both we and the one we are judging are under His appraisal at all times. Making final judgments of others is a presumptuous claim to divine prerogatives. "Who are you to judge the servant of another?" Paul asked the Romans.

Seed Thoughts

1. How can we Christians know with confidence that, whether we live or die, we are the Lord's?
Because Christ died and lived again to be the Lord of both the dead and the living.

2. Why are believers not to judge one another?
Because the Last Judgment is God's alone.

3. What should a Christian do if his or her lifestyle choices truly endanger the faith of another Christian?
No lifestyle choice is as valuable as another's relationship with the Lord.

4. According to Paul, what is the Kingdom of God really about?
"Righteousness, peace and joy in the Holy Spirit."

5. What should the Christians aim be toward other Christians?
Always to encourage and build up the other's relationship with God.

(PLEASE TURN PAGE)

---

1. How can we Christians know with confidence that, whether we live or die, we are the Lord's?

2. Why are believers not to judge one another?

3. What should a Christian do if his or her lifestyle choices truly endanger the faith of another Christian?

4. According to Paul, what is the Kingdom of God really about?

5. What should the Christians aim be toward other Christians?

6. Why did Paul rebuff the critic with the words, "Who are you to judge another's servant?"

7. Regardless of individual decisions about meats and observing days, what common motive should all the Roman Christians have had?

8. If "we do not live and die to ourselves," then to whom?

9. What does Paul, the apostle of grace, have to say about the Last Judgment?

10. Since we will inevitably stand in Judgment as sinners, will we be condemned?

(SEED THOUGHTS--Cont'd)

Because Christ died and lived again to be the Lord of both the dead and the living.

Because the Last Judgment is God's alone.

No lifestyle choice is as valuable as another's relationship with the Lord.

"Righteousness, peace and joy in the Holy Spirit."

Always to encourage and build up the other's relationship with God.

"It is before his own Lord that each one stands or falls."

To glorify God in all things.

"If we live, we live to the Lord, and if we die, we die to the Lord."

That each will be accountable for himself or herself to God.

No, we stand "in Christ," in His life, death and resurrection for us.

---

6. Why did Paul rebuff the critic with the words, "Who are you to judge another's servant?"
"It is before his own Lord that each one stands or falls."

7. Regardless of individual decisions about meats and observing days, what common motive should all the Roman Christians have had?
To glorify God in all things.

8. If "we do not live and die to ourselves," then to whom?
"If we live, we live to the Lord, and if we die, we die to the Lord."

9. What does Paul, the apostle of grace, have to say about the Last Judgment?
That each will be accountable for himself or herself to God.

10. Since we will inevitably stand in Judgment as sinners, will we be condemned?
No, we stand "in Christ," in His life, death and resurrection for us.

May 1, 1994

Delivered From Bondage

Galatians 1:6-7

6 I marvel that ye are so soon removed from him that called you into the grace of Christ unto another gospel:
7 Which is not another, but there be some that trouble you, and would pervert the gospel of Christ.

Galatians 2:11-21

11 But when Peter was come to An'-ti-och, I withstood him to the face, because he was to be blamed.
12 For before that certain came from James, he did eat with the Gentiles: but when they were come. he withdrew and separated himself, fearing them which were of the circumcision.
13 And the other Jews dissembled likewise with him; insomuch that Barnabas also was carried away with their dissimulation.
14 But when I saw that they walked not uprightly according to the truth of the gospel, I said unto Peter before *them* all, If thou, being a Jew, livest after the manner of Gentiles, and not as do the Jews, why compellest thou the Gentiles to live as do the Jews?
15 We *who are* Jews by nature, and not sinners of the Gentiles,
16 Knowing that a man is not justified by the works of the law, but by the faith of Jesus Christ, even we have believed in Jesus Christ, that we might be justified by the faith of Christ, and not by the works of the law for by the works of the law shall no flesh be justified.
17 But if, while we seek to be justified by Christ, we ourselves also are found sinners, *is* therefore Christ the minister of sin? God forbid.
18 For if I build again the things which I destroyed, I make myself a transgressor.
19 For I through the law am dead to the law, that I might live unto God.
20 I am crucified with Christ: nevertheless I live; yet not I, but Christ liveth in me: and the life which I now live in the flesh I live by the faith of the Son of God, who loved me, and gave himself for me.
21 1 do not frustrate the grace of God: for if righteousness *come* by the law, then Christ is dead in vain.

◆◆◆◆◆◆

◀ **Memory Selection**
Galatians 2:20

◀ **Devotional Reading**
1 Timothy 1:12-17

◀ **Background Scripture**
Galatians 1-2

◀ **Printed Scripture**
*Galatians 1:6-7;
2:11-21*

341

Teacher's Target

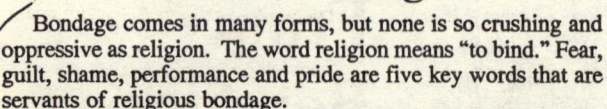

Bondage comes in many forms, but none is so crushing and oppressive as religion. The word religion means "to bind." Fear, guilt, shame, performance and pride are five key words that are servants of religious bondage.

Christ was not a religion. Christ was a revelation of the presence of God in our behalf. He was God doing something for us. Religion was humankind doing something to please or placate God.

God was pleased in Christ Jesus alone. Jesus Christ was the only deity known to humankind who had done an act of love for His devotees before they did something for Him.

What has been your bondage? How has religion bound you? When do you feel free? What does freedom in Christ mean? Can politics really bring about freedom? Was Jesus a political figure?

Lesson Introduction

Many religions claimed to hold the means of salvation. The incipient and insidious religious inclination of all mankind caused people to love religion and hate freedom. Though they talked freedom, they clung to religion. Already religion was robbing the Galatians of their freedom. Some were declaring it was grace in Christ, but that it was grace plus. Paul insisted there was no plus anything. Either Christ paid it all, all at once, or He died in vain.

Paul risked being called a libertine for the sake of liberty in Christ. He stood even against Peter in this point. We say "liberty and justice for all" in our Pledge of Allegiance and that is a good thought, but true liberty comes only in Christ.

Teaching Outline

I. One Gospel: Galatians 1:6-7
   A. God Called You: 6
   B. Christ Brought Grace: 6
   C. Some Pervert Grace: 7
II. Peter's Compromise: Galatians 2:11-14
   A. Jews and Gentiles Free: 11-12a
   B. Peter's Fear: 12b-13
   C. Paul's Rebuke: 14
III. Paul's Conviction: Galatians 2:15-21
   A. Justified by Faith: 15-16
   B. Dead to the Law: 17-19
   C. Crucified with Christ: 20-21

Daily Bible Readings

Mon. Paul Accuses Any Who Dispute Him - *Galatians 1:6-9*
Tue. Paul's Theology Based on Revelation - *Galatians 1:10-17*
Wed. Paul's Revelations Came in Arabia - *Galatians 1:18-24*
Thurs. Paul Had No Teacher of Christian Faith - *Galatians 2:1-10*
Fri. The Law Cannot Justify *Galatians 2:11-16*
Sat. Only Christ Justifies *Galatians 2:17-21*
Sun. Rejoice in the Lord, Always *Philippians 4:4-10*

VERSE BY VERSE

I. One Gospel: Galatians 1:6-7

A. God Called You: 6

6. I marvel that ye are so soon removed from him that called you into the grace of Christ unto another gospel:

The opponents of Paul's presentation of the gospel wanted to emphasize that the way to salvation was grace in Christ plus lawkeeping. Christ was not enough for them. Salvation was seen not as God's gift but man's work. Paul insisted the initiative was with God. People did not earn their place with Him. Neither could they maintain their place by works.

B. Christ Brought Grace: 6

6. I marvel that ye are so soon removed from him that called you into the grace of Christ unto another gospel:

The grace of God was not and could not be earned. Judaism had failed to keep the Law no matter how diligently its efforts. In fact, the harder it tried, the more burdens too heavy to bear were laid upon the people.

Christ and Christ alone brought grace. Law brought condemnation. The people under the Law were alienated from God, from each other and themselves. Christ alone brought salvation in place of condemnation and reconciliation in place of alienation.

C. Some Pervert Grace: 7

7. Which is not another, but there be some that trouble you, and would pervert the gospel of Christ.

Some declared "another gospel" which was no gospel at all. Gospel means "good news." To add keeping of the Law to salvation by grace alone through faith alone was not good news at all.

Some false teachers were playing upon that religious nature in all of us. They offered religion (law) as a shield from self-punishment and God's wrath. The Galatians were becoming their own judge and jury. Self-hatred and self-punishment began once again to reign.

To go back to this after God has freed us is insanity. A perverted gospel, polluted with legalism, judgmentalism, tyranny and bondage is no gospel at all.

II. Peter's Compromise: Gal. 2:11-14

A. Jews and Gentiles Free: 11-12a

11. But when Peter was come to An'-ti-och, I withstood him to the face, because he was to be blamed.

12. For before that certain came from James, he did eat with the Gentiles:

The Jews were free from bondage to the Law. The Gentiles were free from bondage to the appetites of the flesh. They had been released and transferred from the kingdom of darkness into the Kingdom of light.

There was no longer a middle wall between Jew and Gentile (Eph. 2:14-19). Paul and Peter and all the other

Jews in Antioch with them were eating with Gentiles. Peter had been living out the vision of all things being clean before God (Acts 10:9-20).

Theory had been one thing. Practice was another. Earlier, Peter had confirmed Paul's doctrine and his mission to the Gentiles (Acts 15; Gal. 2:1-10), but in the face of possible controversy with fellow Jewish believers who came from James in Jerusalem, he compromised to the hurt of Paul's message and mission. How this hurt the Gentiles and confused them about their acceptability and the truth of Paul's teaching!

B. Peter's Fear: 12b-13

but when they were come. he withdrew and separated himself, fearing them which were of the circumcision.

13. And the other Jews dissembled likewise with him; insomuch that Barnabas also was carried away with their dissimulation.

Peter was the apostle to the circumcision and one of the pillars of the early church (Gal. 2:7-9). What he did would carry great weight with all. How he received and lived among Gentile believers would be a message to all Christians.

Peter's fear was that those of the circumcision would be offended by his "loose behavior," eating with unclean and uncircumcised Gentiles. Paul had no problem with Jewish believers still observing their own tradition so long as it was understood that it was not a basis of justification.

Notice that Paul confronted Peter, he did not tell others or tell people to shun Peter's leadership. He did not make more of it than was necessary. Peter faltered from an unnecessary and undue desire to please men. He was saving the Jewish visitors from embarrassment. In effect, the gospel was compromised. People could not be pleased at the expense of the truth.

C. Paul's Rebuke: 14

14. But when I saw that they walked not uprightly according to the truth of the gospel, I said unto Peter before them all, If thou, being a Jew, livest after the manner of Gentiles, and not as do the Jews, why compellest thou the Gentiles to live as do the Jews?

Paul himself was no stranger to concessions. In Galatians 2:1-5 Paul refused to have Titus circumcised because he was a Gentile. In Acts 16:1-3 Paul allowed Timothy, whose mother was a Jewess, to be circumcised. This Paul did as a concession to the Jews in the area. Paul was willing to become all things to all men in order to win some, but not at the expense of the gospel. Circumstantial concessions were permissible but not core compromises of the gospel truth.

Paul rebuked Peter because it violated the principle of grace alone by faith alone in this setting. The wall between Jew and Gentile must not be rebuilt.

III. Paul's Conviction: Gal. 2:15-21

A. Justified by Faith: 15-16

15. We who are Jews by nature, and not sinners of the Gentiles,

16. Knowing that a man is not justified by the works of the law, but by the faith of Jesus Christ, even we have believed in Jesus Christ, that we might be justified by the faith of Christ, and not by the works of the law for by the works of the law shall no flesh be justified.

Notice that Paul declared first that there is no justification by man's works. Even faith is not a work of man's righteousness. If it were, it would be another form of works. God did His justifying in such a way that no man could boast. Instead He gave grace exceedingly abundantly above that which any could have ever imagined or expected.

B. Dead to the Law: 17-19

17. But if, while we seek to be justified by Christ. we ourselves also are found sinners, is therefore Christ the minister of sin? God forbid.

18. For if I build again the things which I destroyed, I make myself a transgressor.

19. For I through the law am dead to the law, that I might live unto God.

Paul now read the Old Testament through new eyes. God never trusted His plan of mankind's salvation to the Law or man. God rested His plan of justification upon Himself. God provided a way of salvation that depended upon faith in Jesus Christ and not any meritorious activity of humankind. To build up again the things Jesus' cross had torn down would be to become a transgressor.

C. Crucified With Christ: 20-21

20. I am crucified with Christ: nevertheless I live; yet not I, but Christ liveth in me: and the life which I now live in the flesh I live by the faith of the Son of God, who loved me, and gave himself for me.

21. I do not frustrate the grace of God: for if righteousness come by the law, then Christ is dead in vain.

It was important for Paul to communicate when he died with Christ. It was not at the time of Paul's faith, his baptism or his cessation of certain sins. Paul was crucified when Christ was crucified. That is to say, Christ died for us all and all were declared dead to the Law, world, sin and Satan at the cross. The past tense was important. It clarified that Jesus did the work.

Since Paul died with Christ, he could say he no longer lived. By faith in the gracious gift of the work of Christ on the cross, Paul could live the resurrection life by Christ's power. The flesh did not any longer have control over his life. Faith in the Son of God (Gal. 2:20) was what had brought the resurrection power of the Holy Spirit into his life. Knowing this truth Paul would not dare tempt God by teaching that righteousness could in anyway come by the Law. Such a teaching and practice would be to treat Jesus' death as a vain and hollow event.

Evangelistic Emphasis

Even though we have watched it on the television news and read about it in the papers, we do not really understand what freedom has meant to those held hostage for months and years. Few of us have ever had our lives restricted to a small room, with no contact with the outside world, with nothing to read, no one to whom we can voice our complaints, no opportunity to come and go, no privilege of worship with other Christians.

That is not to say that none of us is held hostage. Many people in our society are held captive to drug abuse, sexual problems, work, dysfunctional relationships or to their own consuming emotional and spiritual problems. The gospel of freedom in Christ is truly good news to modern hostages. "You shall know the truth and the truth will set you free," Jesus promised in John 8. The saying has become one of the most familiar in the world. it is sometimes chiseled in stone above buildings at great universities. But Jesus was not talking about academic learning or knowledge in general. He was speaking of our relationship with God. In Him we can come to know God, to find our true humanity as we come into right relationship with Him and receive the life that only He can give. Jesus is good news for us and for the whole world held hostage in the darkness.

♦♦♦♦♦♦

Memory Selection

I am crucified with Christ: nevertheless I live; yet not I but Christ liveth in me: and the life which I now live in the flesh I live by the faith of the Son of God, who loved me, and gave himself for me.
Galatians 2:20

After the first announcement of His coming passion Jesus issued a disturbing invitation. "If any would come after me let him deny himself, take up his cross and follow me" (Mk.8:34). Jesus was going up to Jerusalem to suffer and die in obedience to the Father and in order to redeem mankind. He was not just fulfilling some abstract spiritual exercise, following a religious vocation.

It was deeply personal with him, something between him and his Father. It had to do with Peter, James and John, the Roman centurion, children who were brought to him, and the lepers. Jesus does not call us to give up something for Lent; He calls us to get over ourselves for Him and for others. Paul's life had been turned upside down by his encounter with the crucified and risen Lord. He never was the same after what happened on the Damascus road. He no longer lived for himself. He was free of the tyranny of his own self-interest. Paul had taken Christ's agenda as his own.

May 1, 1994

Weekday Problems

Raymond is addicted-not to alcohol, gambling or perverted sexual practice. His addition is socially acceptable, even encouraged by society and rewarded. He is addicted to work. The symptoms are clear and obvious to everyone but Raymond. He has trouble taking a day off without dropping by the office or at least phoning in. Vacation trips are torture. He gets into heated arguments with his wife because he takes a briefcase full of work. His children try to reach him by asking if they can make an appointment to see him.

The whole family is miserable because Raymond can never really relax, never really get away from his job. He has been programmed to feel that work is the only honorable activity a man can pursue. If he is not working or thinking about working he flagellates himself severely. His father told Raymond many times that the greatest reason for failure, the cardinal sin, is laziness. Responsible people work long hours every day and make the world go 'round, while playboys live like parasites on the fat of the land. To make matters worse, at work Raymond is praised for his dedication, initiative and hard work.

*What should freedom in Christ mean to Raymond?
*What will Raymond do, what will Raymond be, when it comes time to retire?

♦♦♦♦♦♦

Sparkles

A young minister said to an old seasoned warrior for God, "There's a woman who commits fornication and gives her wages in alms."

The old warrior said, "She will not go on committing fornication, for the fruit of faith is appearing in her."

Later the young minister reported, "She has increased her lovers and her alms to the poor."

The old warrior replied, "She will not go on committing fornication."

The young man returned. The woman had wanted to come with him. He was told to bring her on his next visit.

When the woman came and heard the Word of God from the old man, she was filled with repentance and said, "From today forward I shall cling to God and resolve not to commit fornication anymore."

Read John 4:1-42 and John 8:1-11,

DELIVERED FROM BONDAGE

This Lesson In Your Life

Often people think following Christ is a heavy burden and a painful sacrifice. Becoming a Christian means saying goodbye forever to the joy of living. In Galatians 2:20 Paul speaks out of his own profound joy of living with Christ. His relationship to the Lord was the basis of his freedom, his joy, his life. It had not always been that way with Paul. Once young Saul of Tarsus labored with feverish ambition to prove himself worthy of God's love. He strained every sinew for the approval of his teachers and the religious leaders in Jerusalem. He was a young man of promise, on his way to the top. His instrument for this enterprise was the Law of Moses expanded over the centuries into thousands of rules and subrules. If he could walk blameless before the Law, if he could observe the religious practices, if he could master the body of knowledge handed him by the inherited faith he would be on his way. Even that heavy burden was not all of it. Beyond his own commitment to the Law, Saul felt an obligation to bring every other Jew under the yoke as well.

Now, writing to the churches in Galatia as a wandering Christian missionary without status or security, Paul had come to know true joy and freedom for the first time in his life. It had been a painful process, but well worth the anguish. Since the Damascus road Paul had revised every cherished tenet of his faith. If God had actually come in Jesus of Nazareth to serve and suffer, then life was not what Paul had thought. If His own people had rejected Jesus, then the Messiah was not what everyone else thought. Something new and different was at work.

The implications for Paul's life were far reaching and profound. He was not called to advance his own career, cultivate his own contacts, plan his own success. Jesus called him to lay aside his own goals, dreams and ambitions. Paul would be God's instrument by which the news of Golgotha would reach the Gentiles. On the face of it, this was not a prestigious calling. No drum rolls, no trumpet blasts ever announced his arrival. As often as not, Paul was as despised as his Lord had been. Revising his own understanding of God was only part of the challenge. He was called to tell the whole world, Jewish and Gentile, that God was the Servant of servants.

Life and liberty are not what we think. The world around us tells us that happiness is in having position, possessions, feelings and sensations that thrill us. Life is doing just as we please. We are told continually to look out for number one, to love ourselves, to take care of ourselves regardless of what that means to others. Only by pursuing one's own agenda by one's own chosen means can success and true joy be realized. Young Saul of Tarsus believed that, too. The only difference was that he played the religious version of the same self-promotion game.

The good news for us Christians and for all mankind is that it is possible, in God's grace, to be so in love with Christ that His agenda, purposes and dreams matter more to us than our own.

Seed Thoughts

1. What was the "true gospel" the Galatians were forsaking?
That God had already reconciled in the cross all who would believe.

2. Why did Peter withdraw from eating with the Gentile Christians?
Because he was afraid of brotherhood political pressures.

3. How could Peter announce on Pentecost that the gospel was also for those "afar off" and then cave in to the Jews?
Human approval from one's own group is one of life's most compelling motivations.

4. How could Peter observe at the house of Cornelius that "God is no respecter of persons" and then withdraw from the Gentiles?
Like the rest of us, Peter had to be converted again and again to the gospel and its implications.

5. If we are not justified by lawkeeping, is the Law of Moses then of no importance and worth?
No, as revelation, instruction and guide the Law is invaluable. As the means of salvation it is ineffective.

(PLEASE TURN PAGE)

---

1. What was the "true gospel" the Galatians were forsaking?

2. Why did Peter withdraw from eating with the Gentile Christians?

3. How could Peter announce on Pentecost that the gospel was also for those "afar off" and then cave in to the Jews?

4. How could Peter observe at the house of Cornelius that "God is no respecter of persons" and then withdraw from the Gentiles?

5. If we are not justified by lawkeeping, is the Law of Moses then of no importance and worth?

6. How was it possible for Paul to say, "I have been crucified with Christ; it is no longer I who live but Christ lives in me"?

7. What did Paul have to believe in order to say, "It is Christ who lives in me."?

8. What does it say about Jesus Christ if we are able to get right with God by perfect law-keeping?

9. What two freedoms does Paul discuss in this passage?

10. Why would anyone choose salvation by lawkeeping over the free gift of God in Christ?

That God had already reconciled in the cross all who would believe.

Because he was afraid of brotherhood political pressures.

Human approval from one's own group is one of life's most compelling motivations.

Like the rest of us, Peter had to be converted again and again to the gospel and its implications.

No, as revelation, instruction and guide the Law is invaluable. As the means of salvation it is ineffective.

It took many years for Paul fully to adopt Jesus' agenda above his own.

Faith that Jesus was actually God's Son and that Jesus gave His life for Paul.

That His cross was a pointless and meaningless gesture.

Freedom from human approval and freedom from self-salvation by law-keeping.

Why did Adam and Eve eat of the forbidden fruit when the whole garden was theirs? Human pride.

(SEED THOUGHTS--Cont'd)

6. How was it possible for Paul to say, "I have been crucified with Christ; it is no longer I who live but Christ lives in me"?
It took many years for Paul fully to adopt Jesus' agenda above his own.

7. What did Paul have to believe in order to say, "It is Christ who lives in me."?
Faith that Jesus was actually God's Son and that Jesus gave His life for Paul.

8. What does it say about Jesus Christ if we are able to get right with God by perfect law-keeping?
That His cross was a pointless and meaningless gesture.

9. What two freedoms does Paul discuss in this passage?
Freedom from human approval and freedom from self-salvation by law-keeping.

10. Why would anyone choose salvation by lawkeeping over the free gift of God in Christ?
Why did Adam and Eve eat of the forbidden fruit when the whole garden was theirs? Human pride.

May 8, 1994

Adopted as God's Children

Galatians 3:1-5
1 O FOOLISH Ga-la'-tians, who hath bewitched you, that ye should not obey the truth, before whose eyes Jesus Christ hath been evidently set forth, crucified among you?
2 This only would I learn of you, Received ye the Spirit by the works of the law, or by the hearing of faith?
3 Are ye so foolish? having begun in the Spirit, are ye now made perfect by the flesh?
4 Have ye suffered so many things in vain? if *it be* yet in vain.
5 He therefore that ministereth to you in the Spirit, and worketh miracles among you, *doeth he it* by the works of the law, or by the hearing of faith?

Galatians 3:23-4:7
23 But before faith came, we were kept under the law, shut up unto the faith which should afterwards be revealed.
24 Wherefore the law was our schoolmaster to *bring us* unto Christ, that we might be justified by faith.
25 But after that faith is come, we are no longer under a schoolmaster.
26 For ye are all the children of God by faith in Christ Jesus.
27 For as many of you as have been baptized into Christ have put on Christ.
28 There is neither Jew nor Greek, there is neither bond nor free, there is neither male nor female: for ye are all one in Christ Jesus.
29 And if ye *be* Christ's, then are ye Abraham's seed, and heirs according to the promise.
4 NOW I say, *That* the heir, as long as he is child, differeth nothing from a servant, though he be lord of all;
2 But is under tutors and governors until the time appointed of the father.
3 Even so we, when we were children, were in bondage under the elements of the world:
4 But when the fulness of the time was come, God sent forth his Son, made of a woman, made under the law,
5 To redeem them that were under the law, that we might receive the adoption of sons.
6 And because ye are sons, God hath sent forth the Spirit of his Son in your hearts, crying, Ab'-ba, Father.
7 Wherefore thou art no more a servant, but a son; and if a son, then an heir of God through Christ.

◆◆◆◆◆◆

◀ **Memory Selection**
Galatians 4:4-5

◀ **Devotional Reading**
1 Corinthians 12:11-33

◀ **Background Scripture**
Galatians 3:1 - 4:7

◀ **Printed Scripture**
*Galatians 3:1-5,
23 - 29; 4:1-7*

ADOPTED AS GOD'S CHILDREN

Teacher's Target

An old Chinese proverb goes like this. "Fool me once shame on you. Fool me twice shame on me." Paul was concerned that the Galatians who had been fooled by the evil one once would again be deceived and go back into bondage. He was afraid someone had put an "evil-eye" upon them and they were caught in a destructive spell of delusion.

Having been adopted as children of God, what would make the Galatians want to go back under the Law? Paul was horrified. Would they submit again to the Law, or continue in the Spirit which saved them?

Have you ever been fooled, tricked by your own perceptions or another's cleverness of argument? Can there be optical illusions in the spiritual realm? Discuss Paul's putting the law in the category of sorcery. What does adoption mean? Is it hard to believe sonship is real when one is adopted?

Lesson Introduction

Magic was common in the market place in Paul's day. There was and still is a continual stream of hustlers and hucksters in and out of religion. People have always been susceptible to the persuasive influence of clever shysters.

Paul was concerned that the converts in Galatia had become fascinated with teachers who desired to place them under the restrictive life of the law. Paul declared that these teachers of the law were every bit as caught in illusion and Satan's power as any sorcerer (Acts 8:9-11; 13:17). Paul insisted that as surely as they were saved by faith, they could live the Christian life only by faith. These believers knew they began their faith walk in the Spirit. They were about to throw away their faith life in Christ's work for works righteousness on the tottering ladder of Law.

Teaching Outline

I. How Came the Spirit : Galatians 3:1-5
   A. Bewitched or Bequeathed: 1
   B. How Made Perfect: 2-4
   C. Miracles by Faith or Law: 5
II. Under a Custodian : 3:23-29
   A. The Law's Role: 23-24
   B. Faith's Transformation: 25-27
   C. All One in Christ: 28-29
III. Adopted As Sons and Daughters 4:1-7
   A. Child-heir Like a Servant: 1-3
   B. Adoption as Sons: 4-5
   C. Heir of God: 6-7

Daily Bible Readings

Mon. Miracles by Way of Law or Faith - *Galatians 3:1-5*
Tue. People of Faith: Children of Abraham - *Galatians 3:6-10*
Wed. The Spirit Comes Through Faith - *Galatians 3:11-15*
Thurs. The Righteous Live by Faith *Galatians 3:16-22; Habakkuk 2:1-4*
Fri. Christians Are All Children of God - *Galatians 3:23-27*
Sat. No Longer Slaves, but Adopted Children - *Galatians 3:28 -4:7*
Sun. Let Your Faith Rest in God *1 Corinthians 2:1-5*

May 8, 1994

VERSE BY VERSE

I. How Came the Spirit: Gal. 3:1-5

A. Bewitched or Bequeathed: 1

1. O FOOLISH Ga-la'-tians, who hath bewitched you, that ye should not obey the truth, before whose eyes Jesus Christ hath been evidently set forth, crucified among you?

The question that perplexed Paul was how Wisdom's children could so quickly desire to become Fool's slaves. They were enchanted by the seduction of religion which always produced legalistic bondage. In the hands of deluding charlatans, God's law, meant for good, had become an instrument of magic incantation.

The Galatians had been taught freedom in Christ. Knowing the freedom of truth and having feasted on heavenly fare; they were asking for shackles of law and slave rations.

B. How Made Perfect: 2-4

2. This only would I learn of you, Received ye the Spirit by the works of the law, or by the hearing of faith?

3. Are ye so foolish? having begun in the Spirit, are ye now made perfect by the flesh?

4. Have ye suffered so many things in vain? if it be yet in vain.

Paul asked three questions. How did you receive the Spirit? How will you be made perfect? By what power did the one who ministered to you do his ministry? The Galatians knew they received the Spirit by faith.

False teachers had tricked the Galatians into believing they could make their faith visible through the practice of the Law. Paul wanted to know how the Law could make them perfect in the end if it couldn't get them started in the first place! They began in the Spirit by faith, they would walk in the Spirit by faith, and they would be perfected on the last day through the Spirit by faith.

C. Miracles by Faith: 5

5. He therefore that ministereth to you in the Spirit, and worketh miracles among you, doeth he it by the works of the law, or by the hearing of faith?

The third question Paul proposed for the people to consider was how the one who ministered to them (Paul himself) did so. Did he do his ministry by the Spirit or by the Law? Did miracles happen among them by the power of the Spirit or by the law? The answer, or course, was that Paul had ministered to them in the power of the Spirit.

The hearing of faith was the important ingredient, not works of the law. Hearing meant giving ear to, obedience to the truth. That truth was that God in grace had sent His Son Jesus Christ to die on the cross and remove the curse of the Law and sin from all, Jew and Gentile.

II. Under a Custodian: Gal. 3:23-29

A. The Law's Role: 23-24

23. But before faith came, we were kept under the law, shut up unto the faith which should afterwards be revealed.
24. Wherefore the law was our schoolmaster to *bring* us unto Christ, that we might be justified by faith.

The Law had its place, but it never was as important to God's plan as the Jews had made it, Paul declared. Man's sin and desire to justify himself had exalted the law and man's works over God and His grace. To show the relative importance of the law, Paul used the word translated "schoolmaster" in the King James Version of the Bible.

A trusted servant of the household was assigned to be "custodian." He was not a school teacher but had more comprehensive responsibilities to his charge. He was helping the child to grow beyond the need for a custodian.

Now that faith had come, Paul declared, there was no need for the custodial role of the law. The Holy Spirit would be the believer's guide.

B. Faith's Transformation: 25-27

25. But after that faith is come, we are no longer under a schoolmaster.
26. For ye are all the children of God by faith in Christ Jesus.
27. For as many of you as have been baptized into Christ have put on Christ.

The law showed the need of salvation, but did not offer it. Only God's grace had the power to transform people.

Faith and baptism went together like a hand in a glove. When a person professed faith in the early Church, he was baptized. When this occurred, often the candidate for baptism would stand on one side of the water in his old clothes. As he stepped in the water, he would take off his outer garment, be baptized and step out on the other side. When he came up out of the water he would be wrapped in a new white robe. This symbolized putting on Christ's new nature. The way of the world, law and flesh were renounced.

C. All One in Christ: 28-29

28. There is neither Jew nor Greek, there is neither bond nor free, there is neither male nor female: for ye are all one in Christ Jesus.
29. And if ye be Christ's, then are ye Abraham's seed, and heirs according to the promise.

A common Jewish prayer was said by Jewish men as part of their evening prayers. Paul himself had probably said it as a Jew. The prayer went like this, "God, thank you that I was not born a Gentile, a slave or a woman." Paul took this prayer and totally transformed it in verses 28-29 to show the radical newness of Christ and His work of redemption. Paul declared that in Christ there was neither Jew nor Greek, slave nor free, male nor female. All are one in Christ. There were differences, yes, but they were not value judgments.

III. Adopted as Sons and Daughters: Gal. 4:1-7

A. Child-heir Like a Servant: 1-3

1. NOW I say, That the heir, as long as he is child, differeth nothing from a servant, though he be lord of all;
2. But is under tutors and gover-

nors until the time appointed of the father.

3. Even so we, when we were children, were in bondage under the elements of the world:

The child of a family had no more access to the inheritance of the family than a slave or servant. The child was not free but under tutors and governors until the father of the household declared the child an adult and subject to the privileges of a mature person.

Paul used this analogy to illustrate that under the Law the people were treated like children. They were in bondage to the way of the world, law and enforcement.

B. Adoptions of Sons: 4-5

4. But when the fulness of the time was come, God sent forth his Son, made of a woman, made under the law,

5. To redeem them that were under the law, that we might receive the adoption of sons.

Now the fullness of time, the time for the birth of the new order had come. All creation had been groaning in travail for the release of the new creation, like a woman in birth pains. Now Jesus had come and the old order could bind people to it no longer. The Law was of the old order. It now had no hold. In Christ, the Galatians and all believers had been transferred to the new creation and transformed by the Holy Spirit into a new way of life. They were adopted by God Himself as children, not children as minors, but children declared to be partakers of the full privileges of the Kingdom won by their Lord Jesus Christ.

C. Heir of God: 6-7

6. And because Ye are sons, God hath sent forth the Spirit of his Son in your hearts, crying, Ab'-ba, Father.

7. Wherefore thou art no more a servant, but a son; and if a son, then an heir of God through Christ.

Never before had a Jew thought of calling God by the name of "Abba" prior to Jesus' appearance upon the earth. "Abba" was a term of endearment for a father, like that of "Daddy" in our culture. To be so familiar with God was almost blasphemy to a devout Jew. Yet, when Jesus taught His disciples to pray He told them to call God "Abba" (Matt. 6:9-13).

Here Paul declared once again the believer's closeness to the Father. Through Christ all believers have become sons. By faith in that marvelous grace gift of Jesus Christ they were heirs of God. All that was the Father's was theirs through His Son.

ADOPTED AS GOD'S CHILDREN

Evangelistic Emphasis

Everyone wants to belong. No one wants to be completely left outside. Many of us have painful childhood memories of being excluded, chosen last, discounted and discarded. Those painful memories have set some of us off on a lifetime quest for acceptance. All too often we pay an exorbitant price to get inside. There is a resulting loss of self-esteem and personal identity. Everyone wants to be included. Even the least social people who find interpersonal relations painful need to be a part of something. This fact of human nature alone accounts to a considerable extent for the multiplicities of clubs, organizations and associations in our society.

God wants all His children to belong. His great plan for all ages is to bring His wandering children back home to Himself where they belong, where they can know the love and acceptance of the family circle. if unbelievers experience a warm, caring, embracing community of faith when they come to church they will be drawn in to discover the secret. As with those first Christian communities described in Acts, so it is today--the loving family of faith is a powerful instrument for evangelism.

❖❖❖❖❖❖

Memory Selection

God sent forth his Son...to redeem them that were under the law, that we might receive adoption as sons. *Galatians 4:4, 5*

As long as people try to prove themselves and buy God's love they remain outside His family circle. We try to do this by various means: perfect lawkeeping, perfect knowledge, perfect attitudes, perfect feelings, perfect relationships, perfect mental health. Our pride says, "Surely there is something better to barter. Don't you have to bring something with which to bargain and buy your place into the house of God?"

When we admit our need, confess our longing to belong and accept the gift of redemption in God's Son we are welcomed into the family circle. The wonder of it is that arrangements for our adoptions were made long before we were born, long before our grandparents were born. If we can get over our own pride we can belong in the family, have a right to an inheritance, know the joy of being chosen, and experience being loved and included.

May 8, 1994

Weekday Problems

If you asked Sylvia why she is good she would reply, "What do you mean? We Christians are supposed to be good, aren't we?" It's not that she wants to turn people off with her goodness. Yet she does. She obsessively attends every public worship service at her church. She does this not out of joy and a desire to praise God, not for the fellowship of being with other disciples, but because she feels it is expected of her as a Christian.

She will never stray into an extramarital affair. This is not because of loyalty to her husband and the vows she made, but because she knows it is expected of her as a Christian. She would never steal so much as a paper clip from her desk at work. Her devotion to duty would forbid it. She is honest because she is expected to be honest. Her life is governed by others' expectations. If you asked Sylvia, "Do you think you are okay with God?" she would answer, "I hope so, I do the best I can. Different people give different answers to that question. How can one be sure?"

*Does Sylvia's case mean we should discount duty as a motive for Christian ethics and do the right thing only when we feel like it?

*How can Sylvia ever find the joy of living the Christian lifestyle?

◆◆◆◆◆◆

Smiles

Several "uptown" counterfeiters accidentally printed a batch of fifteen dollar bills. Moe asked Joe, "Man, what we gonna do with all these fifteen dollar bills?"

Joe came up with a bright idea. "I got it. We'll drive down to hillbilly country and pawn these bills off on the storekeepers back in the mountains."

Hours later they pulled up to a dilapidated old country store. Moe and Joe winked at each other as they approached an old man behind the counter.

Moe ambled up the man and nonchalantly asked. "Hey, mister, can you make change for a fifteen dollar bill?"

Without batting an eye the old gentleman retorted, "Sure, how do you want it, sonny? Five threes or a seven and an eight?"

This Lesson In Your Life

It's a great relief when struggling with self-salvation to discover grace. Knowing that reconciliation with God is an accomplished fact as a result of Golgotha brings a song to the heart. Then, one day, one finds a new challenge. With freedom comes increased responsibility. We can no longer plead helplessness. The child can say, "I don't know why we moved to California. My parents just told us we were moving." The prisoner does not bear the burden, the warden makes decisions. The co-dependent is relieved to plead, "I can't help it, she wasn't what she ought to have been for me."

Along with freedom comes responsibility for that freedom. The challenges of decision making and consequence bearing sometimes tempts us to go back into captivity. The book of Exodus in the Old Testament is instructive. God saw the Hebrews in Egypt enslaved and mistreated by their masters. Out of compassion He reached down with a strong arm and rescued them. He planned to take them across the desert to a promised land. The way would be tough, they would have to be grown-up about the hardships.

What God had already done for them should have been evidence of His love and power. But when the sand burned their feet, their throats were dry and they couldn't see their way, they began to murmur against Moses and against God. "Why did you bring us out here? Were there no graves in Egypt? Oh, how we wish we were back there right now! At least in Egypt we had three meals a day! We didn't have to pack all our possessions each morning and unpack after a long day's journey. We wish we were back in Egypt!"

It was true, life was much simpler, more predictable, more secure in Egypt. They had no decisions to make. Before long Moses would lead them to Mount Sinai where God would present them with the biggest decision of their lives. Out of His grace, with respect for their own will, God offered them covenant. "I will be your God if you will be my people," He said. He gave them time to ponder the decision, spelled out in detail what being His people would mean. In Egypt they had no such decisions to make. All the important decisions were made for them.

The Galatian Christians were like that. At the beginning they responded to the loving rescue of God in Jesus Christ. They then discovered the rigors of being grown up people in covenant with God. When that happened the old security of legalism looked pretty good. They decided to go back to comfortable slavery, to accept "other gospels."

Some of us were smothered by a legalistic view of God. He seemed to us the stereotypical Marine sergeant who does His best to wash out fresh recruits. We needed to know that our peace with Him has been settled at Golgotha and awaits only our acceptance and signature. But grace presents its own challenges. How do we control and direct our freedoms? How do we live with the consequences of selfish choices? How does the community live regulated just by the rule of God's love for us in Jesus Christ? Maybe being adopted into the family, with all the rights and responsibilities involved is not so wonderful after all. In legalism we are not responsible. There is comfort in that.

Seed Thoughts

1. **Do we receive the Holy Spirit by what we do or by what God does?**
   By believing the gospel and accepting God into our lives.

2. **Is there any place for the Law in our spiritual education?**
   Yes, children must learn the "dos" and "don'ts" before they discover their need for grace.

3. **Why did Jewish legalism mean a wall between Jews and non-Jews?**
   Because the Law was given only to the children of Abraham.

4. **How are all peoples united when they believe in Christ?**
   Jesus' coming, serving, teaching, dying and resurrection were for all God's children.

5. **Does "no longer Jew or Greek, slave or free, male or female" mean early Christians all looked alike?**
   No, it meant the differences didn't matter "in Christ."

(PLEASE TURN PAGE)

---

1. Do we receive the Holy Spirit by what we do or by what God does?

2. Is there any place for the Law in our spiritual education?

3. Why did Jewish legalism mean a wall between Jews and non-Jews?

4. How are all peoples united when they believe in Christ?

5. Does "no longer Jew or Greek, slave or free, male or female" mean early Christians all looked alike?

6. If you are no slave but a legally adopted child God, what is your inheritance?

7. Does grace mean no rules, no limits, and we can do as we please?

8. What if one is a Christian but feels like he or she has never met his or her Father?

9. Why did the Galatians try "finishing in the flesh" after starting in the Holy Spirit?

10. Where, when and how is one adopted into God's family?

(SEED THOUGHTS--Cont'd)

By believing the gospel and accepting God into our lives.

Yes, children must learn the "dos" and "don'ts" before they discover their need for grace.

Because the Law was given only to the children of Abraham.

Jesus' coming, serving, teaching, dying and resurrection were for all God's children.

No, it meant the differences didn't matter "in Christ."

Life forever in the family circle with God and Christ.

No, it means reflecting the unselfish love of Christ in the way we treat others.

One can meet the Father and come to know Him in Jesus Christ (John 14:8).

It is safer, less demanding of maturity to follow a set of rules.

Provisions were made at the cross and the open tomb of Jesus. We receive the gift in baptism (Romans 6).

6. **If you are no slave but a legally adopted child God, what is your inheritance?**
Life forever in the family circle with God and Christ.

7. **Does grace mean no rules, no limits, and we can do as we please?**
No, it means reflecting the unselfish love of Christ in the way we treat others.

8. **What if one is a Christian but feels like he or she has never met his or her Father?**
One can meet the Father and come to know Him in Jesus Christ (John 14:8).

9. **Why did the Galatians try "finishing in the flesh" after starting in the Holy Spirit?**
It is safer, less demanding of maturity to follow a set of rules.

10. **Where, when and how is one adopted into God's family?**
Provisions were made at the cross and the open tomb of Jesus. We receive the gift in baptism (Romans 6).

May 15, 1994

Given the Birthright of Freedom

Galatians 4:8-20

8 Howbeit then, when ye knew not God, ye did service unto them which by nature are no gods.
9 But now, after that ye have known God or rather are known of God, how turn ye again to the weak and beggarly elements, whereunto ye desire again to be in bondage?
10 Ye observe days, and months, and times, and years.
11 I am afraid of you, lest I have bestowed upon you labour in vain.
12 Brethren, I beseech you, be as I *am*; for I *am* as ye *are*: ye have not injured me at all.
13 Ye know how through infirmity of the flesh I preached the gospel unto you at the first.
14 And my temptation which was in my flesh ye despised not, nor rejected; but received me as an angel of God, *even* as Christ Jesus.
15 Where is then the blessedness ye spake of? for I bear you record, that, if *it had been* possible, ye would have plucked out your own eyes, and have given them to me.
16 Am I therefore become your enemy, because I tell you the truth?
17 They zealously affect you, *but* not well; yea, they would exclude you, that ye might affect them.
18 But *it is* good to be zealously affected always in a good *thing*, and not only when I am present with you.
19 My little children, of whom I travail in birth again until Christ be formed in you,
20 I desire to be present with you now, and to change my voice; for I stand in doubt of you.

◆◆◆◆◆◆

Memory Selection
◀ *Galatians 4:9*

Devotional Reading
◀ *Titus 2:11-13; 3:1-8*

Background Scripture
◀ *Galatians 4:8-31*

Printed Scripture
◀ *Galatians 4:8-20*

GIVEN THE BIRTHRIGHT OF FREEDOM

Teacher's Target

By the number of religions and "isms" that pervade the world one could surmise that people are seeking to fill an internal void. Once filled with good or bad, removal of the contents and refilling the void is not an easy task.

God revealed in an ultimate way through Jesus Christ that there was only one health producing filler, God Himself. All else was illusion. Not even the Law, given by God, could be a substitute for God Himself.

What gods consume people in our day? Could patriotism, religion, peer groups, clubs, organizations, family and corporations be as much "gods" as those made of wood or stone? What makes other gods which are no-gods so appealing? Who is in control when God isn't? What have you made a god in your life either now or earlier?

Lesson Introduction

There is a big difference between knowing other gods and being known by God. Usually people attach to the kind of false god that would appeal to their fleshly interest or allay their particular brand of fear. Paul knew these no-gods were the worshiper's fears, phobias and hopes projected onto the gods. The gods had no real life nor real power. The people had bound themselves. But the no-gods had become familiar. Anxiety increased when the familiar was laid aside for a new way.

Those who spied out the Galatians' freedom had played upon this anxiety. They offered "secure" bondage. Paul would not accept this false sense of being in control. He continued to call the people to freedom as Moses had. Paul would contend with the false teachers for the people's freedom.

Teaching Outline

I. Desiring Bondage: Galatians 4:8-11
   A. Serving No-Gods: 8
   B. Return to Beggarly Elements: 9
   C. Observing Times: 10-11
II. A Friend Become Enemy: Galatians 4:12-16
   A. The Bearer of Good News: 12-13
   B. Received with an Infirmity: 13-15
   C. Now Treated as an Enemy: 16
III. Jealous for a Good Thing: Galatians 4:17-20
   A. Manipulated Zeal: 17
   B. Zeal for Christ's Formation: 18-20

Daily Bible Readings

Mon. Christ the Power/Wisdom of God - *1 Corinthians 1:17-25*
Tue. Let Those Who Boast, Boast in God - *1 Corinthians 1:26-31*
Wed. Paul's Demonstrations of the Spirit - *1 Corinthians 2:1-5*
Thurs. No One Comprehends God's Thoughts - *1 Corinthians 2:6-13*
Fri. Paul Reproves Galatians for Immaturity - *Galatians 4:8-11*
Sat. Paul's Eye Problems Blessed *Galatians 4:12-20*
Sun. Allegory of Two Covenants: Hagar, Sarah - *Galatians 4:21-31*

VERSE BY VERSE

I. Desiring Bondage: Galatians 4:8-11

A. Serving No-Gods: 8

8. Howbeit then, when ye knew not God, ye did service unto them which by nature are no gods.

Paul was extremely perplexed. He knew what he had experienced when he met Christ. He knew what gospel he had preached to the Galatians. It was a gospel of grace through faith in Jesus Christ. If the Galatians had received the same Christ, how could they ever go back to serving ideologies and idols, including the Law, that were no-gods?

One of the answers to this question was that the no-gods came in a form that looked and sounded like God to them. That form was the Law. God gave the Law, didn't He? Then it must be good, don't you think? Then it should be kept, shouldn't it? With such arguments the people had been persuaded.

God did not give the Law as a means of salvation. It was a tool not the goal. God did not want law-keepers. God wanted God lovers.

B. Return to Beggarly Elements: 9

9. But now, after that ye have known God or rather are own of God, how turn ye again to the weak and beggarly elements, whereunto ye desire again to be in bondage?

Humankind had rejected the one true God who created them and sustained them. They worshiped gods of their own making. They could not rise above their source. None of these gods were due adoration, praise and exaltation. God alone deserved humankind's devotion.

Transformation had come about through God's revelation of Himself through the gospel. Not even the Law of God had made this change in them. To return to any temporal deity or temporary form of religion or even the Jewish Law was to return to bondage.

C. Observing Times: 10-11

10. Ye observe days, and months, and times, and years.
11. I am afraid of you, lest I have bestowed upon you labour in vain.

Paul knew the impact of the gospel. He was a product of its life-changing power. Seeing the Galatians in their present relapse, he questioned what he had seen at the first. Could he have been fooled as to how well it had been received by the hearers? Neither his ministry nor the power of the gospel were on trial. Paul had labored well. The gospel had the power to save. Had they turned away from that which had the power to save?

Even the Old Testament believers had believed in God, not the Law. They were looking forward to the fulfillment of their hope which finally came in Christ (1 Pet. 1:10-13). To make them a part of salvation would be to defect from the pure and simple truth of the gospel.

II. A Friend Become Enemy: Galatians 4:12-16

A. The Bearer of Good News: 12-13

12. Brethren, I beseech you, be as I am; for I am as ye are: ye have not injured me at all.
13. Ye know how through infirmity of the flesh I preached the gospel unto you at the first.

Notice the affection with which Paul addressed the Galatians. He had been the one who brought them the freeing word of Jesus Christ. His desire was for them to be as free of the Law as he was. They had been freed from idols, and now they were about to submit to the bondage from which he himself had been freed.

The Galatians had not hurt Paul with their freedom. He was not offended by their lack of observance of the Law. They had not drawn him away from his practice of the Law. Rather, Christ had freed him through the gospel. Helping them to hold to their freedom was Paul's purpose in writing to them.

B. Received with an Infirmity 13-15

13. Ye know how through infirmity of the flesh I preached the gospel unto you at the first.
14. And my temptation which was in my flesh ye despised not, nor rejected; but received me as an angel of God, even as Christ Jesus.
15. Where is then the blessedness ye spake of? for I bear you record, that, if it had been possible, ye would have plucked out your own eyes, and have given them to me.

Paul had no quarrel from his side of the relationship with the Galatians. They had been most gracious to him when he appeared among them to preach the gospel. Though he had a physical infirmity, they had not rejected him.

Paul's reproof did not come from private resentment. Paul's deep love of God and desire for their well-being prompted his admonition.

Paul recounted their earlier affection for him. When he first came to them, they respected him and honored him as a messenger of God. So strong was their affection, they would have given their own eyes for him at that time. They went from esteem to contempt for the very person who had their best interest at heart.

C. Now Treated as an Enemy: 16

16. Am I therefore become your enemy, because I tell you the truth?

Telling the truth never has been a popular position with the masses. In fact, it seldom will be because people are attached to their illusions. When truth exposed their illusions, the Galatians, like we, reacted rather defensively to protect their misplaced self-esteem. They sought to save face and hold their position in the face of all truth.

Paul was doing no more than faithfully discharging his responsibility as a minister of the gospel. Yet, this very good and responsible act made him an enemy to the Galatians. Paul knew he could not compromise the truth for the sake of a relationship. Paul's stance showed that often in the face of opposition and misunderstanding the minister must stand for truth. Also, standing for the truth doesn't always make friends.

III. Zealous for a Good Thing: Galatians 4:17-20

A. Manipulated Zeal: 17

17. They zealously affect you, but not well; yea, they would exclude you, that ye might affect them.

Paul had sensed that the Galatians had lost the joy of their salvation (vs. 15). Legalism had robbed them. Shame replaced humility, guilt replaced love. Performance was stressed above relationship.

Here in verse 17 Paul made it plain that the people had been made zealous for a bad thing. The false teachers appealed to the human desire to be right and manipulated the people to their own ends. The teachers' motives were selfish. They would use the people only to further their own fame and position.

B. Zeal for Christ's Formation: 18-20

18. But it is good to be zealously affected always in a good thing, and not only when I am present with you.

19. My little children, of whom I travail in birth again until Christ be formed in you,

20. I desire to be present with you now, and to change my voice; for I stand in doubt of you.

Paul had no objection to zeal. Yet he knew that zeal was like sincerity. One could be zealous but wrong just as surely as a person could be sincere but wrong. He warned the people to test the spirits to be sure that they were zealous for a good thing.

The most important matter that was worthy of their zeal was the formation of Christ in their being. Paul had no desire to he a watch dog over their every move. Nor did Paul need to get the credit and applause for their faithfulness.

Being zealous for Christ to be formed in them meant to have the mind of Christ (Phil. 2:5-11; Col. 3:1-3). The Gospels revealed that Jesus was humble, not prideful. Jesus was self-giving, not selfish. Jesus was obedient, not self-willed. Jesus was obedient to God, not subservient to the Law. To be zealous for Christ looked quite different from legalistic bondage.

Evangelistic Emphasis

Sometimes an unbeliever hesitates to become a Christian because he has known other Christians. "Are you telling me that I should become like you are?...depressed all the time because you live under a cloud of guilt and fear?" What a tragedy it is when the world sees in us only defeat and despair, as if we have no real hope.

When we say that there should be something victorious about the believer's life we are not playing Pollyanna with the realities of life. Christianity takes sin seriously. When one looks at the cross she can see just how seriously. We do not try to laugh off our moral failure, our distorted relationships and the demons within. The bottom line is that God has won the victory in Jesus Christ. The decisive battle was waged centuries ago, in Palestine, between God and the devil. When Jesus died, everyone thought darkness had won. Three days later God's brilliant victory was known.

Satan is still alive, inflicting wounds on people. Yet he is mortally wounded and we know who wins. While we freely and continually admit our failures, we also celebrate God's love and triumph over evil in Jesus Christ. Otherwise, we are just inviting others into a bondage worse than their own.

◆◆◆◆◆◆

Memory Selection

But now, after that ye have known God, or rather are known of God, how turn ye again to the weak and beggarly elements, whereunto ye desire again to be in bondage? *Galatians 4:9*

For years the *Reader's Digest* ran a column entitled, "My Most Unforgettable Character." Sometimes the character sketched was just unique, interesting or amusing. More often the writer told a moving story about his or her encounter with the most unforgettable character. The person described not only arrested one's attention, he or she made a significant difference in the writer's life.

In our memory verse Paul encourages the Galatians. "How, after you have come to know God, or rather to be known by Him, can you go back to the grinding routine of self-salvation you knew before?" From their behavior one might imagine that they had never met God. We need to ask whether we have met God in Christ, whether we have seen His love for us, whether we know that we exist because of Him and whether our relationship with Him makes any real difference in the way we live.

May 15, 1994

Weekday Problems

Within a year after Sam became a Christian he was even more miserable than before. His friends at church had noticed. So did his fellow officers on the force. For awhile after his baptism he was a changed man. He seemed to have a reason for living, he showed real concern for others, spent time trying to help those who were hard up against it. His cynicism disappeared almost completely.

Slowly, like the embers of a campfire left alone, his enthusiasm and joy seemed to cool and die. He became irritable, tense, resentful about petty offenses. He discovered that Christianity was not all about getting, taking, being taken care of. His new faith made claims on his time, energy and money. In some ways it was more burdensome than his old pagan attempts at decency had been. Whereas once he measured his worth by his performance of commonly accepted virtues like honesty, kindness and hard work, now he had tackled a more demanding life. He took seriously Jesus' beatitudes and tried to live them out. Sam tried to live by Jesus redefinition of the Law, beyond one's actions to his deepest thoughts and attitudes. How could he ever measure up perfectly? How could he ever please his Lord?

*Is the Sermon on the Mount a new Law by which Christians will meet God's approval?

*Why was Sam so miserable?

♦♦♦♦♦♦

Sparkles

I watched a little tyke from Texas with his father at a rodeo. He wore a hat like his dad wore. The boots, the belt, the jeans, the western cut shirt, were all identical to his fathers. When he walked, his gait was Dad's gait. Dad was it, in the eyes of this little replica in the flesh. The father crossed his legs. Almost immediately the son followed suit.

These actions were not conscious to either. They were enjoying a rodeo together. An outside observer could see it clearly. That boy would grow up to be a lot like his dad.

In psychological jargon such emulation and incorporation of another's attitudes is called introjection. In his letters Paul continually called for believers to introject Jesus into their being. "Have this mind in you which was in Christ Jesus...."

This Lesson In Your Life

T.S. Eliot wrote to his friend, William Levy, that the religion of his youth had been a matter of legalistic rules and regulations. Righteousness consisted of not playing cards, not dancing and not pursuing the amusements of the world. He observed that the system operated very efficiently. They simply made a list of sins they never committed and then pronounced themselves good. Eliot said that kind of religion, as Jesus told the scribes and Pharisees, is always easier than a genuine concern for love, justice and mercy--the weightier matters of the law.

There is something demanding about grace. It is sometimes so demanding that we Christians are tempted to create for ourselves a simpler and more manageable system of salvation. Grace is a challenge in at least two ways. First, it stretches us to the limit to believe in unmerited favor. As Paul understood it salvation is radically God's doing. We would rather talk of "our part" and "God's part," maybe as a 50/50 proposition. We might concede that it's more like 60 percent God's doing and 40 percent ours. If pushed to the extreme we might agree to a 90/10 breakdown.

Paul would have none of this kind of calculation. What struck his life with force was the realization that salvation is 100 percent God's doing. He made us, He came in Christ to redeem us, He gave us that in which to believe, He gave us the faith to trust, He will redeem us finally when the story is over. According to Paul's new understanding of salvation all is from God. Our obedience and good works are nothing but the appropriate "Thank You" notes given in gratitude for His boundless love.

Grace is also a challenge because God treats us with respect and gives us the responsibility of responding. He did not program Adam and Eve, He gave them a choice. Jesus dealt with people the same way. "I stand at the door and knock," He said, leaving it to the resident to invite Him in or not. Unlike so many religious leaders today who want to spoon-feed followers and keep them dependent, Jesus demanded that His followers grow up and take responsibility for their lives. For example, after telling the parable of the Good Samaritan, Jesus refused to give the inquiring lawyer a legal definition of "neighbor" and to stipulate exactly under which conditions mercy should be meted out. Instead, Jesus gave the challenge: "Now you go and do something like that."

Paul was disturbed because the Galatian Christians had retreated from the sunlight of God's grace in Jesus Christ back into the shadows of a rules and regulations religion. "How could you be enslaved again to salvation by keeping days and observing rules?" Paul asked.

We who are Christians can escape into the simplicity, comfort and irresponsibility of legalism. It's hard to trust God completely and let our whole weight down on His love in Christ. It's hard to grow up, to use our imaginations and creativity in discovering how to show our gratitude for His love. It's easier to let someone else spell it all out for us.

Seed Thoughts

1. Why was Paul shocked at the legalism of the Galatian Christians?
They had come know God in Christ and then reverted to self-salvation.

2. Was Paul saying Christians should not attend church and live moral lives?
No, but he was saying these acts should be in response to salvation, not for the purpose of winning salvation.

3. Why did Paul ask if the Galatians had turned against him personally?
Because some leaders had belittled Paul in order to undermine his teaching.

4. What did Paul mean by yearning for Christ to be "fully formed" in the Galatians?
He longed for them to know and love Christ as he did, to desire more than anything else the Christ-like mind.

5. Are Christian forms of worship arbitrary, empty rituals?
Not if our Lord ordained them, gave them their meaning and we meet Him there.

(PLEASE TURN PAGE)

---

1. Why was Paul shocked at the legalism of the Galatian Christians?

2. Was Paul saying Christians should not attend church and live moral lives?

3. Why did Paul ask if the Galatians had turned against him personally?

4. What did Paul mean by yearning for Christ to be "fully formed" in the Galatians?

5. Are Christian forms of worship arbitrary, empty rituals?

6. Why should Paul express a desire to be with the Galatians?

7. What was Paul's definition of Christian maturity?

8. If the motivating force in legalism is fear and pride, what moves a life of grace?

9. Why does the devoted legalist find it hard to laugh at himself?

10. Why did Paul speak, not just of knowing God, but rather of being known by God?

They had come know God in Christ and then reverted to self-salvation.

No, but he was saying these acts should be in response to salvation, not for the purpose of winning salvation.

Because some leaders had belittled Paul in order to undermine his teaching.

He longed for them to know and love Christ as he did, to desire more than anything else the Christ-like mind.

Not if our Lord ordained them, gave them their meaning and we meet Him there.

Like every other disciple, Paul needed fellowship and encouragement.

Growing more and more like Christ in obedience to God and in love for others.

Gratitude and joy in fellowship with a Father of love.

When one is saving himself by perfectly keeping the rules, it is no laughing matter.

The bedrock of our confidence is not our knowledge of Him but His knowledge of us and His love for us anyway.

(SEED THOUGHTS--Cont'd)

6. Why should Paul express a desire to be with the Galatians?
Like every other disciple, Paul needed fellowship and encouragement.

7. What was Paul's definition of Christian maturity?
Growing more and more like Christ in obedience to God and in love for others.

8. If the motivating force in legalism is fear and pride, what moves a life of grace?
Gratitude and joy in fellowship with a Father of love.

9. Why does the devoted legalist find it hard to laugh at himself?
When one is saving himself by perfectly keeping the rules, it is no laughing matter.

10. Why did Paul speak, not just of knowing God, but rather of being known by God?
The bedrock of our confidence is not our knowledge of Him but His knowledge of us and His love for us anyway.

May 22, 1994

Bear Fruit of the Spirit

Galatians 5:1
1 STAND fast therefore in the liberty wherewith Christ hath made us free, and be not entangled again with the yoke of bondage.

5:13-26
13 For brethren, ye have been called unto liberty; only *use* not liberty for an occasion to the flesh, but by love serve one another.
14 For all the law is fulfilled in one word, *even* in this; Thou shalt love thy neighbour as thyself.
15 But if ye bite and devour one another, take heed that ye be not consumed one of another.
16 *This* I say then, Walk in the Spirit, and ye shall not fulfil the lust of the flesh.
17 For the flesh lusteth against the Spirit, and the Spirit against the flesh: and these are contrary the one to the other: so that ye cannot do the things that ye would.
18 But if ye be led of the Spirit, ye are not under the law.
19 Now the works of the flesh are manifest, which are *these*; Adultery, fornication, uncleanness, lasciviousness,
20 Idolatry, witchcraft, hatred, variance, emulations, wrath, strife, seditions, heresies,
21 Envyings, murders, drunkenness, revellings, and such like: of the which I tell you before, as I have also told *you* in time past, that they which do such things shall not inherit the kingdom of God.
22 But the fruit of the Spirit is love, joy, peace, longsuffering, gentleness, goodness, faith,
23 Meekness, temperance: against such there is no law.
24 And they that are Christ's have crucified the flesh with the affections and lusts.
25 If we live in the Spirit, let us also walk in the Spirit.
26 Let us not be desirous of vain glory, provoking one another, envying one another.

◆◆◆◆◆◆

◀ **Memory Selection**
Galatians 5:22-23

◀ **Devotional Reading**
1 Timothy 6:10-12

◀ **Background Scripture**
Galatians 5

◀ **Printed Scripture**
Galatians 5:1, 13-26

BEAR FRUIT OF THE SPIRIT

Teacher's Target

Freedom came in Christ. Only in freedom could the fruit of the Spirit flow through people. Law and legalism could serve only to increase and reinforce the works of the flesh (Rom. 7:5-11). Freed from shame and guilt through faith in Jesus Christ, humankind could relinquish fear and self-serving.

Freedom could easily be abused if the flesh still held sway. Paul was often accused of a laissez-faire kind of gospel that declared "anything goes." However, Paul knew that only in Christ was there the power to be free and use freedom for good. In Galatians 5:22 Paul listed characteristics of freedom in the Spirit.

Can government and politics bring about the freedom Paul speaks of in Galatians? How have you misused freedom? When have you experienced Christian freedom from others in the form of the fruit of the Spirit?

Lesson Introduction

Paul was well acquainted with both God and human frailty. He recognized how incredibly prone people were to self-deception. our penchant for arrogance did not escape Paul's study of human nature. He was aware of our thinly camouflaged judgments that are continually active in our comparisons one with the other.

Paul also knew how much we are like sheep in spiritual matters. Sheep are unable to find the barn even after the same routine for several years. Humans are unable to find the "authentic center" by themselves. So Paul spelled out what Christian freedom looks like and how it behaves toward others. The flesh would invest in activities that hurt the individual and others. Only Christ has crucified the flesh. Only in Him would freedom be used for healing and not hurt.

Teaching Outline

I. Set Free in Christ:
   Galatians 5:1
   A. Stand Firm: 1
   B. Be Not Entangled: 1
II. Called to Liberty:
    Galatians 5:13-18
    A. No Occasion for Flesh: 13-15
    B. Walk in the Spirit: 16-18
III. Conflict: Flesh vs. Spirit:
     Galatians 5:19-26
     A. Works of the Flesh: 19-21
     B. Fruit of the Spirit: 22-23
     C. No Vain Glory: 24-26

Daily Bible Readings

Mon. Wait for Righteousness
Galatians 5:1-5
Tue. Basic Value: Faith Working Through Love - *Galatians 5:6-12*
Wed. You Were Called to Freedom
Galatians 5:13-17
Thurs. Name the Works of the Flesh
Galatians 5:18-23
Fri. Avoid the Fruits of Darkness
Galatians 5:24-25; Ephesians 5:18-20
Sat. Obtaining the Grace of God
Hebrews 12:12-17
Sun. Bear Fruit in Every Good Work
Colossians 1:3-14

May 22, 1994

VERSE BY VERSE

I. Set Free in Christ: Galatians 5:1

A. Stand Firm: 1

1. STAND fast therefore in the liberty wherewith Christ hath made us free, and be not entangled again with the yoke of bondage.

Paul held to one theme with many variations. That one theme was that the work of Jesus Christ on the cross and in the resurrection had set all people free from the bondage of sin and death. Through faith in this finished work, humankind could experience life more abundant now and hereafter eternal life with God. For Paul, all else could fall away but this much had to remain.

Paul had known bondage under law. He had even been an instrument of the Law to bind others. He knew what he had been set free from in Christ. Out of that awareness he had an eye and an ear for anything that would pull a believer away from the gospel. Faith in Jesus Christ, not righteousness of the Law, needed to be the Galatians' motto.

B. Be Not Entangled: 1

1. STAND fast therefore in the liberty wherewith Christ hath made us free, and be not entangled again with the yoke of bondage.

Paul's call to freedom in Christ was not to a freedom to indulge our passions and desires. The Galatians had been as bound in their flesh from the rejection of God as the Jews had been bound in trying to keep the Law out of their rejection of God. Lawkeeping and lawlessness were both rejections of God.

Paul wanted the Galatians to see that to forsake their lawlessness for the yoke of the Law is to fall off of the other side of the same log. Both are an entanglement in the world's ways and both lead to death. In Christ, people are not just free from law's bondage and sin's enslavement; they are free to be obedient to God and to love their neighbor as themselves.

II. Called to Liberty: Galatians 5:13-18

A. No Occasion for Flesh: 13-15

13. For brethren, ye have been called unto liberty; only use not liberty for an occasion to the flesh, but by love serve one another.
14. For all the law is fulfilled in one word, even in this; Thou shalt love thy neighbour as thyself.
15. But if ye bite and devour one another, take heed that ye be not consumed one of another.

Humankind had always had the freedom to sin. Christ did not need to come to give this possibility. Christ came to give the freedom to love God and honor Him by serving our neighbor.

Paul knew this freedom had been hard won in Christ. It would be hard won over and over again in each indi-

373

vidual who placed his faith in Christ. The struggle between flesh and Spirit is in everyone. Paul urged that when the flesh's strong pull begins to tug within us, to nip it in the bud. Don't play with the flesh's enticements. Give them no foothold. How could such a thing be accomplished?

In all areas of the Christian life, service stands in the good pleasure of the Lord. If believers make themselves available to the Spirit and engage in service to one another, there would be no occasion to judge each other or despise each other. Love looks past faults and draws out good. If the Galatians tore at one another, they would reap what they sowed. The evil spirit that sought destruction of Christ desired to work through them to get them to consume each other.

B. Walk in the Spirit: 16-18

16. This I say then, Walk in the Spirit, and ye shall not fulfil the lust of the flesh.
17. For the flesh lusteth against the Spirit, and the Spirit against the flesh: and these are contrary the one to the other: so that ye cannot do the things that ye would.
18. But if ye be led of the Spirit, ye are not under the law.

Oil and water don't mix. Neither will flesh and Spirit. "Flesh" is used here as a metaphor for our propensity for sin. God can have no part in corruption. Sin corrupts, Jesus saves. Through Him the Galatians had been drawn out of corruption. Now Paul wanted them to realize that they could be kept out of corruption only by the Spirit as well. To go back to the flesh which could not save them as if it could now maintain them was insanity.

The flesh's feelings and the Spirit's leading are not to be confused. Both forces are at work in the believers. Flesh would not check flesh. If it did it would be a house divided against itself. The Spirit quickens the hearts of believers. They must walk in the same source that gave them life. The fruit of the Spirit in Galatians 5:22 is our checklist. To walk in these is life.

III. Conflict: Flesh vs. Spirit: Galatians 5:19-26

A. Works of the Flesh: 19-21

19. Now the works of the flesh are manifest, which are these; Adultery, fornication, uncleanness, lasciviousness,
20. Idolatry, witchcraft, hatred, variance, emulations, wrath, strife, seditions, heresies,
21. Envyings, murders, drunkenness, revellings, and such like: of the which I tell you before, as I have also told you in time past, that they which do such things shall not inherit the kingdom of God.

Each person has natural evil desires that issue out of their condition of sin. There have always been infinite varieties of the same condition. "Sin" with a capital letter manifests itself in many forms of sins, small letter. One of the problems with the Law was that it sought to control the symptoms (sins with a small "s"). it could not remove the condition of bondage (Sin with a capital "S") in which man is hopelessly entangled. Jesus Christ had changed humankind's condition at the cross.

Paul knew how humans could deceive themselves about their condition. So he spells out the works that proceed from flesh's rule in people's lives. Notice that each of the works of the flesh is a perversion of something that was good in and of itself.

B. Fruit of the Spirit: 22-23

22. But the fruit of the Spirit is love, joy, peace, longsuffering, gentleness, goodness, faith,

23. Meekness, temperance: against such there is no law.

All people have always been controlled by something other than their own will. Humankind's will was in bondage, though it would vehemently reject this truth. Paul made this reality clear in Romans 7. What controlled people would produce its issue through them.

Notice that "works" is plural in the phrase "works of the flesh." However, "fruit" is singular in "fruit of the Spirit." These character traits of the Spirit were the possession of all believers, for all believers had the same Holy Spirit. The fruit of the Spirit was not an action or actions. Now the Galatian believers were in Christ. The Holy Spirit was producing fruit in each of them. Out of this would flow actions expressive of God's love through Christ. It was the gift of God which would issue in fruit of the Spirit. Now the intent of the Law could be fulfilled: loving God and our neighbor.

C. No Vain Glory: 24-26

24. And they that are Christ's have crucified the flesh with the affections and lusts.

25. If we live in the Spirit, let us also walk in the Spirit.

26. Let us not be desirous of vain glory, provoking one another, envying one another.

The flesh has its own affections, things it is attracted to; and lusts, things it desires to possess. Christ had crucified these on the cross. Believers, by faith, have nailed their natural desires to His cross. That is to say, believers are crucified with Him (vs. 24). It is a past tense action. Though the flesh might rage and seek to entangle believers once again in law or lawlessness, in Christ flesh is null and void.

The affection that was now most troublesome to the Galatians was the desire for the approval of men. If this was indulged in, they would provoke one another and envy one another. Remember, Paul warned, all glory which comes from humankind is vain glory. What believers could glory in is Christ and Him crucified. Be dead to fleshly glory and alive to Christ's glory. This way provokes no one and arouses no envy.

Evangelistic Emphasis

"The proof of the pudding is in the eating," the old saying goes. People may be impressed by our arguments but they are convinced by the Christian lifestyle. When they see the difference, they sometimes inquire about the source of our lives, what makes us tick. Then we are privileged to explain that it's not what we know, it's who we know that makes all the difference. That is true if we understand Christianity not to be a philosophical school of thought, but as a companionship for life.

The secret is not a movement of which we are a part, a set of principles we espouse, an organization we promote. The secret is God's Spirit moving in and through us. God's creative Spirit enters our lives when we confess faith and are baptized into the death and resurrection of Jesus Christ. We are raised to walk "in newness of life," with His life born in us. The simplest and most effective evangelism has always been a real and informal introduction of the seeker to the Master. We are not instructing people to achieve what we have achieved, to learn what we have learned, to experience what we have experienced. We are inviting them to receive a relationship we have been given.

◆◆◆◆◆◆

Memory Selection

But the fruit of the Spirit is love, joy, peace, patience, kindness, goodness, faithfulness, gentleness, self control; against such there is no law.
Galatians 5:22, 23

Paul contrasts fruit and works to show us two ways of living. When we are in business for ourselves, trying to find life by our own merits, we are working for wages. We imagine we have a business deal with God. There is nothing life-giving or energizing in that. We usually think of the "wages of sin" as payment due a life of gross immorality. In addition to gross sins, Paul here pictures one's moral life without God as hard work earning scant wages. Even when we work hard at being religious, we will collect the wages of alienation from God, from others and from ourselves.

By contrast, when we look to God for our life, take Jesus as our Lord and Savior, invite His Spirit into our hearts, we can taste the delicious fruit of love, joy, patience and so on. Frank Sinatra struck the keynote for our modern American life in his song, "I Did It My Way." One can do it that way. But as the wise man in Proverbs said, "There is a way which seems right to a man, but the end of it is the way of death."

May 22, 1994

Weekday Problems

John grew up in a competitive home. Everything was a race, a contest, a game of competition. He learned to define himself day by day as winner or loser. All the way through school it was the same. For John, academics were a game; and he studied to be the best. He was attracted to the individual events of track and field because of the one-to-one competition. He was on his own, not dependent on teammates. The opportunities and victories were personal and individual. When he dated he went after the quarterback's girl--as much to beat him out as to get to know the girl.

After John finished law school he went to work as one of many young lawyers in the most prestigious firm in Chicago. Seven days a week he worked twelve and fourteen hours a day. He knocked himself out, not to do the job, to serve the clients, or even just to build his own career. More than anything else, he worked hard to win. He wanted to be the youngest partner in the firm's history. When he went to court, his interest was not justice so much as beating the lawyers across the aisle. The ideas of simply making a significant contribution, of sharing human life with others, of serving his clients and of graciously receiving a gift were totally foreign to John.

*How does our society view John— positively or negatively?
*Why did Paul write what he did in Galatians 5:26?

♦♦♦♦♦♦

Sparkles

"Egotism is a conceited insistence on my own particular ways and manners and customs. It is an easily discernible characteristic, and fortunately is condemned straightway by right thinking people. We are inclined to overlook egotism in young people and in ignorant people, but even in them it is of the detestable vicious order."--Oswald Chambers

"Fruit is not the salvation of souls, that is God's work; fruit is the fruit of the Spirit, love, joy, peace, etc."--Oswald Chambers

BEAR FRUIT OF THE SPIRIT

This Lesson In Your Life

In today's passage Paul addresses the final frontier in our personal quests for freedom. Galatians has been called the *Magna Charta* of Christian liberty. Over the centuries it has liberated thousands of enslaved souls and brought life and hope where there was only darkness and despair.

When we speak of the last frontier of freedom, just what is meant is not immediately obvious. In Galatians Paul addresses three aspects of the Christian's freedom. In chapter 1 he defends himself against the charges that he preached a second-hand, borrowed gospel. In the process he affirmed that he was no longer enslaved to human opinion (Gal. 1:10). To live in constant fear of his ratings would be a betrayal of his devotion to Christ.

In the second and third chapters he explained the Christian's second great freedom: liberty from the burden of self-salvation. God's Law was a blessing in that it brought the believer to Christ. It never had functioned as a ladder of achievement by which human beings could climb up to God's throne and demand acceptance. How liberating to know that our reconciliation does not depend on our performance, but upon His grace demonstrated forever at Golgotha!

The third and final frontier of freedom is seldom even recognized. Many who are liberated from the tyranny of human approval, who joyfully accept God's grace in Jesus Christ are still enslaved and do not even know it. The most subtle, powerful and persistent form of bondage is slavery to self. The most difficult liberty to know is freedom from our freedoms. Escape from consuming self-interest is the final work of God's grace in our lives.

Paul says, "Do not use your freedom as a launching pad from which to destroy others." Freedom is a two-edged sword. It must be handled carefully. If I am blindly self-centered in my freedom I will use and abuse you to get what I want, to exercise my rights, to claim what's coming to me.

We never are finally released from this prison of self in which we live here and now. None are totally free of self-centeredness. By God's power we are granted more and more frequent furloughs from ourselves. We are given the joy of getting out of ourselves to show His love to others.

Paul gives two secrets for dealing with runaway self-interest. These were lessons he learned in his own life and revealed in Galatians. First, Paul was continually lifted out of himself by remembering Jesus Christ who, in Paul's words, "loved me and gave himself up for me" (Gal. 2:20). Jesus was not only Paul's Savior, he was also his inspiration and model. Second, our text encourages us to ask for help from beyond ourselves. We can either fight the battles just on our own resources or we can invite God to come into our hearts and help. We have the option of walking in the Spirit.

We Christians are never truly free in Christ when we are just independent of the control of others and liberated from self-salvation. We are fully free when we know Christ lifting us out of ourselves by his love to live as he lived.

Seed Thoughts

1. Why does Paul contrast "works of the flesh" with "fruit of the Spirit"?
Running our lives ourselves is hard work. With God's help the good things come as naturally as fruit.

2. Why did Paul save until last his discussion of our abuse of our freedoms?
Because getting free from our freedoms is the ultimate challenge.

3. What was the "yoke of slavery" the Galatians were tempted to accept again?
Self-salvation by perfect Law-keeping.

4. What is the difference between appropriate self-love and self-indulgence?
Self-love is recognizing that we are made in God's image. Self-indulgence is pretending to be God.

5. What was Paul's summary of ethics according to the Law?
"You shall love your neighbor as yourself."

(PLEASE TURN PAGE)

---

1. Why does Paul contrast "works of the flesh" with "fruit of the Spirit"?

2. Why did Paul save until last his discussion of our abuse of our freedoms?

3. What was the "yoke of slavery" the Galatians were tempted to accept again?

4. What is the difference between appropriate self-love and self-indulgence?

5. What was Paul's summary of ethics according to the Law?

6. Did Paul endorse competition as always healthy?

7. What two possibilities for life tug always at the Christian for allegiance?

8. By "flesh" does Paul mean just bodily sins?

9. Why does Paul say "there is no law against" the fruit of the Spirit?

10. If those "in Christ have crucified the flesh" does that mean Christians should be living the ascetic lifestyle?

Running our lives ourselves is hard work. With God's help the good things come as naturally as fruit.

Because getting free from our freedoms is the ultimate challenge.

Self-salvation by perfect Law-keeping.

Self-love is recognizing that we are made in God's image. Self-indulgence is pretending to be God.

"You shall love your neighbor as yourself."

No, it is possible to be so competitive that we are "consumed by one another."

Life "according to the flesh" and "life in the Spirit."

No, he means all sins, of body and attitude, which express human independence from God.

Because it is not produced by keeping rules but in relationship with God's Spirit.

Some may be called to that. But always all are called to seek God's will more than their own.

(SEED THOUGHTS--Cont'd)

6. Did Paul endorse competition as always healthy?
No, it is possible to be so competitive that we are "consumed by one another."

7. What two possibilities for life tug always at the Christian for allegiance?
Life "according to the flesh" and "life in the Spirit."

8. By "flesh" does Paul mean just bodily sins?
No, he means all sins, of body and attitude, which express human independence from God.

9. Why does Paul say "there is no law against" the fruit of the Spirit?
Because it is not produced by keeping rules but in relationship with God's Spirit.

10. If those "in Christ have crucified the flesh" does that mean Christians should be living the ascetic lifestyle?
Some may be called to that. But always all are called to seek God's will more than their own.

May 29, 1994

Express Christ's Love In All Relationships

Galatians 6:1-10; 14-18

1 Brethren, if a man be overtaken in a fault, ye which are spiritual restore such a one in the spirit of meekness; considering thyself lest thou also be tempted.
2 Bear ye one another's burdens, and so fulfil the law of Christ.
3 For if a man think himself to be something, when he is nothing, he deceiveth himself.
4 But let every man prove his own work, and then shall he have rejoicing in himself alone, and not in another.
5 For every man shall bear his own burden.
6 Let him that is taught in the word communicate unto him that teacheth in all good things.
7 Be not deceived; God is not mocked: for whatsoever a man soweth that shall he also reap.
8 For he that soweth to his flesh shall of the flesh reap corruption; but he that soweth to the Spirit shall of the Spirit reap life everlasting.
9 And let us not be weary in well doing: for in due season we shall reap, if we faint not.
10 As we have therefore opportunity, let us do good unto all *men*, especially unto them who are of the household of faith.
14 But God forbid that I should glory, save in the cross of our Lord Jesus Christ, by whom the world is crucified unto me, and I unto the world.
15 For in Christ Jesus neither circumcision availeth any thing, nor uncircumcision, but a new creature.
16 And as many as walk according to this rule, peace *be* on them, and mercy, and upon the Israel of God.
17 From henceforth let no man trouble me: for I bear in my body the marks of the Lord Jesus.
18 Brethren, the grace of our Lord Jesus Christ *be* with your spirit. A'-men.

◆◆◆◆◆◆

◀ **Memory Selection**
Galatians 6:10

◀ **Devotional Reading**
1 Corinthians 13:1-7

◀ **Background Scripture**
Galatians 6

◀ **Printed Scripture**
Galatians 6:1-10, 14-18

EXPRESS CHRIST'S LOVE IN ALL RELATIONSHIPS

Teacher's Target

A woman who was an atheist watched Rev. Carlyle Marney as he walked to church. He came upon a small child who had had a tricycle accident. The tricycle had lost a wheel and the little girl had skinned her knee. She cried, rubbing her scraped knee. The woman expected Marney to he too busy for the child. Instead, he knelt down, wiped her knee and eyes with a handkerchief, put the wheel and cotter key back in place, and patted her on the head. The girl smiled and rode off. The woman was shaken.

The next Sunday, the woman joined the church. She asked to speak. "It wasn't Marney's great preaching that impressed me," she said. Then she told about the little girl. She concluded, "If a man as important as Marney could take time for that little girl, there might be something to this Christ after all."

Have class members share similar events that have affected their walk with Christ. Have them discuss negative examples as well.

Lesson Introduction

Being a Christian does not mean being exempt from trouble or from ever falling into sin again. In fact, the warfare and its intensity seem to escalate with each new decision to relinquish our lives into Christ's keeping. Everything in the world wars against such faith and wants us to decide the cost is too great.

No one is an island. In fact, when we get isolated from other believers we are more susceptible to falling. We are so constituted that we need each other for support, correction and comfort. Community means we will act as priests to each other.

Community can be created only by adhering to the truth of Christ which will work compassion and sincere interest in each other. Tireless love will reap a harvest (Gal. 6:9).

Teaching Outline

I. The Law of Christ:
Galatians 6:1-6
  A. Restoring and Bearing: 1-3
  B. Testing and Sharing: 4-6

II. Sowing to the Spirit:
Galatians 6:7-10
  A. Reap Eternal Life: 7-8
  B. Not Grow Weary: 9
  C. Do Good to All: 10

III. Glorying in the Cross:
Galatians 6:14-18
  A. World Crucified: 14
  B. New Creation: 15-16
  C. Bear Christ's: 17-18

Daily Bible Readings

Mon. Bear One Another's Burdens
Galatians 6:1-5
Tue. Let Us Do Good to All People
Galatians 6:6-10
Wed. In the Cross of Christ I Glory
Galatians 6:11-18
Thurs. God Desires All Persons Be Saved - *I Timothy 2:1-7*
Fri. "Fight the Good Fight"
2 Timothy 4:1-5
Sat. "Fulfill Your Ministry"
2 Timothy 4:1-5
Sun. "I Have Kept the Faith"
2 Timothy 4:6-18

May 29, 1994

VERSE BY VERSE

I. The Law of Christ: Galatians 6:1-6

A. Restoring and Rearing: 1-3

1. Brethren, if a man be overtaken in a fault, ye which are spiritual restore such a one in the spirit of meekness; considering thyself lest thou also be tempted.
2. Bear ye one another's burdens, and so fulfil the law of Christ.
3. For if a man think himself to be something, when he is nothing, he deceiveth himself.

No one is beyond temptation. No one is beyond falling. The word used to talk about restoring a fallen believer has the meaning of setting a broken bone or dislocated joint. Paul admonishes us to treat a relapse into sin as an injury. With gentle and appropriate council set the fallen one back in proper place. Philippians 2:3 parallels what is said here and in verse 3.

No wrath or malice is to be in the restoration, no gloating over the fallen one. How could this be accomplished? Remember how easily temptation could befall them.

Bearing one another's burdens does not mean to remove the person from his or her own responsibility. The instruction is based on the realization that all burdens are lightened by someone who makes himself present for others even if he can do nothing else to remove the burden.

B. Testing and Sharing: 4-6

4. But let every man prove his own work, and then shall he have rejoicing in himself alone, and not in another.
5. For every man shall bear his own burden.
6. Let him that is taught in the word communicate unto him that teacheth in all good things.

One of the great preventions for self-conceit and condemning judgment of others was presented in verse 4. If each will examine his own work by the standard of the law of Christ, which is love, conceit will flee and judgment desist. Paul wanted the Galatians each to do his own homework and leave all rewarding and judging to God.

All believers belong to God. What business does anyone have in judging a servant that is not his? Also, not a single believer is adequate to be a standard by which anyone is judged.

On the final day, God will not hold any accountable for anyone but himself. Testing self is enough to occupy anyone.

Another part of the law of Christ is sharing. Test self; share with others. Especially be generous with those who are seeking to teach them the faith.

II. Sowing to the Spirit: Galatians 6:7-10

A. Reap Eternal Life: 7-8

7. Be not deceived; God is not mocked: for whatsoever a man soweth that shall he also reap.

8. For he that soweth to his flesh shall of the flesh reap corruption; but he that soweth to the Spirit shall of the Spirit reap life everlasting.

God did not go to sleep on the job. Whatever He did was in plain view of His overseeing presence. One might have mocked parents by doing what was not acceptable behind their backs, but God was ever vigilant. If one invested in the flesh, the flesh would yield its reward. If one invested in the Spirit, the Spirit would yield its reward. Corruption came by the flesh. Eternal life by the Spirit. This was not a judgment by Paul, but a warning. Any god could only deliver to devotees what that god had to give. For example, alcohol or drugs can only deliver a buzz or a high. Power can only give power, fame can only give one fame, etc.

B. Not Grow Weary: 9

9. And let us not be weary in well doing: for in due season we shall reap, if we faint not.

The harvest of the spirit is eternal life. The power of the Spirit is not to grow weary, and the benefit of the Spirit is to do good to all. No one could sustain good works out of his own humanity for very long. Flesh works on the principle of immediate gratification. Without the power of the Spirit humanitarian good deeds were streaky and faddish.

The Spirit gives the power to stay in the trenches when popular opinion and current fads pass by. Judson was seven years at his post in Burma without a single convert. Then the Spirit's harvest blossomed forth. What if Judson had grown weary in the sixth year? God could have still done His mighty deed. He was not dependent upon Judson. The reverse was true, Judson was dependent on Him. Judson would have missed the blessing of God's great harvest.

C. Do Good to All: 10

10. As we have therefore opportunity, let us do good unto all men, especially unto them who are of the household of faith.

Paul desired the Galatians never to underestimate their value to God's work. They would never know what nor when God was doing a mighty thing through them. All men and women are important to God. Therefore, none should be slighted. Especially, Paul urges us to take care of the household of faith.

III. Glorying in the Cross: Gal. 6:14-18

A. World Crucified: 14

14. But God forbid that I should glory, save in the cross of our Lord Jesus Christ, by whom the world is crucified unto me, and I unto the world.

When the Galatians gloried in the world, it had their hearts. They expected the world's rewards for their devotion and loyalty. Now they had seen a whole new order of existence that had broken into the old order. The world's way had been exposed as illusion. The Kingdom of God had been revealed as reality. Those who worshiped at the world's shrine sooner or later came to know only futility and despair.

All this had changed for Paul. The only power to which he yielded was the cross of Christ. This was the power of holy, humble, self-giving love. He was dead to the charms of the world that once fascinated him.

Now He was alive to God's revelation of Himself in Christ.

B. New Creation: 15-16

15. For in Christ Jesus neither circumcision availeth any thing, nor uncircumcision, but a new creature.
16. And as many as walk according to this rule, peace be on them, and mercy, and upon the Israel of God.

Jews held to the Law. Circumcision was the external sign of one's allegiance to it. The Gentiles held to their investment in lawlessness. Uncircumcision was the external sign of their exclusion from those who adhered to the Law. Now Christ had come and declared there was no advantage to circumcision or uncircumcision. Both were adherents to this world's ways of reckoning and valuing existence. In Christ there had come a more excellent way. Now those of the circumcision and those of the uncircumcision could be citizens of the new creation. All divisions and distinctions that made for natural enemies were broken down.

C. Bear Christ's Marks: 17-18

17. From henceforth let no man trouble me: for I bear in my body the marks of the Lord Jesus.
18. Brethren, the grace of our Lord Jesus Christ be with your spirit. A'-men.

When one glories in Christ the world is crucified and the believer is unimpressed and unaffected by its pomp and ceremony any longer. When one glories in Christ one has "moved out" of the world into the new creation in Christ. He or she still lives in Adam's carcass but a new person is being formed inside.

When one glories in Christ a third thing bound to happen in this age. The believer will bear the marks of Christ on his body. Paul had scars from the beatings and wounds he had received because of his devotion to Christ. Others' marks for Christ might not be as numerous or as visible, but they will be evident to eyes of faith. All who serve Jesus Christ in this age will be treated as the world treated Him. Paul closes out his letter by stating that his scars testified that he was willing to pay the price for following Christ. The false teachers that troubled them were the ones who had not paid the price. So don't argue with me anymore, Paul declared. Judge for yourself whether my witness in life bears out my profession.

Evangelistic Emphasis

Through this whole quarter we have stressed the power of the believing community to attract unbelievers to Christ. This observation should not be taken as a glorification of the Church in itself, as if the institution by itself provides answers. Our goal should not be to convert people primarily to the Church. While the Church is not the gospel, the fruit of the gospel should be visible in the Church. It is a shame when we hear someone say, "To tell the truth, I have closer relationships at work than I do at church. People are more real, more concerned for one another, more forgiving than I find them at church."

Paul urges the Galatians to live their lives by the "law of Christ." He was not speaking of a legal, written code. He spoke of the life Jesus lived and calls us to live in obedience to God and in concern for one another. Unbelievers can come to inquire about our secret when they see Christians loving one another, restoring each other, bearing one another's burdens, and taking responsibility for their own burdens. Most striking of all, the seeker sees those displaying honest humility, each confessing his or her own need for God.

♦♦♦♦♦♦

Memory Selection

As we have therefore opportunity, let us do good to all men, especially unto them who are of the household of faith. *Galatians 6:10*

Throughout the Bible God's people are referred to as a family of faith. In the New Testament we find frequent references to our Father and to Jesus, our older brother. In turn, we are instructed to love and care for one another as brothers and sisters in the Lord. Many modern Christians have little or no time for fellowship. "I don't come to church for fellowship, I come to worship God!" is a heard from time to time.

In 1 Corinthians 11 Paul reminded a confused church about the meaning of the Lord's Supper. In Corinth it had degenerated into a come-and-go affair, small groups exclusive to themselves shut others out. "If you partake without really observing the body of Christ, the church assembled, you eat and drink damnation to yourselves," Paul warned. We are to see, notice and care for one another as the people of God. We should be eager to meet any human need, especially of those who are in the family of faith.

May 29, 1994

Weekday Problems

Carol hoped that she could live a self-centered life and not become self-centered. Unconsciously she assumed, as someone has said, that two plus two do not always make four. Carol went to church each Sunday and rated the worship experience according to how well it met her needs. She made friends and graded them on their attentiveness and devotion to her. Others at the office were getting involved with various service projects. Some were working at the new center for the homeless downtown. Others were contributing their time to the back to school program at the welfare center. They helped make it possible for every child to begin school with two changes of clothing, books and school supplies.

Carol didn't get involved. She was incensed when her friend Barbara told of her wild lost weekends and the parties she enjoyed. "You are just flushing your life down the drain," Carol scolded. But, despite all her religion, she was really no happier than Barbara.

*Why should Christians saved by grace devote themselves to good works?
*What would it take for Carol to get out of herself to help others?

◆◆◆◆◆◆

Sparkles

A jester, known as a fool, came before the king. "Why do you dare to disturb His Majesty?" the king asked.

"I come to be your teacher," the fool responded.

"How?" asked the king with laughter.

"See, already you have asked me a question," said the fool.

"You offered me a clever response but have not answered my question," said the king.

"Only a fool has all the answers," the fool said with a smile.

"But, what would others say if they knew the king had a fool for a teacher?"

"Better to have a fool for a teacher than a fool for a king," said the fool.

Shaken, the king said, "Now I do feel like a fool."

"No," said the fool, "It is only a fool who has never felt like one."

EXPRESS CHRIST'S LOVE IN ALL RELATIONSHIPS

This Lesson In Your Life

Asking the right questions is an important key to life. One of the most penetrating questions is: In what do I take the greatest joy? We might get at the same idea in other ways. Of all my achievements and blessings, what moves me most deeply? If I had only one chance at "Show and Tell," what would I talk about?

Many answers come to mind. "If you have your health you have everything." Thousands are most proud of their bodies and their good health. Others are proud of those moments of high achievement in our lives, whether in academics, sports, the arts, career or whatever. It is not insignificant that we have worked hard and achieved. Many would talk about home and family, about marriage, children and grandchildren. Through the ups and downs it has all been worth it. Being with family is the supreme joy of life for many people.

For the legalistic Judaizing teachers of Galatia the answer was clear. "We are most proud of our heritage and of our devotion to that heritage. We have always been God's people. Circumcision is the sign of our election. It is our calling which sets us apart from all other peoples. Therefore, we must keep the Law perfectly in every detail in order to please God and to remain His special people." They were also secretly proud that they had the power to influence others of the rightness of their case, to force them into compliance with their regulations.

Paul's main intent in Galatians was to focus on God, not on any religion performed by mankind. He had something to share, something for which he was willing to die if necessary. It certainly was not his heritage, the Law of Moses, least of all his own record of performance. "Far be it from me to glory, except in the cross of Christ through which the world has been crucified unto me and I unto the world."

To many in Paul's day, that pride appears odd, even twisted. How could anyone take pride in a crucified Lord? How could one brag about a master who died a death of shame, a criminal's death? Paul took pride in God's incredible love. It was fantastic that God would come here, assume the role of a servant and willingly suffer to reconcile His lost children to Himself! No human achievement could compare with that. Nothing in the annals of human history could even begin to measure up. One can see God revealed in the cross. The Creator reveals Himself in nature. He communicated Himself in the history of Israel, in the covenant and the Law. But God revealed Himself most clearly, most profoundly in the cross.

The effects for Paul's life were dramatic. In Galatians 6:14 he mentioned three crosses. Jesus died on the first. As a result, the world with all its beautiful enticements to self-seeking died on the second. Paul's own ambition and runaway ego died on the third.

This lesson in our lives is probing. We should each stop to ask, of what am I most proud? In what do I find my greatest joy? If I had only one opportunity to share, what would I talk about? Many wonderful and beautiful secondary blessings fall away when we see God on the cross for us. "God was in Christ reconciling the world unto Himself" (2 Cor. 5:19).

Seed Thoughts

1. Why would Paul encourage Christians to help when others failed? Doesn't that suggest negative thinking and expectations?
No, Christianity is a realistic faith. Christians will fall and need help getting up again.

2. How does "bearing one another's burden" "fulfill the law of Christ?"
Jesus came and gave Himself to lift our burdens.

3. What two principles about burden-bearing do we find in Galatians 6:1-5?
Christians should bear one another's burdens and at the same time each must bear his own burden.

4. Why did Paul warn the burden-bearing Christian about temptation?
Because one is especially vulnerable when he feels spiritually superior.

5. When Paul writes "you will reap what you have sown," was he forsaking salvation by grace for works?
No, if one insists on running away from God she will discover that she is godforsaken.

(PLEASE TURN PAGE)

---

1. Why would Paul encourage Christians to help when others failed? Doesn't that suggest negative thinking and expectations?

2. How does "bearing one another's burden" "fulfill the law of Christ?"

3. What two principles about burden-bearing do we find in Galatians 6:1-5?

4. Why did Paul warn the burden-bearing Christian about temptation?

5. When Paul writes "you will reap what you have sown," was he forsaking salvation by grace for works?

6. If Christians are called to do good does that make them "do-gooders"?

7. What incentive should Christians have for persistence in doing good?

8. Why did Paul say that neither circumcision nor uncircumcision is anything in God's Kingdom?

9. Why should Christians have a special degree of care for other Christians in trouble?

10. Of what was Paul most proud?

(SEED THOUGHTS--Cont'd)

No, Christianity is a realistic faith. Christians will fall and need help getting up again.

Jesus came and gave Himself to lift our burdens.

Christians should bear one another's burdens and at the same time each must bear his own burden.

Because one is especially vulnerable when he feels spiritually superior.

No, if one insists on running away from God she will discover that she is godforsaken.

No, the good we do should be neither to impress others nor to elevate them but to glorify God.

God promises the harvest if we do not give up.

Because acceptance with God is based on faith in His grace on Golgotha.

In addition to the kinship we feel in the family of mankind, we know that other Christians are also in the family of Christ.

That he and all human beings were so loved that God came to die on a cross to provide reconciliation.

6. If Christians are called to do good does that make them "do-gooders"?
No, the good we do should be neither to impress others nor to elevate them but to glorify God.

7. What incentive should Christians have for persistence in doing good?
God promises the harvest if we do not give up.

8. Why did Paul say that neither circumcision nor uncircumcision is anything in God's Kingdom?
Because acceptance with God is based on faith in His grace on Golgotha.

9. Why should Christians have a special degree of care for other Christians in trouble?
In addition to the kinship we feel in the family of mankind, we know that other Christians are also in the family of Christ.

10. Of what was Paul most proud?
That he and all human beings were so loved that God came to die on a cross to provide reconciliation.

June 5, 1994

God Remembers

Exodus 1:8-11a

8 Now there arose up a new king over Egypt, which knew not Joseph.
9 And he said unto his people, Behold, the people of the children of Israel *are* more and mightier than we:
10 Come on, let us deal wisely with them; lest they multiply, and it come to pass, that, when there falleth out any war, they join also unto our enemies, and fight against us, and so get them up out of the land.
11 Therefore they did set over them taskmasters to afflict them with their burdens. And they built for Pharaoh treasure cities, Pi'-thom and Ra-am'-ses.

Exodus 2:1-9a

2 AND there went a man of the house of Levi and took *to wife* a daughter of Levi.
2 And the woman conceived, and bare a son: and when she saw him that he *was* a goodly *child* she hid him three months.
3 And when she could not longer hide him, she took for him an ark of bulrushes, and daubed it with slime and with pitch, and put the child therein; and she laid *it* in the flags by the river's brink.
4 And his sister stood afar off, to wit what would be done to him.
5 And the daughter of Pharaoh came down to wash *herself* at the river and her maidens walked along by the river's side; and when she saw the ark among the flags, she sent her maid to fetch it.
6 And when she had opened *it* she saw the child: and behold, the babe wept. And she had compassion on him, and said, This *is one* of the Hebrews' children.
7 Then said his sister to Pharaoh's daughter, Shall I go and call to thee a nurse of the Hebrew women, that she may nurse the child for thee?
8 And Pharaoh's daughter said to her, Go. And the maid went and called the child's mother.
9 And Pharaoh's daughter said unto her, Take this child away, and nurse it for me, and I will give *thee* thy wages. And the woman took the child, and nursed it.

Exodus 2:23-25

23 And it came to pass in process of time, that the king of Egypt died: and the children of Israel sighed by reason of the bondage, and they cried, and their cry came up unto God by reason of the bondage.
24 And God heard their groaning, and God remembered his covenant with Abraham, with Isaac, and with Jacob.
25 And God looked upon the children of Israel, and God had respect unto *them*.

◆◆◆◆◆

◀ **Memory Selection**
Exodus 2:24

◀ **Devotional Reading**
Exodus 2:16-23, 24

◀ **Background Scripture**
Exodus 1-2

◀ **Printed Scripture**
*Exodus 1:8-11a,
2:1-9a, 23-25*

GOD REMEMBERS

Teacher's Target

This world does not help the believer know that God has His hand on the throttle. Sometimes it seems we are on a runaway train. Everything in the world's system wars against faith. In fact, to forget about God is often advantageous in the world.

Circumstances, trials, adversities and temptations can cause us to feel forgotten. Children are afraid of being abandoned. old people are afraid they will not be remembered. All ages in between are afraid they will not fit in or belong anywhere.

Scripture says that God remembers when all others forget. Jesus, on the cross, had faith that He could put His Spirit in the Father's care. Here in Exodus the children of Israel are shown that God remembers. When have you been afraid of being forgotten? How did you come to know God remembered you?

Lesson Introduction

Joseph arranged for his father and brothers to move to Egypt. There they prospered. They became an influential voice in Egypt. As time passed, the Egyptians feared the Hebrews' power. Joseph's generation was gone. The Egyptians forgot his contributions.

A new Pharaoh, who knew not Joseph, sought to eliminate the children of Israel. First they were enslaved. Such affliction did not slow their increase in population. Finally, Pharaoh decreed to kill every male child born to an Israelite. The midwives feared God. They saved the male children.

Moses was one such child. His family devised an ingenious plan for his continued safety. He would be raised in Pharaoh's own house. Moses' own mother got to be his nurse! Saved by Pharaoh's house, he would save his people from Pharaoh.

Teaching Outline

I. Changing of the Guard: Exodus 1:8-11a
   A. New King: 8
   B. New Plot: 9-10
   C. New Punishment: 11
II. A Way of Preservation: Exodus 2:1-9a
   A. A Concealed Birth: 1-2
   B. A Planned Adoption: 3-6
   C. A Provision for Nature: 7-9a
III. A People Remembered: Exodus 2:23-25
   A. A King Died: 23
   B. A People Cried: 24
   C. God Looked and Heard: 25

Daily Bible Readings

Mon. A New, Harsh King Ruled Egypt - *Exodus 1:5-10*
Tue. More Oppressed, More Hebrews! *Exodus 1:11-16*
Wed. Midwives Feared the Lord, Not Pharaoh - *Exodus 1:17-21*
Thurs. Mother Made a Basket; Sister Watched - *Exodus 1:22-2:4*
Fri. Princess Called for Nurse for Moses *Exodus 2:5-9*
Sat. Moses Killed an Egyptian *Exodus 2:10-14*
Sun. Moses Fled to Midian, Married Zipporah - *Exodus 2:15-23*

VERSE BY VERSE

I. Changing of the Guard: Exodus 1:8-11a

A. New King: 8

8. Now there arose up a new king over Egypt, which knew not Joseph.

Thomas Merton once said he did not need to read the newspaper because he could read the Bible and know exactly what was on the front page of the paper. The only thing that would change would be the names of the characters. He was right. What occurred in Egypt had been and continues to be repeated in history. Whatever is a threat or a presumed threat to the powers that be will be in for a hard time. In Exodus, a pharaoh that was threatened by the might and numbers of the Hebrew people plotted their destruction.

B. New Plot: 9-10

9. And he said unto his people, Behold, the people of the children of Israel are more and mightier than we:

10. Come on, let us deal wisely with them; lest they multiply, and it come to pass, that, when there falleth out any war, they join also unto our enemies, and fight against us, and so get them up out of the land.

A minority was becoming a majority. The fear of an overthrow and exodus prompted the king to plot a way to diminish the Hebrew power. An exodus would mean the loss of the work force.

A policy was proposed to prohibit the Israelite's increase. First, they would be worked to death. The second stage of the plan was to kill the male children at birth. The third stage was for Egyptians to destroy all male Hebrew babies by throwing them into the river.

C. New Punishment: Exodus 1:11

11. Therefore they did set over them taskmasters to afflict them with their burdens. And they built for Pharaoh treasure cities, Pi'-thom and Ra-am'-ses.

Hard labor could not destroy God's elect people. Thinking themselves wise, the Egyptians were foolish. Wickedness is never wisdom regardless of the hand that performs it.

The Hebrews remained peaceable and inoffensive in behavior. Their work produced great cities and plentiful crops. They served and suffered but did not look to man for their solace. They cried out to God. The adversity fanned the fires of their resolve and hope for deliverance. The Psalmist said it well when he declared that those who plot against the Lord and His people do so in vain (Ps. 2:1-6).

II. A Way of Preservation: Exodus 2:1-9a

A. A Concealed Birth: 1-2

1. AND there went a man of the house of Levi and took to wife a daughter of Levi.

2. And the woman conceived, and bare a son: and when she saw him that he was a goodly child she hid him three months.

Affliction could not destroy the Hebrews. The midwives had protected their male children. Now the Hebrews were pressed even harder. The Israelites became adept in hiding their offspring. Moses' story was an example of such ingenuity. As the children grew they could not be easily concealed. Moses' family devised a strategy to prevent his death at the hands of the Egyptians.

Notice that already God was working to relieve His people's suffering. No one could see in the birth of this one child what was to issue from it. God moved in His own mysterious way and time to fulfill His purposes. As was stated in the New Testament, the Kingdom of God does not come with observation (Luke 17:20).

B. A Planned Adoption: 3-6

3. And when she could not longer hide him, she took for him an ark of bulrushes, and daubed it with slime and with pitch, and put the child therein; and she laid it in the flags by the river's brink.
4. And his sister stood afar off, to wit what would be done to him.
5. And the daughter of Pharaoh came down to wash herself at the river and her maidens walked along by the river's side; and when she saw the ark among the flags, she sent her maid to fetch it.
6. And when she had opened it she saw the child: and behold, the babe wept. And she had compassion on him, and said, This is one of the Hebrews' children.

Evidently Moses' mother and sister had observed Pharaoh's daughter bathing at this spot on the river. They could not be sure what would be done to the child when found. They could only hide the child in the reeds and wait.

Now all involved were placed in a situation where they were faced with observing God's providence and the wonder of His ways. Faith had to be exercised.

Pharaoh's daughter's maidens retrieved the baby in the ark from the bulrushes at the river's edge. She knew it was a Hebrew baby. Still she had compassion on the child when he cried. Here God provided a friend to this Hebrew child right in Pharaoh's own family. She would be responsible for raising the deliver of Israel. What ironic humor accompanies the ways of God at times.

C. A Provision for Nurture: 7-9a

7. Then said his sister to Pharaoh's daughter, Shall I go and call to thee a nurse of the Hebrew women, that she may nurse the child for thee?
8. And Pharaoh's daughter said to her, Go. And the maid went and called the child's mother.
9. And Pharaoh's daughter said unto her, Take this child away, and nurse it for me, and I will give thee thy wages. And the woman took the child, and nursed it.

Moses' sister acted quickly. As soon as Pharaoh's daughter showed a compassionate side toward the baby, she volunteered to find a Hebrew woman to nurse the baby.

This approach of Miriam, Moses' sister, could have been dangerous. She had no way of knowing how she would be received. Again, faith had to be the only safety net for God's people. Like Abraham going out not knowing whither, Miriam and her mother acted not knowing the outcome.

Not only was Miriam sent to bring her mother to nurse Moses, but Pharaoh's daughter was going to pay her wages for the task. A double blessing had come to the family through these circumstances of adversity.

III. A People Remembered: Exodus 2:23-25

A. A King Died: 23

23. And it came to pass in process of time, that the king of Egypt died: and the children of Israel sighed by reason of the bondage, and they cried, and their cry came up unto God by reason of the bondage.

What had seemed like an eternity to a tormented people had ended. The killing of their male children probably ended with this Pharaoh's death.

The "process of time" and the learning of patience (endurance) was not man's desired way. Hurry was ever Adam's sin. He wanted what he wanted now. Humankind since has been no different. How painful it must continually be for God to have to observe His people disturbed by circumstances rather than content through faith. Israel again proved this. Once they were free they grumbled against God. He was not moving fast enough for them. However, God was right on His schedule. His ways were not mankind's ways.

B. A People Cried: 24

24. And God heard their groaning, and God remembered his covenant with Abraham, with Isaac, and with Jacob.

The grinding of time had not just been moving closer to God's deliverance. The duration of the children of Israel's oppression had caused them finally to begin to remember their God. They had been serving idols (Ezek. 20:8). None of them had rescued them or relieved their anguish. They had focused on the human predicament and human resources. The situation seemed impossible. Humanly it was. Finally, the oppression was causing them to remember God.

Circumstances had displaced God from the place in Israel's heart reserved for Him. Only an adjustment of their focus from horizontal to vertical, from human to divine, could provide a vision of liberation.

C. God Looked and Heard: 25

25. And God looked upon the children of Israel, and God had respect unto them.

A bruised reed, God will not break. A smoldering ember, He will not quench. This was and is the nature of God. Four phrases describe His kind intentions toward Israel. He heard their groaning. He remembered His covenant. He looked upon them in their distress with compassion. He claimed them unto Himself.

In these three verses the name of God was used five times. When the major character in the story changed, the story itself changed. Such repetition of God's name was an indication that something new and mighty was about to occur.

Evangelistic Emphasis

Moses thought no one knew that he had slain the Egyptian, until a fellow Hebrew asked if he intended to do him in "as thou killedst the Egyptian" (Ex. 2:14). Seeing that the deed had caught up with him, Moses fled. No doubt he thought that both the Egyptians and his own people were against him. God was waiting for Moses in Midian; and instead of rebuking him, He gave him a challenging task to accomplish.

Many unbelievers stay in perpetual flight for similar reasons. Because of their sins they flee from God, from others, and from their best self. Even if their wrong-doings are better hidden than Moses', their own conscience accuses them. Assuming that God and His people would condemn them, they may spend a lifetime seeking a wilderness in which to hide.

God is in their wilderness, just as He is in the promptings of their conscience. He waits there not to hurl thunderbolts of judgment, but to tell them, as He told Moses, that He has work for them to do!

Some of our best opportunities for evangelism arise when we are sensitive to the tender conscience of those "on the run" from God, and surprise them with our own warmth and caring acceptance. If we project only judgmentalism and suspicion, they may remain fugitives. Only when we portray God as seeking them in love instead of turning His back on them can we say we have shared the Good News. If we show confidence in their being useful to Him, perhaps they will stop running away.

♦♦♦♦♦♦

Memory Selection

And God heard their groaning, and God remembered his covenant with Abraham, with Isaac, and with Jacob. *Exodus 2:24*

One reason "the good ol' days" were good is that a man's word was his bond, and a handshake was as good as a contract. We should remember that this kind of faithfulness is rooted in the God who keeps covenant with His people.

How discouraging it would be if God kept His promises like so many of us do today. If He kept His word only to this extent, He would have turned His back on Israel's groaning in Egypt, and gone on to bless someone who could keep himself out of trouble.

In a fallen world, circumstances can seemingly require us to reconsider our promises, asking if changed circumstances have changed the underlying meaning of the promise. Nevertheless, it is reassuring to recall that God blesses the one who "swears to his own hurt and does not change" (Ps. 15:4, NKJV). After all, we serve a God who keeps His own covenants like that.

June 5, 1994

Weekday Problems

Edward is a dedicated Christian businessman, a mid-level executive with a large mattress factory. He has worked for the same firm for twenty-five years, willingly putting in extra hours, and taking advantage of every possible in-service educational opportunity and management training course. He believes in God's providence, and that He will preserve the deserving for special service, as He saved Moses to deliver Israel from Egypt.

The president and CEO of the firm will retire in six months. Because of a long-standing policy of promoting from within, Edward and many of his coworkers believe that the board will select him to fill this top management post. Suddenly he learns that the board believes the firm needs new blood, and that they are going outside to hire a younger man for the job. Edward is being passed over.

*Has anything like this ever happened to you or to someone you know?

*What should Edward do? Appeal the board's decision? Resign and seek work elsewhere? Tough it out until retirement?

*Sometimes we seem challenged to believe two seemingly contradictory "truths"--that "life isn't fair," and that "God provides." Can such views be harmonized?

Sparkles

A carpenter came to the wise old man in his village. "I have built houses for others. Now I desire to build one for myself. Have you any advice?"

"I am not a craftsman like you, but the wisdom of our fathers says that a house must have a window and a door."

The carpenter smiled and said, "All know this."

"Yes, but do you know why a house must have a window and a door?" asked the wise man. The carpenter fell silent in humble anticipation of the answer.

"Your house must have a door for you to enter yourself and a window to see beyond yourself." With a pause and a more serious countenance the wise man continued, "Remember the only difference between a house and a coffin is a door."

# This Lesson In Your Life
MOTIVATION BY THREATS OR PRAISE?

Had Pharaoh been to a business seminar where he learned "management by intimidation"? He was threatened because God blessed the children of Israel and caused them to prosper and multiply. Since Joseph was dead now, they had no protection in the upper echelons of Egyptian government.

Pharaoh thought he knew just what to do. Not only did he enslave them; he made their tasks so difficult as to be impossible, fearing that if they enjoyed life too much they would make poor subjects, or even revolt.

Many people today have had a supervisor or a spouse that had a similar philosophy: If people aren't intimidated and kept off-balance by unreasonable demands, they may not do their best work. If they become too secure in their position they may become complacent and unproductive. The antidote for this problem is supposed to be to keep them off-balance and just a little afraid they might lose the job.

Under this kind of leadership, a workplace or a home can become a "sweat-shop." Morale sags. People lack incentive to do their best work. They become suspicious of each other. Back-biting and tale-bearing can appear to be the only way to advance. Leadership in the rank and file isn't encouraged, because top-management perceives it to be a threat.

In one office, a secretary who was having trouble at home flew into tears over a trivial issue. One supervisor called her into his office to see if he could help. Another supervisor apparently had been to the same school of management Pharaoh had. He called his fellow-supervisor on the carpet for "coddling" the woman, saying: "Leave her to stew in her own juice. We need to let her go anyway; maybe if things get tough enough for her, she'll quit."

How much better it is when a home or a work situation is affirming instead of intimidating! It's not that it just makes the people involved feel better. Many studies have shown that people are more productive at their work in such an atmosphere. When management encourages leadership, new ideas are generated, costs are often cut, and production increases.

If a worker does need to be let go, how much more straightforward and honest to say, after suitable attempts to bring his work up to par, "This just isn't working out for either of us. It's time for you to get other work." At least such an approach enables the worker to pinpoint deficiencies, instead of wondering why the boss is cross.

The irony facing the pharaohs of the world is that God has a way of looking after right-hearted people. In our lesson, the cries of injustice reached the divine throne. In response, God saw to it that the life of the infant Moses was spared. In His providence Moses had the upbringing that would enable him one day to respond to the commission, "Let my people go!" Eventually, the people who had been enslaved to make them more productive and less of a threat threw off their yoke—and Pharaoh had no more slave labor to build his cities and his pyramids.

The story becomes a forecast of the classic standoff between labor and management, in which both causes suffer. It doesn't have to be the norm. Workers can do their job "not with eyeservice, as menpleasers; but as the servants of Christ, doing the will of God from the heart; with good will doing service, as to the Lord, and not to men" (Eph. 6:6-7). Supervisors can "forbear threatening, knowing that they have a Master also" (vs. 9). They can learn that most people are better motivated by praise than by threats and intimidation.

Seed Thoughts

1. List the twelve tribal heads of Israel who migrated to Egypt.
   Reuben, Simeon, Levi, Judah, Issachar, Zebulun, Benjamin, Dan, Naphtali, Gad, Asher, and Joseph (Ex. 1:1-5).

2. Have you ever worked in a situation in which a supervisor made the work as difficult as possible?
   (Encourage discussion of what to do in such situations.)

3. In addition to hard physical labor, what emotional burden did the Egyptians heap on the Hebrews?
   They "made their lives bitter." (Discuss similar experiences among class members.)

4. How did God bless the Hebrew midwives for sparing the lives of newborn males?
   He "made them houses"--either literally, or perhaps blessed their families so that they grew in strength and numbers.

5. Of what tribe was Moses born, and what later significance would this tribe have?
   He was of the tribe of Levi, which would later become the tribe from whom priests were chosen in the Jewish system of worship.

(PLEASE TURN PAGE)

---

1. List the twelve tribal heads of Israel who migrated to Egypt.

2. Have you ever worked in a situation in which a supervisor made the work as difficult as possible?

3. In addition to hard physical labor, what emotional burden did the Egyptians heap on the Hebrews?

4. How did God bless the Hebrew midwives for sparing the lives of newborn males?

5. Of what tribe was Moses born, and what later significance would this tribe have?

6. What "good news/bad news" or bittersweet experience befell the mother of Moses?

7. What indication is given that Moses knew his identity--that he was a Hebrew instead of an Egyptian prince?

8. What strength of body and character did Moses exhibit at the well in Midian?

9. What is the "covenant" referred to in Exodus 2:24?

10. According to Acts 7:23, how old was Moses when he returned to Egypt from Midian?

(SEED THOUGHTS--Cont'd)

Reuben, Simeon, Levi, Judah, Issachar, Zebulun, Benjamin, Dan, Naphtali, Gad, Asher, and Joseph (Ex. 1:1-5).

(Encourage discussion of what to do in such situations.)

They "made their lives bitter." (Discuss similar experiences among class members.)

He "made them houses"--either literally, or perhaps blessed their families so that they grew in strength and numbers.

He was of the tribe of Levi, which would later become the tribe from whom priests were chosen in the Jewish system of worship.

She got to nurse her own son instead of his being killed, but later had to give him up to Pharaoh's daughter to be raised as an Egyptian.

Exodus 2:11 refers to Moses going out to the Hebrew slaves, "his brethren."

He defended the daughters of the priest of Midian against opposing shepherds, so they could water their flocks.

That God would bless the "seed" or descendants of Abraham, Isaac, and Jacob (see Gen. 12:1-3).

Age forty.

6. **What "good news/bad news" or bittersweet experience befell the mother of Moses?**
She got to nurse her own son instead of his being killed, but later had to give him up to Pharaoh's daughter to be raised as an Egyptian.

7. **What indication is given that Moses knew his identity--that he was a Hebrew instead of an Egyptian prince?**
Exodus 2:11 refers to Moses going out to the Hebrew slaves, "his brethren."

8. **What strength of body and character did Moses exhibit at the well in Midian?**
He defended the daughters of the priest of Midian against opposing shepherds, so they could water their flocks.

9. **What is the "covenant" referred to in Exodus 2:24?**
That God would bless the "seed" or descendants of Abraham, Isaac, and Jacob (see Gen. 12:1-3).

10. **According to Acts 7:23, how old was Moses when he returned to Egypt from Midian?**
Age forty.

June 12, 1994

God Calls and Moses Responds

Exodus 3:10-15a

10 Come now therefore, and I will send thee unto Pharaoh, that thou mayest bring forth my people the children of Israel out of Egypt.
11 And Moses said unto God, Who *am* I, that I should go unto Pharaoh, and that I should bring forth the children of Israel out of Egypt?
12 And he said, Certainly I will be with thee; and this *shall be* a token unto thee, that I have sent thee; When thou hast brought forth the people out of Egypt, ye shall serve God upon this mountain.
13 And Moses said unto God, Behold, *when* I come unto the children of Israel, and shall say unto them, The God of your fathers hath sent me unto you; and they shall say to me, What is his name? what shall I say unto them?
14 And God said unto Moses, I AM THAT I AM: and he said, Thus shalt thou say unto the children of Israel, I AM hath sent me unto you.
15 And God said moreover to Moses, Thus shalt thou say unto the children of Israel, The LORD God of your fathers, the God of Abraham, the God of Isaac, and the God of Jacob, hath sent me unto you; this *is* my name forever, and this is my memorial unto all generations.

Exodus 4:1-5

1 AND Moses answered and said. But, behold, they will not believe me, nor hearken unto my voice: for they will say, The LORD hath not appeared unto thee.
2 And the LORD said unto him, What *is* that in thine hand? And he said, A rod.
3 And he said, Cast it on the ground. And he cast it on the around, and it became a serpent; and Moses fled from before it.
4 And the LORD said unto Moses, Put forth thine hand and take it by the tail. And he put forth his hand, and caught it, and it became a rod in his hand:
5 That they may believe that the Lord God of their fathers, the God of Abraham, the God of Isaac, and the God of Jacob, hath appeared unto thee.

Exodus 4:10-12

10 And Moses said unto the LORD, O my Lord, I *am* not eloquent, neither heretofore, nor since thou hast spoken unto thy servant: but I *am* slow of speech, and of a slow tongue.
11 And the LORD said unto him, Who hath made man's mouth? or who maketh the dumb, or deaf, or the seeing, or the blind? have not I the LORD?
12 Now therefore go, and I will be with thy mouth, and teach thee what thou shalt say.

◆◆◆◆◆◆

◀ **Memory Selection**
Exodus 3:10

◀ **Devotional Reading**
Exodus 3:16

◀ **Background Scripture**
Exodus 3:1-4:17

◀ **Printed Scripture**
Exodus 3:10-15a
4:1-5. 10-12

GOD CALLS AND MOSES RESPONDS

Teacher's Target

Who is worthy to be a spokesman for God? The answer is no one. Yet the paradox is that all people of the earth seem to have a penchant for clamoring for power, fame and fortune. Most of us overreach our grasp. Read the Book. It will confirm this reality.

Moses had once worked to deliver his people. His way resulted in the murder of an Egyptian at his hands. Now he was not so sure of his adequacy.

An evangelist had a two-week protracted meeting. Only one convert came forward, a young boy. He thought the revival a failure. The young boy was Billy Graham. Who could have known what God would do through him?

What is God asking you to do? Who will provide what you need for the task? What causes such hesitancy to follow the leading of the Lord. How can you know it is God who is calling?

Lesson Introduction

Moses had been forty years on the back side of Midian. He had fled there after slaying an Egyptian for being cruel to a Hebrew. Moses' bright future as one raised in Pharaoh's palace was ended in a moment of rage. Now he tended sheep. Little did he know his experiences in Pharaoh's house and in tending sheep were all preparation for a shining hour in the service of His Lord.

Did Moses not know who it was that summoned him? If God called, why wouldn't a person know that there was nothing to fear? Wouldn't he know that God would provide? The Scripture reveals repeatedly that sight of self and surroundings stagger and stunt faith in God and His sufficiency. Moses was no exception. "I AM" had called, yet Moses could not get his eyes off of his own shortcomings.

Teaching Outline

I. A Rescue Planned: Exodus 3:10-15
   A. God Enlists: 10
   B. God Enables: 11-12
   C. God Reveals: 13-15

II. A Man Empowered: Exodus 4:1-5,10-12
   A. Questions Asked: 1,10
   B. Questions Answered: 2-5
   C. Presence Promised: 11-12

Daily Bible Readings

Mon. God Speaks to Moses *Exodus 3:1-6*
Tue. God Came to Deliver Israel *Exodus 3:7-10*
Wed. But, Who Are You? *Exodus 3:11-15*
Thurs. God of Abraham, Isaac, and Jacob - *Exodus 3:16-22*
Fri. Take Your Rod - Cast It Away *Exodus 4:1-5*
Sat. If Rod and Leprosy Fail, Pour Water - *Exodus 4:6-17*
Sun. Moses and Aaron Go to Israel's Elders - *Exodus 4: 18-31*

June 12, 1994

VERSE BY VERSE

I. A Rescue Planned: Exodus 3:10-15

A. God Enlists: 10

10. Come now therefore, and I will send thee unto Pharaoh, that thou mayest bring forth my people the children of Israel out of Egypt.

"If God is for us who can be against us?" made a nice slogan. However, remembering that truth was never was an easy task. One answer to this question could be Pogo's answer: "We have found the enemy and it is us."

Moses heard God's call. He saw the burning bush. He knew who was in charge. He recognized might and power when he saw it. Still, being incorporated into the divine plan put another slant on things. Life would change. old forgotten and ignored fears would have to be faced. Old memories and powerful enemies would have to be confronted. God called, but Moses would have to be the one to walk through the valley. How could he know he would be adequate for the task?

B. God Enables: 11, 12

11. And Moses said unto God, Who am I, that I should go unto Pharaoh, and that I should bring forth the children of Israel out of Egypt?

12. And he said, Certainly I will be with thee; and this shall be a token unto thee, that I have sent thee; When thou hast brought forth the people out of Egypt, ye shall serve God upon this mountain.

The truth was, Moses was not adequate. He had shortcomings both physical and emotional. The other part of the truth was that God wasn't counting on Moses' adequacy. All God desired from Moses was a willingness to put all of who he was at God's disposal. God plus Moses' willingness would be adequate. God would enable Moses to accomplish far more than Moses could have ever thought possible.

God never asked any of His servants to work alone. He provided other human resources such as Aaron. Most of all God promised Moses that He Himself would be with him. Moses had God Himself and all the resources of all creation at His fingertips. The God who spoke a world into existence surely could enable a man to lead a people out of bondage.

C. God Reveals: 13-15

13. And Moses said unto God, Behold, when I come unto the children of Israel, and shall say unto them, The God of your fathers hath sent me unto you; and they shall say to me, What is his name? what shall I say unto them?

14. And God said unto Moses, I am that I am: and he said, Thus shalt thou say unto the children of Israel, I am hath sent me unto you.

15. And God said moreover to Moses, Thus shalt thou say unto the

children of Israel, The LORD God of your fathers, the God of Abraham, the God of Isaac, and the God of Jacob, hath sent me unto you; this is my name forever, and this is my memorial unto all generations.

Moses knew the Egyptian culture and its religions. They had many gods with many names. Also, he was aware that the Hebrews had adopted some of these gods as their own. Moses wanted to know how he could clearly distinguish the one true God from the many counterfeits. Likewise, how could he name God so that the Hebrews would hear the call back to the faith of their fathers? How could he get them to accept the promise of their lineage? God gave Moses the answer.

God revealed himself as "I AM." This was the one that was before all things, not created, not made. As "I AM," God declared Himself to be the one constant in a world of instability, insecurity and continual change. Furthermore, God told Moses to declare that "I AM" was the God of Abraham, Isaac and Jacob. This designation could fan the memory of God's promise to the fathers of their nation. How could Moses fail with the God who promised to be constant security and stability for all generations on his side?

II. A Man Empowered: Exodus 4:1-5, 10-12

A. Questions Asked: 1, 10

1. AND Moses answered and said. But, behold, they will not believe me, nor hearken unto my voice: for they will say, The LORD hath not appeared unto thee.

10. And Moses said unto the LORD, O my Lord, I am not eloquent, neither heretofore, nor since thou hast spoken unto thy servant: but I am slow of speech, and of a slow tongue.

Moses still had fear of failure (vs. 1). He could not imagine that the people of Israel would listen to a shepherd from Midian. He had been gone forty years. He had no standing nor platform to speak to these people. How could he believe that these people would authorize him to speak to them, much less allow him to lead them?

Besides, Moses had a speech problem (vs. 10). He would embarrass himself and God. From Moses' human point of view it would be better for God to find Himself another man.

No one who is called to do a mission for God small or great, knows in advance how he or she will be received. We do not know in advance that we have the goods for the task. Moses had lived long enough to know well his inadequacies. All God asked was for Moses to take the first step of faith, just to yield himself into God's hands. Only such yielding would remove the questioning fear and relieve the anxiety generated by his human inadequacy.

B. Questions Answered: 2-5

2. And the LORD said unto him, What is that in thine hand? And he said, A rod.

3. And he said, Cast it on the ground. And he cast it on the ground, and it became a serpent; and Moses fled from before it.

4. And the LORD said unto Moses, Put forth thine hand and take it by the tail. And he put forth his hand, and caught it, and it became a rod in his hand:

5. That they may believe that the Lord God of their fathers, the God of Abraham, the God of Isaac, and the God of Jacob, hath appeared unto thee.

Some might put the emphasis upon the miracles of the rod changing into a snake or a hand becoming leprous. What the people would understand from this may be more important. A serpent was a symbol of evil. For Moses to throw down the rod and it to become a snake, pick it up in his hand and it change into a useful rod, spoke a message to the people. This event would picture for the people that Moses had the power over evil on his side. Without any magical incantations, the power of the one true God is revealed to be with Moses. He would have the power of God with him to overcome evil and turn all things for good. Likewise the leprous hand being cleansed signifies the power of God with Moses to cleanse His people from the leprosy of their abandonment of the one true God.

God continually uses ordinary objects such as a rod and people with impediments to teach profound lessons about who He is and what He is about in the world. God comes into the people's world. He knows they could not get into His. He speaks in ways they can comprehend, ways in which His person and work would best he revealed. He does not expect people to grasp His ways. They are too high for humankind. God condescends and speaks on the human level in ways appropriate for the time and place. He did not speak the same way to all people. God was always context and culture appropriate. Otherwise the people would have missed His message. People had a hard enough time hearing and seeing God's revelation even with His incarnational methods.

C. Presence Promised: 11-12

11. And the LORD said unto him, Who hath made man's mouth? or who maketh the dumb, or deaf, or the seeing, or the blind? have not I the LORD?

12. Now therefore go, and I will be with thy mouth, and teach thee what thou shalt say.

God had condescended to Moses' every doubt and every need. He had been patient and reassuring. Still Moses was hesitant. In verse 14 the Scripture even declares that God was angry with Moses for lingering on his handicaps and misgivings. Still God reasoned with Moses and did not act out His anger upon him. In verses 10 and 11 God begins to declare the reality of His power.

He asks questions of Moses much like He did Job. Moses is worried about his speech. God asks, "Who do you think made your mouth?" Moses is worried about the people hearing. God says, "Who do you think gave them ears with which to hear?" God's point is that if He could create the mouth and the ears then He had the power to open mouths to speak clearly and ears to hear and eyes to see clearly?

Having assured Moses that "I AM" would go with him, God says to Moses, "Get on with the mission." What an instructor and what a prompter! "I will be with thy mouth, and teach thee what thou shalt say" (vs. 12). Finally, Moses moves. Slowly in every age, people in every period in history have taken that first step into their anxiety and found that God was sufficient for their hour, too.

Evangelistic Emphasis

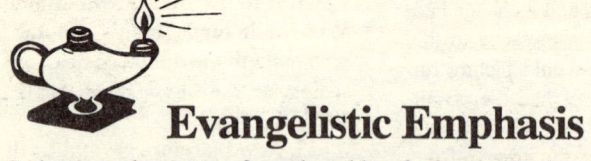

God appeared to Moses from the midst of a burning bush to commission him to take the message of deliverance to the Hebrew captives. It's remarkable how often Scripture and Christian history use *fire* to symbolize such missions.

The prophet Jeremiah tried to stop delivering God's message, but found that "his word was in mine heart as a burning fire shut up in my bones ... and I could not stay" (Jer. 20:9). On the first Pentecost after Christ's resurrection, flames of fire hovered above the heads of the disciples bearing the message of salvation through the risen Lord. Jonathan Edwards, the early Puritan preacher, echoed Jeremiah when he spoke of how "divine things would often, of a sudden, kindle, as it were, a sweet burning in my heart, an ardor of soul."

These evangelistic fires have been dampened in the hearts of many Christians today. Perhaps we have been intimidated by the powerful voices of unbelief all about us. We are embarrassed by the moral failures of a few evangelistic types with high visibility. As Quaker philosopher Elton Trueblood has said, "there is something faintly embarrassing about all evangelism."

But the bush is still burning! It was not consumed when God spoke to Moses from it, and its urgency still glows hot today. Let us pray that the burning need to tell others of the deliverance and hope available in Christ will be rekindled in our hearts.

◆◆◆◆◆◆

Memory Selection

Come now therefore, and I will send thee to Pharaoh, that thou mayest bring forth my people the children of Israel out of Egypt. *Exodus 3:10*

Often the task facing the church seems as overwhelming as releasing the Hebrew captives must have seemed to Moses. We are faced with liberating a world in bondage to immorality and injustice. Even within the church, complacency, division, financial needs and personal problems can daunt all but the boldest. With Moses, we may feel inadequate for the task.

If we identify with Moses' reluctance to rise to the challenge, can we also identify with the way God overcame it? One by one, Moses' fears were calmed, and his inadequacies supplied. Armed with God's strong presence and miraculous powers, and with his brother Aaron as spokesman, Moses was able to accomplish what had seemed impossible.

Surely we can take heart, too, knowing that "where God guides, God provides." He does not require anything of us that He does not empower us, through His Spirit, to accomplish.

June 12, 1994

Weekday Problems

Elizabeth and her husband James are having trouble in their marriage. They seem to be locked in a power struggle. She feels that James makes all the decisions for the family, including how to budget and spend their money, how to discipline the children, where to go on vacation—even where to eat out. One of her major complaints is that she has no funds she can call her own.

During counseling, it has emerged that Elizabeth often handles problems with the children by saying, "Just wait 'til your father gets home. He'll give you what for!" James told the counselor that he had tried to turn the checkbook over to Elizabeth, but that she had trouble keeping it balanced. When he asks her such questions as "Where do you want to eat?" she often replies, "I don't care. You decide."

*Like Moses in Exodus 3, does it sound as though Elizabeth needs to be reassured of the personal resources and power she has, in order to feel more "powerful"?

*Do you think it would help for Elizabeth to earn her own money outside the home?

*How do you or others you know of divide the decision-making responsibility/authority in your home?

*Personal power, like personal accomplishments, is hard for some people to "internalize," or feel deep inside. Make up a possible scenario explaining why this is true of Elizabeth. (Did some failure in the past make her fear responsibility? Was she rebuked as a child for over-stepping her bounds?)

♦♦♦♦♦♦

Smiles

A minister visited the home of a member who was ill. He was met at the door by the man's wife who said, "Oh, he is improving, but he is still in the expensive-care unit."

One thing not to say in a hospital is: "You look fine. I hardly recognized you at all."

A surgeon was talking about anesthetics with a prospective surgery patient. "Would you prefer a local anesthetic?" the surgeon asked.

"Well, I can afford the best," replied the patient. "Why don't you get something imported."

GOD CALLS AND MOSES RESPONDS

This Lesson In Your Life

God's patient and reassuring responses to Moses' repeated reluctance to return to Egypt contains special words of encouragement for us today when we face difficult challenges, and feel inadequate for the task.

The first word of reassurance was that the great "I AM" would be with Moses (Ex. 3:14; see the commentary portion of this lesson). Whatever the precise meaning of this phrase, its general reference to the being of God is fundamental to our belief that He can help us in our weakness.

The late theologian Paul Tillich spoke of God as "the ground of being." By this he meant that the reality of God undergirds all our questions and personal problems, all our doubts and fears. As Isaiah put it, "Underneath are the everlasting arms" (Deut. 33:27). This means that our doubts about who we are, and what we can do in our own strength, can be "shored up" by remembering who God is. Our own strength may be dubious and short-lived. If we rely on "the I AM," we are in touch not with mere beings, but with the power of being itself. If we align our lives with the divine Life, we are in touch with unlimited and inexhaustible Strength.

Another source of reassurance is in trusting the God of signs and wonders. The rod's becoming a serpent and Moses' hand becoming leprous—then both resuming normalcy—were forecasts of the mighty works that God would do through Moses to convince both Moses and Pharaoh that God was truly behind the message, "Let my people go!"

A similar situation existed when the early disciples of Christ were sent out on "the Great Commission." Jesus promised, "And these signs shall follow them that believe" (Mk. 16:17; see also vss. 18-20). Today, we may wish we could see more miraculous evidence that God is with us in His work. We should recall that even in Bible times such evidences were limited to a few basic periods. There are the miracles of creation, the saving of Noah and the covenant through Abraham, the prophetic activities in late Judaism, and the signs and wonders accompanying the life of Christ. Most of the rest of the time, people had to do without miracles—they were called simply to trust in a wonder-working God. So are we.

Again, Moses was reluctant to go to Egypt because he was insecure about his speaking ability. This time God reassured him by saying he could use his brother Aaron as a spokesperson, since he could "speak well" (Ex. 4:14).

Today, not all of us are so fortunate as to have a silver-tongued brother! So it's important that we hear God's word to Moses before He agreed to let Aaron help: "Who hath made man's mouth? or who maketh the dumb, or deaf, or the seeing, or the blind? have not I the Lord?" (4:11). How could Moses doubt that the God who invented speech would be able to enable Moses to speak! How can we balk at tackling even the most challenging task when we remember that both we and the task have come from the same God?

Finally, Moses is given the reassurance that God will be at work not only in his life, and in Aaron's; He will also be working on Pharaoh, by hardening his heart in order to set up the great scene of deliverance God has planned.

Was God unfair to do so? Not in view of the fact that the Bible says that Pharaoh hardened his own heart (Ex. 8:15, 39). When people had rather not be obedient to God, He merely promises to assist in their own self-destructive tendencies (see 2 Thess. 2:10-12).

The point is that God not only empowers us to meet high challenges; he works within the situation itself to accomplish His will through His servants. The story of Moses' inadequacies being supplanted one by one with the adequacies of God reassures us that "If God be for us, who can against us?" (Rom. 8:31).

Seed Thoughts

1. What significance will Mount Horeb, where God spoke to Moses in Exodus 3:1, 12, have later?
Horeb is also called Mount Sinai, where Moses received the Law on tables of stone (see Ex. 19, 20).

2. Noting Moses' response when God called his name (Ex. 3:4), can you recall other instances when someone answered God in this way?
Young Samuel, in 1 Samuel 3:4; and Isaiah (6:8).

3. What does Exodus 3:7 have to say to us when we are burdened by sorrows no one else knows about?
We can be assured that God knows, and understands.

4. Several times in this section God reminds Moses that he is caught up in a cause larger than himself. What is this reminder? (See 3:6, 8, 15-16.)
That God is not just Moses' God, but the God who promised to bless the descendants of Abraham, Isaac and Jacob.

5. Under what conditions today do people sometimes reject God's messengers?
When we don't want to hear what they have to say; or when the messenger's life doesn't match his message.

(PLEASE TURN PAGE)

---

1. What significance will Mount Horeb, where God spoke to Moses in Exodus 3:1, 12, have later?

2. Noting Moses' response when God called his name (Ex. 3:4), can you recall other instances when someone answered God in this way?

3. What does Exodus 3:7 have to say to us when we are burdened by sorrows no one else knows about?

4. Several times in this section God reminds Moses that he is caught up in a cause larger than himself. What is this reminder? (See 3:6, 8, 15-16.)

5. Under what conditions today do people sometimes reject God's messengers?

6. Why would Paul become so earthy as to care what the Roman Christians did with the "members" of their bodies?

7. Why does Paul speak of being "slaves to righteousness?"

8. Why does Paul continually refer to the death, burial and resurrection of Jesus?

9. According to Romans 6, what is the mainspring of Christian ethics?

10. According to Paul, what is the best safeguard against "cheap grace" and loose, libertine ethics?

Horeb is also called Mount Sinai, where Moses received the Law on tables of stone (see Ex. 19, 20).

Young Samuel, in 1 Samuel 3:4; and Isaiah (6:8).

We can be assured that God knows, and understands.

That God is not just Moses' God, but the God who promised to bless the descendants of Abraham, Isaac and Jacob.

When we don't want to hear what they have to say; or when the messenger's life doesn't match his message.

Because his heart was hardened; and because his magicians seemed to be able to work miracles also.

Only if people had a heart to believe in the first place. See Luke 16:29-31.

(Encourage class sharing and discussion.)

Apparently that the words Moses would tell Aaron to say would be God's words.

Although God is sovereign, this is doubtful.(See John 7:17.)

(SEED THOUGHTS--Cont'd)

6. Why did Moses' miracles not convince Pharaoh that God had sent him?
Because his heart was hardened; and because his magicians seemed to be able to work miracles also.

7. Do you think more miracles today would make more believers?
Only if people had a heart to believe in the first place. See Luke 16:29-31.

8. Do you know someone who has had a powerful witness for Christ even though, like Moses, he was not eloquent?
(Encourage class sharing and discussion.)

9. What did God mean by telling Moses that he would be as a god to his brother Aaron? (4:16)
Apparently that the words Moses would tell Aaron to say would be God's words.

10. Do you think that God would "harden" the heart of anyone who would otherwise do His will if left alone?
Although God is sovereign, this is doubtful.(See John 7:17.)

God Redeems Israel

Exodus 6:5-7

5 And I have also heard the groaning of the children of Israel, whom the Egyptians keep in bondage; and I have remembered my covenant.

6 Wherefore say unto the children of Israel, I am the Lord, and I will bring you out from under the burdens of the Egyptians, and I will rid you out of their bondage, and I will redeem you with a stretched out arm, and with great judgments;

7 And I will take you to me for a people, and I will be to you a God; and ye shall know that I am the Lord your God, which bringeth you out from under the burdens of the Egyptians.

Exodus 11:1

11 And the Lord said unto Moses, Yet will I bring one plague more upon Pharaoh, and upon Egypt; afterwards he will let you go hence: when he shall let you go, he shall surely thrust you out hence altogether.

Exodus 12:29-33

29 And it came to pass, that at midnight the Lord smote all the firstborn in the land of Egypt, from the firstborn of the Pharaoh that sat on his throne unto the firstborn of the captive that was in the dungeon; and all the firstborn cattle.

30 And the Pharaoh rose up in the night, he, and all his servants, and all the Egyptians; and there was a great cry in Egypt; for there was not a house where there was not one dead.

31 And he called for Moses and Aaron by night, and said, Rise up, and get you forth from among my people, both ye and the children of Israel; and go, serve the Lord, as ye have said.

32 Also take your flocks and your herds, as ye have said, and be gone; and bless me also.

33 And the Egyptians were urgent upon the people, that they might send them out of the land in haste; for they said, We be all dead men.

◆◆◆◆◆◆

◀ **Memory Selection**
Exodus 6:6-7

◀ **Devotional Reading**
Exodus 5:1-9

◀ **Background Scripture**
Exodus 6:2-9; 11:1-3; 12:21-36

◀ **Printed Scripture**
Exodus 6:5-7; 11:1; 12:29-33

GOD REDEEMS ISRAEL

Teacher's Target

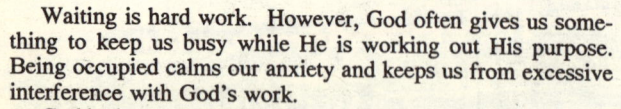

Waiting is hard work. However, God often gives us something to keep us busy while He is working out His purpose. Being occupied calms our anxiety and keeps us from excessive interference with God's work.

God had not purposed the devastating and demoralizing treatment of the Hebrews, but He had given them a task to occupy them and allow them to be productive in the midst of their suffering. Now they would focus their attention on preparations for their exodus while God worked out their deliverance.

The Egyptians practiced denial and persisted in their patterns of behavior. In the face of nine plagues they would not change.

How do you handle waiting? What old patterns of behavior have hurt you? Have you ever practiced denial? How has God delivered you?

Lesson Introduction

The situation of the Hebrews is a specific example of our universal condition. The Hebrews could solve small problems of daily living but the larger problem of the human predicament of suffering, pain, bondage and death was beyond their human capacity. God told Adam this was so. Adam didn't listen, and no one since learned from his mistake. We seem to have to repeat it for ourselves. However, with the help of God's revelation believers can begin to hear and see their helplessness and need of God's guidance.

It took Israel many times around the same track to learn what God was seeking to teach them. In the case of Egypt, extreme and heartrending pain befell them before their denial fell away. The Lord wanted to attain His purpose with minimum discomfort for the Hebrews and Egyptians alike. Human willfulness intensified the agony in Egypt.

Teaching Outline

I. The Way of Redemption: Exodus 6:5-7
   A. God Remembers: 5
   B. God Acts: 6
   C. God Adopts: 7
II. The Way of Denial: Exodus 11:1
   A. Truth Resisted: 1
   B. Opportunities to Learn: 1
III. The Pain of Reality: Exodus 12:29-33
   A. Defenses Penetrated: 29
   B. Sorrowful Resolve: 30-32
   C. Urgent Relief: 33

Daily Bible Readings

Mon. I will Redeem You with Great Acts - *Exodus 6:2-9*
Tue. Hebrews Ask Egyptians for Gold/Silver - *Exodus 6:10-13; 11:1-3*
Wed. Preparations for Passover Meal *Exodus 12:1-6*
Thurs. The Lord Will Pass Over Israelite Homes - *Exodus 12:7-13*
Fri. The "Pass-over" Is a Memorial Day - *Exodus 12:14-20*
Sat. Hebrews Saved; Egyptians Slain *Exodus 12:21-32*
Sun. The Hebrews Despoiled the Egyptians - *Exodus 12:33-39*

June 19, 1994

VERSE BY VERSE

I. The Way of Redemption: Exodus 6:5-7

A. God Remembers: 5

5. And I have also heard the groaning of the children of Israel, whom the Egyptians keep in bondage; and I have remembered my covenant.

Moses was like the rest of us. In Exodus 5:22, 23 he had complained that God mistreated His people. Moses was thinking along the lines of his human timetable. Like all people, Moses expected quick results and few problems. God seems undaunted by Moses' complaints. He knew Moses had a disadvantaged perspective of things. He could not see the whole thing from heaven's view.

Scripture declares that God was not slow to act, though it appeared slow to His people. Adversity gave opportunity to develop patience (endurance) and strong character. God knew His way. God knew His people. He had not abandoned Israel.

The groans of God's people were not in vain. God had not forgotten His covenant. He had large miracles to perform for His people to see and remember. Not only did God remember, but Israel's remembrance of these events would shape their whole history and faith from this point on.

B. God Acts: 6

6. Wherefore say unto the children of Israel, I am the Lord, and I will bring you out from under the burdens of the Egyptians, and I will rid you out of their bondage, and I will redeem you with a stretched out arm, and with great judgments;

Notice the "I" in this verse. God is the one speaking. He would do the work of redemption for His people. He would deliver them out of the cruel hand of their Egyptian rulers. Listen to God's word to the Hebrews: "I will bring you out from under the burdens...I will rid you of their bondage...I will redeem you with a stretched out arm...."

This is the same language used to speak about our ultimate redemption in Christ. He bore the burden of sin in His own body. He released humankind from the bondage of sin. He redeemed us by His stretched out arm and pronounced judgment upon all evil that would destroy us.

God was the same in the beginning and at the end. Always He had the same pattern and the same goal for His people. He would act in their behalf in the midst of their helplessness and they would be able to rejoice in seeing His mighty miracles worked in their midst.

C. God Adopts: 7

7. And I will take you to me for a people, and I will be to you a God; and ye shall know that I am the Lord your God, which bringeth you out from under the burdens of the Egyptians.

Being released from prison was one thing. Not knowing how to live in freedom was another. Many an inmate released from prison after serving time has returned in short order because he could not handle freedom. Israel would be no different. Bondage had become a way of life. They had no experience in living free of their burdens and bondage.

God knew that to release them was not sufficient in itself. They needed nurture and instruction. only God had the wisdom necessary to enable the Hebrews to live in freedom. God adopted them as His own. He would he their God and they would he His people. He would claim them as His own, like a father, and teach them the truth that could keep them free. They would know that it was God and God alone that could affect and maintain their freedom.

II. The Way of Denial: Exodus 11:1

A. Truth Resisted: 1

1. And the Lord said unto Moses, Yet will I bring one plague more upon Pharaoh, and upon Egypt; afterwards he will let you go hence: when he shall let you go, he shall surely thrust you out hence altogether.

God had been patient with Pharaoh. He had shown His superiority in the least intrusive ways possible. He had no desire to harm Pharaoh or his people. God would allow Pharaoh to remain where he wanted to be, even allow him to have power in that realm. God only desired to have the Hebrews released from Pharaoh's crushing control.

Acknowledging the truth of God's superior authority was all that was required of Pharaoh. This truth was like bitter gall to Pharaoh. He would not yield his rule to any other power. Still God was patient and slow to bring calamity upon the Egyptian people.

B. Opportunities to Learn: 1

1. And the Lord said unto Moses, Yet will I bring one plague more upon Pharaoh, and upon Egypt; afterwards he will let you go hence: when he shall let you go, he shall surely thrust you out hence altogether.

God had given many opportunities for Pharaoh to learn that his power was nothing in comparison to the God of creation. The consequences of Pharaoh's refusal to heed God's entreaties to him had become increasingly severe. Now God declares the consequence of Pharaoh's hard heart. This was not God's original desire. At first, God's desire was simply for the release of His people. What God declared here is the ultimate consequence of Pharaoh's refusal to yield the field to God. After this final plague, all Egypt would scream for the Hebrews to leave.

How like all of us to resist opportunities to learn what God is seeking to teach us in gentle ways. Opportunities to learn are missed until the consequences of our stubborn refusal to yield to truth become painful instructors.

III. The Pain of Reality: Exodus 12:29-33

A. Defenses Penetrated: 29

29. And it came to pass, that at midnight the Lord smote all the firstborn in the land of Egypt, from the firastborn of the Pharaoh that sat on his throne unto the firstborn of the captive that was in the dungeon; and all the firstborn cattle.

Pharaoh had strong defenses against the truth. He holds to his illusion of superiority and invulnerability in the face of much hardship which was self-imposed by his refusal to hear and see the truth.

Now God penetrates these defenses. No one was ever born that could keep cracks from developing in his defense mechanisms. Most could repair their illusions quickly, but at some moments, sometimes painful moments, truth would pierce the heart through. The death of the firstborn in Egypt crumbles the defensive wall. Why did it take such extreme consequences for Egypt to acknowledge the truth?

B. Sorrowful Resolve: 30-32

30. And the Pharaoh rose up in the night, he, and all his servants, and all the Egyptians; and there was a great cry in Egypt; for there was not a house where there was not one dead.
31. And he called for Moses and Aaron by night, and said, Rise up, and get you forth from among my people, both ye and the children of Israel; and go, serve the Lord, as ye have said.
32. Also take your flocks and your herds, as ye have said, and be gone; and bless me also.

The night was filled with anguish. It crept into the homes of the Egyptians like a thief in the night. The firstborn of every Egyptian and the first born of the cattle were dead. This anguish, at least temporarily, elicits an acknowledgement of defeat. Pharaoh even asks Moses to bless him before leaving (vs. 32).

Pharaoh resolves to allow the children of Israel to leave. He even instructs that they take their herds with them. He wants to be rid of them and any reminder of what calamity had befallen him.

C. Urgent Relief: 33

33. And the Egyptians were urgent upon the people, that they might send them out of the land in haste; for they said, We be all dead men.

Pharaoh is not alone in his resolve. The Egyptian people are insistent that the Hebrews leave. They could not be rid of this people fast enough, whereas before they had been insistent that the Hebrews stay to do their work for them. Now they are urgent for them to be gone, regardless of the cost.

Death had walked among them and taken their firstborn. They knew their helplessness to stave off death. Their mortality looked back at them as they looked at the dead all around them. Finally, they had to see the truth that all men and women die. They could project their own death now. They feared lest it come soon if the Hebrews stayed in their land.

Evangelistic Emphasis

The Exodus is the event above all others that formed the descendants of Abraham, Isaac and Jacob into a unified people (see Ex. 6:7). Actually, those who fled Egypt by the mighty deliverance of God were not all Israelites. "A mixed multitude" fled with them (Ex. 12:38). They may have sensed some kinship with each other as slaves, in a kind of fellowship of suffering; but it was not until they shared the experience of deliverance that they were welded into a single nation.

Today, a powerful part of the Christian message is that as we are delivered from the bondage of sin we experience peoplehood. While salvation is personal, God promises to save "the Body" (Eph. 5:23). Even now we enjoy the blessings of being in God's family. We weep with those who weep, and rejoice with those who rejoice. We no longer think that some are second-class citizens of the Kingdom because of gender or race, for we are "all one in Christ Jesus" (Gal. 3:28).

The power of our message is not realized when we limit it to a "Me and Jesus" appeal. Instead, we offer people who have no family, or who feel estranged and lonely, the loving support of Christian fellowship and community. To those who feel cut off from others we offer the privilege of being incorporated ("embodied") into the family of God. To those who feel unproductive and useless, we offer the honor of becoming a working member of the Body. We are delivered from bondage in a mighty Exodus--together.

◆◆◆◆◆◆

Memory Selection

I will redeem you with a stretched out arm, and with great judgments: And I will take you for a people, and I will be to you a God. *Exodus 6:6-7*

"Great acts of judgment"? Can we hear this word, in a world that places such a high premium on being "accepting" and "non-judgmental"? Can't we just hear about salvation, without condemnation?

Frankly, no. The fact that Israel needed to be redeemed implies God's judgment upon their being enslaved. The plagues suffered by the oppressors were as surely a word from God as was the deliverance He offered the oppressed. The fact that God formed Israel into a people implies His disapproval of the kind of radical individualism that separates people from each other.

Of course this is no license for mere humans to presume to judge in the place of God. It is a call for us to realize that evil has consequences. It is a summons to stand for God's positives so stalwartly that Satan's negatives feel our presence...to stand for justice so firmly that injustice is routed...for love so consistently that hatred is put to flight.

June 19, 1994

Weekday Problems

James and Elizabeth Franklin have had a streak of unhappy events. They have come to think of them as "plagues" like those rained down on Pharaoh and the Egyptians for not letting the Israelites leave Egypt. Two months ago, James was laid off from work. Then both children got "strep throat." Their car's water pump went out, stranding Elizabeth on a busy freeway. They are wondering what they did to deserve such misfortune.

James and Elizabeth finally "unloaded" on Harold, a Christian neighbor and friend. They essentially told him they were angry at God for allowing all this to happen. Harold expressed hurt and surprise at their attitude, and told them they should not feel that way.

*Do you agree with what Harold told the Franklins?

*How would you respond if the Franklins shared their feelings with you? Would you speak of what's happened as "bad luck" or would you encourage them to examine themselves to see if God is punishing them for some wrong in their lives?

*How does Matthew 5:45 (the latter part of the verse) affect your view of such matters?

*How does Hebrews 12:3-6 affect your view of suffering?

*What Old Testament book is quoted in Hebrews 12:5b? What is that book's general insight into the problem of undeserved suffering?

♦♦♦♦♦♦

Sparkle

A rich man came to the wise old sage. He asked, "Why does Scripture teach that I must give to the poor?"

The wise one said, "Because they are responsible for your freedom."

"How can they be responsible for my freedom? They have nothing to give me," the man replied.

"Oh?," responded the old sage, "either the key to your wallet is in your heart or the key to your heart is in your wallet. Unless you give to the poor, you will remain locked in your greed."

This Lesson In Your Life

DEALING WITH DISASTER

How would we have reacted if we had been in Pharaoh's sandals during the disastrous plagues in Egypt? Here are some ways many people deal with disaster.

<u>Denial</u>. Up until the last plague, the death of the firstborn children, Pharaoh was able to tell himself that God was not really working through Moses to obtain the release of the captive Hebrews. Of course not all disasters indicate God's displeasure; but even after his magicians admitted, "This is the finger of God" (Ex. 8:19), Pharaoh could not bring himself to look objectively at the evidence.

George's wife Jill left him abruptly, after twenty years of marriage. After talking with Jill, a counselor told George to prepare for the fact that she had her mind made up: she was filing for a divorce. George, a salesman, had adopted a "positive thinking" approach to life, training himself to allow no negatives to cloud his optimistic view. Three days later he asked the counselor, "How can I deal with my <u>separation</u>?"

George had simply refused to let the word "divorce" penetrate his view of reality. When the divorce was eventually made final, he was devastated because he had not allowed himself to admit the reality of what was happening. Denial had not only made the divorce a shock; it insulated George from the healing touch of his friends and of God. It's very hard to be healed while denying that you're wounded.

<u>Blaming</u>. At one point, Pharaoh apparently was able to accept responsibility for the disaster of the plagues. He told Moses, "I have sinned...I and my people are wicked" (9:27). As soon as the plague was lifted, however, he repented of repenting; he hardened his heart.

In George's case, his early denial soon turned to wrath. "How could she do this to me?" he raged. "It's her fault our marriage is a wreck." For awhile, he found comfort in convincing himself that he shared none of the responsibility for the failure of the marriage. As for Jill, George's blaming spirit only convinced her more strongly that she had made the right decision.

<u>Accepting responsibility</u>. Unfortunately, Pharaoh died in the sea before he could come clean with God and really mean it when confessing, "I have sinned." Fortunately, George came to himself in time to keep from "drowning" in his own self-pity. Reluctantly, at first, he admitted to the counselor that his affair two years earlier played a large part in Jill's being unable to continue the marriage. Admitting this to Jill did not bring her back; but it cleared the rubbish from George's own thinking, enabling him to forgive himself--as well as to stop blaming Jill.

George's new-found ability to accept responsibility for his part in the breakdown of the marriage was so strengthening that he overcame his tendency to hand over to Jill the power to make him happy or miserable. He stopped making "make-feel" statements such as "She makes me so mad!" and "She makes me feel so guilty."

"Do you really want to give anyone that kind of power over the way you feel?" the counselor asked. While he still loved Jill, George was soon able to express his feelings openly, but to attribute them to himself. By "owning" his feelings, he also discovered that he could control them better. He learned that dealing with life's negatives by denying them and blaming others really doesn't deal with life at all.

Seed Thoughts

1. By what name does God say He had been known to the patriarchs? (Ex. 6:2-3; see a Bible dictionary or the footnote in some versions.)
El Shaddai, which means "God Almighty."

2. What covenant, referred to in 6:5-8, did God honor by bringing the Hebrews out of captivity?
His promise to give the "seed" of Abraham a homeland, and to make of them a great people (Gen. 17:1-8).

3. Why did the Hebrews not hear Moses at first? How can this still be a problem today?
Their emotional pain apparently blocked their ears (Ex. 2:9). Even today, emotional pain can deafen us to attempts to help.

4. List the ten plagues visited on the land of Egypt.
Rivers turned to blood; frogs; lice; flies; cattle were stricken; people suffered boils; a "pestilence"; hail and fire; locusts; darkness; the death of the firstborn.

5. Explain the origins of the Passover feast.
It was instituted in memory of the night the Lord "passed over" the marked houses of the Hebrews. (Ex. 12).

(PLEASE TURN PAGE)

---

1. By what name does God say He had been known to the patriarchs? (Ex. 6:2-3; see a Bible dictionary or the footnote in some versions.)

2. What covenant, referred to in 6:5-8, did God honor by bringing the Hebrews out of captivity?

3. Why did the Hebrews not hear Moses at first? How can this still be a problem today?

4. List the ten plagues visited on the land of Egypt.

5. Explain the origins of the Passover feast.

6. What did the unleavened bread of the Passover feast commemorate?

7. Who else was the Passover open to?

8. What vengeance did the Hebrews take on their captors just before leaving Egypt?

9. How long were the Hebrews in Egypt?

10. What was the dedication of firstborn children and animals to remind the Hebrews of?

(SEED THOUGHTS--Cont'd)

El Shaddai, which means "God Almighty."

His promise to give the "seed" of Abraham a homeland, and to make of them a great people (Gen. 17:1-8).

Their emotional pain apparently blocked their ears (Ex. 2:9). Even today, emotional pain can deafen us to attempts to help.

Rivers turned to blood; frogs; lice; flies; cattle were stricken; people suffered boils; a "pestilence"; hail and fire; locusts; darkness; the death of the firstborn.

It was instituted in memory of the night the Lord "passed over" the marked houses of the Hebrews. (Ex. 12).

The haste of the Hebrews when preparing to leave Egypt, causing them to take up the dough before it was leavened (Ex. 12:34).

Any servant, stranger or "sojourner" among the Hebrews, as long as he was willing to be circumcised (Ex. 12:43-49).

They took spoils of jewelry and rich clothing (Ex. 12:35-36).

According to Exodus 12:40 and Galatians 3:17, 430 years. Stephen rounds it off to 400 years in Acts 7:6.

Of the slaying of the firstborn among the Egyptians, which finally freed the Israelites (Ex. 13:1-2, 11-16).

6. What did the unleavened bread of the Passover feast commemorate?
The haste of the Hebrews when preparing to leave Egypt, causing them to take up the dough before it was leavened (Ex. 12:34).

7. Who else was the Passover open to?
Any servant, stranger or "sojourner" among the Hebrews, as long as he was willing to be circumcised (Ex. 12:43-49).

8. What vengeance did the Hebrews take on their captors just before leaving Egypt?
They took spoils of jewelry and rich clothing (Ex. 12:35-36).

9. How long were the Hebrews in Egypt?
According to Exodus 12:40 and Galatians 3:17, 430 years. Stephen rounds it off to 400 years in Acts 7:6.

10. What was the dedication of firstborn children and animals to remind the Hebrews of?
Of the slaying of the firstborn among the Egyptians, which finally freed the Israelites (Ex. 13:1-2, 11-16).

June 26, 1994

God Brings Victory

Exodus 14:21-31

21 And Moses stretched out his hand over the sea; and the LORD caused the sea to go back by a strong east wind all that night and made the sea dry land and the waters were divided.
22 And the children of Israel went into the midst of the sea upon the dry ground: and the waters were a wall unto them on their right hand, and on their left.
23 And the Egyptians pursued, and went in after them to the midst of the sea, even all Pharaoh's horses, his chariots, and his horsemen.
24 And it came to past, that in the morning watch the LORD looked unto the host of the Egyptians through the pillar of fire and of the cloud, and troubled the host of the Egyptians.
25 And took off their chariot wheels, that they drave them heavily; so that the Egyptians said, Let us flee from the face of Israel; for the Lord fighteth for them against the Egyptians.
26 And the LORD said unto Moses, Stretch out thine hand over the sea, that the waters may come again upon the Egyptians upon their chariots, and upon their horsemen.
27 And Moses stretched forth his hand over the sea, and the sea returned to his strength when the morning appeared; and the Egyptians fled against it; and the Lord overthrew the Egyptians in the midst of the sea.
28 And the waters returned, and covered the chariots, and the horsemen, and all the host of Pharaoh that came into the sea after them; there remained not so much as one of them.
29 But the children of Israel walked upon dry land in the midst of the sea; and the waters were a wall unto them on their right hand, and on their left.
30 Thus the Lord saved Israel that day out of the hand of the Egyptians; and Israel saw the Egyptians dead upon the sea shore.
31 And Israel saw that great work which the LORD did upon the Egyptians: and the people feared the LORD, and believed the Lord, and his servant Moses.

◆◆◆◆◆◆

◀ **Memory Selection**
Exodus 14:30-31

◀ **Background Scripture**
Exodus 13:17 - 14:31

◀ **Devotional Reading**
Exodus 15:22-27

◀ **Printed Scripture**
Exodus 14:21-31

GOD BRINGS VICTORY

Teacher's Target

Every suspense movie, every western movie that is a credit to its genre, has a scene where it seems impossible for the heroes to emerge victorious. The Bible is not fiction, but it has stories of real life as suspenseful as any Hollywood creation.

Your own life may have some events that were as hopeless as Israel's in Egypt. All of us have had moments when we saw no answer to a dilemma.

God was and is about victory over our terrors. He is a constant help in time of trouble. When have you seen God's hand at work in your time of trouble? What did He do? How did He do it? What was so different from the outcome you had expected?

Lesson Introduction

Pharaoh had let the people go. But the reality of who he was up against faded quickly. He reconstructed his illusion of great power. Illusion back in place, he went after God's people. The chase scene was on!

Like a rear guard sniper, God waited for the right moment to act. He was sure that the Hebrews were safe on dry ground. He released the waters just as the riverbed filled with Egyptians. It was too late for escape. The waters washed over them until not one of the soldiers in the river lived.

God did this mighty act of deliverence so that all Israel could see His care for them and believe in Him. Captivity was ended but the ordeal was not over. The people would need to trust God and His messenger Moses to survive.

Teaching Outline

I. God Opens the Way: Exodus 14:21-22
  A. Moses' Hand: 21
  B. God's Power: 21
  C. A Way Provided: 22
II. God Defends the Way: Exodus 14:23-28
  A. Pharaoh Pursued: 23-26
  B. Moses' Hand: 27a
  C. God's Power: 27b-28
III. God Shows the Way: Exodus 14:29-31
  A. The Way Experienced: 29
  B. God the Lord: 30-31
  C. Moses the Servant: 30-31

Daily Bible Readings

Mon. Passover: "Night of Watching" *Exodus 12:40-51*
Tue. Conservation of Israel's First Born: Man/Beast - *Exodus 13:1-10*
Wed. Ask: "What Does This Mean?" *Exodus 13:11-16*
Thurs. God leads Israel by Cloud and Fire - *Exodus 13:17-22*
Fri. Fear Not, Stand Firm, See Salvation - *Exodus 14:10-23*
Sat. Israel Walks on Dry Land *Exodus 14:26-31*
Sun. Miriam Leads Women in Singing/Dancing - *Exodus 15:13-21*

422

June 26, 1994

VERSE BY VERSE

I. God Opens the Way:
   Exodus 14:21-22

A. Moses' Hand: 21

21. And Moses stretched out his hand over the sea; and the LORD caused the sea to go back by a strong east wind all that night and made the sea dry land and the waters were divided.

God did very little without using a human representative even in the Old Testament. This was magnified in the New Testament by the incarnation of Jesus Christ. Here Moses is the human sign. Humankind could not stand to encounter God directly. So, He used Moses as His messenger and instrument of deliverance.

Moses stretches out his hand in obedience to God's command. This is a sign to all that God honors His word and can and will act in His people's best interest as He leads them toward the fulfilment of His promises.

B. God's Power: 21

21. And Moses stretched out his hand over the sea; and the LORD caused the sea to go back by a strong east wind all that night and made the sea dry land and the waters were divided.

Moses was visible. He lifted his hand. The people could see this happen. Moses was not the power. A strong east wind is the natural sign that symbolizes the power of God. There was no doubt that the wind did not come from Moses' hand. However, it would be possible for the people to conclude that the forces of nature obeyed Moses. Some would so interpret the events. The very opposite was true. Moses was the one obeying. He was obeying His God's command. Moses knew God was the power. He knew who had told him to stretch out his hand. He knew to whom he and the wind answered.

C. A Way Provided: 22

22. And the children of Israel went into the midst of the sea upon the dry ground: and the waters were a wall unto them on their right hand, and on their left.

No difficulty is too great for God's sufficiency. There was no visible means of escape when the children of Israel reached the Red Sea. Where were the boats? Didn't someone plan ahead? These human questions or some similar ones would not be unexpected from people when they were in dire straits such as these.

God had always planned ahead even when it was not evident to the people. That is what faith was all about. "Faith is evidence of things not seen." Moses could not see a way either, but he obeyed by lifting his hand. When he did, God provided a way that was more creative and disturbing than anyone could have expected. He parted the waters! Dry land was there for the Hebrews to walk on. One greater than Pharaoh had delivered them.

II. God Defends the Way:
    Exodus 14:23-28

423

A. Pharaoh Pursued: 23-26

23. And the Egyptians pursued, and went in after them to the midst of the sea, even all Pharaoh's horses, his chariots, and his horsemen.

24. And it came to past, that in the morning watch the LORD looked unto the host of the Egyptians through the pillar of fire and of the cloud, and troubled the host of the Egyptians.

25. And took off their chariot wheels, that they drave them heavily; so that the Egyptians said, Let us flee from the face of Israel; for the Lord fighteth for them against the Egyptians.

26. And the LORD said unto Moses, Stretch out thine hand over the sea, that the waters may come again upon the Egyptians upon their chariots, and upon their horsemen.

Pharaoh's memory was short. His pride of power, his desire to save face, his refusal to yield resurfaces. He had said, "I know not the Lord." Now he shows this to be true. He had horses and chariots. He had superior soldiers. Israel is on foot and unarmed. How could he fail if he pursued them to destroy them?

Pharaoh's presumption killed him. He was blinded by his rage and his presumption of power. He brought about his own destruction. He charged headlong into the Red Sea with no thought of peril. Never did he consider that the God of Israel was the source of the divided sea. He was mightier than these slaves. if the waters were parted for them they certainly would stay parted for me, thought Pharaoh.

B. Moses' Hand: 27a

27. And Moses stretched forth his hand over the sea, and the sea returned to his strength when the morning appeared;

Pharaoh had mocked Moses to his own hurt. The messenger of God would not be mocked, for God is not mocked. The contrast is extreme between Pharaoh and Moses. Pharaoh had the army and the weapons. Moses had the slaves and empty hands. Pharaoh barked commands. Moses lifted his hand. Pharaoh had been proud and insolent with Moses. God's messenger had been meek and humble, yet bold, before Pharaoh.

Pharaoh's heart had hardened in his obstinance to God. His people were like him. Moses had yielded all that he was to God. He could lead God's people. He once again obeys the command of God. His raised hand symbolizes the obedience. How sad that the people, still caught in their own hardness, put more stock in Moses power with God than God's power with Moses.

C. God's Power: 27b-28

and the Egyptians fled against it; and the Lord overthrew the Egyptians in the midst of the sea.

28. And the waters returned, and covered the chariots, and the horsemen, and all the host of Pharaoh that came into the sea after them; there remained not so much as one of them.

Again it is God's power that defends the children of Israel. He had provided the way. Now He protects them from sure death at the hands of the Egyptians. Moses is the people's leader, but God is their salvation. "And the Lord overthrew the Egyptians in the midst of the sea."

Pharaoh had defied all God's warnings. He had plunged headlong into combat with God Himself. Pride truly went before a fall. All that Pharaoh had boasted of is of no value in the battle with God. Horsemen, chariots and weapons of human intervention all fail. All is lost at the Red Sea.

III. God Shows the Way:

Exodus 14:29-31

A. The Way Experienced: 29

29. But the children of Israel walked upon dry land in the midst of the sea; and the waters were a wall unto them on their right hand, and on their left.

For the children of Israel, after all their suffering at the hands of the Egyptians, God's way of deliverance experienced. They walk across on dry land. They see the waters take the Egyptians. Now they observe the protective care of God in a mighty act.

Moses had obeyed. The people had followed the Word the Lord sent through Moses. Their faith in that Word had been confirmed before their eyes. The God of their fathers had confirmed His superiority to Pharaoh and all his gods.

B. God the Lord: 30-31

30. Thus the Lord saved Israel that day out of the hand of the Egyptians; and Israel saw the Egyptians dead upon the sea shore.

31. And Israel saw that great work which the LORD did upon the Egyptians: and the people feared the LORD, and believed the Lord, and his servant Moses.

The visible sight leaves no doubt as to who is truly in charge. God, the Lord, is the author and finisher of the days of men. The bodies of the Egyptians are thrown upon the shore. The shame of human pride is evident. A people who had a great heritage of pomp and ceremony were buried in ignominy.

God broke the Egyptians' pride at the point of their strength. War and battle were their way. They never got to display their prowess. God, the Lord of all, shows the futility of their reliance upon their own strength. The weak, Israel, has been made strong by the mighty hand of God.

C. Moses the Servant: 30-31

30. Thus the Lord saved Israel that day out of the hand of the Egyptians; and Israel saw the Egyptians dead upon the sea shore.

31. And Israel saw that great work which the LORD did upon the Egyptians: and the people feared the LORD, and believed the Lord, and his servant Moses.

Moses had doubted his ability to lead the Hebrews. He knew his weakness. He alone would not have been sufficient. What he had a hard time accepting was what God could do when all was put at God's disposal.

The peoples' doubt is being washed away. In the face of this awesome event they begin to fear the Lord. This fear means reverence and awe. For the moment, they believed God. They would follow Moses, their leader. However, they would soon forget. God knew human nature well. They would need continual reinforcement of their faith. He would need a servant like Moses on the scene to call them back to the way when they strayed.

Evangelistic Emphasis

Of course everyone knows that whatever the explanation of the parting of the Red Sea, God doesn't work such wonders today....Or does he?

When Christians speak to unbelievers of a God as One who can deliver them from the grips of addiction, of unloving relationships—of sin—we speak of a God just as powerful as the One who delivered the Israelites by parting the waters. Anyone who has ever seen a life so changed knows that the God of the exodus still works miracles of deliverance.

When we live lives of calm confidence in the midst of personal problems and social and political chaos, we bear eloquent testimony to the power of God over the storms of life. Many former unbelievers testify that this kind of silent witness drew them to a God who can still enable His people to emerge victoriously from waters that threaten to engulf them.

When we stand before modern anti-Christian influences with the courage of a Moses standing with raised rod over the Red Sea, the world knows that the God of Israel can still empower His people.

Why are such spiritual "deliverances" any less marvelous than the Hebrews' crossing on the dry of the sea? If we will allow the God of the exodus to work in our lives, we can still be a witness to Him who delivered His people from Egypt with outstretched arm.

❖❖❖❖❖❖

Memory Selection

Thus the Lord saved Israel that day out of the hand of the Egyptians....And Israel saw that great work which the Lord did upon the Egyptians: and the people feared the Lord, and believed the Lord, and his servant Moses. *Exodus 14:30-31.*

The motley band of Semitic slaves were not only welded together into one people by the exodus. As they watched God deliver them through the same waters that destroyed Pharaoh's armies, they also began a long tradition of "fearing the Lord."

The pagans round about these early Israelites knew well the kind of fear of the gods that was terror, for their gods were unpredictable and harsh. In the Hebrew term for the fear of the Lord there is more reverence than terror. This is the fear that causes His people to bow in adoration, rather than to cringe in dread. This is the fear that is "the beginning of wisdom" (Prov. 1:7)—the only apprehension in it is of our own ability to guide our steps without Him.

Truly "God-fearing" people are those who are driven to their knees not in horror of God, but in awe and wonder at His mighty works.

June 26, 1994

Weekday Problems

Freda and Dorothy, who are neighbors, are also business partners, operating a small food service and catering business out of their homes. They supply sandwiches and coffee to a few nearby businesses at lunchtime, and cater a few small private parties.

An economic slump caused one of the businesses they served to close down--amounting to a 20 percent reduction in their income. Furthermore, Dorothy's husband happened to work for that business, and now he is unemployed.

Freda wants to meet this situation by running some ads in the local paper, hoping to pick up customers to replace the loss. But, especially since her husband is out of work, Dorothy is against spending any extra money on advertising at the very time their business is struggling.

As the two partners discuss what to do, it's clear that Dorothy's motto is: "God will provide." On the other hand Freda counters with her own motto: "God helps those who help themselves."

*Do these two attitudes represent a "right" and a "wrong" approach to life, or just two different personality types?

*Do you identify more with Freda or Dorothy?

*Is Freda being sensitive enough to Dorothy's personal finances, with her husband being unemployed?

*What compromise could you suggest that might resolve the argument?

♦♦♦♦♦♦

Smiles

A man fell into a lake, and a friend pulled him out. It was suggested to him that he should give his friend at least $20 for saving his life.

The man replied, "Could I make it $10? I was half-dead when he pulled me out!"

People today appear to he concerned about the higher things in life--like prices.

A boss asked an employee, "Why were you trying to go over my head for a raise?"

The employee denied it, saying, "I did not! "

The boss then asked, "You were praying for a raise, weren't you?"

427

This Lesson In Your Life
'STAND STILL'—WHILE MARCHING!

Historically, Christians have sometimes been separated by a gulf as threatening as the waters that separated the Israelites from Egypt, after crossing the Red Sea. Theologically, it is the argument about grace vs. works--historically labeled "Calvinism" vs. "Arminianism." At the level of personality, it's the argument between those who say "Let go and let God," and those who protest, like Freda ("This Lesson in Your Life"), "God helps those who help themselves."

A "prooftext" approach to our lesson could even pit these two viewpoints against each other from the biblical story. The "God does it all" folk could seize on Moses' command, "Stand still, and see the salvation of the Lord" (Ex. 14:13). The "We have to do our part" camp could counter that the Israelites in fact did *not* "stand still"--they had to march across the river bed or else they would have remained in Egypt.

Tension between these two viewpoints divides not only Christians but our own minds. Many people, facing a personal problem, are torn between wanting to "take responsibility for their own life" on the one hand, and realizing their total dependence upon God on the other.

Two heart patients were hospitalized in the same room. They were advised by the doctor to relax, and to accept calmly what was happening in order for their mental state to cooperate with the medication, and with the body's own capacity to heal itself. One man did just that—and died (but very relaxed!). The second man would do no such thing: he met his disease kicking and screaming and waving his fist in the face of death—and the doctor said his will to live brought him through.

Of course we have all heard other stories in which acceptance meant life, and agitation death. Human experience is simply too varied to lend itself to sweeping conclusions about whether it's human action or God's grace that is at work in specific situations.

Without pretending to bridge this chasm with such a long history in a single lesson, can we still honor the Bible's affirmation that "there is one body"—and not separate over these differing viewpoints? Would it be weak and unduly compromising to admit elements of truth in both positions? Can we work in harmony with those who don't see it our way?

Perhaps we can agree that apart from God's gracious deliverance, both Israel and we are in a hopeless state; and that without trusting His grace enough to walk in the path He clears for us, we nullify that grace. Israel did not earn God's deliverance: He brought them out of Egypt not because they were a mighty or a moral people, but simply because He loved them (Deut.7:7-8). Yet, seeing His mighty acts, they—we—are called to "stand still" by marching!

Similarly, the apostle Paul affirms that no one is saved by keeping the works of the Law. "For by grace are ye saved through faith; and that not of yourselves: it is the gift of God: Not of works, lest any man should boast" (Eph. 2:8-9). Yet, seeing what God has done through Christ, we do respond in faithful works, "For we are his workmanship, created in Christ Jesus unto good works" (Eph. 2:10). Again, we "stand still" by marching.

By the way—we should be careful about quoting James at this point, affirming that "by works a man is justified, and not by faith only" (Jas. 2:24). In Ephesians (and in Romans), Paul speaks of how to move from being lost to being saved—it's by accepting God's grace, not by working our way to heaven. On the other hand, James addresses those who have already done that; now they are to work because they have been saved, not *in order* to be saved.

Practically speaking, perhaps it is enough to affirm the adage that is so familiar it's a part of Christian folk wisdom: *"I will work as though all depended on me; and I will pray as though all depended on God."*

Seed Thoughts

1. According to Exodus 13 why did God not lead Israel directly to the promised land?
Because the immediate transition from slaves to soldiers might discourage them.

2. What other delay would the Israelites experience?
They would wander in the wilderness for forty years because of their lack of faith (see Num. 14:27-33).

3. How did God show the Israelites the way through the wilderness after leaving Egypt?
With a pillar of cloud by day, and a pillar of fire by night (Ex. 14:21-22).

4. Why did some Israelites wish they had not followed Moses out of Egypt?
Because they feared Pharaoh's pursuing army 14:1-12).

5. According to Exodus 14:19-20, how did God protect Israel? How does He do this today?
His angel, and the cloud, stood between them and the Egyptians. Today, He hears our prayers and otherwise "stands between" the faithful and Satan.

(PLEASE TURN PAGE)

---

1. According to Exodus 13 why did God not lead Israel directly to the promised land?

2. What other delay would the Israelites experience?

3. How did God show the Israelites the way through the wilderness after leaving Egypt?

4. Why did some Israelites wish they had not followed Moses out of Egypt?

5. According to Exodus 14:19-20, how did God protect Israel? How does He do this today?

6. How did Moses and Miriam celebrate the defeat of the Egyptians?

7. What evidence in the Psalms indicates the impact of the Exodus on Israel's worship? (See Ps. 105.)

8. What physical or "natural" means did God use to accomplish the supernatural parting of the waters?

9. What "natural" condition might explain the problem with the chariot wheels referred to in 14:25?

10. Some scholars explain that the arm of the sea at this point was very shallow--a "Reed Sea." Even so, how deep does the account require it to be?

(SEED THOUGHTS--Cont'd)

Because the immediate transition from slaves to soldiers might discourage them.

They would wander in the wilderness for forty years because of their lack of faith (see Num. 14:27-33).

With a pillar of cloud by day, and a pillar of fire by night (Ex. 14:21-22).

Because they feared Pharaoh's pursuing army 14:1-12).

His angel, and the cloud, stood between them and the Egyptians. Today, He hears our prayers and otherwise "stands between" the faithful and Satan.

By singing a psalm recounting the mighty deliverance of the Lord (Ex. 15:1-22)

This poetic recollection of the events of the Exodus appears in what might be called Israel's "hymnbook."

A strong east wind that apparently not only divided the waters but dried out the bed of the sea.

Perhaps the sea bed was dry enough to walk across but still damp enough to mire the chariots.

Deep enough to cover the armies of Pharaoh when the walls of water came crashing back together (14:28).

6. How did Moses and Miriam celebrate the defeat of the Egyptians?
By singing a psalm recounting the mighty deliverance of the Lord (Ex. 15:1-22)

7. What evidence in the Psalms indicates the impact of the Exodus on Israel's worship? (See Ps. 105.)
This poetic recollection of the events of the Exodus appears in what might be called Israel's "hymnbook."

8. What physical or "natural" means did God use to accomplish the supernatural parting of the waters?
A strong east wind that apparently not only divided the waters but dried out the bed of the sea.

9. What "natural" condition might explain the problem with the chariot wheels referred to in 14:25?
Perhaps the sea bed was dry enough to walk across but still damp enough to mire the chariots.

10. Some scholars explain that the arm of the sea at this point was very shallow--a "Reed Sea." Even so, how deep does the account require it to be?
Deep enough to cover the armies of Pharaoh when the walls of water came crashing back together (14:28).

July 3, 1994

Bread From Heaven

Exodus 16:2-7

2 And the whole congregation of the children of Israel murmured against Moses and Aaron in the wilderness:
3 And the children of Israel said unto them, Would to God we had died by the hand of the Lord in the land of Egypt, when we sat by the flesh pots, and when we did eat bread to the full; for ye have brought us forth into this wilderness, to kill this whole assembly with hunger.
4 Then said the LORD unto Moses, Behold, I will rain bread from heaven for you; and the people shall go out and gather a certain rate every day, that I may prove them, whether they will walk in my law, or no.
5 And it shall come to pass, that on the sixth day they shall prepare that which they bring in; and it shall be twice as much as they gather daily.
6 And Moses and Aaron said unto all the children of Israel, At even, then ye shall know that the LORD hath brought you out from the land of Egypt:
7 And in the morning, then ye shall see the glory of the LORD; for that he heareth your murmurings against the LORD: and what are we, that ye murmur against us?

Exodus 13-18

13 And it came to pass that at even the quails came up, and covered the camp: and in the morning the dew lay round about the host.
14 And when the dew that lay was gone up, behold, upon the face of the wilderness there lay a small round thing, as small as the hoar frost on the ground.
15 And when the children of Israel saw it, they said one to another, It is man'-na: for they wist not what it was. And Moses said unto them, This is the bread which the LORD hath given you to eat.
16 This is the thing which the LORD hath commanded, Gather of it every man according to his eating, an o'-mer for every man, according to the number of your persons; take ye every man for them which are in his tents.
17 And the children of Israel did so, and gathered, some more, some less.
18 And when they did mete it with an o'-mer, he that gathered much had nothing over, and he that gathered little had no lack; they gathered every man according to his eating.

◆◆◆◆◆◆

◀ **Memory Selection**
Exodus 16:4

◀ **Devotional Reading**
Exodus 17:1-13

◀ **Background Scripture**
Exodus 16

◀ **Printed Scripture**
Exodus 16:2-7, 13-18

BREAD FROM HEAVEN

Teacher's Target

Not only are people fickle, they have short memories. A person who is a hero today can easily be the object of cruel jokes tomorrow. What God has done for us in the past can quickly slip out of our awareness in a short time. History is replete with such stories.

The city of Sardis was conquered when they thought themselves so secure that there was no need for a night watch. You might expect this overconfidence once, but the same scenario happened a second time in their history. John in Revelation used these events as a background to tell the people of Sardis to be watchful (Rev 3:1-6).

Has God provided for you? Have you ever forgotten some care or answer to prayer that you thought you would never forget? Give examples of how God has provided for you.

Lesson Introduction

How long did it take for the children of Israel to experience memory loss? Scripture states that on the fifteenth day of the second month after their deliverance from Egypt they began to murmur (Ex. 16:1). It seems that enough provisions for a month had been packed when they left Egypt. Now the supplies were gone. Their bellies began to speak.

Moses had been listening to God and guiding the people at God's direction. He thought they were with him now. They had seen God's mighty acts. Surely they would not lose heart. But they had experienced little more than suffering. Maybe they thought this just a different trick by a different leader to cause them even more suffering. Maybe once again their hopes would be in a god who only healed to hurt once again.

Teaching Outline

I. Hope Fails: Exodus 16:2-3
   A. People Murmur: 2
   B. Hearts Turn Back: 3
II. God Intervenes: Exodus 16:4-7
   A. God Instructs: 4-5
   B. Moses Reassures: 6-7
III. Provisions Arrive:
Exodus 16:13-17
   A. Quail at Evening: 13
   B. Manna at Dawn: 14-16
   C. People Gather: 17

Daily Bible Readings

Mon. Spring of Water; 70 Palm Trees *Exodus 15:22-27*
Tue. God Will Rain Bread from Heaven - *Exodus 16:1-5*
Wed. Each Morning Look for God's Glory - *Exodus 16:6-10*
Thurs. In Evenings, Eat Flesh; Mornings, Bread - *Exodus 16:11-15*
Fri. The People Gathered According to Needs - *Exodus 16:16-27*
Sat. A Double Supply the Sixth Day *Exodus 16:22-30*
Sun. Keep a Jar Full of Manna *Exodus 16:31-36*

July 3, 1994

VERSE BY VERSE

I. Hope Fails: Exodus 16:2-3

A. People Murmur: 2

2. And the whole congregation of the children of Israel murmured against Moses and Aaron in the wilderness:

Mutiny is at hand. These are a frightened and beaten people. All they were accustomed to was abuse. They cannot see that if God had desired to kill them He had His chance at the Red Sea. They can only think of their present predicament. Their circumstances had filled their hearts. Hope departed. Now they are hungry. They do not know the skills needed to survive in the wilderness. Their past experience colors their interpretation of the present. The flesh pots of Egypt look better to them than the unknown ahead of them. God had been leading them, but where? Were they delivered only to die in the wilderness?

B. Hearts Turn Back: 3

3. And the children of Israel said unto them, Would to God we had died by the hand of the Lord in the land of Egypt, when we sat by the flesh pots, and when we did eat bread to the full; for ye have brought us forth into this wilderness, to kill this whole assembly with hunger.

Even Jesus said the spirit is willing but the flesh is weak. The people of Israel had seen a great miracle also. Truth was having a hard time gaining a foothold in their hearts. No promised land is in sight. Only wilderness and hunger are visible to them. At least in Egypt they could have died with a full stomach. What kind of God would lead them to such desolation? If He wanted to kill them why did He not do it there? Their minds are overriding their faith. They cannot see that if God had desired their death, He would not have gone to such lengths to rescue them.

In our own history there was the great march of the Cherokee called the "trail of tears." Also there was the Bataan death march in World War II. Given their short experience with God to this point, the children of Israel could not apply their faith over their fear. To them this could have looked very much like a death march. This would not be the last time people had such difficulty seeing beyond the visible present.

II. God Intervenes: Exodus 16:4-7

A. God Instructs: 4-5

4. Then said the LORD unto Moses, Behold, I will rain bread from heaven for you; and the people shall so out and gather a certain rate every day, that I may prove them, whether they will walk in my law, or no.

5. And it shall come to pass, that on the sixth day they shall prepare that which they bring in; and it shall be twice as much as they gather daily.

We learn to follow by following. Moses and Aaron had been doing so longer than the others. God had not left Himself without a witness. He instructs Moses about His plan for the people's welfare.

God reassures Moses that a constant and plentiful supply of food would be provided. He has not forgotten that His people were flesh. Better than any, He knows their need. He would supply their want.

God also knows the people need to learn obedience and discipline. He does not want simply to indulge their flesh. He desires to make this a learning experience. They are to gather as he instructed. Through the need of the flesh He would teach them to live one day at a time. He would seek to show them that they did not need to borrow trouble from tomorrow (Matt. 6). Moses is instructed to tell the people when and how much to gather.

B. Moses Reassures: 6-7

6. And Moses and Aaron said unto all the children of Israel, At even, then ye shall know that the LORD hath brought you out from the land of Egypt:

7. And in the morning, then ye shall see the glory of the LORD; for that he heareth your murmurings against the LORD: and what are we, that ye murmur against us?

Moses is the prophet, Aaron the pastor. Later, in verse 9, Moses directs Aaron to speak to the people. But Moses is the leader to whom God had given the heavier share of the load of leading the Hebrew children. Here he reassures the people that in the morning they would see the glory of the Lord.

Moses had feelings as did the people. Often the people forgot that their leaders could be hurt by them. Often they did not care. Their own need consumed their compassion. Moses lets the people know that it was not just him and Aaron that they murmured against. It was ultimately God with whom they contended.

God and His leaders do not refuse a hearing to the murmuring. These were a new undisciplined people weak in faith. They had experienced much pain and loss. They could be heard, but such murmuring was not to be their constant practice. Men murmur, but God silences the murmuring with grace sufficient for their need.

III. Provisions Arrive: Exodus 16:13-17

A. Quail at Evening: 13

13. And it came to pass that even the quails came up, and covered the camp: and in the morning the dew lay round about the host.

The people are willing to return to Egypt and flesh pots and bread. God provides a banquet at evening that would go far beyond mere necessity. God wants the people to know that serving Him would have its delights, even though the way might at times be arduous.

How easily men at all times have held to the visible and immediate. God desires the people to risk adventure with Him over the dull and burdensome life offered by the world. Seeking first His kingdom would not mean denial of human needs. All of these He would provide in His own way if they would not yearn to return to the clutches of the world. His arms would be everlasting. The hand of man would be fleeting and only bind those who served it. God's outstretched arm would provide freedom.

B. Manna at Dawn: 14-16

14. And when the dew that lay was gone up, behold, upon the face of the wilderness there lay a small round thing, as small as the hoar frost on the ground.

15. And when the children of Israel saw it, they said one to another, It is man'-na: for they wist not what it was. And Moses said unto them, This is the bread which the LORD hath given you to eat.

16. This is the thing which the LORD hath commanded, Gather of it every man according to his eating,

an o'-mer for every man, according to the number of your persons; take ye every man for them which are in his tents.

The manna comes with the dew. This was God's doing. He would nourish, strengthen and enliven them. Egypt had fed them only to bear burdens while killing their spirits.

God knew what and how much they needed. The people's tendency would have been to gorge themselves. This would not have been conducive to travel. Nor would it have been good for their digestive system. After a life of heavy labor and poor treatment there is need for a steady but not heavy provision for their hunger and nutrition.

God's storehouse could not be emptied. As with the feeding of the 5,000 at the hands of Jesus, so in this case God would not run out. How much He wanted his people to know His sufficiency!

C. People Gather: 17-18

17. And the children of Israel did so, and gathered, some more, some less.

18. And when they did mete it with an o'-mer, he that gathered much had nothing over, and he that gathered little had no lack; they gathered every man according to his eating.

Always God had something for the people to do. They prepared the quail. They gather the manna. As Jesus later said, How much more precious are people to God than the birds of the air or the lilies of the field. Unlike the birds and lilies, humans can tend flocks, till the land and gather harvest. God's intent is always for humankind to be in cooperation with Him under His instruction.

When God is obeyed there is plenty for all. All were not the same size nor did they all burn up their meal at the same rate. Each man has plenty in proportion to his capacity and need for food.

Evangelistic Emphasis

The manna and quail God provided the Hebrews in the wilderness were in one sense supernatural miracles. In another sense, they are only expressions of the quite natural concern God has for His people. Just as it is of the nature of love to give to the beloved, it is of the very nature of God to supply believers with what they need. He is a God who delights in answering the prayer, "Give us this day our daily bread"--both literally and spiritually.

So it is with confidence that we say to a hungry world, "Come with us, and feast on the good things of God." It has been well said that evangelism is one hungry person telling another where he can find bread. As the psalmist expressed it, "O taste and see that the Lord is good...for there is no want to them that fear him. The young lions do lack, and suffer hunger: but they that seek the Lord shall not want any good thing" (Ps. 34:8-10).

Yet, even as we emphasize this truth we must also be aware of a danger. In our day of marketing expertise and consumer-oriented sales, it is easy for this message to degenerate into *pandering*--appealing to that part of human nature that asks, "What's in it for me?" A self-centered person who comes to Christ only to have certain needs met hasn't really experienced the change of heart Christ seeks--he is still self-centered. The key is to affirm that Christ provides our needs not just to benefit us, but in order for those who have tasted the good things of God to offer them to others.

◆◆◆◆◆◆

Memory Selection

I will rain bread from heaven for you; and the people shall go out and gather a certain rate every day, that I may prove them, whether they will walk in my law, or no. *Exodus 16:4*

Does it strike you as unusual that God would consider a blessing such as the manna in the wilderness as a "test"? It's more common for difficulties--such as those suffered by Job--to be seen as tests of our faith. More than one believer has been tempted to abandon faith as they stood at the grave of a loved one and asked, also with Job, Why, Lord?

On second thought we realize that faith is also put to the test in times when life seems kinder to us. We can plunge so headlong into the banquet that we forget to say Thanks to the host. We can so easily connect financial success with our own hard work that we forget who empowers us to work, and who showers us with blessings. We can take peace so much for granted that it takes war to shock us into acknowledging our need for God in both good times and bad.

Let us never allow the very blessings of God to obscure the Hand and Heart from which they flow.

July 3, 1994

Weekday Problems

The Branscombs--Harvey and Annette--have been faithful members of First Church for twenty years. Their church involvement has included regular financial contributions. They believe that God blesses those who put Him and His work first. In fact, they can point to specific instances where they feel that God blessed them financially for maintaining their giving during times when Harvey's business was slow.

Now, with their children grown and married, Harvey and Annette are making long-range plans for retiring. Recently one of their investments had a stock split that resulted in an unexpected return of $10,000 overnight. The Branscombs are discussing what to do with this windfall.

"Let's just roll it over and keep it there earning money toward our retirement," Harvey said.

"Don't you think that's leaving the Lord out of it?" Annette responded. "Why don't we give it to that medical mission in Africa?"

"Well," said Harvey, "I think God wants us to think of the future. We certainly don't want the kids to have to care for us in our old age."

*How do you handle your own decisions about contributing to the church? How would you advise the Branscombs?

*What do you think about tithing?

*Do you think most people overdo, or slight, the matter of planning for future financial needs?

♦♦♦♦♦♦

Sparkles

One wise man was speaking on possessions. He said, "The desire of possessions is dangerous and terrible, knowing no satiety; it drives the soul which it controls to the heights of evil. Therefore, let us drive it away vigorously from the beginning. For once it has become master it cannot he overcome."

What does it gain a man if he gains the whole world and loses his soul? God knows we have need of the necessities of life. He will provide.

This Lesson In Your Life
SATISFYING THE SOUL

Manna and quail from heaven—wouldn't it gladden our hearts to receive our food in this way? Not necessarily. It didn't gladden the hearts of the Hebrews. The free gift of manna merely made some want more—in gathering more than their allotment, against the commandment of God, they demonstrated not contentment and a grateful heart, but only the insatiable desire for more. Some recipients of this bread from heaven soon tired of it, saying, "Our soul loatheth this light bread" (Num. 21:5).

On and on it goes—and we don't have to look at the Israelites in the wilderness to see that provisions for the flesh do not always satisfy the soul. We ourselves know the experience of gaining externals while experiencing inner poverty. Not only Scripture but life itself teaches that "He that loveth silver shall not be satisfied with silver; nor he that loveth abundance with increase" (Eccl. 5:10).

It's not that bread and money and material goods are wrong. Religion that teaches that there is no value in the material--and even that there is evil in material goods—is not biblical religion. Scripture does teach the danger of excessive wealth, but it frankly acknowledges the value of the material. A wise person prays for balance: "Give me neither poverty nor riches..lest I be full, and deny thee, and say Who is the Lord? or lest I be poor, and steal, and take the name of my God in vain" (Prov. 30:8-9).

What escapes many of us is neither material nor spiritual blessings, but the ability to be satisfied by them. We admire the stage of development in the apostle Paul, who said, "I have learned, in whatsoever state I am, therewith to be content" (Philip. 4:11). (No, it's not that Paul had learned to be happy even when in Texas or Alabama or New York--he's speaking of a state of mind, here!)

In contrast, we are too often anxious about having enough money to buy things that soon lose their appeal—fulfilling the prophecy of Leviticus 26:26: "Ten women shall bake your bread...and ye shall eat, and not be satisfied." How much better to put ourselves in a frame of mind where the opposite is true, in which we can "eat and be satisfied" (Deut. 14:29).

How can we discover such a state?

Perhaps it would help if we could adjust our *expectations* to fit our situation. It is inappropriate—and asking for frustration—to have heavenly expectations of an earthly situation. In one sense, as St. Augustine reminds us, our hearts will be restless until they find their rest in God. Or, as the poet asks, "What's a heaven for?" God help us not to project divine expectations on the mere human we live and work with...or to expect total fulfillment from our careers...or total ecstasy from joys that are framed by the limitations of time and mortality.

Another insight is given to us in Psalm 107:8—"Oh that men would praise the Lord for his goodness, and for his wonderful works to the children of men! For he satisfieth the longing soul, and filleth the hungry soul with goodness." It's amazing how much more fulfilling it is to lift our voices in praise and thanksgiving to God for what He has done for us, than it is to list the things we wish He had done.

The prophet Isaiah gives us another key to the door of genuine contentment: "If thou draw out thy soul to the hungry, and satisfy the afflicted soul...the Lord shall guide thee continually, and satisfy thy soul" (Isa. 58:10-11). It is in tending to the needs of others that are own inner needs are met. The soul's satisfaction is not to be found in sitting back wishing the Lord would fill our cup, but in filling someone else's.

Seed Thoughts

1. Murmuring about the lack of food was the second time the Israelites fleeing Egypt had complained to Moses. What was their first complaint?
   That Pharaoh and his armies were about to attack (Ex. 14:10).

2. Give an illustration of the feeling that it would be better to be fed in captivity than to be hungry though free (as in Ex. 16:3).
   (Encourage class discussion. Example: steady though confining work vs. free-lancing.)

3. Why were the people to gather on the sixth day enough manna for two days?
   In order to observe the Sabbath by resting instead of gathering food.

4. What common human failing is indicated by the Israelites who gathered more than their daily allotment of manna?
   A lack of faith that God will provide for our needs.

5. How can complaints against religious leaders be distinguished from complaints against God? (See Ex. 16:8b.)
   One way is to measure the complaint against an objective value-base such as the Bible.

(PLEASE TURN PAGE)

---

1. Murmuring about the lack of food was the second time the Israelites fleeing Egypt had complained to Moses. What was their first complaint?

2. Give an illustration of the feeling that it would be better to be fed in captivity than to be hungry though free (as in Ex. 16:3).

3. Why were the people to gather on the sixth day enough manna for two days?

4. What common human failing is indicated by the Israelites who gathered more than their daily allotment of manna?

5. How can complaints against religious leaders be distinguished from complaints against God? (See Ex. 16:8b.)

6. What does the word "manna" mean? (See the footnote in many Bibles, or a Bible dictionary.)

7. How was the miracle of the manna to be commemorated for later generations?

8. What arrangement indicated God's concern for those who were too weak or ill to gather much manna?

9. What was the third murmuring among the Israelites about?

10. Now did God publicly confirm Moses' authority in the battle with the Amalekites?

439

(SEED THOUGHTS--Cont'd)

That Pharaoh and his armies were about to attack (Ex. 14:10).

(Encourage class discussion. Example: steady though confining work vs. free-lancing.)

In order to observe the Sabbath by resting instead of gathering food.

A lack of faith that God will provide for our needs.

One way is to measure the complaint against an objective value-base such as the Bible,

"What is that?", "What is it?", or "It is a portion."

A bowl or pot of it was to be kept for a remembrance (Ex. 16:33; later carried in the Ark of the Covenant--Heb. 9:4).

"He that gathered much had nothing over, and he that gathered little had no lack" (Ex. 16:18).

A lack of water in the desert (Ex. 17:1-3).

God caused the battle to go well for Israel as long as Moses' arms were raised (Ex. 17:11-12).

---

6. What does the word "manna" mean? (See the footnote in many Bibles, or a Bible dictionary.)
"What is that?", "What is it?", or "It is a portion."

7. How was the miracle of the manna to be commemorated for later generations?
A bowl or pot of it was to be kept for a remembrance (Ex. 16:33; later carried in the Ark of the Covenant--Heb. 9:4).

8. What arrangement indicated God's concern for those who were too weak or ill to gather much manna?
"He that gathered much had nothing over, and he that gathered little had no lack" (Ex. 16:18).

9. What was the third murmuring among the Israelites about?
A lack of water in the desert (Ex. 17:1-3).

10. Now did God publicly confirm Moses' authority in the battle with the Amalekites?
God caused the battle to go well for Israel as long as Moses' arms were raised (Ex. 17:11-12).

July 10, 1994

Leadership For Meeting Needs

Exodus 18:13-25

13 And it came to pass on the morrow, that Moses sat to judge the people: and the people stood by Moses from the morning unto the evening.

14 And when Moses' father in law saw all that he did to the people, he said, What is this that thou doest to the people? why sittest thou thyself alone, and all the people stand by thee from morning unto even?

15 And Moses said unto his father in law, Because the people come unto me to enquire of God:

16 When they have a matter, they come unto me; and I judge between one and another, and I make them know the statutes of God, and his laws.

17 And Moses' father in law said unto him, The thing that thou doest is not good.

18 Thou wilt surely wear away, both thou, and this people that is with thee: for this thing is too heavy for thee; thou art not able to perform it thyself alone.

19 Hearken now unto my voice, I will give thee counsel and God shall be with thee: Be thou for the people to Godward, that thou mayest bring the causes unto God:

20 And thou shalt teach them ordinances and laws, and shalt shew them the way wherein they must walk and the work that they must do.

21 Moreover thou shalt provide out of all the people able men, such as fear God, men of truth, hating covetousness; and place such over them, to be rulers of thousands, and rulers of hundreds, rulers of fifties, and rulers of tens:

22 And let them judge the people at all seasons: and it shall be, that every great matter they shall bring unto thee, but every small matter they shall judge: so shall it be easier for thyself, and they shall bear the burden with thee.

23 If thou shalt do this thing, and God command thee so then thou shalt be able to endure, and all this people shall also go to their place in peace.

24 So Moses hearkened to the voice of his father in law, and did all that he had said.

25 And Moses chose able men out of all Israel, and made them heads over the people, rulers of thousands, rulers of hundreds, rulers of fifties, and rulers of tens.

◆◆◆◆◆◆

◀ **Memory Selection**
Exodus 18:21

◀ **Devotional Reading**
Exodus 18:1-12

◀ **Background Selection**
Exodus 18

◀ **Printed Scripture**
Exodus 18:13-25

LEADERSHIP FOR MEETING NEEDS

Teacher's Target

Being a leader is a delicate balancing act. one has to be willing to put ideas and plans before the people with the risk of being rejected. Also, leaders have to make judgment calls about what course to follow and between conflicting ideas and opinions.

Leaders have to accept that they cannot please all the time. They must accept responsibility even for their subordinates' actions. They need tough skins and compassionate hearts. They must know their own mind and be willing to stick to their course in the face of criticism and controversy.

Beyond that, leaders need help. They cannot do it all. For some, relinquishing control is hard. When have you been a leader? How did you like the responsibility? What would you do differently? How did you share responsibility?

Lesson Introduction

Moses had much responsibility. Just leading out of Egypt a tired, physically weak, beaten down, broken spirited multitude of slaves unaccustomed to their own rule was problematic enough. Now he had them on a journey and needed to rule between them and keep order.

The Hebrews were like small children. They went to Moses for everything. Few among them were as yet self-starters.

Age can and often does lend itself to wisdom. Moses' father-in-law, Jethro, had the chance to observe the situation as Moses sat hour after hour making decisions. The lines were so long. The people got discouraged. A one-man system of counsel was not very responsive to such a multitude.

Moses felt the burden of his responsibility. He had Aaron, but where else could he turn?

Teaching Outline

I. A Problem Spotted: Exodus 18:13-18
   A. An Older Man Observed: 13
   B. An Older Man Listened: 14-15
   C. An Older Man Advised: 17-18

II. A Problem Diagnosed: Exodus 18:19-23
   A. A Solution Proposed: 19
   B. A Leader's Role Defined: 20-21
   C. A Cooperative System Formed: 22-23

III. A Problem Solved: Exodus 18:24-25
   A. A Leader Listened: 24
   B. A System Implemented: 25
   C. A Leadership Multiplied: 25

Daily Bible Readings

Mon. Moses: "The People Will Stone Me." - *Exodus 17:1-5*
Tue. "Strike the Rock!" and Water Flows - *Exodus 17:6-12*
Wed. Moses' Family Reunited *Exodus 18:1-5*
Thurs. Jethro Rejoiced for Moses' Good News - *Exodus 18:6-10*
Fri. Jethro Offered Sacrifices to God *Exodus 18:11-18*
Sat. Jethro Suggested a Better Way *Exodus 18:19-27*
Sun. "O That I Were Judge" *2 Samuel 15:1-5*

VERSE BY VERSE

I. A Problem Spotted: Exodus 18:13-18

A. An Older Man Observed: 13

13. And it came to pass on the morrow, that Moses sat to judge the people: and the people stood by Moses from the morning unto the evening.

Early in the morning Moses began the laborious task of making rulings among his followers. He was the one they looked to for guidance, civil and spiritual. The lines were so long that at the end of the day he still was not through. The people become bored, restless and discouraged as they wait for Moses to hear their case or concern.

Jethro, Moses' father-in-law, was not on the hot seat of responsible judging. This gives him the chance to have an objective stance from which to view the situation. He also had wisdom gained from years of living and experiencing the nature of people and the need for shared responsibility. Being the head of a family had taught him much.

B. An Older Man Listened: 14-16

14. And when Moses' father in law saw all that he did to the people, he said, What is this that thou doest to the people? why sittest thou thyself alone, and all the people stand by thee from morning unto even?

15. And Moses said unto his father in law, Because the people come unto me to enquire of God:

16. When they have a matter, they come unto me; and I judge between one and another, and I make them know the statutes of God, and his laws.

Jethro shows his wisdom by not barging in with directives and advice for Moses. He goes to Moses with questions. His desire is not to usurp Moses' authority but to assist him with it. There is no attempt to dictate to or dominate Moses.

Jethro begins by finding out what Moses is seeking to accomplish. Moses is not put off by such an inquiry. He has not been put in a corner where he has either to reject Jethro's suggestion or comply unwillingly.

Moses describes for Jethro the nature of his business. He also tells him why he is doing it. The people look to him for direction from God. Moses is the vice regent for God to this people. They had authorized him to rule among them.

C. An Older Man Advised: 17-18

17. And Moses' father in law said unto him, The thing that thou doest is not good.

18. Thou wilt surely wear away, both thou, and this people that is with thee: for this thing is too heavy for thee; thou art not able to perform it thyself alone.

Jethro can see the weariness of Moses and the people. He knows that if this continues Moses will be entangled in another occasion for murmuring. Moses would not only be weary from the work, the people would stop appreciating him, and begin to form cliques of criticism and unrest.

Most older men have come to know the meaning of human limitations. Jethro knows there is just so much energy any one man could expend without collapsing.

Often leaders have failed even though they had a good heart and good skills because they overextended themselves. Like a fine race horse, Moses knows how to run, but he needs a jockey to tell him when to quit before he bursts his heart. Just because God is with him does not make Moses superhuman. Jethro advises a modification in Moses' style of leadership.

II. A Problem Diagnosed: Exodus 18:19-23

A. A Solution Proposed: 19

19. Hearken now unto my voice, I will give thee counsel and God shall be with thee: Be thou for the people to God-ward, that thou mayest bring the causes unto God:

Jethro asks to be heard. He has a solution to Moses' problem that he believes would alleviate the strain and be pleasing to God. He reinforces Moses' need to take all matters before God. He too knew that his wisdom had come from God.

Had Jethro not been a godly man he might have been more dictatorial with Moses. Also, he might have given him very unwise counsel. There was no desire for ascendancy over Moses. Jethro had his turn at the wheel. His humility of person under God allowed him to share out of his own authority of person without overriding Moses' authority.

B. A Leader's Role Defined: 20-21

20. And thou shalt teach them ordinances and laws, and shalt shew them the way wherein they must walk and the work that they must do.

21. Moreover thou shalt provide out of all the people able men, such as fear God, men of truth, hating covetousness; and place such over them, to be rulers of thousands, and rulers of hundreds, rulers of fifties, and rulers of tens:

Moses was having to wear too many hats. He needed to be assisted in defining his role more clearly. This did not mean giving up his authority, but sharing it so that he would be free to invest his energy where it was truly needed.

Moses was to teach the people that they could learn leadership and self-rule. Multiplying teaching of what he knew of God and His way was the goal. Moses would not always be around. Who would lead when he was gone if he kept all he knew close to the vest?

Moses was to be guide, instructor and overseer. He was to listen for God's voice, follow God's guidance and teach this to the people. They would then know how to order their private and public lives and what to put their hands to as their task.

C. A Cooperative System Formed: 22-23

22. And let them judge the people at all seasons: and it shall be, that every great matter they shall bring unto thee, but every small matter they shall judge: so shall it be easier for thyself, and they shall bear the burden with thee.

23 If thou shalt do this thing, and God command thee so then thou shalt be able to endure, and all this people shall also go to their place in peace.

Jethro proposes a system of rulers of thousands, leaders of hundreds, rulers of fifties and rulers of ten. These would bear the burden of leadership with Moses. They would rule in small and easier matters, and Moses would decide only in the harder and weightier matters. This would free Moses for his other responsibilities and give him time for counsel with God.

Not all were ready to be rulers of thousands. For this system to work, each ruler needed to he content with the role he was given. Jealousy of position would lead to dissension.

III. A Problem Solved: Exodus 18:24-25

A. A Leader Listened: 24

24. So Moses hearkened to the voice of his father in law, and did all that he had said.

One cannot lead unless he can follow. One cannot teach unless he will be taught. One cannot be given authority to speak unless he will listen. Moses listens to Jethro. He takes it before God and he is relieved of a wearisome burden.

Moses is not afraid to be a man under the authority of men and of God. He knows his role and his gifts, and knowing who he is and to whom he belongs he can accept wise counsel. Moses listens and God is pleased.

B. A System Implemented: 25

25. And Moses chose able men out of all Israel, and made them heads over the people, rulers of thousands, rulers of hundreds, rulers of fifties, and rulers of tens.

Moses looks among his people and chooses able men. As their leader, Moses had a vantage point from which to see them that no one else had. Only the one who has the big picture of what is necessary could make the decision about who would rule well at the different levels of leadership. Some would grow in ability and replace those who were over them at the appropriate time. God would continue to guide Moses in his solution and raise up those who could help.

When God has a task He does not leave His leaders without resources. When God's purposes are followed the resources followed on the heels of godly men's obedience.

C. A Leadership Multiplied: 25

25. And Moses chose able men out of all Israel, and made them heads over the people, rulers of thousands, rulers of hundreds, rulers of fifties, and rulers of tens.

Where once there was one, now there are many. The children of Israel are moving from a disordered mass to an ordered community.

A tension between authority and freedom would always exist in the history of God's people. It is true that too much organization could become bureaucracy. Also too little could become chaos.

Martin Luther stated that the continual struggle of God's people would he between Spirit and structure. Structure over Spirit would kill. Always it was to be Spirit over structure. However, structure that facilitated the functioning of the Spirit and the well being of the people was and is always necessary.

Evangelistic Emphasis

We might have expected Jethro, Moses' father-in-law, to be only a country rustic since he hailed from the sheep country of Midian. But his wise advice to Moses shows a sophisticated sense of organizational and managerial principles. The various levels of government he suggested, each with a carefully selected leader in charge, helped transform a rag-tag mob of slaves into an efficiently organized socio-political entity.

God's people today also have their forms of organization or polity. As we consider the evangelistic implications of this lesson, the question arises: Can we structure evangelism as efficiently as Jethro's scheme?

Some churches have visitation teams that make regular calls on people who visit their services, or who are new in the community. Others have a small group program in which friends and neighbors--some of whom might be reluctant to attend a formal worship service at church--are invited for Bible study and fellowship.

On the other hand, some Christians prefer less structure, feeling that evangelism should be more spontaneous.

How do you feel about it? What ways of reaching the unchurched have you seen practiced? Could some organization or structure help your church be more intentional about sharing the message of Christ?

♦♦♦♦♦♦

Memory Selection

Moreover thou shalt provide out of all the people able men, such as fear God, men of truth, hating covetousness; and place such over them, to be rulers of thousands, and rulers of hundreds, rulers of fifties, and rulers of tens. *Exodus 18:21*

It has been said that in a democracy people have the leadership they deserve. There is a sense in which the Church—the earthly expression of the Kingdom of God—is not a democracy: Jesus Christ is its King. In another sense, however, "democratic" principles guided Christians from the beginning. The whole people were told to "look ye out among you seven men of honest report, full of the Holy Ghost and wisdom, whom we may appoint over this business" (Acts 6:3).

It's no accident that similar qualifications were sought in the leaders whom Moses appointed. They were to be God-fearing, truthful and above taking a bribe.

Even today it is incumbent upon Christians to take the selection of leaders—whether in local and national politics or in the Church—just as seriously. In our nation and among the people of God: Do we have the leaders we deserve?

July 10, 1994

Weekday Problems

James Osterman is chairman of his church's board of elders. Lately he has been worried about Pastor Elliott Duncan. The minister has looked tired lately, and has shown other signs of strain. one of the ladies of the church came to James recently and complained that at an education committee meeting Rev. Duncan had snapped at her for wanting to take on a task, saying that it was his job, and that he needed no help.

James wonders if the minister is showing signs of burn-out. Yet he is hesitant to talk to the minister. After all, Elliott is the professional, while Jim is only a layman. The minister probably even counsels people suffering burn-out, James reasoned. Furthermore, he knows that the minister is sensitive, and he isn't sure he could bring the matter up without sounding critical.

*Have you ever experienced "burn-out" in your job, or as a Sunday School teacher, or in other responsibilities? What are some signs?

*Some psychologists say that ministers are especially susceptible to burn-out. Why is this?

*If you were in James Osterman's shoes, how would you approach Rev. Duncan so he doesn't feel attacked?

*Suppose the two men agree that burn-out is a real possibility. What constructive steps can be taken to deal with burn-out? How can it be prevented?

◆◆◆◆◆◆

Sparkles

Three men went to speak and visit with one of the wise fathers of the faith. Two of these men discussed their thoughts and the salvation of their souls with him. However, the third man remained silent and did not ask him anything. After several visits over a long period of time, the wise old man said to the third man, "You often come here to see me, but you never ask me anything."

The man replied, "It is enough for me to see and be with you."

Not much can be learned when our mouths are open all the time. Also, let us so live that many can learn of God through our manner of being.

LEADERSHIP FOR MEETING NEEDS

This Lesson In Your Life

Few organizations can rise above the level of their leadership. Americans have diverse views about leadership styles, from authoritarian to more "participatory" leadership that invites the involvement of a number of people. All can agree that in the church, the community, and at every level of government, good leaders are required to get the job done.

Can leadership be taught, so we might instill in young people qualities that will enable them to be good leaders in the future? Or are leaders born, and not made?

No doubt some character traits that make an effective leader are natural endowments. But many communities have proved that they can also be developed. Cities have founded programs--often in connection with a local college or university--that expose bright youth to political processes, and some have gone on to become elected or appointed officials. Churches have sought out young people who show the potential for leadership. Bible colleges and seminaries are dedicated not only to providing appropriate training, but to screening out those whose gifts may lie elsewhere.

What qualities do we look for in our leaders? As Jethro suggested to Moses, we hope for them to be able and truthful. Should a country such as ours, in which a majority are at least "inclined" toward Christianity, also seek to name to office only those with Christian values? Would this be fair to minority faiths? Should leaders also protect the rights of those with no faith?

As far as leadership in the church is concerned, the "Pastoral Epistles" contain interesting qualifications that might even provide some guidelines for leaders in the body politic. The young minister Timothy was told to seek out leaders who were of good reputation, responsible in family relationships, alert and able teachers. They were to be sober and self-controlled, not drunkards or hot-tempered. Like the leaders Moses appointed, they were not to covet the job for financial gain. They were to be experienced instead of green, truthful instead of given to lying, discreet instead of delighting in slander. (See 1 Timothy 3:1-12; Titus 1:5-9.)

Let us not become so cynical about political leaders that we wonder if these are qualities of angels instead of people on earth. There is some evidence that, with proper checks and balances, a nation's populace can require of their leaders the kind of behavior they need. This is to say that followers have roles as important as leaders. In a democracy, it is the people's responsibility to seek out the good and to weed out the bad. Let us dedicate ourselves to searching out the kind of leadership envisioned in these inspirational words:

> God give us men! A time like this demands
> Strong minds, great hearts, true faith and ready hands;
> Men whom the lust of office does not kill;
> Men whom the spoils of office cannot buy;
> Men who possess opinions and a will;
> Men who have honor--men who will not lie;
> Men who can stand before a demagogue
> And damn his treacherous flatteries without winking;
> Tall men, sun-crowned, who live above the fog
> In public duty and in private thinking;
> For while the rabble, with their thumb-worn creeds,
> Their large professions and their little deeds,
> Mingle in selfish strife, lo! Freedom weeps,
> Wrong rules the land, and waiting Justice sleeps.
> --Josiah Gilbert Holland, 1819-1881

Seed Thoughts

1. How do we know that Jethro, Moses' father-in-law, was a religious man?
He was a priest (Ex. 2:16; note that Jethro is also called Ruel, 2:18; and Raguel, Num. 10:29).

2. What was Jethro's reaction to the news that God had delivered Moses and the people from Egypt?
He rejoiced at the way God had blessed them (Ex. 18:8-9).

3. What did this apparently do for Jethro's primitive faith?
Apparently it elevated Jehovah above other "gods" he may have known, and even worshiped (vs. 11).

4. What sign of peace was there between Jethro's people and the Israelites?
A sacrifice was offered and a meal was shared among Jethro and the leaders in Israel (vs. 12).

5. What role had Moses assumed among the people of Israel?
That of judge, and interpreter of the will of God (vss. 15-16).

(PLEASE TURN PAGE)

---

1. How do we know that Jethro, Moses' father-in-law, was a religious man?

2. What was Jethro's reaction to the news that God had delivered Moses and the people from Egypt?

3. What did this apparently do for Jethro's primitive faith?

4. What sign of peace was there between Jethro's people and the Israelites?

5. What role had Moses assumed among the people of Israel?

6. What concerns did Jethro have about the way Moses was going about this work?

7. What "small matters" may have been considered appropriate for "lower-level" judges, and what "hard causes" may have been reserved for Moses? (See vs. 26.)

8. How does this incident show that Moses was secure in his self-image as a leader?

9. Can an organization (political, church, business) become so highly structured as to become less efficient instead of more efficient?

(SEED THOUGHTS--Cont'd)

He was a priest (Ex. 2:16; note that Jethro is also called Ruel, 2:18; and Raguel, Num. 10:29).

He rejoiced at the way God had blessed them (Ex. 18:8-9).

Apparently it elevated Jehovah above other "gods" he may have known, and even worshiped (vs. 11).

A sacrifice was offered and a meal was shared among Jethro and the leaders in Israel (vs. 12).

That of judge, and interpreter of the will of God (vss. 15-16).

That both Moses and the people would find his "caseload" too heavy, and would grow weary (vss. 17-18).

Encourage class discussion. Conjectures might include a dispute over ownership of a goat as a "small matter," while a question concerning the observation of the Sabbath may have been brought to Moses.

He could not have delegated responsibility as Jethro suggested if he had been easily threatened or insecure.

Encourage class discussion. Nearly everyone can think of an example where "bureaucracy" got in the way.

6. What concerns did Jethro have about the way Moses was going about this work?
That both Moses and the people would find his "caseload" too heavy, and would grow weary (vss. 17-18).

7. What "small matters" may have been considered appropriate for "lower-level" judges, and what "hard causes" may have been reserved for Moses? (See vs. 26.)
Encourage class discussion. Conjectures might include a dispute over ownership of a goat as a "small matter," while a question concerning the observation of the Sabbath may have been brought to Moses.

8. How does this incident show that Moses was secure in his self-image as a leader?
He could not have delegated responsibility as Jethro suggested if he had been easily threatened or insecure.

9. Can an organization (political, church, business) become so highly structured as to become less efficient instead of more efficient?
Encourage class discussion. Nearly everyone can think of an example where "bureaucracy" got in the way.

July 17, 1994

A Covenant to Keep

Exodus 19:4-6
4 Ye have seen what I did unto the Egyptians, and *how* I bare you on eagles' wings, and brought you unto myself.
5 Now therefore, if ye will obey my voice indeed, and keep my covenant, then ye shall be a peculiar treasure unto me above all people: for all the earth is mine:
6 And ye shall be unto me a kingdom of priests, and an holy nation.

Exodus 20:2-4
2 I *am* the LORD thy God, which have brought thee out of the land of Egypt, out of the house of bondage.
3 Thou shalt have no other gods before me.
4 Thou shalt not make unto thee any graven image, or any likeness *of any thing* that *is* in heaven above, or that *is* in the earth beneath, or that *is* in the water under the earth:

Exodus 20:7-17
7 Thou shalt not take the name of the LORD thy God in vain; for the Lord will not hold him guiltless that taketh his name in vain.
8 Remember the sabbath day, to keep it holy.
9 Six days shalt thou labor, and do all thy work:
10 But the seventh day *is* the sabbath of the LORD thy God: *in it* thou shalt not do any work, thou, nor thy son, nor thy daughter, thy manservant, nor thy maidservant, nor thy cattle, nor thy stranger that *is* within thy gates.
11 For *in* six days the LORD made heaven and earth, the sea, and all that in them *is*, and rested the seventh day: wherefore the LORD blessed the sabbath day, and hallowed it.
12 Honour thy father and thy mother. that thy days may be long upon the land which the LORD thy God giveth thee.
13 Thou shalt not kill.
14 Thou shalt not commit adultery.
15 Thou shalt not steal.
16 Thou shalt not bear false witness against thy neighbour.
17 Thou shalt not covet thy neighbour's house, thou shalt not covet thy neighbour's wife, nor his manservant. nor his maidservant, nor his ox, nor his ass, nor any thing that is thy neighbour's.

◆◆◆◆◆◆

◀ **Memory Selection**
Exodus 19:5

◀ **Devotional Reading**
Deuteronomy 5:2-20

◀ **Background Scripture**
Exodus 19:1 - 20:17

◀ **Printed Scripture**
Exodus 19:4-6: 20:2-4, 7-17

A COVENANT TO KEEP

Teacher's Target

Becoming a family or a nation with order and dignity is not easy. Nothing just takes care of itself. Gardens and vineyards, houses and buildings all need tending. Without constant vigil weeds take gardens and decay destroys buildings. God knows what is needed. He gives clear and reasonable instructions for our well-being. When they are followed a peace can settle in us and over our land.

Every parent knows how difficult it is to stay with a routine in a household. It is the one thing necessary and the one thing most resisted by all. Something in us tends toward chaos.

What routine for life are you seeking to establish? How do you recognize your own resistance to routine? What could be done to help you remember the good instruction that God has given?

Lesson Introduction

Learn, keep and do. These three words made a good formula for making any instructions a part of your daily living. Learning what the instructions were was the first step for Israel. Keeping them came next. By that Moses meant reminding themselves daily what they were. Then doing them was essential. Practice would make these instructions a part of their being. Over time they would become second nature to the people of Israel.

God did not give His laws to Israel in order to dominate them. He gave them to insure their health and well being. God was not the author of confusion, nor was He the author of bondage and anxiety. God desired order and peace for His people. He wanted nothing less than joy and contentment for His own. His way was a pattern for true justice and mercy for all in the land.

Teaching Outline

I. Moses Reminds: Deuteronomy 5:2-5
   A. Who Gave the Covenant: 2
   B. To Whom It Was Given: 3
   C. The Experience of the Giving: 4-5

II. Moses Instructs: Deuteronomy 5:6-20
   A. Instruction About God: 6-11
   B. Instructions About Community: 12-20

Daily Bible Readings

Mon. Yahweh Offers a Covenant with Israel - *Exodus 19:1-6*
Tue. Kingdom of Priests and Holy Nation - *Exodus 19:7-15*
Wed. Moses Brings People to Meet God - *Exodus 19:16-20*
Thurs. Moses Takes Aaron to God *Exodus 19:21-25*
Fri. God Comes Down to Meet Israel - *Exodus 24:1-8*
Sat. The Ten Commandments *Exodus 20:1-17*
Sun. Instruction for Making Earthen Altars - *Exodus 20:18-26*

July 17, 1994

VERSE BY VERSE

I. Moses Reminds: Deuteronomy 5:2-5

A. Who Gave the Covenant: 2

2. The LORD our God made a covenant with us in Horeb.

Moses never forgot to whom he belonged. He never forgot that the people he served as leader were not his possession. He was a steward of God's people. He knew the source of his strength and the true protector of the people.

Also, Moses continually reminded himself and the people about Who established the covenant with them. He had not done it. The people had not done it. God Himself had established the covenant with them in Horeb.

Moses was carrying out his formula for learning presented in verse one. Learn the instructions. Remind yourself continually of them. Apply them in daily living. The most important instruction to remember was with whom the people had a relationship. It was none other than the Living God, the Great "I AM."

B. To Whom It Was Given: 3

3. The LORD made not this covenant with our fathers, but with us, even us, who are all of us here alive this day.

Moses wanted the people to know this was no distant God of the past. They knew the history of God with their forefathers. They also knew that Moses declared this same God had delivered and provided for them in their escape from Egypt. Now Moses wants them always remember that God is always present. God had made His covenant with them, not with their fathers only. Many among them were present when Moses received God's commandments at Sinai. God was still speaking to His people.

God would always be present. He would reestablish His covenant with each generation. God never intended to give the law and walk away. He knew He could not leave any people alone with His law and expect them to use it properly. He knew that without a relationship with Him, renewed daily, the people would be slaves to their lower nature. Without this relationship with Him, the very good thing God had given, the law, would be used for base and destructive ends.

C. The Experience of the Giving: 4-5

4. The LORD talked with you face to face in the mount out of the midst of the fire,

5. (I stood between the LORD and you at that time, to shew you the word of the LORD; for ye were afraid by reason of the fire, and went not up into the mount;) saying,

Moses is the mediator but God is the Speaker. Moses wants no mistake about this. He may have been the one who went up on the mountain but God is in charge. Also, God doesn't just speak to him. God spoke to all the people through him.

Moses had the experience of the burning bush to draw on. He was willing to approach the fire of God's presence. The people had been afraid of the presence of God. Moses had stood between God and the people. He had been willing to assume the awesome task of speaking for God.

Moses could never forget this experience. The people had not been on the mountain. They had seen his shining face but still they could turn upon Moses and declare it was only his instruction. Moses knew this rationalization was possible. He desired to drive home his point time and again. God, the "I AM," was the one whom he experienced on Mount Sinai. He and He alone was their Eternal Leader and Giver of Truth.

II. Moses Instructs: Deuteronomy 5:6-20

A. Instruction About God: 6-11

6. I am the LORD thy God, which brought thee out of the land of Egypt, from the house of bondage.

7. Thou shalt have none other gods before me.

8. Thou shalt not make thee any graven image, or any likeness of any thing that is in heaven above, or that is in the earth beneath, or that is in the waters beneath the earth;

9. Thou shalt not bow down thyself unto them, nor serve them; for I the LORD thy God am a jealous God, visiting the iniquity of the fathers upon the children unto the third and fourth generation of them that hate me,

10. And shewing mercy unto thousands of them that love me and keep my commandments.

11. Thou shalt not take the name of the LORD thy God in vain; for the LORD will not hold him guiltless that taketh his name in vain.

Repetition was a rule for learning. This would not change. What had been said once and written would need to be repeated time and again. The truth needed to be preserved in the people and impressed upon them at every opportunity.

The first important teaching is about God. Whatever was first in the lives of the people was their god. Moses wants the people to have no doubt about who they would put first.

Moses realized that the people could build their lives around almost anything. They would name it and then create a god to represent it. Only one God, the "I AM," had come to them from outside themselves. All the other gods of any people had arisen from within their own hearts and humankind's heart was deceitfully wicked.

Only God could cast out all other desires as primary. He alone could enable the people to put all of life in proper order. Only God could enable the people not to destroy themselves with their own wayward desires. No other God could be placed before Him.

Because He was the Living God nothing He created could adequately represent Him. Also, He could not be boxed up in a locale nor captured in any image that could come forth from man's imagination. The best man's imagination could do was, under God's revelation, to create word pictures and verbal images of His majesty and character. No graven images are allowed. God is beyond the capacity of any image to contain Him or property to represent Him.

God declares Himself to be a jealous God. He is not jealous in the sense of envious, but in the sense of desiring His people to be with Him and jealous to provide for their best interests. He is jealous to give them good things and to enjoy His relationship with them. Should they refuse such jealous love, God would allow them their self-destruction and it would continue from generation to generation.

For those who loved God, there would be no end to the blessings that would flow from His steadfast love. Therefore, they are not to be vain in their use of His name. They are to revere and respect Him as a child respects and reveres his father.

B. Instructions About Community: 12-20

12. Keep the sabbath day to sanctify it, as the LORD thy God hath commanded thee.
13. Six days thou shalt labour, and do all thy work;
14. But the seventh day is the sabbath of the LORD thy God; in it thou shalt not do any work, thou, nor thy son, nor thy daughter, nor thy manservant, nor thy maidservant, nor thine ox, nor thine ass, nor any of thy cattle, nor thy stranger that is within thy gates; that thy manservant and thy maidservant may rest as well as thou.
15. And remember that thou wast a servant in the land of Egypt, and that the LORD thy God brought thee out thence through a mighty hand and by a stretched out arm: therefore the LORD thy God commanded thee to keep the sabbath day.
16. Honour thy father and thy mother, as the LORD thy God hath commanded thee; that thy days may be prolonged, and that it may go well with thee, in the land which the LORD thy God giveth thee.
17. Thou shalt not kill.
18. Neither shalt thou commit adultery.
19. Neither shalt thou steal.
20. Neither shalt thou bear false witness against thy neighbour.

God is clear as to where the learning process had its strongest impact. What occurred in the home as one grew into adulthood would shape values and mindsets for life. Beginning with an ordered and compassionate home where father and mother lead in such a way that the natural honor of a child is nurtured and not destroyed was a must. Proper recognition of the awesome task laid upon the parents is highlighted as a major building block for wholesome community to become reality.

All of God's instructions about human relations found in His law were meant to create and enhance community. One could not steal from another and at the same time build community with him. Neither could one lie, nor covet another's spouse nor material possessions and create goodwill at the same time. Killing a person would surely not be an act of concern. Bearing false witness would only create distrust.

A day of reminder and instruction about God is established. Man's first day on earth was a day of rest. Out of rest and reflection upon God all of man's efforts were to flow. Such rest and time with God would focus the energies of people for good and not ill.

Evangelistic Emphasis

The middle-aged couple at dinner were discussing a cult-like religious group. "They're so strict they have rules for every little detail," they warned. "They'll tell you who you can date and when. Their legalism obviously shows they have no concept of grace."

A young doctor at the table listened thoughtfully for a few moments, then spoke up. "Wait a minute," he said. "A group like that is the reason I'm a Christian!" As an undergraduate he had been rootless and rule-less, into drugs and other forms of rebellion. The firm rules and expectations of a campus group were not legalistic to him; they brought the order and structure he needed to experience God's grace.

Unfortunately, rules like the Ten Commandments--the focus of our lesson--are often viewed legalistically. In the time of Paul, some had made keeping the commandments so burdensome that no one could live up to their expectations. Even today, some unbelievers fear coming to Christ lest they be "saddled" with so many laws and rules that they lose their freedom.

The fact is, the Law was originally a part of God's act of freeing Israel from slavery. God knew that these undisciplined former slaves would never have the freedom to grow into the people of God without the kind of structure the Law offered. Likewise, the message of Christ liberates--"My yoke is easy and my burden is light." As we share that message, let us present it as the pathway to freedom, not another set of rules that are just as heavy as Israel's bonds in Egypt. Where's the "Good News" in that?

♦♦♦♦♦♦

Memory Selection

Now therefore, if ye will obey my voice indeed, and keep my covenant, then ye shall be a peculiar treasure unto me above all people: for all the earth is mine. *Exodus 19:5*

The apostle Peter must have had this or a similar Old Testament passage in mind when he described Christians as "a chosen generation, a royal priesthood, an holy nation, a peculiar people" (1 Pet. 2:9). As has often been pointed out, more recent translations show that Christians aren't really called to be peculiar in the sense of "odd." Instead, we are to think of the way peculiar is used when we say, "The melting pot theory is largely peculiar to the U. S." That is, few nations have treasured different kinds of people in the way that is a special characteristic of our nation.

Here is the key to understanding our own "peculiar" nature as God's people. He treasures us because we belong to Him, rather than to the world. He hears us confess no one else as Lord. Our allegiance is "peculiarly" His. What a grace to be treasured! What a treasure to be shared!

July 17, 1994

Weekday Problems

Breakfast at the Harrelson's was chaos last Friday, with the whole family in an uproar. Fifteen-year-old Jason was out past his curfew the previous night. When his mother asked him about it at breakfast, he was sullen and wouldn't discuss it, saying he was late for school.

The twins, Robert and Roberta, age twelve, wanted to go to summer band camp, but they had quit their paper routes two months ago and didn't have the money. They loudly insisted that their parents pay their way, even though the rule was that such extras had to come from their own earnings.

"You kids know the rule," Mr. Harrelson said. "No pay, no play!" To Jason the word was, "You know the rule about when to come in at night. You're grounded."

Amid howls of protest, Jason shouted in his still-changing voice as he stormed out the door: "Rules, rules! I hate your old rules!"

*Can families operate without rules?

*What appropriate measures would you suggest in the situation described?

*How can parents enforce rules in ways that avoid the scene at the Harrelsons? (Do you have ideas and techniques to share about how to motivate children?)

*How can a family's rules become something other than the <u>parents'</u> rules, as Jason put it?

◆◆◆◆◆◆

Sparkle

One of the marks of a saint for the desert fathers was a person who did not judge. The desert fathers made it their aim to practice no judgment of any. One, Macarius, was said to be like God in this matter. "God is one who shields the world and hears the sin of all, and Macarius is like him. He shields the brethren and when anyone sins he will not hear or see it," they said.

How good for us to apply the principle of non-judgment in our own lives. We do not know what a man has experienced nor how far he has come in his spiritual journey. From where one started he may be far down the road while we are caught judging that he has not come far enough.

This Lesson In Your Life

CHRISTIANS AND THE TEN COMMANDMENTS

It would be hard to overstate the significance of the Ten Commandments, which are the heart of the old Covenant. Like a great Bedouin shiek, God enters into a "treaty" or covenant with His chosen people, Israel, promising to protect them and bless them. For their part, Israel is to "obey my voice...and keep my covenant" (Ex. 19:5).

But these simple commandments have proved too profound to confine them to Sinai, or to Israel. Part of their timelessness is due to the way they speak to the universal need of persons to relate both to God and to each other. The first four Commandments focus on the "vertical" relationship. They forbid the worship of other gods (vs. 3), making visible representations of the true but invisible God (vs. 4) and using His name in frivolous, demeaning or insincere ways (vs. 7); and they require the observance of His day, the Sabbath (vss. 8-11). Then come six commandments applicable to "horizontal" relationships--interactions among people. Parents are to be honored (vs. 12); murder is forbidden (vs. 13), as are adultery (vs. 14), theft (vs. 15), lying (vs. 16), and coveting (vs. 17).

How are Christians, who have been "freed from the law" (see Rom. 8:2-3), to relate to these universal principles? Differing answers have been given to this question almost from the beginning of the Church. The apostle Paul went to great lengths to show that "the Law," with its emphasis on works, has been superceded or fulfilled, by the "law" (or principle) of salvation by grace through Christ (see esp. Rom. 3:28; Gal. 3:24-25; 5:4; Eph- 2:15). This teaching was directed against those who would make of the Law a system of salvation by works--in effect saying they kept the Commandments so perfectly they had no need of Christ. Some hold that only the "ceremonial" law was superceded with Christ, and that the "moral law," including the Ten Commandments, still applies.

Furthermore, it is often observed that each of the Ten Commandments, with the exception of Sabbath-keeping, is repeated in principle in the New Covenant writings. In other words, there is really no cause for the attitude of the nineteenth-century English minister who, upon hearing that a visitor believed he was no longer bound by the Ten Commandments, told his servant, "John, show that man the door, and keep your eye upon him until he is beyond the reach of every article of wearing apparel or other property in the hall"!

Similarly, Paul's emphasis on freedom over law was considered "antinomian" (lit. "lawless") by some in the early church. One faction insisted that people had to come to Christ through Moses and the Law. Others went to the other extreme of true antinomianism, contending that all that mattered was to have Christ in the heart; deeds or works or keeping commandments were irrelevant.

A part of Paul's thought grows out of the fact that "rule-keeping" focuses on a limited list of do's and don'ts, instead of emphasizing the Christian's responsibility to behave responsibly in an infinite number of situations no list could encompass. We must admit that the little old lady had a point when she objected to reading and re-reading the Ten Commandments "because they put such bad ideas in my head!" As Paul said, "I had not known sin, but by the law" (Rom. 7:7).

Yet Paul emphasized the importance of obedience in the very letter he emphasized salvation by grace. Anticipating the antinomian question, he asked rhetorically of Christians who are under grace, "Shall we continue in sin, that grace may abound? God forbid" (Rom. 6:12). For Paul, Christians have freedom from sin, but not freedom to sin. The fact that Christ has "fulfilled" the law, results in their being "filled full"--full of a new Spirit, a new heart for obedience. Only their attitude is no longer, "See how well I have kept the Commandments!" but "Speak, Lord, thy servant heareth; command, and I will obey!"

Seed Thoughts

1. How did God use the <u>setting</u> to emphasize the importance of the Law given through Moses?
  He spoke from a thick cloud and amid thunder, lightning, and smoke (Ex. 19:9, 16-18).

2. Did Israel have trouble keeping the first commandment?
  Frequently. For example, they worshiped the golden calf (Ex. 32); and Ba'al, a Canaanite god (Judg. 2:11).

3. How are pictures of Jesus (as in our Sunday School literature or art) different from the "images" forbidden by the second commandment?
  They are not objects of worship or substitutes for the living Lord.

4. Song of Solomon 8:6 says that jealousy is "cruel." Now can this be a characteristic of God, as in Exodus 20:5?
  God is not jealous in the sense of being envious or petty, but in the sense of demanding our loyalty.

5. What constitutes taking God's name "in vain"?
  Using it carelessly or in a derogatory way; taking an oath in God's name when we have no intention of keeping it.

(PLEASE TURN PAGE)

---

1. How did God use the <u>setting</u> to emphasize the importance of the Law given through Moses?

2. Did Israel have trouble keeping the first commandment?

3. How are pictures of Jesus (as in our Sunday School literature or art) different from the "images" forbidden by the second commandment?

4. Song of Solomon 8:6 says that jealousy is "cruel." Now can this be a characteristic of God, as in Exodus 20:5?

5. What constitutes taking God's name "in vain"?

6. Is Sunday correctly referred to as "the Christian sabbath"?

7. Reconcile "Thou shalt not kill" with Paul's statement that government has the power of the sword against wrongdoers, in Romans 13:1-4?

8. What does Paul mean in Galatians 3:24-25 by saying that the Law was our "schoolmaster"?

9. Explain the purpose of the Law stated in Romans 7:7.

He spoke from a thick cloud and amid thunder, lightning, and smoke (Ex. 19:9, 16-18).

Frequently. For example, they worshiped the golden calf (Ex. 32); and Ba'al, a Canaanite god (Judg. 2:11).

They are not objects of worship or substitutes for the living Lord.

God is not jealous in the sense of being envious or petty, but in the sense of demanding our loyalty.

Using it carelessly or in a derogatory way; taking an oath in God's name when we have no intention of keeping it.

Although popular usage allows it, the sabbath was the seventh day of the week, while the early Christians met on the first day of the week (see Acts 20:7).

Apparently Paul distinguished between murder and the execution of those officially proved guilty.

That it was appropriate at an earlier stage in man's spiritual development. (Compare other translations.)

Conscience isn't enough. Just as a parent must explain right and wrong to a child, the Law puts such labels on deeds, so that we are "without excuse."

(SEED THOUGHTS--Cont'd)

6. Is Sunday correctly referred to as "the Christian sabbath"?
Although popular usage allows it, the sabbath was the seventh day of the week, while the early Christians met on the first day of the week (see Acts 20:7).

7. Reconcile "Thou shalt not kill" with Paul's statement that government has the power of the sword against wrong-doers, in Romans 13:1-4?
Apparently Paul distinguished between murder and the execution of those officially proved guilty.

8. What does Paul mean in Galatians 3:24-25 by saying that the Law was our "schoolmaster"?
That it was appropriate at an earlier stage in man's spiritual development. (Compare other translations.)

9. Explain the purpose of the Law stated in Romans 7:7.
Conscience isn't enough. Just as a parent must explain right and wrong to a child, the Law puts such labels on deeds, so that we are "without excuse."

Restoration After Wrongdoing

Exodus 32:15-19

15 And Moses turned, and went down from the mount, and the two tables of the testimony *were* in his hand: the tables *were* written on both their sides; on the one side and on the other *were* they written.
16 And the tables *were* the work of God, and the writing *was* the writing of God, graven upon the tables.
17 And when Joshua heard the noise of the people as they shouted, he said unto Moses, *There is* a noise of war in the camp.
18 And he said, *It is* not the voice of *them that* shout for mastery, neither *is it* the voice of *them that* cry for being overcome: *but* the noise of *them that* sing do I hear.
19 And it came to pass, as soon as he came nigh unto the camp that he saw the calf, and the dancing: and Moses' anger waxed hot, and he cast the tables out of his hands, and brake them beneath the mount.

Exodus 32:30-34

30 And it came to pass on the morrow, that Moses said unto the people, Ye have sinned a great sin: and now I will go up unto the LORD; peradventure I shall make an atonement for your sin.
31 And Moses returned unto the LORD, and said, Oh, this people have sinned a great sin, and have made them gods of gold.
32 Yet now, if thou wilt forgive their sin--; and if not, blot me, I pray thee, out of thy book which thou hast written.
33 And the LORD said unto Moses, Whosoever hath sinned against me, him will I blot out of my book.
34 Therefore now go, lead the people unto *the place* of which I have spoken unto thee: behold, mine Angel shall go before thee: nevertheless in the day when I visit I will visit their sin upon them.

Exodus 34:4-6

4 And he hewed two tables of stone like unto the first; and Moses rose up early in the morning, and went up unto mount Si'-nai, as the LORD had commanded him, and took in his hand the two tables of stone.
5 And the LORD descended in the cloud, and stood with him there, and proclaimed the name of the LORD.
6 And the LORD passed by before him, and proclaimed The LORD, The LORD God. merciful and gracious, longsuffering, and abundant in goodness and truth.

◆◆◆◆◆◆

◀ **Memory Selection**
Exodus 34:6

◀ **Devotional Reading**
Numbers 12:1-16

◀ **Background Scripture**
Exodus 32; 34:1-10

◀ **Printed Scripture**
Exodus 32:15-19, 30-34; 34:4-6

RESTORATION AFTER WRONGDOING

Teacher's Target

God is a jealous God. Not in the sense of envy, but in desiring a committed, exclusive relationship as the only God. It is like the commitment of one man to one woman in marriage. God knows our need and His sufficiency. He wants no other priority to inform our way of life.

God is also a just God. He longs to teach all people how to emulate His nature with one another. He grieves when He observes what our wayward behavior does to diminish our growth toward wholeness and our energy for service.

God is a merciful God. When intercession and repentance are practiced He forgives and forgets our wrongs. He acts graciously to heal, restore and redirect.

How have you experienced God's jealousy? What caused you to turn to God? How did He respond?

Lesson Introduction

Moses had gone up on the Mount to converse with God. The people grew restless in Moses' absence. Their leader who could hold them accountable and chart their spiritual course was not present. Without their leader they broke loose and began to revert to their former ways.

God had to teach His people personal boundaries. They needed a center or a core around which to develop their spiritual formation. This core was the law for life. Leaving behind old ways was not easy for the people. They had no experience in self-regulation and self-control.

God had been gracious to the people before their request for an idol. God sternly disciplined them to call them back to His way. Yet even in this stern discipline He listened to Moses' intercession and would not destroy them from the face of the earth.

Teaching Outline

I. Moses' Anger: Exodus 32:15-19
   A. Moses Descends: 15-16
   B. Moses Observes: 17-19
   C. Moses Reacts: 19
II. Moses' Intercession: Exodus 32:30-34
   A. Moses Rebukes: 30
   B. Moses Intercedes: 31-32
   C. God Answers: 33-34
III. God's Steadfastness: Exodus 34:4-6
   A. Moses Makes Tablets: 4
   B. God Comes: 5
   C. God Proclaims: 6

Daily Bible Readings

Mon. What Happened to Aaron's Faith? - *Exodus 32:1-6*
Tue. Is the Molten Calf Your Savior? *Exodus 32:7-14*
Wed. Moses Destroys the Golden Calf - *Exodus 32:15-20*
Thurs. "Out Came This (Golden) Calf" - *Exodus 32:21-24*
Fri. Who is on the Lord's Side? *Exodus 32:25-35*
Sat. God Makes a Distinct People *Exodus 33:12-23*
Sun. God Abounds in Love and Faithfulness - *Exodus 34:1-10*

July 24, 1994

VERSE BY VERSE

I. Moses' Anger: Exodus 32:15-19

A. Moses Descends: 15-16

15. And Moses turned, and went down from the mount, and the two tables of the testimony were in his hand. the tables were written on both their sides; on the one side and on the other were they written.

16. And the tables were the work of God, and the writing was the writing Of God, graven upon the tables.

Moses comes down from the mount with God's Word for the people. He had been in the presence of the great "I AM." This had been a high moment for Moses. He returns with a good word for the guidance of his people. What could have been richer than to receive instruction straight form God? He is anxious to share the way of life.

Joshua had waited as near to Moses as he could venture. Moses did not tell Joshua what God had told him the people were doing. Joshua thought the people were preparing for war and would need their leadership. Moses feared a worse fate at the camp. He recognized the sounds for what they were. God had warned Moses what to expect. He waited for Joshua to see for himself.

B. Moses Observes: 17-19

17. And when Joshua heard the noise of the People as they shouted, he said unto Moses, There is a noise of war in the camp.

18. And he said, *It is* not the voice of them that shout for mastery, neither *is it* the voice of them that cry for being overcome: but the noise of them that sing do I hear.

19. And it came to pass, as soon as he came nigh unto the camp that he saw the calf, and the dancing: and Moses' anger waxed hot, and he cast the tables out of his hands, and brake them beneath the mount.

Moses, a good leader, waits until he can confront the offenders themselves. He is full of his experience with God. He knows what good God intended. His heart is heavy with anguish over the inability of the people to wait and their affront to such a gracious and giving God.

What Moses observes is a great iniquity. The people had begun to rely upon a false god. They were practicing spiritual adultery, unfaithfulness to God.

C. Moses Reacts: 19

19. And it came to pass, as soon as he came nigh unto the camp that he saw the calf, and the dancing: and Moses' anger waxed hot, and he cast the tables out of his hands, and brake them beneath the mount.

Some believe Moses sinned in his anger. Others believe it was righteous indignation that caused him to withhold the word from God by breaking the tablets. Possibly he wanted them to see the great blessing they had lost. Also they would see that the god they worshiped could not protect them from the consequences of their sin. There could be no greater consequence of the peoples' sin than to have the word of God withdrawn from their midst. Possibly this act by Moses pictured in visible and human form God's great hurt and anger that they should so easily and quickly turn from His guidance.

II. Moses' Intercession: Exodus 32:30-34

A. Moses Rebukes: 30

30. And it came to pass on the morrow, that Moses said unto the people, Ye have sinned a great sin: and now I will go up unto the LORD; peradventure I shall make an atonement for your sin.

The principal offenders had been dealt with harshly as though a surgeon were removing cancerous cells. God had to root out those who clung to the old gods and practices.

Now Moses rebukes the people for their sin. one of his least pleasurable and yet necessary tasks as their leader is to point out their iniquity. All who lead God's people are burdened with the unwanted task of confronting God's people with their waywardness.

Moses lets the people know that it would take a mighty intercession for them to be pardoned. Out of his great love for them he would once again go before God to plead in their behalf.

B. Moses Intercedes: 31-32

31. And Moses returned unto the LORD, and said, Oh, this people have sinned a great sin, and have made them gods of gold.

32. Yet now, if thou wilt forgive their sin--; and if not, blot me, I pray thee, out of thy book which thou hast written.

Moses had been obedient. He had gone to God for counsel. He had no part in what had occurred. Yet his great character and compassion for the people were manifest in his willingness to face God and plead for the people who had sinned.

God does not allow Moses to bear their sin. However, He does listen to Moses' intercession. God would deal justly and mercifully with the situation. His desire was not to destroy but to save.

Moses could not be the people's savior. He was human, like them. He could be their leader, bring conviction to their souls and convey God's mercy to them.

C. God Answers: 33-34

33. And the LORD said unto Moses, Whosoever hath sinned against me, him will I blot out of my book.

34. Therefore now go, lead the people unto the place of which I have spoken unto thee: behold, mine Angel shall go before thee: nevertheless in the day when I visit I will visit their sin upon them.

Moses is instructed concerning God's decision. Moses had interceded, but God would act in accord with His nature. He would allow a plague to come upon the people for their sin (vs. 35) but He would not forsake them. Moses would lead. God's ministering angels would go before him to prepare the place God had promised.

III. God's Steadfastness: Exodus 34:4-6

A. Moses Makes Tablets: 4

4. And he hewed two tables of stone like unto the first; and Moses rose up early in the morning, and went up unto mount Si'-nai, as the LORD had commanded him, and took in his hand the two tables of stone.

In chapter 33 God had indicated that He would allow Israel to reconcile with Him. God has always been reconciled to the people, working for their well-being.

God comes to Moses to start again the process of establishing His covenant with the people. Moses was to hew out tablets of stone like the ones he broke. He was to rise early and go to commune with God. Moses would be the spokesman for God and the mediator for the people. Even Moses could not see God. The people could not be in God's presence. As Moses tarried with God it would be revealed as to whether the people had learned anything about waiting.

B. God Comes: 5

5. And the LORD descended in the cloud, and stood with him there, and proclaimed the name of the LORD.

God makes Himself known to Moses in an appropriate manner when Moses gets to the top of the mountain. Always God is the God who comes. He had come to Moses in the burning bush. He continued to come and instruct him as he was told to make the tablets. Then He "stooped" (brought Himself down to Moses' human level to speak). God condescends to come to humankind in forms and manners that they can comprehend. God in His essence is too High for mankind. His ways are not man's and His ways are beyond human understanding. Even what was revealed to Moses and in the Scripture was not and is not all that God will reveal of Himself when the New Heaven and the New Earth appear (Rev. 21, 22). What God continued to do with humankind was revealed to them where they were in life. He gave them what they could handle at a given time. Even then it would be a stretch for them to comprehend. It would take an act of faith to understand what was revealed.

C. God Proclaims: 6

6. And the LORD passed by before him, and proclaimed The LORD, The LORD God. merciful and gracious, longsuffering, and abundant in goodness and truth.

After sin and its consequences had occurred, the people needed to know they were not forsaken by God. Moses is given a word of reassurance from God. He proclaims His steadfastness. First God names Himself. He alone is Lord. Then He declares the kind of Lord they could expect Him to be. Merciful, gracious, longsuffering and abundant in goodness and truth would be His manner in dealing with the people. Verse 7 goes on to say that He would forgive iniquity, transgression and sin. However, the consequences of such acts would still be evident among them.

God knew humankind's weakness and instability. He knew what the fall of man had done to their nature. He knew that as long as the world stood the evidence of our need of Him and His steadfast nature would ever be present. Humankind would continually need to call upon this Steadfast One to work in their midst, even in the midst of their sin, to reclaim who they were and repair what they did. Man's way would ever tend toward destruction, but God would use even this to work His purposes for their good. God would not be thwarted in His redemption of His creation.

Evangelistic Emphasis

There are several parallels between Moses, whose leadership is nowhere more admirable than in this lesson, and Jesus Christ.

Both men were Jews--Moses of the tribe of Levi, son of Jacob, and Jesus of the tribe of Judah.

Both Moses and Christ came out of Egypt--Moses in the exodus, and Christ after His parents fled there to escape the persecution of Herod.

Both Moses and Jesus were commissioned to reveal God's covenant to the people--Moses was given the Old Covenant, while the New Covenant came through Christ.

Both figures stood on a mountain or hillside to deliver important messages--Moses on Sinai and Christ in the Sermon on the Mount (Mt. Olivet).

Perhaps the most important parallel emerges from the way Moses interceded for the people after they had committed idolatry in worshiping the golden calf. He went so far as to pray that God would remove his name out of His book if it would mean the salvation of the people (Ex. 32:32). How like Jesus, who, in the central evangel proclaimed ever since, was willing to go to the Cross, giving up His life in behalf of the sins of the world.

◆◆◆◆◆◆

Memory Selection

And the Lord passed by before him, and proclaimed, "the Lord, the Lord God, merciful and gracious, longsuffering, and abundant in goodness and truth." *Exodus 34:6*

It is just as tempting to contrast the God of the Old Testament with the God of the New, as it is to draw parallels between Moses and Christ. Doesn't the old Testament portray an angry God who strikes down the disobedient, as in the case of those who worshiped the golden calf? Isn't this a far different picture from the loving father in the parable of the prodigal son?

Not according to our memory selection. The Old Testament God did hold impenitent and stubborn people responsible for their sin--but the New Testament also speaks of a God coming to render righteous judgment against the disobedient (as in 2 Thess. 1:6-9). It is not just the New Testament God who is a God of love. Even in Exodus, He is a God of mercy, grace, and patience.

The Lord our God is one God. We can count on His consistent nature in both the Old Testament and the New.

July 24, 1994

Weekday Problems

Elaine sat at her desk, her head in her hands. The divorce was such a strain. She tried to pray, but God didn't seem very real just then....

The Israelites milled restlessly about near the foothills of Sinai. Moses, the towering figure who had emboldened them to flee Egypt, had vanished. And where was this God of which he spoke so often?

Oh, yes--it was easy enough for the elders to explain that Moses was off somewhere communing with God. <u>What</u> God? These Hebrews had little memory of the God of their forefathers, the invisible God who could appear to Abraham, Isaac and Jacob whenever He wished, but who was essentially and mysteriously intangible.

Now the gods of Egypt--<u>there</u> were gods who knew how to <u>look</u> like gods. So, from the jewelry they had "borrowed" from their Egyptian captors, the impatient Israelites made an Egyptian god--a calf like the pagan god Apis, the bull-god who could be seen and touched and counted on to be there when he was needed....

*Honestly now--do you ever feel that God is not present, since He can't be seen?

*On the other hand, what disadvantages are there in having a god that can be seen (apart from its simply being <u>false</u>!)?

*How can we explain the invisible nature of God to young children? How can we remind ourselves that He is present?

◆◆◆◆◆◆

Smiles

A little boy prayed, "Lord, if you can't make me a better boy, don't worry about it. I'm having a real good time like I am!"

Minister: "So your mother says your prayers for you each night? What does she say?"
"Thank God, he's in bed!"

A four-year-old fashioned his prayer after what he thought he heard in church. "And forgive us our trashbaskets as we forgive those who put trash in our baskets."

This Lesson In Your Life

THE GOD OF SECOND CHANCES

The most striking element in the story of the golden calf is not how an angry God dealt sternly with the idolaters. We would expect any God worthy of the name to come down hard on those who violated His will so flagrantly.

What is remarkable is that this same God was willing to issue another set of laws after Moses, in his own wrath, broke the originals! What is striking is that God gave these faithless Israelites another chance, saying, "I will write upon these tables the words that were in the first tables, which (he said, speaking to Moses) thou brakest" (Ex. 34:1).

"Which thou brakest." Of course we understand that the tragedy is not just that the stone tablets were broken, but the very law of God. The idolatry and pagan revelry to which Moses returned after receiving the first stone tables were the real indication that the Commandments had been broken. Even before they had seen the engraved Word against worshiping idols, God held them accountable for going against what Moses had already taught them about His nature, and how it contrasts with "the gods."

Yet, in issuing the second set of tablets, God was also giving the people a second chance.

In some ways this is a scandal. <u>Grace</u> is a scandal. "Don't talk to me about your Christian God," said a Buddhist to a Christian. "You'll tell me that His Son Jesus took our sins upon Himself out of pure grace, not counting their wrongs against them. The world can't work on that principle. People have to be held responsible for their deeds. They can't be saved by what someone else does for them." The man was scandalized by grace, by the God of the second chance.

The scandal becomes more radical when we realize that most of us need not merely a second chance, but a third ... or more. The apostle Peter, radical that he was, mustered enough graciousness of spirit to ask Jesus if we should go so far as to forgive an offender <u>seven</u> times--only to hear Jesus explode the principle of grace far beyond what even Peter imagined. Forgiveness is a matter of attitude, not numbers; God gives us not a second chance, or a seventh chance, but seventy times seven--an infinity of chances! (Matt. 18:21-22.)

The grumpy workers who had toiled all day resented the later chances given to the "eleventh hour" workers (Matt. 20:1-16). Suspicious disciples wondered whether a man so vicious as Saul of Tarsus could really be given the opportunity to become the apostle Paul (see Acts 9:26-27).

Won't people take advantage of such largesse? That was the Buddhist's fear. Perhaps a realistic view of humanity must admit the possibility. Those who really know the value of forgiveness will not trade on grace. No matter how often they stumble, they will not try to tough it out or bluff it through on their own goodness. They will return again and again to the God who replaces broken tables of stone with new ones, and broken lives with renewed spirits.

The question is not whether He can give us second chances, but whether we will have the faith to act on and respond responsibly to His promise of grace.

Seed Thoughts

1. Why do you think Moses' absence was so upsetting to the Israelites? Do similar reactions occur today?
They were insecure without their leader. (Compare the chaos in the former Soviet Union when the strong centralized leadership fell.)

2. What leader took the initiative in gathering the jewelry and forging the golden calf?
Surprisingly, it was Aaron, Moses' own brother and the head of the priesthood, which would develop later (Ex. 32:2-4).

3. What is the primary error in idolatry, if Exodus 32:8 is any indication?
Attributing the power of which only God is capable (here, deliverance from Egypt) to false gods.

4. What insight did Moses have into probable Egyptian reaction to any wholesale slaughter of the Israelites?
He implied that the Egyptians would attribute it to a capricious or mean-spirited God (32:12).

5. What did Moses remind God of, in begging Him not to destroy the Israelites?
Of the covenant He had made with their forefathers, Abraham, Isaac, and

(PLEASE TURN PAGE)

---

1. Why do you think Moses' absence was so upsetting to the Israelites? Do similar reactions occur today?

2. What leader took the initiative in gathering the jewelry and forging the golden calf?

3. What is the primary error in idolatry, if Exodus 32:8 is any indication?

4. What insight did Moses have into probable Egyptian reaction to any wholesale slaughter of the Israelites?

5. What did Moses remind God of, in begging Him not to destroy the Israelites?

6. If God is sinless, how can it be said that He "repented," as in 32:14? (See Gen. 6:6.)

7. What did Moses require the Israelites to do, in punishment for their idolatry?

8. What lame excuse did Aaron make for this incident?

9. Who served as executioners to put the main culprits to death?

10. After this incident, what reassurance did God give to Israel through Moses?

They were insecure without their leader. (Compare the chaos in the former Soviet Union when the strong centralized leadership fell.)

Surprisingly, it was Aaron, Moses' own brother and the head of the priesthood, which would develop later (Ex. 32:2-4).

Attributing the power of which only God is capable (here, deliverance from Egypt) to false gods.

He implied that the Egyptians would attribute it to a capricious or mean-spirited God (32:12).

Of the covenant He had made with their forefathers, Abraham, Isaac, and Jacob (32:13).

Repentance basically means to change one's mind. In Genesis 6:6 God had "second thoughts" about having created people; here, about destroying Israel.

He had the idol burned, then ground into powder, which he sprinkled in their water and made them drink.

He maintained that he merely threw the people's jewelry into the fire, "and there came out this calf."

The "sons of Levi" (32:27-28), who would become the priests in the Old Testament system of worship.

God renewed His covenant, promising to bless them and protect them (34:10).

(SEED THOUGHTS--Cont'd)

Jacob (32:13).

6. If God is sinless, how can it be said that He "repented," as in 32:14? (See Gen. 6:6.)
Repentance basically means to change one's mind. In Genesis 6:6 God had "second thoughts" about having created people; here, about destroying Israel.

7. What did Moses require the Israelites to do, in punishment for their idolatry?
He had the idol burned, then ground into powder, which he sprinkled in their water and made them drink.

8. What lame excuse did Aaron make for this incident?
He maintained that he merely threw the people's jewelry into the fire, "and there came out this calf."

9. Who served as executioners to put the main culprits to death?
The "sons of Levi" (32:27-28), who would become the priests in the Old Testament system of worship.

10. After this incident, what reassurance did God give to Israel through Moses?
God renewed His covenant, promising to bless them and protect them (34:10).

July 31, 1994

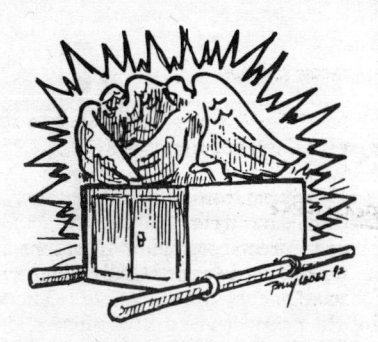

God's Constant Presence

Exodus 25:1-8

1 AND the LORD spake unto Moses, saying,
2 Speak unto the children of Israel, that they bring me an offering: of every man that giveth it willingly with his heart ye shall take my offering.
3 And this *is* the offering which ye shall take of them; gold, and silver, and brass,
4 And blue, and purple, and scarlet, and fine linen, and goats' *hair,*
5 And rams' skins dyed red, and badgers' skins, and shit'-tim wood,
6 Oil for the light, spices for anointing oil, and for sweet incense,
7 Onyx stones, and stones to be set in the e'-phod, and in the breastplate.
8 And let them make me a sanctuary; that I may dwell among them.

Exodus 29:42-46

42 *This shall be* a continual burnt offering throughout your generations *at* the door of the tabernacle of the congregation before the LORD: where I will meet you, to speak there unto thee.
43 And there I will meet with the children of Israel, and *the tabernacle* shall be sanctified by my glory.
44 And I will sanctify the tabernacle of the congregation, and the altar. I will sanctify also both Aaron and his sons, to minister to me in the priest's office.
45 And I will dwell among the children of Israel, and will be their God.
46 And they shall know that I *am* the LORD their God, that brought them forth out of the land of Egypt, that I may dwell among them: I *am* the LORD their God.

Exodus 40:33c-38

Moses finished the work.
34 Then a cloud covered the tent of the congregation, and the glory of the LORD filled the tabernacle.
35 And Moses was not able to enter into the tent of the congregation, because the cloud abode thereon, and the glory of the LORD filled the tabernacle.
36 And when the cloud was taken up from over the tabernacle, the children of Israel went onward in all their journeys:
37 But if the cloud were not taken up, then they journeyed not till the day that it was taken up.
38 For the cloud of the LORD *was* upon the tabernacle by day, and fire was on it by night, in the sight of all the house of Israel, throughout all their journeys.

◆◆◆◆◆◆

◀ **Memory Selection**
Exodus 29:45

◀ **Devotional Reading**
Exodus 33:12-16

◀ **Background Scripture**
Exodus 25:1-9; 29:38-46; 40:16-38

◀ **Printed Scripture**
Exodus 25:1-8; 29:42-46; 40:33c-38

GOD'S CONSTANT PRESENCE

Teacher's Target

A principle that appears to be true is that until we can learn a lesson on the human plane we cannot ~~posit~~ experience the same truth about the spiritual plane. For example, until we learn to accept and respect human authority and learn how to be under authority we can not be under God's authority. God desired all the human plane relationships to be visible symbols of our relationship to Him. Through them we could learn of His presence and trustworthiness. In 1 John we are told that if we don't love our neighbor whom we have seen we can't love God whom we haven't seen (1 John 4:20).

One of the things we fear the most is being alone. How has God let you know you are not alone? How are you reassured of His presence with you? When has His presence been most evident to you? *Even when we make mistakes God tells us to get up, brush ourselves off and start again. He wants our companionship + we need His.*

Lesson Introduction

God wanted the people to learn of their dependence upon Him and to acknowledge their thankfulness for His steadfast presence with them. He did not need their offerings. The people needed to give the offerings to know that possessions, flocks and fields were not their sufficiency. Also, they needed to know His gracious provision for them would not run out. They needed to learn that they did not need to hoard for themselves, but rather they could give the first and very best back to God and still there would be enough.

A visible symbol of God's presence was provided. Exodus 25-31 describes the tabernacle. The beauty and grandeur of the tabernacle was to represent God's greatness. The fact that there was no representation of God was to depict His transcendence. His glory being present was His immanence (His being in their midst).

Teaching Outline

I. The Tabernacle: Exodus 25:1-8
   A. The Offering: 1-7
   B. The Purpose: 8
II. The Meeting: Exodus 29:42-46
   A. The Burnt Offering: 42
   B. The Service: 43
   C. The Ministry: 44-46
III. The Cloud; Exodus 40:33c-38
   A. The Glory: 33c-35
   B. The Journey: 36
   C. The Rest: 37-38

Daily Bible Readings

Mon. Those Whose Hearts Are Willing - *Exodus 25:1-9*
Tue. Make a Beautiful Sanctuary *Exodus 25:10-22*
Wed. Priests to Wear Beautiful Robes *Exodus 28:1-5*
Thurs. Service for Ordaining Priests *Exodus 29:1-13*
Fri. Service for Consecrating Priests *Exodus 29:38-46*
Sat. The Erection of the Tabernacle *Exodus 40:16-29*
Sun. The Glory of the Lord *Exodus 40:30-38*

July 31, 1994

VERSE BY VERSE

I. The Tabernacle: Exodus 25:1-8

A. The Offering: 1-7

1. AND the LORD spake unto Moses, saying,
2. Speak unto the children of Israel, that they bring me an offering: of every man that giveth it willingly with his heart ye shall take my offering.
3. And this is the offering which ye shall take of them; gold, and silver, and brass,
4. And blue, and purple, and scarlet, and fine linen, and goats' hair,
5. And rams' skins dyed red, and badgers' skins, and shit'-tim wood,
6. Oil for the light, spices for anointing oil, and for sweet incense,
7. Onyx stones, and stones to be set in the e'-phod, and in the breastplate.

Moses enters the cloud and hears and experiences God's mighty truth. On this occasion Moses is instructed concerning the tabernacle. All of the materials that were to he offered to God were the trappings of royalty. The very finest materials among them would be used to build a habitation (a palace) for royalty. None was more royal than God. His grandeur, transcendence, holiness (separateness) and might would he represented by this place of His dwelling. These were to be voluntary gifts as tokens of their voluntary acceptance of God as their Lord. Always God desires willing gifts given from the heart. Generosity is the nature of God's grace. He wants His people to be like-minded.

B. The Purpose: 8

8. And let them make me a sanctuary; that I may dwell among them.

In verse 8 God discloses the purpose of the offering of such finery. He wanted to tabernacle (tent) with His people. He desired they know who He was in His transcendence but He wanted them to realize He was with them and for them.

God's holiness, His separateness, is symbolized by the veil around the Holy of Holies. However, this separateness is not to be interpreted as distance. God is not a distant deity. He is in their midst. He desires them to enjoy His presence as He delights in His people and provides good things for them continually.

II. The Meeting: Exodus 29:42-46

A. The Burnt Offering: 42

42. This *shall* be a continual burnt offering throughout your generations at the door of the tabernacle of the congregation before the LORD: where I will meet you, to speak there unto thee.

God gives detailed instruction about the sacrifices to be performed in His presence. This yielding and coming before Him was to be daily. They were to be as aware of Him on the ordinary days as in the high moments and low moments of life. Such a routine was meant to be a comfort to the people not a burden. Their daily sins would be covered and their daily mercies would be acknowledged.

Whatever their task, none was more important than keeping themselves in touch with their need and God's sufficiency. As surely as they needed daily bread they needed daily spiritual renewal. To neglect this would be to starve their souls and shrivel their lives. Duty would become drudgery and enjoyments would become diversions.

B. The Service: 43

43. And there I will meet with the children of Israel, and the tabernacle shall be sanctified by my glory.

All through Scripture the message resounds: God wants to meet with His people. As a parent can anticipate with joy the meeting of children when they return home, this is a small indicator of God's joy in meeting with those who love Him. As a child can anticipate jumping into the outstretched arms of a parent, this is a small reminder of the kind of joy that should accompany our meetings with God.

God did not set appointed times for such a meeting to cramp our style or clutter our days. He did so to reassure the people that He would be there waiting. God wanted them to know He would not abandon them. Also, they could be assured of a reception and a blessing when they came. They had set times to meet at table for meals. God had a set time that they could count on feeding upon His glory.

C. The Ministry: 44-46

44. And I will sanctify the tabernacle of the congregation, and the altar. I will sanctify also both Aaron and his sons, to minister to me in the priest's office.

45. And I will dwell among the children of Israel, and will be their God.

46. And they shall know that I am the LORD their God, that brought them forth out of the land of Egypt, that I may dwell among them: I am the LORD their God.

God has no hands and feet, no face, no arms, no bodily presence. He has his ministers to flesh out His presence and activity among the people. These were not better men than the others. They were simply those singled out as representatives before God and to the people. They would show the people the way of praise, adoration and prayer. These would be seen as signs of every person's dependence upon God and obedience to God.

Aaron and his sons had no power in themselves. Scripture makes it clear that God was the One who brought them out of Egypt and He would continue to be the power and presence in their midst (vs. 46). There was to be no minister or ministry worshiped as it were a replacement for God Himself. "I AM the Lord their God" (vs. 46) was to be what all ministers and ministries point toward as the true source of nurture and blessing.

III. The Cloud: Exodus 40:33c-38

A. The Glory: 33c-35

Moses finished the work.
34. Then a cloud covered the tent of the congregation, and the glory of the LORD filled the tabernacle.
35. And Moses was not able to enter into the tent of the congregation, because the cloud abode thereon, and the glory of the LORD filled the tabernacle.

Moses had finished his work. All was ready for habitation. The cloud covers the tent and the glory of the Lord enters the tabernacle. Heavenly royalty had taken up residence in their midst.

Though this awesome presence had entered, the tabernacle is not consumed. As with the burning bush, God's presence illumines and empowers and warms their lives but does not seek their destruction.

Moses could not enter the tent, so great was the Force inside. It is an awesome experience to stand in the presence of the Living God. He was and is a consuming fire. This fire's intent was to remove the dross and allow the gold to remain.

B. The Journey: 36

36. And when the cloud was taken up from over the tabernacle, the children of Israel went onward in all their journeys:

God not only is present, He leads the people. When the cloud ascends, the people move forward on their journey. God knows their restlessness and their need of rest. He would lead in the manner best for the company of Hebrew pilgrims. Left to themselves, they would become so restless that they would outstrip their energy, grow weary and irritable, maybe even give up. God knew their limits as well as their stamina for the march.

C. The Rest: 37-38

37. But if the cloud were not taken up, then they journeyed not till the day that it was taken up.
38. For the cloud of the LORD was upon the tabernacle by day, and fire was on it by night, in the sight of all the house of Israel, throughout all their journeys.

Nothing seems to have been done by God without rest. He was never in a hurry and He gave the first day of humankind's existence over to rest. Jesus was continually going aside to rest.

When the cloud did not ascend the people did not journey. So long as the cloud was not taken up the people camped. Physical rest was needed but possibly there was more. It takes time to build relationships and community. It takes time to visit and be together, to remember and share. God provided time for the people to be united and strengthened in their understanding of each other and their common heritage and purpose.

GOD'S CONSTANT PRESENCE

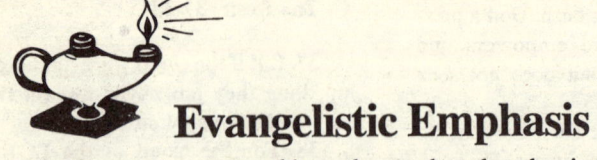

Evangelistic Emphasis

One difference between earth's northern and southern hemispheres is the appearance of the night sky. Standing outside at night in Australia, one can see fewer stars than in North America. In the "nullarbor," Australia's vast, treeless plain, far away from city lights, a moonless night is the darkest scene imaginable.

Well, not quite. The very darkest scene imaginable is the life that is unlit by the presence of God. Pagans in the time of Moses knew what that darkness was like. The children of Israel, during those times when they shut the eyes of faith and grumbled in the wilderness, knew that darkness. Modern pagans--those who know nothing of the light of forgiving grace--know the despair of groping through the darkness of self-condemnation and hopelessness.

In the wilderness, God sent a flame of fire to light the night. It sat over the tabernacle, that great tent of meeting, itself a beacon in its own way, with its gorgeous trappings and its oil lamps. All this was to proclaim to those with ears to hear, "All is not darkness. Here, God is present. Here, there is light."

Can we do less than to proclaim to our own world that darkness need not rule? May our own lives be tabernacles in the wilderness, showing forth Christ as the light of the world.

♦♦♦♦♦♦

Memory Selection

I will dwell among the children of Israel, and will be their God. *Exodus 29:45*

In some ways, faith is a very personal matter. No one can believe for us. The capacity of every person, regardless of status or circumstance, to relate individually to God is a precious heritage in Christianity.

Yet this very blessing can become a curse if we forget the corporate nature of the faith. our memory selection reminds us that God promises not only to dwell in the individual heart but, in a special way, among His people. God called Abraham not just to make him glow with the warmth of a chummy relationship, but to make of him a people. In the wilderness, the tabernacle served as a focus to unite Israel's gaze at the God who dwelt among them as a body.

All this should make us cherish the privilege of being a part of God's people, the Church. For He promises: "I will dwell in them, and walk in them; and I will be their God, and they shall be my people" (2 Cor. 6:16). As has been well said, Christianity is personal; but it is not private.

July 31, 1994

Weekday Problems

First Church has been enjoying a period of growth. Its Sunday School is bursting at the seams, and attendance at worship has required two services to accommodate the crowds. The church's leadership has decided it's time to launch a new building program.

Economic conditions in the community pose a problem. Some 10 percent of the church's bread-winners are out of work. Where will the money for a new building come from?

"We're not contributing sacrificially," said one deacon at a meeting to discuss the problem. He had his Bible open at Exodus 25:2. "In the Bible, resources for a building program were there when people gave willingly, from the heart; and we're not doing that at First Church. If the preacher will just preach it as the Good Book says, the money will be there."

*Do you agree with this application of Exodus 25:2?

*Do you make a practice of deciding beforehand how much to contribute regularly, or do you put in the plate whatever is available or seems appropriate at the moment?

*Do you think the church places too much or too little emphasis on sacrificial giving?

*In your experience, are building programs a good way to generate interest in the church?

♦♦♦♦♦♦

It seems we only go to God when we are really in need.

Smiles

Two men were shipwrecked. One of them started to pray, "Dear Lord, I've broken most of the Commandments. I've been an awful sinner all my days. Lord, if you'll spare me I'll. . . "

The other man shouted, "Hold on, don't commit yourself. I think I see a boat!"

"Do you say your prayers at night, little boy?" inquired the preacher.

"Yes, sir," answered the lad.

"And do you always say them in the morning, too?"

"No, sir," responded the lad, "I ain't scared in the daytime."

477

This Lesson In Your Life
PRACTICING THE PRESENCE OF GOD

The rich trappings of the tabernacle in the wilderness made it one of the wonders of the ancient world. Its dyed tapestries and animal skins, ornate appointments of jewels and precious metals and somber offerings and sacrifices provided an awesome setting that said to the worshiper, "This is a holy place. God Himself is here. Come to this place to be filled with His presence and power."

Do special places or settings give you this sense of the presence of God? A famous historian of religions described primitive people's awe-struck reaction to the presence of the divine as the "mysterium tremendum"--and we can grasp something of what he meant even without knowing the Latin. It is the experience described by Job's friend Eliphaz:

In thoughts from the visions of the night, when deep sleep falleth on men, fear came upon me, and trembling, which made all my bones to shake. Then a spirit passed before my face; the hair of my flesh stood up: It stood still, but I could not discern the form thereof: an image was before mine eyes, there was silence, and I heard a voice ... (Job 4:13-17).

While the element of fright implied here need not be a part of our experience, even moderns long to experience the presence of God. We may sense His nearness on a quiet morning at a distant lake, with the birds awakening to the dawn. Great cathedrals have been constructed with spires and buttresses sweeping heavenward in order for the setting of worship to remind us of God's presence. Many people find that great musical works like Handel's "Messiah" communicate the presence of the divine in their midst. Others have felt God's presence in a time of revival, or in quiet meditation and contemplative prayer.

As valid as these avenues for experiencing the holy are, we cannot always be at a distant lake or in a great cathedral or in the presence of great music or on our knees. Fortunately, God promises to be with us in less dramatic but no less significant ways.

The apostle Paul says that God dwells in the individual Christian through the Holy Spirit: "Know ye not that your body is the temple of the Holy Ghost?" (1 Cor. 6:19). This means--wonder of wonders!--that the Christian carries around his own "temple" everywhere he goes. As was noted in the discussion at the Memory Selection, God also promises to dwell among His people in a collective sense. Again Paul writes, "Know ye not that ye (the Greek is plural) are the temple of God, and that the Spirit of God dwelleth in you?" This means that God dwells in the universal Church in a way similar to the way He designated the tabernacle as His dwelling.

How seldom we are aware of Christ within, or of the joy of Christian fellowship, in a way that thrills us like the experience at the lake or in the cathedral or in revival. Of course our work, and the concerns of others, need our attention. Concerning God's presence in the Church, would a holy God really dwell among folk as flawed as we know church folk to be?

Yes, if we believe His promise! Perhaps we simply need to practice the presence of God. This is the title of a famous devotional title by "Brother Lawrence," a seventeenth-century monk. This man had so focused on God's presence that he could say, "The time of business does not with me differ from the time of prayer; and in the noise and clatter of my kitchen, while several persons are at the same time calling for different things, I possess God in as great tranquility as if I were upon my knees" (Brother Lawrence, The Practice of the Presence of God (Old Tappan, NJ: Fleming H. Revell, 1958).

Can we practice making a temple of our work and other daily activities, so that any moment we can pause, and experience His presence?

Seed Thoughts

1. What fundamental lesson was Israel to learn in the precise details God gave for the tabernacle? (see Heb 8:5b.)
   The principle of obedience--carrying out God's instructions "according to the pattern."

2. Looking back at the tabernacle's sacrifices, what does Hebrews 9:11-12 compare them to?
   To the ultimate sacrifice, Jesus Christ.

3. Why do you think Jesus was called "the lamb of God" (as in John 1:29)?
   To compare Him with the lambs of atonement sacrificed under the old Covenant.

4. What group of people were set apart to serve as priests in the tabernacle worship?
   Aaron and his sons, the Levites, descendants of Levi, son of Jacob (Ex. 29:44).

5. What inadequacy does the New Testament find with this sacrificial system, and what remedy does it offer?
   Whereas the priests had to offer and reoffer sacrifices, the sacrifice of Christ was effective in only one offering.

(PLEASE TURN PAGE)

---

1. What fundamental lesson was Israel to learn in the precise details God gave for the tabernacle? (see Heb 8:5b.)

2. Looking back at the tabernacle's sacrifices, what does Hebrews 9:11-12 compare them to?

3. Why do you think Jesus was called "the lamb of God" (as in John 1:29)?

4. What group of people were set apart to serve as priests in the tabernacle worship?

5. What inadequacy does the New Testament find with this sacrificial system, and what remedy does it offer?

6. Do you experience God's presence at church, as the Israelites were promised would occur at the tabernacle?

7. Have you experienced God's presence in a special way in another setting? Can it be duplicated?

8. What did the Ark of the Covenant contain?

9. What was the laver for, and what did this symbolize? (See Ex. 40:30-32, and Heb. 10:22.)

10. What was symbolized by the cloud that alternately hovered over the tabernacle and led Israel on the journey?

The principle of obedience--carrying out God's instructions "according to the pattern."

To the ultimate sacrifice, Jesus Christ.

To compare Him with the lambs of atonement sacrificed under the old Covenant.

Aaron and his sons, the Levites, descendants of Levi, son of Jacob (Ex. 29:44).

Whereas the priests had to offer and reoffer sacrifices, the sacrifice of Christ was effective in only one offering.

Encourage discussion. Point out that while the church is really the people, not the building, the setting of worship can affect our sense of God's presence.

Encourage sharing and discussion.

The tables of the Law, a pot of manna and Aaron's rod that budded (Ex. 40:20; Heb. 9:4.).

Ceremonial washing, a symbol of spiritual purity.

God's "glory" or presence.

(SEED THOUGHTS--Cont'd)

6. Do you experience God's presence at church, as the Israelites were promised would occur at the tabernacle?
Encourage discussion. Point out that while the church is really the people, not the building, the setting of worship can affect our sense of God's presence.

7. Have you experienced God's presence in a special way in another setting? Can it be duplicated?
Encourage sharing and discussion.

8. What did the Ark of the Covenant contain?
The tables of the Law, a pot of manna and Aaron's rod that budded (Ex. 40:20; Heb. 9:4.).

9. What was the laver for, and what did this symbolize? (See Ex. 40:30-32, and Heb. 10:22.)
Ceremonial washing, a symbol of spiritual purity.

10. What was symbolized by the cloud that alternately hovered over the tabernacle and led Israel on the journey?
God's "glory" or presence.

August 7, 1994

Celebrate God's Ownership

Leviticus 25:8-10
8 And thou shalt number seven sabbaths of years unto thee, seven times seven years; and the space of the seven sabbaths of years shall be unto thee forty and nine years.
9 Then shalt thou cause the trumpet of the jubile to sound on the tenth *day* of the seventh month, in the day of atonement shall ye make the trumpet sound throughout all your land.
10 And ye shall hallow the fiftieth year, and proclaim liberty throughout *all* the land unto all the inhabitants thereof: it shall be a jubile unto you; and ye shall return every man unto his possession, and ye shall return every man unto his family.

Leviticus 25:23-28
23 The land shall not be sold forever for the land *is* mine; for ye *are* strangers and sojourners with me.
24 And in all the land of your possession ye shall grant a redemption for the land.
25 If thy brother be waxen poor, and hath sold away *some* of his possession, and if any of his kin come to redeem it, then shall he redeem that which his brother sold.
26 And if the man have none to redeem it, and himself be able to redeem it;
27 Then let him count the years of the sale thereof, and restore the overplus unto the man to whom he sold it; that he may return unto his possession.
28 But if he be not able to restore *it* to him, then that which is sold shall remain in the hand of him that hath bought it until the year of jubile: and in the jubile it shall go out, and he shall return unto his possession.

Leviticus 25:39-42
39 And if thy brother that *dwelleth* by thee be waxen poor, and be sold unto thee; thou shalt not compel him to serve as a bondservant:
40 *But* as an hired servant, *and* as a sojourner, he shall be with thee, *and* shall serve thee unto the year of jubile:
41 And *then* shall he depart from thee, *both* he and his children with him, and shall return unto his own family, and unto the possession of his fathers shall he return.
42 For they *are* my servants, which I brought forth out of the land of Egypt: they shall not be sold as bondmen.

◆◆◆◆◆◆

◀ **Memory Selection**
Leviticus 25:23

◀ **Devotional Reading**
Deuteronomy 3:5-9

◀ **Background Scripture**
Leviticus 25

◀ **Printed Scripture**
*Leviticus 25:8-10.
23-28, 39-42*

CELEBRATE GOD'S OWNERSHIP

JUBILEE

Teacher's Target

Ownership is a concept fraught with promise and problem. Owning property involves taking responsibility for the property. Some people have realized that at times property can begin to own them rather than the other way around. As property becomes a burden, its worth diminishes.

God knew both humankind and our desire to possess. He knew our desire for security quickly slid over into greed. He knew our tendency to over-burden ourselves in an attempt to gain life through material things. Because of this, God devised a plan to limit our grasping and relieve our stress from over-reaching our limits.

When has property been a burden to you? Does ownership make a person more important or better? Does ownership reduce people's awareness of to whom all things really belong?

Lesson Introduction

Our all-wise God knew that there was no more effective way for us to demean each other than by how we use property. With this in mind He instructed the children of Israel concerning property. Had His instructions been followed, a society without permanent poverty would have been established. However, there is no indication in the Bible or in historical records that the jubilee concept was ever implemented.

God desired the people to realize that He was the true owner of all. Humankind was a temporary overseer of what God had created. All that mankind could boast of creating was made from something God alone created. Everything was on loan to the human race.

To protect the poor from the rich and the rich from their riches, God planned an equitable leveling process every 50 years. He called it jubilee.

Teaching Outline

I. Jubilee Established: Leviticus 25:8-10
   A. Numbering the Years: 8-9
   B. The Hallowed Year: 10
II. Jubilee and Real Estate: Leviticus 25:23-28
   A. Land on Loan: 23
   B. Land Redemption Policy: 24-28
III. Jubilee and Servitude: Leviticus 25:39-42
   A. Brother No Bond Servant: 39
   B. Time of Service: 40-41
   C. True Owner: 42

Daily Bible Readings

Mon. The Land Shall Keep Sabbatical Year - *Leviticus 25:1-7*
Tue. Hallow the Fiftieth Year *Leviticus 25:8-12*
Wed. Land Cannot Be Sold in Perpetuity - *Leviticus 25:13-23*
Thurs. Property is the Lord's Land *Leviticus 25:24-28*
Fri. Levites May Redeem Property Any Time - *Leviticus 25:29-34*
Sat. Jubilee Sets Slaves Free *Leviticus 25:35-43*
Sun. Israel is God's Servant - Not Slave - *Leviticus 25:44-55*

VERSE BY VERSE

I. Jubilee Established: Leviticus 25:8-10

A. Numbering the Years: 8-9

8. And thou shalt number seven sabbaths of years unto thee, seven times seven years; and the space of the seven sabbaths of years shall be unto thee forty and nine years.
9. Then shalt thou cause the trumpet of the jubile to sound on the tenth day of the seventh month, in the day of atonement shall ye make the trumpet sound throughout all your land.

Because our culture is so radically different from that of early Israel, we often miss the significance of the legal instructions of Leviticus. Wall Street rules in America. Material possession is the basis of our economic structure and our consumerism. This basis may also be one of the contributing factors to a society with perpetual and growing poverty problems.

In any case, God's principle of jubilee, which was never carried out, was wiser than man's wisdom. Humankind did not have enough faith to carry through with God's program. Foolishly, humankind labors to put through its own faulty constructions of economic health. Most often each new construct was designed to favor the economic group making the proposal.

In our text for today, people had to number the years. That is to say, they were to be aware of how long they would yet have the land and what year they would release the land to its original caretaker. Surely it would have made a difference in attitude toward the land, the original owner and the use and care of the land had such a policy been followed.

God knew all people needed protection from themselves and each other, especially in matters of property. He knew there was need for responsible stewardship and also relaxation and release from the burden of ownership. Every person paid a price for his station in life, the landowner no less than the hired servant. They simply had different prices to pay. Jubilee would have been a leveling effect where each could get a new start.

B. The Hallowed Year: 10

10. And ye shall hallow the fiftieth year, and proclaim liberty throughout all the land unto all the inhabitants thereof: it shall be a jubile unto you; and ye shall return every man unto his possession, and ye shall return every man unto his family.

"To hallow" meant to make holy or to venerate. The Sabbath was a hallowed day. Now God establishes a hallowed year. The fiftieth year is to be the sabbath of years. The Sabbath was a day of rest and jubilee was a year of rest (Levit. 25:11-12). God was big on rest. What a contrast to the way His people lived!

What was God's intent? Part of His desire was for the people to know themselves to be caretakers for God and not owners of property or other people. All ownership was to be recognized as temporary. Also, God desired no one to be in a position to place others in poverty. Nor did he want any to be in poverty even when they had been poor managers. Redemption was His desire. They could be hired servants for a time but they would also receive another chance at overseeing their portion of the land in the year of jubilee.

II. Jubilee and Real Estate: Leviticus 25:23-28

A. Land on Loan: 23

23. The land shall not be sold for ever for the land is mine; for ye are strangers and sojourners with me.

God's goal was not materialism, but community and relationship. Materialism divided into class and clique. Community united family and friends as of equitable worth. There was to be enough for all. All was to be placed at God's disposal not at the disposal of a few privileged people or a privileged class of people.

God wanted communion with Him to have precedence over possession of property. Nothing was to be cut off or hoarded as one's own apart from God.

B. Land Redemption Policy: 24-28

24. And in all the land of your possession ye shall grant a redemption for the land.
25. If thy brother be waxen poor, and hath sold away some of his possession, and if any of his kin come to redeem it, then shall he redeem that which his brother sold.
26. And if the man have none to redeem it, and himself be able to redeem it;
27. Then let him count the years of the sale thereof, and restore the overplus unto the man to whom he sold it; that he may return unto his possession.
28. But if he be not able to restore it to him, then that which is sold shall remain in the hand of him that hath bought it until the year of jubile: and in the jubile it shall go out, and he shall return unto his possession.

Each man could redeem his land when he became able to do so. The price was to be settled based upon the number of years since the sale and before the jubilee. No one could be refused this opportunity of redeeming his land.

If a person could not redeem his own land, a kinsman could do so. Then the man could work as a hired servant to reclaim the land, or in the jubilee year it would be restored to him.

Houses within the city were treated somewhat differently from land (vs. 30). One of the reasons for this policy was to encourage strangers and proselytes to settle among them.

Such a practice allowed for everyone to have dignity and a sense of place. All knew that many things could happen beyond the control of the person. Also, the person's own failings could cause the need to sell the land. They all knew none was exempt from calamity from self or outside forces. Also, none would be refused the opportunity to reclaim what was his.

III. Jubilee and Servitude: Leviticus 25:39-42

A. Brother, No Bond Servant: 39

39. And if thy brother that dwelleth by thee be waxen poor, and be sold unto thee; thou shalt not compel him to serve as a bondservant:

God desired His people to be a free people. A man could be another's hired servant but he could not be bound to him in servitude. No fellow-Jew could be treated as a captive of war. He was never to be property to be used, sold or willed to another.

The children of Israel were to be God's servants. No man was to own them. They had been redeemed out of bondage in Egypt and they were not to be slaves to the world again.

The Hebrews were to honor each other as brother and sister. No one was to become the possessor of another's soul or diminish his dignity. The Hebrew as hired servant was to have work and treatment that was honorable for a child of Abraham. God did not make servants slaves, and neither were the people to do so with each other.

B. Time of Service: 40-41

40. But as an hired servant, and as a sojourner, he shall be with thee, and shall serve thee unto the year of jubile:

41. And then shall he depart from thee, both he and his children with him, and shall return unto his own family, and unto the possession of his fathers shall he return

This service to another had its limit. At the year of jubilee the person would be released from his duties. His land would be restored to him and a fresh start would be before him.

A person who had hired servants would ever be aware that one day the servant would be free. One day he would be likely to face him as a neighbor with his own land. How he had treated him while a hired servant would affect future relations and the unity of the community as a whole.

C. True Owner: 42

42. For they are my servants, which I brought forth out of the land of Egypt: they shall not be sold as bondmen.

God made clear in verse 42 who was the true owner of the Hebrews. He alone had brought them out of Egypt. He held them as His people. He alone knew how to treat them properly. His was a way of mercy, wisdom and compassion. He did not make His yoke heavy upon His people. He desired to lighten their burden. He expected this same treatment from His people toward each other.

God had been the bestower of dignity and honor upon mankind from the beginning. Every instruction, injunction and intervention on God's part was aimed at crowning humankind with the likeness of His image. How sad that we have allowed the evil one to deceive us into the practice of destroying our own and others' dignity through our pride of superiority.

CELEBRATE GOD'S OWNERSHIP

Evangelistic Emphasis

When Jesus came proclaiming the Good News, He did so in the spirit of the Old Testament "jubilee." The year of jubilee came every fiftieth year. It was a time of emphasis on freedom--from debt, and even, in the case of slaves, from human ownership.

In Luke 4, when Jesus emerged from His temptations ready to go to work, He came with this very emphasis: "The Spirit of the Lord is upon me, because he hath anointed me to preach the gospel to the poor; he hath sent me to heal the brokenhearted, to preach deliverance to the captives, and recovering of sight to the blind, to set at liberty them that are bruised, to preach the acceptable year of the Lord" (Luke 4:18-19).

The Good News about Jesus means that jubilee is here! The good news is that in Him we are no longer slaves of sin; we are free! Even those bound by bodily weaknesses such as blindness can finally "see the light" in Christ. Those "possessed" by sorrow and disappointment and heart-break are invited to "possess the land" themselves--to stake out the claim God has reserved for them in His kingdom.

Christians who are aware of their blessings in Christ approach the world with the awareness Christ did: that they have a message of liberation and freedom too important to hide under a bushel. Jesus means jubilee!

◆◆◆◆◆◆

Memory Selection

The land shall not be sold for ever: for the land is mine; for ye are strangers and sojourners with me.
Leviticus 25:23

Strangers and sojourners? Even after God had given Israel the Land of Promise? Would there ever be a time when they could become settled inhabitants and landowners?

These are not unlike questions people often ask today, when it seems as though the only unchanging fact of life is change itself. Our work takes us to a new city. Our children grow up. our health declines. Our relationships change-- "You're not the man (or woman) I married!" is a familiar refrain in many households.

If life seems to be a continual pilgrimage, we could ask for no better traveling companion! God does not leave us consigned to the wilderness as lonely wanderers. Instead, He promises that we will be sojourners *with Him*. Through all the changes, undergirding all the uncertainties, throughout life's ever-varying pilgrimage, "underneath are the everlasting arms."

August 7, 1994

Weekday Problems

Dave Schultz is an assistant superintendent at Green Forest Industries, a lumber mill. Dave is a Christian, and has recently become interested in whether the Bible speaks to principles of land and resources management. The emphasis in Genesis 1:28 on "replenishing the earth" says to Dave that we should be good stewards of the resources--such as timber--that God has provided.

Recently the lumber mill superintendent announced long-range plans for clear-cutting a thousand acres of Ponderosa pines on property the company owns. An environmental group has protested that this would destroy the habitat of forest animals, and that it would leave the land subject to erosion. They are seeking an injunction to stop the cutting.

Dave's problem is that he finds himself on the side of the environmental group. If he speaks out, he is sure to be fired--and the unemployment rate is high in the mountain town where he lives. If he doesn't say what he thinks, he wonders if he can live with his conscience.

*What would you do if you were Dave?

*Do you agree with the common perception that environmentalists value nature above people, while industry values people (jobs) above nature?

*Do you think there is tension between Genesis 1:28's command, on the one hand, to "replenish" the earth, and, on the other, to "subdue" it?

♦♦♦♦♦♦

Sparkles

A missionary deep in the jungle, came upon a witch doctor who was pounding heavily on a drum. "What is the drumming about?" asked the missionary.

"We have no water," replied the witch doctor.

"Oh, I see," said the missionary, "So you are praying for rain?"

"No," the man answered, "I am sending for the plumber."

A missionary learned of a native with five wives. "You are violating one of God's laws," he instructed the man. "You must go and tell four of those women they can no longer live with you and consider you their husband."

The native man thought for a moment. Then he said "Me wait here. You tell 'em!"

This Lesson In Your Life

THE JUBILEE PRINCIPLE

Would we have been able to live by the principles of the sabbath year and jubilee? Apparently many Jews themselves had difficulty doing so, since there is no record of letting land lie untilled every seventh year, and returning land to its original owner every fiftieth year. Yet some of the concerns and principles reflected in this ancient tradition might well inform Christian attitudes today. What are these principles?

The world belongs to God, not humans (Lev. 25:23). Although our culture prizes the freedom to own private property, this should not lead us to forget that all that we have comes from God.

Several implications arise from the fact that we are really only tenants leasing God's property, rather than landowners "in perpetuity." For one thing, we have the responsibility of caring for the landlord's world as good stewards. We should follow the old principle of camping: leave the campground in as good or better shape as you found it.

We should share our bounty with the less fortunate. The "Look out for No. 1" syndrome is sub-Christian. God said through Isaiah, "Woe unto them that join house to house, that lay field to field, till there be no place, that they may be placed alone in the midst of the earth!" (Isa. 5:8). We harvest partly in order to give others something to glean (Lev. 19:10). We work partly to have something to give to the needy (Eph 4:28).

Values extend into the future. The jubilee principle tied land values to the number of years left before it was to revert to the original owner. Financial decisions we make today impact the future. For example, do we violate the rights and freedom of our unborn heirs when we create a national debt that will burden them, while we enjoy life to their hurt?

Too often we have the attitude of Hezekiah, who said, when warned of a dark future for his children, "Is it not good, if peace and truth be in my days?" (2 Kings 20:19). Too many of us want our children to learn the principle of "delayed gratification," while we are quite willing to gratify ourselves at the future's expense.

We should use what we have wisely, in view of our temporary ownership. If I will have this piece of land only forty-nine years, let me (a) put it to its best and highest use now--"I must work the works of him that sent me, while it is day: the night cometh, when no man can work" (John 9:4); and (b) let me respect the next owner enough not to abuse it and render it unusable.

There is a connection between how we treat the earth and how God blesses us. If Israel would obey God in observing the jubilee principle, He promised that the land shall yield her fruit, and ye shall eat your fill, and dwell therein in safety" (Lev. 25:19). The apostle Paul would later link human sinfulness and injustice to an earth that "groaneth and travaileth in pain" (Rom. 8:22). An abused environment will in turn make misery for its abusive inhabitants.

Being good stewards is a joy, not a burden. Sometimes practicing good principles of conservation can be made to sound like a burden, a lessening of life, a joyless existence. Nineteenth century black Americans sang of "jubilee" as a joyous time. The word literally refers to a "blast" (as from a ram's horn). Serving the God of creation by caring for His creation, including each other, is not a burden, but a blessing.

Seed Thoughts

1. How often was Israelite land to be allowed to lie fallow?
   Every seventh year (Lev. 25:1-4).

2. What was to be done with any yield from the land that came up "volunteer"?
   It was to be used as food not only for the landowner but for servants and for both domesticated and wild animals (vss. 6-7).

3. How often did the year of "jubilee" occur, and on what day was it?
   Every fiftieth year, on the day of atonement (vss. 8-9).

4. How were land values to be determined during the forty-nine years before a jubilee year?
   According to the number of years remaining until the fiftieth, when it would revert back to the original owner (vss. 14-16).

5. What guarantee of food did the Israelites have for the year of jubilee, when they were not to sow or reap?
   God promised to make the land fruitful enough to make up even for three years (vss. 20-22).

(PLEASE TURN PAGE)

---

1. How often was Israelite land to be allowed to lie fallow?

2. What was to be done with any yield from the land that came up "volunteer"?

3. How often did the year of "jubilee" occur, and on what day was it?

4. How were land values to be determined during the forty-nine years before a jubilee year?

5. What guarantee of food did the Israelites have for the year of jubilee, when they were not to sow or reap?

6. On what basis did Israelites occupy land, and why did God arrange it in this way?

7. What advantage did this system give to the poor? Would this be a good idea in modern times?

8. What exceptions were made to the reversion of the land to the original owner?

9. What other economic measure helped those who had to go into debt? (see vs. 36).

10. What restrictions on using fellow-Israelites for labor were provided?

(SEED THOUGHTS--Cont'd)

Every seventh year (Lev. 25:1-4).

It was to be used as food not only for the landowner but for servants and for both domesticated and wild animals (vss. 6-7).

Every fiftieth year, on the day of atonement (vss. 8-9).

According to the number of years remaining until the fiftieth, when it would revert back to the original owner (vss. 14-16).

God promised to make the land fruitful enough to make up even for three years (vss. 20-22).

It was like a forty-nine year lease, to remind Israel that God actually owned the land (vss. 23-24).

It gave the poor a fresh start. (Encourage class discussion of whether the system would be good now.)

Houses within walled cities could be redeemed within a year, but if they weren't they were exempt from the jubilee principle (vss. 29-31).

Usury, or charging interest on money loaned, was forbidden.

They were to be paid wages as servants instead of serving as slaves; and they were to be released at the year of jubilee (vss. 39-41).

6. **On what basis did Israelites occupy land, and why did God arrange it in this way?**
It was like a forty-nine year lease, to remind Israel that God actually owned the land (vss. 23-24).

7. **What advantage did this system give to the poor? Would this be a good idea in modern times?**
It gave the poor a fresh start. (Encourage class discussion of whether the system would be good now.)

8. **What exceptions were made to the reversion of the land to the original owner?**
Houses within walled cities could be redeemed within a year, but if they weren't they were exempt from the jubilee principle (vss. 29-31).

9. **What other economic measure helped those who had to go into debt? (see vs. 36).**
Usury, or charging interest on money loaned, was forbidden.

10. **What restrictions on using fellow-Israelites for labor were provided?**
They were to be paid wages as servants instead of serving as slaves; and they were to be released at the year of jubilee (vss. 39-41).

August 14, 1994

Accept God's Guidance

Numbers 13:25-28
25 And they returned from searching of the land after forty days.
26 And they went and came to Moses, and to Aaron, and to all the congregation of the children of Israel, unto the wilderness of Pa'ran, to Ka-desh; and brought back word unto them, and unto all the congregation, and shewed them the fruit of the land.
27 And they told him, and said, We came unto the land whither thou sentest us, and surely it floweth with milk and honey; and this *is* the fruit of it.
28 Nevertheless the people *be* strong that dwell in the land, and the cities *are* walled, *and* very great: and moreover we saw the children of A'-nak there.

Numbers 13:30-31
30 And Caleb stilled the people before Moses, and said, Let us go up at once, and possess it; for we are well able to overcome it.
31 But the men that went up with him said, We be not able to go up against the people; for they *are* stronger than we.

Numbers 14:6-10a
6 And Joshua the son of Nun, and Caleb the son of Jephun'neh, *which were* of them that searched the land, rent their clothes:
7 and they spake unto all the company of the children of Israel, saying, The land, which we passed through to search *is* an exceeding good land.
8 If the LORD delight in us, then he will bring us into this land, and give it us; a land which floweth with milk and honey.
9 Only rebel not ye against the LORD, neither fear ye the people of the land; for they *are* bread for us: their defense is departed from them, and the LORD *is* with us: fear them not.
10 But all the congregation bade stone them with stones.

Numbers 14:28-30
28 Say unto them, *As truly as* I live, saith the LORD, as ye have spoken in mine ears, so will I do to you:
29 Your carcases shall fall in this wilderness; and all that were numbered of you, according to your whole number, from twenty years old and upward, which have murmured against me,
30 Doubtless ye shall not come into the land, *concerning* which I sware to make you dwell therein, save Caleb the son of Je-phun'-neh, and Joshua the son of Nun.

◆◆◆◆◆◆

◀ **Memory Selection**
Numbers 14:8-9

◀ **Devotional Reading**
Numbers 23:18-23

◀ **Background Scripture**
Numbers 13-14

◀ **Printed Scripture**
Numbers 13:25-28, 30-31; 14:6-10a, 28-30

ACCEPT GOD'S GUIDANCE

Teacher's Target

Our greatest gifts often become our greatest nemesis. Sight is a wonderful blessing. It is a source of joy and wonder. Yet we hinder ourselves in faith through the over use of this means of accessing the world and acquiring information. We rely on the natural attributes too heavily. In regard to sight our motto often is: "What we see is what is." We are blind to our tendency toward reductionism. Often we see only what we want to see.

God continually warns His people about living by sight rather then faith. Any listening is hard work. Listening to God harder still. Yet faith is the evidence of things unseen and this faith comes by the hearing of God's word.

When have you relied on what you saw later to be proven wrong? How can this "sight sureness" be corrected?

Lesson Introduction

God had promised the people a land rich and plentiful with all they needed and desired. He had promised His assistance in making the land their own. Moses knew that in any new venture one needed to know certain information. He sent spies into the land to gain this information.

Moses sent twelve tribal leaders ahead. When they returned they bore good news and bad news. The land was all that they had been promised. There was a hitch in the works, however. There were giants in the land and the cities were fortified.

Ten of the spies could only focus on the obstacles to possession of the land. For them the glass was half empty, not half full. Two remembered God's promise of assistance. In all situations there is always one significant unseen factor, God Himself.

Teaching Outline

I. The Report: Numbers 13:25-28,30-31
   A. Good News: 25-27
   B. Bad News: 28
   C. The Crossroad: 30-31
II. The Rebellion: Numbers 14:6-10a
   A. The Plea of the Visionary: 6-9
   B. The Resistance of the Fainthearted: 10
III. The Result: Numbers 14:28-30
   A. Fear Fulfilled: 28-29
   B. Faith Honored: 30

Daily Bible Readings

Mon. Miriam and Aaron Rebuked by God - *Numbers 12:1-15*
Tue. Moses Sends Spies to Canaan *Numbers 13:1-2, 17-24*
Wed. Two Spies Vote to Enter Canaan - *Numbers 13:25-31*
Thurs. Fear Dominated the Majority *Numbers 13:33-14:3*
Fri. Only Caleb and Joshua Confident *Numbers 14:4-19*
Sat. Ten Spies Die of Plagues *Numbers 14:20-35*
Sun. Doubters: The Lord Is Not Among You - *Numbers 14:36-45*

VERSE BY VERSE

I. The Report: Numbers 13:25-28, 30-31

A. Good News: 25-27

25. And they returned from searching of the land after forty days.
26. And they went and came to Moses, and to Aaron, and to all the congregation of the children of Israel, unto the wilderness of Pa'ran, to Ka-desh; and brought back word unto them, and unto all the congregation, and shewed them the fruit of the land.
27. And they told him, and said, We came unto the land whither thou sentest us, and surely it floweth with milk and honey; and this is the fruit of it.

The people were waiting with Moses for forty days. Anticipation mounted. The spies return and confirm the report that all that had been promised was true. Evidence in the form of fruit from the land is brought back. The returning spies cannot contain themselves as they speak of this land of milk and honey. Even those who would quickly give a negative report cannot deny the bountiful nature of the land.

The vision is confirmed. God's promise of such a land was as true as His promise to deliver them from Egypt. Already they had experienced the fulfillment of many promises to them. Now the Promise Land is theirs for the taking. Well, almost!

B. Bad News: 28

28. Nevertheless the people be strong that dwell in the land, and the cities are walled, and very great: and moreover we saw the children of A'-nak there.

Just as it seems the next step in the story would be to take the land promised, ten of the spies balk. Their courage flags as they focus on the size of their adversaries and the strength of their cities. They carry the people along with them. Again fear won out over faith. God was weary with their wavering.

The ten spies allowed their focus to fall on the negative even though they had already overcome much greater obstacles such as Egypt's might and a sea of water. They never considered their own strength (600,000 men) and the Lord's promise of help. All they could see were the giants in the land and the fortified cities. They saw themselves as grasshoppers in comparison to the giants (vs. 33). How cowardly they became when they failed to remember God and His faithfulness.

C. The Crossroad: 30-31

30. And Caleb stilled the people before Moses, and said, Let us go up at once, and possess it; for we are well able to overcome it.
31. But the men that went up with him said, We be not able to go up against the people; for they are stronger than we.

In this decisive event there comes a

"crossroad" moment. The avenues are open and clearly seen. A decision as to which road would be taken stares them in the face. Fear stares them down. On this occasion the hard road appears too formidable to the Hebrews. Their desire for safety and security overrides their sense of adventure. They lose the best by settling for something less.

Israel faced a crossroad about entering the Promise Land. It was good to be cautious. Caution is one thing. Cowardice is another. Fear made cowards of the majority.

Caleb stills the people and gives a clarion call for an overcoming outlook. But the majority of the voices are more numerous and ring louder in the ears of the people. Defeatism carries the day. Conquest would have to wait for another generation to rise and possess the land.

II. The Rebellion: Numbers 14:6-10a

A. The Plea of the Visionary: 6-9

6. And Joshua the son of Nun, and Caleb the son of Jephun'neh, *which were* of them that searched the land, rent their clothes:

7. and they spake unto all the company of the children of Israel, saying, The land, which we passed through to search it, *is* an exceeding good land.

8. If the LORD delight in us, then he will bring us into this land, and give it us; a land which floweth with milk and honey.

9. Only rebel not ye against the LORD, neither fear ye the people of the land; for they *are* bread for us: their defense is departed from them, and the LORD is with us: fear them not.

It is the same old story. The prophet, the visionary, the one with an eye and an ear for God, stands and declares the certainty of God's promise. This one, (and in this instance two, Joshua and Caleb) would have brought healing to their fearful hearts. They desire to save Israel from its own ruin.

The story never changed in Israel. Neither does it change for any other people for that matter. People continually resist change in all ages. The prophet speaks and the people rebel. Even with Joshua and Caleb telling them, "Only do not rebel against the Lord..." (vs. 9), still they refuse to hear and act on faith.

Only a remnant seemed ever to come forth from the majority and follow the prophet of God. In this instance Joshua and Caleb stood alone. No remnant stepped out of the crowd.

B. The Resistance of the Fainthearted: 10

10. But all the congregation bade stone them with stones.

"But all the congregation bade stone them with stones" (vs. 10). What Jesus was later to say is on the verge of happening here. "You stoned the prophets" (Matt. 21:33-46).

The people's fears had been stirred up. The most ardent appeal is made to still the storm in their hearts. However, overwrought with fear, they cannot or will not understand the truth that would secure their peace.

Moses and Aaron, Joshua and Caleb had done their pleading in vain (vss. 5-9). The noise of the voices of fear shout down the calm voice of reassurance. The still small voice for God cannot be heard in the din of confusion and chaos generated by the fearmongers. Fear causes the fainthearted people to resist and disbelieve God. Fear of abandonment even in the face of answered prayers and fulfilled promises holds their hearts in a grip of death. What a strong defense to faith was fear!

III. The Result: Numbers 14:28-30

A. Fear Fulfilled: 28-29

28. Say unto them, As truly as I live, saith the LORD, as ye have spoken in mine ears, so will I do to you:

29. Your carcases shall fall in this wilderness; and all that were numbered of you, according to your whole number, from twenty years old and upward, which have murmured against me,

In verse 22 of this chapter God told Moses that Israel had failed ten times to trust Him (Ex. 14:11, 12; 15:24; 16:3; 16:20; 16:27-29; 17:2, 3; 32:7-10; Num. 11:1; 11:4; 14:1-4). Now God allows what they had feared to come upon them. The children of Israel had feared they would die in the wilderness. Now they would. For forty years they would wander in the wilderness. Their children whom they thought would be prey in the land if they entered it would in fact be the conquerors of the land they refused. Despising God's deliverance resulted in dull and deadly drudgery.

B. Faith Honored: 30

30. Doubtless ye shall not come into the land, concerning which I sware to make you dwell therein, save Caleb the son of Je-phun'-neh, and Joshua the son of Nun.

God had first threatened immediate death to the people (Num. 14:12). He repented to allow them to wander aimlessly without purpose instead. Even this was not to be a permanent consequence. His purposes would not be thwarted by man's failure. Another generation would enter the land.

Nor does God forget His faithful. He knows all that Joshua and Caleb have done to save the people from themselves. God would have to ask them to wander with the people. The people would need their leadership. These two had a different spirit from the rest (Num. 14:24). Joshua and Caleb had that ability to hold a vision in their hearts and minds long after it had passed. They were men of faith in the faithfulness of God. The faithfulness of God would confirm their faith.

ACCEPT GOD'S GUIDANCE

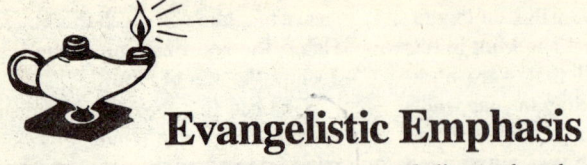

Evangelistic Emphasis

There is no more powerful testimony to unbelievers than the effect Christ has on the life of believers. When we allow ourselves to be nourished on the abundant blessings of the fruit of the promised land--the forgiveness of sins--we demonstrate the truth of God's promise.

The fruits that Israel's spies brought back from their mission included a cluster of grapes so huge it had to be carried on a pole between two men. Christians have the opportunity to reap even more impressive fruits from their life in Christ. Paul calls them the "fruit of the spirit"--love, joy, peace, longsuffering, gentleness, goodness, faith, meekness and temperance (Gal. 5:22-23).

This fruit is not provided to Christians merely for their personal nourishment. Incorporated into our actual lives, these character traits become evidence to unbelievers of the faithfulness of God, reassuring them that He means what He says.

When we are unfruitful, our witness is likely to have the effect Moses warned of when he said that the Egyptians would think that God was too impotent to usher the people into the Land of Promise (Num. 14:13-16). We dare not project a picture of God as weak simply because we, His people, declined to partake of His promises.

Memory Selection

If the Lord delight in us, then he will bring us into this land, and give it us; a land which floweth with milk and honey. Only rebel not ye against the Lord. *Numbers 14:8-9a.*

How big is the "If" with which this verse begins? Is there really any doubt that the Lord "delights in us"? Is receiving His blessings dependent upon His whim, so that if He "likes" us He gives us "the promised land," but if He gets up in a bad mood some morning and finds us distasteful or irritating, then He changes His mind?

Of course not. The "if" is only a rhetorical phrase. God is always ready to bless His children. The only "if" involved lies in our own courage to lay hold on His promises, our own willingness to obey. God has already given us "all spiritual blessings" through His Son. He has already made us "kings and priests." All that remains is for us to become what we are. God delights to bless us richly. He only waits to see whether we have the faith to accept, and the willingness not to rebel.

August 14, 1994

Weekday Problems

Regina is thirty-five now, and is still only a teller at the bank even though she has been there for six years. Her husband Sam is an accountant, and very satisfied with his work at a firm he joined right out of college. They have no children.

Regina is bored and restless. She remembers how Jake, to whom she was engaged before meeting Sam, offered her that job with his marketing firm. It would have probably led to marriage; but Regina broke off the engagement because she felt both Jake and the job were unstable. Life with Sam had looked safer.

Looking back, Regina wonders if she made the right choice. She and Sam are doing fine, financially. Although her teller's job doesn't pay a lot, it has good fringe benefits. Sam keeps reminding her of its excellent retirement plan; but at her age this just exasperates Regina. Is thinking about retirement at her age all that important? she wonders. Does safe have to be so dull?

*How can Regina's job restlessness be dealt with before it becomes a marriage problem, too?

*Would you advise her to make a career move at this point in her life?

*Before doing so, what factors should she consider?

*How can couples with different levels of risk-taking capabilities work out their differences?

♦♦♦♦♦♦

Say It Right

Paran:	Pay-rahn
Kadesh:	Kay-desh
Anak:	Ay-nack
Caleb:	Kay-leb
Jephunneh:	Jef-fun-nuh
Joshua:	Josh-ue-uh
Amalekites:	Am-a-lek-ites
Negeb:	Neh-gev
Hittites:	Hit-tights
Jebusites:	Jeb-you-sites
Amorites:	Am-or-ites
Canaanites:	Kay-nuh-nites

ACCEPT GOD'S GUIDANCE

This Lesson In Your Life

FAITH AS A DECISION

Optimists, the saying goes, see half a glass of water and say it's half full, while pessimists say it's half empty. If ever there was a life illustration of this principle, it was when Israel spied out the Promised Land. Ten of the spies saw a half-empty glass, and reported that the venture was simply too risky. Only two saw the half-full glass, and affirmed with faith that they could possess the land.

Are these two different viewpoints merely different personality types? Or were the ten fearful spies perhaps mistreated by their parents, and therefore handicapped as adults by being unable to trust? No doubt there can be an element of truth in both possibilities. The "natural" bent toward trust or doubt is well-illustrated by the story of the two boys whose dad gave his pessimistic son a pony, only to receive the dour prediction, "He'll just mess up the yard." Dad led the other boy, the natural optimist, to a pile of manure, and the lad immediately begin to dig furiously, crying, "There's got to be a pony in here somewhere!"

Another truth is often over-looked: *Faith is a decision.*

This is not to deny that faith has some objective elements. The empty tomb occured in a real and rational world, and is a firm basis for rational faith. What makes the difference between one believer whose outlook is cramped and distrusting, and another who is open to possibility, optimism and trust? Often it's the determination to choose to live that way.

There are plenty of trade-offs between good and evil in the world. As philosopher A. N. Whitehead said, "The fairies dance, and Christ is crucified on the cross." Faith in dancing and joy and possibility over crucifixion is more than a matter of cool examination of the evidence. It requires a choice, a decision--and that choice can be made both by naturally optimistic and pessimistic people.

The two faithful spies, Caleb and Joshua, exemplify the person who chooses faith. Over forty years after bringing back his favorable report from the mission to spy out the land, Caleb still maintained this determination. By then, he was eighty-five years old--old enough to have a crochety spirit and to blame it on old age if he wished. He wasn't just a Polyanna--he admitted that there were obstacles--"giants" in the land. Yet the choice to choose still burned in Caleb, and he said, "Give me this mountain...if so be the Lord will be with me, then I shall be able to drive them out, as the Lord said" (Josh. 14:12).

Still later, Joshua issued the challenge that still stands as a bold and inspirational challenge to believe by choice: "Choose you this day whom ye will serve...but as for me and my house, we will serve the Lord" (Josh. 24:15).

The rewards of such daring faith are rich. We catch a glimpse of them from these words by a Canadian pilot who refused to be content with earth-bound existence:

> Oh I have slipped the surly bonds of earth,
> And danced the skies on laughter-silvered wings;
> Sunward I've climbed and joined the tumbling mirth
> Of sun-split clouds--and done a hundred things
> You have not dreamed of--wheeled and soared and swung
> High in the sunlit silence.
> . . .
> And, while, with silent, lifting mind I've trod
> The high untrespassed sanctity of space,
> Put out my hand, and touched the face of God.

Seed Thoughts

1. Why were exactly twelve men sent to spy out the land of Canaan?
Apparently to represent each of the twelve tribes of Israel (see Num. 13:3-15).

2. If, as Numbers 13:2 says, God had already given the land to Israel, why spy it out in view of an invasion?
The gift of the land was God's part. It remained for the people to show the courage to do what was necessary to actually occupy it.

3. Draw a parallel to everyday life from this principle.
(Encourage discussion of God's benevolence and grace, along with our responsibility to "become what we are.")

4. What elements of the land were the spies to investigate?
The character and strength of the people; whether the soil was good or bad and its produce plentiful or scarce; and the fortifications of its cities.

5. Did Moses' commission suggest a preconceived perspective from which the spies should view the land?
Yes: "Be ye of good courage" (13:20).

(PLEASE TURN PAGE)

---

1. Why were exactly twelve men sent to spy out the land of Canaan?

2. If, as Numbers 13:2 says, God had already given the land to Israel, why spy it out in view of an invasion?

3. Draw a parallel to everyday life from this principle.

4. What elements of the land were the spies to investigate?

5. Did Moses' commission suggest a preconceived perspective from which the spies should view the land?

6. What was the nature of "the children of Anak" referred to in 13:28? (See vs. 33.)

7. What figurative "giants" sometimes test our own courage in conquering our problems?

8. What reaction did the report of the ten fearful spies produce among the people?

9. Compare the way Moses responded to God's intent to destroy Israel with the work of Christ.

10. What punishment was earned by the people who doubted God in the matter of the conquest of Canaan?

(SEED THOUGHTS--Cont'd)

Apparently to represent each of the twelve tribes of Israel (see Num. 13:3-15).

The gift of the land was God's part. It remained for the people to show the courage to do what was necessary to actually occupy it.

(Encourage discussion of God's benevolence and grace, along with our responsibility to "become what we are.")

The character and strength of the people; whether the soil was good or bad and its produce plentiful or scarce; and the fortifications of its cities.

Yes: "Be ye of good courage" (13:20).

The "Anakim" were a race of huge people--giants like Goliath (see also Deut. 2:21; 1 Sam. 17:4-7).

(Encourage discussion of problems that can overwhelm us if we have no more faith than the ten spies.)

Complaints, fear, regret that they had been led out of Egypt only to die, and a clamor to return (14:1-4).

Moses, as Christ, served as mediator and intercessor between the people and God (14:11-19).

They wandered forty years in the wilderness, until all but Caleb and Joshua died (14:27-35).

6. What was the nature of "the children of Anak" referred to in 13:28? (See vs. 33.)
The "Anakim" were a race of huge people--giants like Goliath (see also Deut. 2:21; 1 Sam. 17:4-7).

7. What figurative "giants" sometimes test our own courage in conquering our problems?
(Encourage discussion of problems that can overwhelm us if we have no more faith than the ten spies.)

8. What reaction did the report of the ten fearful spies produce among the people?
Complaints, fear, regret that they had been led out of Egypt only to die, and a clamor to return (14:1-4).

9. Compare the way Moses responded to God's intent to destroy Israel with the work of Christ.
Moses, as Christ, served as mediator and intercessor between the people and God (14:11-19).

10. What punishment was earned by the people who doubted God in the matter of the conquest of Canaan?
They wandered forty years in the wilderness, until all but Caleb and Joshua died (14:27-35).

August 21, 1994

Love the Lord Your God

Deuteronomy 6:1-13

1 NOW these are the commandments, the statutes, and the judgments, which the Lord your God commanded to teach you, that ye might do them in the land whither ye go to possess it:

2 That thou mightest fear the Lord thy God to keep all his statutes and commandments, which I command thee, thou, and thy son, and thy son's son, all the days of thy life; and that thy days mat be prolonged.

3 Hear therefore, O Israel, and observe to do it, that it may be well with thee, and that ye may increase mightily, as the Lord God of thy fathers hath promised thee, in the land that floweth with milk and honey.

4 Hear, O Israel: The Lord our God is one Lord:

5 And thou shalt love the LORD thy God with all thine heart and with all thy soul, and with all thy might.

6 And these words, which I command thee this day shall be in thine heart:

7 And thou shalt teach them diligently unto thy children, and shalt talk of them when thou sittest in thine house, and when thou walkest by the way, and when thou liest down, and when thou risest up.

8 And thou shalt bind them for a sign upon thine hand, and they shall be as frontlets between thine eyes.

9 And thou shalt write them upon the posts of thy house, and on thy gates.

10 And it shall be, when the LORD thy God shall have brought thee into the land which he sware unto thy fathers, to Abraham, to Isaac, and to Jacob, to give thee great and goodly cities, which thou buildedst not,

11 And houses full of all good things, which thou filledst not, and wells digged, which thou diggedst not, vineyards and olive trees, which thou plantedst not; when thou shalt have eaten and be full;

12 Then beware lest thou forget the Lord, which brought thee forth out of the land of Egypt, from the house of bondage.

13 Thou shalt fear the LORD thy God, and serve him, and shalt swear by his name.

◆◆◆◆◆◆

◀ **Memory Selection**
Deuteronomy 6:4-5

◀ **Devotional Reading**
Deuteronomy 7:6-9, 12

◀ **Background Scripture**
Deuteronomy 6

◀ **Printed Scripture**
Deuteronomy 6:1-13

LOVE THE LORD YOUR GOD

Teacher's Target

Boundaries between nations, states and persons are continual reasons for conflict and strife. Also, knowing one's identity is a basic necessity for a healthy integrated self. A strong sense of identity grows out of a feeling of personal worth and a sense of belonging. In order for this to occur each of us needs a "constant object" in our life from childhood through maturity. This constant object needs to mirror back to us who we are. Also this person must be someone we respect and admire. The one true God desires to be this object. Father and mother are meant to be this for a time in a child's life. Others assist us along the way until God becomes all in all.

Who has helped you know who you are? Is God a constant source of identity for you? How stable is your identity? Who and what define your boundaries?

Lesson Introduction

In Deuteronomy six, Moses was instructing the children of Israel about how to keep their relationship with God constant when they entered Canaan. Holding to their identity would be hard as they mingled with other cultures and religions. Their boundaries as a people and as individuals would be challenged. Only if they allowed God continually to remind them and reinforce them as to their heritage and destiny would they escape pollution of their heritage. Should they forget their identity it would lead to the disintegration of their unity.

Moses knew that unless the people loved God with all their heart they would look in other directions for objects by which to define themselves. He also knew that God alone was constant. He had their best interest at heart. God also knew what boundaries were necessary.

Teaching Outline

I. Boundaries: Deuteronomy 6:1-3
  A. Precepts: 1
  B. Practice: 2
  C. Performance: 3
II. Transcendent Presence: Deuteronomy 6:4-5
  A. A Supreme Authority of Love: 4
  B. A Continual Obedience of Love: 5
III. Identity: Deuteronomy 6:6-13
  A. Mirrored Image: 6
  B. Constant Reminder: 7-9
  C. Consistent Practice: 10-13

Daily Bible Readings

Mon. Heads of Tribes Hear God's Word - *Deuteronomy 5:22-27*
Tue. The Lord Hears Israel's Words *Deuteronomy 5:28-6:3*
Wed. Israel, Hear God's Words: Shema - *Deuteronomy 6:4-9*
Thurs. "You Shall Fear, Love, Serve God" - *Deuteronomy 6:10-17*
Fri. Do What Is Right and Good *Deuteronomy 6:18-25*
Sat. The Covenanted People *Deuteronomy 7:6-14*
Sun. Remember Ways God Has Led You - *Deuteronomy 8:1-7*

August 21, 1994

VERSE BY VERSE

I. Boundaries: Deuteronomy 6:1-3

A. Precepts: 1

1. NOW these are the commandments, the statutes, and the judgments, which the Lord your God commanded to teach you, that ye might do them in the land whither ye go to possess it:

The Israelites were about to enter a strange new land. They would be bombarded by new concepts, ideologies and ways of living. Their own way would need to he clear and deeply embedded in their being. They would have to be strong to resist the temptation to throw off their own manner and become like the inhabitants of the land. The old adage, "When in Rome do as the Romans do," could easily have been for the Jews, "When in Canaan do as the Canaanites do."

Moses knew they would need commandments, statutes and judgments. He did all in his power to fix their affection on God and to teach them the practice of godliness.

B. Practice: 2

2. That thou mightest fear the Lord thy God to keep all his statutes and commandments, which I command thee, thou, and thy son, and thy son's son, all the days of thy life; and that thy days may be prolonged.

Moses knew that only continued practice of the presence of God with them would result in a God-oriented life. The primary need in this area would be the awareness of their need of God. When he commands in verse two that they fear God, this is the point. They are to fear being without God and His loving guidance. Theirs is not to be the fear of a cruel and unjust god like the pagan gods of their neighbors. What they are to fear is the loss of God's presence with them. They could withstand the loss of property, possessions and other people, but they could not be without God and have prolonged and prosperous lives. Only a consistent practice of the presence of God would sustain them and protect them from the perils and pitfalls ahead.

C. Performance: 3

3. Hear therefore, O Israel, and observe to do it, that it may be well with thee, and that ye may increase mightily, as the Lord God of thy fathers hath promised thee, in the land that floweth with milk and honey.

The key to Israel's successful possession and inhabiting of the land would be to do the precepts of God in the defined way. Success for His people was not measured by God in the accumulation of material goods. For God and His people, success means a full and rich life of peace and joy. There could be no success of this nature without staying close to the God who could instill this in their hearts. This would require daily practice of what God had

503

taught them. Also, this righteous way would have to be modeled before each generation for it to become their way as well.

II. Transcendent Presence: Deuteronomy 6:4-5

A. A Supreme Authority of Love: 4

4. Hear, O Israel: The Lord our God is one Lord:

Moses presses home that there is but one God who loved them and desired their well being. All other gods are false. These would bring the people to ruin, not righteousness. Only God rules as a Being of love and justice. He alone knows humankind's needs, limits and potential. He alone can give them the heart and mind to become what He had intended them to be from the beginning. With Him, the people could find contentment, peace and prosperity.

B. A Continual Obedience of Love: 5

5. And thou shalt love the LORD thy God with all thine heart and with all thy soul, and with all thy might.

When someone had loved as God loved Israel, the response hoped for was a reciprocal love. However, there would be no such affection unless the ways of the authoritative lover were accepted, practiced and experienced as good for the one loved. The people, by faith, would have to invest their whole heart, soul and strength in loving God and His way. God had done His part to show His love to His people. Now they must realize Who had preserved them and cherish Him as deeply as He cherished them.

For the Jews these two verses (4 and 5) are the core of the Old Testament Scriptures. They wrote them on their phylacteries and said them morning and evening. They knew this love of God was the way of life abundant and rich in purpose and meaning.

III. Identity: Deuteronomy 6:6-13

A. Mirrored Image: 6

6. And these words, which I command thee this day shall be in thine heart:

One of the great needs of humankind is to know identity and place. "Who am I?" and "Where do I belong?" are questions Israel raised along with the rest of mankind. God is aware of this yearning in mankind. His Word held up a mirror to reflect to His people who they were. His commandments would continually remind them who they were intended to be and could be in relationship to God. This mirrored image was to be hidden deep in their hearts. God mirrored the greatness that was His intent for man from the beginning. God created man to be free of covetousness and destructive behavior, full of peace with God and fellow man.

B. Constant Reminder: 7-9

7. And thou shalt teach them diligently unto thy children, and shalt talk of them when thou sittest in thine house, and when thou walkest by the way, and when thou liest down, and when thou risest up.

8. And thou shalt bind them for a sign upon thine hand, and they shall be as frontlets between thine eyes.

9. And thou shalt write them upon the posts of thy house, and on thy gates.

For the image of Israel's potential to become reality, they would need continual reminders. Many other voices besides God's would fill their ears with ideas. God's instructions would have to be embedded in the very fabric of their daily lives. Children would need to be taught from childhood. God's truth would need to be an important part of their conversations. Significant scriptures should be written in prominent places to keep God and His presence ever before them.

Without continual reinforcement, the Word of God would wither and fall away from the people's hearts. Their houses would not be full of His presence and peace. Daily conversation with God's word and practice of His instruction were the evidence of their loving God with their whole heart, soul and might. Laziness in this matter would result in decay and destruction in personal and communal life.

C. Consistent Practice: 10-13

10. And it shall be, when the LORD thy God shall have brought thee into the land which he sware unto thy fathers, to Abraham, to Isaac, and to Jacob. to give thee great and goodly cities, which thou buildedst not,

11. And houses full of all good things, which thou filledst not, and wells digged, which thou diggedst not, vineyards and olive trees, which thou plantedst not; when thou shalt have eaten and be full;

12. Then beware lest thou forget the Lord, which brought thee forth out of the land of Egypt, from the house of bondage.

13. Thou shalt fear the LORD thy God, and serve him, and shalt swear by his name.

God desired the very best for his people. He would keep His promise and give them the land. They would have houses full of all good things, wells which they had not had to dig, vineyards and olive trees they did not plant. They would be full.

However, God has a warning for them. Beware of forgetting the Lord. He is the One who provides all the bounty they would enjoy. How easy it would be to enjoy the blessings and forget the Blesser. (Don't We?)

The deceit of humankind's heart never escaped God's attention. He continually reminds His people to beware of betraying themselves out of their own hearts. Israel is never to forget that their joy and peace are due to their relationship with God, not what they had or enjoyed in the world. Without Him, none of the rest would satisfy or protect them from their own destructive deterioration.

LOVE THE LORD YOUR GOD

Evangelistic Emphasis

"Our church family will gather at the park for a picnic."
"Do you have a church home"?

Such language has become more or less familiar in all churches. It speaks, like Deuteronomy, of the close relationship between communities of faith and the family. The relationship used to be emphasized even more, in the days when people used "brother" and "sister" more in referring to others in the church.

While the language as we use it implies warm and caring relationships more than Deuteronomy's emphasis on learning the Law, there is the same healthy implication that there is a homeliness about God's people.

We need to be aware that many people lack this sense of connection between faith and family. They find modern life impersonal and cold, offering none of the qualities of home life with its sense of security and acceptance. For some who live alone, a close-knit fellowship can become the surrogate family they need, not only to bolster their faith but to share their joys and sorrows, triumphs and pain.

First Timothy 3:15 speaks of "the house of God, which is the church of the living God." Are we tending to this "house" in a way that makes it attractive to those who have no "church home"?

♦♦♦♦♦♦

Memory Selection

Hear, O Israel: The Lord our God is one Lord: and thou shalt love the Lord thy God with all thine heart, and with all thy soul, and with all thy might.
Deuteronomy 6:5

Monotheism--the idea that there is only one God instead of many--was an important distinctive in Israel's faith, just as it is in Christianity. It is important to remember that it has definite implications for the way God's people are to live, not just for what we are to teach about the nature of God.

The apostle John wrote, "as he [God] is, so are we in this world" (1 John 4:17). John's point is that since God is love, His children are to act in loving ways. Otherwise, we reflect badly on His very nature.

Deuteronomy 6:5 makes the same point in a slightly different way. Since God is one, we are, to respond as one whole person--heart, soul and mind. We are not to allow the flesh to go in one direction and the heart in another (another way of saying we are not to sit in church wishin' we were fishin'!). We are not to present a split personality to God, spiritually speaking, but to be whole-hearted in our devotion.

August 21, 1994

Weekday Problems

Unfortunately, it's Sunday morning as usual at the Van Camp household, only worse. Sixteen-year-old Oscar has just announced, "I'm not going to Sunday School. That's for kids."

His sister Flora, who is fourteen, chimes in, "Well if he's not, I'm not either. I'm almost as old as he is. Besides--our class is boring."

Even eight-year-old Elizabeth, who loves Sunday School, has caught some of the disease. Dawdling over breakfast, she'll have trouble getting ready on time.

"That's enough!" snaps Mom, as she turns a pleading look to husband John.

"Snap to it, kids!" John says sternly. They move off slowly to their rooms to dress, but John wonders how long his sternness will work--especially with his oldest son.

*How is it at your home? Are your children glad to take part in church activities?

*What are some ways to motivate children at various ages to receive the religious instruction we want them to have?

*What can be done by the home--apart from the church--to impart Bible knowledge or Christian values to our children?

*How can Sunday School be made more appealing to children?

◆◆◆◆◆◆

Sparkles

Fame can inflate and fragment a person's being. One must seek a center inside one's being to guard against disintegration of personhood.

One wise sage who experienced much attention continually sought life in the commonplace. The more his reputation was inflated the more he sought to make himself less. He cherished his moments alone. He listened and observed deeply the commonest things. From waiting for the water to boil in a teapot he learned patience. From listening to the teapot whistle he learned to listen for God's call. He had to pay attention and act when the call came. Patience, calm, attention and action were the lessons of the teapot for him. From the empty cup after his tea, he learned to abide in the silent center of his being and know the peace of God.

This Lesson In Your Life

WILL HE FIND FAITH?

The amazing persistence of the Jewish faith through the centuries--often in the face of persecution--is partly due to the power of family "traditioning" such as that described in Deuteronomy 6. In Orthodox Judaism even today, religious practice in the home continues to exercise a powerful influence, as illustrated in the novels of Chaim Potok (for example, The Chosen).

How strong is this element of family life among Christians? Jesus asked a poignant question about the durability of the faith at the close of his parable on persistent prayer: "When the Son of man cometh, shall he find faith on the earth?" (Luke 18:8).

Deuteronomy 6 reminds us of one way this question can be answered in the affirmative--by maintaining a consistent witness to the faith in the home, instructing children in the ways of faith.

Of course, as many parents have discovered, the process of handing along faith to our children is far from inevitable. In an age of open communication and transportation, many outside influences can counter our attempts to "teach your children diligently" (Deut. 6:7). Still, some surveys show that eighty percent of children eventually affirm the faith and values of their parents, even though they may go through a period of questioning and even rebellion. Our children deserve to see their parents consistently living their faith, and communicating it to them as best they can.

All this is to say that faith can be taught, not just caught. If Jesus finds faith when He returns, it will be a faith that is communicated and practiced by others, in community. Homes and churches will be found living out the faith interactively, not just meditating about it in private. Parents will be found modeling faith as well as "posting it on the doorposts." Oases will be found where the principles of faith--not just the offerings of commerical TV--will be intentionally inserted into the "communications atmosphere"--"Thou...shalt talk of them when thou sittest in thine house" (Deut. 6:7).

Will He find faith? Jesus' parable suggests also that long-lasting faith depends on persistence through questioning. The mistreated widow fought her way through to justice only by stubbornly persisting in asking for it.

Any attempts to make the home and the church places for handing along the faith must allow for questions and exploration. Authoritarian attempts to make the kids sit still while we pour doctrine down them are doomed to failure. Fearful protectionism that will not allow questions only makes youth wonder what we have to fear and to hide.

The work of religious educator James Fowler has shown that this approach to passing along faith can actually stifle it. His research indicates that we grow and mature in faith only as we confront--like the widow of Luke 18--problems that challenge us to apply our faith to new situations (see James Fowler, Stages of Faith (San Francisco: Harper & Row, Publishers, 1981]).

Youth have a better opportunity to affirm the faith if they are allowed to explore its implications among people who have asked their own questions, and still have faith. Some people abandon faith when they look about them and see injustice reigning, as in the widow's experience. Giving up on God merely because of undeserved poverty and oppression is too easy; it does not take into account the fact that evil is loose in the world, as well as good. If Christ finds faith still flourishing when He comes again, it will be because we hang tough in tough times, refusing to let the fact that some skirmishes seem to be won by Satan tempt us to give away the whole battle. It will be because some persistently ask God to intervene, and insistently work for justice in the world.

When Jesus comes again, will he find faith?

Seed Thoughts

1. Why were such concepts as "commandments, statutes, and judgments" (Deut. 6:1) important for Israel at this time?
   Israel was being formed into a nation, and nations cannot long exist without rules.

2. What condition among the pagans in the promised land makes the first commandment emphasized here crucial?
   The concept of one God (monotheism) would be crucial to maintain in the face of pagan polytheism.

3. What "heartfelt" element in keeping the Law shows that it was to go deeper than just checking off rules?
   The commands were to be "in thine heart," not just in tables of stone (Deut. 6:6).

4. In what ways were the commandments to be kept before the Israelites in personal and everyday ways, not just in worship?
   They were to be taught to the children, talked about in the home and in daily activities, posted on the doorways, and worn on the person (vss. 6-9).

5. How did Moses emphasize that the promised land was a gift of grace instead of "salvation by works"?
   He reminded them that they would be enjoying cities, houses, wells and fields built by others.

(PLEASE TURN PAGE)

---

1. Why were such concepts as "commandments, statutes, and judgments" (Deut. 6:1) important for Israel at this time?

2. What condition among the pagans in the promised land makes the first commandment emphasized here crucial?

3. What "heartfelt" element in keeping the Law shows that it was to go deeper than just checking off rules?

4. In what ways were the commandments to be kept before the Israelites in personal and everyday ways, not just in worship?

5. How did Moses emphasize that the promised land was a gift of grace instead of "salvation by works"?

6. Is it common for people to "forget the Lord" when they are blessed with an abundance of material goods?

7. How did Israel's subsequent behavior break the law of 6:14, and what does this show about the influence of others about us?

8. What temptation at Massah is referred to in 6:16?

9. Although the promised land was a gift from God, what were the people to do in order to possess it?

10. What crucial event was Israel to keep alive throughout succeeding generations?

(SEED THOUGHTS--Cont'd)

Israel was being formed into a nation, and nations cannot long exist without rules.

The concept of one God (monotheism) would be crucial to maintain in the face of pagan polytheism.

The commands were to be "in thine heart," not just in tables of stone (Deut. 6:6).

They were to be taught to the children, talked about in the home and in daily activities, posted on the doorways, and worn on the person (vss. 6-9).

He reminded them that they would be enjoying cities, houses, wells and fields built by others.

Yes. We see it all the time. (On the other side of the coin, statistics show that in the U.S., church attendance grows during times of stress, such as war.)

They would frequently fall into worshiping Ba'al or other false gods, showing the tendency to conform to our current social environment.

That was the place where the people complained about a lack of water (Ex. 17:1-7).

They were to drive out the inhabitants of the land (who had polluted it with idolatrous worship).

How God had brought them out of Egypt and had given them the land of Canaan (vss. 20-24).

6. Is it common for people to "forget the Lord" when they are blessed with an abundance of material goods?
Yes. We see it all the time. (On the other side of the coin, statistics show that in the U.S., church attendance grows during times of stress, such as war.)

7. How did Israel's subsequent behavior break the law of 6:14, and what does this show about the influence of others about us?
They would frequently fall into worshiping Ba'al or other false gods, showing the tendency to conform to our current social environment.

8. What temptation at Massah is referred to in 6:16?
That was the place where the people complained about a lack of water (Ex. 17:1-7).

9. Although the promised land was a gift from God, what were the people to do in order to possess it?
They were to drive out the inhabitants of the land (who had polluted it with idolatrous worship).

10. What crucial event was Israel to keep alive throughout succeeding generations?
How God had brought them out of Egypt and had given them the land of Canaan (vss. 20-24).

August 28, 1994

Choose To Obey

Deuteronomy 28:1-6

1 And it shall come to pass, if thou shalt harken diligently unto the voice of the LORD thy God, to observe *and* to do all his commandments which I command thee this day, that the LORD thy God will set thee on high above all nations of the earth:
2 And all these blessings shall come on thee, and overtake thee, if thou shalt hearken unto the voice of the LORD thy God.
3 Blessed *shalt* thou *be* in the city, and blessed *shalt* thou *be* in the field.
4 Blessed *shall be* the fruit of thy body, and the fruit of thy ground, and the fruit of thy cattle, the increase of thy kine, and the flocks of thy sheep
5 Blessed *shall be* thy basket and thy store.
6 Blessed *shalt* thou *be* when thou comest in, and blessed *shalt* thou *be* when thou goest out.

Deuteronomy 28:15-19

15 But it shall come to pass if thou wilt not hearken unto the voice of the LORD thy God, to observe to do all his commandments and his statutes which I command thee this day; that all these curses shall come upon thee, and overtake thee:
16 Cursed *shalt* thou *be* in the city, and cursed *shalt* thou *be* in the field.
17 Cursed *shall be* thy basket and thy store.
18 Cursed *shall be* the fruit of thy body, and the fruit of thy land, the increase of thy kine, and the flocks of thy sheep.
19 Cursed *shalt* thou *be* when thou comest in, and cursed *shalt* thou *be* when thou goest out.

Deuteronomy 28:64-66

64 And the LORD shall scatter thee among all people, from the one end of the earth even unto the other and there thou shalt serve other gods, which neither thou nor thy fathers have known, *even* wood and stone.
65 And among these nations shalt thou find no ease, neither shall the sole of thy foot have rest: but the LORD shall give thee there a trembling heart, and failing of eyes, and sorrow of mind:
66 And thy life shall hang in doubt before thee; and thou shalt fear day and night, and shalt have none assurance of thy life:

◆◆◆◆◆◆

◀ **Memory Selection**
Deuteronomy 28:2

◀ **Devotional Reading**
Deuteronomy 29:10-18a

◀ **Background Scripture**
Deuteronomy 28

◀ **Printed Scripture**
Deuteronomy 28:1-6, 15-19, 64-66

CHOOSE TO OBEY

Teacher's Target

Obedience is a dirty word within many circles of our culture today. Doing our own thing has become our trademark as we have moved from what was called the modern era to the post-modern era. We have moved to a day where each person is encouraged to write his or her own script and make up his or her own meaning. Anything goes because nothing matters.

We have freedom to choose almost any kind of lifestyle, but we do not have the spiritual maturity to know how to choose one thing over another. No one is subject to anyone, and all actions and values are relative. Part of the story of how we got to this point is the belief that there are no absolutes and there is no ultimate authority.

What is your authority? To whom are you obedient? Do you believe in a foundation for life? What do you center life around?

Lesson Introduction

The blessings of God were listed before the curses in Deuteronomy. This reflected God's nature. He is a merciful God, slow to become angry with His people and swift to move to their rescue. Also God desires to woo His people with love. He has no desire to have them clinging to Him out of a groveling fear of destruction.

God desires faith which is obedience. Trusting God's Word enough to listen (obedience means "to give ear") is God's desire. Realizing that only God had the Word of life should have made obedience come easy. However the will of man weakened by sin was and is fickle and faltering.

God promised and warned. He knew humankind needed both. He also knew it would be hard for them to believe either. What a complicated piece of work humankind had become since the day of Adam's and Eve's fall!

Teaching Outline

I. Blessing: Deuteronomy 28:1-6
   A. Listening: 1
   B. Stability in Labor: 2-5
   C. Stability in Self: 6
II. Warning: Deuteronomy 28:15-19
   A. Not Listening: 15
   B. No Stability in Labor: 16-18
   C. No Stability in Self: 19
III. Trembling: Deuteronomy 28: 64-66
   A. Scattered: 64
   B. Restless: 65
   C. Fearful: 66

Daily Bible Readings

Mon. Count Your Many Blessings, Name Them - *Deuteronomy 28:1-9*
Tue. Obedience to God Brings Prosperity - *Deuteronomy 28:10-14*
Wed. Curses Come if Disobedient *Deuteronomy 28:15-24*
Thurs. No One Will Offer to Help *Deuteronomy 28:29-34*
Fri. Curses Come Through Disobedience *Deuteronomy 28:36-37, 43-46*
Sat. Practice Obedience to God's Purposes - *Deuteronomy 28:47, 58, 62-65*
Sun. Only a Fool Refuses God's Law *Deuteronomy 29:1-13*

August 28, 1994

VERSE BY VERSE

I. Blessing: Deuteronomy 28:1-6

A. Listening: 1

1. And it shall come to pass, if thou shalt harken diligently unto the voice of the LORD thy God, to observe and to do all his commandments which I command thee this day, that the LORD thy God will set thee on high above all nations of the earth:

To "hearken diligently to the voice of the Lord means to listen attentively and act diligently. This is obedience. This is faith. There was no sight of God. Only His word was present to be taken by faith and applied by faith. Anyone who lived like God had instructed would be able to stand among others and before God. No shame would shadow the believer's days upon the earth.

Listening attentively was the hard part. Especially since humankind had turned each to his own ways. Placing self where only God was intended to be enthroned had impaired people's hearing.

B. Stability in Labor: 2-5

2. And all these blessings shall come on thee, and overtake thee, if thou shalt hearken unto the voice of the LORD thy God.

3. Blessed shalt thou be in the city, and blessed shalt thou be in the field.

4. Blessed *shall be* the fruit of thy body, and the fruit of thy ground, and the fruit of thy cattle, the increase of thy kine, and the flocks *of* thy sheep.

5. Blessed shall be thy basket and thy store.

Obeying God once was not enough. Obeying Him diligently and daily would be the only means of health and well being. Knowing their identity before God and their boundaries and limits as human beings would produce an energy within and a freedom without.

Notice that all the ways of humankind were dependent upon God. He was the one staple they could not do without in their daily diet. + neither can we.

C. Stability in Self: 6

6. Blessed shalt thou be when thou comest in, and blessed shalt thou be when thou goest out.

When the people went out they would know a sense of security. When they came in they would know the same. In a crowd in the marketplace they knew who they were and what they were about. When they were alone their fears did not overwhelm them for they knew they had God's presence with them.

Obedience produced stability and security. When one knew he was observing God's way he was stable within. Likewise, he was secure in his endeavors and among the people.

II. Warning: Deuteronomy 28:15-19

A. Not Listening: 15

15. But it Shall come to pass if thou wilt not hearken unto the voice

513

of the LORD thy God, to observe to do all his commandments and his statutes which I command thee this day; that all these curses shall come upon thee, and overtake thee:

God was not threatening the people with His power. He was not conjuring up fear of what He would do to wayward children. He was warning them of what they would do to themselves if they failed to heed His word. As is said in the book of James, "a double-minded man is unstable in all his ways" (James 1:8).

When God was not heard and His Word acted upon there was no stability within His people. They could not find a center within themselves. They had no direction, and fear overtook them. Their habit of life became erratic and their endeavors faltered and failed. The lack of the practice of godliness (God's foundation of life) caused them to deteriorate and come to destruction.

B. No Stability in Labor: 16-18

16. Cursed shalt thou be in the city, and cursed shalt thou be in the field.
17. Cursed shall be thy basket and thy store.
18. Cursed shall be the fruit of thy body, and the fruit of thy land, the increase of thy kine, and the flocks of thy sheep.

Knowing who they were and to whom they belonged and what their purpose was--this was the source of Israel's quality of living. Without this they placed themselves under the curse of this world: disintegration of person, divided loyalties, misdirected energy and dismantled purposes. A disoriented life would produce as much misery as obedient listening had produced blessing. They could seek quality life in a city or the country and they would not find it. Life was not in a place or an endeavor but in God.

The warning was not against trivial miscues. Despising God and refusing to relate to and listen to Him was the issue. God did not discard His people. They discarded Him.

C. No Stability in Self: 19

19. Cursed shalt thou be when thou comest in, and cursed shalt thou be when thou goest out.

The destructive sin above all others was placing something, anything, above God. When the heart's affection was set on something other than God the downfall had begun.

Only God was big enough to become a center for an individual's life or a people's life in community. He alone could stabilize personal life and communal living. One could run to the country or hide in the city but the disintegration went with him everywhere. Humankind could not flee himself.

III. Trembling: Deuteronomy 28:64-66

A. Scattered: 64

64. And the LORD shall scatter thee among all people, from the one end of the earth even unto the other and there thou shalt serve other gods, which neither thou nor thy fathers have known, even wood and stone.

Sin and disobedience disintegrate. They disintegrate personhood and people. The person divided within himself seeks dominance of or isolation from others. He cannot create community.

Allow a whole people to practice disobedience and they will eventually self-destruct. What they have built in obedience will fall in disobedience. They will scatter and long for connection and relationship but find none.

B. Restless: 65

65. And among these nations shalt thou find no ease, neither shall the

sole of thy foot have rest: but the LORD shall give thee there a trembling heart, and failing of eyes, and sorrow of mind:

A people who knew the way of God could not move from it without great terror coming upon them. They would find no rest for their bodies. They would be continually on the move in hope of some gain in a new place or in flight due to fear of persecution. They would he a wandering people with no sense of place due to God's presence.

Worse than even the lack of bodily rest was the lack of rest for the mind which would produce a trembling heart. When the mind could not he renewed by the presence of God it was open to the assault of rapacious thoughts. The mind was plundered with fear and the courage went out of the person. The disobedient would be on the move inside themselves and out, but no escape from their fearful and trembling heart would be found except in a return to God.

C. Fearful: 66

66. And thy life shall hang in doubt before thee; and thou shalt fear day and night, and shalt have none assurance of thy life:

A quiet mind stayed upon God welcomed the night and the light. One obedient to God could look forward to the task of the day with confidence and purpose. Likewise the night would bring rest and repose.

For the disobedient it was not so. They would he a torment to themselves. Terror accompanied their days and nights. They would fear the failure of their labor by day and fear the silence with themselves at night. Life would seem futile and the task burdensome. Their hearts would tremble, eyes fail them, and sorrow would fill their minds (vs. 65). They would fear both life and death. Also, their uneasiness with themselves would be a vexation to all around them as well.

Let the obedient walk in faith that can calm their hearts, clear their eyes and heal their minds was the warning. only God would rule in love. If this would not be received then the people would be ruined by the world that entered their hearts and held them captive to corruption.

Evangelistic Emphasis

A powerful witness for evangelism is tucked away in Deuteronomy 28:9-10--"The Lord shall establish thee an holy people unto himself, as he hath sworn unto thee...and all people of the earth shall see that thou art called by the name of the Lord."

Holiness is an endangered species these days. For one thing, purity of life is widely disdained as an old-fashioned relic of Puritanism. We have only to note the media's reluctance to speak of sexual abstinence as a means of educating people about the danger of AIDS. It's much more popular to speak of "safe sex" than of having moral fiber.

Holiness has also been given bad press because of its abuse by religious folk themselves. Highly visible representatives of the faith have proved less than exemplary in their private lives. At the other extreme, some Christians seem to take so much pride in their holiness that others are put off by their smugness.

Somewhere in all this there is room for people who are quietly determined to march to the beat of Christ's drum, to be holy without "letting their good be evil spoken of." God promises to establish such people as a city set on a hill, as lamps that cannot be hidden, lighting the pathway to God.

♦♦♦♦♦♦

Memory Selection

And all these blessings shall come on thee, and overtake thee, if thou shalt hearken unto the voice of the Lord thy God. *Deuteronomy 28:2*

The blessings God has for those who follow Him are so rich as to defy description. Believers enjoy the forgiveness of sins, citizenship in the Kingdom, the fellowship of the faithful, the indwelling Spirit giving them victory over the problems of life and the incomparable thrill of actually dwelling with Christ forever.

This storehouse of blessings is so stunning that it inevitably raises the question Satan asked about Job: "Doth Job fear God for nought?" (Job 1:9). Do we serve the Lord just because of rewards such as those promised in Deuteronomy 28? Or are we faithful just to avoid the curses?

At their best, Christians are less concerned about such rewards and punishments than they are awed by the unearned grace that calls them into obedience. They recall that the best reward for following Him is not *for* obeying, but *in* obeying.

August 28, 1994

Weekday Problems

Pastor McGaughey had worked in the town of Ashton for fifteen years. He was a likable person, with good seminary training. His preaching was consistently positive, his board found him cooperative and responsive to their suggestions. He was active in several community programs.

But Pastor McGaughey was discouraged. Despite his hard work through the years, there were still only forty-five members in the congregation.

"What am I doing wrong?" he asked his wife Margaret.

"I think you do everything right," his wife said reassuringly. She had always tried to be supportive.

"But where is the evidence?" her husband asked. "God promises to bless faithful work with fruitfulness. I must have misinterpreted His call to the ministry. I'm going to submit my resignation at the board meeting tomorrow night."

*Does a healthy church always grow numerically?
*Do ministers serve people or God? Or do they serve both?
*Was Jeremiah a successful person? (See Jer. 38:5-6.)
*What would you say to Pastor McGaughey if you were on the church's board?

♦♦♦♦♦♦

Smiles

A lady was trying to impress those at the party with her family origin. "My family's ancestry is very old," she boasted. "It dates back to the days of King James."

Then she turned to a lady next to her and asked with a condescending air, "How old is your family, my dear?"

"Well," the lady said with a slight smile, "I can't really say. All our family records were lost in the Flood."

After the service the rabbi looked despondent. "What took the wind out of your sails?" his wife asked.

He replied, "I tried to tell them it was the duty of the rich to help the poor."

"And did you convince them?"

"Only half. I convinced the poor!"

This Lesson In Your Life

GODLINESS AND THE GOOD LIFE

God's covenant with Israel establishes a firm connection between obedience to God and receiving His blessings. His people were told to expect good crops, large families and a favored position among the nations when they honor God; and famine, closed wombs, plagues, and captivity if they are disobedient. Although this expectation is spelled out most sharply in Deuteronomy 28, it was imbedded in God's promise to Abraham from the beginning. It is a clear part of the Ten Commandments, which promise, for example, a long life as a result of honoring father and mother (Ex. 20:12).

To what extent are we today to count on such a close connection between living the godly life and enjoying the good life? "Prosperity" theologies would have us believe that the connection is automatic--do right and grow rich seems to be an automatic principle. The other side of the coin seems to be that if we're not wealthy we are guilty of disobedience.

Job, the classic sufferer, saw it differently. God rebuked Job's friends for insisting that his suffering was due to some secret sin in his life. Rather, his plight is to be traced to a sovereign God who wants to prove to Satan that Job serves God for just the opposite reason--"though he slay me, yet will I serve Him."

Furthermore, as Jesus said, God makes the rain fall on the just and the unjust (Matt. 5:45). The lives of faithful but persecuted believers show that serving God doesn't always guarantee that we will experience His blessings in the form of material goods or success in this life. Many faithful heroes have died not having received the promise (Heb. 11:39).

Yet Job and the martyrs are "boundary" situations. The general rule is that there is a close relationship between wholeness and holiness. It's similar to the general feeling of well-being experienced by those who exercise regularly. We usually receive back in better health more than enough to make the discipline and expended effort worthwhile. Likewise, those who discipline themselves to "fear" or obey the Lord often testify to a joy that is worth more than any material or visible reward they can imagine.

This reciprocal relationship between heaven and earth flows the other way, too. Not only is our earthly existence often blessed in obeying; it reflects Him whom we obey. In the classic story, "The Great Stone Face," a man is fascinated by the admirable features he imagines he sees in a natural, face-like stone outcropping. Eventually the townspeople notice that the ideals the man took from the rock somehow fashioned themselves within the man--until, sure enough, his very countenance resembled what he admired.

People tend to become like the one they worship--the divinity takes shape in their humanity. Pagans whose gods demanded human sacrifices often had little respect themselves for human life. Ancient Greeks whose gods were adulterers often called their own sexual promiscuity "worship."

This principle has a special application when we reflect on the implications of the oneness of God emphasized in Deuteronomy 6:5. God's oneness is to be reflected in the unity of His people. Paul says that just as there is one God, there is "one body," or Church (Eph. 4:4; 1:22-23). Any other state in the Body of Christ reflects badly on the oneness of God. A critical pagan might look at a divided church full of back-biting and quarreling as an indication that we serve plural and warring gods!

There really is an intimate connection between serving God, and life here on earth. Only let us not presume always to see it in forms and at times we ourselves dictate. Let us leave it in the hands of the Sovereign God.

Seed Thoughts

1. In general, on what do all the "blesseds" in Deuteronomy 28 depend?
On "hearkening," to the voice of the Lord, and keeping (obeying) His commandments (see vss. 1-2).

2. Why were large families ("the fruit of thy body," vss. 4, 11) an important part of God's promised blessing?
Because the covenant included the promise of many descendants (see Gen. 15:5).

3. Are you aware of blessings as a Christian that may be similar to those listed in Deuteronomy 28?
(Encourage sharing.)

4. What example of the promise in vs. 10 is recounted in Joshua 10:1-2?
The king of Jerusalem heard of Israel's victory over the city of Ai, and feared them.

5. What example of the curse in vs. 25 is recorded in Joshua 7:1-5, 10-12?
Ironically, it concerned again the city of Ai, which defeated Israel because of disobedience.

(PLEASE TURN PAGE)

---

1. In general, on what do all the "blesseds" in Deuteronomy 28 depend?

2. Why were large families ("the fruit of thy body," vss. 4, 11) an important part of God's promised blessing?

3. Are you aware of blessings as a Christian that may be similar to those listed in Deuteronomy 28?

4. What example of the promise in vs. 10 is recounted in Joshua 10:1-2?

5. What example of the curse in vs. 25 is recorded in Joshua 7:1-5, 10-12?

6. What events back in Egypt show God's impartiality in enforcing the curse of vss. 21-22?

7. What event in Daniel 4:24-33 shows God's impartiality in sending the curse of vss. 28-29?

8. How was the prophecy of vss. 36, 49-51 fulfilled? (See 2 Chron. 36:2-7, 14-20.)

9. The term "dispersion" is often used to describe the later fate of the Israelites. How does vs. 65 define this term?

10. What common human temperament is described in vs. 67?

On "hearkening," to the voice of the Lord, and keeping (obeying) His commandments (see vss. 1-2).

Because the covenant included the promise of many descendants (see Gen. 15:5).

(Encourage sharing.)

The king of Jerusalem heard of Israel's victory over the city of Ai, and feared them.

Ironically, it concerned again the city of Ai, which defeated Israel because of disobedience.

The plagues God brought against the Egyptians when they at first refused to release the Israelite slaves (see also Deut. 28:27-28).

King Nebuchadnezzer was driven into the field, mad, for not attributing his success to God's favor.

By the captivity of Judah by the king of Babylon.

It describes the "scattering" of disobedient Israel to the far corners of the earth. (See evidence for this in Acts 2:1-11.)

The restlessness that causes us always to wish we were at another time or place.

(SEED THOUGHTS--Cont'd)

6. What events back in Egypt show God's impartiality in enforcing the curse of vss. 21-22?
The plagues God brought against the Egyptians when they at first refused to release the Israelite slaves (see also Deut. 28:27-28).

7. What event in Daniel 4:24-33 shows God's impartiality in sending the curse of vss. 28-29?
King Nebuchadnezzer was driven into the field, mad, for not attributing his success to God's favor.

8. How was the prophecy of vss. 36, 49-51 fulfilled? (See 2 Chron. 36:2-7, 14-20.)
By the captivity of Judah by the king of Babylon.

9. The term "dispersion" is often used to describe the later fate of the Israelites. How does vs. 65 define this term?
It describes the "scattering" of disobedient Israel to the far corners of the earth. (See evidence for this in Acts 2:1-11.)

10. What common human temperament is described in vs. 67?
The restlessness that causes us always to wish we were at another time or place.